Unshelved™
Volume 1

Unshelved™
Volume 1

Bill Barnes and Gene Ambaum

OVERDUE MEDIA
Seattle

ISBN: 0-9740353-0-0

First printing: May 2003
Second printing: October 2004

Printed in Canada.

Be gentle.

That's what we tell ourselves whenever we're brave enough to wade through our own archives. When we started this project Bill hadn't drawn in years and Gene had never written a comic strip. And it shows. But we were lucky enough to be supported at an early stage by our families, friends, and an extremely forgiving readership which cheered us on, told their friends about us, and urged us to publish this book. We were also given incredibly sound cartooning advice by Brian Basset and Michael Jantze. Buy their books too.

Bill would especially like to thank Sara, who made him go through with it. Gene is similarly grateful to his or her spouse, who does not have a pen name at this time.

A comic strip about a library? Is that really such a good idea? Here's your chance to find out. But please, be gentle.

Bill Barnes and Gene Ambaum
April, 2003

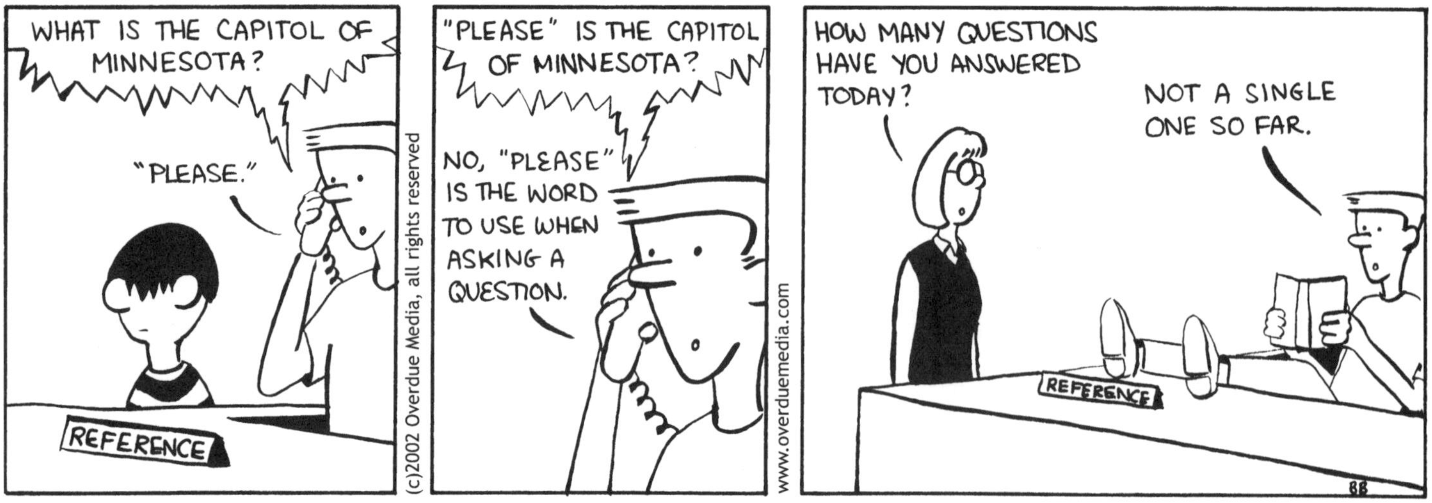
WHAT IS THE CAPITOL OF MINNESOTA?
"PLEASE."
REFERENCE
(c)2002 Overdue Media, all rights reserved
"PLEASE" IS THE CAPITOL OF MINNESOTA?
NO, "PLEASE" IS THE WORD TO USE WHEN ASKING A QUESTION.
www.overduemedia.com
HOW MANY QUESTIONS HAVE YOU ANSWERED TODAY?
NOT A SINGLE ONE SO FAR.
REFERENCE
BB

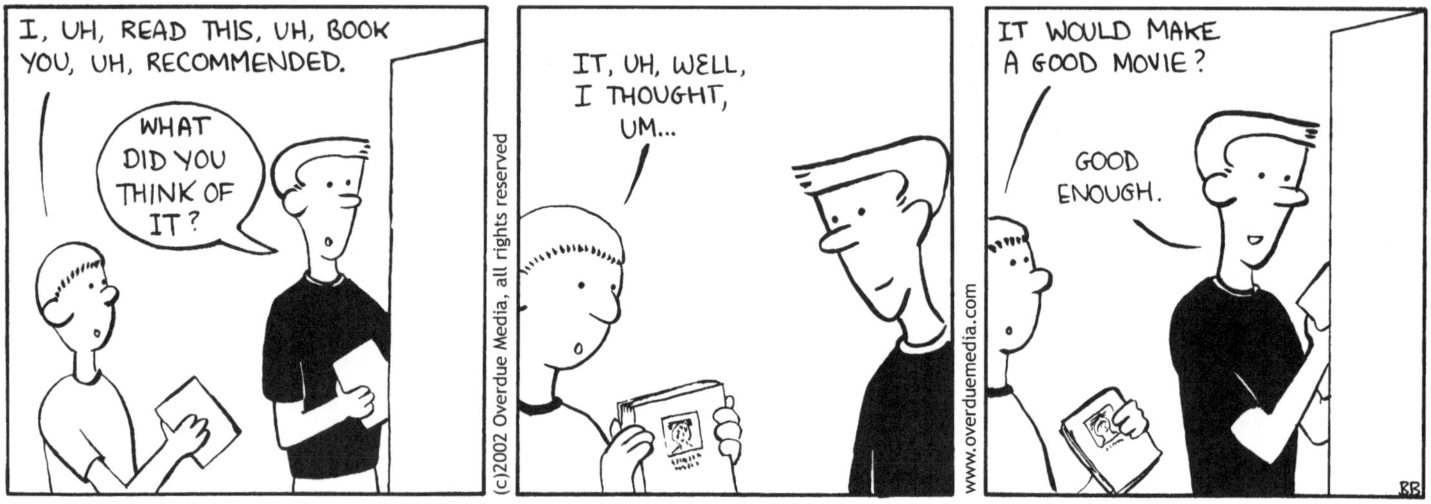
I, UH, READ THIS, UH, BOOK YOU, UH, RECOMMENDED.
WHAT DID YOU THINK OF IT?
(c)2002 Overdue Media, all rights reserved
IT, UH, WELL, I THOUGHT, UM...
www.overduemedia.com
IT WOULD MAKE A GOOD MOVIE?
GOOD ENOUGH.
BB

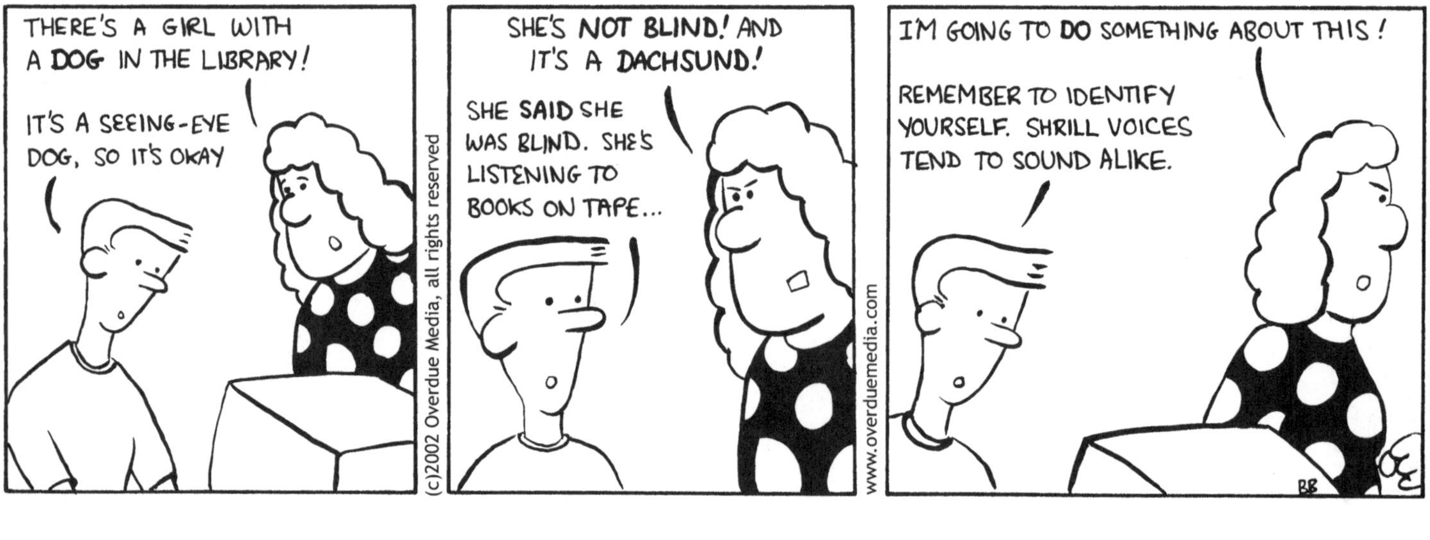
THERE'S A GIRL WITH A DOG IN THE LIBRARY!
IT'S A SEEING-EYE DOG, SO IT'S OKAY
(c)2002 Overdue Media, all rights reserved
SHE'S NOT BLIND! AND IT'S A DACHSUND!
SHE SAID SHE WAS BLIND. SHE'S LISTENING TO BOOKS ON TAPE...
www.overduemedia.com
I'M GOING TO DO SOMETHING ABOUT THIS!
REMEMBER TO IDENTIFY YOURSELF. SHRILL VOICES TEND TO SOUND ALIKE.
BB

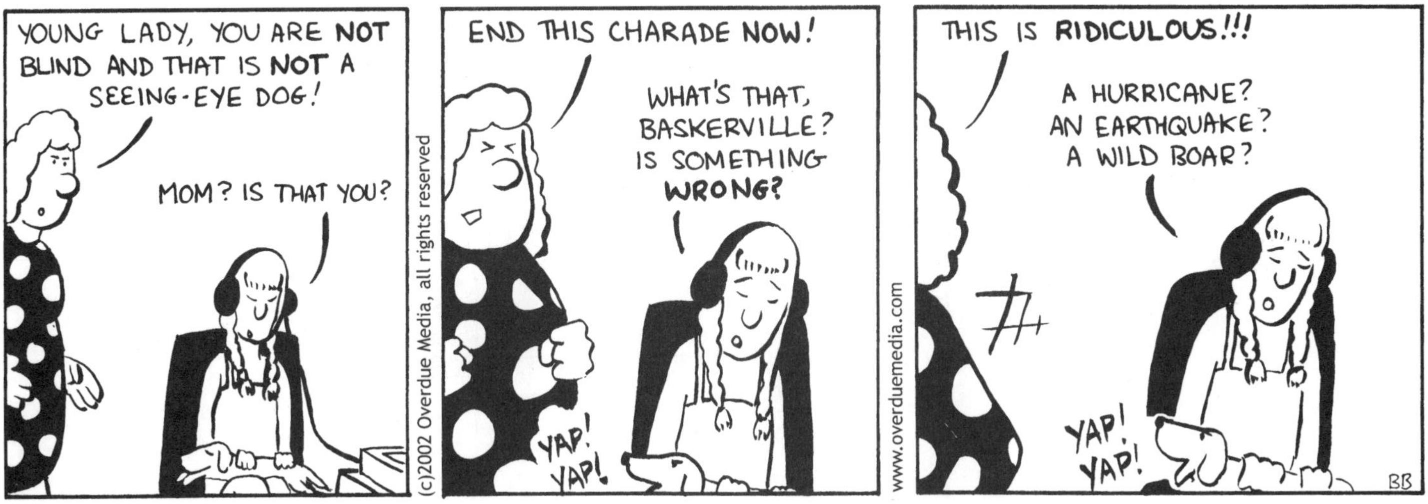
YOUNG LADY, YOU ARE NOT BLIND AND THAT IS NOT A SEEING-EYE DOG!
MOM? IS THAT YOU?
END THIS CHARADE NOW!
WHAT'S THAT, BASKERVILLE? IS SOMETHING WRONG?
YAP! YAP!
THIS IS RIDICULOUS!!!
A HURRICANE? AN EARTHQUAKE? A WILD BOAR?
YAP! YAP!
BB
(c)2002 Overdue Media, all rights reserved
www.overduemedia.com

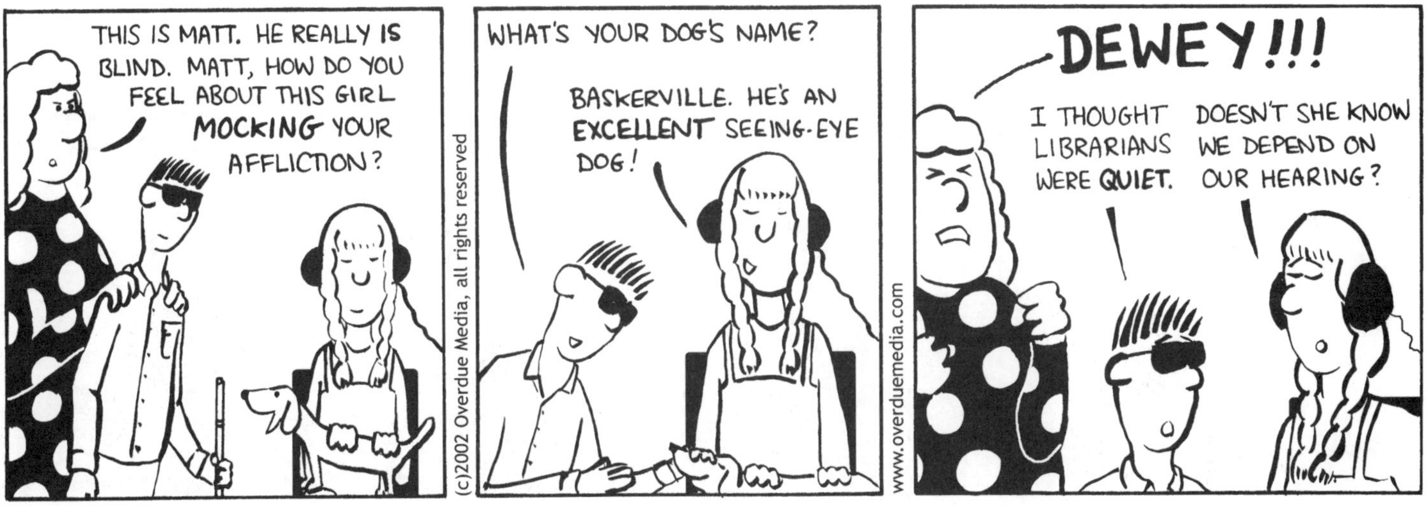
THIS IS MATT. HE REALLY IS BLIND. MATT, HOW DO YOU FEEL ABOUT THIS GIRL MOCKING YOUR AFFLICTION?
WHAT'S YOUR DOG'S NAME?
BASKERVILLE. HE'S AN EXCELLENT SEEING-EYE DOG!
DEWEY!!!
I THOUGHT LIBRARIANS WERE QUIET.
DOESN'T SHE KNOW WE DEPEND ON OUR HEARING?
(c)2002 Overdue Media, all rights reserved
www.overduemedia.com

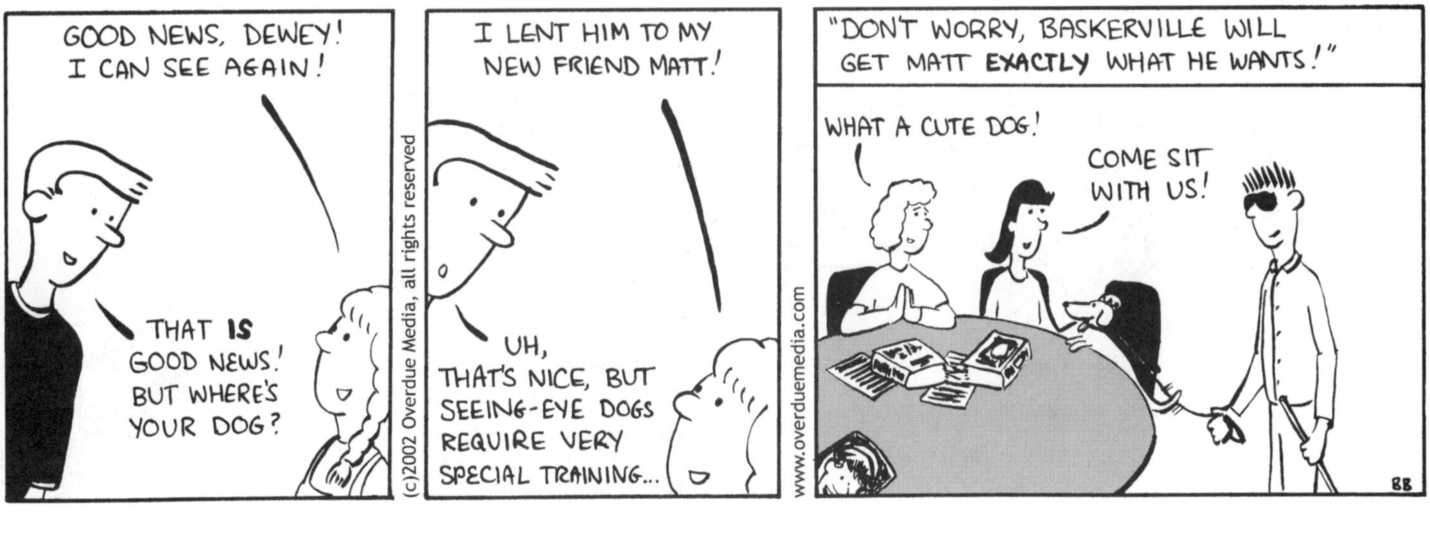
GOOD NEWS, DEWEY! I CAN SEE AGAIN!
THAT IS GOOD NEWS! BUT WHERE'S YOUR DOG?
I LENT HIM TO MY NEW FRIEND MATT!
UH, THAT'S NICE, BUT SEEING-EYE DOGS REQUIRE VERY SPECIAL TRAINING...
"DON'T WORRY, BASKERVILLE WILL GET MATT EXACTLY WHAT HE WANTS!"
WHAT A CUTE DOG!
COME SIT WITH US!
BB
(c)2002 Overdue Media, all rights reserved
www.overduemedia.com

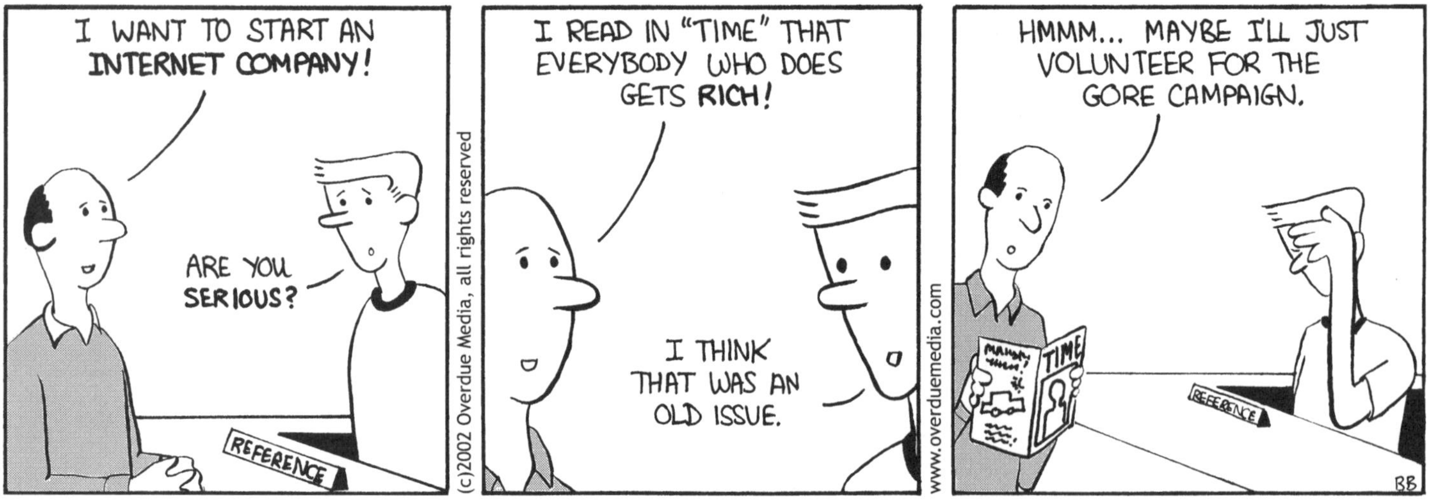
I WANT TO START AN INTERNET COMPANY!
ARE YOU SERIOUS?
REFERENCE
I READ IN "TIME" THAT EVERYBODY WHO DOES GETS RICH!
I THINK THAT WAS AN OLD ISSUE.
(c)2002 Overdue Media, all rights reserved
HMMM... MAYBE I'LL JUST VOLUNTEER FOR THE GORE CAMPAIGN.
TIME
REFERENCE
www.overduemedia.com
BB

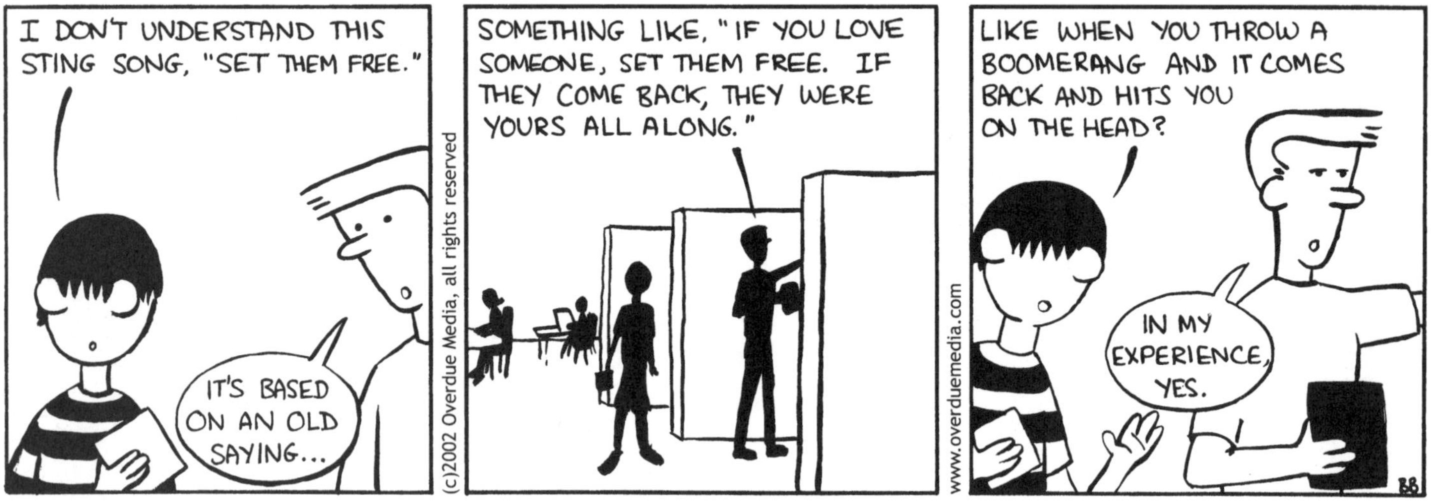
I DON'T UNDERSTAND THIS STING SONG, "SET THEM FREE."
IT'S BASED ON AN OLD SAYING...
(c)2002 Overdue Media, all rights reserved
SOMETHING LIKE, "IF YOU LOVE SOMEONE, SET THEM FREE. IF THEY COME BACK, THEY WERE YOURS ALL ALONG."
LIKE WHEN YOU THROW A BOOMERANG AND IT COMES BACK AND HITS YOU ON THE HEAD?
IN MY EXPERIENCE, YES.
www.overduemedia.com
BB

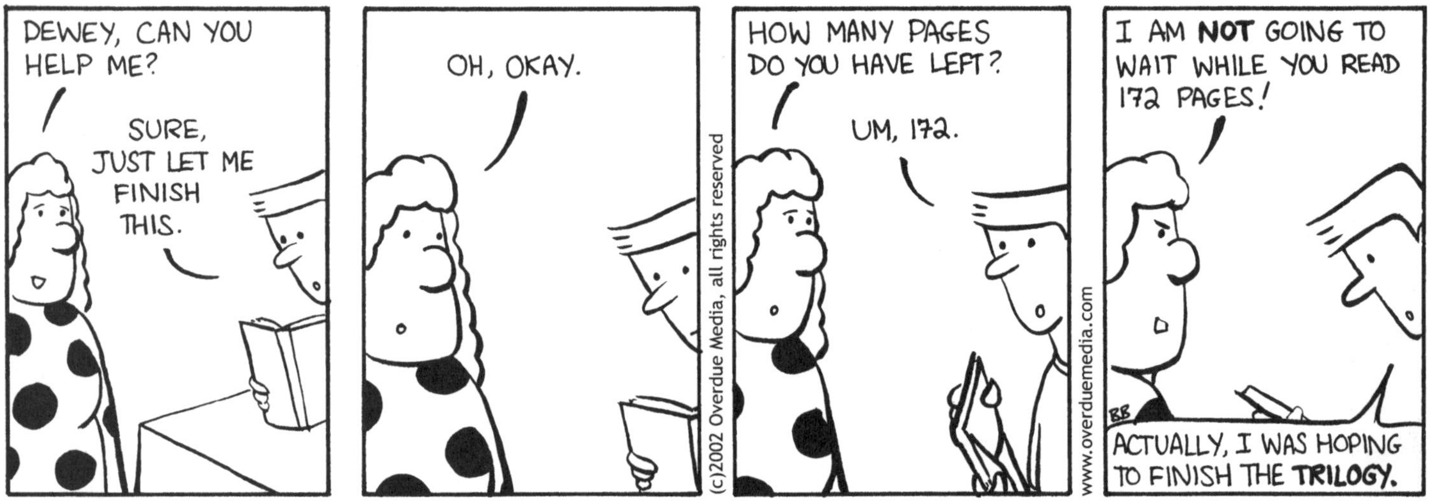
DEWEY, CAN YOU HELP ME?
SURE, JUST LET ME FINISH THIS.
OH, OKAY.
(c)2002 Overdue Media, all rights reserved
HOW MANY PAGES DO YOU HAVE LEFT?
UM, 172.
www.overduemedia.com
I AM NOT GOING TO WAIT WHILE YOU READ 172 PAGES!
BB
ACTUALLY, I WAS HOPING TO FINISH THE TRILOGY.

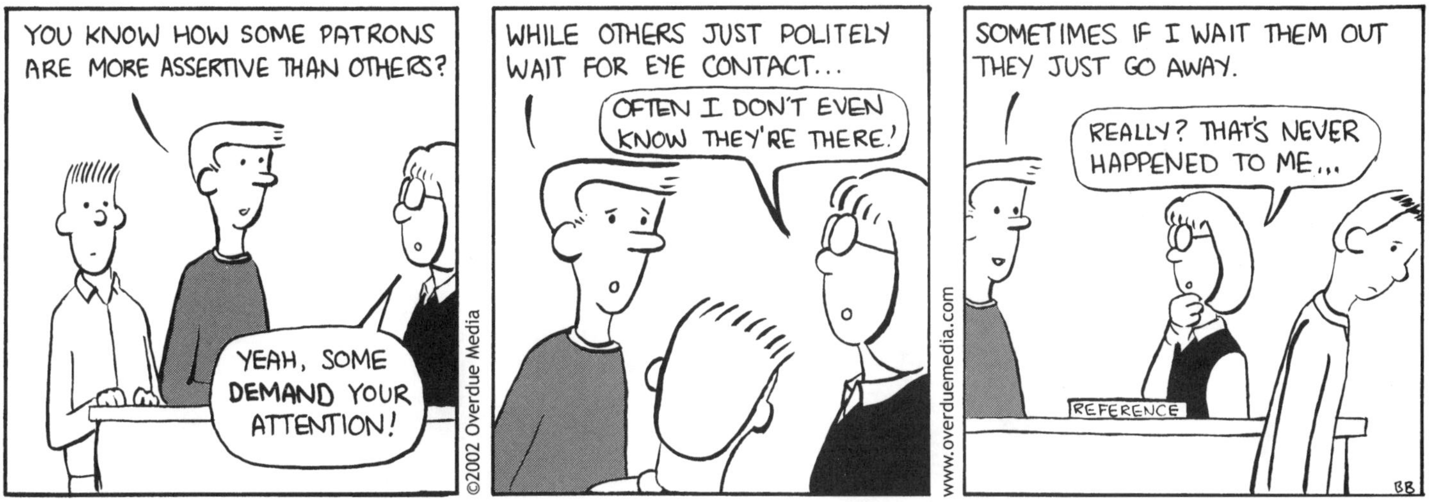

YOU KNOW HOW SOME PATRONS ARE MORE ASSERTIVE THAN OTHERS?
YEAH, SOME DEMAND YOUR ATTENTION!
©2002 Overdue Media
WHILE OTHERS JUST POLITELY WAIT FOR EYE CONTACT...
OFTEN I DON'T EVEN KNOW THEY'RE THERE!
www.overduemedia.com
SOMETIMES IF I WAIT THEM OUT THEY JUST GO AWAY.
REALLY? THAT'S NEVER HAPPENED TO ME...
REFERENCE
BB

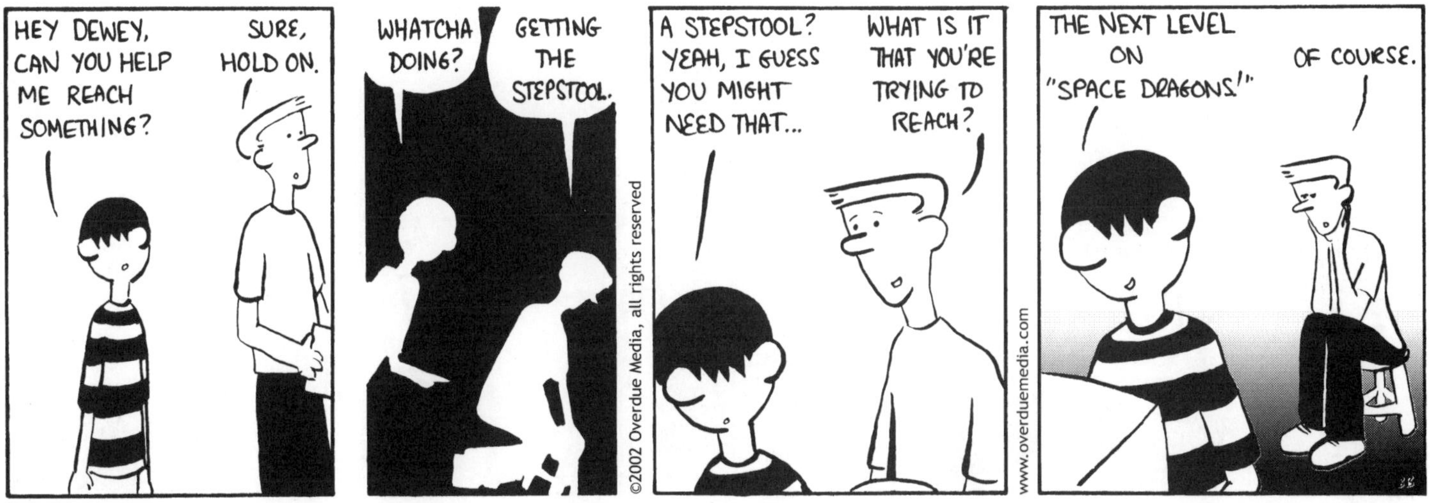

HEY DEWEY, CAN YOU HELP ME REACH SOMETHING?
SURE, HOLD ON.
WHATCHA DOING?
GETTING THE STEPSTOOL.
©2002 Overdue Media, all rights reserved
A STEPSTOOL? YEAH, I GUESS YOU MIGHT NEED THAT...
WHAT IS IT THAT YOU'RE TRYING TO REACH?
www.overduemedia.com
THE NEXT LEVEL ON "SPACE DRAGONS!"
OF COURSE.
BB

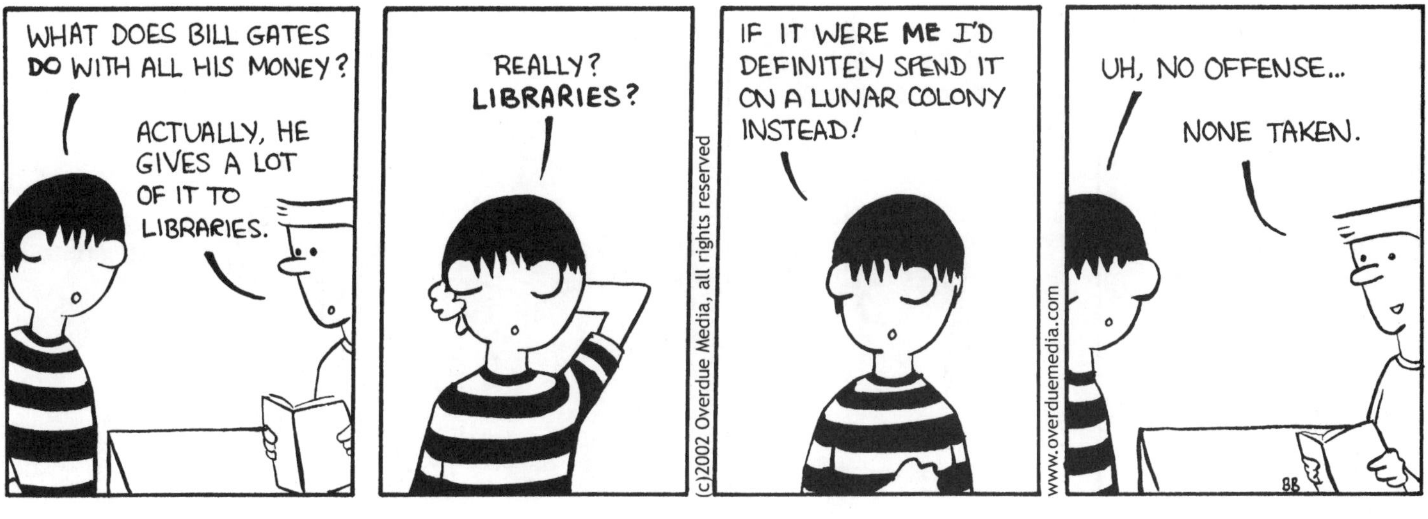

WHAT DOES BILL GATES DO WITH ALL HIS MONEY?
ACTUALLY, HE GIVES A LOT OF IT TO LIBRARIES.
REALLY? LIBRARIES?
(c)2002 Overdue Media, all rights reserved
IF IT WERE ME I'D DEFINITELY SPEND IT ON A LUNAR COLONY INSTEAD!
www.overduemedia.com
UH, NO OFFENSE...
NONE TAKEN.
BB

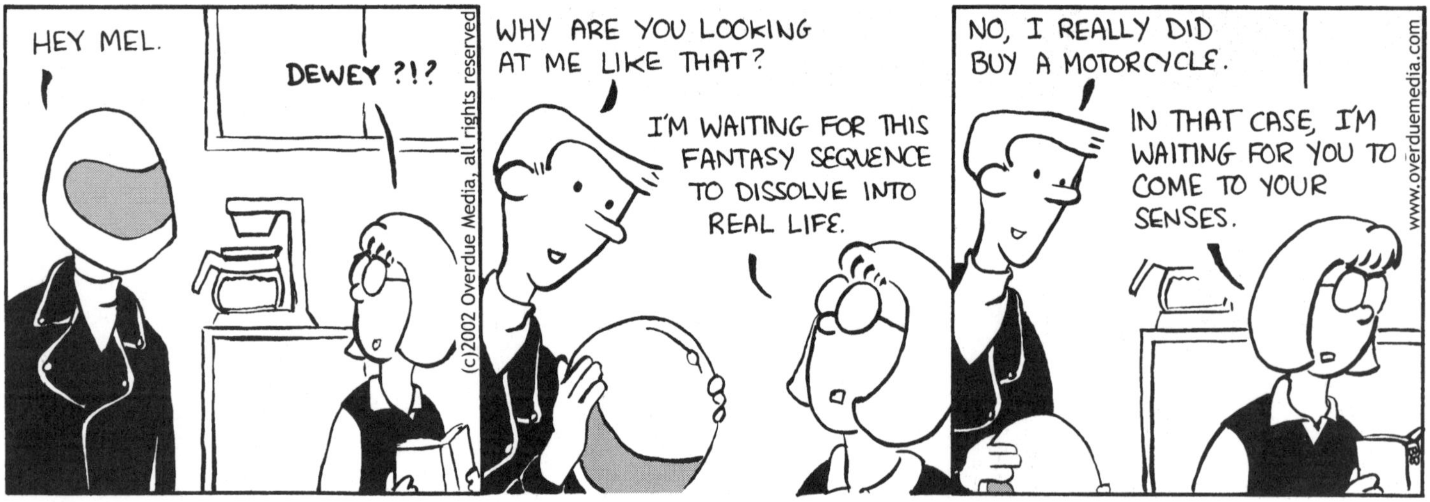
HEY MEL.
DEWEY ?!?
(c)2002 Overdue Media, all rights reserved
WHY ARE YOU LOOKING AT ME LIKE THAT?
I'M WAITING FOR THIS FANTASY SEQUENCE TO DISSOLVE INTO REAL LIFE.
NO, I REALLY DID BUY A MOTORCYCLE.
IN THAT CASE, I'M WAITING FOR YOU TO COME TO YOUR SENSES.
www.overduemedia.com
BB

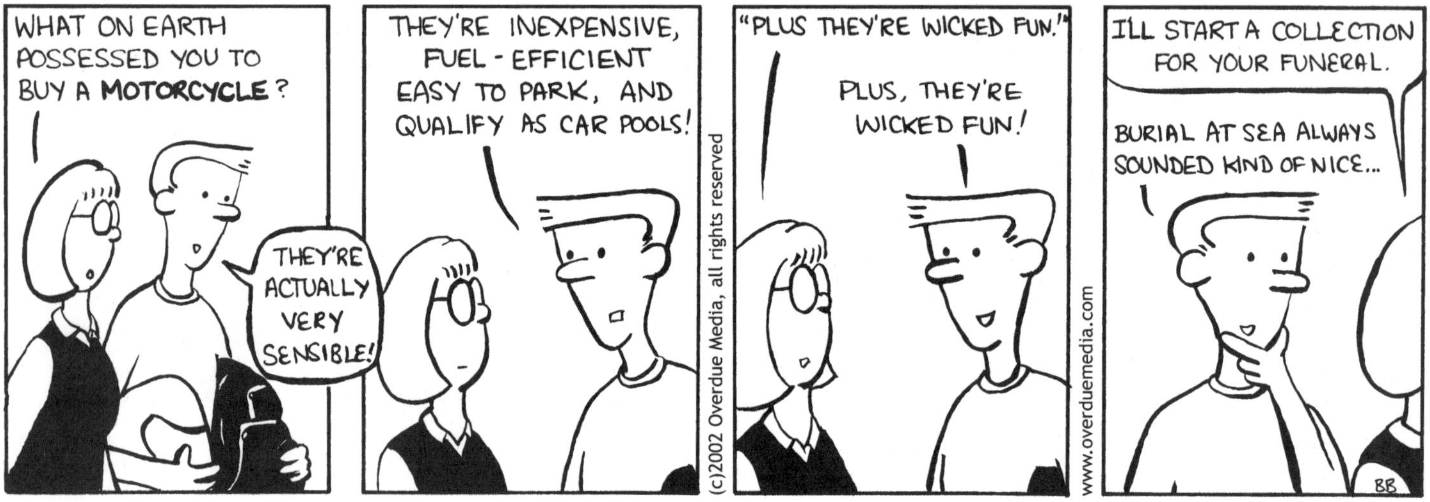
WHAT ON EARTH POSSESSED YOU TO BUY A **MOTORCYCLE**?
THEY'RE ACTUALLY VERY SENSIBLE!
THEY'RE INEXPENSIVE, FUEL-EFFICIENT EASY TO PARK, AND QUALIFY AS CAR POOLS!
(c)2002 Overdue Media, all rights reserved
"PLUS THEY'RE WICKED FUN."
PLUS, THEY'RE WICKED FUN!
www.overduemedia.com
I'LL START A COLLECTION FOR YOUR FUNERAL.
BURIAL AT SEA ALWAYS SOUNDED KIND OF NICE...
BB

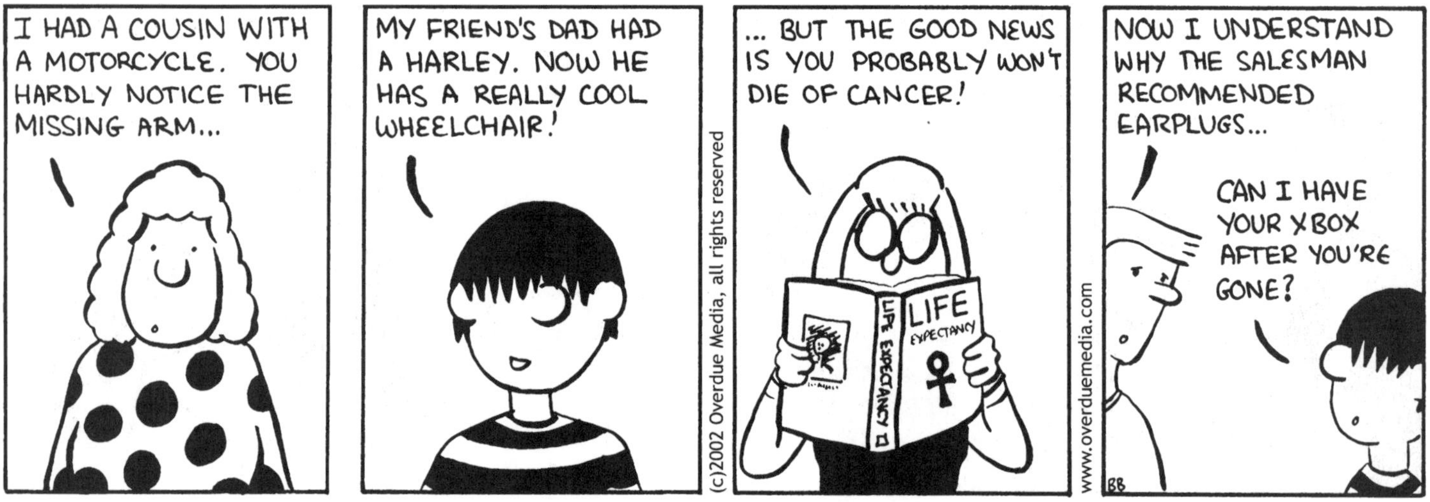
I HAD A COUSIN WITH A MOTORCYCLE. YOU HARDLY NOTICE THE MISSING ARM...
MY FRIEND'S DAD HAD A HARLEY. NOW HE HAS A REALLY COOL WHEELCHAIR!
(c)2002 Overdue Media, all rights reserved
... BUT THE GOOD NEWS IS YOU PROBABLY WON'T DIE OF CANCER!
LIFE EXPECTANCY
www.overduemedia.com
NOW I UNDERSTAND WHY THE SALESMAN RECOMMENDED EARPLUGS...
CAN I HAVE YOUR XBOX AFTER YOU'RE GONE?
BB

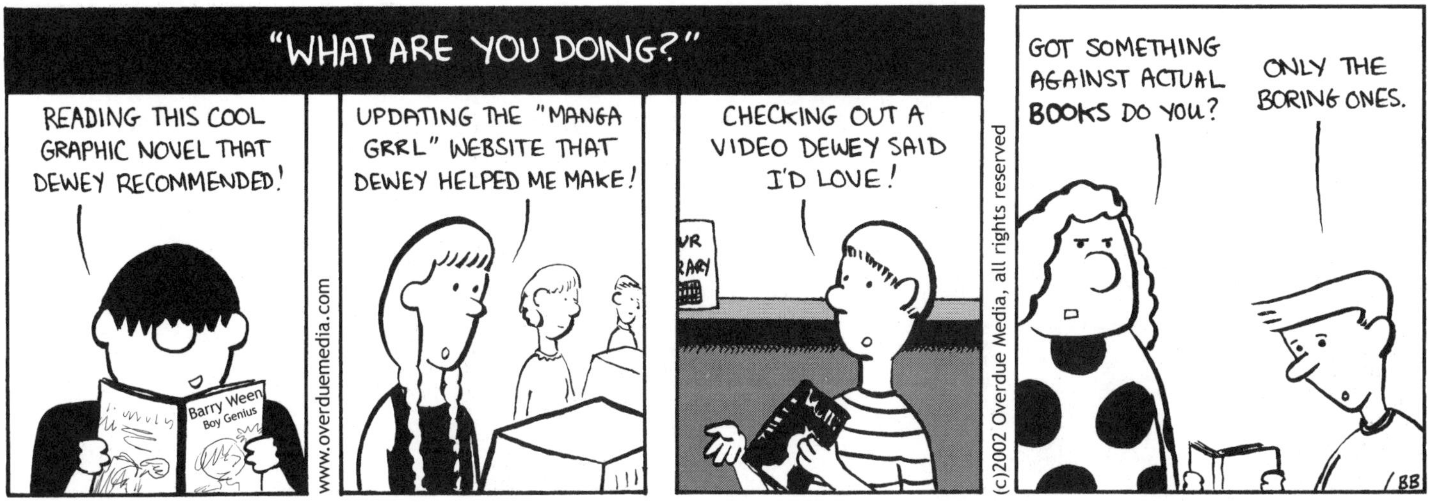
"WHAT ARE YOU DOING?"
READING THIS COOL GRAPHIC NOVEL THAT DEWEY RECOMMENDED!
Barry Ween Boy Genius
UPDATING THE "MANGA GRRL" WEBSITE THAT DEWEY HELPED ME MAKE!
CHECKING OUT A VIDEO DEWEY SAID I'D LOVE!
GOT SOMETHING AGAINST ACTUAL **BOOKS** DO YOU?
ONLY THE BORING ONES.
www.overduemedia.com
(c)2002 Overdue Media, all rights reserved
BB

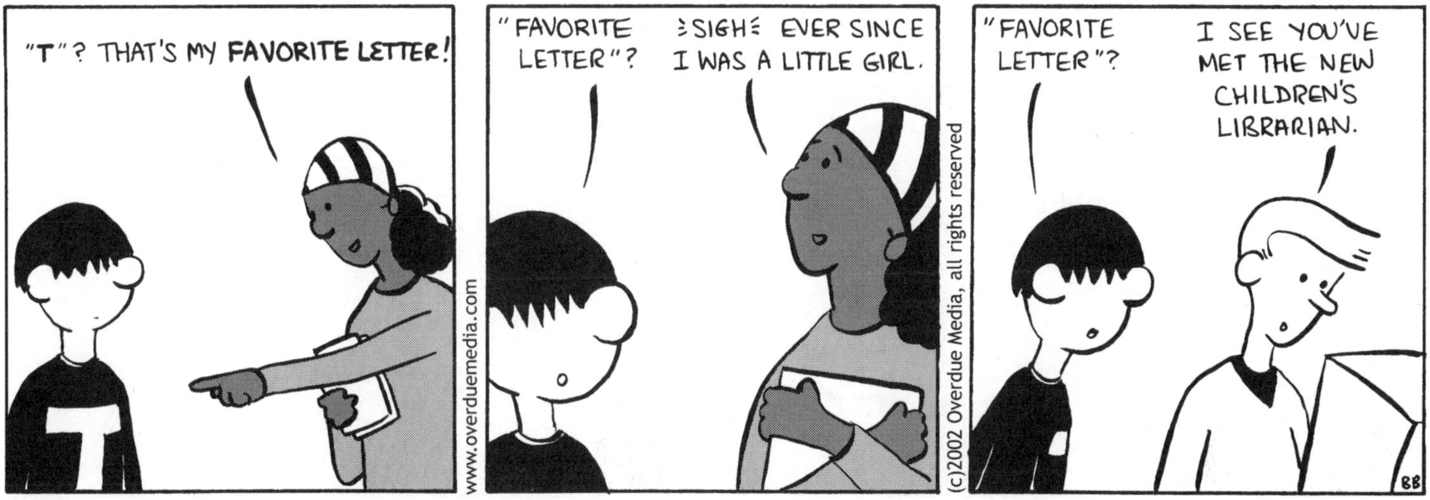
"**T**"? THAT'S MY **FAVORITE LETTER**!
"FAVORITE LETTER"?
⋛SIGH⋚ EVER SINCE I WAS A LITTLE GIRL.
"FAVORITE LETTER"?
I SEE YOU'VE MET THE NEW CHILDREN'S LIBRARIAN.
www.overduemedia.com
(c)2002 Overdue Media, all rights reserved
BB

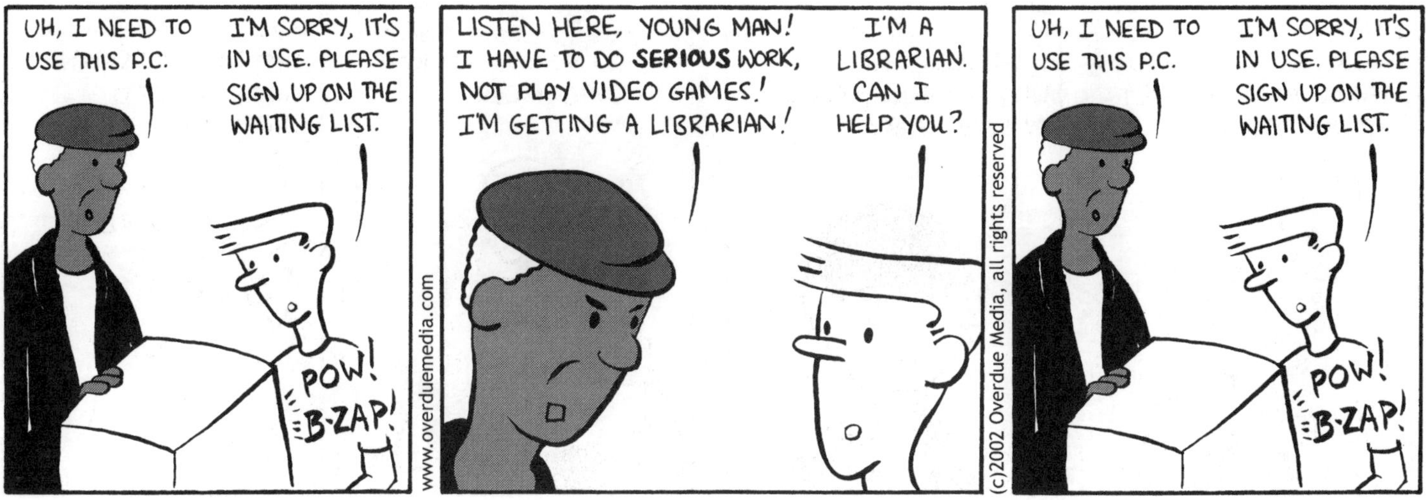
UH, I NEED TO USE THIS P.C.
I'M SORRY, IT'S IN USE. PLEASE SIGN UP ON THE WAITING LIST.
POW! B-ZAP!
LISTEN HERE, YOUNG MAN! I HAVE TO DO **SERIOUS** WORK, NOT PLAY VIDEO GAMES! I'M GETTING A LIBRARIAN!
I'M A LIBRARIAN. CAN I HELP YOU?
UH, I NEED TO USE THIS P.C.
I'M SORRY, IT'S IN USE. PLEASE SIGN UP ON THE WAITING LIST.
POW! B-ZAP!
www.overduemedia.com
(c)2002 Overdue Media, all rights reserved

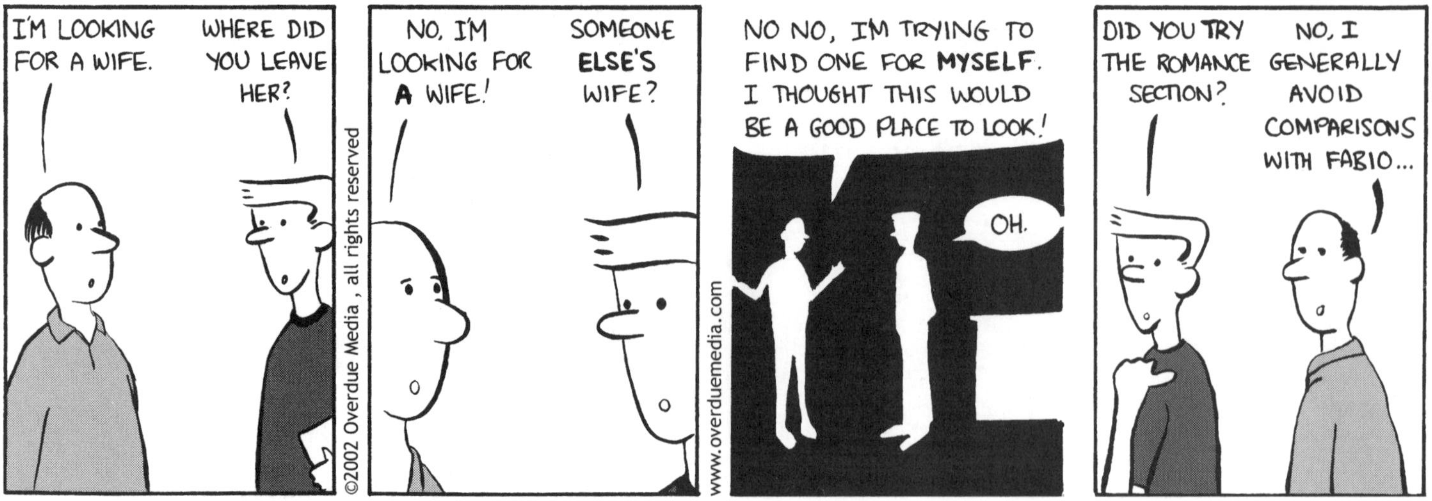
I'M LOOKING FOR A WIFE.
WHERE DID YOU LEAVE HER?
©2002 Overdue Media , all rights reserved
NO, I'M LOOKING FOR **A** WIFE!
SOMEONE **ELSE'S** WIFE?
www.overduemedia.com
NO NO, I'M TRYING TO FIND ONE FOR **MYSELF**. I THOUGHT THIS WOULD BE A GOOD PLACE TO LOOK!
OH.
DID YOU **TRY** THE ROMANCE SECTION?
NO, I GENERALLY AVOID COMPARISONS WITH FABIO...

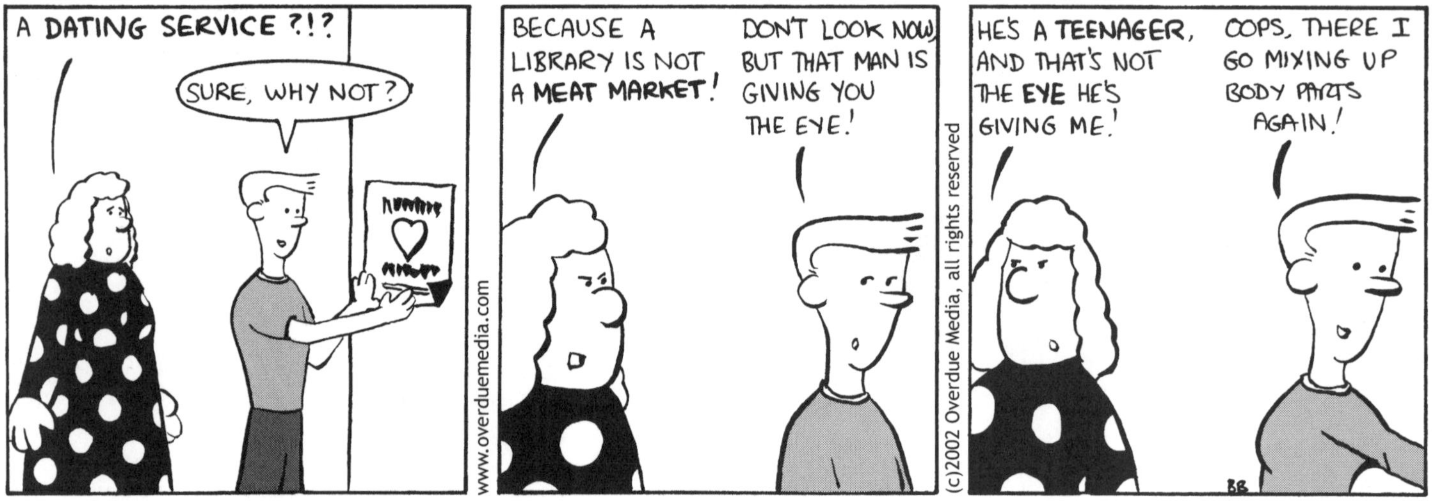
A **DATING SERVICE** ?!?
SURE, WHY NOT?
www.overduemedia.com
BECAUSE A LIBRARY IS NOT A **MEAT MARKET**!
DON'T LOOK NOW, BUT THAT MAN IS GIVING YOU THE EYE!
(c)2002 Overdue Media, all rights reserved
HE'S A **TEENAGER**, AND THAT'S NOT THE **EYE** HE'S GIVING ME!
OOPS, THERE I GO MIXING UP BODY PARTS AGAIN!
BB

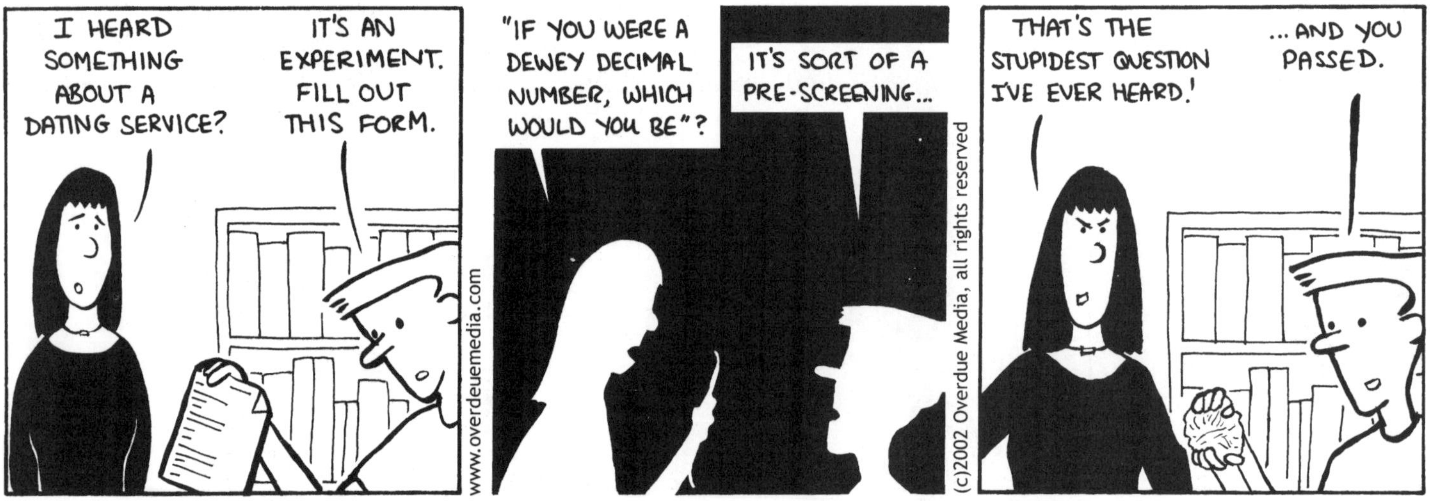
I HEARD SOMETHING ABOUT A DATING SERVICE?
IT'S AN EXPERIMENT. FILL OUT THIS FORM.
www.overduemedia.com
"IF YOU WERE A DEWEY DECIMAL NUMBER, WHICH WOULD YOU BE"?
IT'S SORT OF A PRE-SCREENING...
(c)2002 Overdue Media, all rights reserved
THAT'S THE STUPIDEST QUESTION I'VE EVER HEARD!
...AND YOU PASSED.

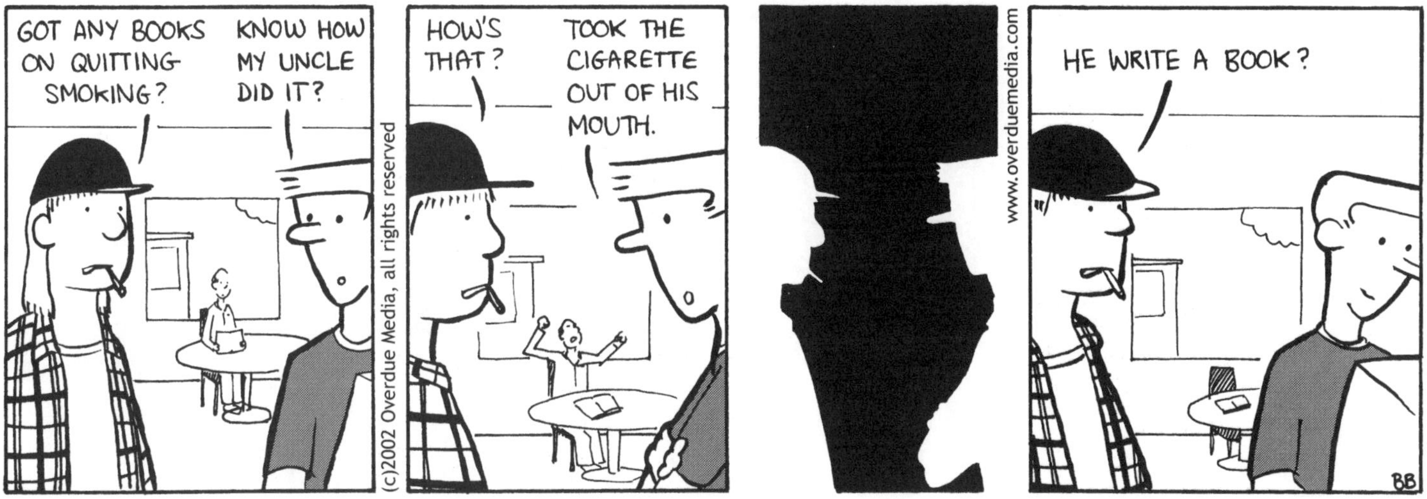
GOT ANY BOOKS ON QUITTING SMOKING?
KNOW HOW MY UNCLE DID IT?
(c)2002 Overdue Media, all rights reserved
HOW'S THAT?
TOOK THE CIGARETTE OUT OF HIS MOUTH.
www.overduemedia.com
HE WRITE A BOOK?
BB

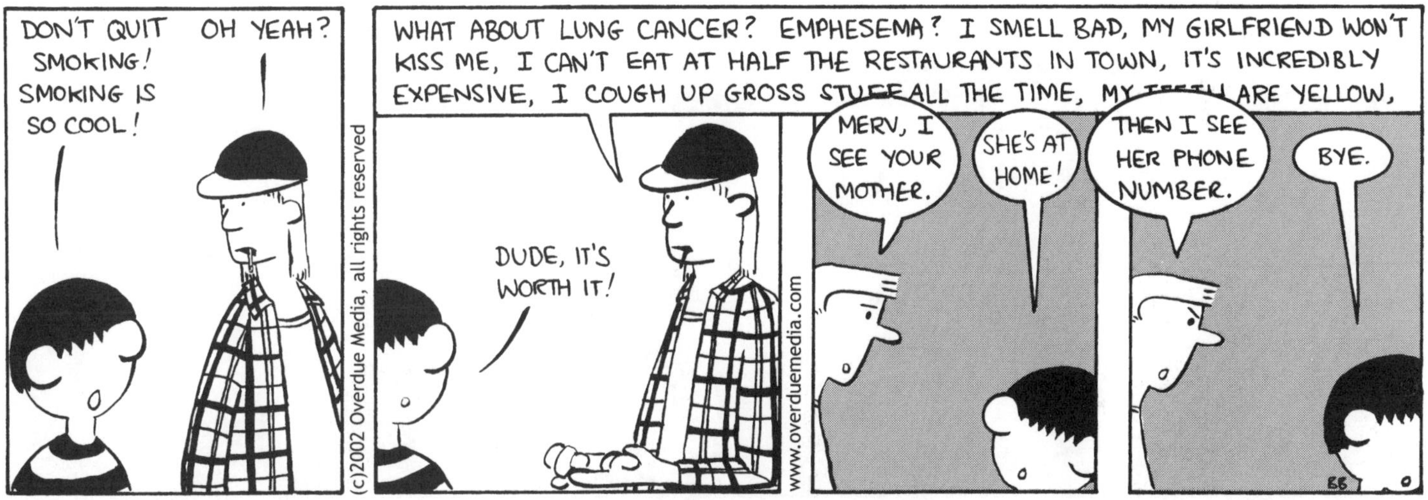
DON'T QUIT SMOKING! SMOKING IS SO COOL!
OH YEAH?
(c)2002 Overdue Media, all rights reserved
WHAT ABOUT LUNG CANCER? EMPHESEMA? I SMELL BAD, MY GIRLFRIEND WON'T KISS ME, I CAN'T EAT AT HALF THE RESTAURANTS IN TOWN, IT'S INCREDIBLY EXPENSIVE, I COUGH UP GROSS ALL THE TIME, MY ARE YELLOW,
DUDE, IT'S WORTH IT!
www.overduemedia.com
MERV, I SEE YOUR MOTHER.
SHE'S AT HOME!
THEN I SEE HER PHONE NUMBER.
BYE.
BB

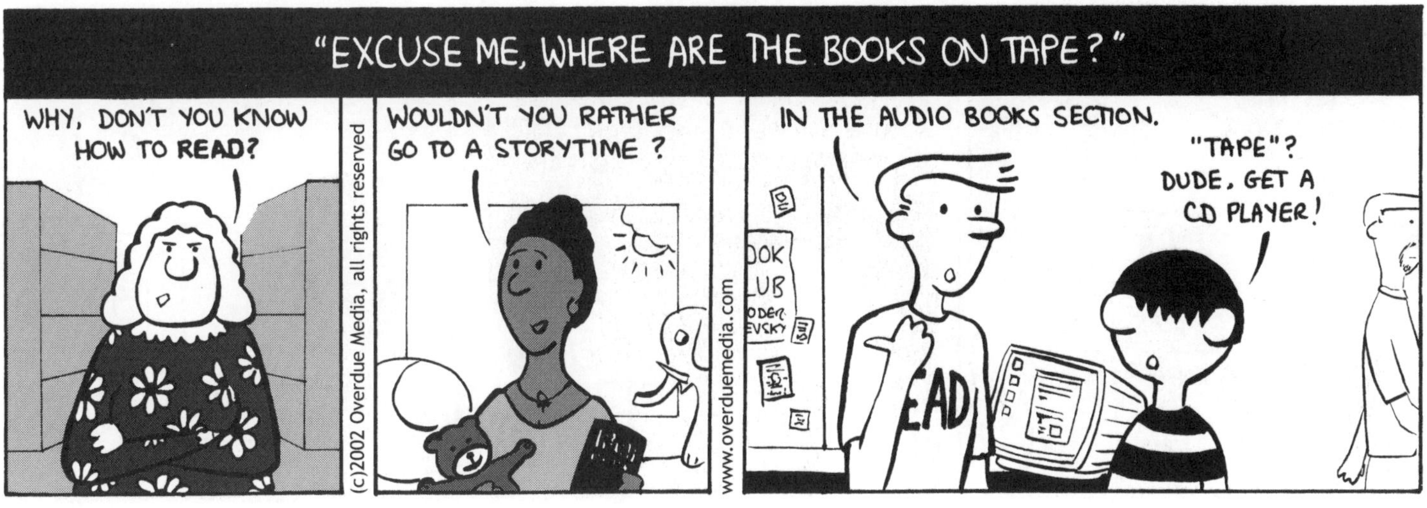
"EXCUSE ME, WHERE ARE THE BOOKS ON TAPE?"
WHY, DON'T YOU KNOW HOW TO READ?
(c)2002 Overdue Media, all rights reserved
WOULDN'T YOU RATHER GO TO A STORYTIME?
www.overduemedia.com
IN THE AUDIO BOOKS SECTION.
"TAPE"? DUDE, GET A CD PLAYER!

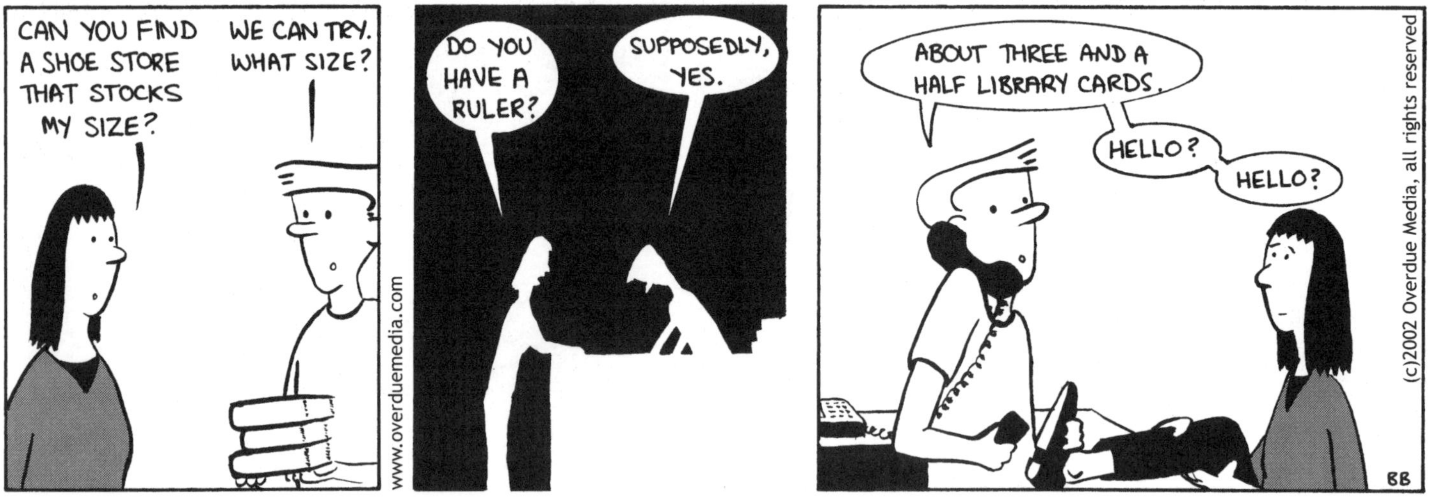
CAN YOU FIND A SHOE STORE THAT STOCKS MY SIZE?
WE CAN TRY. WHAT SIZE?
www.overduemedia.com
DO YOU HAVE A RULER?
SUPPOSEDLY, YES.
ABOUT THREE AND A HALF LIBRARY CARDS.
HELLO?
HELLO?
(c)2002 Overdue Media, all rights reserved
BB

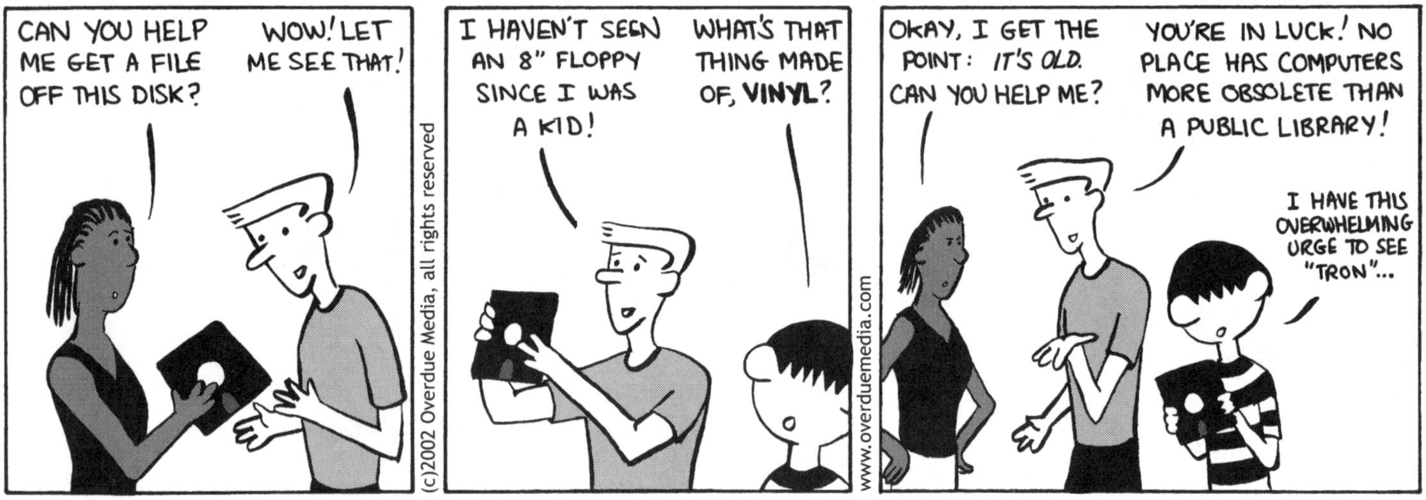
CAN YOU HELP ME GET A FILE OFF THIS DISK?
WOW! LET ME SEE THAT!
(c)2002 Overdue Media, all rights reserved
I HAVEN'T SEEN AN 8" FLOPPY SINCE I WAS A KID!
WHAT'S THAT THING MADE OF, VINYL?
www.overduemedia.com
OKAY, I GET THE POINT: IT'S OLD. CAN YOU HELP ME?
YOU'RE IN LUCK! NO PLACE HAS COMPUTERS MORE OBSOLETE THAN A PUBLIC LIBRARY!
I HAVE THIS OVERWHELMING URGE TO SEE "TRON"...

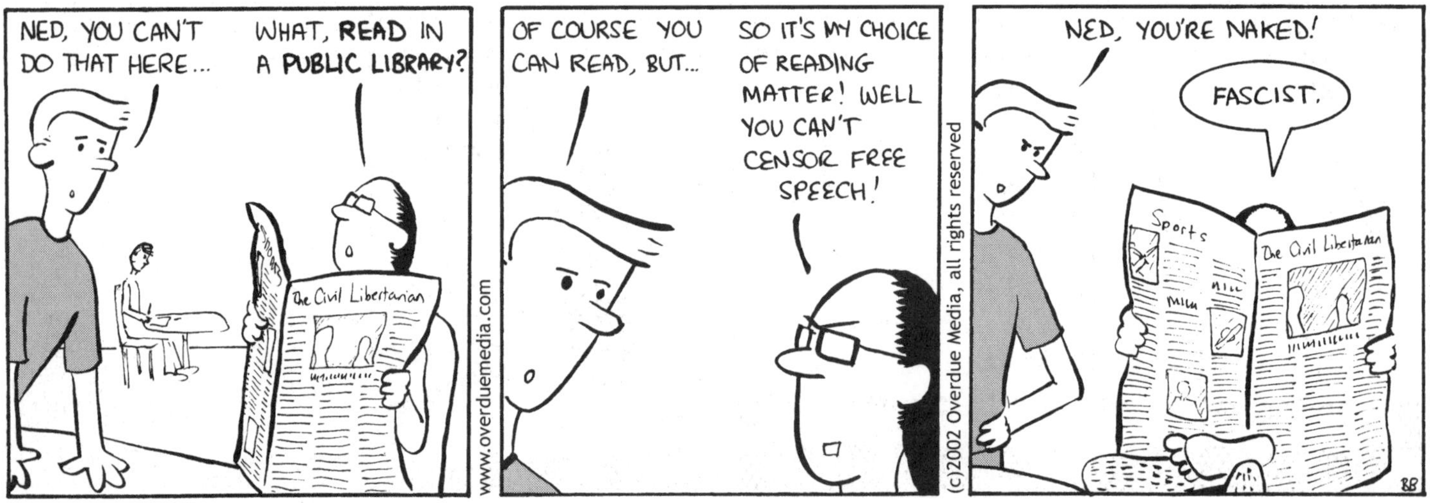
NED, YOU CAN'T DO THAT HERE...
WHAT, READ IN A PUBLIC LIBRARY?
The Civil Libertarian
www.overduemedia.com
OF COURSE YOU CAN READ, BUT...
SO IT'S MY CHOICE OF READING MATTER! WELL YOU CAN'T CENSOR FREE SPEECH!
(c)2002 Overdue Media, all rights reserved
NED, YOU'RE NAKED!
FASCIST.
Sports
The Civil Libertarian
BB

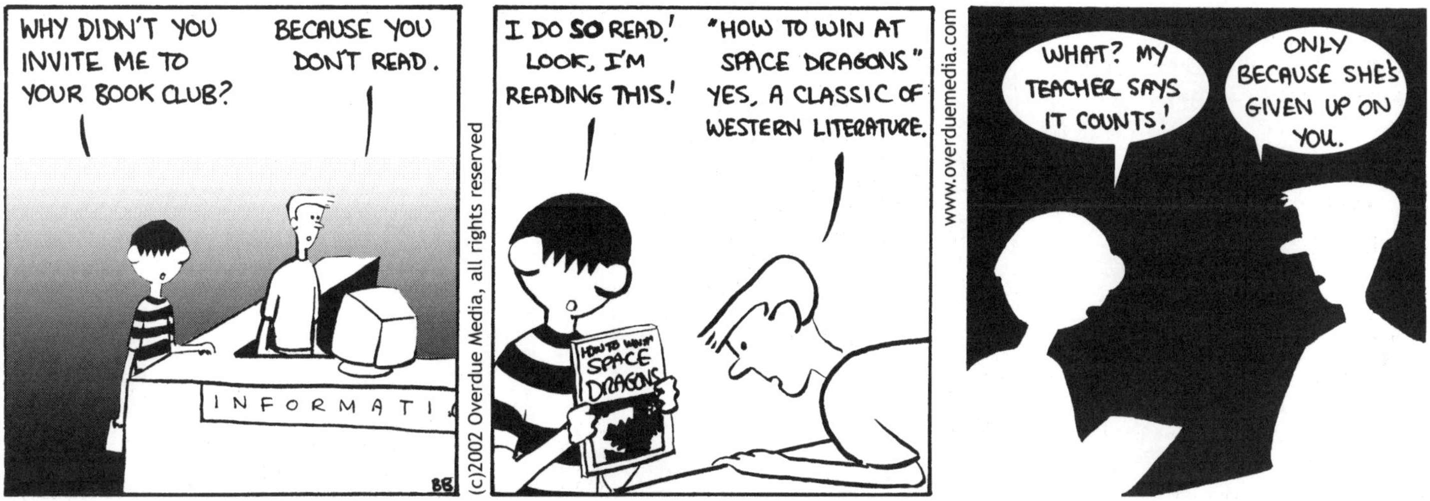
WHY DIDN'T YOU INVITE ME TO YOUR BOOK CLUB?
BECAUSE YOU DON'T READ.
INFORMATI
BB
(c)2002 Overdue Media, all rights reserved
I DO SO READ! LOOK, I'M READING THIS!
HOW TO WIN AT SPACE DRAGONS
"HOW TO WIN AT SPACE DRAGONS" YES, A CLASSIC OF WESTERN LITERATURE.
www.overduemedia.com
WHAT? MY TEACHER SAYS IT COUNTS!
ONLY BECAUSE SHE'S GIVEN UP ON YOU.

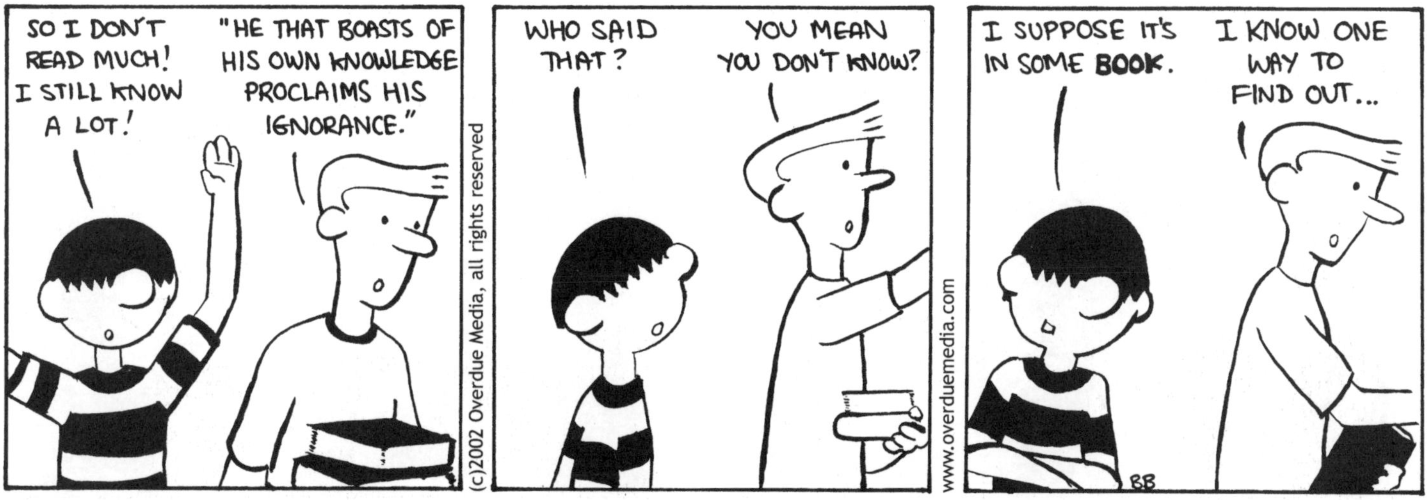
SO I DON'T READ MUCH! I STILL KNOW A LOT!
"HE THAT BOASTS OF HIS OWN KNOWLEDGE PROCLAIMS HIS IGNORANCE."
(c)2002 Overdue Media, all rights reserved
WHO SAID THAT?
YOU MEAN YOU DON'T KNOW?
www.overduemedia.com
I SUPPOSE IT'S IN SOME BOOK.
I KNOW ONE WAY TO FIND OUT...
BB

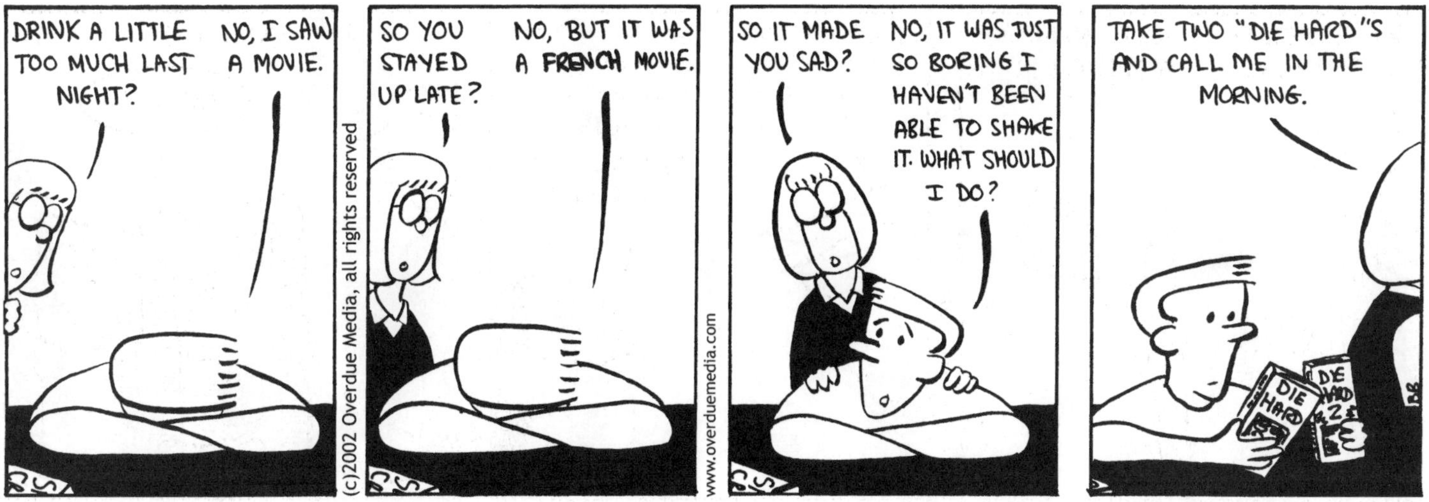
DRINK A LITTLE TOO MUCH LAST NIGHT?
NO, I SAW A MOVIE.
(c)2002 Overdue Media, all rights reserved
SO YOU STAYED UP LATE?
NO, BUT IT WAS A FRENCH MOVIE.
www.overduemedia.com
SO IT MADE YOU SAD?
NO, IT WAS JUST SO BORING I HAVEN'T BEEN ABLE TO SHAKE IT. WHAT SHOULD I DO?
TAKE TWO "DIE HARD"S AND CALL ME IN THE MORNING.
DIE HARD
DIE HARD 2
BB

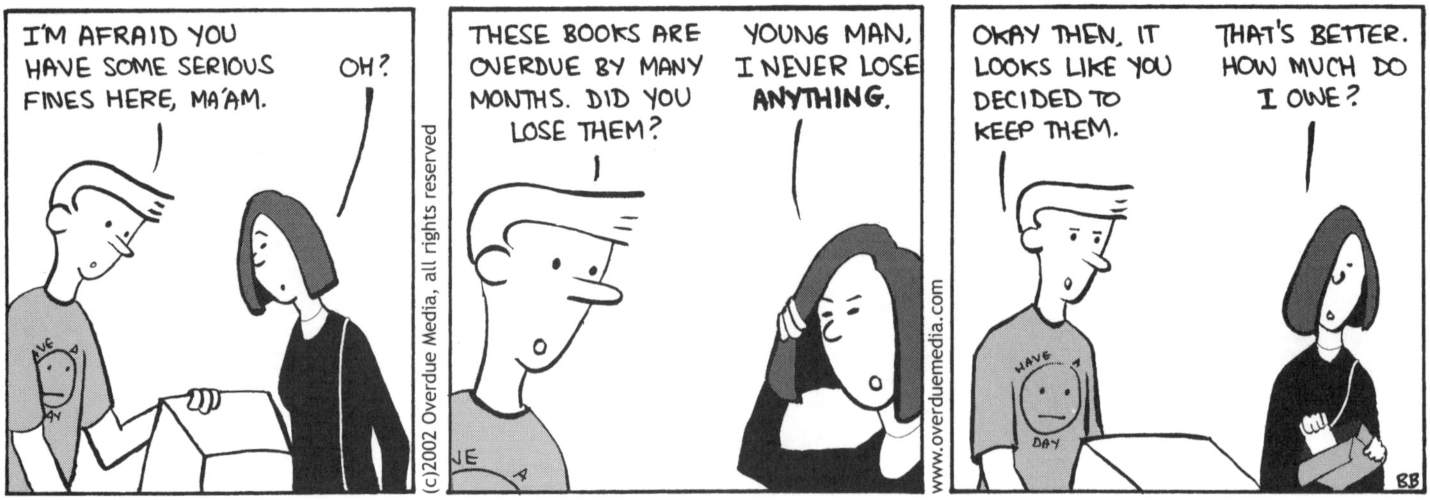
I'M AFRAID YOU HAVE SOME SERIOUS FINES HERE, MA'AM.
OH?
THESE BOOKS ARE OVERDUE BY MANY MONTHS. DID YOU LOSE THEM?
YOUNG MAN, I NEVER LOSE **ANYTHING**.
OKAY THEN, IT LOOKS LIKE YOU DECIDED TO KEEP THEM.
THAT'S BETTER. HOW MUCH DO I OWE?
BB

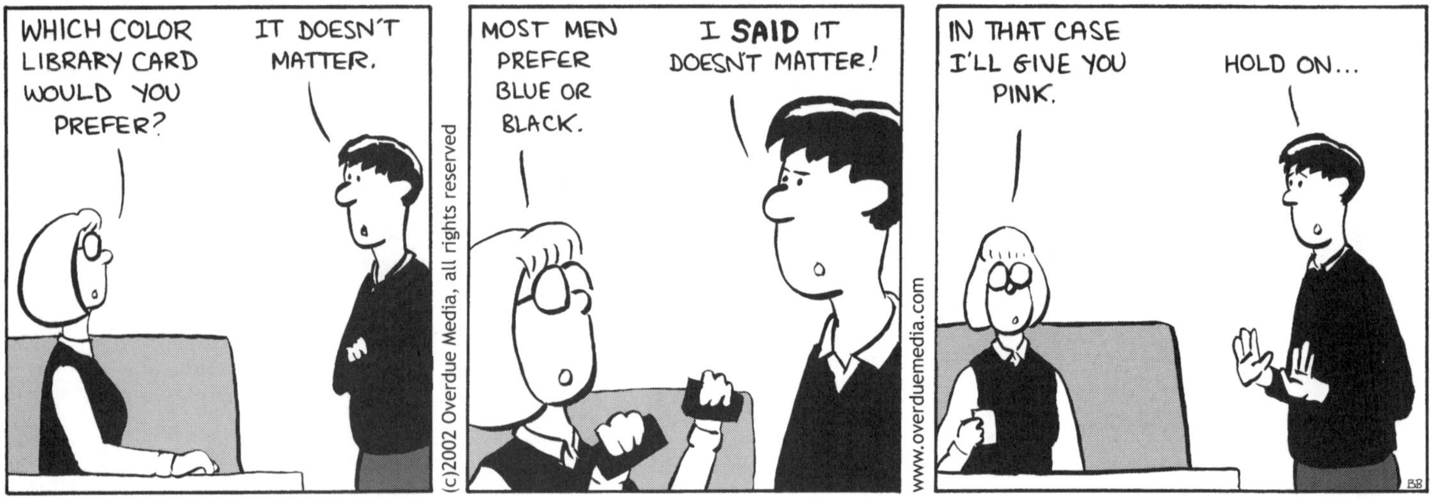
WHICH COLOR LIBRARY CARD WOULD YOU PREFER?
IT DOESN'T MATTER.
MOST MEN PREFER BLUE OR BLACK.
I **SAID** IT DOESN'T MATTER!
IN THAT CASE I'LL GIVE YOU PINK.
HOLD ON...
BB

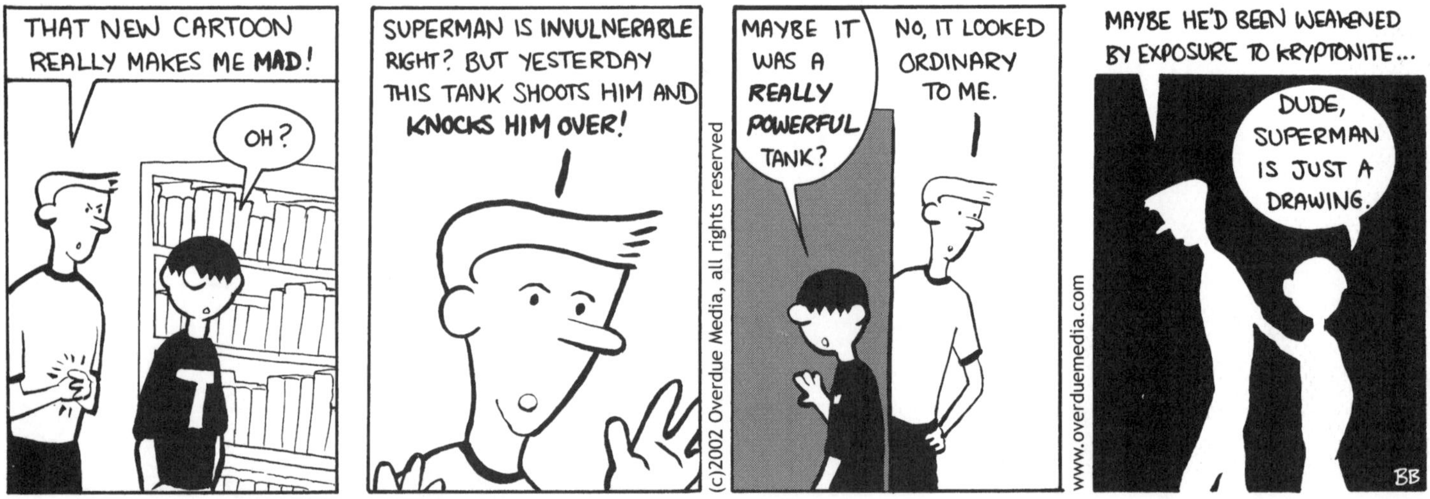
THAT NEW CARTOON REALLY MAKES ME **MAD**!
OH?
SUPERMAN IS **INVULNERABLE** RIGHT? BUT YESTERDAY THIS TANK SHOOTS HIM AND **KNOCKS HIM OVER**!
MAYBE IT WAS A ***REALLY POWERFUL*** TANK?
NO, IT LOOKED ORDINARY TO ME.
MAYBE HE'D BEEN WEAKENED BY EXPOSURE TO KRYPTONITE...
DUDE, SUPERMAN IS JUST A DRAWING.
BB

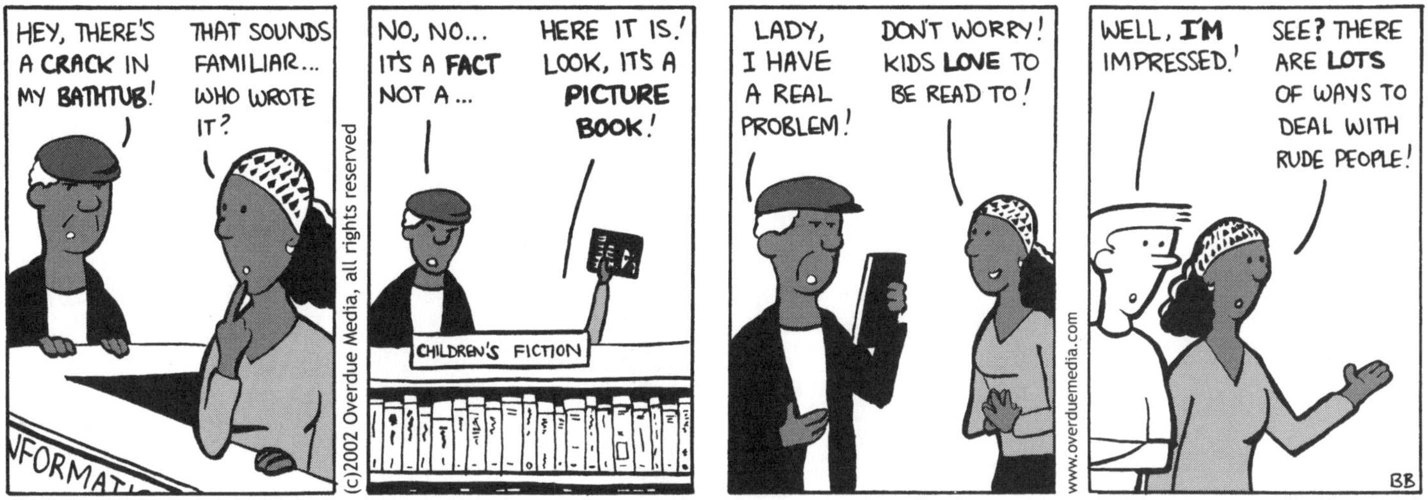
HEY, THERE'S A **CRACK** IN MY **BATHTUB**!
THAT SOUNDS FAMILIAR... WHO WROTE IT?
NO, NO... IT'S A **FACT** NOT A ...
HERE IT IS! LOOK, IT'S A **PICTURE BOOK**!
CHILDREN'S FICTION
LADY, I HAVE A REAL PROBLEM!
DON'T WORRY! KIDS **LOVE** TO BE READ TO!
WELL, **I'M** IMPRESSED!
SEE? THERE ARE **LOTS** OF WAYS TO DEAL WITH RUDE PEOPLE!
BB
(c)2002 Overdue Media, all rights reserved
www.overduemedia.com

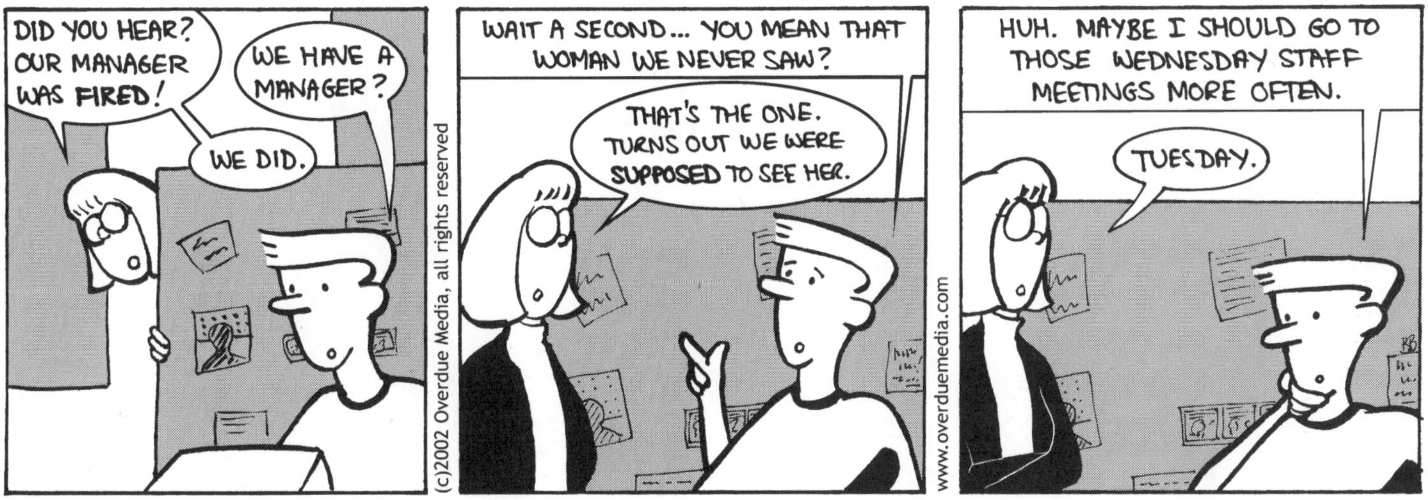
DID YOU HEAR? OUR MANAGER WAS **FIRED**!
WE HAVE A MANAGER?
WE DID.
WAIT A SECOND... YOU MEAN THAT WOMAN WE NEVER SAW?
THAT'S THE ONE. TURNS OUT WE WERE **SUPPOSED** TO SEE HER.
HUH. MAYBE I SHOULD GO TO THOSE WEDNESDAY STAFF MEETINGS MORE OFTEN.
TUESDAY.
BB
(c)2002 Overdue Media, all rights reserved
www.overduemedia.com

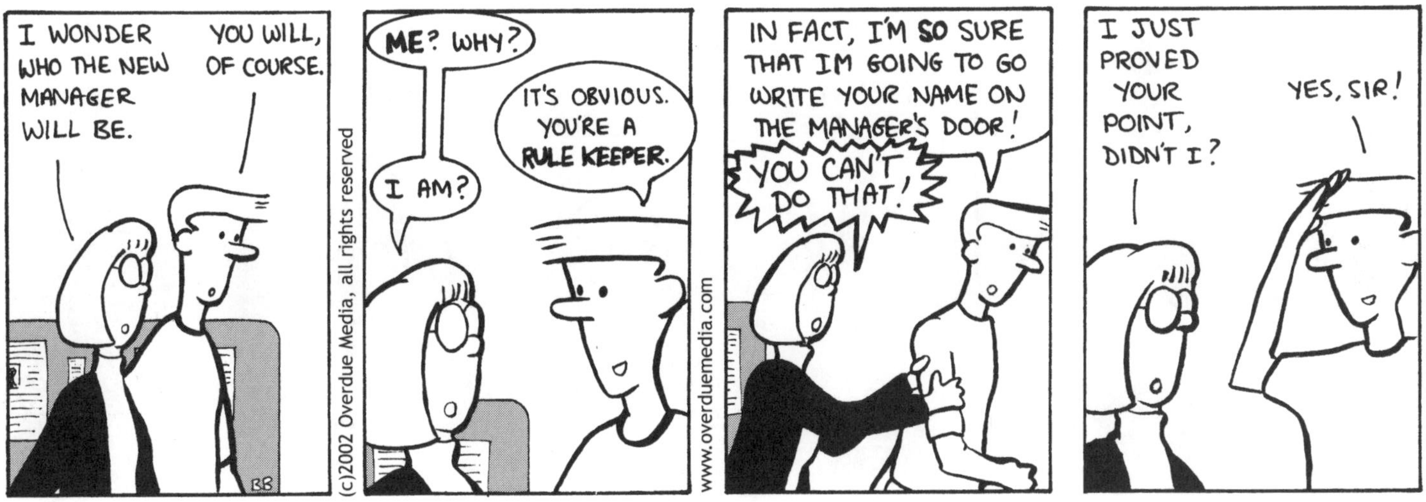
I WONDER WHO THE NEW MANAGER WILL BE.
YOU WILL, OF COURSE.
BB
ME? WHY?
I AM?
IT'S OBVIOUS. YOU'RE A **RULE KEEPER**.
IN FACT, I'M **SO** SURE THAT IM GOING TO GO WRITE YOUR NAME ON THE MANAGER'S DOOR!
YOU CAN'T DO THAT!
I JUST PROVED YOUR POINT, DIDN'T I?
YES, SIR!
(c)2002 Overdue Media, all rights reserved
www.overduemedia.com

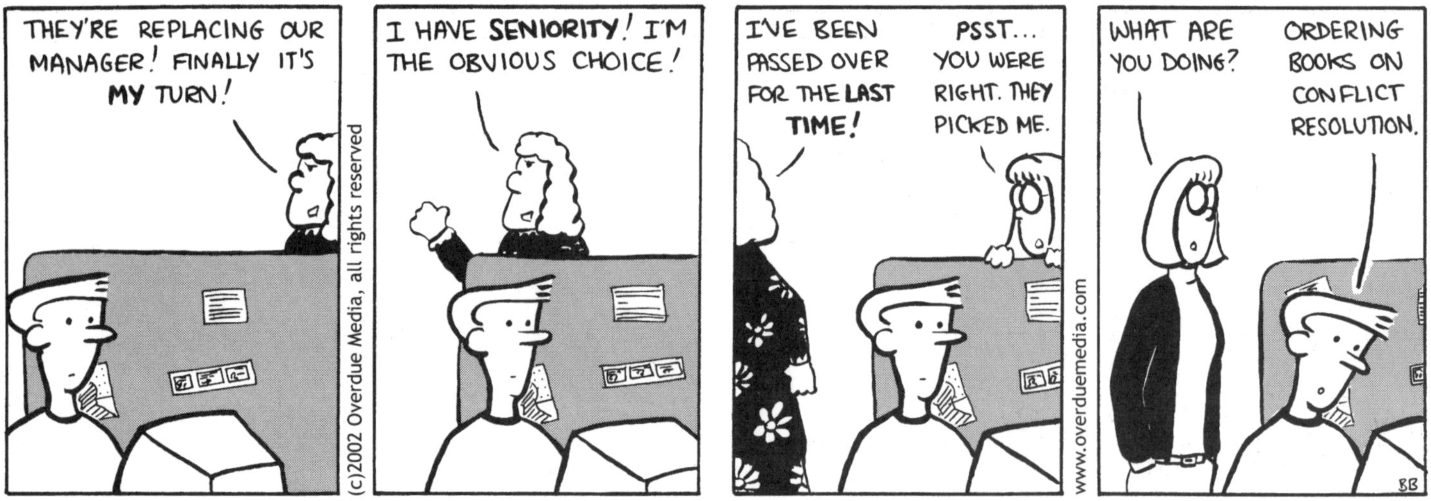
THEY'RE REPLACING OUR MANAGER! FINALLY IT'S **MY** TURN!
I HAVE **SENIORITY**! I'M THE OBVIOUS CHOICE!
I'VE BEEN PASSED OVER FOR THE **LAST TIME**!
PSST... YOU WERE RIGHT. THEY PICKED ME.
WHAT ARE YOU DOING?
ORDERING BOOKS ON CONFLICT RESOLUTION.
(c)2002 Overdue Media, all rights reserved
www.overduemedia.com
BB

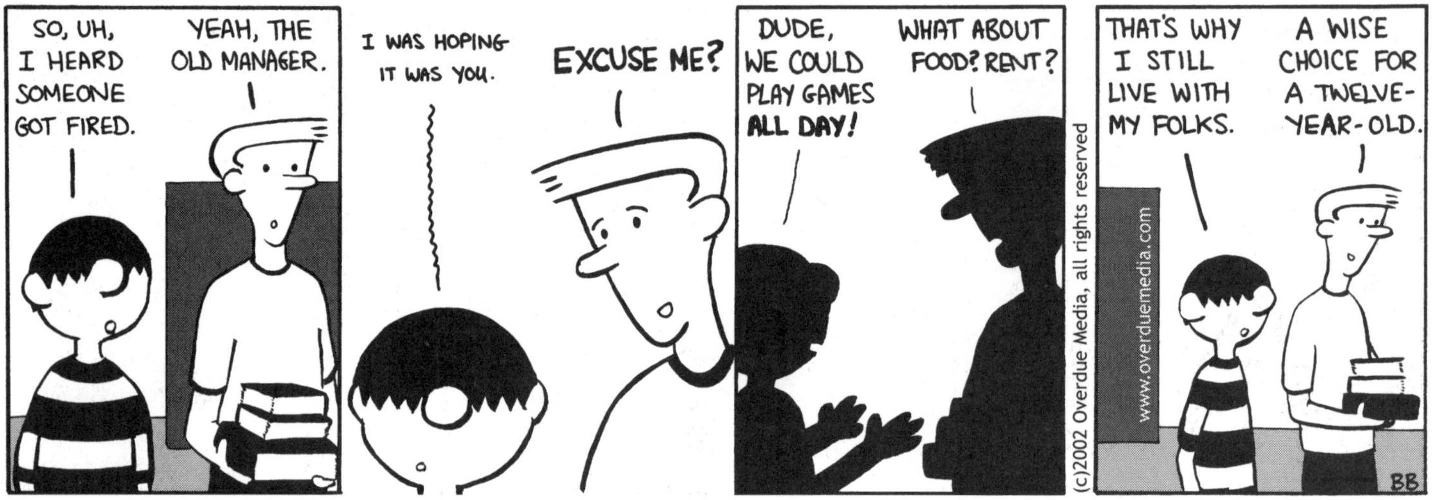
SO, UH, I HEARD SOMEONE GOT FIRED.
YEAH, THE OLD MANAGER.
I WAS HOPING IT WAS YOU.
EXCUSE ME?
DUDE, WE COULD PLAY GAMES **ALL DAY**!
WHAT ABOUT FOOD? RENT?
THAT'S WHY I STILL LIVE WITH MY FOLKS.
A WISE CHOICE FOR A TWELVE-YEAR-OLD.
(c)2002 Overdue Media, all rights reserved
www.overduemedia.com
BB

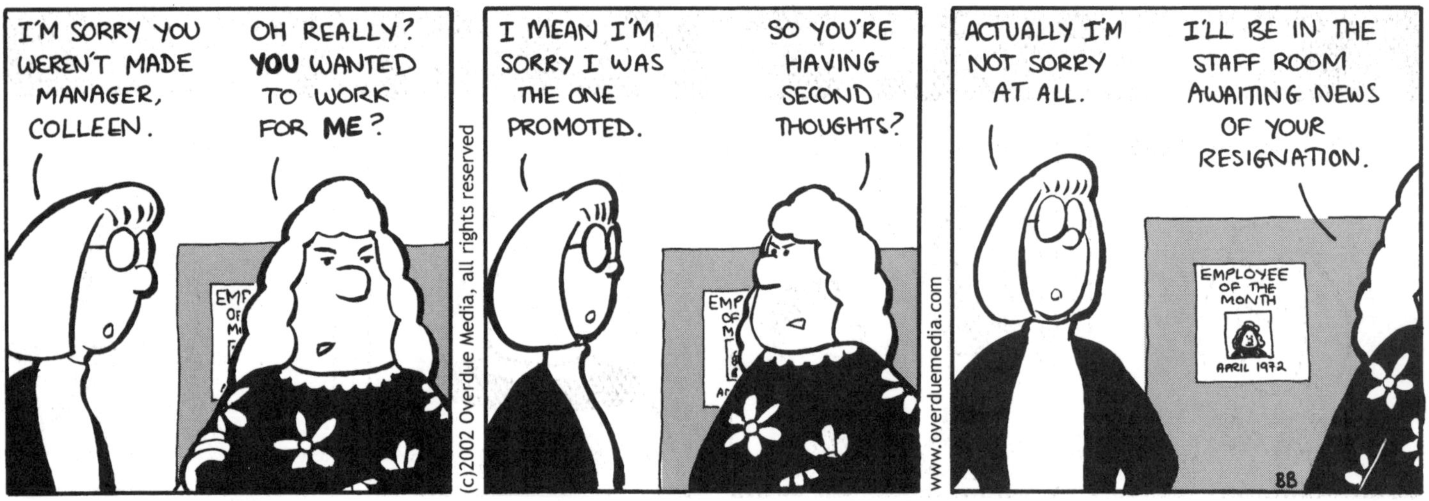
I'M SORRY YOU WEREN'T MADE MANAGER, COLLEEN.
OH REALLY? **YOU** WANTED TO WORK FOR **ME**?
I MEAN I'M SORRY I WAS THE ONE PROMOTED.
SO YOU'RE HAVING SECOND THOUGHTS?
ACTUALLY I'M NOT SORRY AT ALL.
I'LL BE IN THE STAFF ROOM AWAITING NEWS OF YOUR RESIGNATION.
EMPLOYEE OF THE MONTH
APRIL 1972
(c)2002 Overdue Media, all rights reserved
www.overduemedia.com
BB

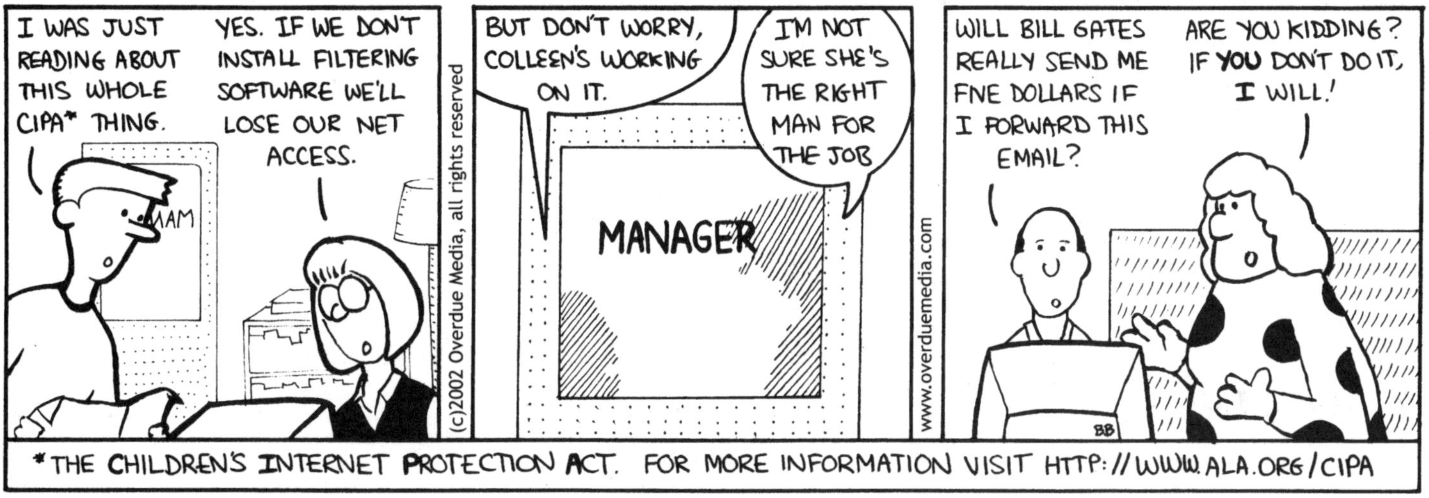
I WAS JUST READING ABOUT THIS WHOLE CIPA* THING.
YES. IF WE DON'T INSTALL FILTERING SOFTWARE WE'LL LOSE OUR NET ACCESS.
(c)2002 Overdue Media, all rights reserved
BUT DON'T WORRY, COLLEEN'S WORKING ON IT.
I'M NOT SURE SHE'S THE RIGHT MAN FOR THE JOB
MANAGER
www.overduemedia.com
WILL BILL GATES REALLY SEND ME FIVE DOLLARS IF I FORWARD THIS EMAIL?
ARE YOU KIDDING? IF YOU DON'T DO IT, I WILL!
BB
* THE CHILDREN'S INTERNET PROTECTION ACT. FOR MORE INFORMATION VISIT HTTP://WWW.ALA.ORG/CIPA

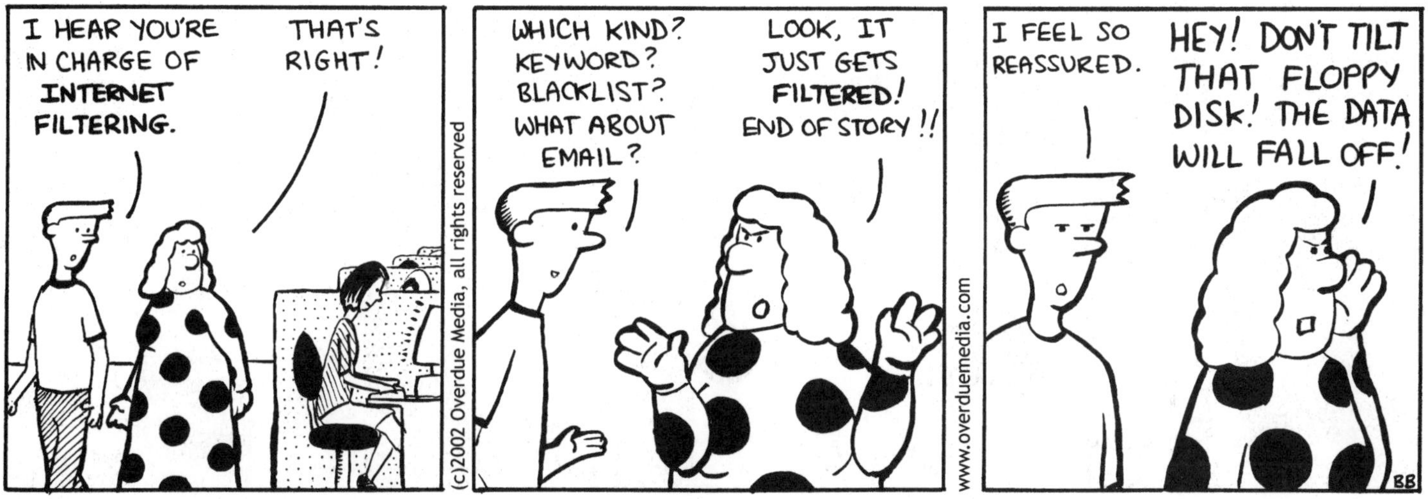
I HEAR YOU'RE IN CHARGE OF INTERNET FILTERING.
THAT'S RIGHT!
(c)2002 Overdue Media, all rights reserved
WHICH KIND? KEYWORD? BLACKLIST? WHAT ABOUT EMAIL?
LOOK, IT JUST GETS FILTERED! END OF STORY!!
www.overduemedia.com
I FEEL SO REASSURED.
HEY! DON'T TILT THAT FLOPPY DISK! THE DATA WILL FALL OFF!
BB

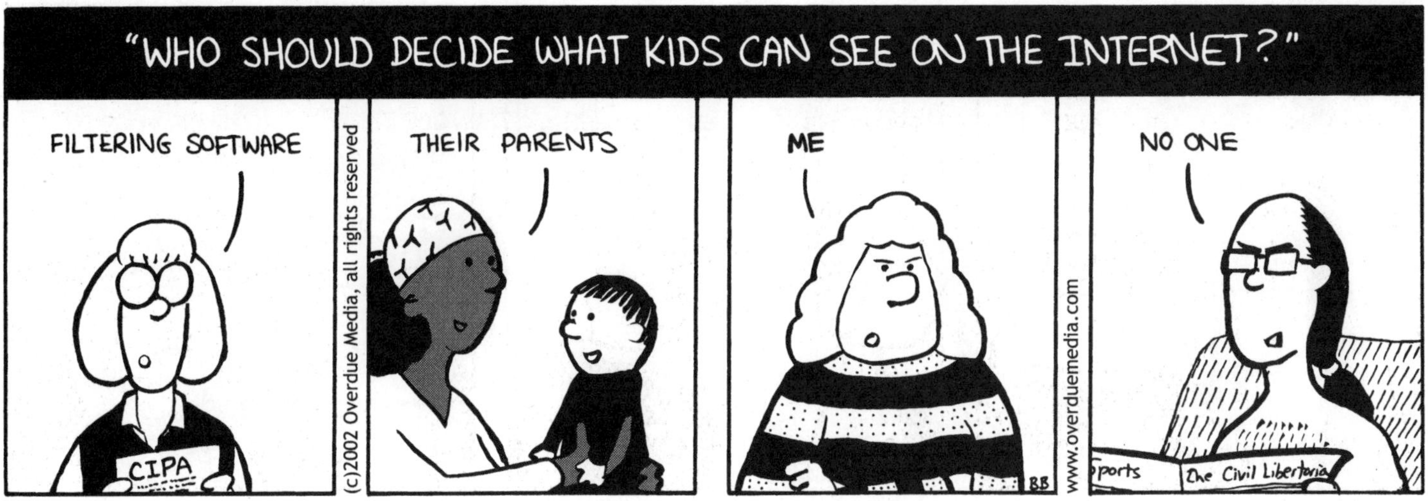
"WHO SHOULD DECIDE WHAT KIDS CAN SEE ON THE INTERNET?"
FILTERING SOFTWARE
CIPA
(c)2002 Overdue Media, all rights reserved
THEIR PARENTS
ME
BB
www.overduemedia.com
NO ONE

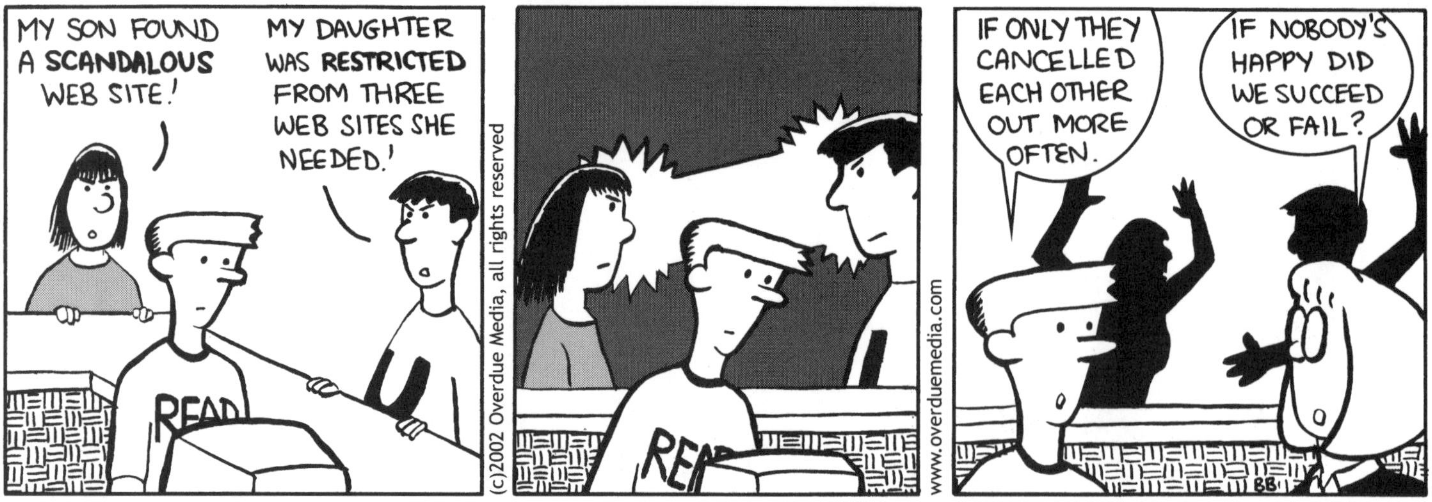
MY SON FOUND A **SCANDALOUS** WEB SITE!
MY DAUGHTER WAS **RESTRICTED** FROM THREE WEB SITES SHE NEEDED!
READ
(c)2002 Overdue Media, all rights reserved
www.overduemedia.com
IF ONLY THEY CANCELLED EACH OTHER OUT MORE OFTEN.
IF NOBODY'S HAPPY DID WE SUCCEED OR FAIL?
BB

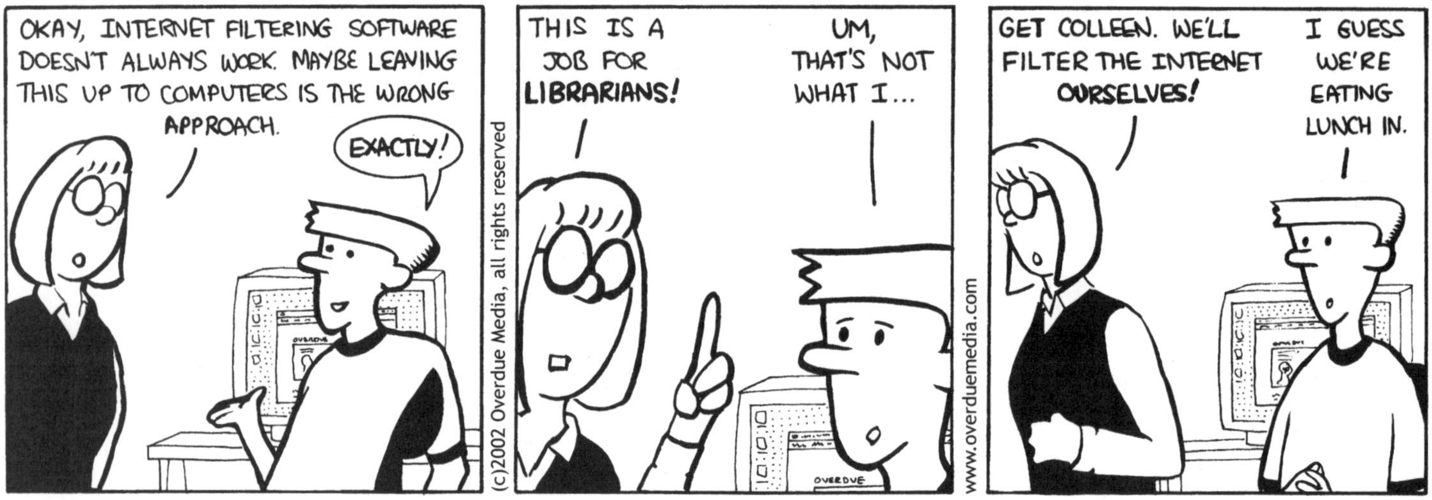
OKAY, INTERNET FILTERING SOFTWARE DOESN'T ALWAYS WORK. MAYBE LEAVING THIS UP TO COMPUTERS IS THE WRONG APPROACH.
EXACTLY!
(c)2002 Overdue Media, all rights reserved
THIS IS A JOB FOR **LIBRARIANS!**
UM, THAT'S NOT WHAT I...
www.overduemedia.com
GET COLLEEN. WE'LL FILTER THE INTERNET **OURSELVES!**
I GUESS WE'RE EATING LUNCH IN.

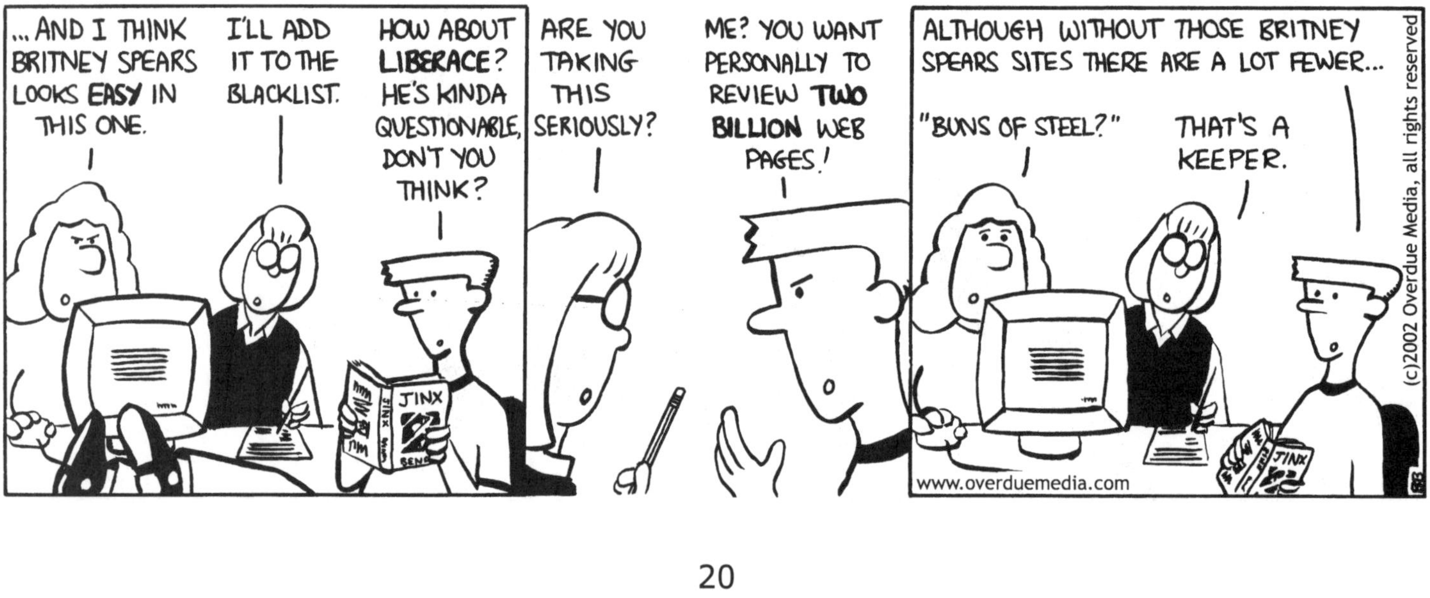
...AND I THINK BRITNEY SPEARS LOOKS **EASY** IN THIS ONE.
I'LL ADD IT TO THE BLACKLIST.
HOW ABOUT **LIBERACE**? HE'S KINDA QUESTIONABLE, DON'T YOU THINK?
JINX
ARE YOU TAKING THIS SERIOUSLY?
ME? YOU WANT PERSONALLY TO REVIEW **TWO BILLION** WEB PAGES!
ALTHOUGH WITHOUT THOSE BRITNEY SPEARS SITES THERE ARE A LOT FEWER...
"BUNS OF STEEL?"
THAT'S A KEEPER.
(c)2002 Overdue Media, all rights reserved
www.overduemedia.com

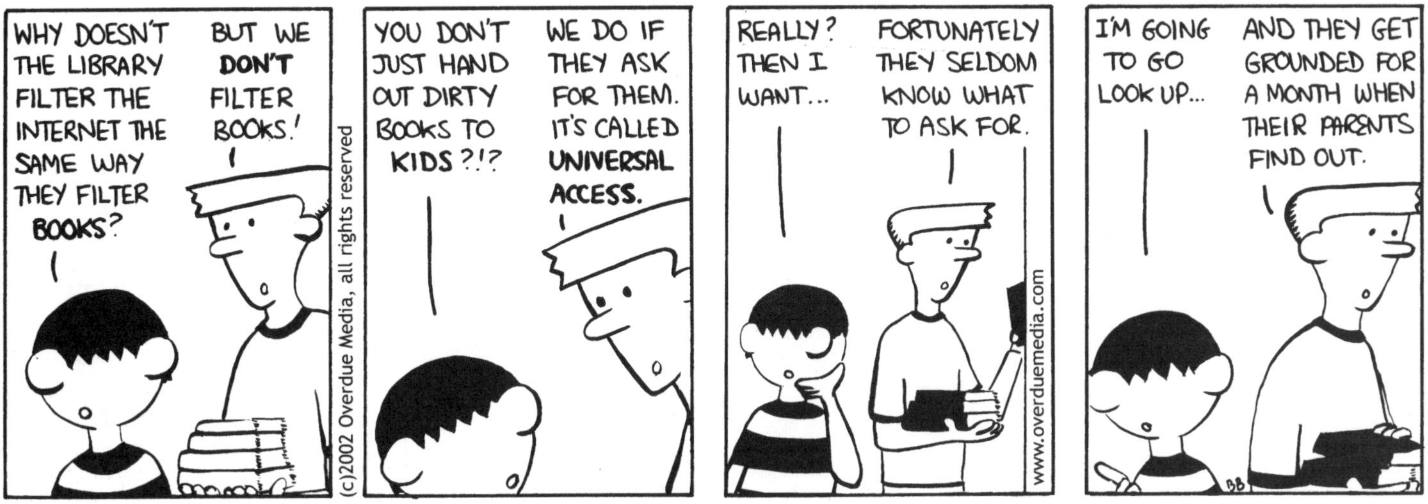
WHY DOESN'T THE LIBRARY FILTER THE INTERNET THE SAME WAY THEY FILTER BOOKS?
BUT WE DON'T FILTER BOOKS!
(c)2002 Overdue Media, all rights reserved
YOU DON'T JUST HAND OUT DIRTY BOOKS TO KIDS?!?
WE DO IF THEY ASK FOR THEM. IT'S CALLED UNIVERSAL ACCESS.
REALLY? THEN I WANT...
FORTUNATELY THEY SELDOM KNOW WHAT TO ASK FOR.
www.overduemedia.com
I'M GOING TO GO LOOK UP...
AND THEY GET GROUNDED FOR A MONTH WHEN THEIR PARENTS FIND OUT.
BB

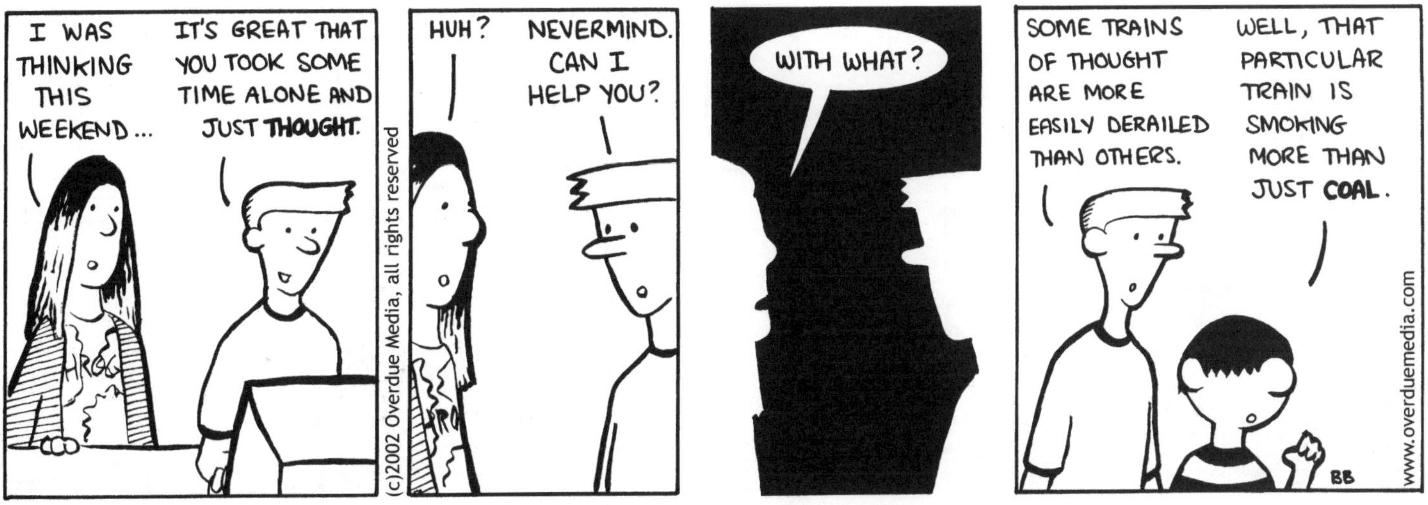
I WAS THINKING THIS WEEKEND...
IT'S GREAT THAT YOU TOOK SOME TIME ALONE AND JUST THOUGHT.
(c)2002 Overdue Media, all rights reserved
HUH?
NEVERMIND. CAN I HELP YOU?
WITH WHAT?
SOME TRAINS OF THOUGHT ARE MORE EASILY DERAILED THAN OTHERS.
WELL, THAT PARTICULAR TRAIN IS SMOKING MORE THAN JUST COAL.
www.overduemedia.com
BB

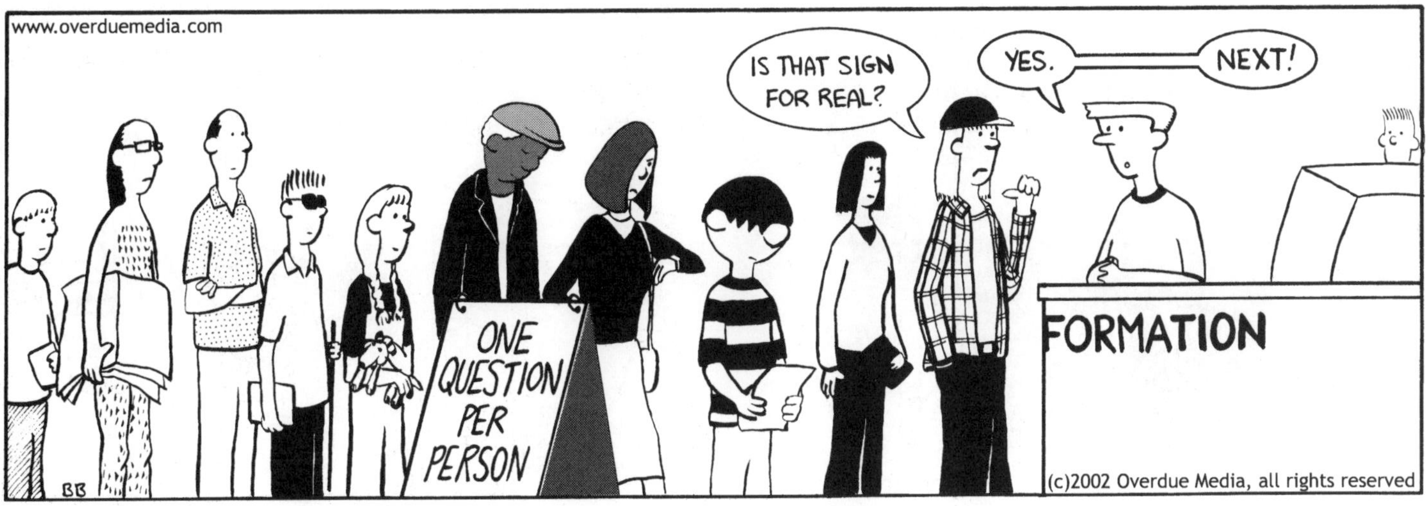
www.overduemedia.com
IS THAT SIGN FOR REAL?
YES.
NEXT!
ONE QUESTION PER PERSON
FORMATION
BB
(c)2002 Overdue Media, all rights reserved

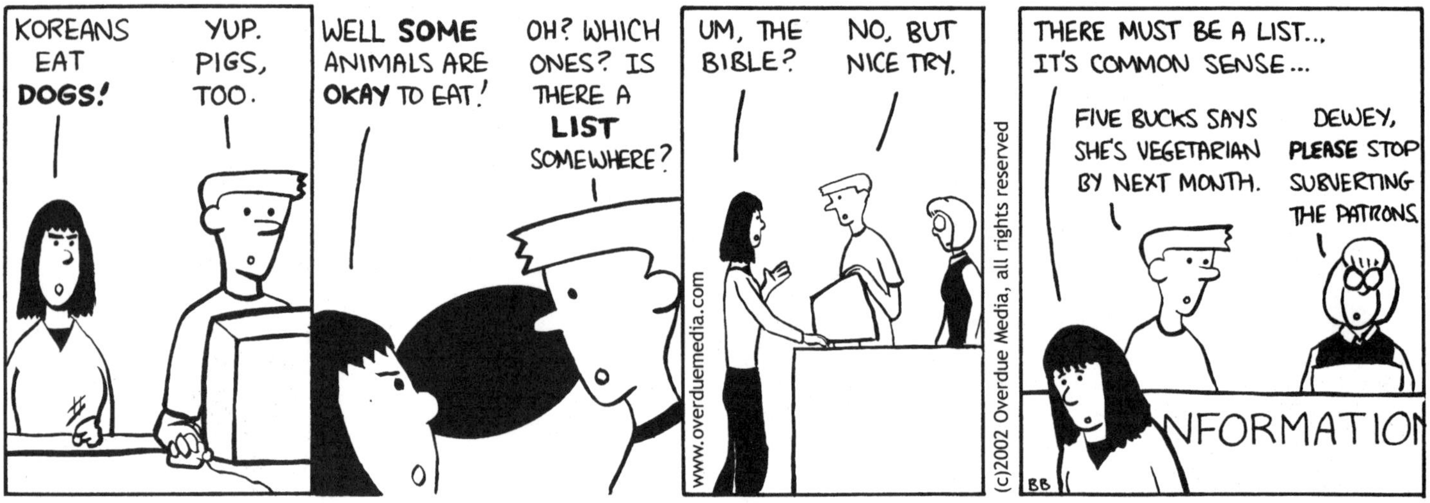
KOREANS EAT DOGS!
YUP. PIGS, TOO.
WELL SOME ANIMALS ARE OKAY TO EAT!
OH? WHICH ONES? IS THERE A LIST SOMEWHERE?
UM, THE BIBLE?
NO, BUT NICE TRY.
www.overduemedia.com
(c)2002 Overdue Media, all rights reserved
THERE MUST BE A LIST... IT'S COMMON SENSE...
FIVE BUCKS SAYS SHE'S VEGETARIAN BY NEXT MONTH.
DEWEY, PLEASE STOP SUBVERTING THE PATRONS.
NFORMATION
BB

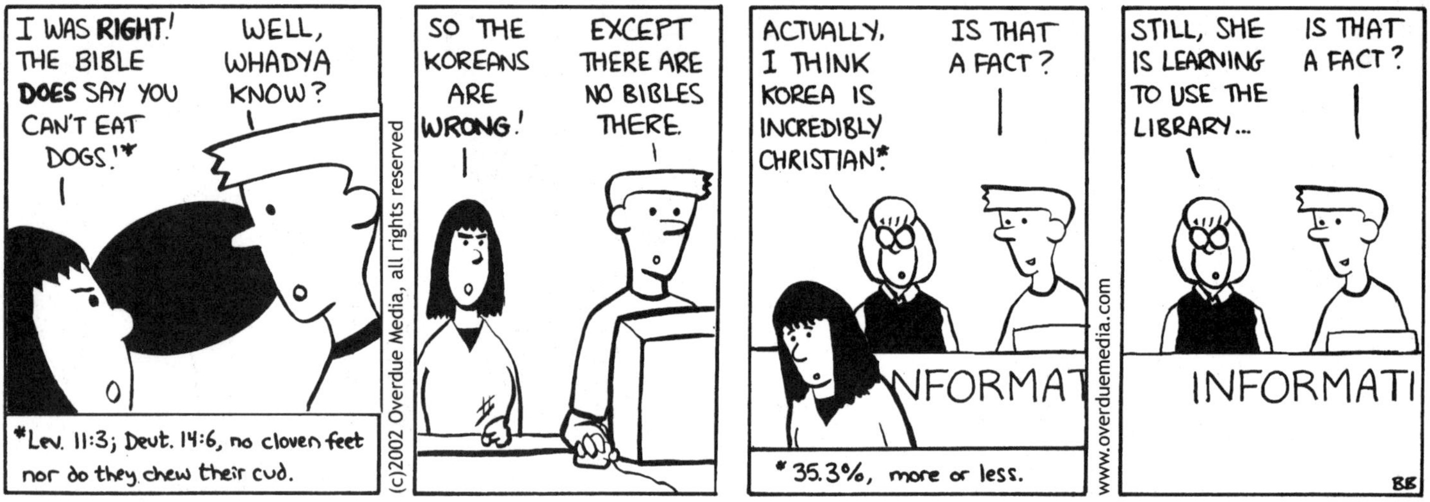
I WAS RIGHT! THE BIBLE DOES SAY YOU CAN'T EAT DOGS!*
WELL, WHADYA KNOW?
*Lev. 11:3; Deut. 14:6, no cloven feet nor do they chew their cud.
(c)2002 Overdue Media, all rights reserved
SO THE KOREANS ARE WRONG!
EXCEPT THERE ARE NO BIBLES THERE.
ACTUALLY, I THINK KOREA IS INCREDIBLY CHRISTIAN*.
IS THAT A FACT?
NFORMAT
* 35.3%, more or less.
www.overduemedia.com
STILL, SHE IS LEARNING TO USE THE LIBRARY...
IS THAT A FACT?
INFORMATI
BB

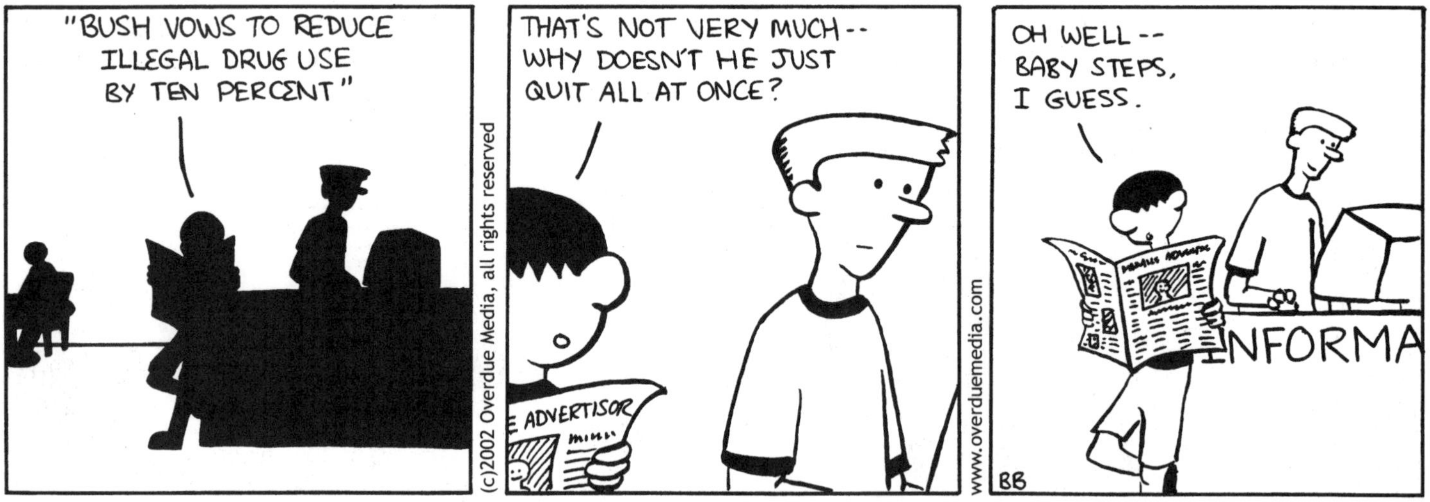
"BUSH VOWS TO REDUCE ILLEGAL DRUG USE BY TEN PERCENT"
(c)2002 Overdue Media, all rights reserved
THAT'S NOT VERY MUCH -- WHY DOESN'T HE JUST QUIT ALL AT ONCE?
ADVERTISOR
www.overduemedia.com
OH WELL -- BABY STEPS, I GUESS.
INFORMA
BB

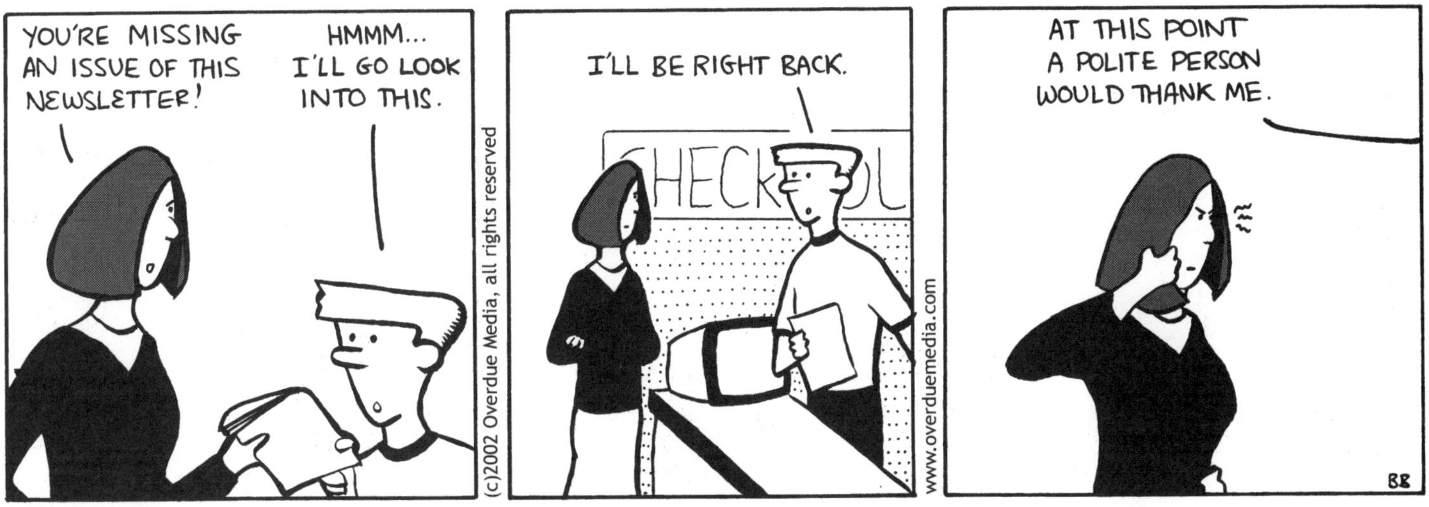
YOU'RE MISSING AN ISSUE OF THIS NEWSLETTER!
HMMM... I'LL GO LOOK INTO THIS.
(c)2002 Overdue Media, all rights reserved
I'LL BE RIGHT BACK.
CHECK OU
www.overduemedia.com
AT THIS POINT A POLITE PERSON WOULD THANK ME.
BB

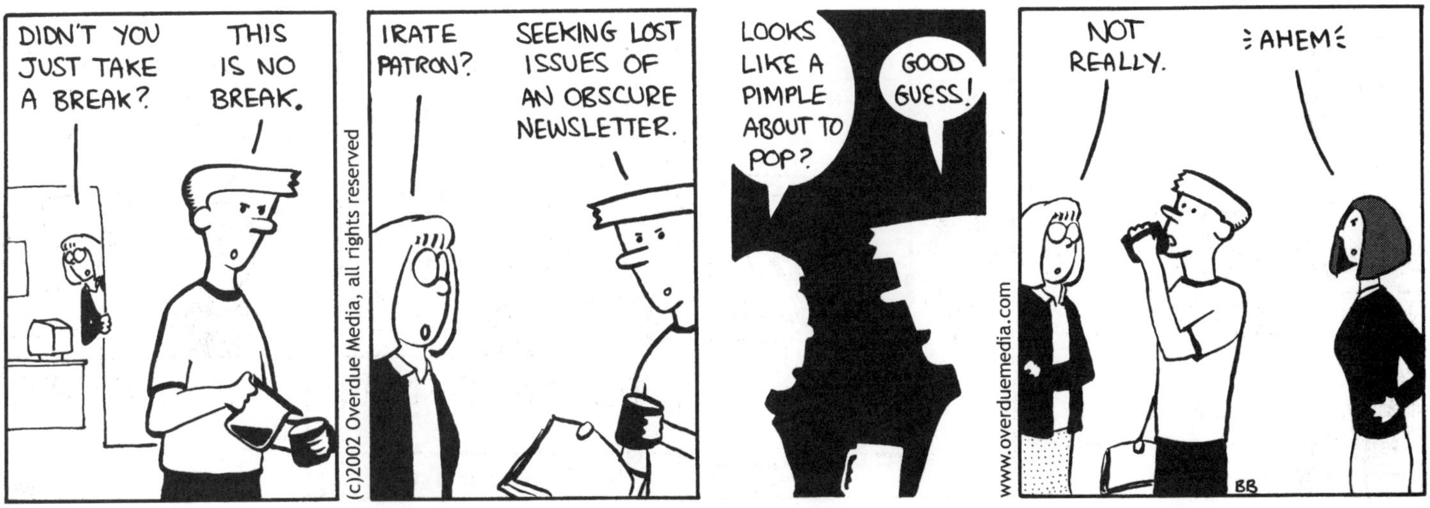
DIDN'T YOU JUST TAKE A BREAK?
THIS IS NO BREAK.
(c)2002 Overdue Media, all rights reserved
IRATE PATRON?
SEEKING LOST ISSUES OF AN OBSCURE NEWSLETTER.
LOOKS LIKE A PIMPLE ABOUT TO POP?
GOOD GUESS!
www.overduemedia.com
NOT REALLY.
AHEM
BB

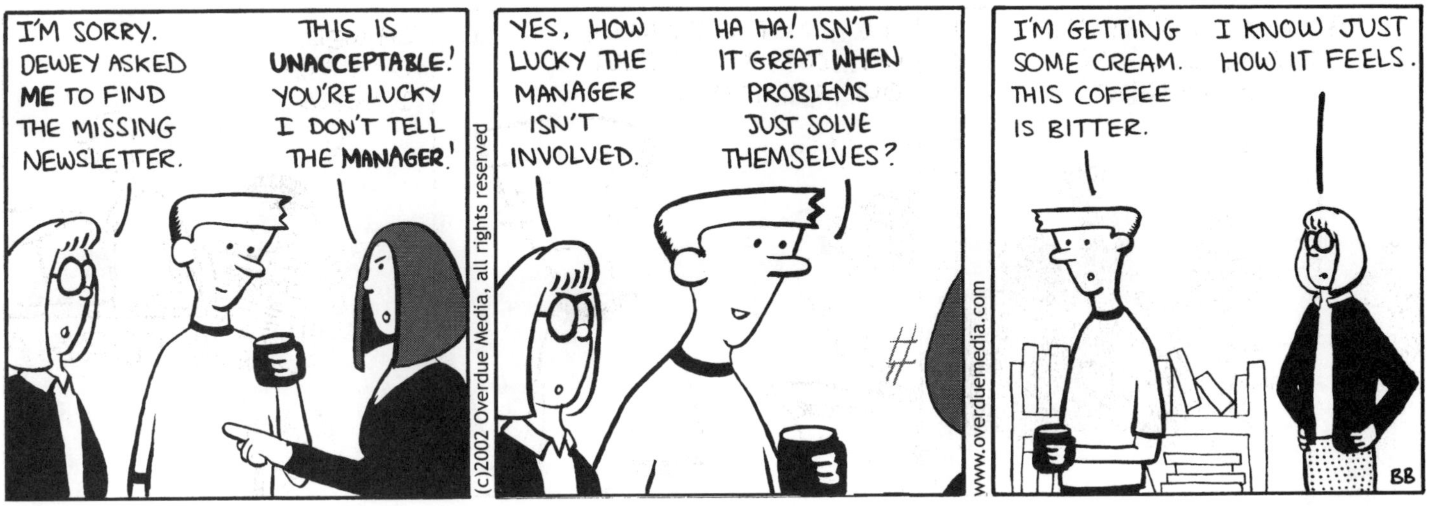
I'M SORRY. DEWEY ASKED ME TO FIND THE MISSING NEWSLETTER.
THIS IS UNACCEPTABLE! YOU'RE LUCKY I DON'T TELL THE MANAGER!
(c)2002 Overdue Media, all rights reserved
YES, HOW LUCKY THE MANAGER ISN'T INVOLVED.
HA HA! ISN'T IT GREAT WHEN PROBLEMS JUST SOLVE THEMSELVES?
www.overduemedia.com
I'M GETTING SOME CREAM. THIS COFFEE IS BITTER.
I KNOW JUST HOW IT FEELS.
BB

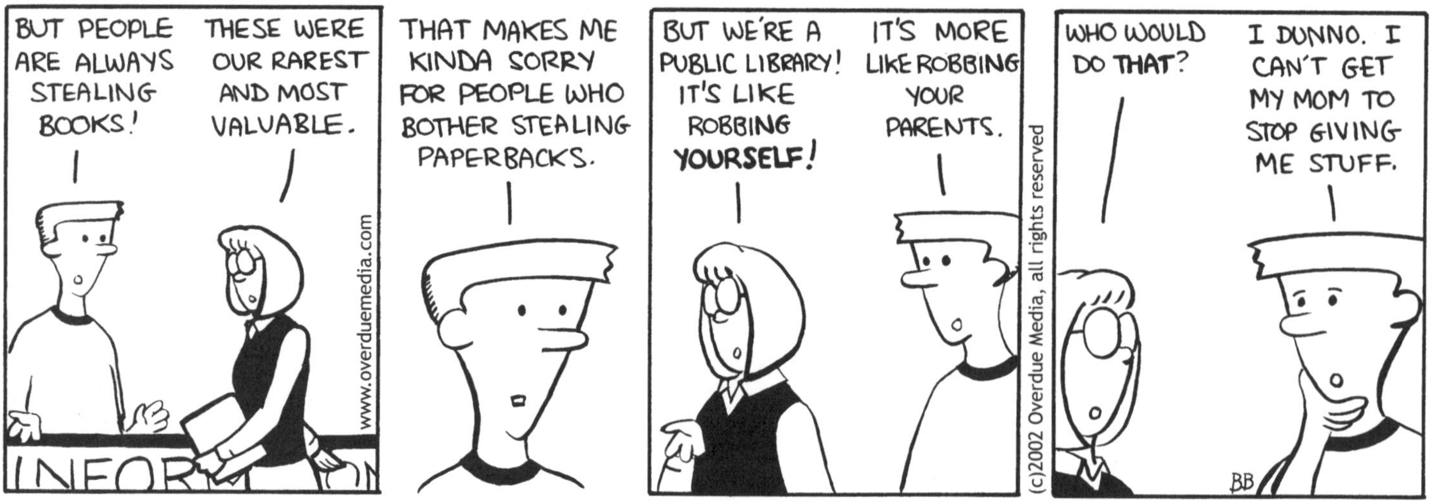
BUT PEOPLE ARE ALWAYS STEALING BOOKS!
THESE WERE OUR RAREST AND MOST VALUABLE.
THAT MAKES ME KINDA SORRY FOR PEOPLE WHO BOTHER STEALING PAPERBACKS.
BUT WE'RE A PUBLIC LIBRARY! IT'S LIKE ROBBING **YOURSELF**!
IT'S MORE LIKE ROBBING YOUR PARENTS.
WHO WOULD DO **THAT**?
I DUNNO. I CAN'T GET MY MOM TO STOP GIVING ME STUFF.
www.overduemedia.com
(c)2002 Overdue Media, all rights reserved
BB

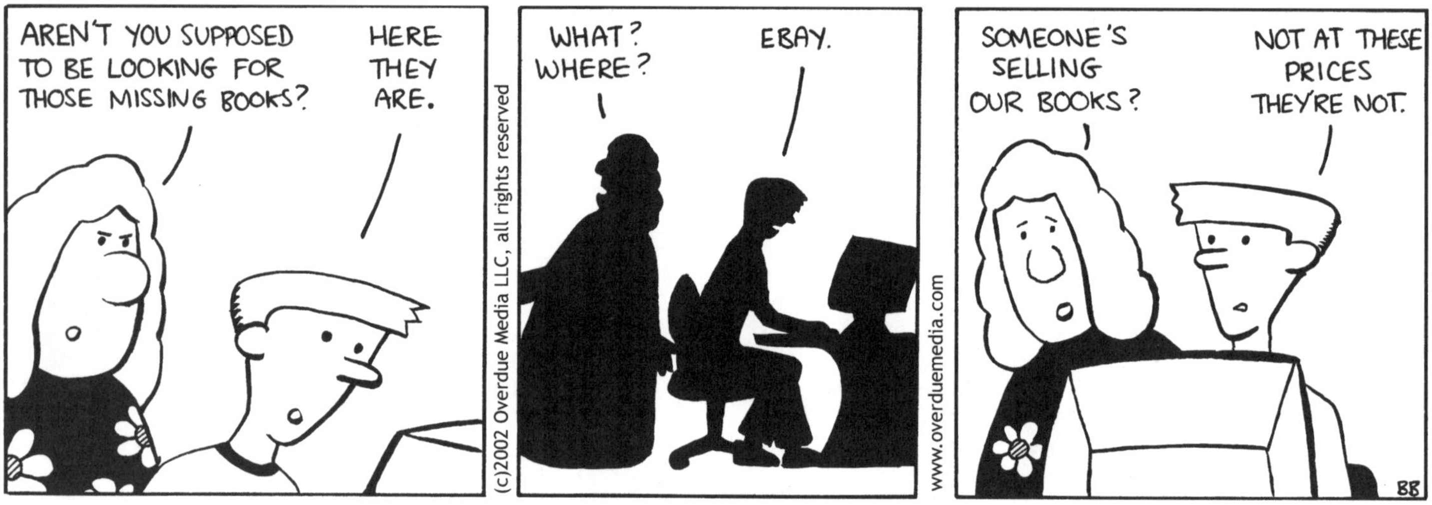
AREN'T YOU SUPPOSED TO BE LOOKING FOR THOSE MISSING BOOKS?
HERE THEY ARE.
WHAT? WHERE?
EBAY.
SOMEONE'S SELLING OUR BOOKS?
NOT AT THESE PRICES THEY'RE NOT.
(c)2002 Overdue Media LLC, all rights reserved
www.overduemedia.com
BB

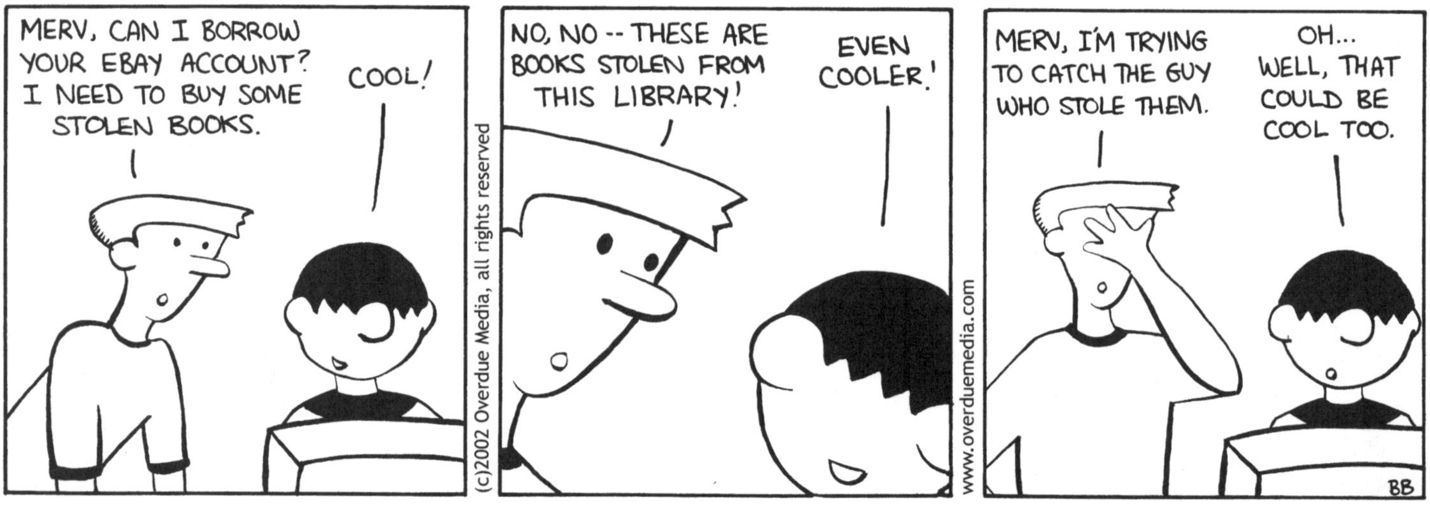
MERV, CAN I BORROW YOUR EBAY ACCOUNT? I NEED TO BUY SOME STOLEN BOOKS.
COOL!
NO, NO -- THESE ARE BOOKS STOLEN FROM THIS LIBRARY!
EVEN COOLER!
MERV, I'M TRYING TO CATCH THE GUY WHO STOLE THEM.
OH... WELL, THAT COULD BE COOL TOO.
(c)2002 Overdue Media, all rights reserved
www.overduemedia.com
BB

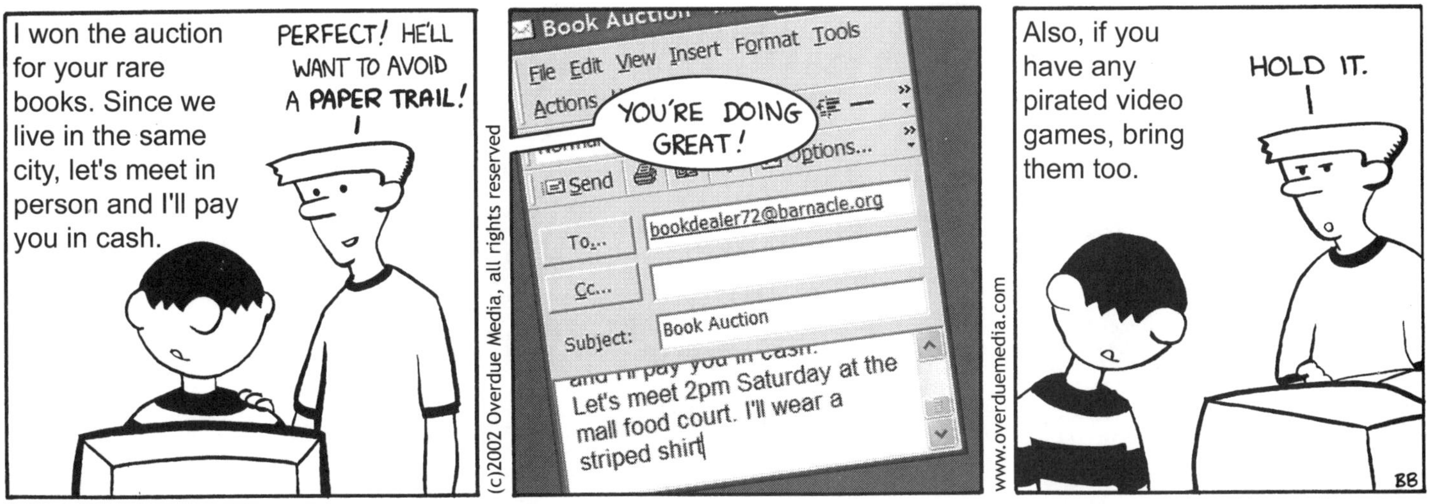
I won the auction for your rare books. Since we live in the same city, let's meet in person and I'll pay you in cash.
PERFECT! HE'LL WANT TO AVOID A **PAPER TRAIL**!
(c)2002 Overdue Media, all rights reserved
Book Auction
File Edit View Insert Format Tools
Actions
YOU'RE DOING GREAT!
Options...
Send
To...
bookdealer72@barnacle.org
Cc...
Subject:
Book Auction
Let's meet 2pm Saturday at the mall food court. I'll wear a striped shirt
www.overduemedia.com
Also, if you have any pirated video games, bring them too.
HOLD IT.
BB

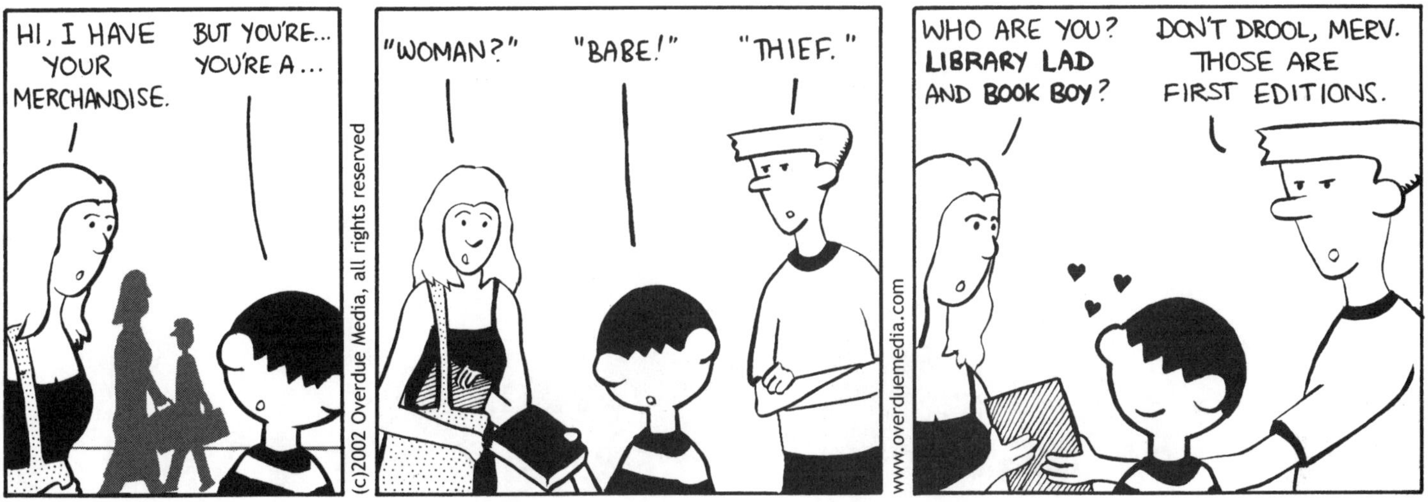
HI, I HAVE YOUR MERCHANDISE.
BUT YOU'RE... YOU'RE A...
(c)2002 Overdue Media, all rights reserved
"WOMAN?"
"BABE!"
"THIEF."
www.overduemedia.com
WHO ARE YOU? **LIBRARY LAD** AND **BOOK BOY**?
DON'T DROOL, MERV. THOSE ARE FIRST EDITIONS.

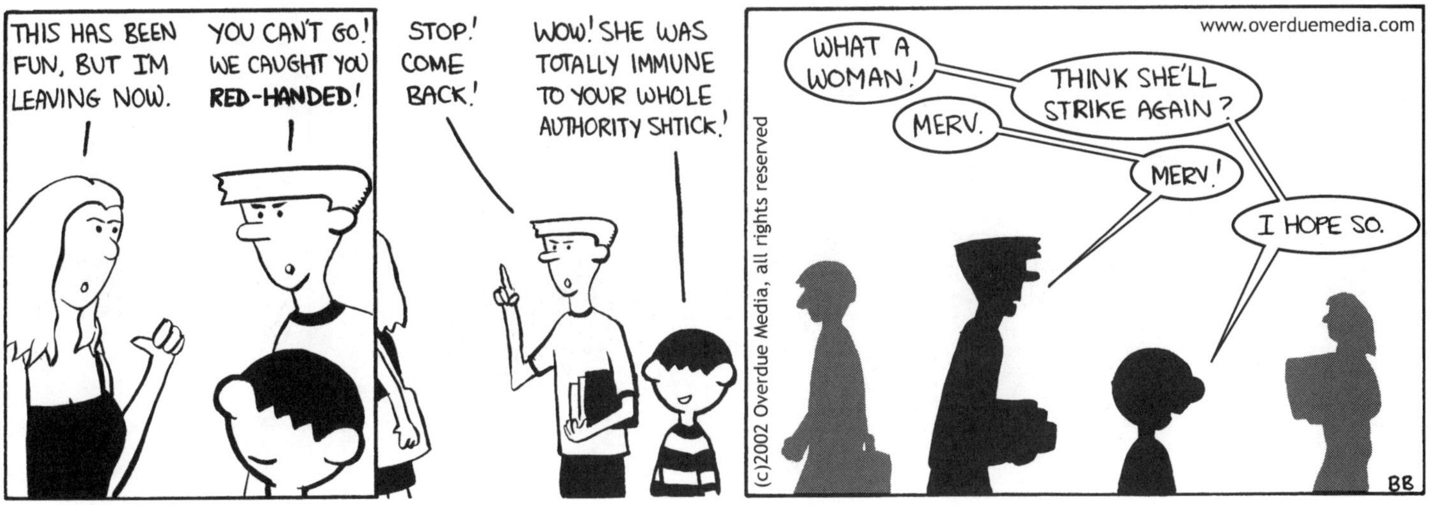
THIS HAS BEEN FUN, BUT I'M LEAVING NOW.
YOU CAN'T GO! WE CAUGHT YOU **RED-HANDED**!
STOP! COME BACK!
WOW! SHE WAS TOTALLY IMMUNE TO YOUR WHOLE AUTHORITY SHTICK!
(c)2002 Overdue Media, all rights reserved
www.overduemedia.com
WHAT A WOMAN!
THINK SHE'LL STRIKE AGAIN?
MERV.
MERV!
I HOPE SO.
BB

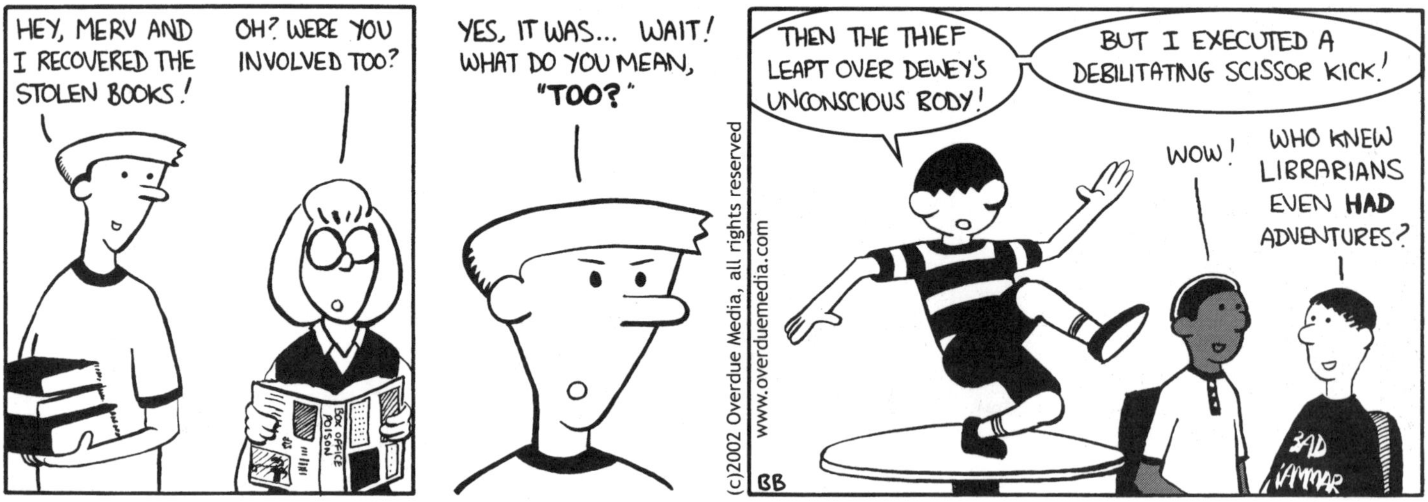
HEY, MERV AND I RECOVERED THE STOLEN BOOKS!
OH? WERE YOU INVOLVED TOO?
YES, IT WAS... WAIT! WHAT DO YOU MEAN, "TOO?"
THEN THE THIEF LEAPT OVER DEWEY'S UNCONSCIOUS BODY!
BUT I EXECUTED A DEBILITATING SCISSOR KICK!
WOW!
WHO KNEW LIBRARIANS EVEN HAD ADVENTURES?
(c)2002 Overdue Media, all rights reserved
www.overduemedia.com
BB

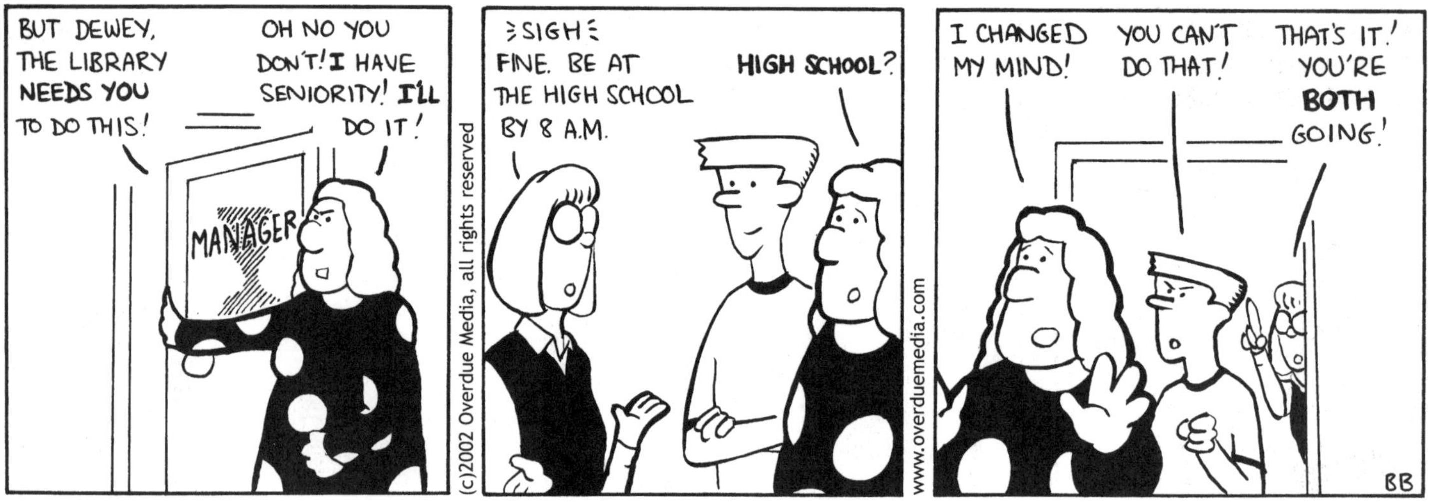
BUT DEWEY, THE LIBRARY NEEDS YOU TO DO THIS!
OH NO YOU DON'T! I HAVE SENIORITY! I'LL DO IT!
MANAGER
(c)2002 Overdue Media, all rights reserved
≋SIGH≋ FINE. BE AT THE HIGH SCHOOL BY 8 A.M.
HIGH SCHOOL?
www.overduemedia.com
I CHANGED MY MIND!
YOU CAN'T DO THAT!
THAT'S IT! YOU'RE BOTH GOING!
BB

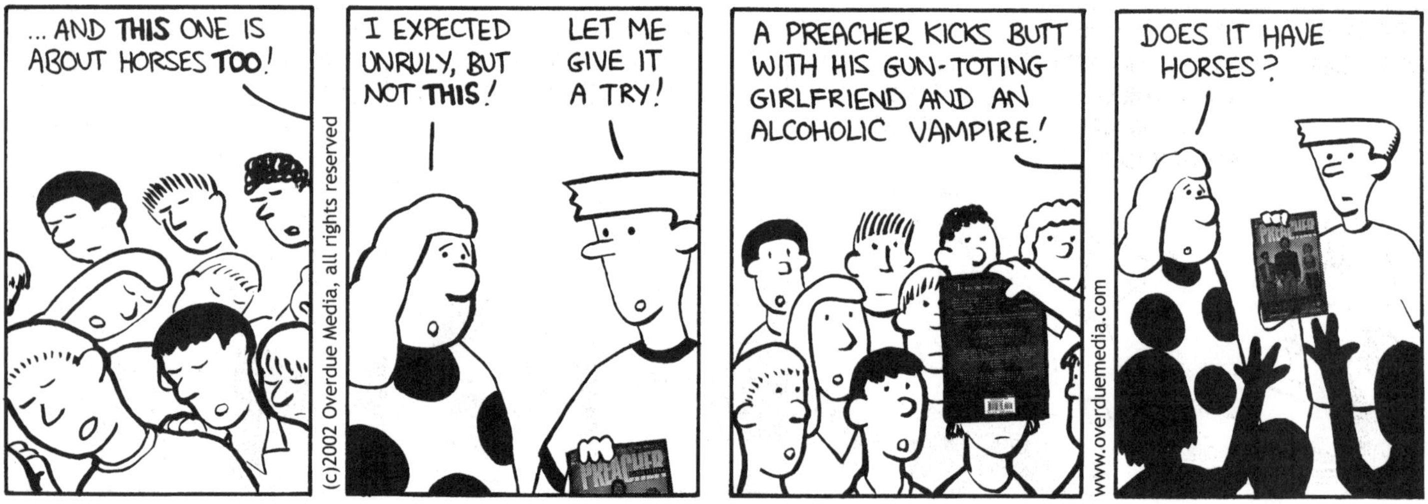
...AND THIS ONE IS ABOUT HORSES TOO!
(c)2002 Overdue Media, all rights reserved
I EXPECTED UNRULY, BUT NOT THIS!
LET ME GIVE IT A TRY!
A PREACHER KICKS BUTT WITH HIS GUN-TOTING GIRLFRIEND AND AN ALCOHOLIC VAMPIRE!
www.overduemedia.com
DOES IT HAVE HORSES?

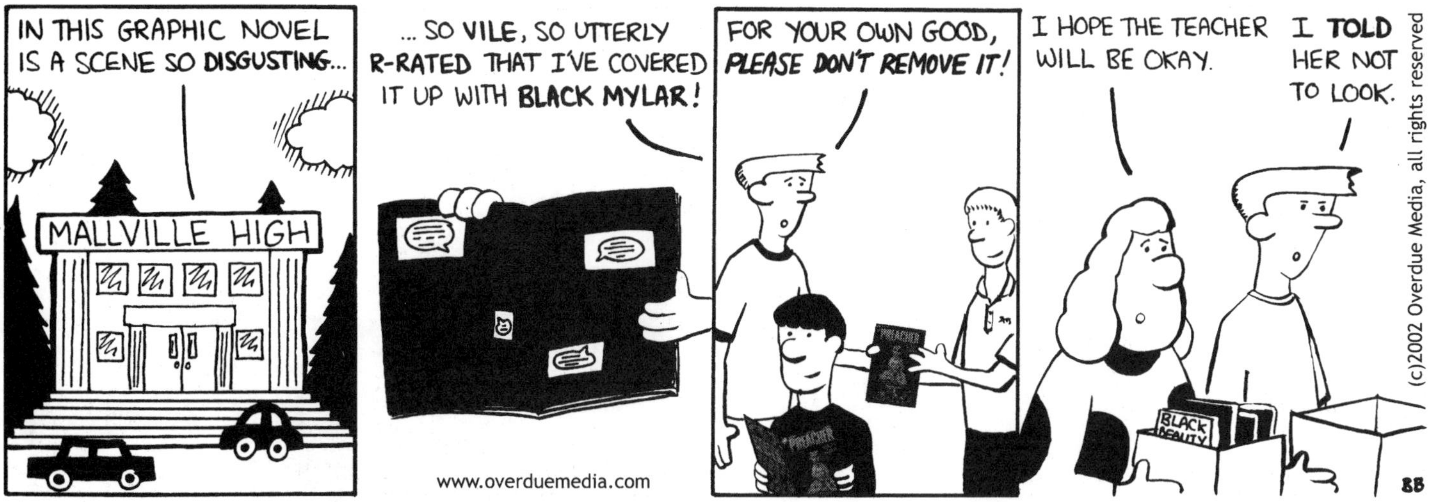
IN THIS GRAPHIC NOVEL IS A SCENE SO **DISGUSTING**...
MALLVILLE HIGH
... SO **VILE**, SO UTTERLY **R-RATED** THAT I'VE COVERED IT UP WITH **BLACK MYLAR**!
www.overduemedia.com
FOR YOUR OWN GOOD, ***PLEASE DON'T REMOVE IT!***
PREACHER
I HOPE THE TEACHER WILL BE OKAY.
I **TOLD** HER NOT TO LOOK.
BLACK BEAUTY
(c)2002 Overdue Media, all rights reserved
BB

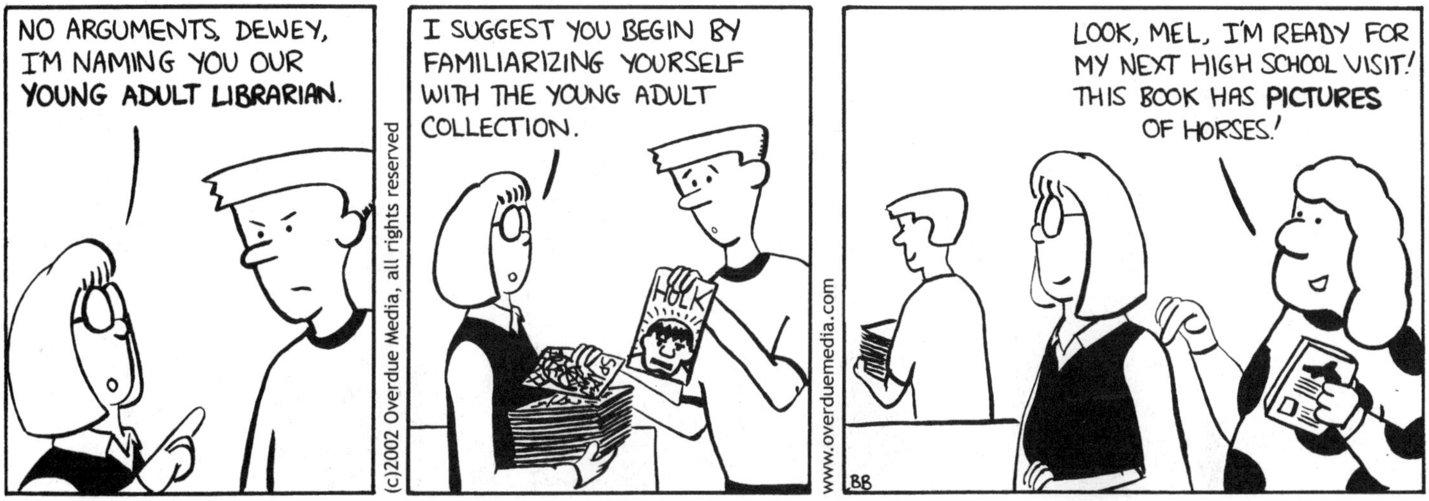
NO ARGUMENTS, DEWEY, I'M NAMING YOU OUR **YOUNG ADULT LIBRARIAN**.
(c)2002 Overdue Media, all rights reserved
I SUGGEST YOU BEGIN BY FAMILIARIZING YOURSELF WITH THE YOUNG ADULT COLLECTION.
HULK
www.overduemedia.com
LOOK, MEL, I'M READY FOR MY NEXT HIGH SCHOOL VISIT! THIS BOOK HAS **PICTURES** OF HORSES!
BB

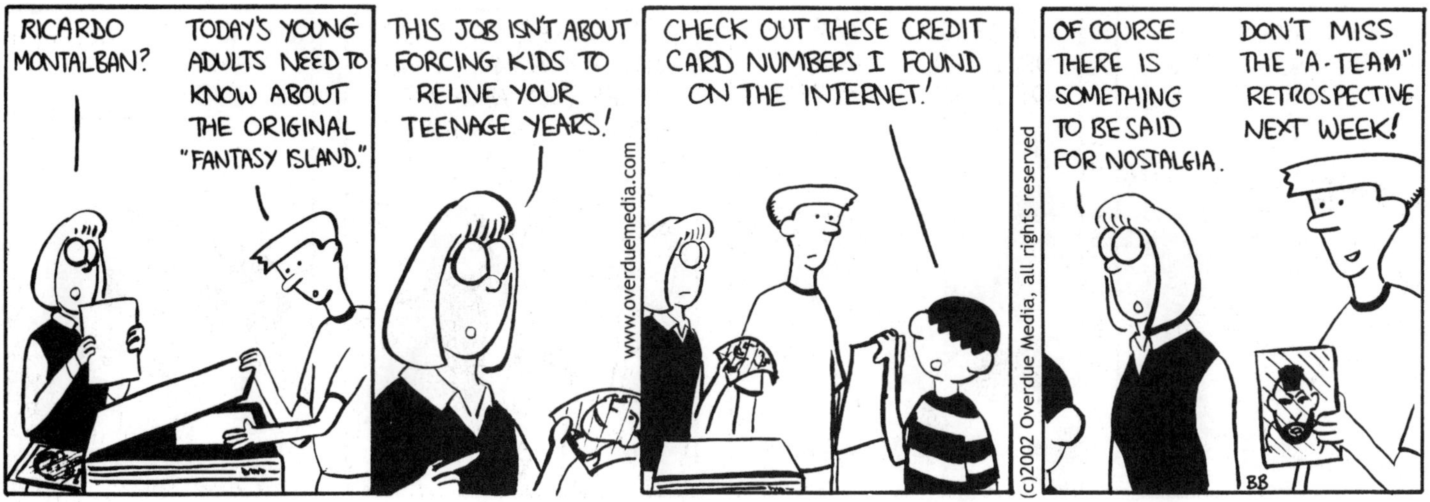
RICARDO MONTALBAN?
TODAY'S YOUNG ADULTS NEED TO KNOW ABOUT THE ORIGINAL "FANTASY ISLAND."
THIS JOB ISN'T ABOUT FORCING KIDS TO RELIVE YOUR TEENAGE YEARS!
www.overduemedia.com
CHECK OUT THESE CREDIT CARD NUMBERS I FOUND ON THE INTERNET!
(c)2002 Overdue Media, all rights reserved
OF COURSE THERE IS SOMETHING TO BE SAID FOR NOSTALGIA.
DON'T MISS THE "A-TEAM" RETROSPECTIVE NEXT WEEK!
BB

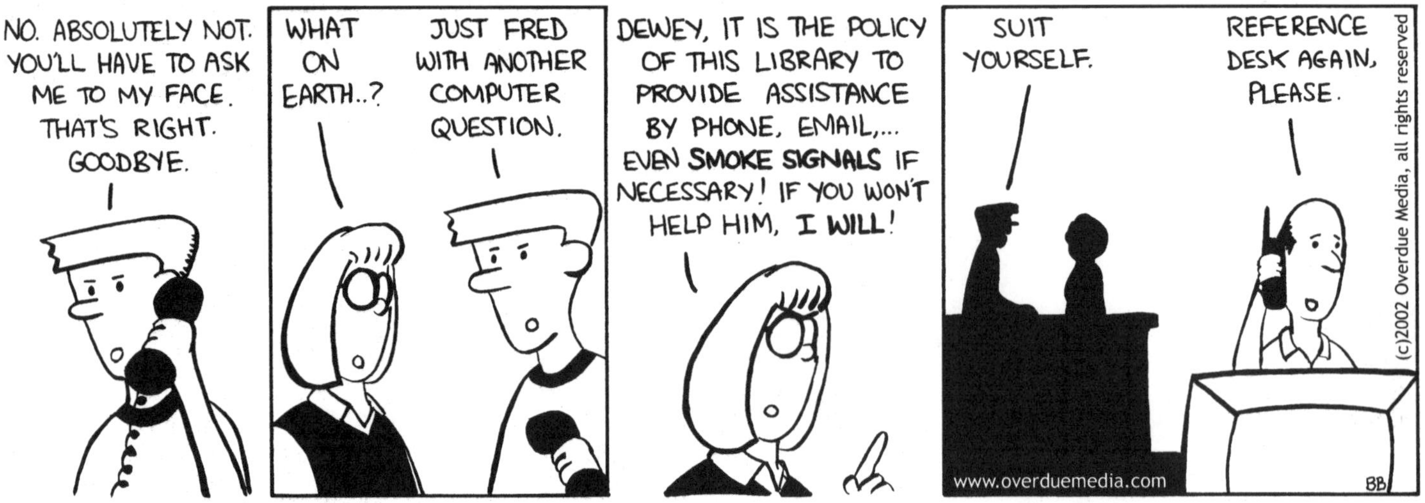
NO. ABSOLUTELY NOT. YOU'LL HAVE TO ASK ME TO MY FACE. THAT'S RIGHT. GOODBYE.
WHAT ON EARTH..?
JUST FRED WITH ANOTHER COMPUTER QUESTION.
DEWEY, IT IS THE POLICY OF THIS LIBRARY TO PROVIDE ASSISTANCE BY PHONE, EMAIL,... EVEN SMOKE SIGNALS IF NECESSARY! IF YOU WON'T HELP HIM, I WILL!
SUIT YOURSELF.
REFERENCE DESK AGAIN, PLEASE.
(c)2002 Overdue Media, all rights reserved
www.overduemedia.com
BB

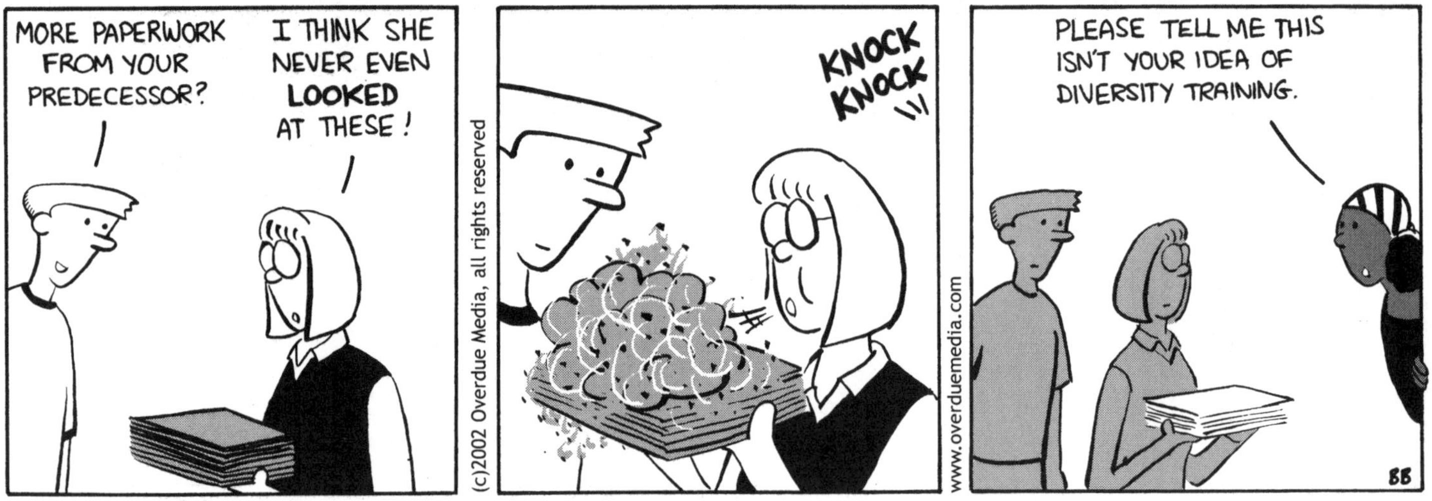
MORE PAPERWORK FROM YOUR PREDECESSOR?
I THINK SHE NEVER EVEN LOOKED AT THESE!
(c)2002 Overdue Media, all rights reserved
KNOCK KNOCK
www.overduemedia.com
PLEASE TELL ME THIS ISN'T YOUR IDEA OF DIVERSITY TRAINING.
BB

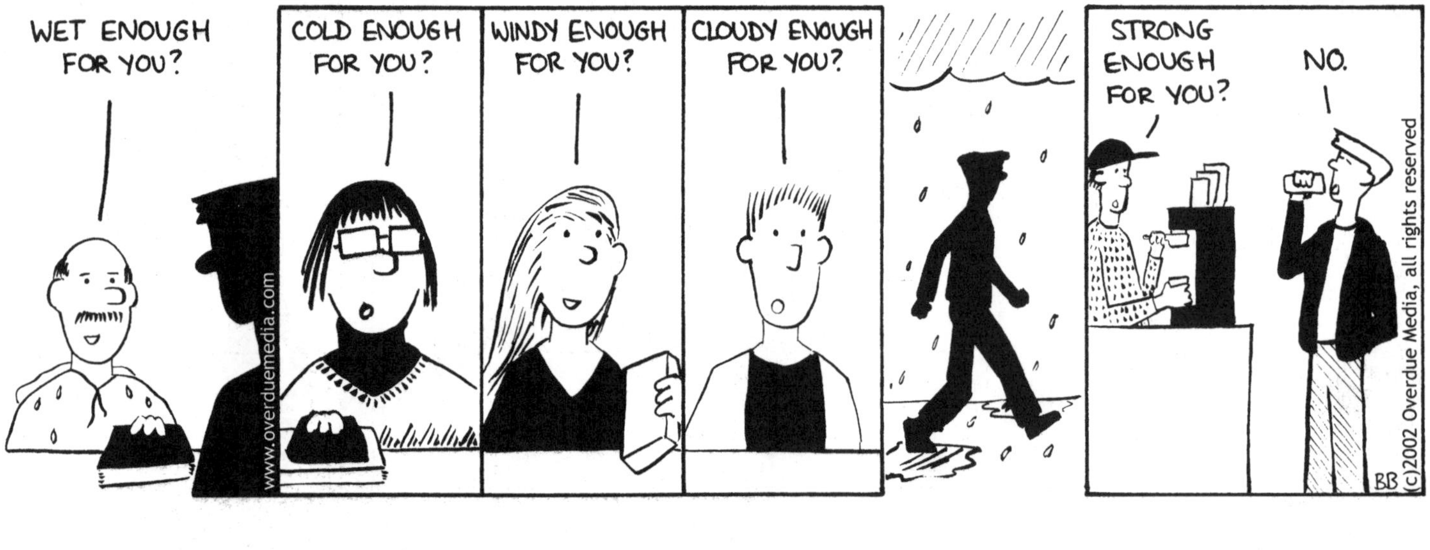
WET ENOUGH FOR YOU?
www.overduemedia.com
COLD ENOUGH FOR YOU?
WINDY ENOUGH FOR YOU?
CLOUDY ENOUGH FOR YOU?
STRONG ENOUGH FOR YOU?
NO.
BB
(c)2002 Overdue Media, all rights reserved

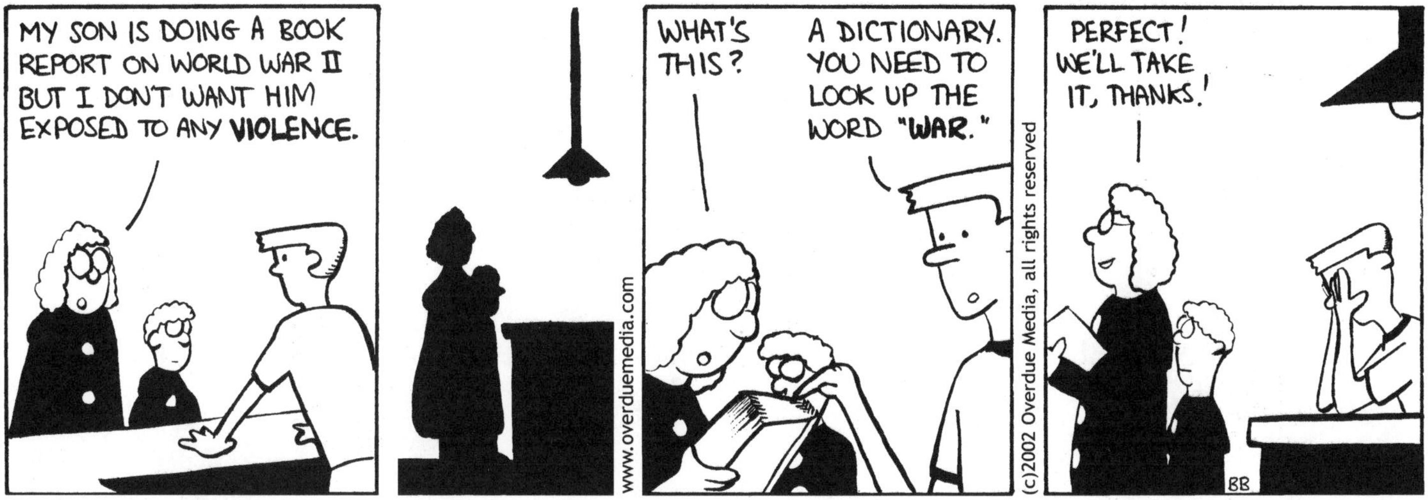
MY SON IS DOING A BOOK REPORT ON WORLD WAR II BUT I DON'T WANT HIM EXPOSED TO ANY **VIOLENCE**.
www.overduemedia.com
WHAT'S THIS?
A DICTIONARY. YOU NEED TO LOOK UP THE WORD "**WAR**."
(c)2002 Overdue Media, all rights reserved
PERFECT! WE'LL TAKE IT, THANKS!
BB

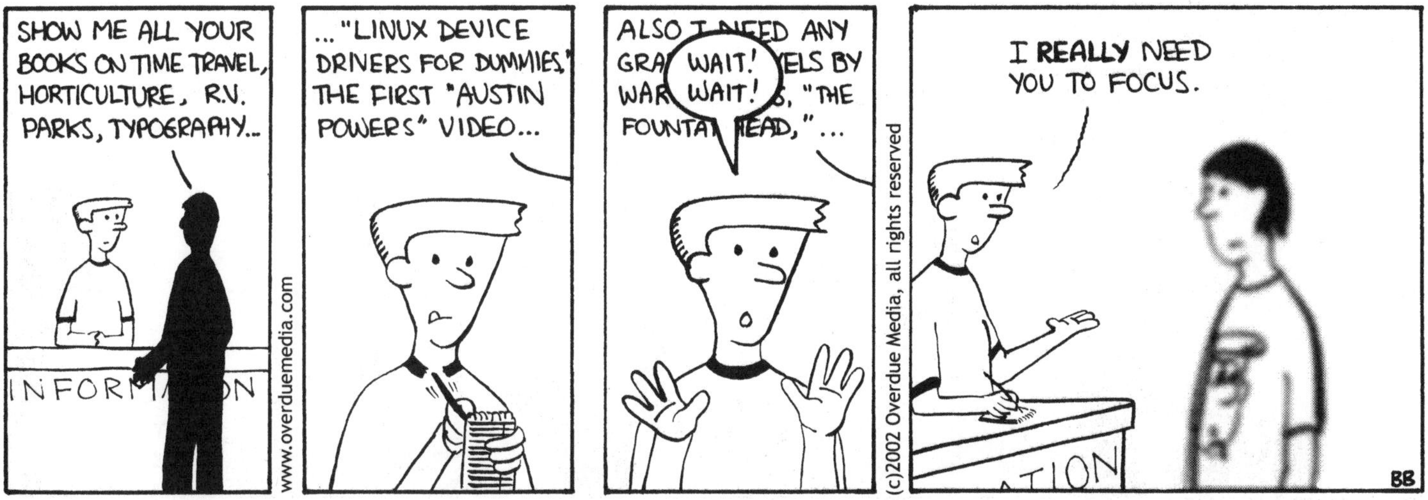
SHOW ME ALL YOUR BOOKS ON TIME TRAVEL, HORTICULTURE, R.V. PARKS, TYPOGRAPHY...
INFORM ON
www.overduemedia.com
..."LINUX DEVICE DRIVERS FOR DUMMIES," THE FIRST "AUSTIN POWERS" VIDEO...
ALSO I NEED ANY GRA ELS BY WAR S, "THE FOUNTA EAD," ...
WAIT! WAIT!
(c)2002 Overdue Media, all rights reserved
I **REALLY** NEED YOU TO FOCUS.
ATION
BB

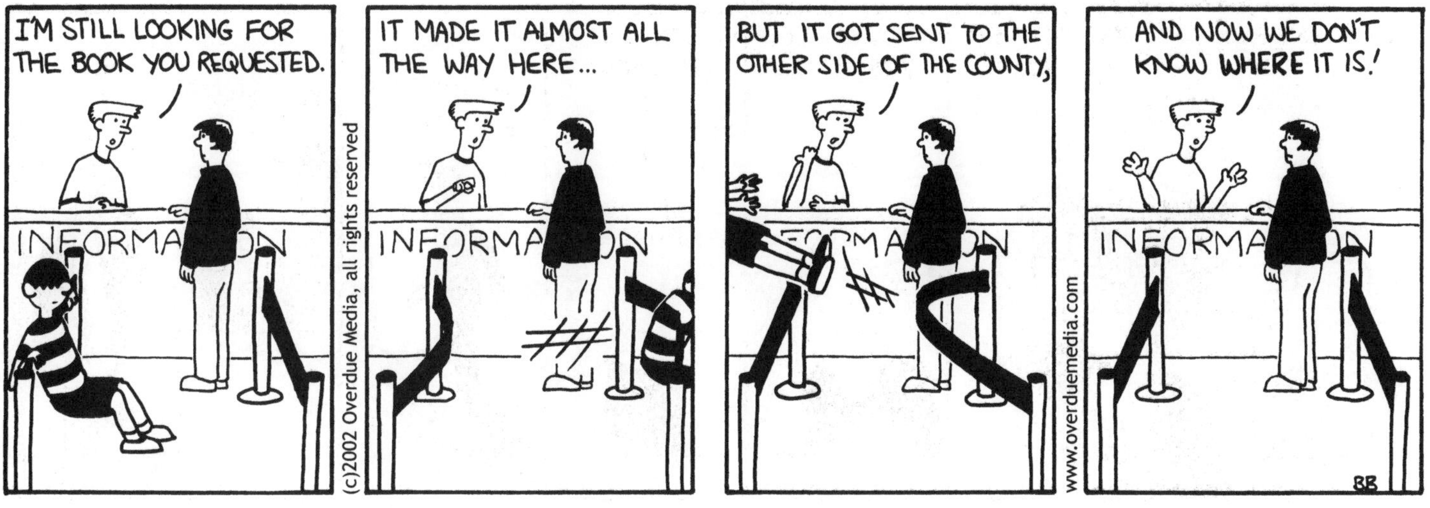
I'M STILL LOOKING FOR THE BOOK YOU REQUESTED.
INFORMA ON
(c)2002 Overdue Media, all rights reserved
IT MADE IT ALMOST ALL THE WAY HERE...
INFORMA ON
BUT IT GOT SENT TO THE OTHER SIDE OF THE COUNTY,
ORMA ON
www.overduemedia.com
AND NOW WE DON'T KNOW **WHERE** IT IS!
INFORMA ON
BB

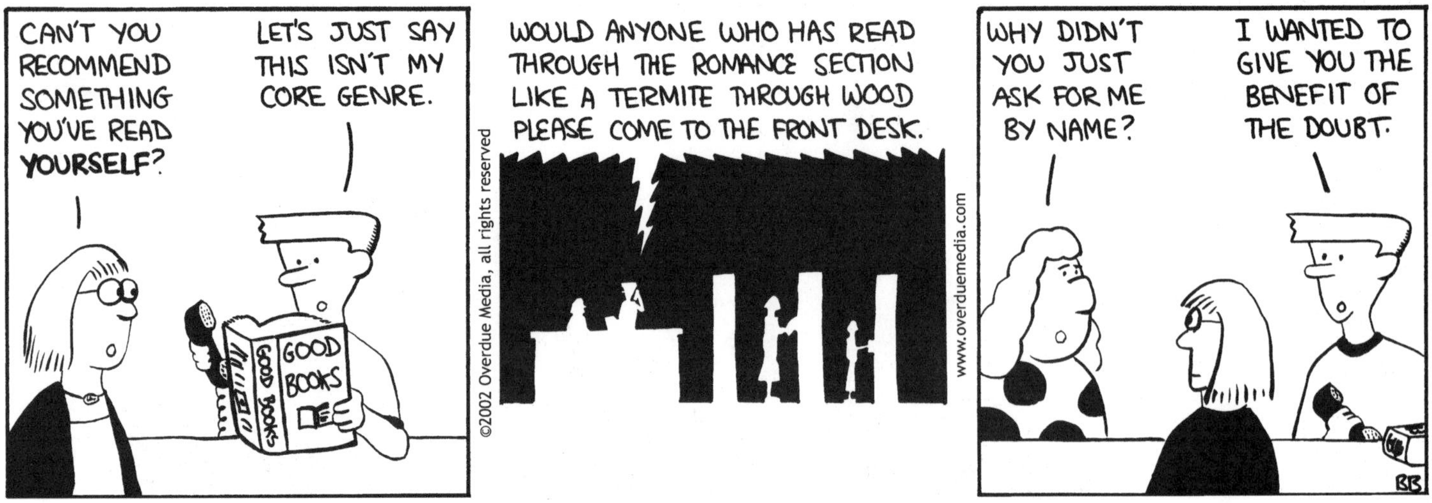
CAN'T YOU RECOMMEND SOMETHING YOU'VE READ **YOURSELF**?
LET'S JUST SAY THIS ISN'T MY CORE GENRE.
GOOD BOOKS
©2002 Overdue Media, all rights reserved
WOULD ANYONE WHO HAS READ THROUGH THE ROMANCE SECTION LIKE A TERMITE THROUGH WOOD PLEASE COME TO THE FRONT DESK.
www.overduemedia.com
WHY DIDN'T YOU JUST ASK FOR ME BY NAME?
I WANTED TO GIVE YOU THE BENEFIT OF THE DOUBT.
BB

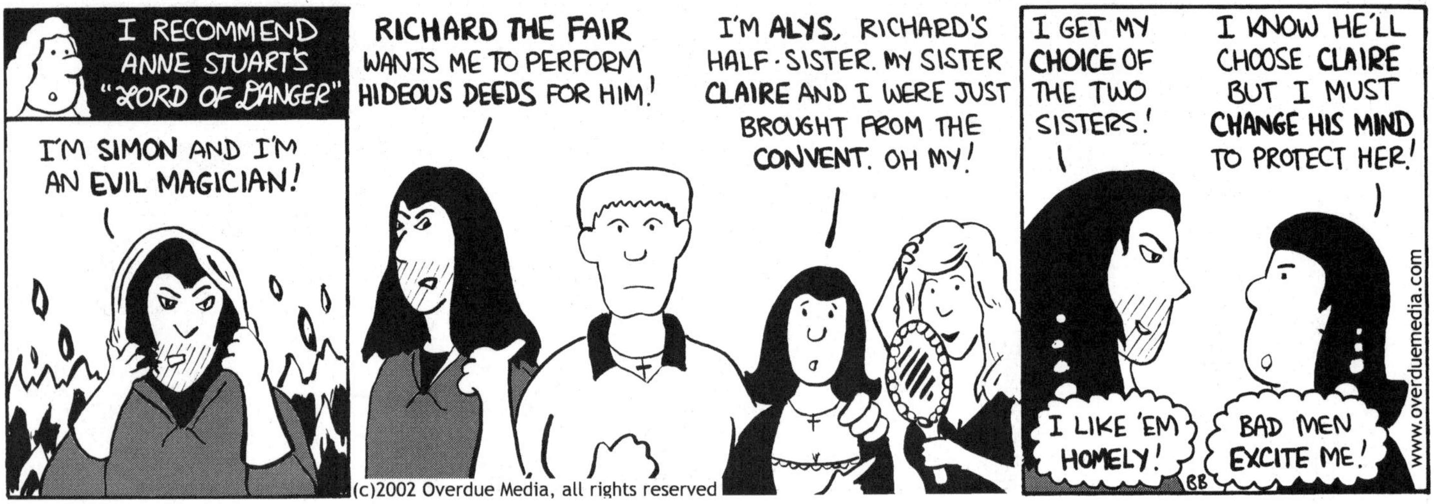
I RECOMMEND ANNE STUART'S "LORD OF DANGER"
I'M **SIMON** AND I'M AN **EVIL MAGICIAN**!
RICHARD THE FAIR WANTS ME TO PERFORM **HIDEOUS DEEDS** FOR HIM!
I'M **ALYS**, RICHARD'S HALF-SISTER. MY SISTER **CLAIRE** AND I WERE JUST BROUGHT FROM THE **CONVENT**. OH MY!
(c)2002 Overdue Media, all rights reserved
I GET MY **CHOICE** OF THE TWO SISTERS!
I KNOW HE'LL CHOOSE **CLAIRE** BUT I MUST **CHANGE HIS MIND** TO PROTECT HER!
I LIKE 'EM **HOMELY**!
BAD MEN **EXCITE** ME!
BB
www.overduemedia.com

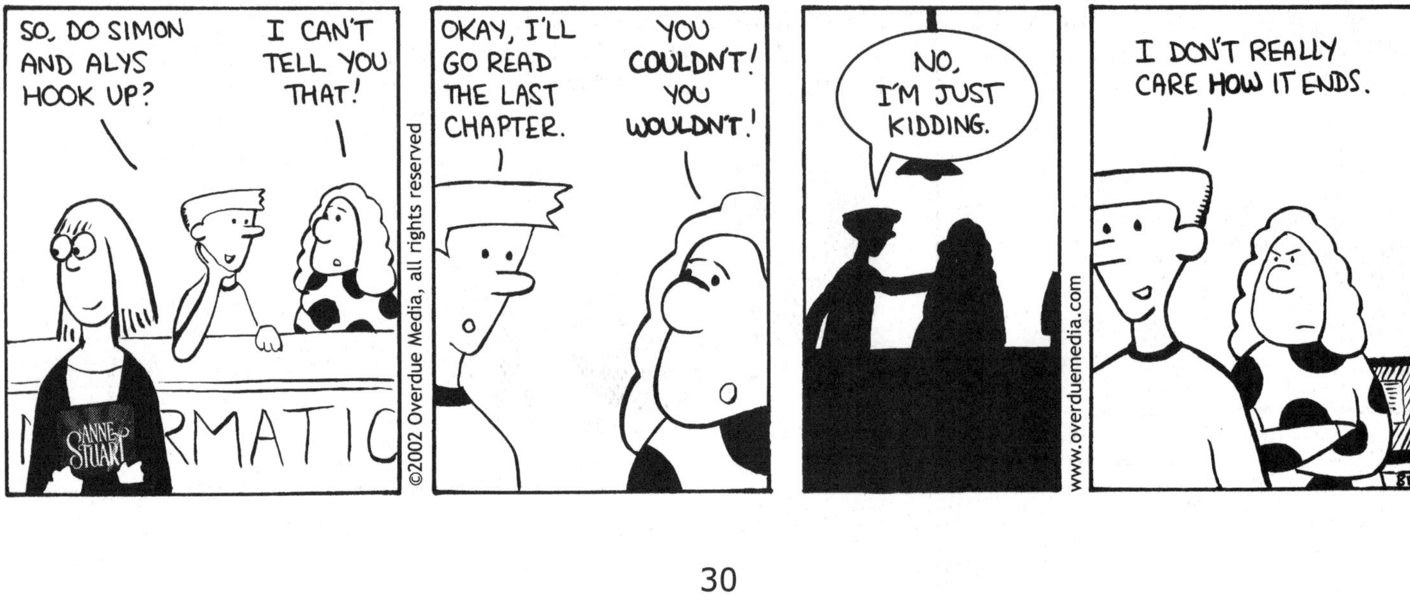
SO, DO SIMON AND ALYS HOOK UP?
I CAN'T TELL YOU THAT!
ANNE STUART
RMATIC
©2002 Overdue Media, all rights reserved
OKAY, I'LL GO READ THE LAST CHAPTER.
YOU **COULDN'T**! YOU **WOULDN'T**!
NO, I'M JUST KIDDING.
www.overduemedia.com
I DON'T REALLY CARE **HOW** IT ENDS.
BB

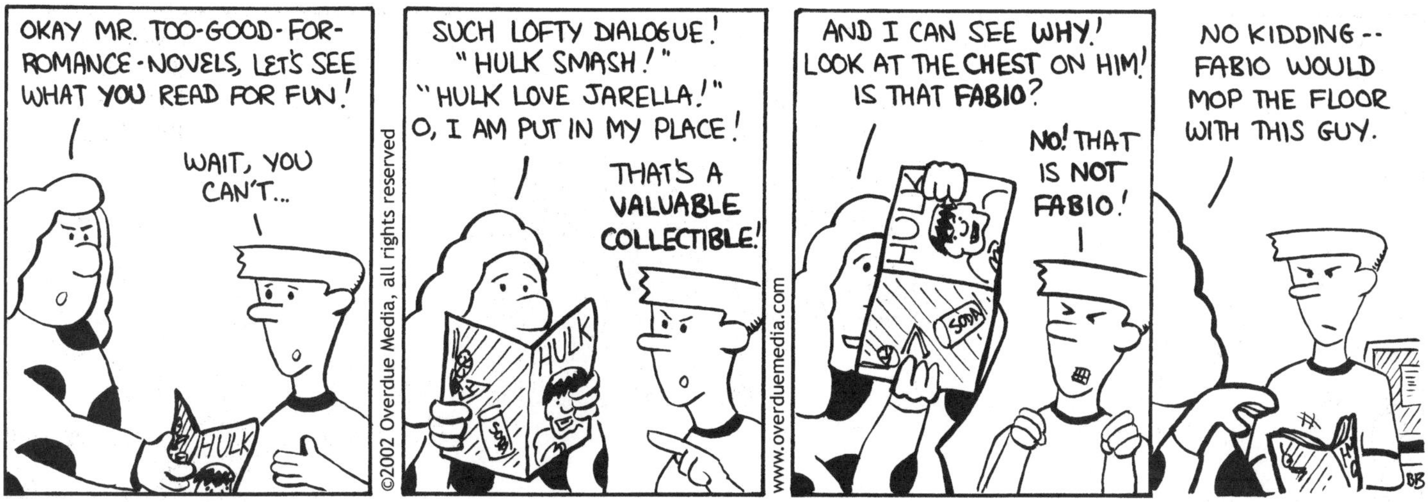
OKAY MR. TOO-GOOD-FOR-ROMANCE-NOVELS, LET'S SEE WHAT YOU READ FOR FUN!
WAIT, YOU CAN'T...
SUCH LOFTY DIALOGUE! "HULK SMASH!" "HULK LOVE JARELLA!" O, I AM PUT IN MY PLACE!
THAT'S A VALUABLE COLLECTIBLE!
AND I CAN SEE WHY! LOOK AT THE CHEST ON HIM! IS THAT FABIO?
NO! THAT IS NOT FABIO!
NO KIDDING -- FABIO WOULD MOP THE FLOOR WITH THIS GUY.
©2002 Overdue Media, all rights reserved
www.overduemedia.com

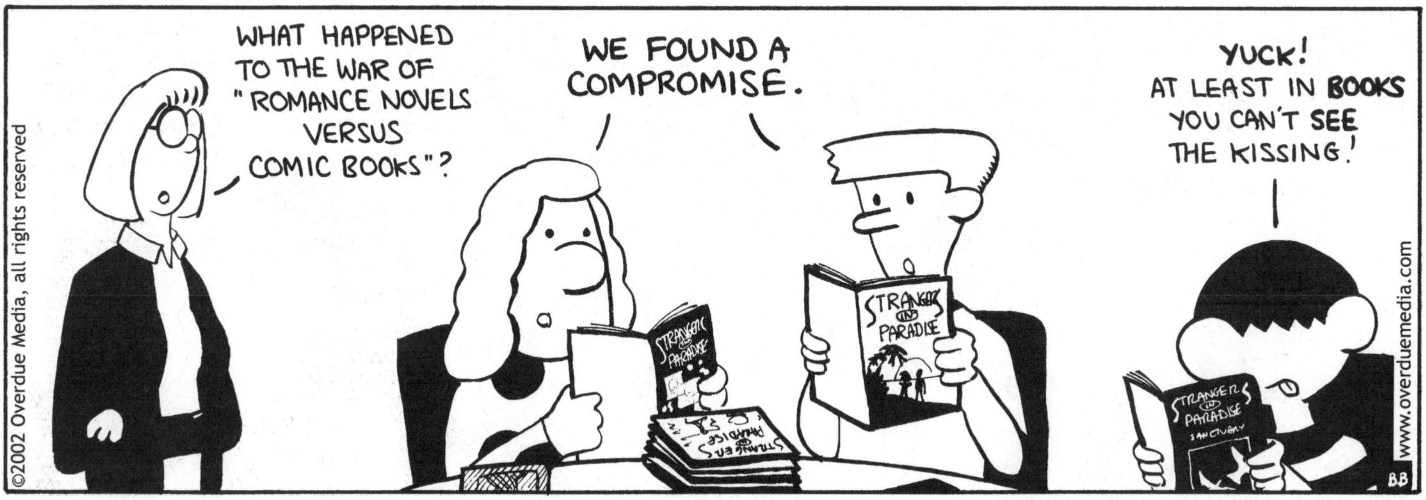
WHAT HAPPENED TO THE WAR OF "ROMANCE NOVELS VERSUS COMIC BOOKS"?
WE FOUND A COMPROMISE.
YUCK! AT LEAST IN BOOKS YOU CAN'T SEE THE KISSING!
©2002 Overdue Media, all rights reserved
www.overduemedia.com

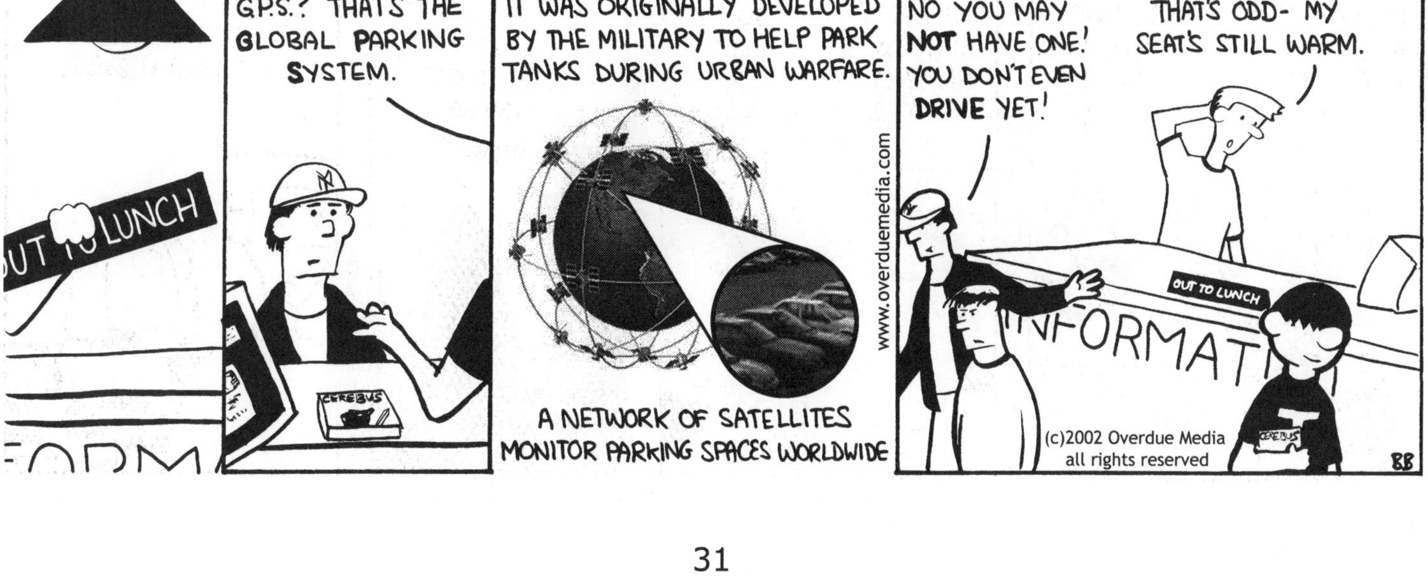
G.P.S.? THAT'S THE GLOBAL PARKING SYSTEM.
IT WAS ORIGINALLY DEVELOPED BY THE MILITARY TO HELP PARK TANKS DURING URBAN WARFARE.
A NETWORK OF SATELLITES MONITOR PARKING SPACES WORLDWIDE
NO YOU MAY NOT HAVE ONE! YOU DON'T EVEN DRIVE YET!
THAT'S ODD- MY SEAT'S STILL WARM.
OUT TO LUNCH
www.overduemedia.com
(c)2002 Overdue Media all rights reserved

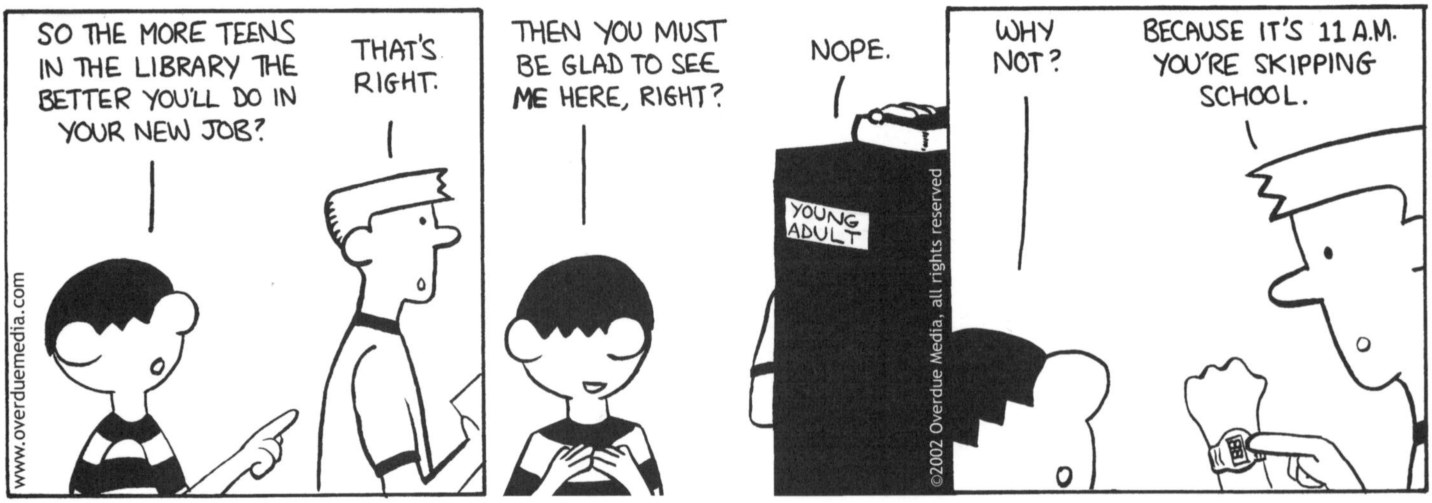
SO THE MORE TEENS IN THE LIBRARY THE BETTER YOU'LL DO IN YOUR NEW JOB?
THAT'S RIGHT.
THEN YOU MUST BE GLAD TO SEE **ME** HERE, RIGHT?
NOPE.
YOUNG ADULT
WHY NOT?
BECAUSE IT'S 11 A.M. YOU'RE SKIPPING SCHOOL.
www.overduemedia.com
©2002 Overdue Media, all rights reserved

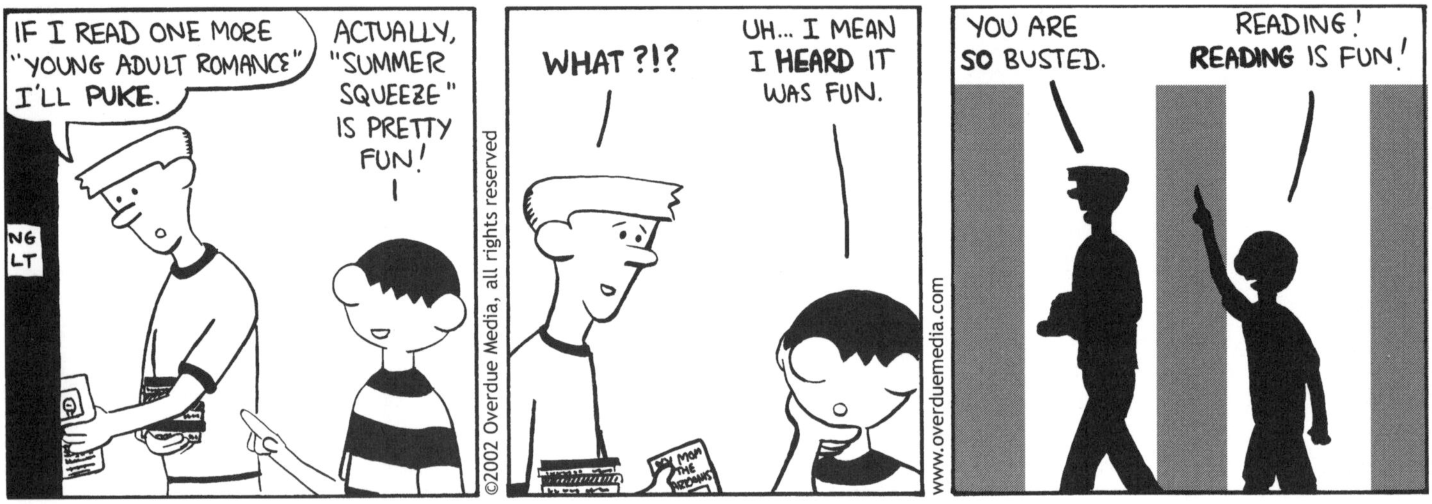
IF I READ ONE MORE "YOUNG ADULT ROMANCE" I'LL **PUKE**.
ACTUALLY, "SUMMER SQUEEZE" IS PRETTY FUN!
WHAT?!?
UH... I MEAN I **HEARD** IT WAS FUN.
YOU ARE **SO** BUSTED.
READING! **READING** IS FUN!
©2002 Overdue Media, all rights reserved
www.overduemedia.com

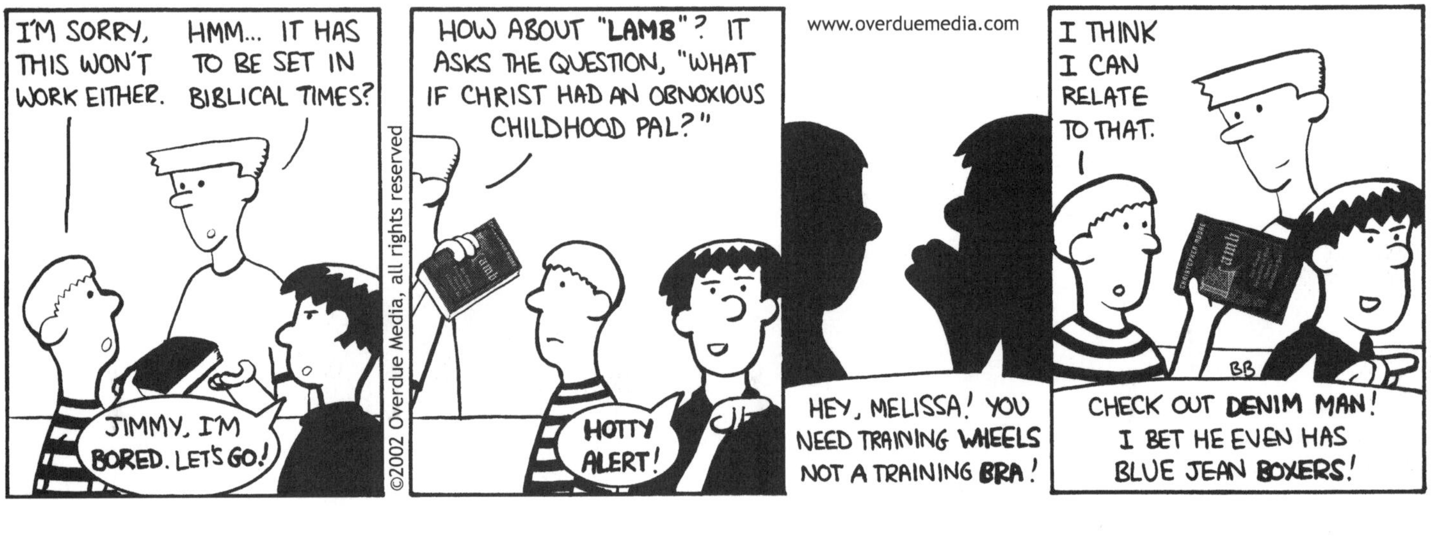
I'M SORRY, THIS WON'T WORK EITHER.
HMM... IT HAS TO BE SET IN BIBLICAL TIMES?
JIMMY, I'M **BORED**. LET'S **GO**!
HOW ABOUT "**LAMB**"? IT ASKS THE QUESTION, "WHAT IF CHRIST HAD AN OBNOXIOUS CHILDHOOD PAL?"
HOTTY ALERT!
HEY, MELISSA! YOU NEED TRAINING **WHEELS** NOT A TRAINING **BRA**!
I THINK I CAN RELATE TO THAT.
CHECK OUT **DENIM MAN**! I BET HE EVEN HAS BLUE JEAN **BOXERS**!
BB
©2002 Overdue Media, all rights reserved
www.overduemedia.com

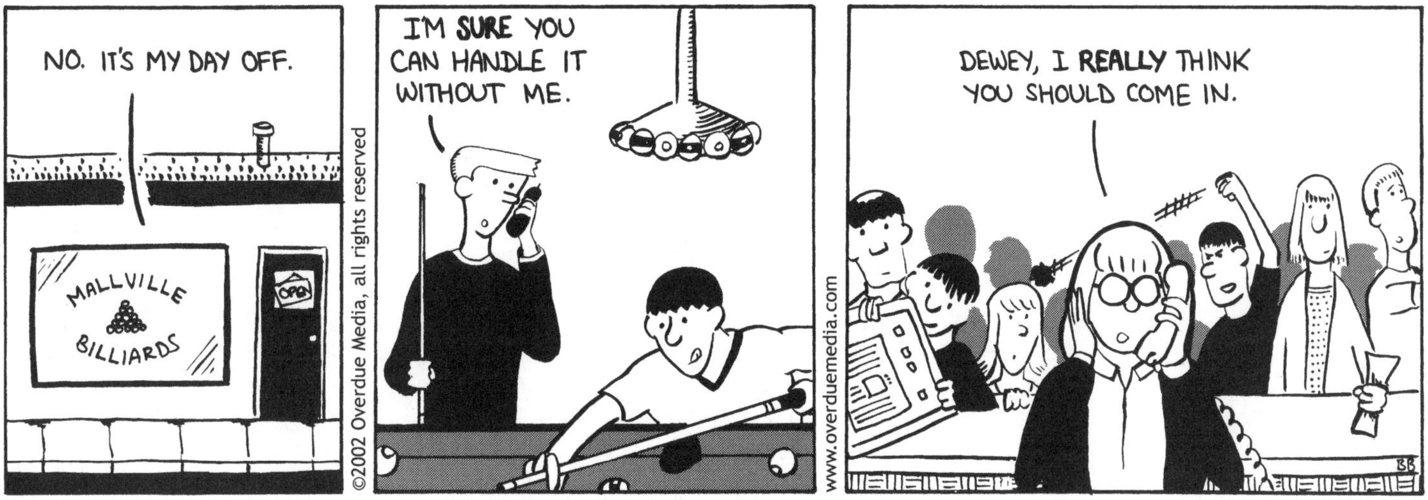
NO. IT'S MY DAY OFF.
MALLVILLE BILLIARDS
OPEN
I'M SURE YOU CAN HANDLE IT WITHOUT ME.
©2002 Overdue Media, all rights reserved
DEWEY, I REALLY THINK YOU SHOULD COME IN.
www.overduemedia.com
BB

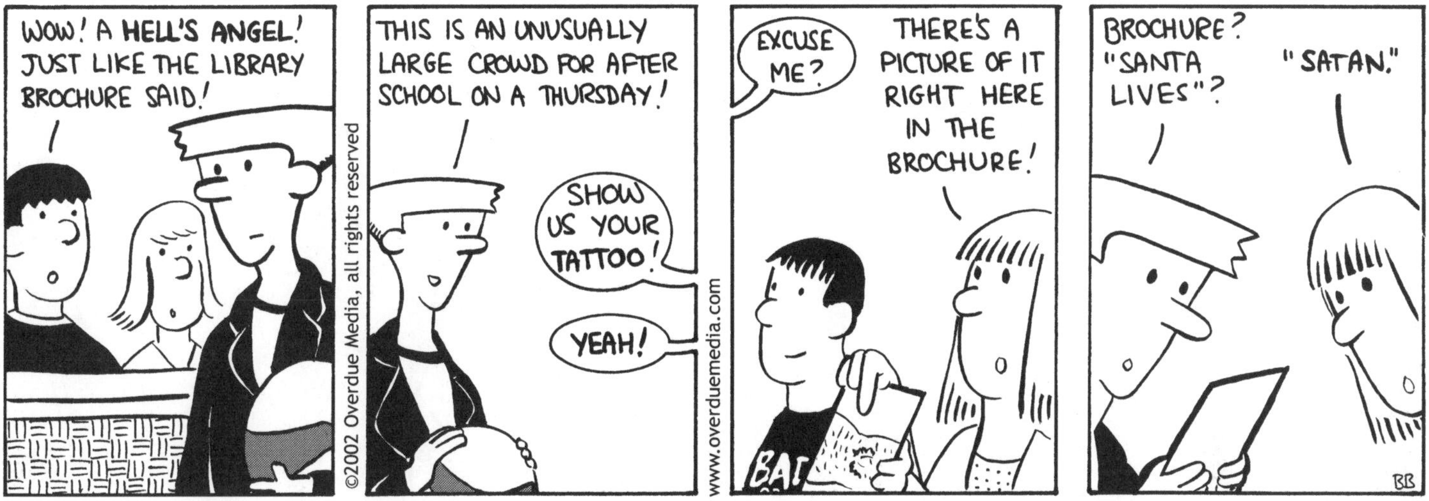
WOW! A HELL'S ANGEL! JUST LIKE THE LIBRARY BROCHURE SAID!
©2002 Overdue Media, all rights reserved
THIS IS AN UNUSUALLY LARGE CROWD FOR AFTER SCHOOL ON A THURSDAY!
SHOW US YOUR TATTOO!
YEAH!
www.overduemedia.com
EXCUSE ME?
THERE'S A PICTURE OF IT RIGHT HERE IN THE BROCHURE!
BROCHURE? "SANTA LIVES"?
"SATAN."
BB

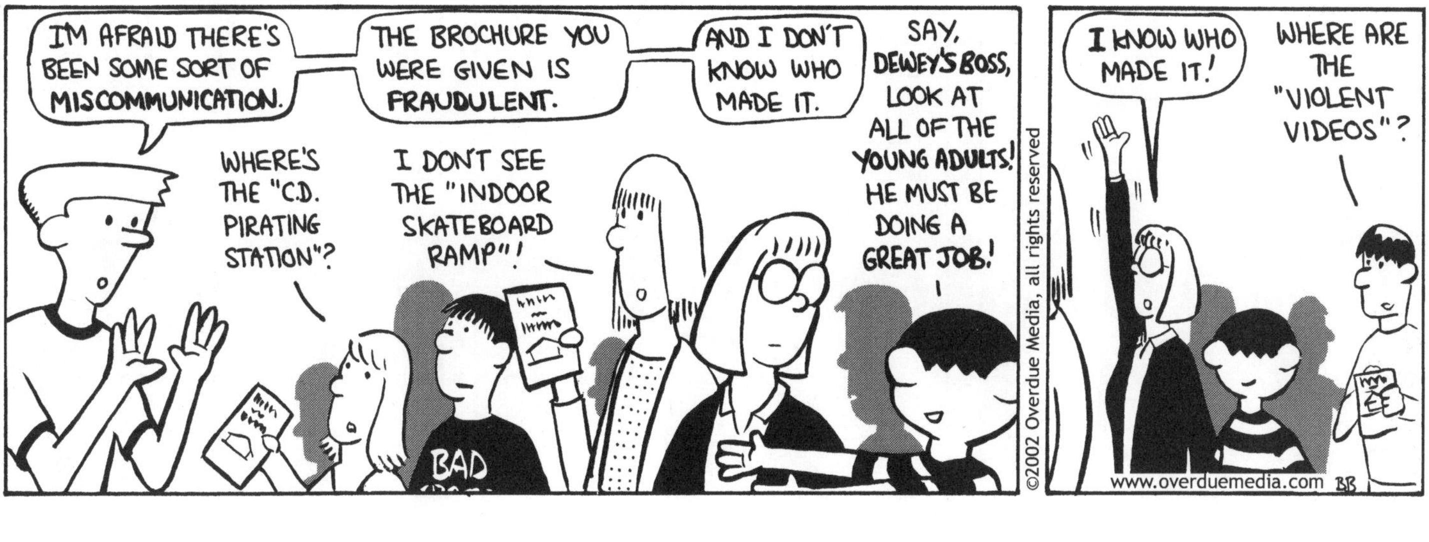
I'M AFRAID THERE'S BEEN SOME SORT OF MISCOMMUNICATION.
THE BROCHURE YOU WERE GIVEN IS FRAUDULENT.
AND I DON'T KNOW WHO MADE IT.
WHERE'S THE "C.D. PIRATING STATION"?
I DON'T SEE THE "INDOOR SKATEBOARD RAMP"!
SAY, DEWEY'S BOSS, LOOK AT ALL OF THE YOUNG ADULTS! HE MUST BE DOING A GREAT JOB!
BAD
©2002 Overdue Media, all rights reserved
I KNOW WHO MADE IT!
WHERE ARE THE "VIOLENT VIDEOS"?
www.overduemedia.com
BB

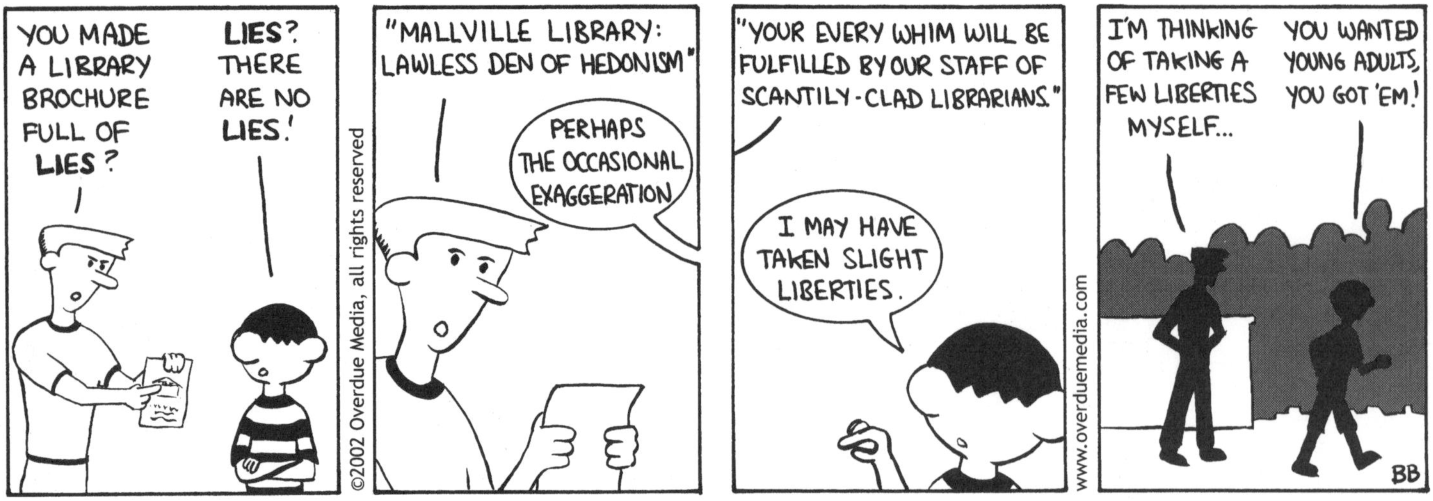
YOU MADE A LIBRARY BROCHURE FULL OF LIES?
LIES? THERE ARE NO LIES!
©2002 Overdue Media, all rights reserved
"MALLVILLE LIBRARY: LAWLESS DEN OF HEDONISM"
PERHAPS THE OCCASIONAL EXAGGERATION
"YOUR EVERY WHIM WILL BE FULFILLED BY OUR STAFF OF SCANTILY-CLAD LIBRARIANS."
I MAY HAVE TAKEN SLIGHT LIBERTIES.
www.overduemedia.com
I'M THINKING OF TAKING A FEW LIBERTIES MYSELF...
YOU WANTED YOUNG ADULTS, YOU GOT 'EM!
BB

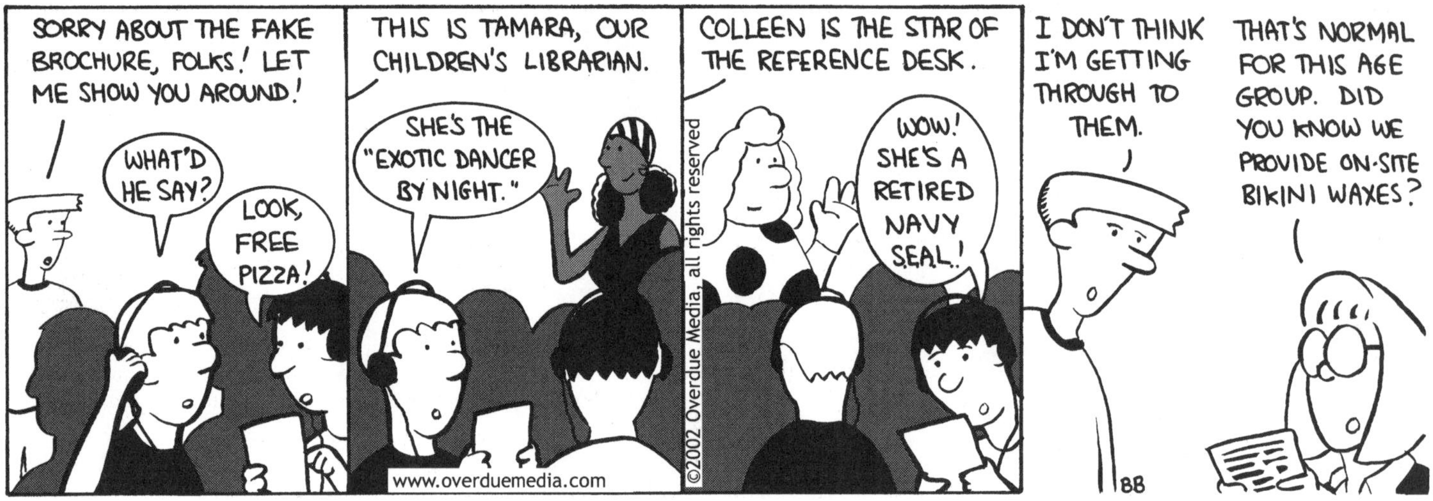
SORRY ABOUT THE FAKE BROCHURE, FOLKS! LET ME SHOW YOU AROUND!
WHAT'D HE SAY?
LOOK, FREE PIZZA!
THIS IS TAMARA, OUR CHILDREN'S LIBRARIAN.
SHE'S THE "EXOTIC DANCER BY NIGHT."
www.overduemedia.com
COLLEEN IS THE STAR OF THE REFERENCE DESK.
WOW! SHE'S A RETIRED NAVY SEAL!
©2002 Overdue Media, all rights reserved
I DON'T THINK I'M GETTING THROUGH TO THEM.
THAT'S NORMAL FOR THIS AGE GROUP. DID YOU KNOW WE PROVIDE ON-SITE BIKINI WAXES?
BB

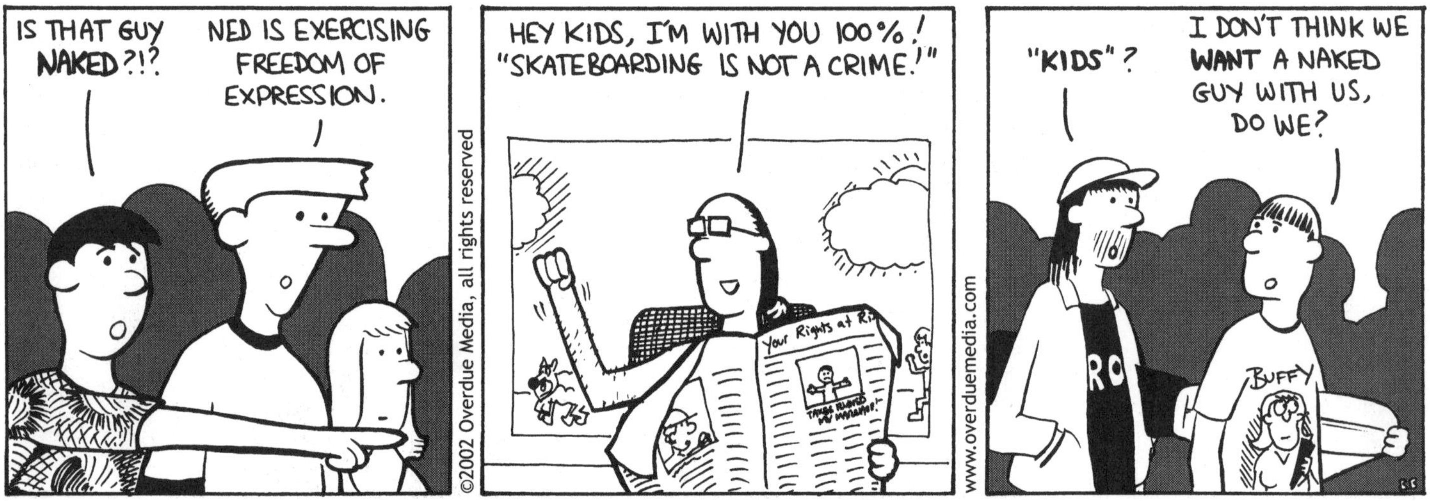
IS THAT GUY NAKED?!?
NED IS EXERCISING FREEDOM OF EXPRESSION.
©2002 Overdue Media, all rights reserved
HEY KIDS, I'M WITH YOU 100%! "SKATEBOARDING IS NOT A CRIME!"
www.overduemedia.com
"KIDS"?
I DON'T THINK WE WANT A NAKED GUY WITH US, DO WE?
BUFFY

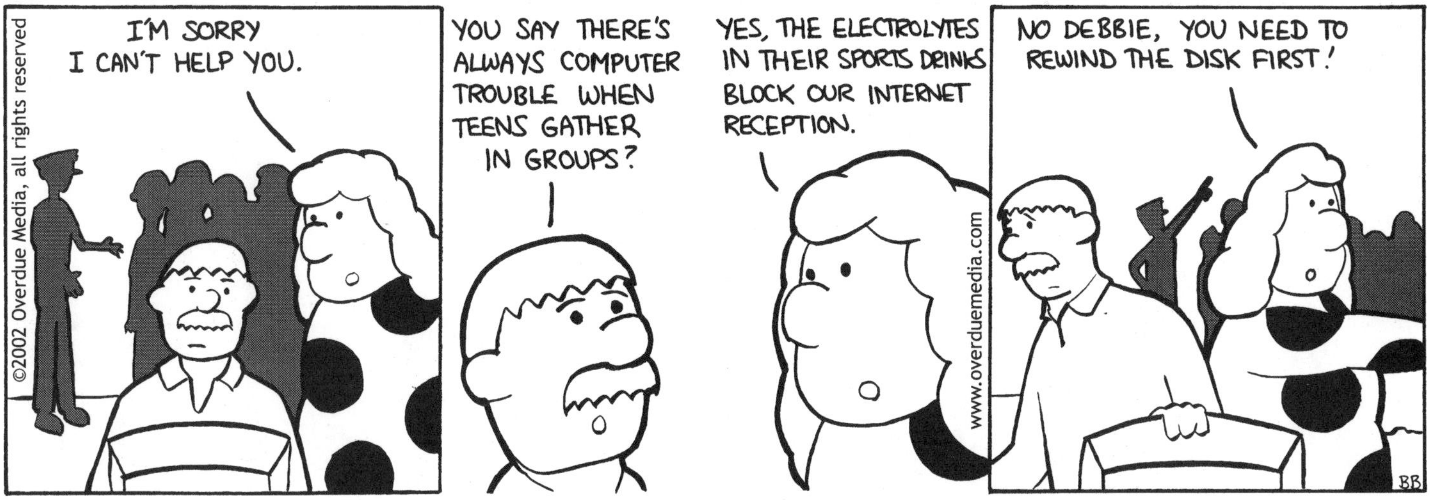
©2002 Overdue Media, all rights reserved
I'M SORRY I CAN'T HELP YOU.
YOU SAY THERE'S ALWAYS COMPUTER TROUBLE WHEN TEENS GATHER IN GROUPS?
YES, THE ELECTROLYTES IN THEIR SPORTS DRINKS BLOCK OUR INTERNET RECEPTION.
www.overduemedia.com
NO DEBBIE, YOU NEED TO REWIND THE DISK FIRST!
BB

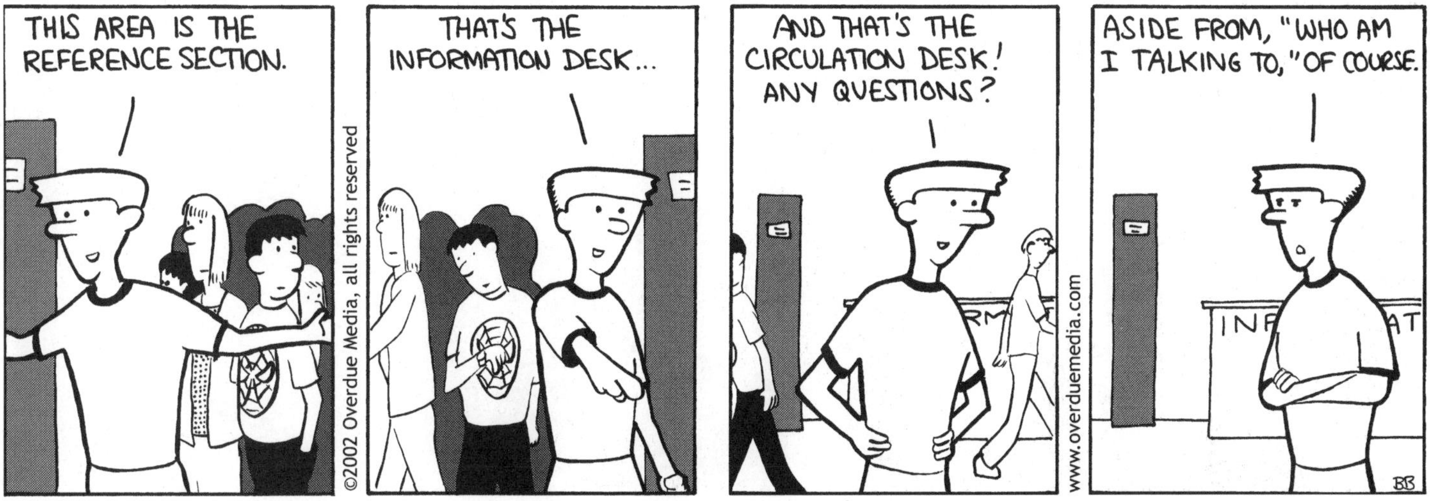
THIS AREA IS THE REFERENCE SECTION.
©2002 Overdue Media, all rights reserved
THAT'S THE INFORMATION DESK...
AND THAT'S THE CIRCULATION DESK! ANY QUESTIONS?
www.overduemedia.com
ASIDE FROM, "WHO AM I TALKING TO," OF COURSE.
BB

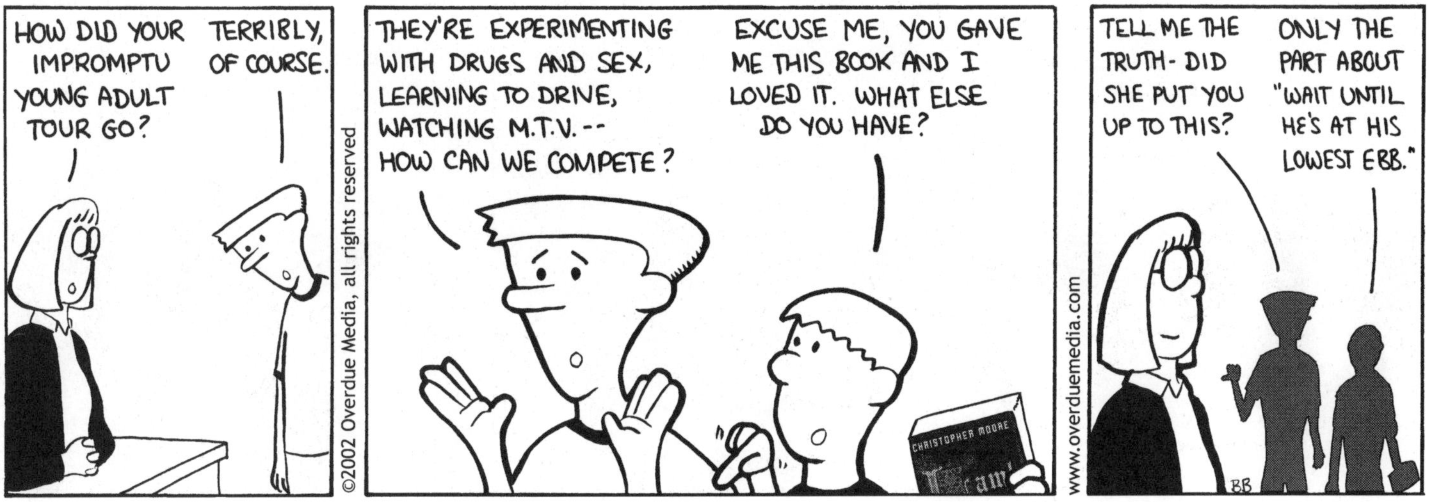
HOW DID YOUR IMPROMPTU YOUNG ADULT TOUR GO?
TERRIBLY, OF COURSE.
©2002 Overdue Media, all rights reserved
THEY'RE EXPERIMENTING WITH DRUGS AND SEX, LEARNING TO DRIVE, WATCHING M.T.V. -- HOW CAN WE COMPETE?
EXCUSE ME, YOU GAVE ME THIS BOOK AND I LOVED IT. WHAT ELSE DO YOU HAVE?
CHRISTOPHER MOORE
www.overduemedia.com
TELL ME THE TRUTH- DID SHE PUT YOU UP TO THIS?
ONLY THE PART ABOUT "WAIT UNTIL HE'S AT HIS LOWEST EBB."
BB

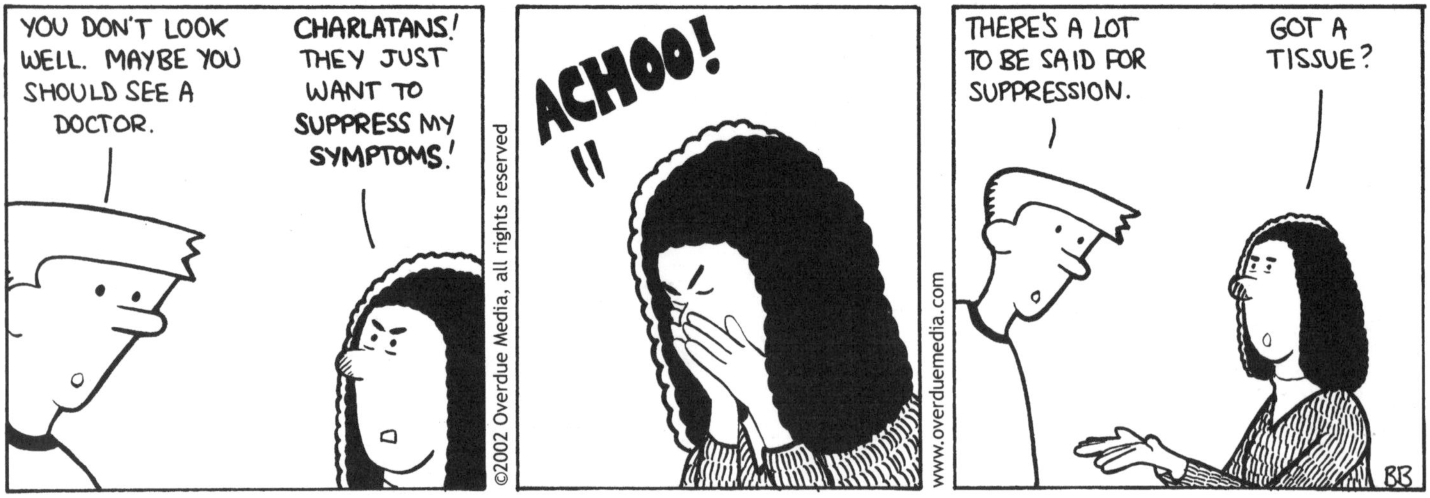
YOU DON'T LOOK WELL. MAYBE YOU SHOULD SEE A DOCTOR.
CHARLATANS! THEY JUST WANT TO SUPPRESS MY SYMPTOMS!
©2002 Overdue Media, all rights reserved
ACHOO!!
www.overduemedia.com
THERE'S A LOT TO BE SAID FOR SUPPRESSION.
GOT A TISSUE?
BB

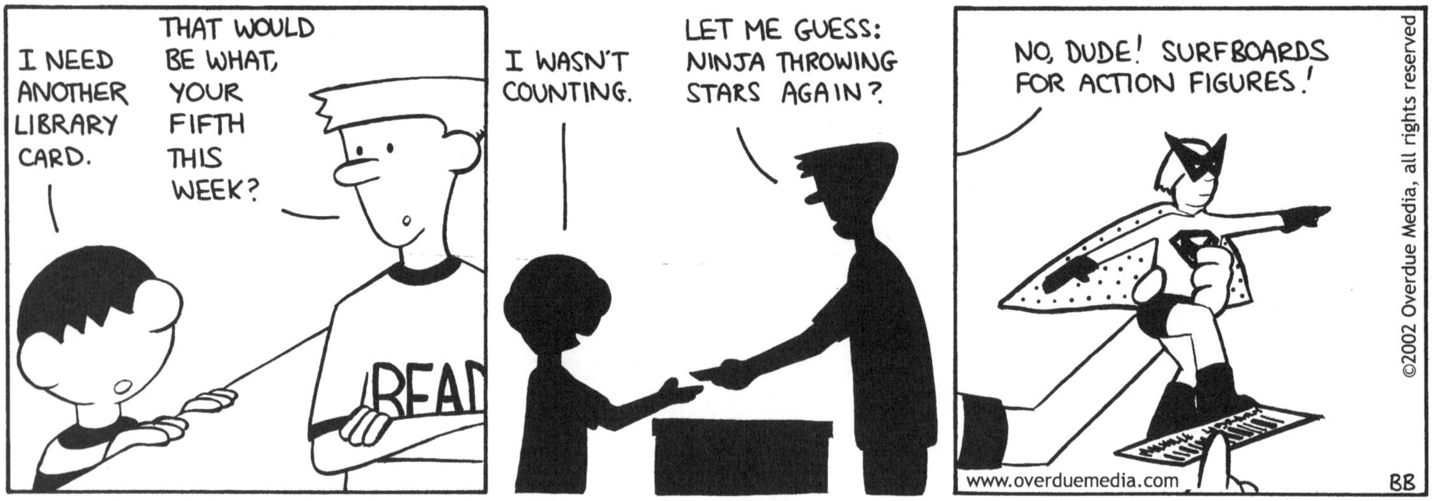
I NEED ANOTHER LIBRARY CARD.
THAT WOULD BE WHAT, YOUR FIFTH THIS WEEK?
READ
I WASN'T COUNTING.
LET ME GUESS: NINJA THROWING STARS AGAIN?
NO, DUDE! SURFBOARDS FOR ACTION FIGURES!
©2002 Overdue Media, all rights reserved
www.overduemedia.com
BB

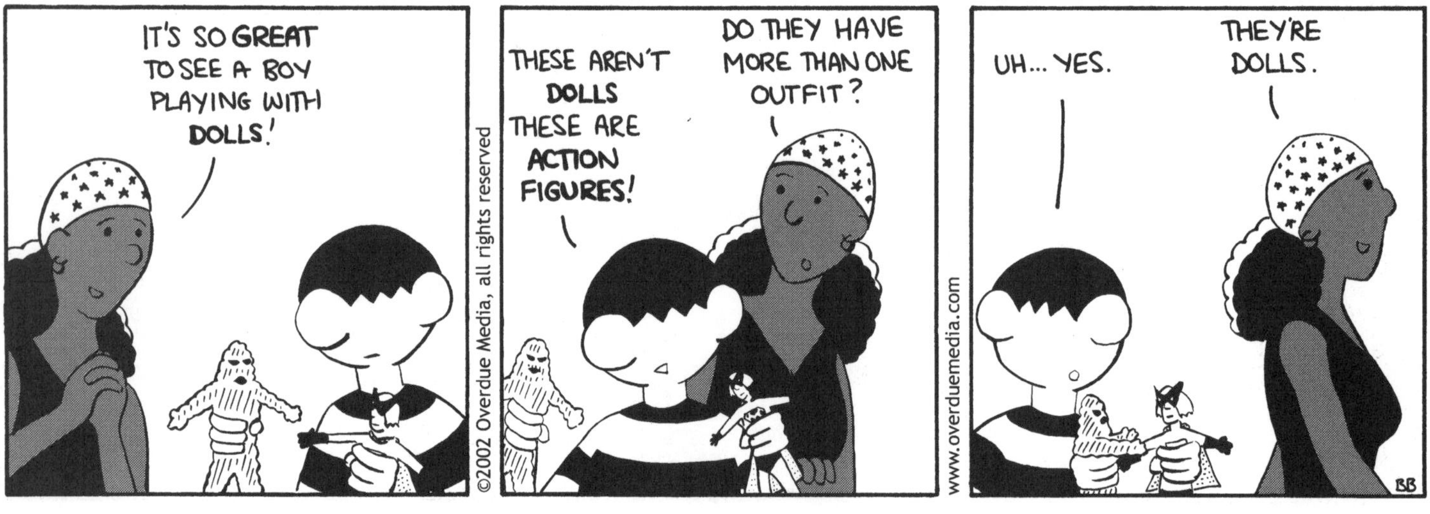
IT'S SO GREAT TO SEE A BOY PLAYING WITH DOLLS!
©2002 Overdue Media, all rights reserved
THESE AREN'T DOLLS THESE ARE ACTION FIGURES!
DO THEY HAVE MORE THAN ONE OUTFIT?
www.overduemedia.com
UH... YES.
THEY'RE DOLLS.
BB

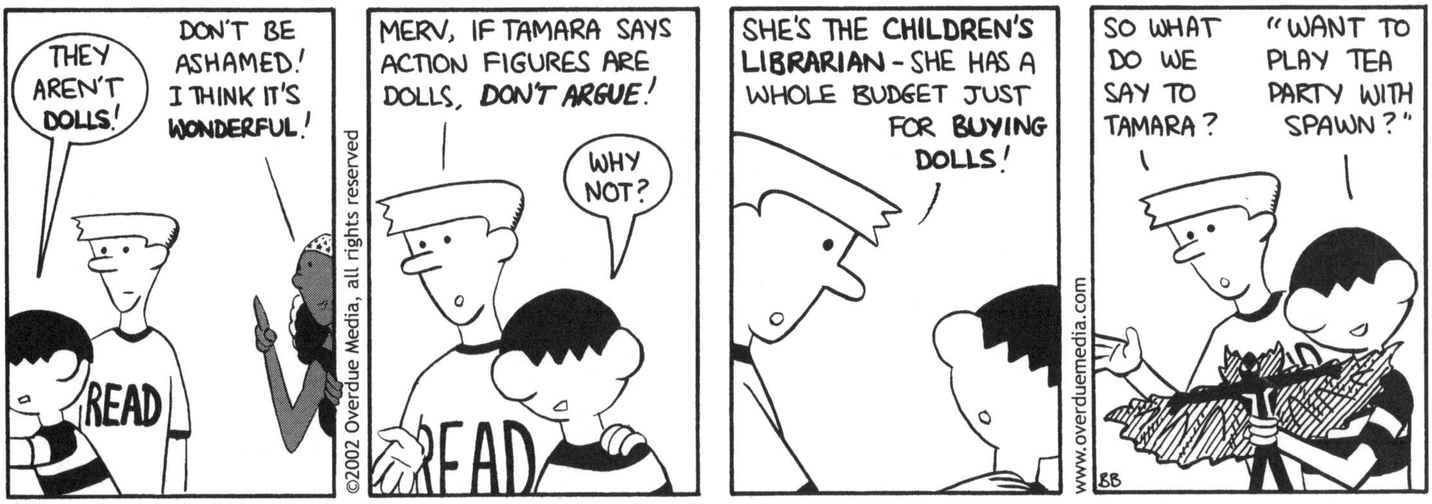
THEY AREN'T DOLLS!
DON'T BE ASHAMED! I THINK IT'S WONDERFUL!
©2002 Overdue Media, all rights reserved
MERV, IF TAMARA SAYS ACTION FIGURES ARE DOLLS, DON'T ARGUE!
WHY NOT?
SHE'S THE CHILDREN'S LIBRARIAN - SHE HAS A WHOLE BUDGET JUST FOR BUYING DOLLS!
www.overduemedia.com
SO WHAT DO WE SAY TO TAMARA?
"WANT TO PLAY TEA PARTY WITH SPAWN?"
BB

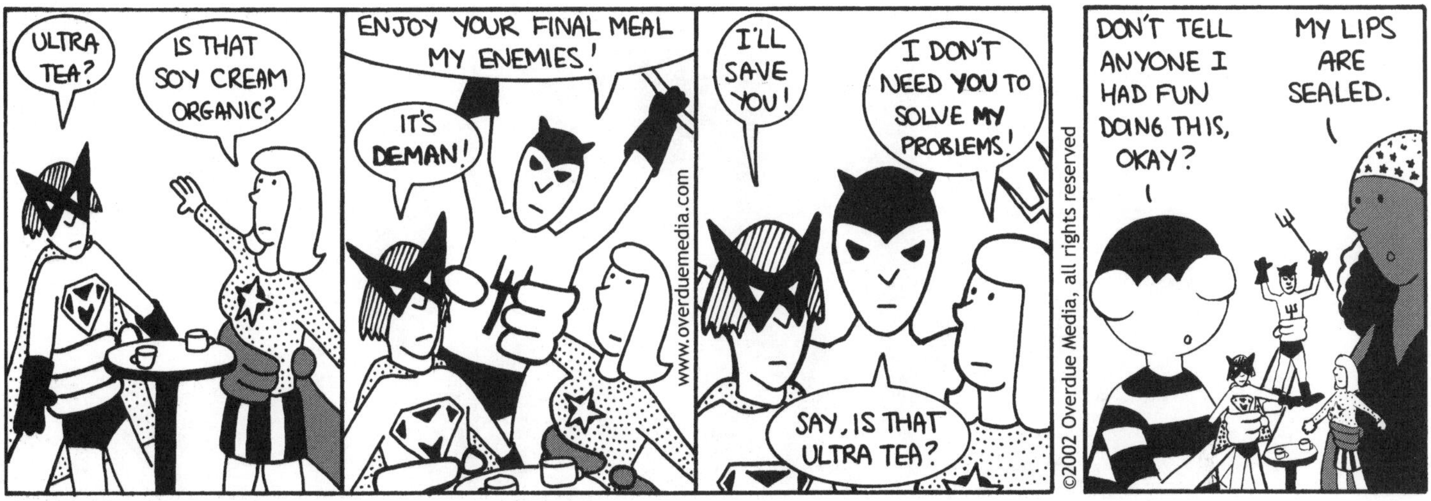
ULTRA TEA?
IS THAT SOY CREAM ORGANIC?
ENJOY YOUR FINAL MEAL MY ENEMIES!
IT'S DEMAN!
www.overduemedia.com
I'LL SAVE YOU!
I DON'T NEED YOU TO SOLVE MY PROBLEMS!
SAY, IS THAT ULTRA TEA?
©2002 Overdue Media, all rights reserved
DON'T TELL ANYONE I HAD FUN DOING THIS, OKAY?
MY LIPS ARE SEALED.

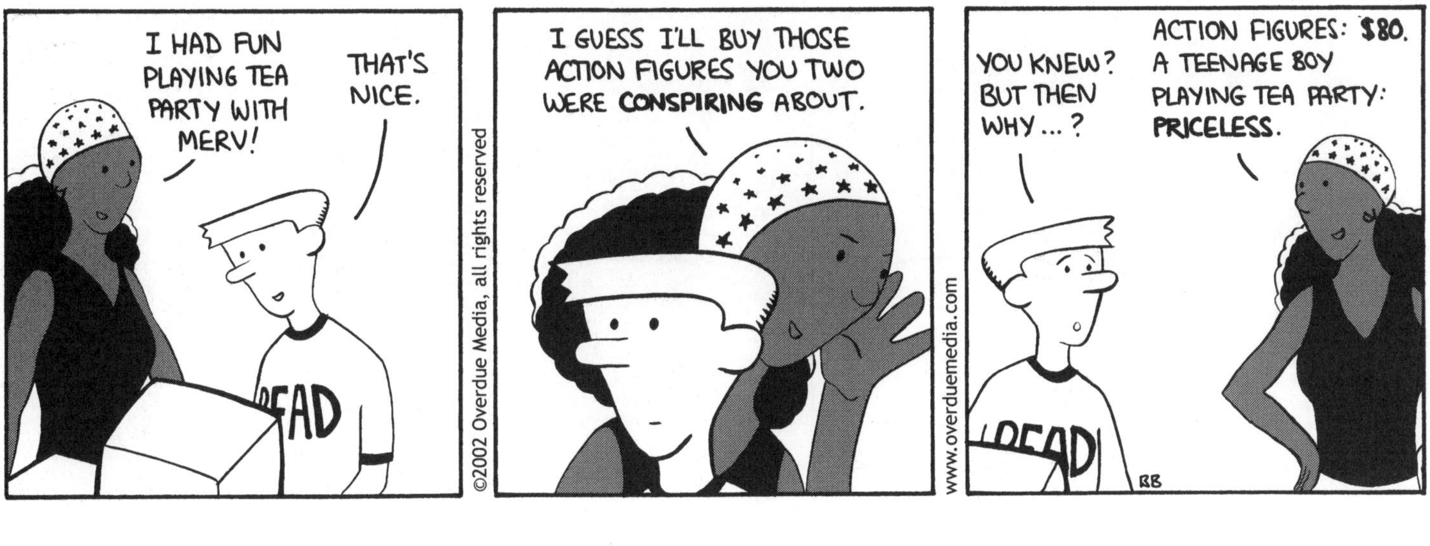
I HAD FUN PLAYING TEA PARTY WITH MERV!
THAT'S NICE.
©2002 Overdue Media, all rights reserved
I GUESS I'LL BUY THOSE ACTION FIGURES YOU TWO WERE CONSPIRING ABOUT.
www.overduemedia.com
YOU KNEW? BUT THEN WHY...?
ACTION FIGURES: $80. A TEENAGE BOY PLAYING TEA PARTY: PRICELESS.
BB

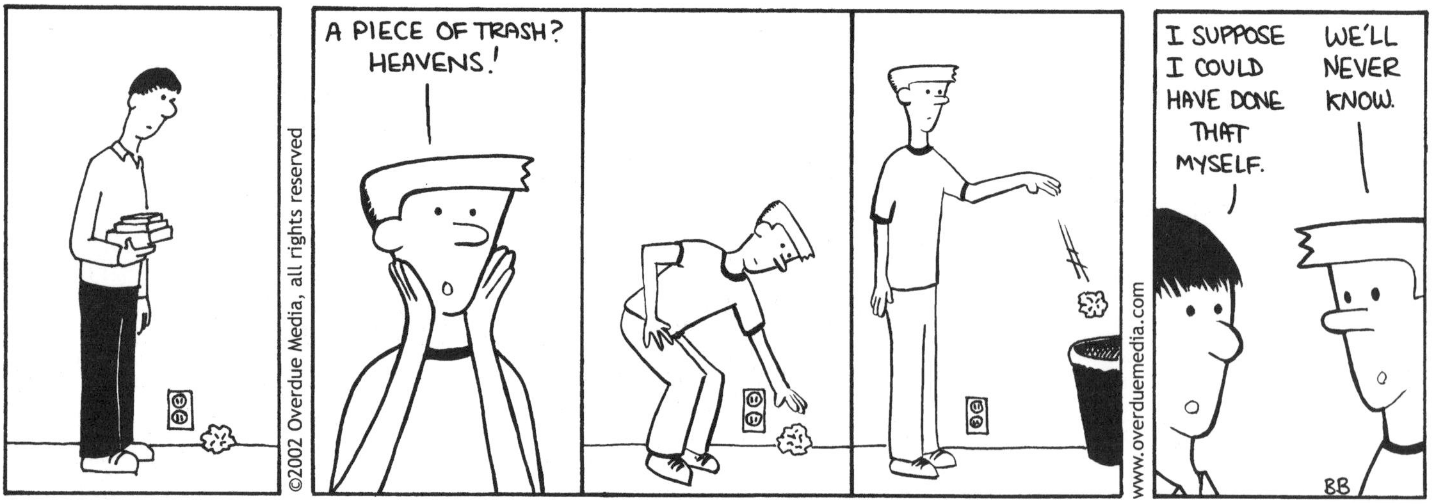
©2002 Overdue Media, all rights reserved
A PIECE OF TRASH? HEAVENS!
www.overduemedia.com
I SUPPOSE I COULD HAVE DONE THAT MYSELF.
WE'LL NEVER KNOW.
BB

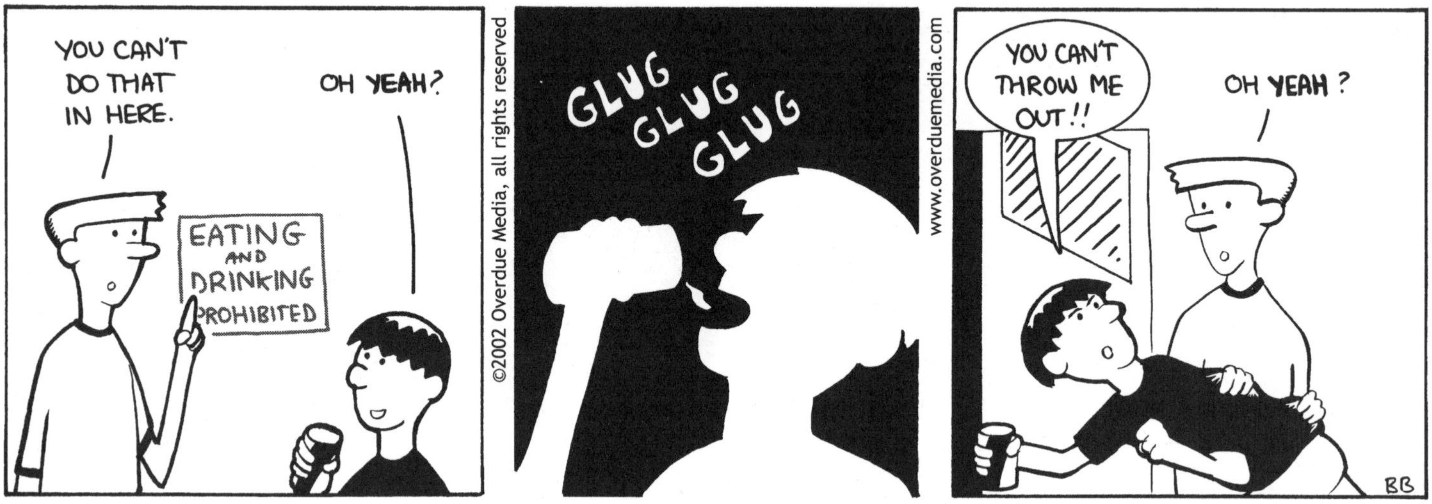
YOU CAN'T DO THAT IN HERE.
EATING AND DRINKING PROHIBITED
OH YEAH?
©2002 Overdue Media, all rights reserved
GLUG GLUG GLUG
www.overduemedia.com
YOU CAN'T THROW ME OUT!!
OH YEAH?
BB

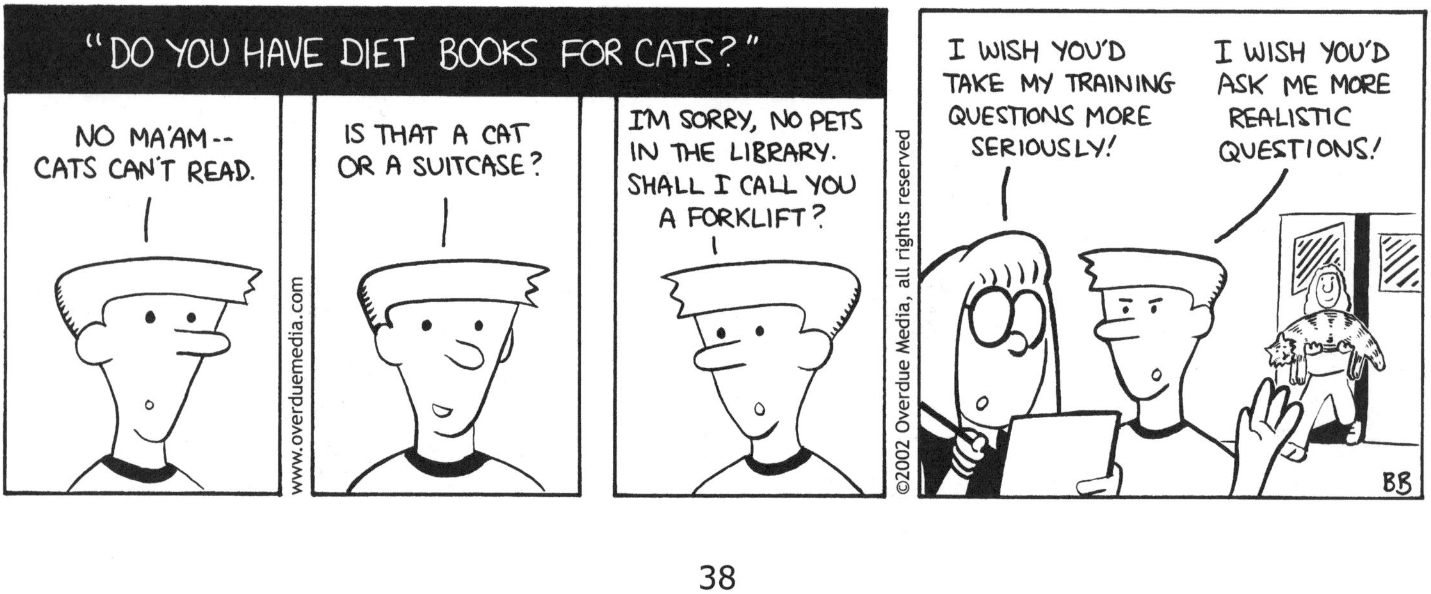
"DO YOU HAVE DIET BOOKS FOR CATS?"
NO MA'AM-- CATS CAN'T READ.
www.overduemedia.com
IS THAT A CAT OR A SUITCASE?
I'M SORRY, NO PETS IN THE LIBRARY. SHALL I CALL YOU A FORKLIFT?
©2002 Overdue Media, all rights reserved
I WISH YOU'D TAKE MY TRAINING QUESTIONS MORE SERIOUSLY!
I WISH YOU'D ASK ME MORE REALISTIC QUESTIONS!
BB

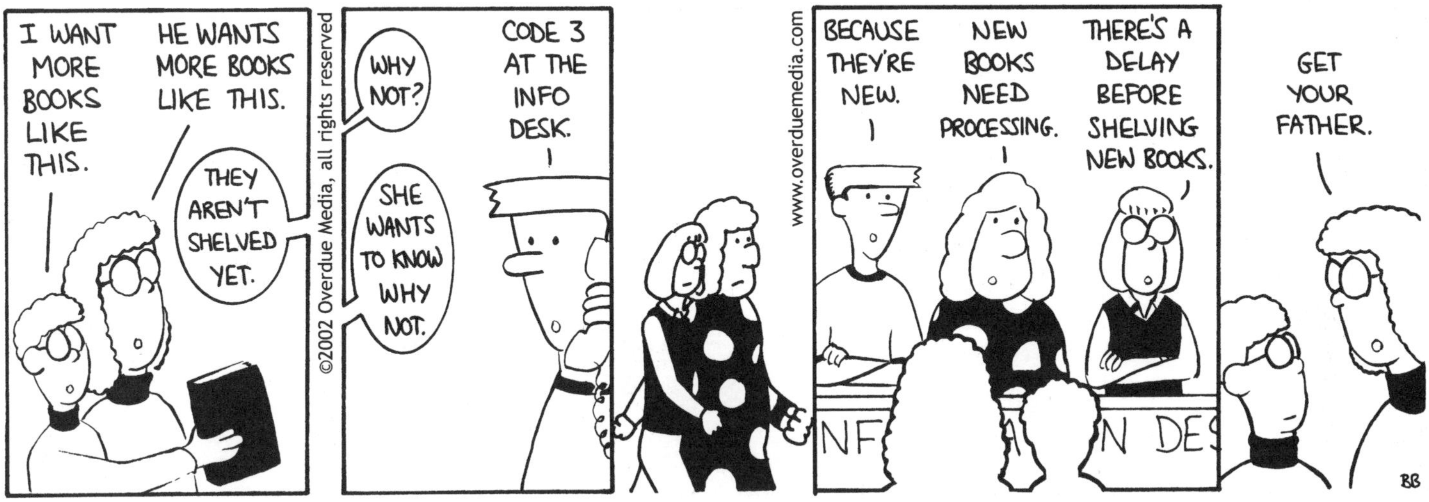
I WANT MORE BOOKS LIKE THIS.
HE WANTS MORE BOOKS LIKE THIS.
THEY AREN'T SHELVED YET.
©2002 Overdue Media, all rights reserved
WHY NOT?
SHE WANTS TO KNOW WHY NOT.
CODE 3 AT THE INFO DESK.
www.overduemedia.com
BECAUSE THEY'RE NEW.
NEW BOOKS NEED PROCESSING.
THERE'S A DELAY BEFORE SHELVING NEW BOOKS.
GET YOUR FATHER.
BB

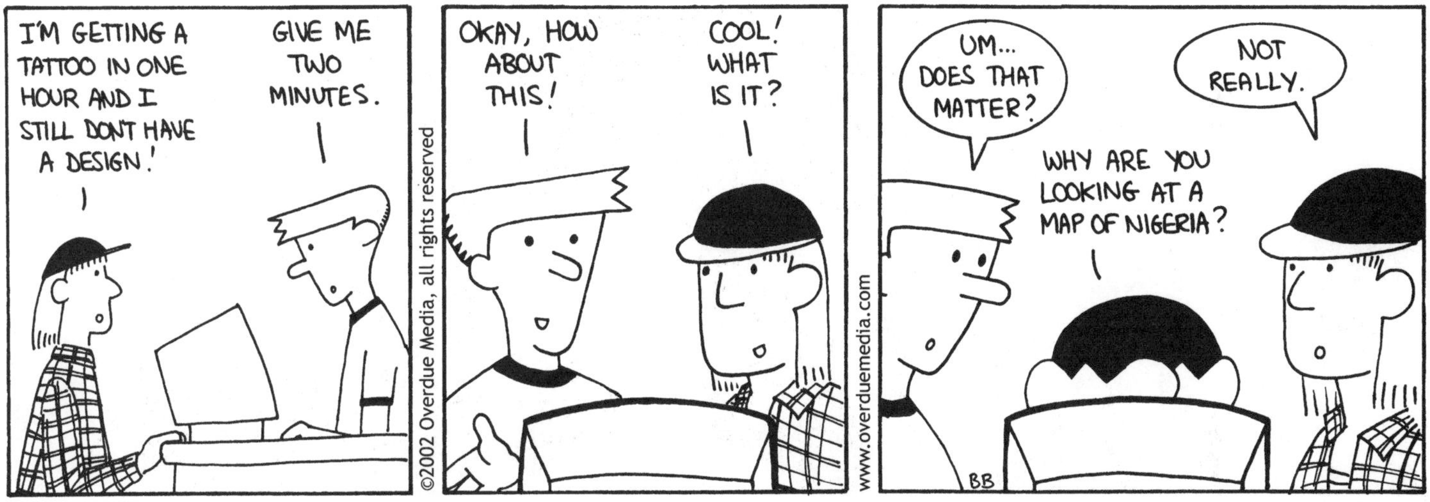
I'M GETTING A TATTOO IN ONE HOUR AND I STILL DON'T HAVE A DESIGN!
GIVE ME TWO MINUTES.
©2002 Overdue Media, all rights reserved
OKAY, HOW ABOUT THIS!
COOL! WHAT IS IT?
www.overduemedia.com
UM... DOES THAT MATTER?
NOT REALLY.
WHY ARE YOU LOOKING AT A MAP OF NIGERIA?
BB

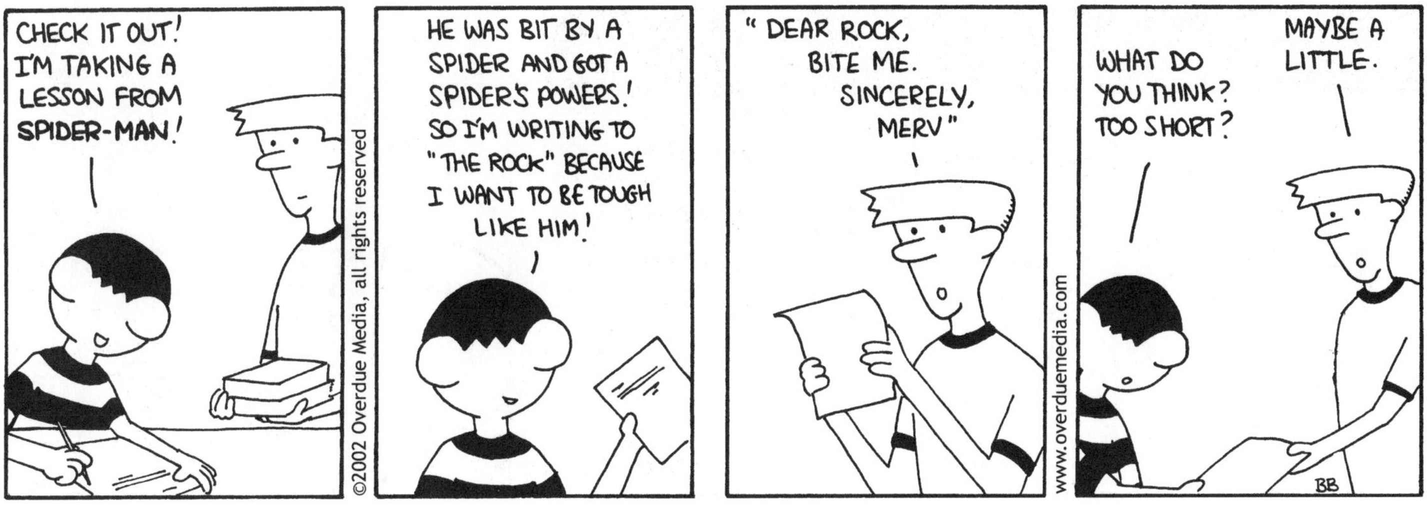
CHECK IT OUT! I'M TAKING A LESSON FROM SPIDER-MAN!
©2002 Overdue Media, all rights reserved
HE WAS BIT BY A SPIDER AND GOT A SPIDER'S POWERS! SO I'M WRITING TO "THE ROCK" BECAUSE I WANT TO BE TOUGH LIKE HIM!
" DEAR ROCK, BITE ME. SINCERELY, MERV "
www.overduemedia.com
WHAT DO YOU THINK? TOO SHORT?
MAYBE A LITTLE.
BB

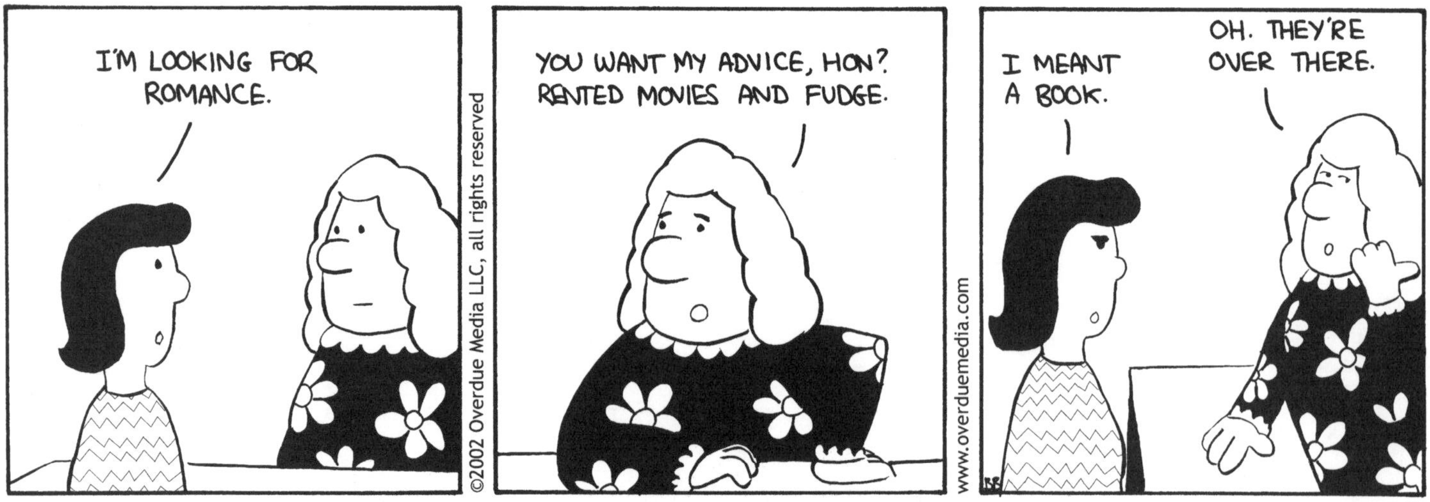
I'M LOOKING FOR ROMANCE.
©2002 Overdue Media LLC, all rights reserved
YOU WANT MY ADVICE, HON? RENTED MOVIES AND FUDGE.
www.overduemedia.com
I MEANT A BOOK.
OH. THEY'RE OVER THERE.

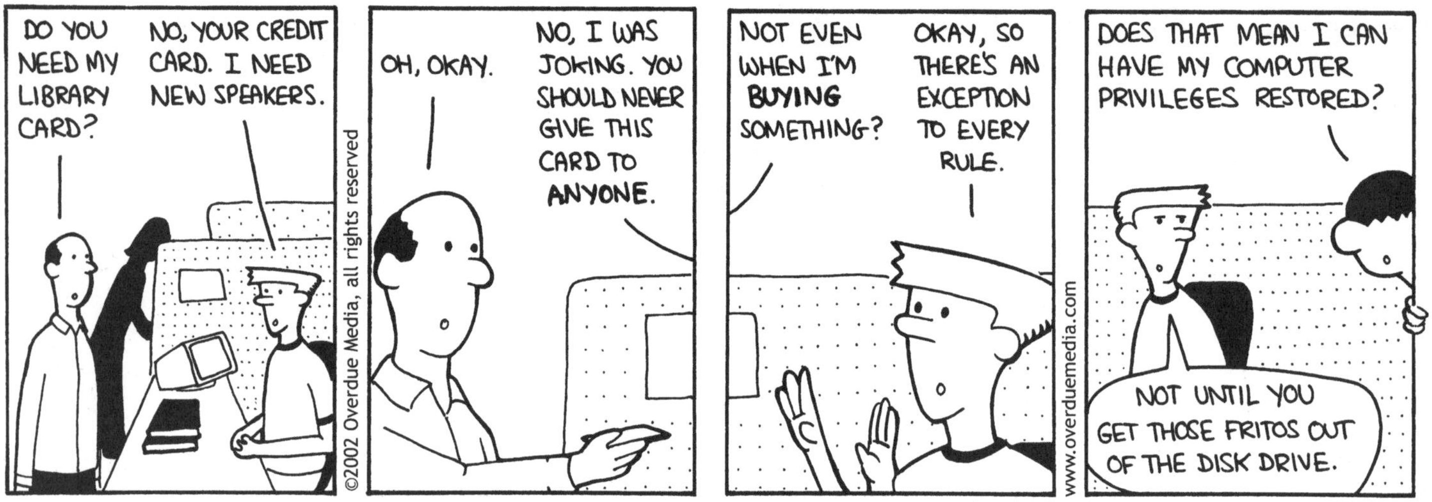
DO YOU NEED MY LIBRARY CARD?
NO, YOUR CREDIT CARD. I NEED NEW SPEAKERS.
©2002 Overdue Media, all rights reserved
OH, OKAY.
NO, I WAS JOKING. YOU SHOULD NEVER GIVE THIS CARD TO **ANYONE**.
NOT EVEN WHEN I'M **BUYING** SOMETHING?
OKAY, SO THERE'S AN EXCEPTION TO EVERY RULE.
www.overduemedia.com
DOES THAT MEAN I CAN HAVE MY COMPUTER PRIVILEGES RESTORED?
NOT UNTIL YOU GET THOSE FRITOS OUT OF THE DISK DRIVE.

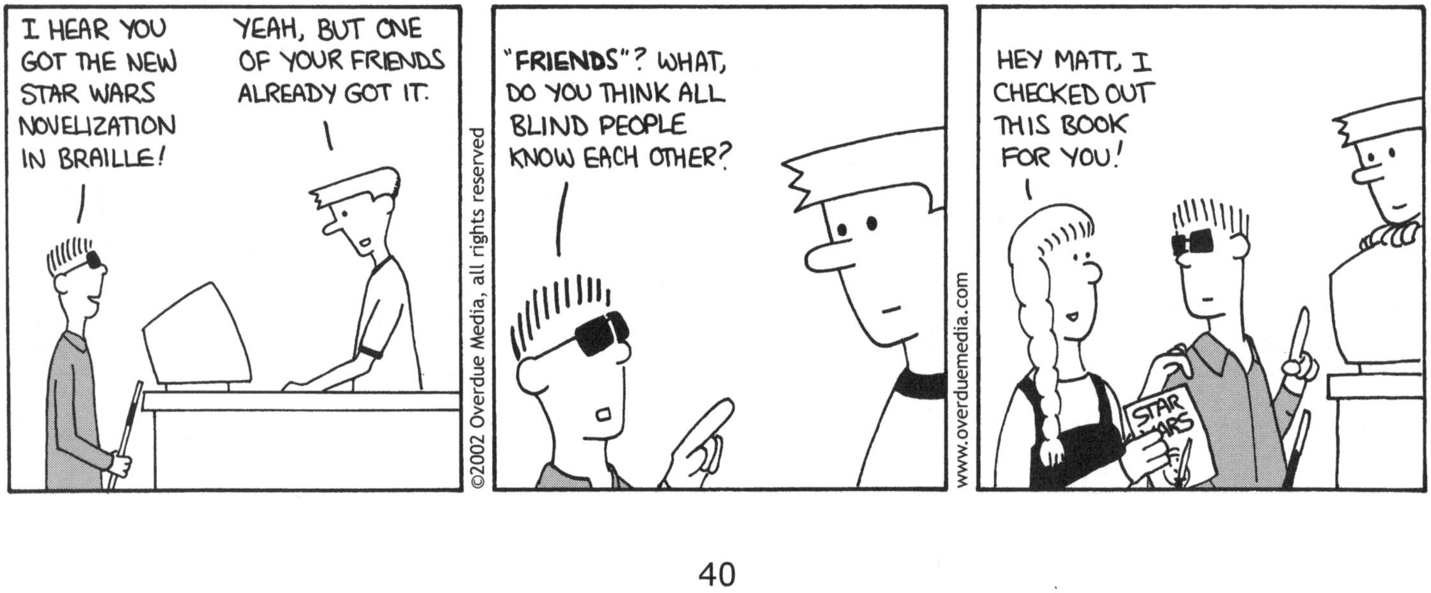
I HEAR YOU GOT THE NEW STAR WARS NOVELIZATION IN BRAILLE!
YEAH, BUT ONE OF YOUR FRIENDS ALREADY GOT IT.
©2002 Overdue Media, all rights reserved
"**FRIENDS**"? WHAT, DO YOU THINK ALL BLIND PEOPLE KNOW EACH OTHER?
www.overduemedia.com
HEY MATT, I CHECKED OUT THIS BOOK FOR YOU!
STAR WARS

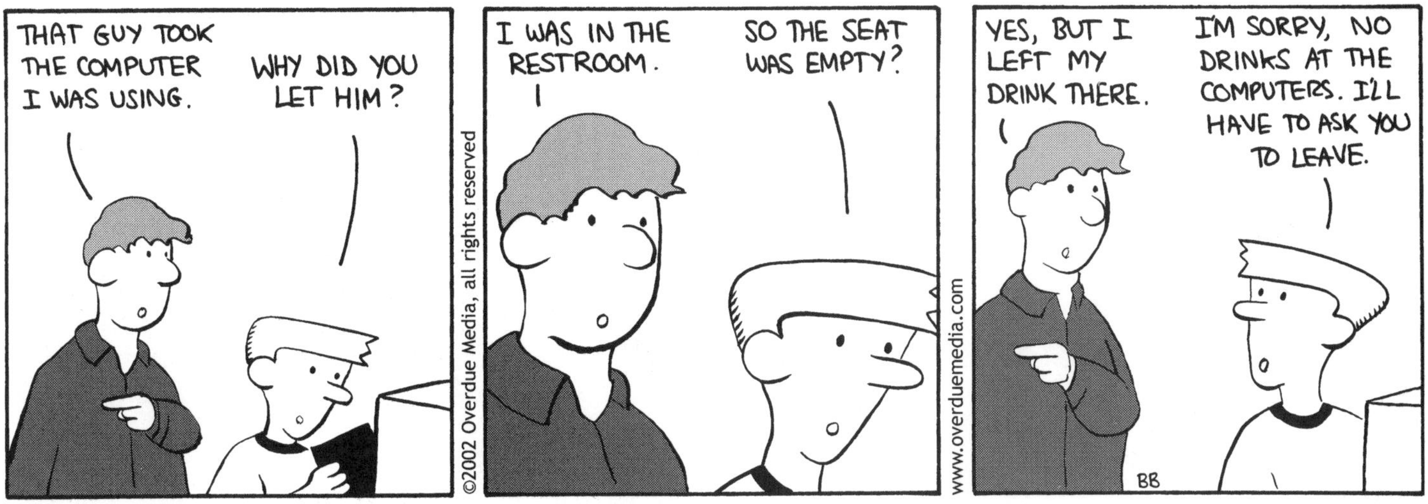
THAT GUY TOOK THE COMPUTER I WAS USING.
WHY DID YOU LET HIM?
©2002 Overdue Media, all rights reserved
I WAS IN THE RESTROOM.
SO THE SEAT WAS EMPTY?
www.overduemedia.com
YES, BUT I LEFT MY DRINK THERE.
I'M SORRY, NO DRINKS AT THE COMPUTERS. I'LL HAVE TO ASK YOU TO LEAVE.
BB

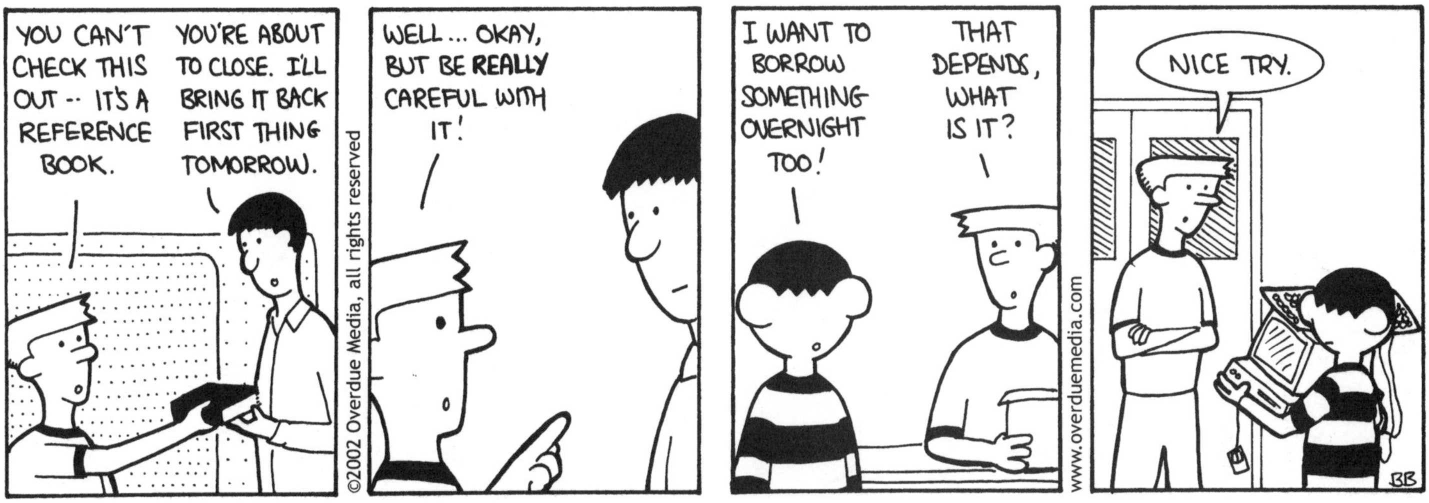
YOU CAN'T CHECK THIS OUT -- IT'S A REFERENCE BOOK.
YOU'RE ABOUT TO CLOSE. I'LL BRING IT BACK FIRST THING TOMORROW.
©2002 Overdue Media, all rights reserved
WELL... OKAY, BUT BE REALLY CAREFUL WITH IT!
I WANT TO BORROW SOMETHING OVERNIGHT TOO!
THAT DEPENDS, WHAT IS IT?
www.overduemedia.com
NICE TRY.
BB

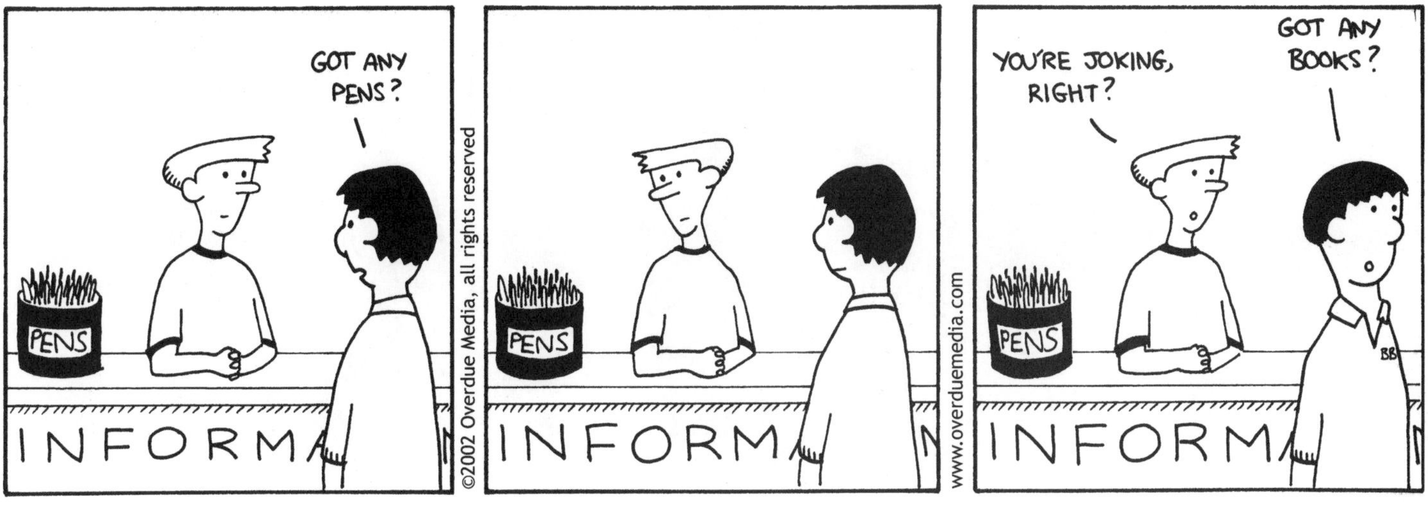
PENS
GOT ANY PENS?
INFORMA
©2002 Overdue Media, all rights reserved
PENS
INFORMA
www.overduemedia.com
PENS
YOU'RE JOKING, RIGHT?
GOT ANY BOOKS?
INFORMA
BB

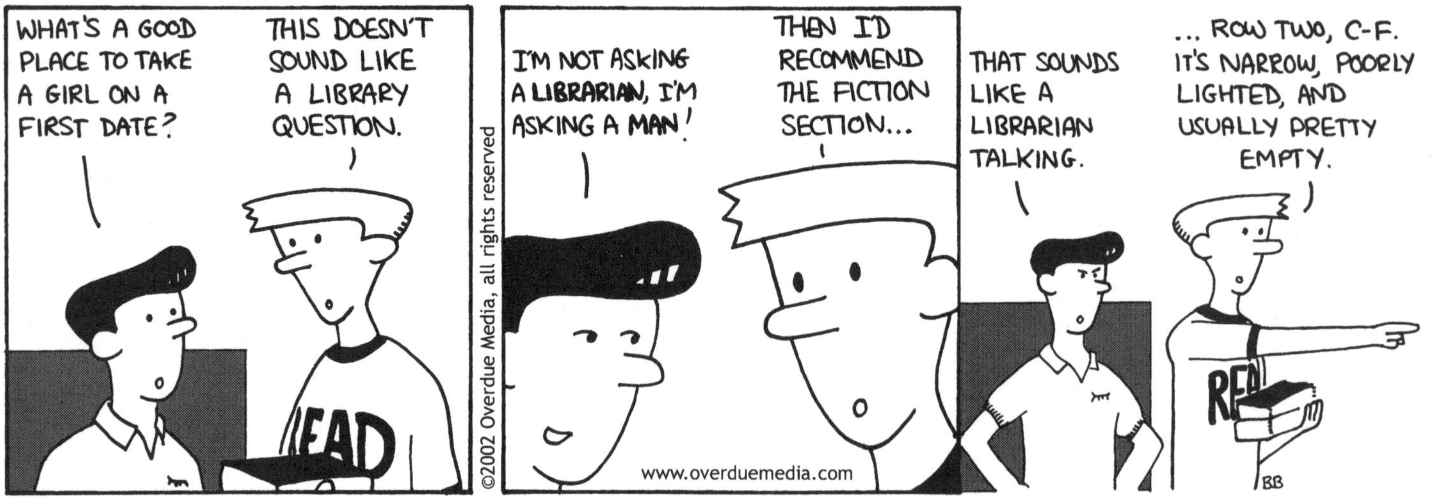
WHAT'S A GOOD PLACE TO TAKE A GIRL ON A FIRST DATE?
THIS DOESN'T SOUND LIKE A LIBRARY QUESTION.
I'M NOT ASKING A LIBRARIAN, I'M ASKING A MAN!
THEN I'D RECOMMEND THE FICTION SECTION...
THAT SOUNDS LIKE A LIBRARIAN TALKING.
... ROW TWO, C-F. IT'S NARROW, POORLY LIGHTED, AND USUALLY PRETTY EMPTY.
©2002 Overdue Media, all rights reserved
www.overduemedia.com
BB

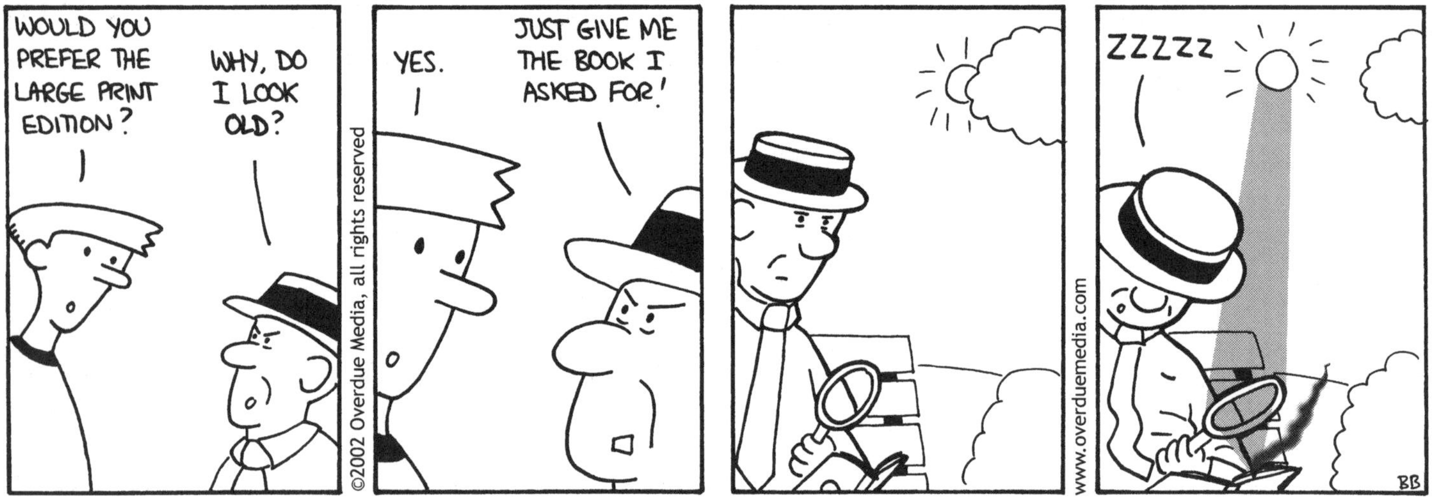
WOULD YOU PREFER THE LARGE PRINT EDITION?
WHY, DO I LOOK OLD?
YES.
JUST GIVE ME THE BOOK I ASKED FOR!
ZZZZZ
©2002 Overdue Media, all rights reserved
www.overduemedia.com
BB

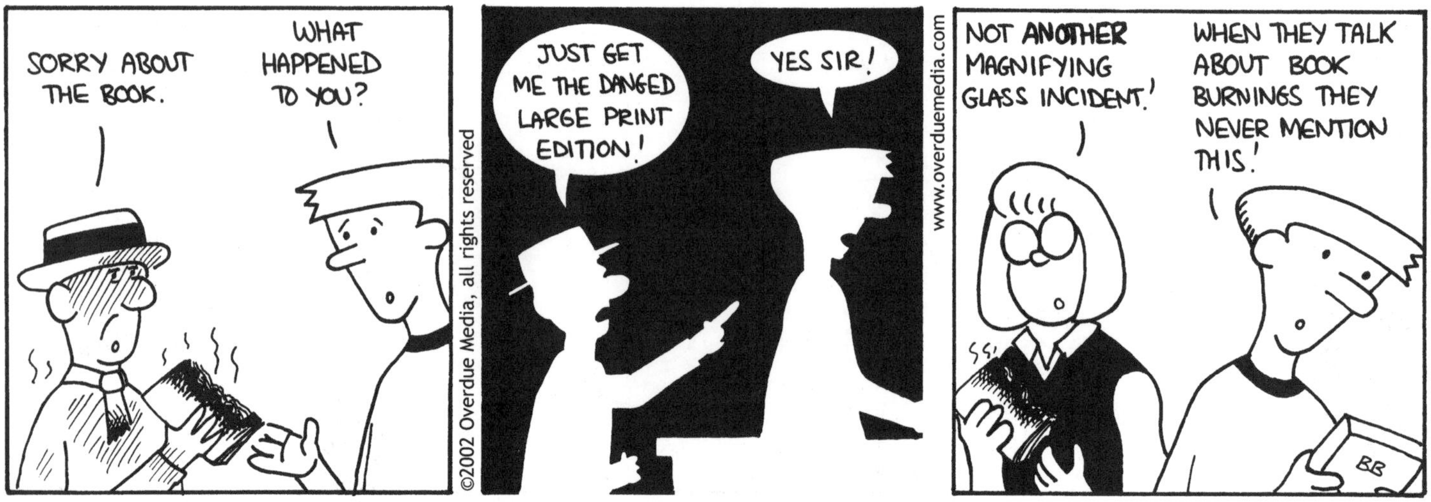
SORRY ABOUT THE BOOK.
WHAT HAPPENED TO YOU?
JUST GET ME THE DANGED LARGE PRINT EDITION!
YES SIR!
NOT ANOTHER MAGNIFYING GLASS INCIDENT!
WHEN THEY TALK ABOUT BOOK BURNINGS THEY NEVER MENTION THIS!
©2002 Overdue Media, all rights reserved
www.overduemedia.com
BB

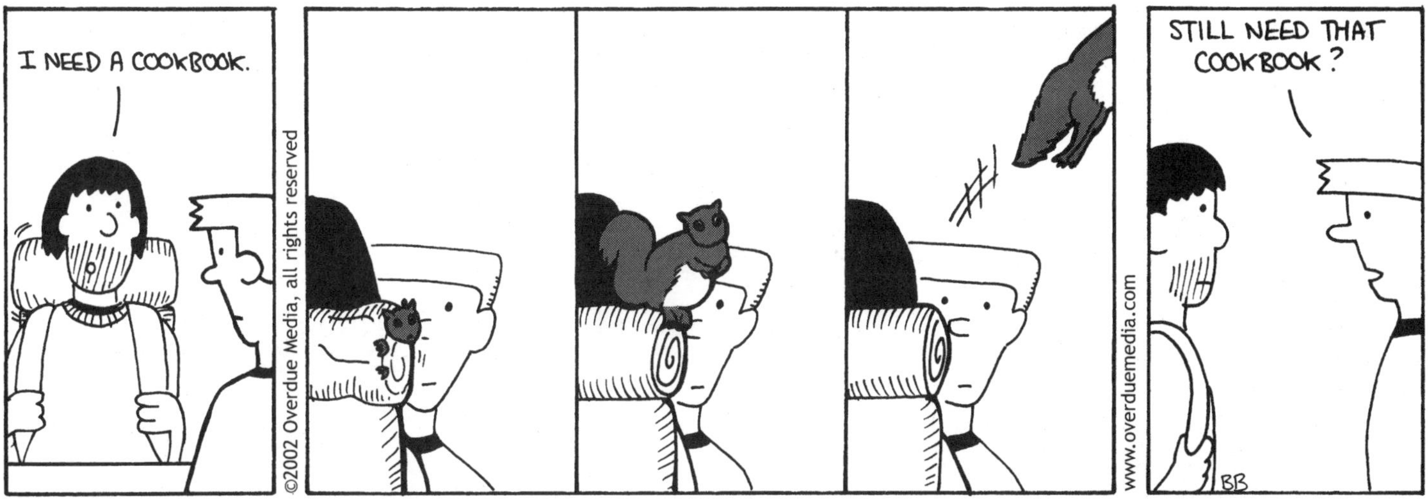
I NEED A COOKBOOK.
STILL NEED THAT COOKBOOK?
©2002 Overdue Media, all rights reserved
www.overduemedia.com
BB

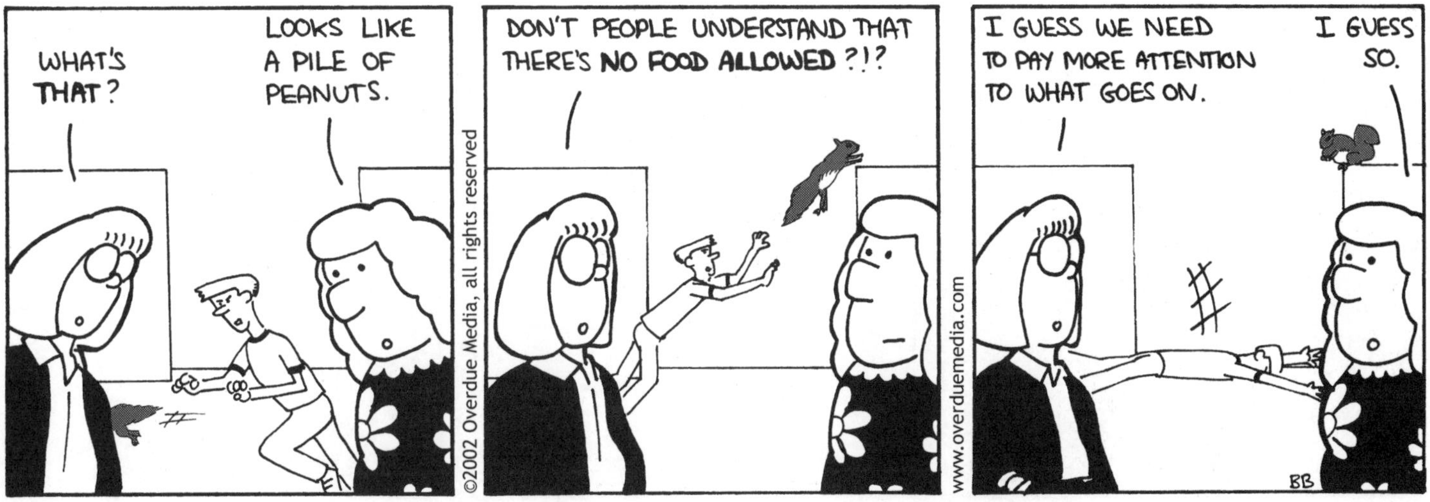
WHAT'S **THAT**?
LOOKS LIKE A PILE OF PEANUTS.
DON'T PEOPLE UNDERSTAND THAT THERE'S **NO FOOD ALLOWED**?!?
I GUESS WE NEED TO PAY MORE ATTENTION TO WHAT GOES ON.
I GUESS SO.
©2002 Overdue Media, all rights reserved
www.overduemedia.com
BB

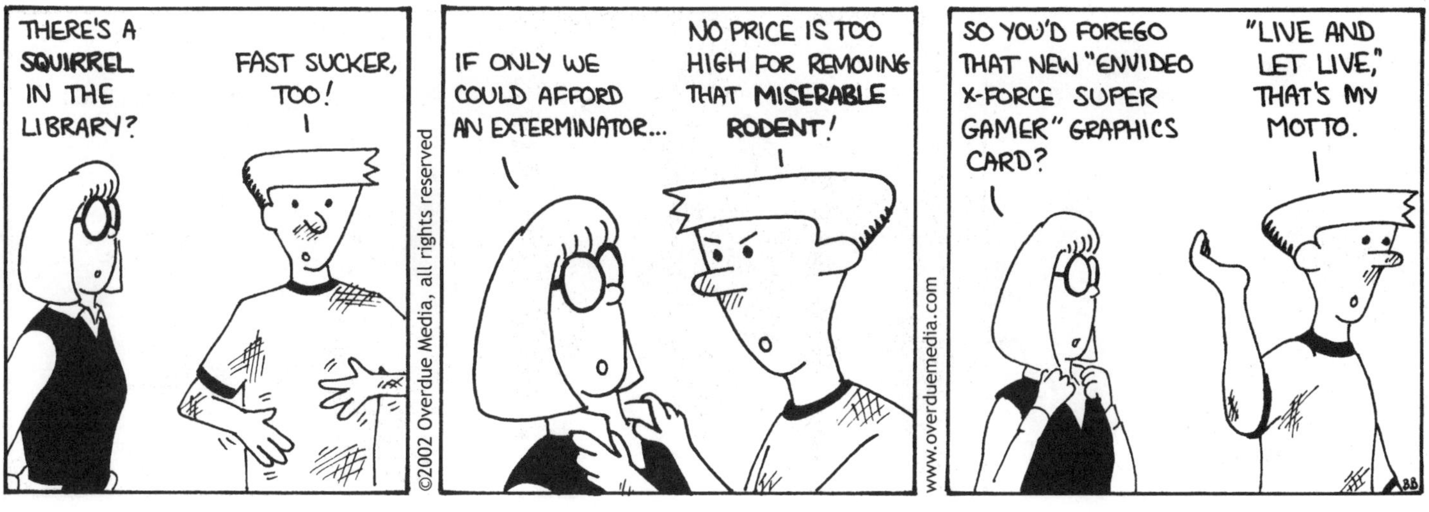
THERE'S A **SQUIRREL** IN THE LIBRARY?
FAST SUCKER, TOO!
IF ONLY WE COULD AFFORD AN EXTERMINATOR...
NO PRICE IS TOO HIGH FOR REMOVING THAT **MISERABLE RODENT**!
SO YOU'D FOREGO THAT NEW "ENVIDEO X-FORCE SUPER GAMER" GRAPHICS CARD?
"LIVE AND LET LIVE," THAT'S MY MOTTO.
©2002 Overdue Media, all rights reserved
www.overduemedia.com
BB

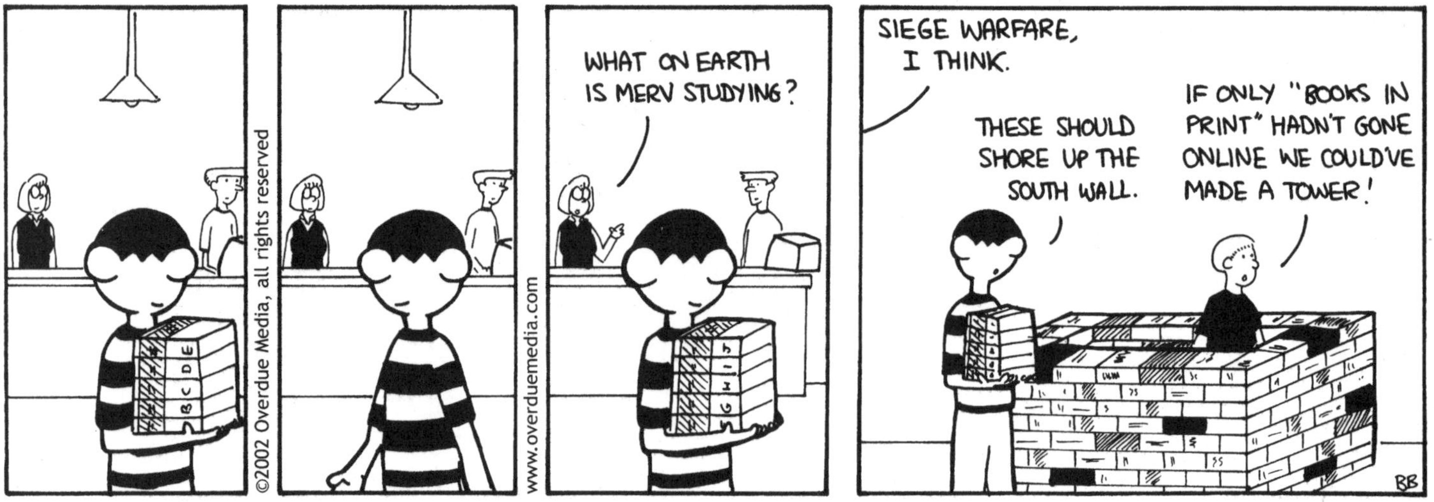
©2002 Overdue Media, all rights reserved
www.overduemedia.com
WHAT ON EARTH IS MERV STUDYING?
SIEGE WARFARE, I THINK.
THESE SHOULD SHORE UP THE SOUTH WALL.
IF ONLY "BOOKS IN PRINT" HADN'T GONE ONLINE WE COULD'VE MADE A TOWER!
BB

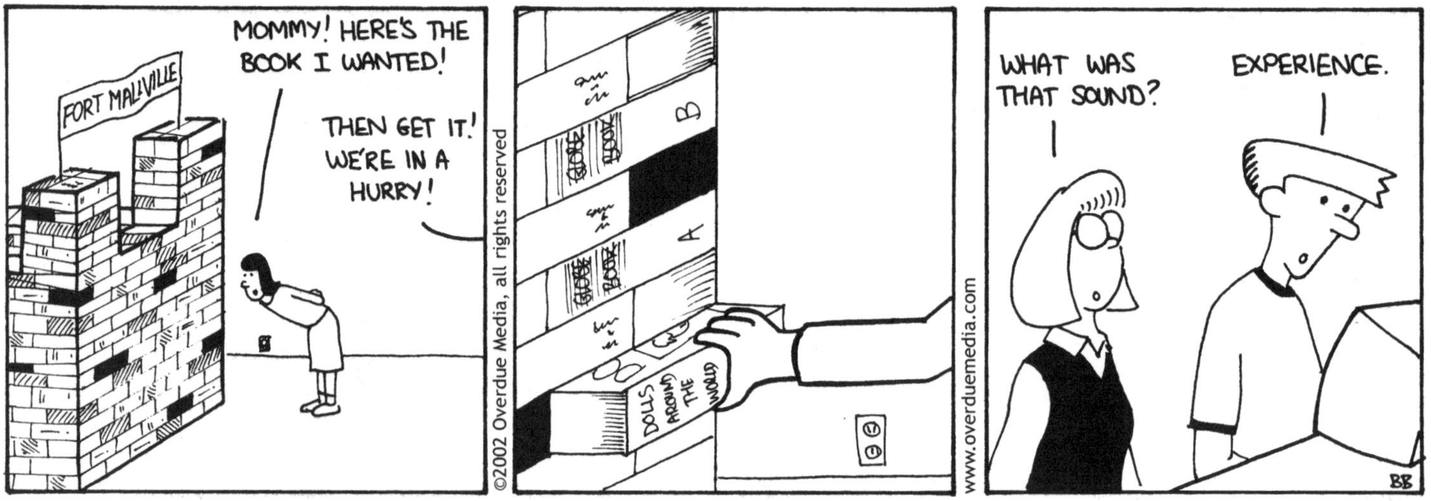
FORT MALLVILLE
MOMMY! HERE'S THE BOOK I WANTED!
THEN GET IT! WE'RE IN A HURRY!
©2002 Overdue Media, all rights reserved
DOLLS AROUND THE WORLD
www.overduemedia.com
WHAT WAS THAT SOUND?
EXPERIENCE.
BB

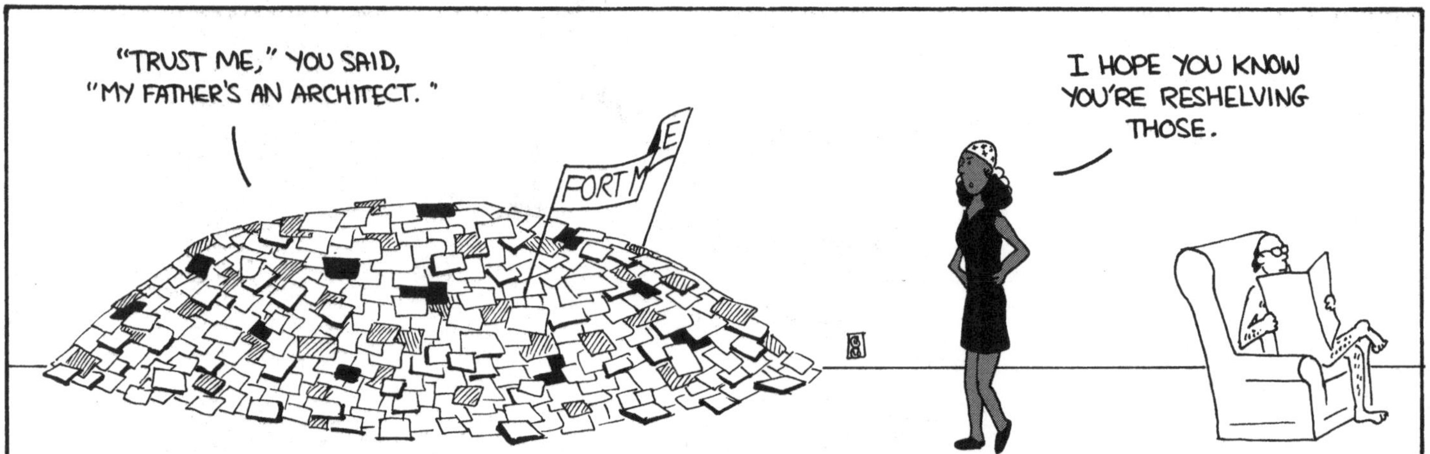
"TRUST ME," YOU SAID, "MY FATHER'S AN ARCHITECT."
FORT M E
I HOPE YOU KNOW YOU'RE RESHELVING THOSE.
©2002 Overdue Media, all rights reserved
www.overduemedia.com
BB

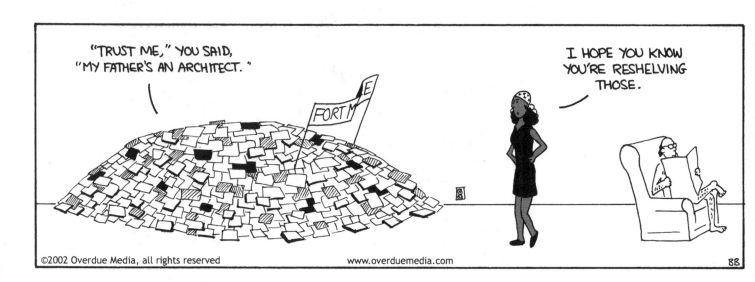

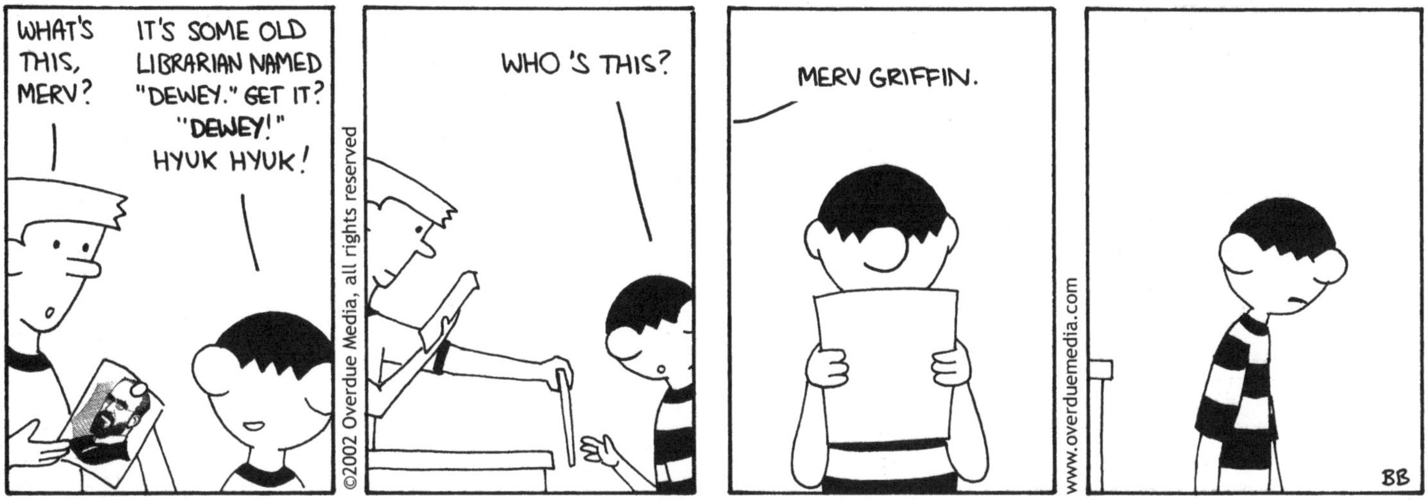
WHAT'S THIS, MERV?
IT'S SOME OLD LIBRARIAN NAMED "DEWEY." GET IT? "DEWEY!" HYUK HYUK!
©2002 Overdue Media, all rights reserved
WHO'S THIS?
MERV GRIFFIN.
www.overduemedia.com
BB

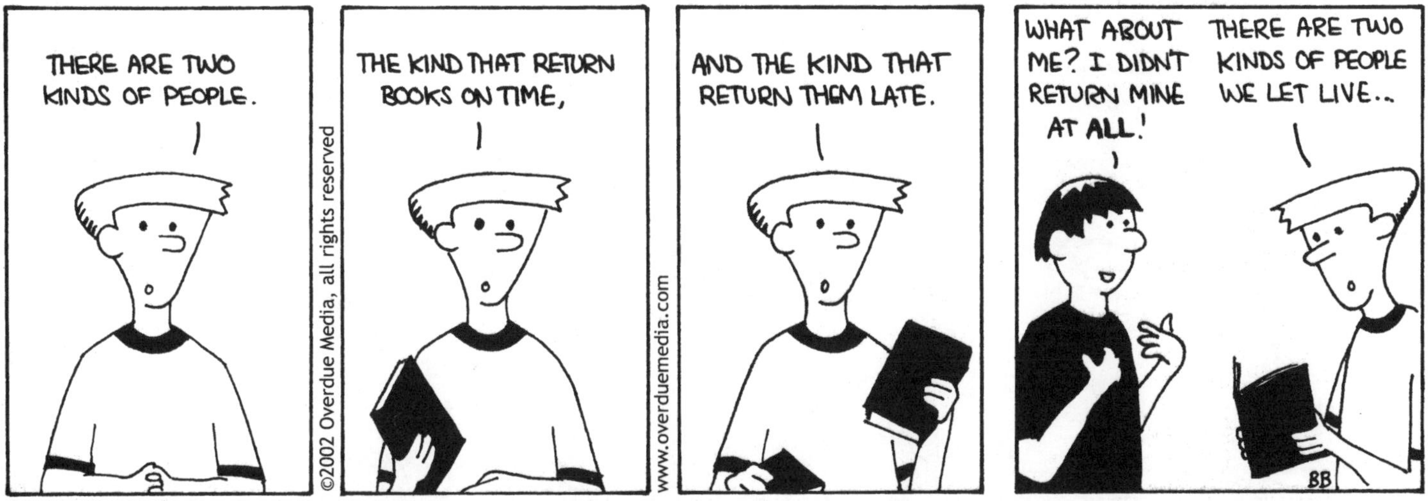
THERE ARE TWO KINDS OF PEOPLE.
©2002 Overdue Media, all rights reserved
THE KIND THAT RETURN BOOKS ON TIME,
www.overduemedia.com
AND THE KIND THAT RETURN THEM LATE.
WHAT ABOUT ME? I DIDN'T RETURN MINE AT ALL!
THERE ARE TWO KINDS OF PEOPLE WE LET LIVE...
BB

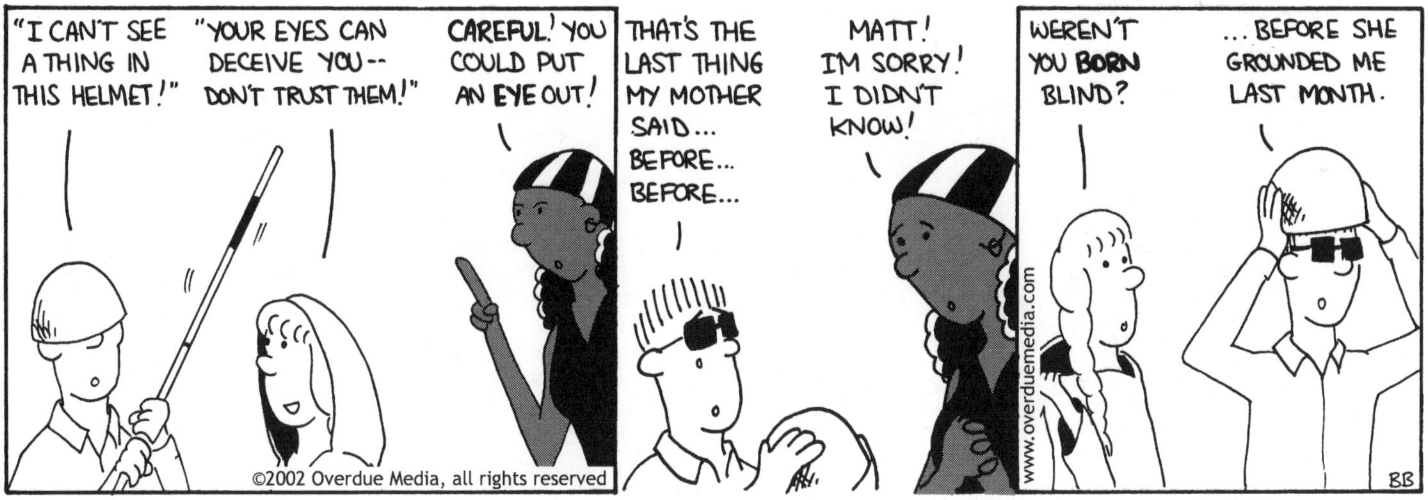
"I CAN'T SEE A THING IN THIS HELMET!"
"YOUR EYES CAN DECEIVE YOU-- DON'T TRUST THEM!"
CAREFUL! YOU COULD PUT AN EYE OUT!
©2002 Overdue Media, all rights reserved
THAT'S THE LAST THING MY MOTHER SAID... BEFORE... BEFORE...
MATT! I'M SORRY! I DIDN'T KNOW!
www.overduemedia.com
WEREN'T YOU BORN BLIND?
...BEFORE SHE GROUNDED ME LAST MONTH.
BB

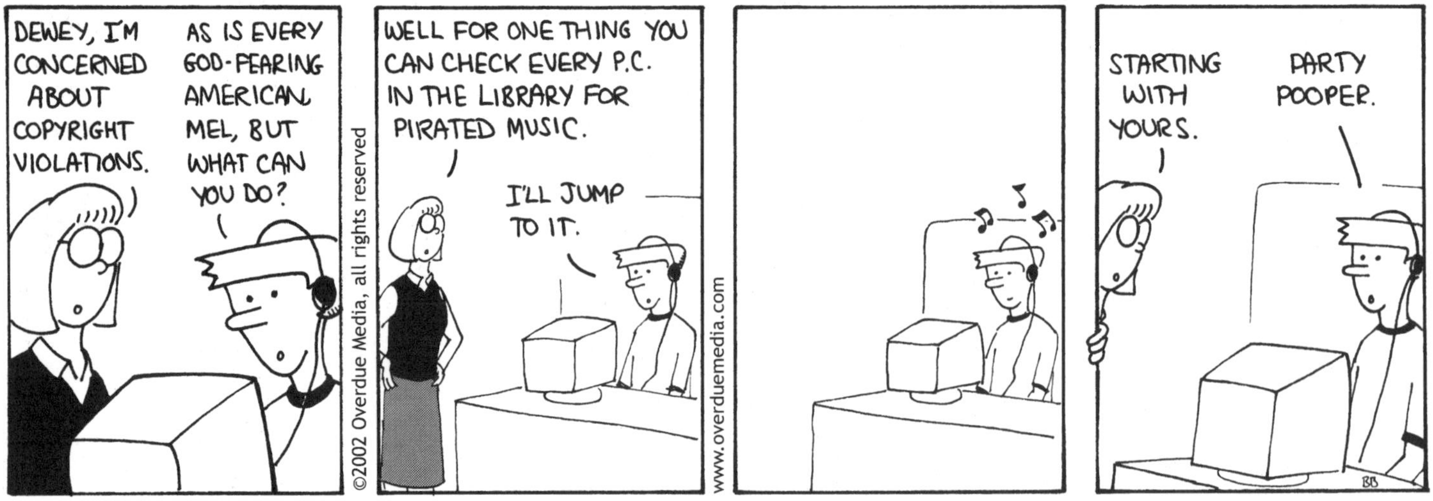
DEWEY, I'M CONCERNED ABOUT COPYRIGHT VIOLATIONS.
AS IS EVERY GOD-FEARING AMERICAN, MEL, BUT WHAT CAN YOU DO?
©2002 Overdue Media, all rights reserved
WELL FOR ONE THING YOU CAN CHECK EVERY P.C. IN THE LIBRARY FOR PIRATED MUSIC.
I'LL JUMP TO IT.
www.overduemedia.com
STARTING WITH YOURS.
PARTY POOPER.
BB

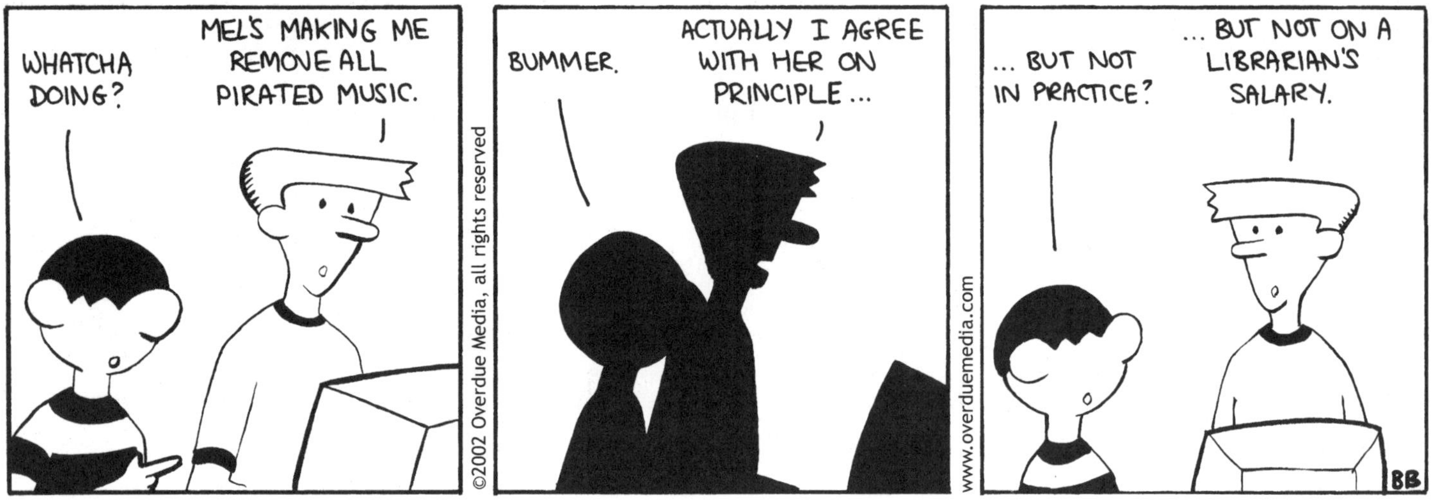
WHATCHA DOING?
MEL'S MAKING ME REMOVE ALL PIRATED MUSIC.
©2002 Overdue Media, all rights reserved
BUMMER.
ACTUALLY I AGREE WITH HER ON PRINCIPLE...
www.overduemedia.com
... BUT NOT IN PRACTICE?
... BUT NOT ON A LIBRARIAN'S SALARY.
BB

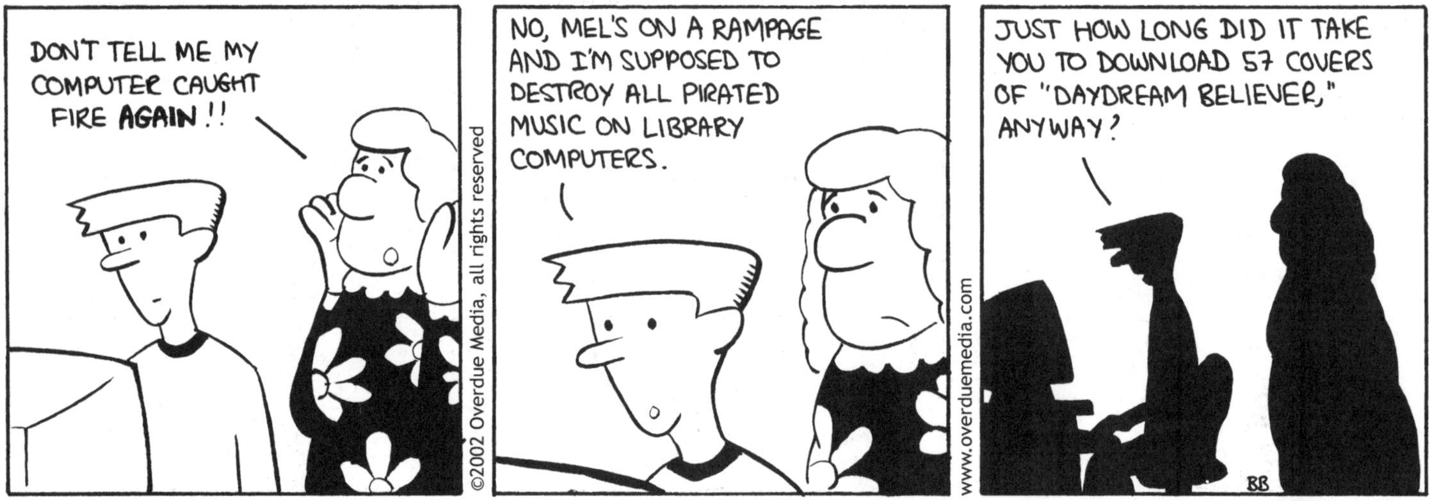
DON'T TELL ME MY COMPUTER CAUGHT FIRE AGAIN!!
©2002 Overdue Media, all rights reserved
NO, MEL'S ON A RAMPAGE AND I'M SUPPOSED TO DESTROY ALL PIRATED MUSIC ON LIBRARY COMPUTERS.
www.overduemedia.com
JUST HOW LONG DID IT TAKE YOU TO DOWNLOAD 57 COVERS OF "DAYDREAM BELIEVER," ANYWAY?
BB

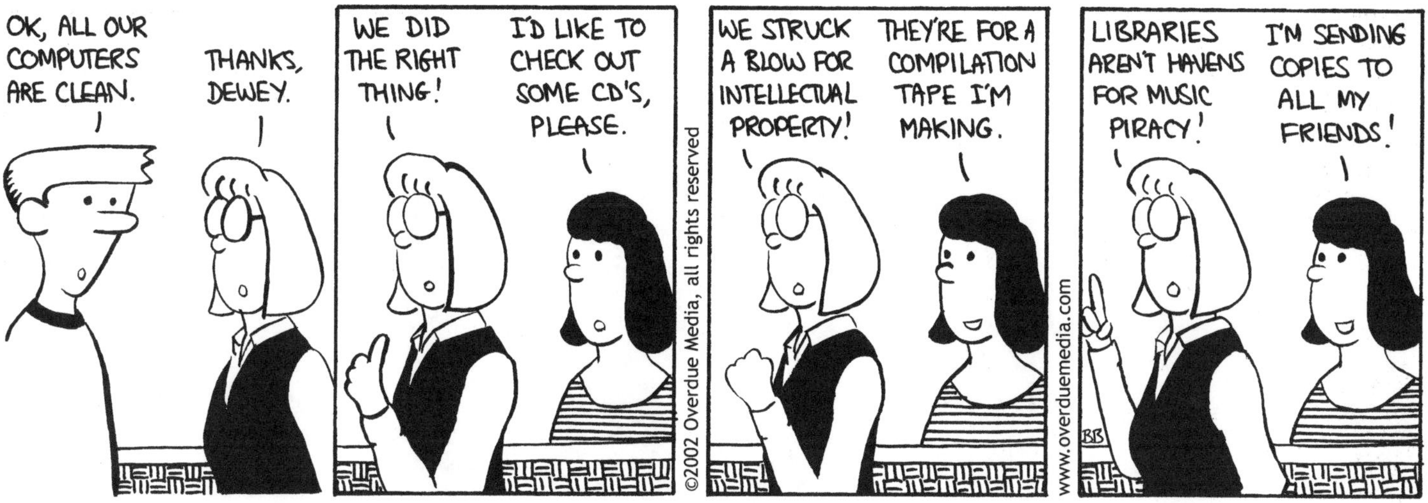
OK, ALL OUR COMPUTERS ARE CLEAN.
THANKS, DEWEY.
WE DID THE RIGHT THING!
I'D LIKE TO CHECK OUT SOME CD'S, PLEASE.
©2002 Overdue Media, all rights reserved
WE STRUCK A BLOW FOR INTELLECTUAL PROPERTY!
THEY'RE FOR A COMPILATION TAPE I'M MAKING.
www.overduemedia.com
LIBRARIES AREN'T HAVENS FOR MUSIC PIRACY!
I'M SENDING COPIES TO ALL MY FRIENDS!
BB

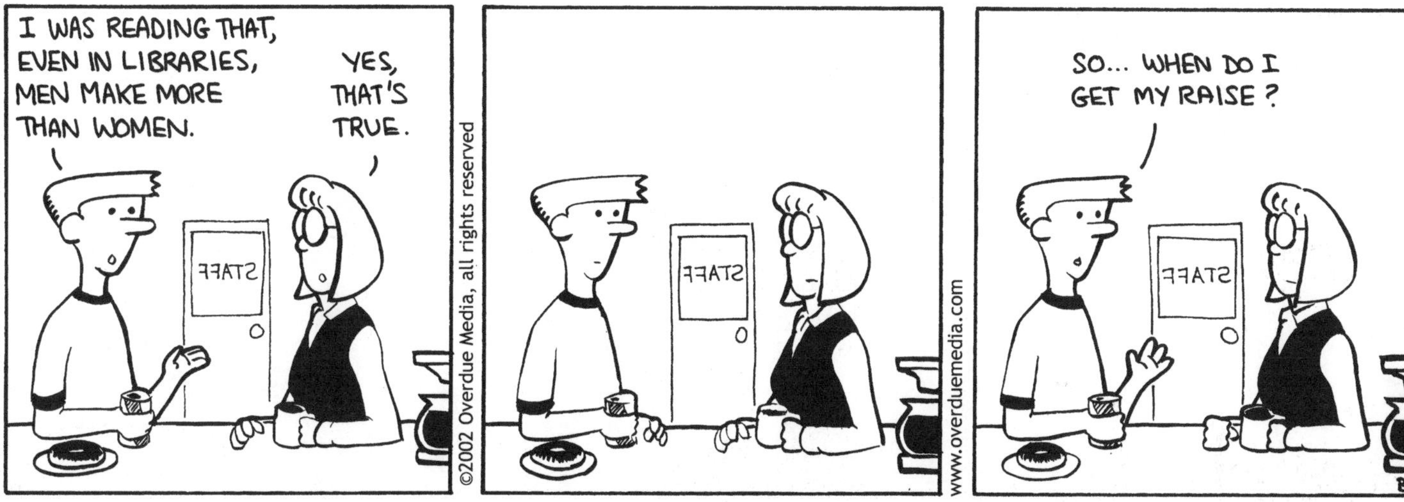
I WAS READING THAT, EVEN IN LIBRARIES, MEN MAKE MORE THAN WOMEN.
YES, THAT'S TRUE.
STAFF
©2002 Overdue Media, all rights reserved
www.overduemedia.com
SO... WHEN DO I GET MY RAISE?
BB

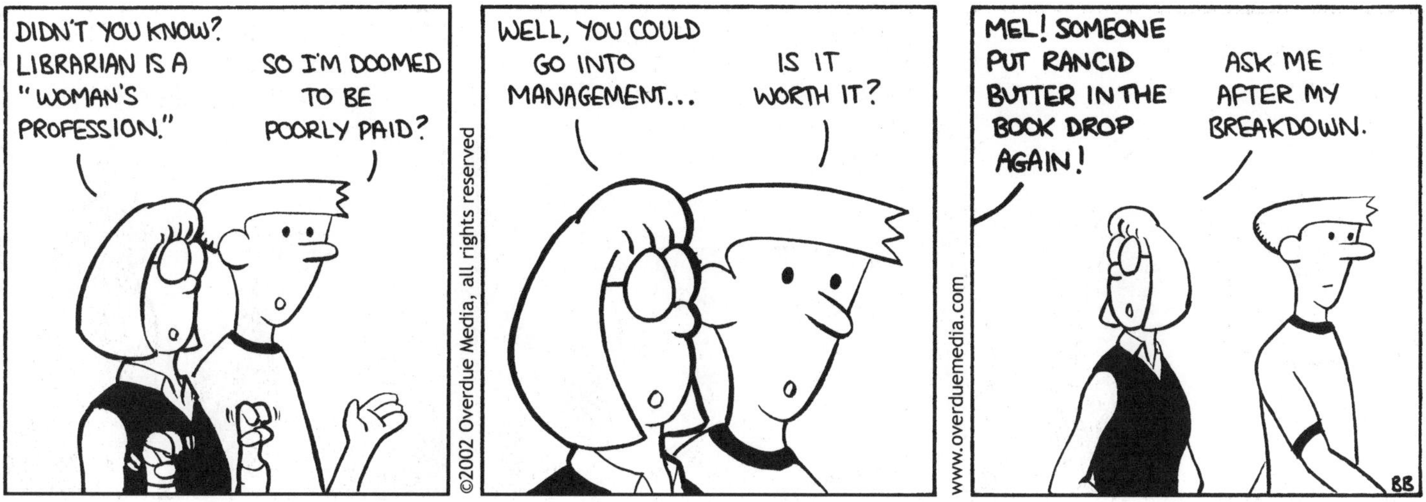
DIDN'T YOU KNOW? LIBRARIAN IS A "WOMAN'S PROFESSION."
SO I'M DOOMED TO BE POORLY PAID?
©2002 Overdue Media, all rights reserved
WELL, YOU COULD GO INTO MANAGEMENT...
IS IT WORTH IT?
www.overduemedia.com
MEL! SOMEONE PUT RANCID BUTTER IN THE BOOK DROP AGAIN!
ASK ME AFTER MY BREAKDOWN.
BB

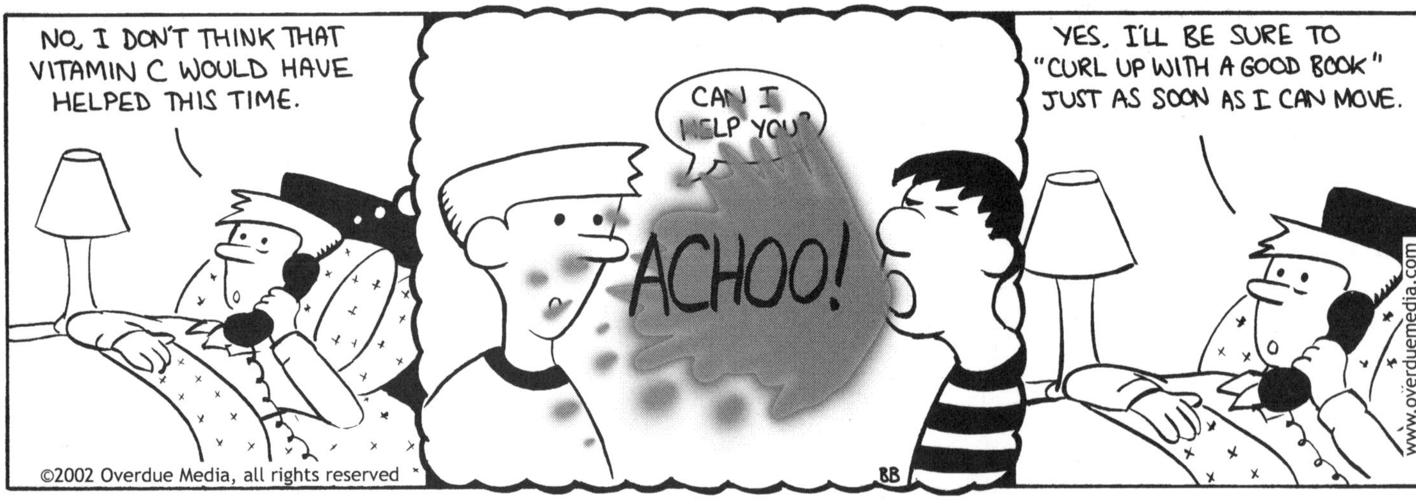
NO, I DON'T THINK THAT VITAMIN C WOULD HAVE HELPED THIS TIME.
©2002 Overdue Media, all rights reserved
CAN I HELP YOU?
ACHOO!
BB
YES, I'LL BE SURE TO "CURL UP WITH A GOOD BOOK" JUST AS SOON AS I CAN MOVE.
www.overduemedia.com

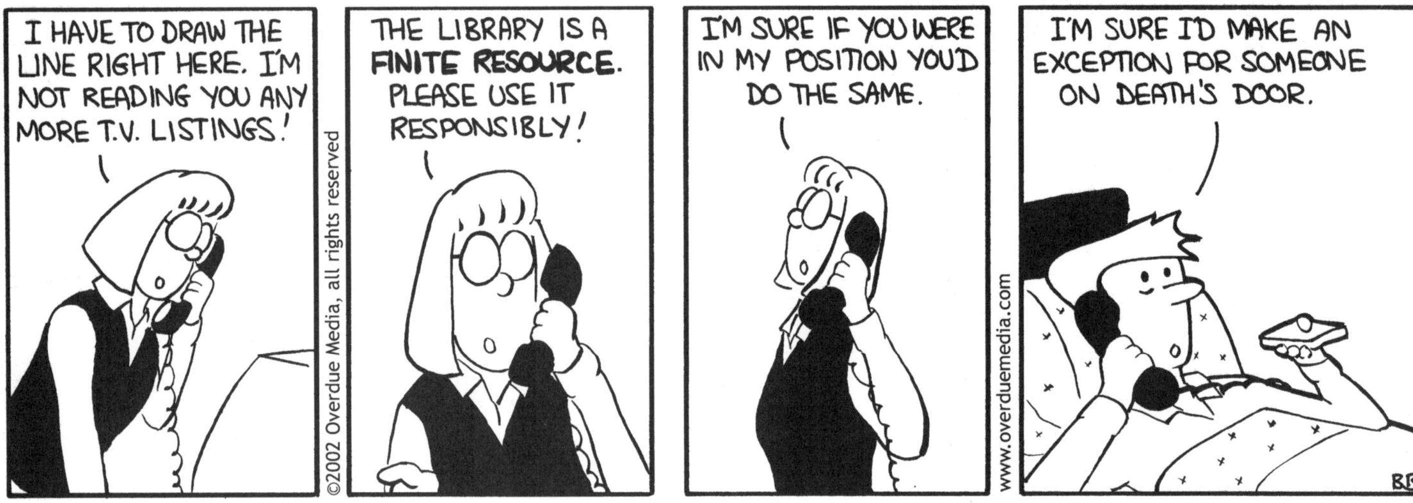
I HAVE TO DRAW THE LINE RIGHT HERE. I'M NOT READING YOU ANY MORE T.V. LISTINGS!
©2002 Overdue Media, all rights reserved
THE LIBRARY IS A **FINITE RESOURCE**. PLEASE USE IT RESPONSIBLY!
I'M SURE IF YOU WERE IN MY POSITION YOU'D DO THE SAME.
www.overduemedia.com
I'M SURE I'D MAKE AN EXCEPTION FOR SOMEONE ON DEATH'S DOOR.
BB

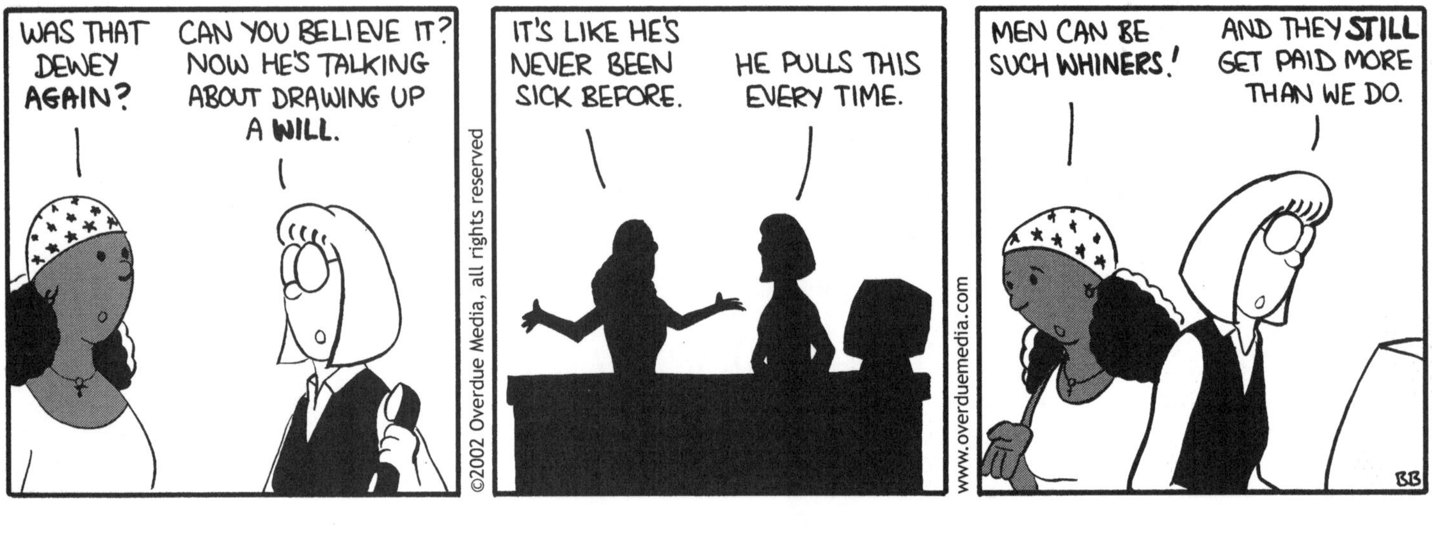
WAS THAT DEWEY **AGAIN**?
CAN YOU BELIEVE IT? NOW HE'S TALKING ABOUT DRAWING UP A **WILL**.
©2002 Overdue Media, all rights reserved
IT'S LIKE HE'S NEVER BEEN SICK BEFORE.
HE PULLS THIS EVERY TIME.
www.overduemedia.com
MEN CAN BE SUCH **WHINERS**!
AND THEY **STILL** GET PAID MORE THAN WE DO.
BB

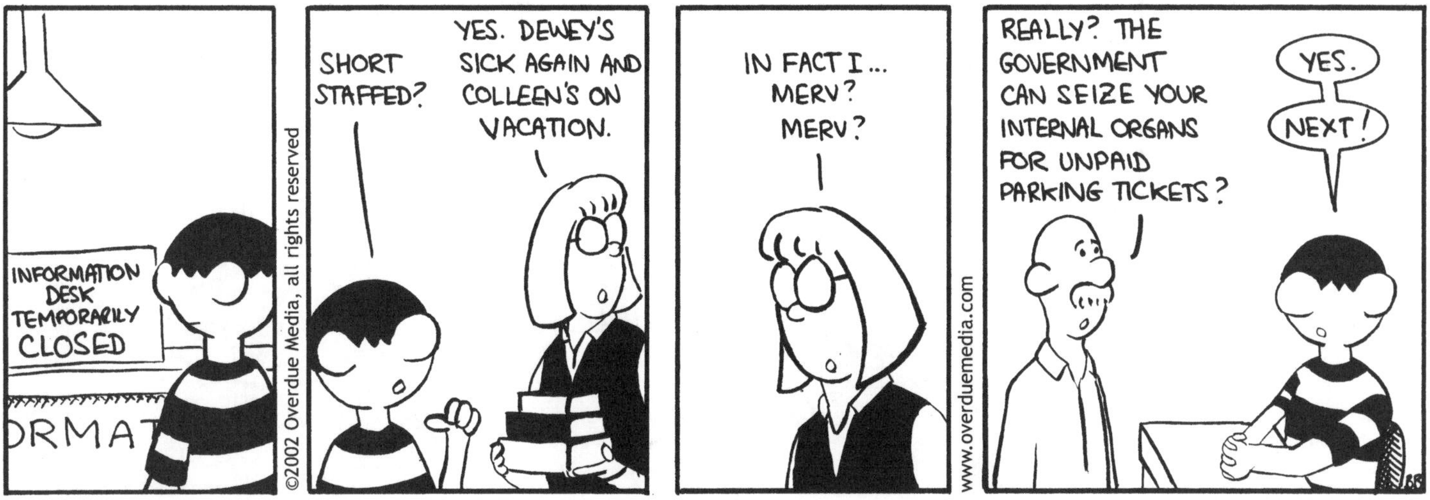
INFORMATION DESK TEMPORARILY CLOSED
ORMAT
©2002 Overdue Media, all rights reserved
SHORT STAFFED?
YES. DEWEY'S SICK AGAIN AND COLLEEN'S ON VACATION.
IN FACT I... MERV? MERV?
www.overduemedia.com
REALLY? THE GOVERNMENT CAN SEIZE YOUR INTERNAL ORGANS FOR UNPAID PARKING TICKETS?
YES.
NEXT!
BB

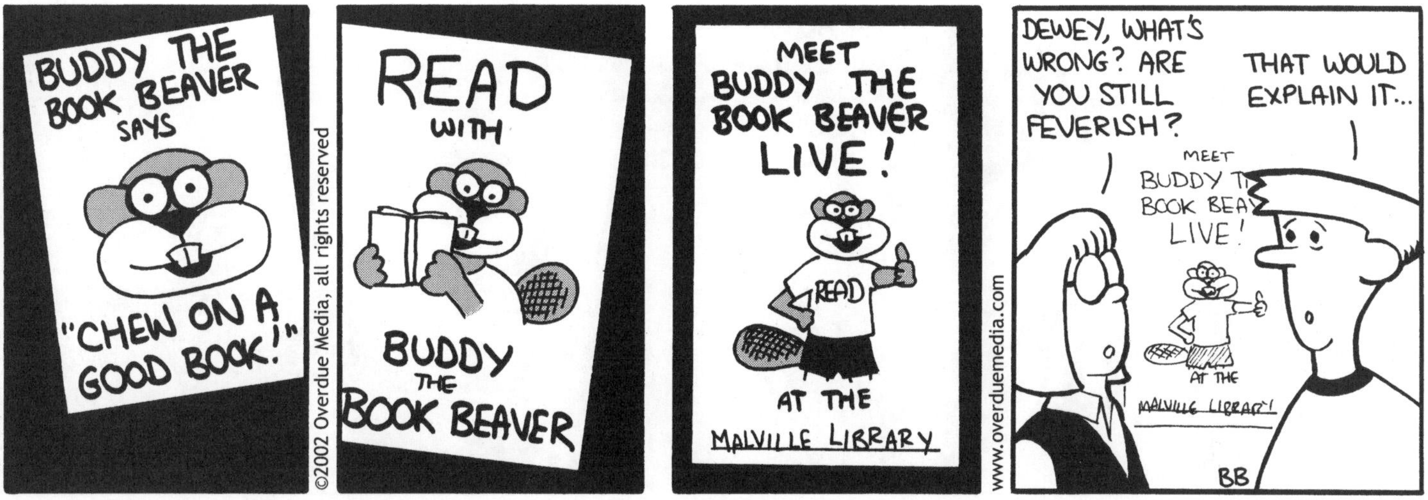
BUDDY THE BOOK BEAVER SAYS "CHEW ON A GOOD BOOK!"
©2002 Overdue Media, all rights reserved
READ WITH BUDDY THE BOOK BEAVER
MEET BUDDY THE BOOK BEAVER LIVE!
READ
AT THE MALVILLE LIBRARY
www.overduemedia.com
DEWEY, WHAT'S WRONG? ARE YOU STILL FEVERISH?
THAT WOULD EXPLAIN IT...
BB

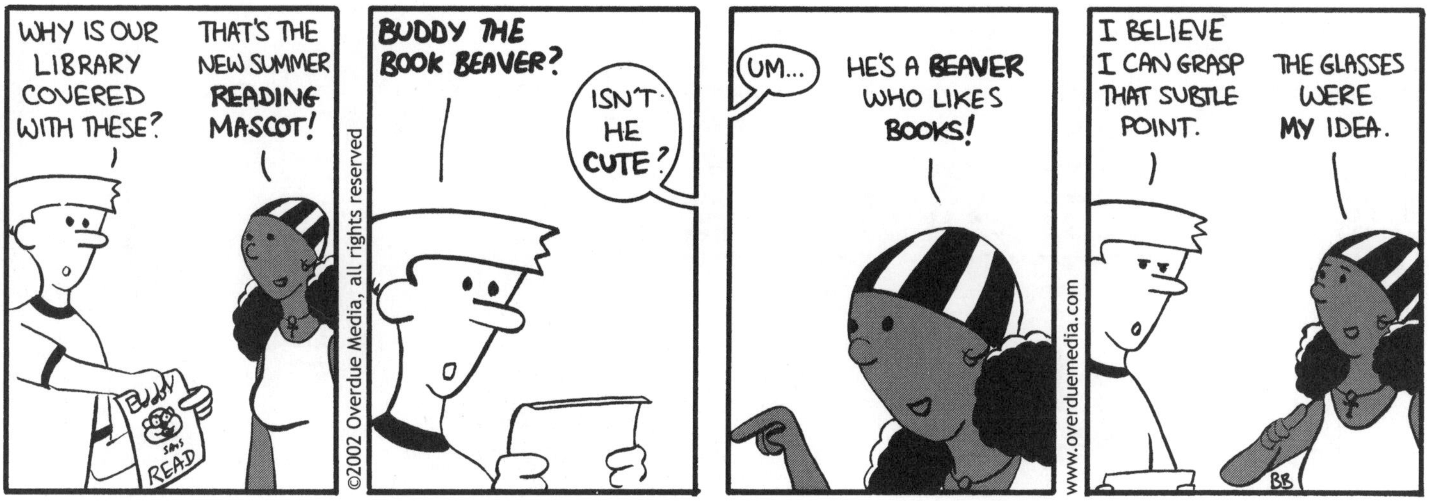
WHY IS OUR LIBRARY COVERED WITH THESE?
THAT'S THE NEW SUMMER READING MASCOT!
READ
©2002 Overdue Media, all rights reserved
BUDDY THE BOOK BEAVER?
ISN'T HE CUTE?
UM...
HE'S A BEAVER WHO LIKES BOOKS!
www.overduemedia.com
I BELIEVE I CAN GRASP THAT SUBTLE POINT.
THE GLASSES WERE MY IDEA.
BB

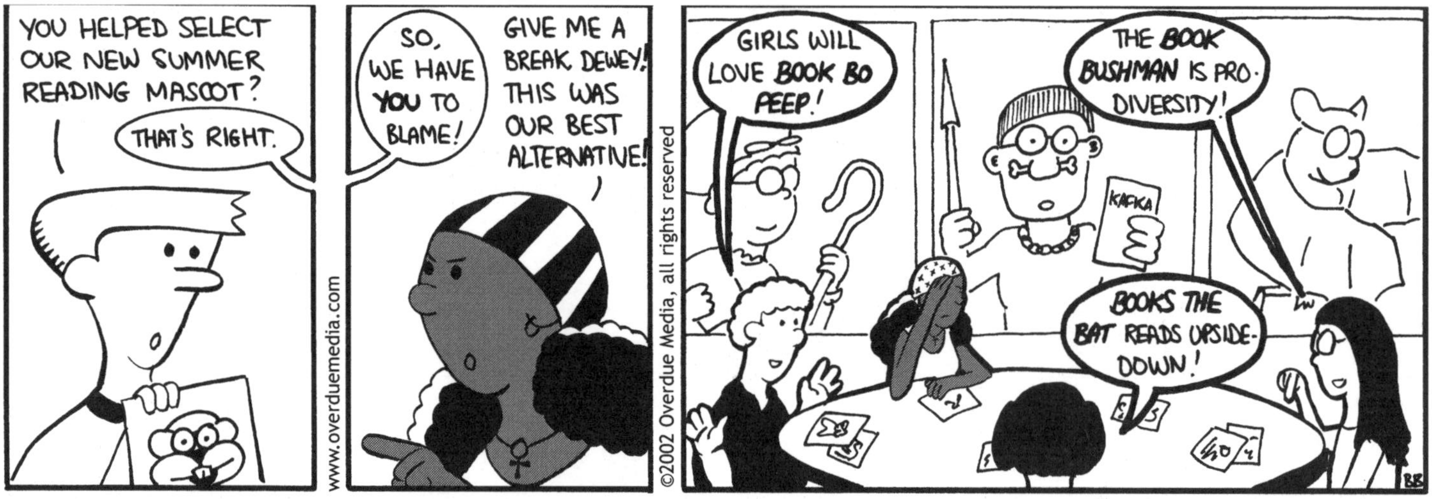
YOU HELPED SELECT OUR NEW SUMMER READING MASCOT?
THAT'S RIGHT.
www.overduemedia.com
SO, WE HAVE YOU TO BLAME!
GIVE ME A BREAK, DEWEY! THIS WAS OUR BEST ALTERNATIVE!
©2002 Overdue Media, all rights reserved
GIRLS WILL LOVE BOOK BO PEEP!
THE BOOK BUSHMAN IS PRO-DIVERSITY!
KAFKA
BOOKS THE BAT READS UPSIDE-DOWN!
BB

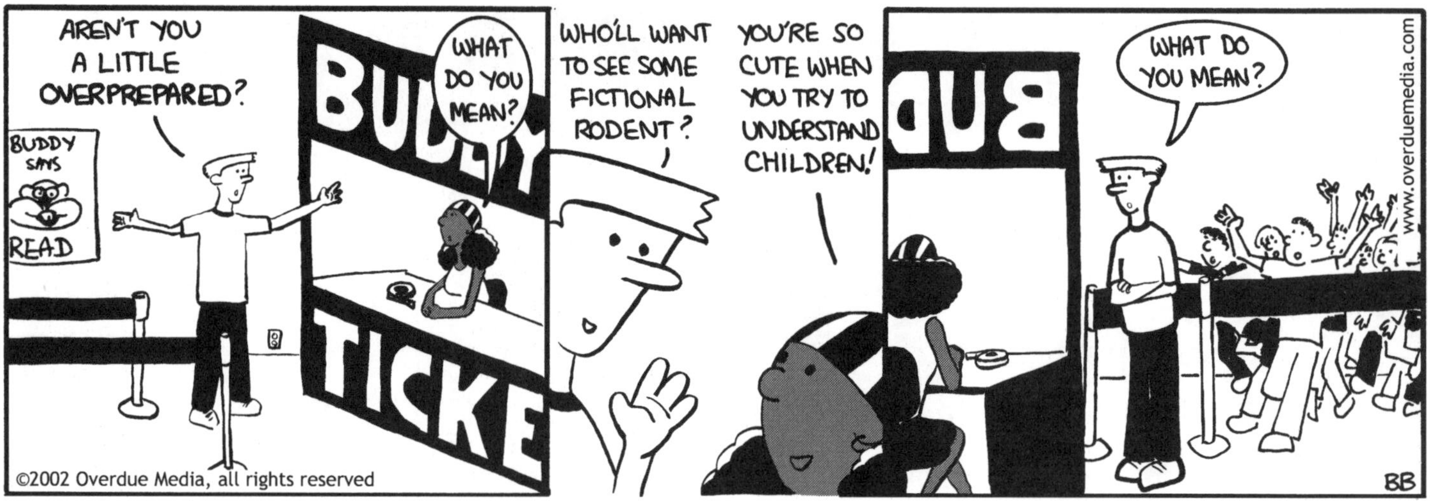
AREN'T YOU A LITTLE OVERPREPARED?
BUDDY SAYS READ
BUDDY
TICKE
WHAT DO YOU MEAN?
©2002 Overdue Media, all rights reserved
WHO'LL WANT TO SEE SOME FICTIONAL RODENT?
YOU'RE SO CUTE WHEN YOU TRY TO UNDERSTAND CHILDREN!
WHAT DO YOU MEAN?
www.overduemedia.com
BB

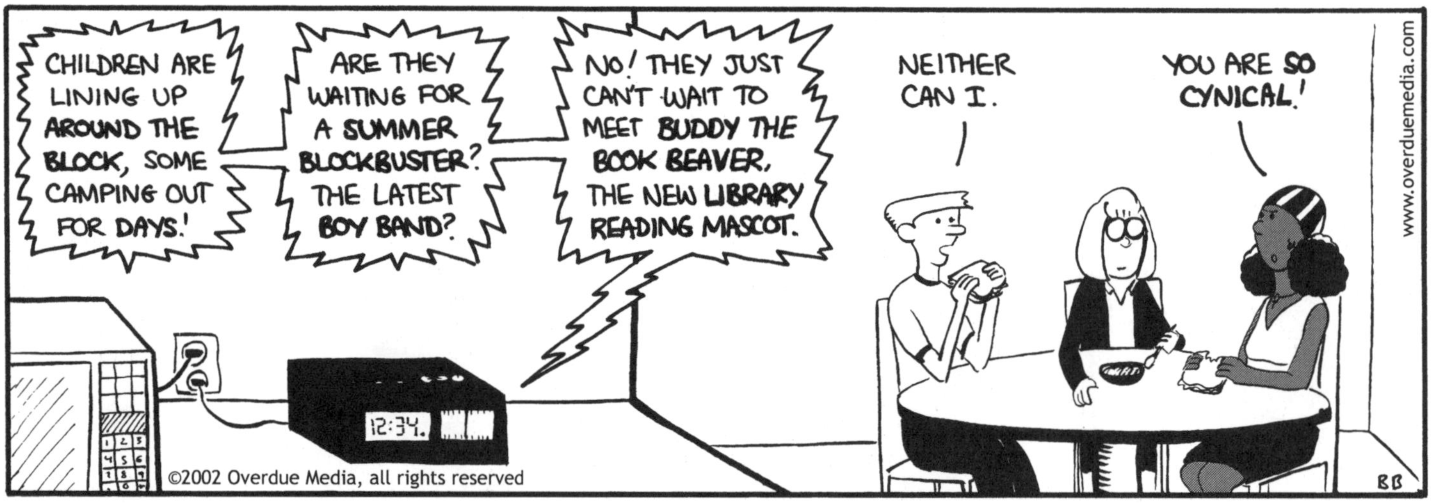
CHILDREN ARE LINING UP AROUND THE BLOCK, SOME CAMPING OUT FOR DAYS!
ARE THEY WAITING FOR A SUMMER BLOCKBUSTER? THE LATEST BOY BAND?
NO! THEY JUST CAN'T WAIT TO MEET BUDDY THE BOOK BEAVER, THE NEW LIBRARY READING MASCOT.
12:34.
©2002 Overdue Media, all rights reserved
NEITHER CAN I.
YOU ARE SO CYNICAL!
www.overduemedia.com
BB

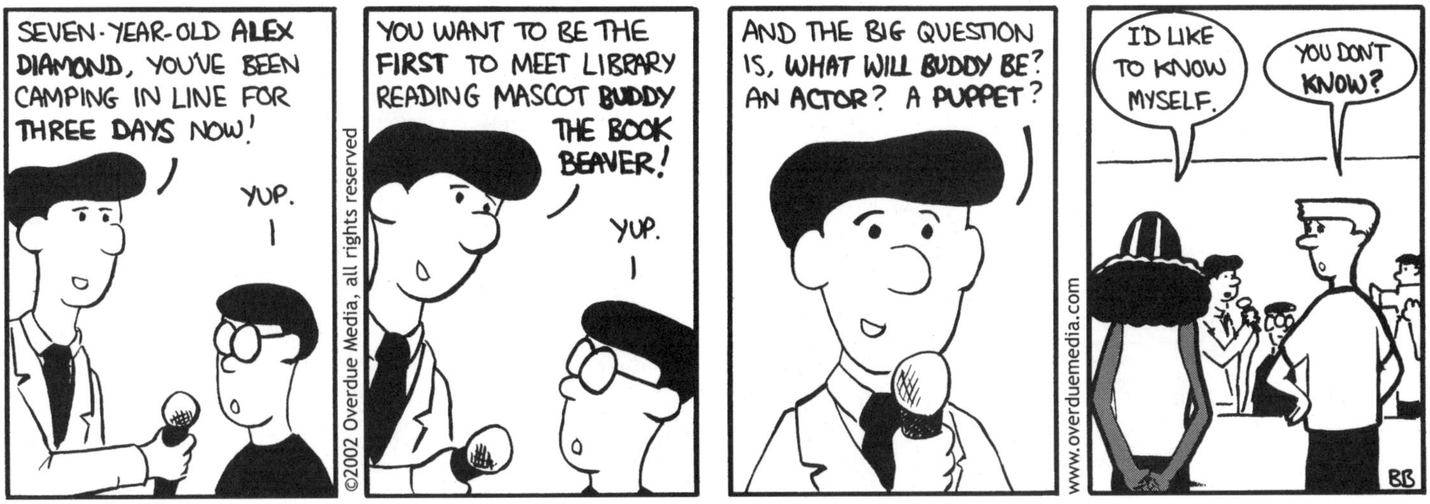
SEVEN-YEAR-OLD ALEX DIAMOND, YOU'VE BEEN CAMPING IN LINE FOR THREE DAYS NOW!
YUP.
©2002 Overdue Media, all rights reserved
YOU WANT TO BE THE FIRST TO MEET LIBRARY READING MASCOT BUDDY THE BOOK BEAVER!
YUP.
AND THE BIG QUESTION IS, WHAT WILL BUDDY BE? AN ACTOR? A PUPPET?
www.overduemedia.com
I'D LIKE TO KNOW MYSELF.
YOU DON'T KNOW?
BB

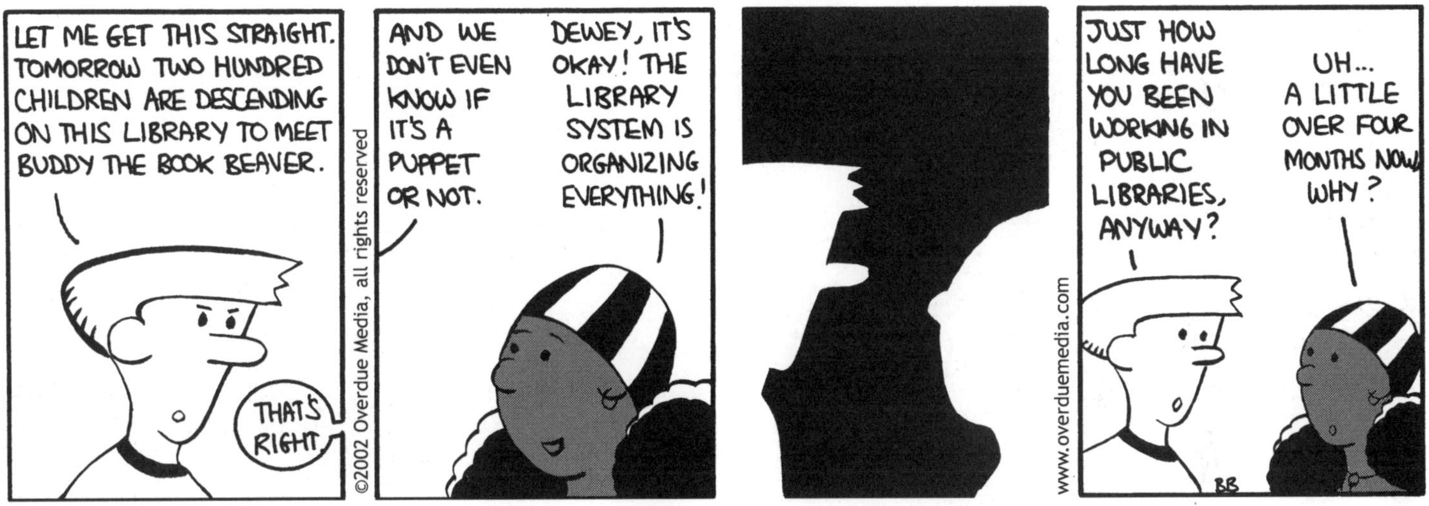
LET ME GET THIS STRAIGHT. TOMORROW TWO HUNDRED CHILDREN ARE DESCENDING ON THIS LIBRARY TO MEET BUDDY THE BOOK BEAVER.
THAT'S RIGHT.
©2002 Overdue Media, all rights reserved
AND WE DON'T EVEN KNOW IF IT'S A PUPPET OR NOT.
DEWEY, IT'S OKAY! THE LIBRARY SYSTEM IS ORGANIZING EVERYTHING!
www.overduemedia.com
JUST HOW LONG HAVE YOU BEEN WORKING IN PUBLIC LIBRARIES, ANYWAY?
UH... A LITTLE OVER FOUR MONTHS NOW. WHY?
BB

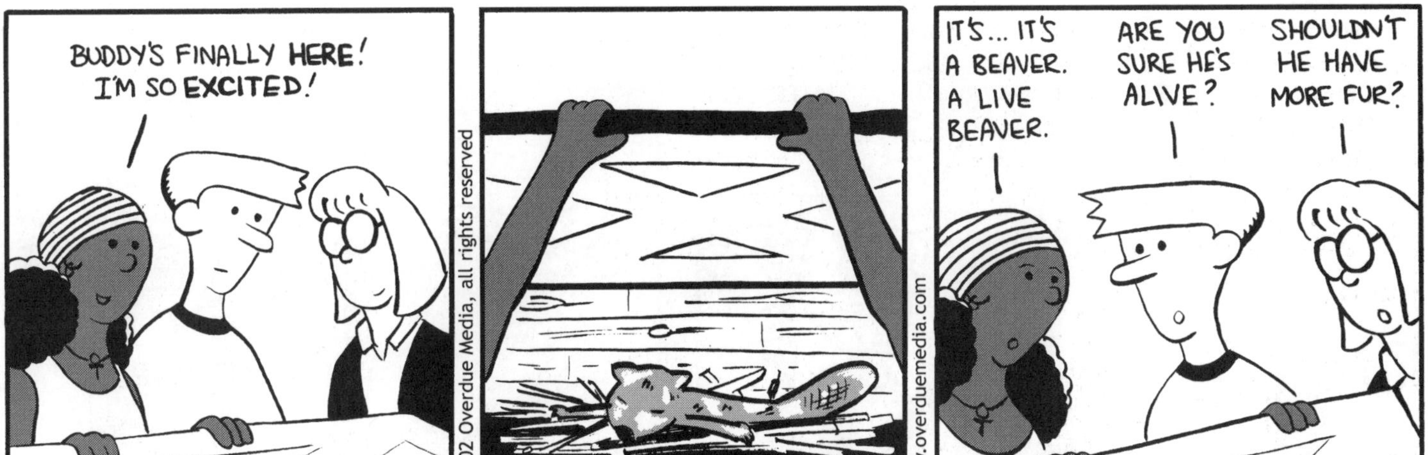
BUDDY'S FINALLY HERE! I'M SO EXCITED!
©2002 Overdue Media, all rights reserved
www.overduemedia.com
IT'S... IT'S A BEAVER. A LIVE BEAVER.
ARE YOU SURE HE'S ALIVE?
SHOULDN'T HE HAVE MORE FUR?
BB

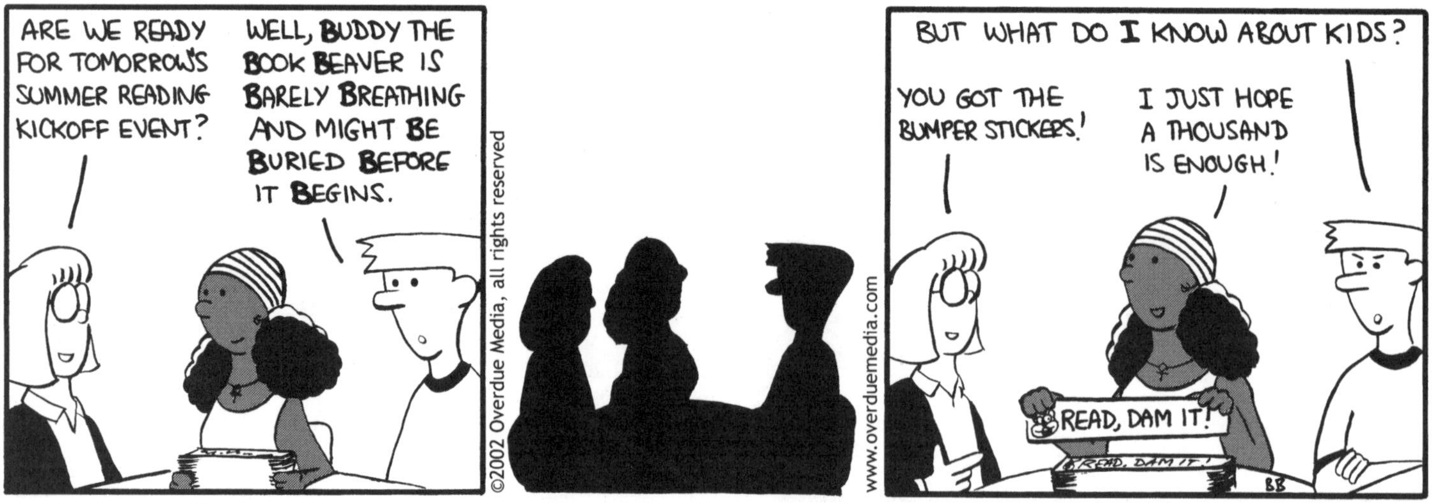
ARE WE READY FOR TOMORROW'S SUMMER READING KICKOFF EVENT?
WELL, BUDDY THE BOOK BEAVER IS BARELY BREATHING AND MIGHT BE BURIED BEFORE IT BEGINS.
©2002 Overdue Media, all rights reserved
www.overduemedia.com
BUT WHAT DO I KNOW ABOUT KIDS?
YOU GOT THE BUMPER STICKERS!
I JUST HOPE A THOUSAND IS ENOUGH!
READ, DAM IT!
READ, DAM IT!
BB

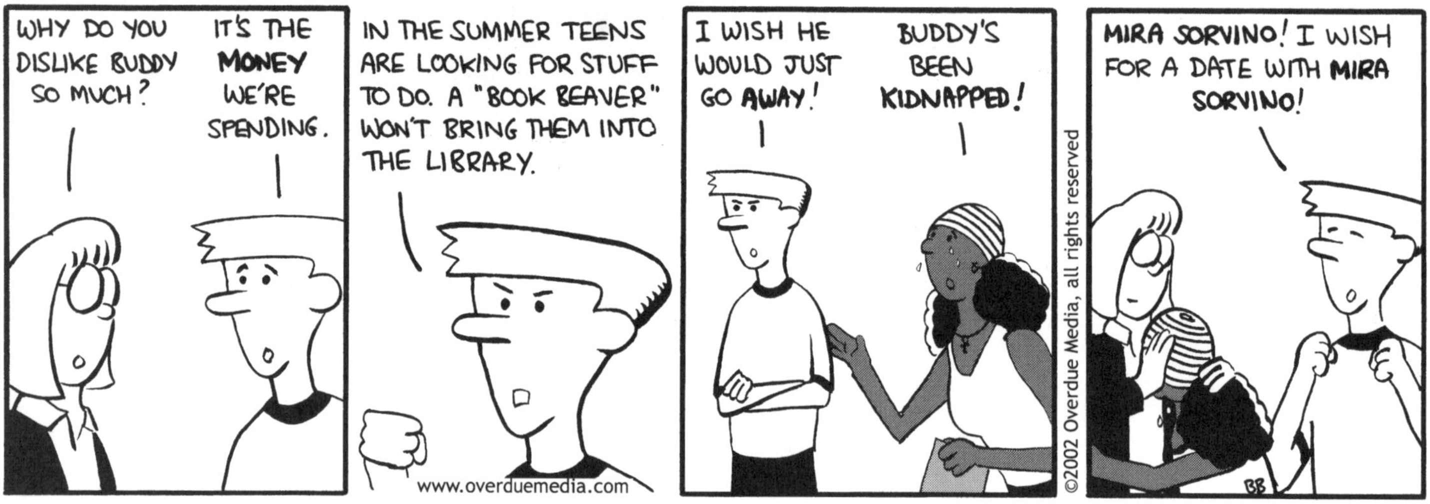
WHY DO YOU DISLIKE BUDDY SO MUCH?
IT'S THE MONEY WE'RE SPENDING.
IN THE SUMMER TEENS ARE LOOKING FOR STUFF TO DO. A "BOOK BEAVER" WON'T BRING THEM INTO THE LIBRARY.
www.overduemedia.com
I WISH HE WOULD JUST GO AWAY!
BUDDY'S BEEN KIDNAPPED!
©2002 Overdue Media, all rights reserved
MIRA SORVINO! I WISH FOR A DATE WITH MIRA SORVINO!
BB

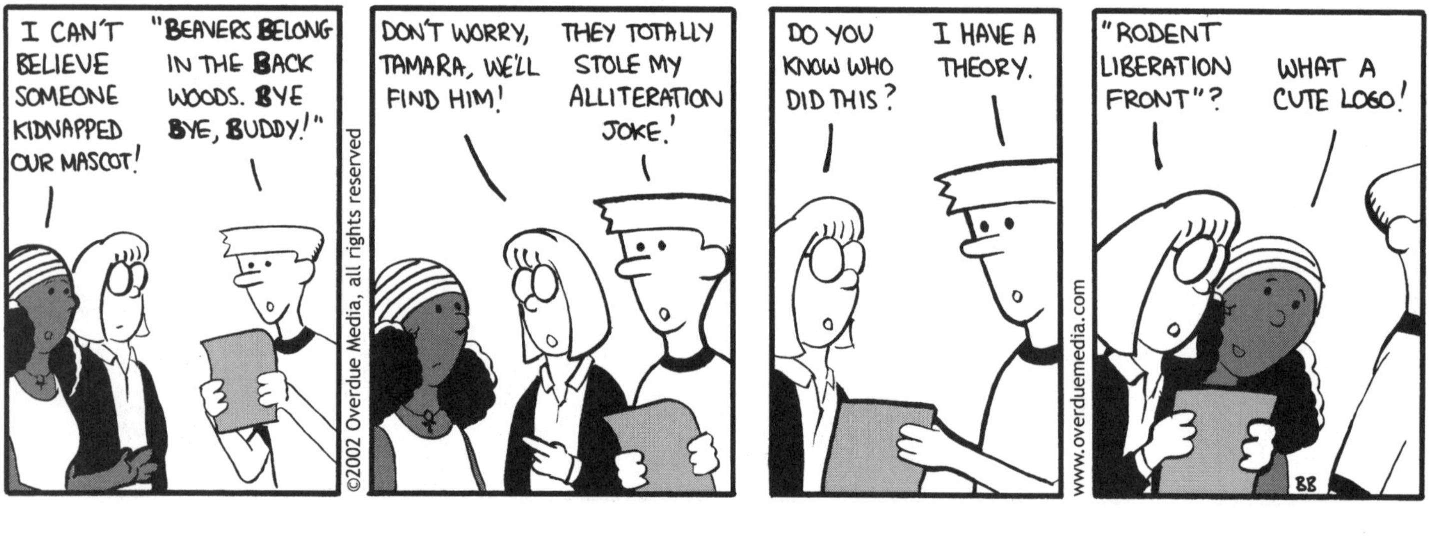
I CAN'T BELIEVE SOMEONE KIDNAPPED OUR MASCOT!
"BEAVERS BELONG IN THE BACK WOODS. BYE BYE, BUDDY!"
©2002 Overdue Media, all rights reserved
DON'T WORRY, TAMARA, WE'LL FIND HIM!
THEY TOTALLY STOLE MY ALLITERATION JOKE!
DO YOU KNOW WHO DID THIS?
I HAVE A THEORY.
www.overduemedia.com
"RODENT LIBERATION FRONT"?
WHAT A CUTE LOGO!
BB

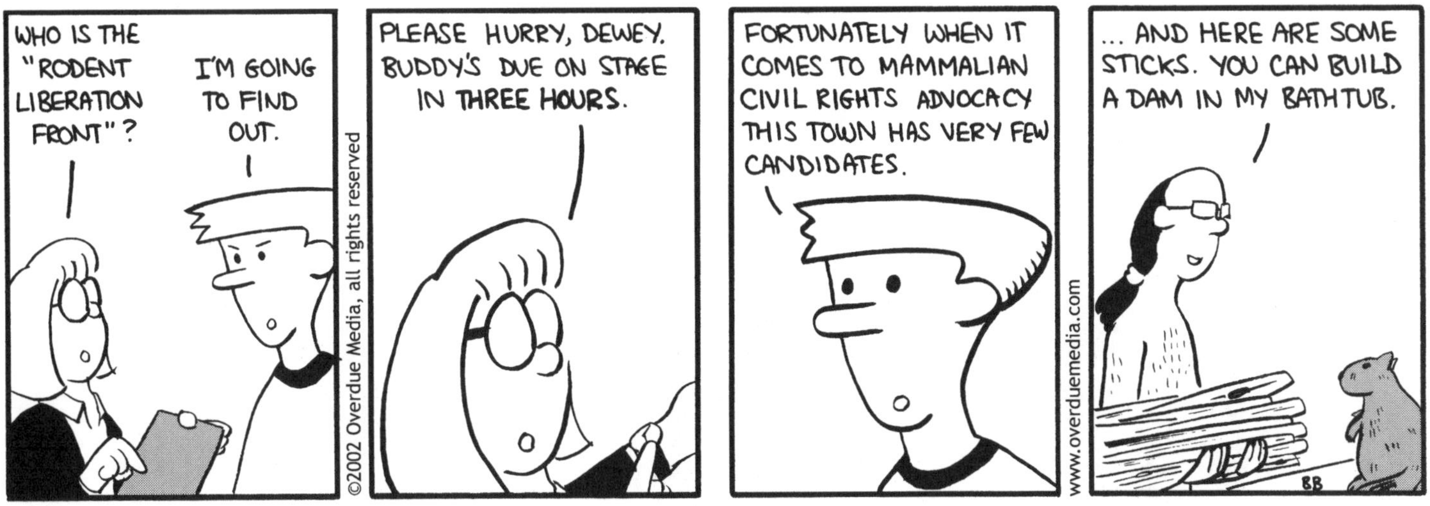
WHO IS THE "RODENT LIBERATION FRONT"?
I'M GOING TO FIND OUT.
©2002 Overdue Media, all rights reserved
PLEASE HURRY, DEWEY. BUDDY'S DUE ON STAGE IN THREE HOURS.
FORTUNATELY WHEN IT COMES TO MAMMALIAN CIVIL RIGHTS ADVOCACY THIS TOWN HAS VERY FEW CANDIDATES.
www.overduemedia.com
... AND HERE ARE SOME STICKS. YOU CAN BUILD A DAM IN MY BATHTUB.
BB

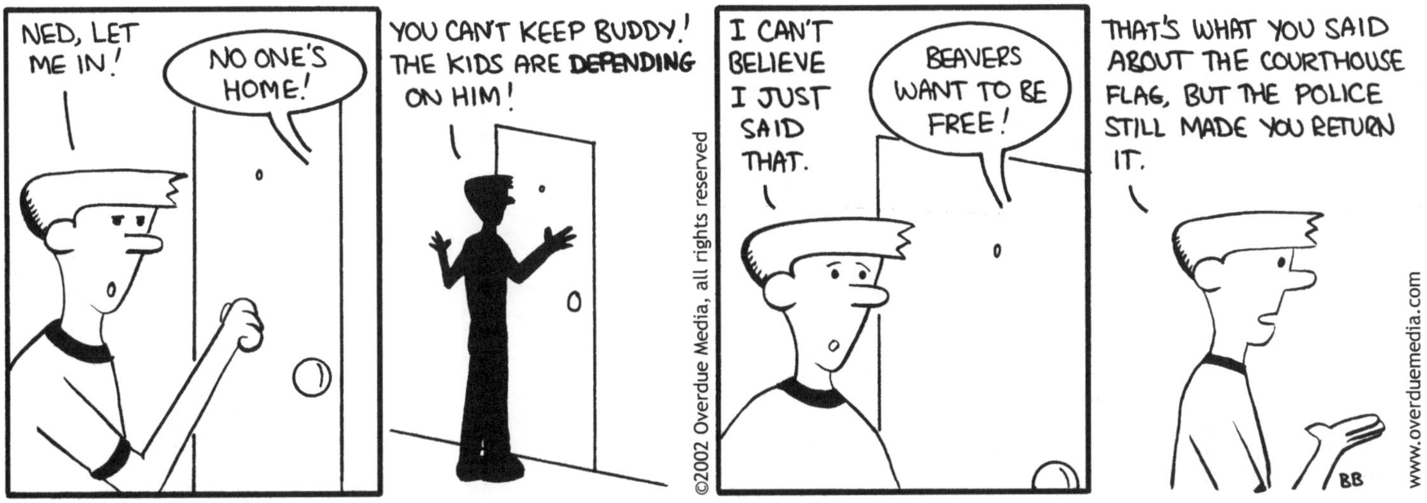
NED, LET ME IN!
NO ONE'S HOME!
YOU CAN'T KEEP BUDDY! THE KIDS ARE DEPENDING ON HIM!
©2002 Overdue Media, all rights reserved
I CAN'T BELIEVE I JUST SAID THAT.
BEAVERS WANT TO BE FREE!
THAT'S WHAT YOU SAID ABOUT THE COURTHOUSE FLAG, BUT THE POLICE STILL MADE YOU RETURN IT.
BB
www.overduemedia.com

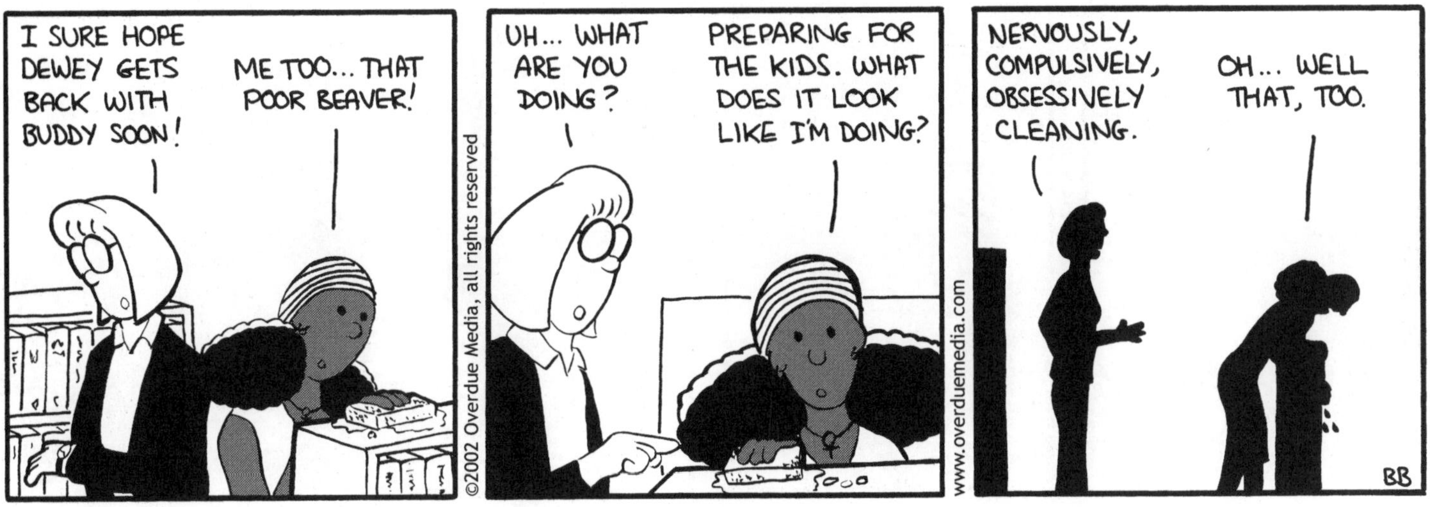
I SURE HOPE DEWEY GETS BACK WITH BUDDY SOON!
ME TOO... THAT POOR BEAVER!
©2002 Overdue Media, all rights reserved
UH... WHAT ARE YOU DOING?
PREPARING FOR THE KIDS. WHAT DOES IT LOOK LIKE I'M DOING?
www.overduemedia.com
NERVOUSLY, COMPULSIVELY, OBSESSIVELY CLEANING.
OH... WELL THAT, TOO.
BB

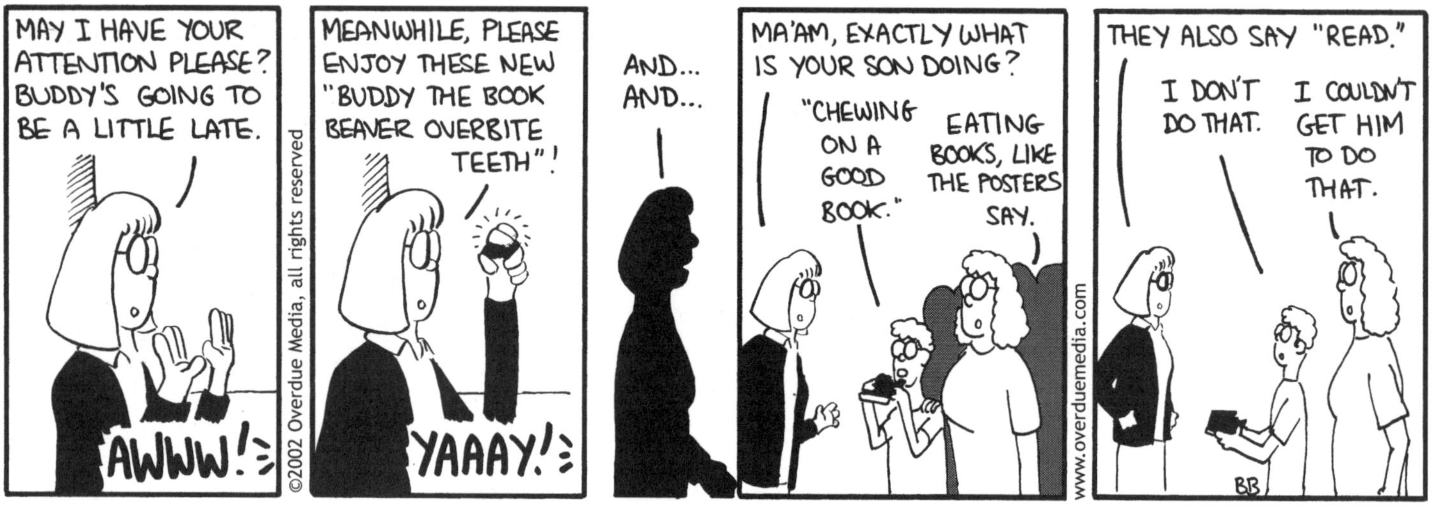
MAY I HAVE YOUR ATTENTION PLEASE? BUDDY'S GOING TO BE A LITTLE LATE.
AWWW!
©2002 Overdue Media, all rights reserved
MEANWHILE, PLEASE ENJOY THESE NEW "BUDDY THE BOOK BEAVER OVERBITE TEETH"!
YAAAY!
AND... AND...
MA'AM, EXACTLY WHAT IS YOUR SON DOING?
"CHEWING ON A GOOD BOOK."
EATING BOOKS, LIKE THE POSTERS SAY.
www.overduemedia.com
THEY ALSO SAY "READ."
I DON'T DO THAT.
I COULDN'T GET HIM TO DO THAT.
BB

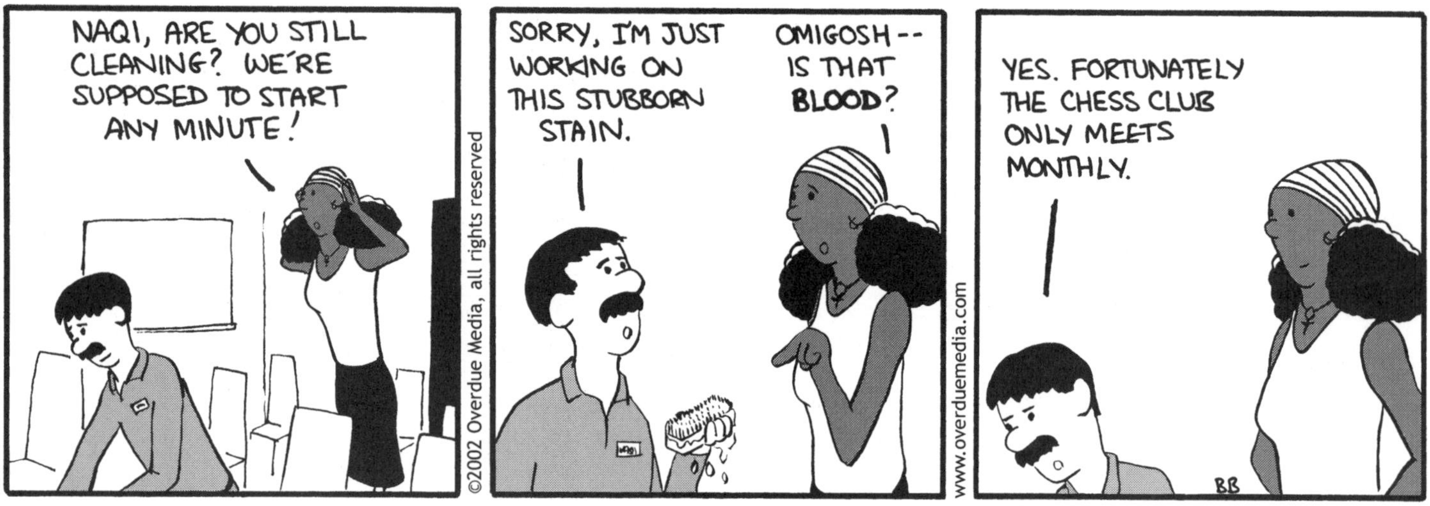
NAQI, ARE YOU STILL CLEANING? WE'RE SUPPOSED TO START ANY MINUTE!
©2002 Overdue Media, all rights reserved
SORRY, I'M JUST WORKING ON THIS STUBBORN STAIN.
OMIGOSH-- IS THAT BLOOD?
www.overduemedia.com
YES. FORTUNATELY THE CHESS CLUB ONLY MEETS MONTHLY.
BB

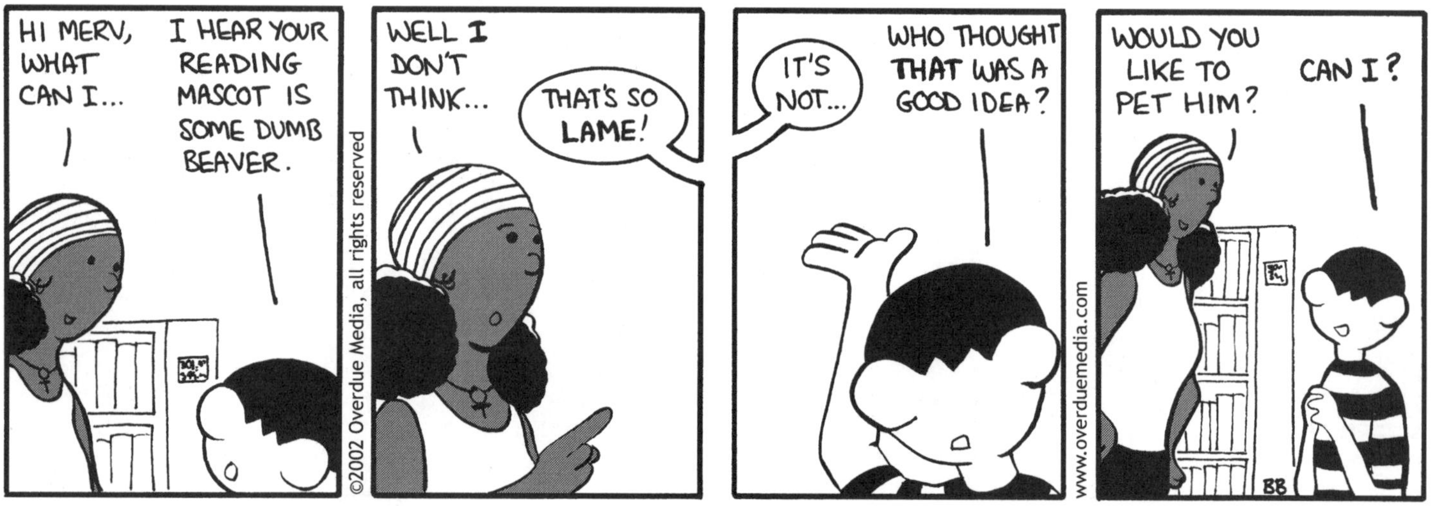
HI MERV, WHAT CAN I...
I HEAR YOUR READING MASCOT IS SOME DUMB BEAVER.
©2002 Overdue Media, all rights reserved
WELL I DON'T THINK...
THAT'S SO LAME!
IT'S NOT...
WHO THOUGHT THAT WAS A GOOD IDEA?
www.overduemedia.com
WOULD YOU LIKE TO PET HIM?
CAN I?
BB

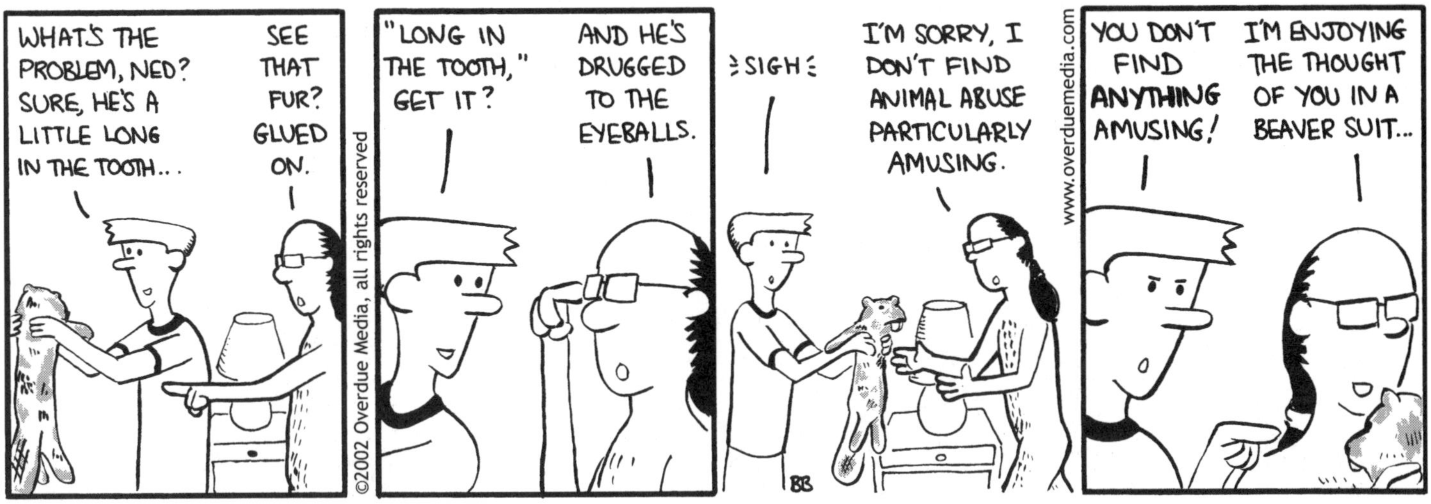
WHAT'S THE PROBLEM, NED? SURE, HE'S A LITTLE LONG IN THE TOOTH...
SEE THAT FUR? GLUED ON.
©2002 Overdue Media, all rights reserved
"LONG IN THE TOOTH," GET IT?
AND HE'S DRUGGED TO THE EYEBALLS.
SIGH
I'M SORRY, I DON'T FIND ANIMAL ABUSE PARTICULARLY AMUSING.
BB
www.overduemedia.com
YOU DON'T FIND **ANYTHING** AMUSING!
I'M ENJOYING THE THOUGHT OF YOU IN A BEAVER SUIT...

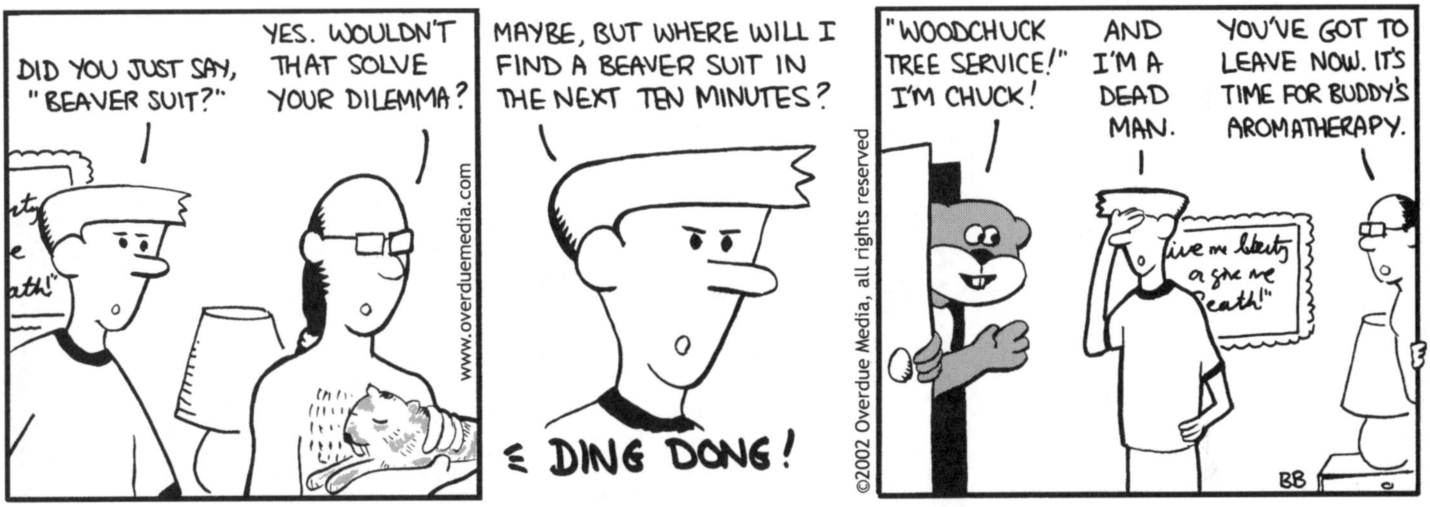
DID YOU JUST SAY, "BEAVER SUIT?"
YES. WOULDN'T THAT SOLVE YOUR DILEMMA?
www.overduemedia.com
MAYBE, BUT WHERE WILL I FIND A BEAVER SUIT IN THE NEXT TEN MINUTES?
DING DONG!
©2002 Overdue Media, all rights reserved
"WOODCHUCK TREE SERVICE!" I'M CHUCK!
AND I'M A DEAD MAN.
YOU'VE GOT TO LEAVE NOW. IT'S TIME FOR BUDDY'S AROMATHERAPY.
BB

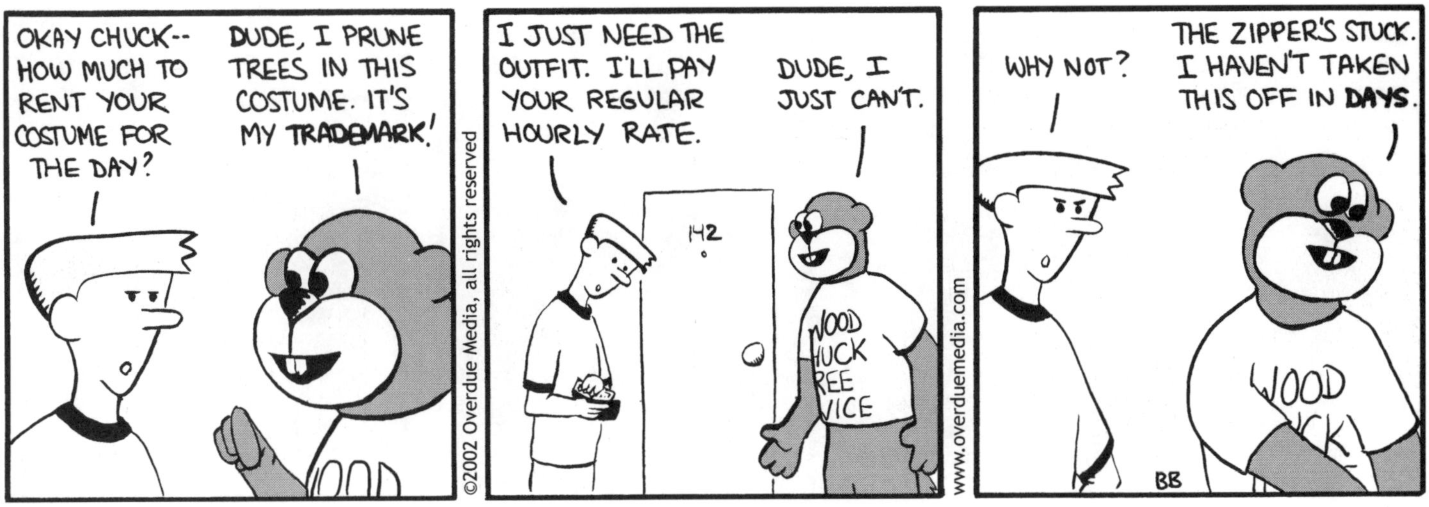
OKAY CHUCK-- HOW MUCH TO RENT YOUR COSTUME FOR THE DAY?
DUDE, I PRUNE TREES IN THIS COSTUME. IT'S MY **TRADEMARK**!
©2002 Overdue Media, all rights reserved
I JUST NEED THE OUTFIT. I'LL PAY YOUR REGULAR HOURLY RATE.
DUDE, I JUST CAN'T.
142
www.overduemedia.com
WHY NOT?
THE ZIPPER'S STUCK. I HAVEN'T TAKEN THIS OFF IN **DAYS**.
BB

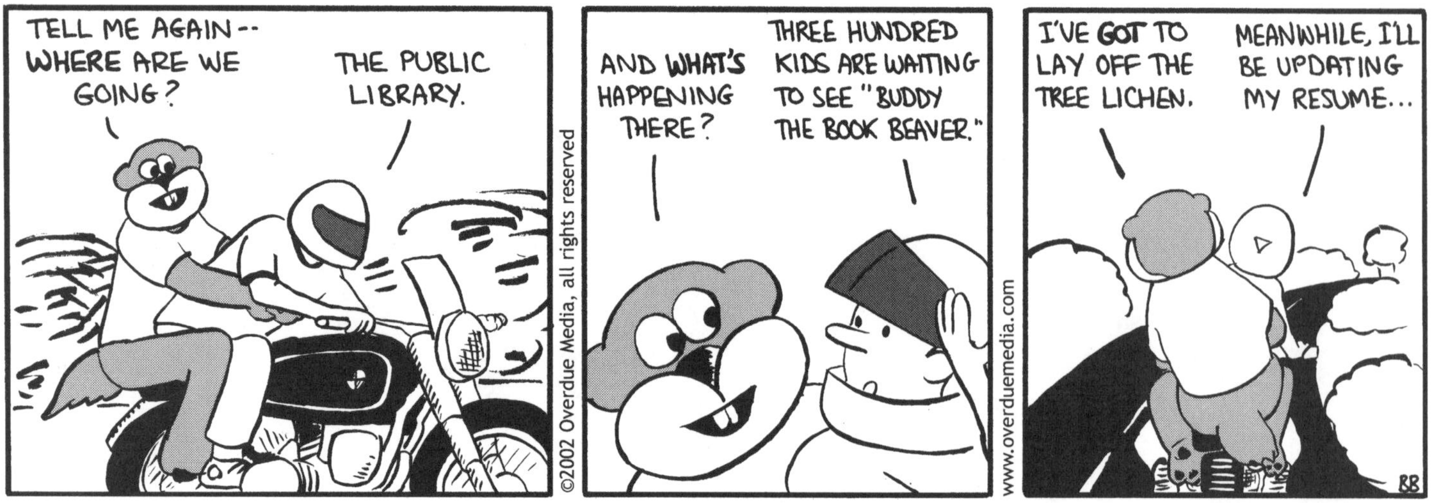
TELL ME AGAIN -- WHERE ARE WE GOING?
THE PUBLIC LIBRARY.
©2002 Overdue Media, all rights reserved
AND WHAT'S HAPPENING THERE?
THREE HUNDRED KIDS ARE WAITING TO SEE "BUDDY THE BOOK BEAVER."
www.overduemedia.com
I'VE GOT TO LAY OFF THE TREE LICHEN.
MEANWHILE, I'LL BE UPDATING MY RESUME...
BB

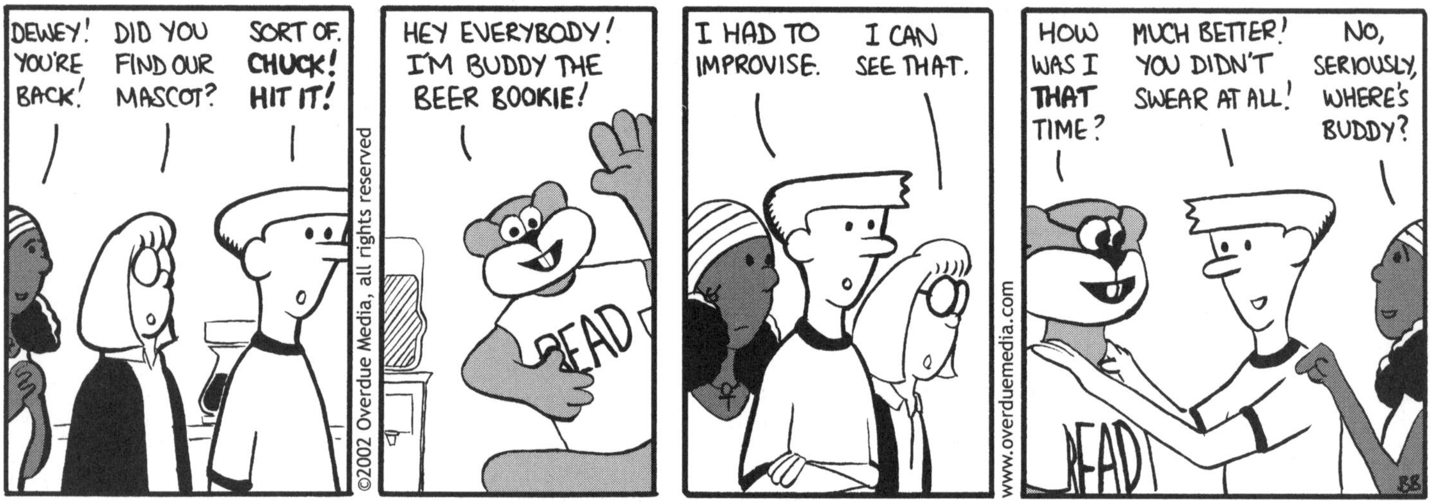
DEWEY! YOU'RE BACK!
DID YOU FIND OUR MASCOT?
SORT OF. CHUCK! HIT IT!
©2002 Overdue Media, all rights reserved
HEY EVERYBODY! I'M BUDDY THE BEER BOOKIE!
READ
I HAD TO IMPROVISE.
I CAN SEE THAT.
www.overduemedia.com
HOW WAS I THAT TIME?
MUCH BETTER! YOU DIDN'T SWEAR AT ALL!
NO, SERIOUSLY, WHERE'S BUDDY?
READ
BB

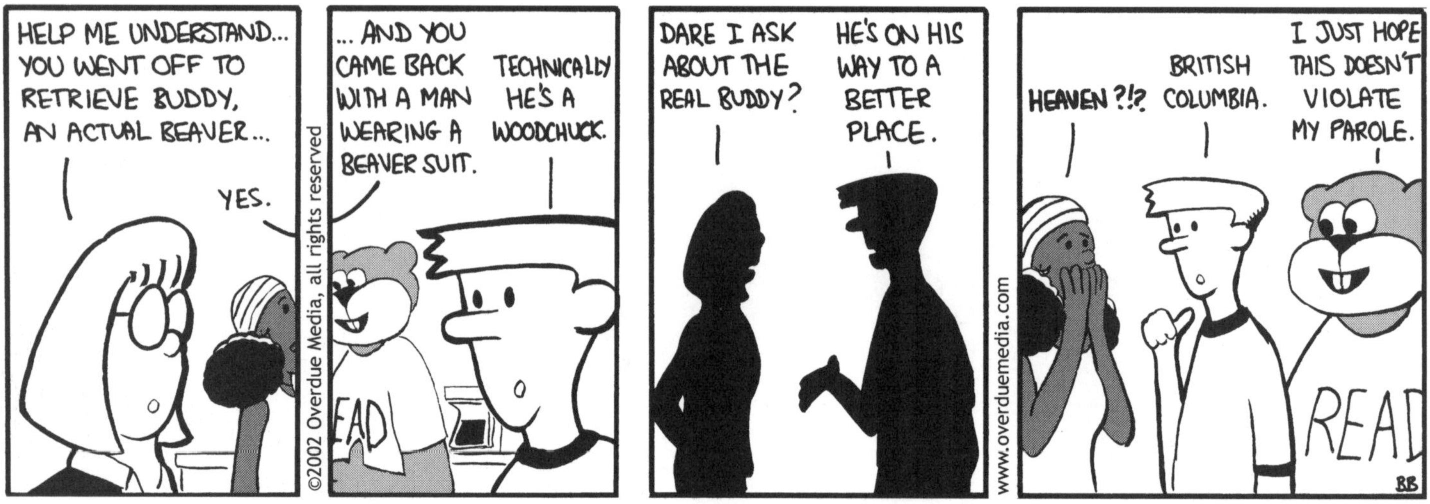
HELP ME UNDERSTAND... YOU WENT OFF TO RETRIEVE BUDDY, AN ACTUAL BEAVER...
YES.
©2002 Overdue Media, all rights reserved
... AND YOU CAME BACK WITH A MAN WEARING A BEAVER SUIT.
TECHNICALLY HE'S A WOODCHUCK.
EAD
DARE I ASK ABOUT THE REAL BUDDY?
HE'S ON HIS WAY TO A BETTER PLACE.
www.overduemedia.com
HEAVEN?!?
BRITISH COLUMBIA.
I JUST HOPE THIS DOESN'T VIOLATE MY PAROLE.
READ
BB

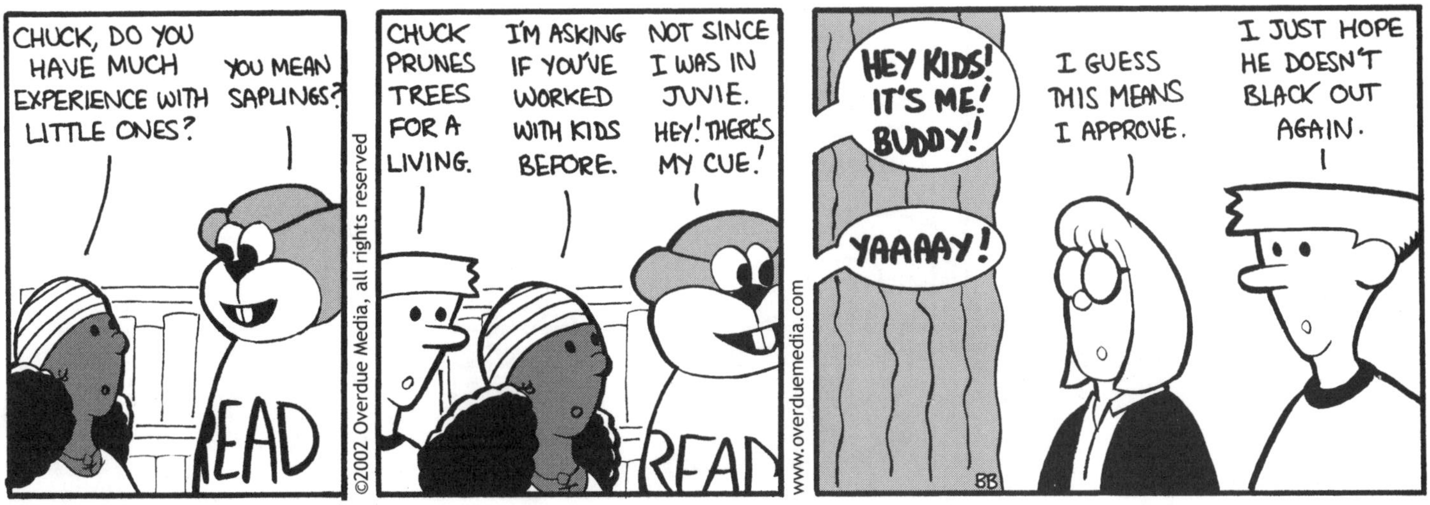
CHUCK, DO YOU HAVE MUCH EXPERIENCE WITH LITTLE ONES?
YOU MEAN SAPLINGS?
READ
CHUCK PRUNES TREES FOR A LIVING.
I'M ASKING IF YOU'VE WORKED WITH KIDS BEFORE.
NOT SINCE I WAS IN JUVIE. HEY! THERE'S MY CUE!
HEY KIDS! IT'S ME! BUDDY!
YAAAAY!
I GUESS THIS MEANS I APPROVE.
I JUST HOPE HE DOESN'T BLACK OUT AGAIN.
BB

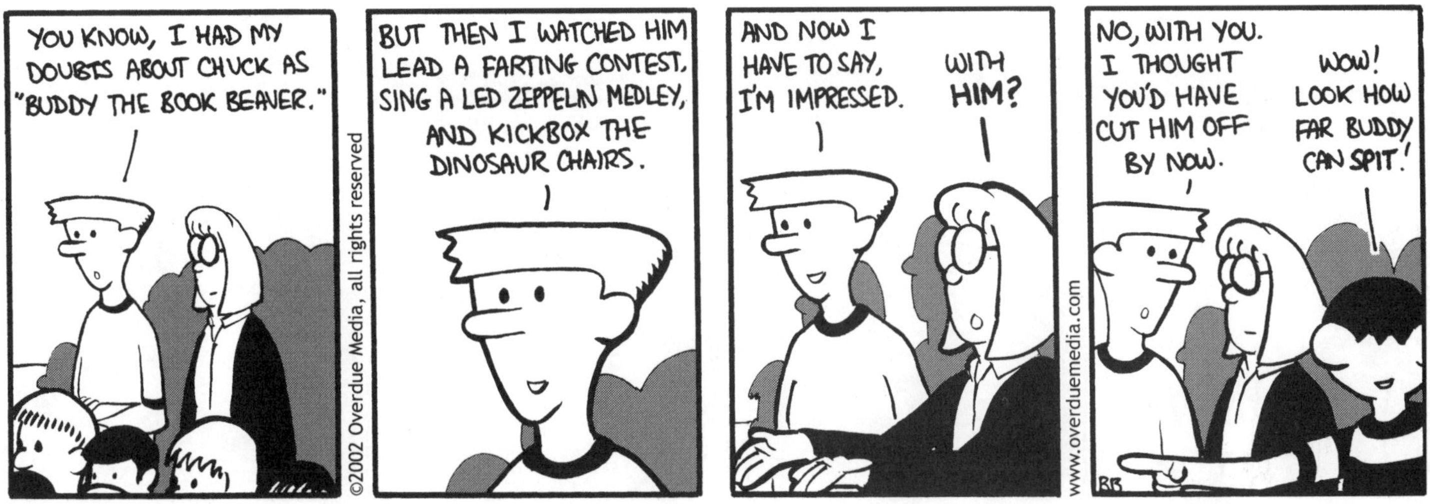
YOU KNOW, I HAD MY DOUBTS ABOUT CHUCK AS "BUDDY THE BOOK BEAVER."
BUT THEN I WATCHED HIM LEAD A FARTING CONTEST, SING A LED ZEPPELIN MEDLEY, AND KICKBOX THE DINOSAUR CHAIRS.
AND NOW I HAVE TO SAY, I'M IMPRESSED.
WITH **HIM**?
NO, WITH YOU. I THOUGHT YOU'D HAVE CUT HIM OFF BY NOW.
WOW! LOOK HOW FAR BUDDY CAN **SPIT**!
BB

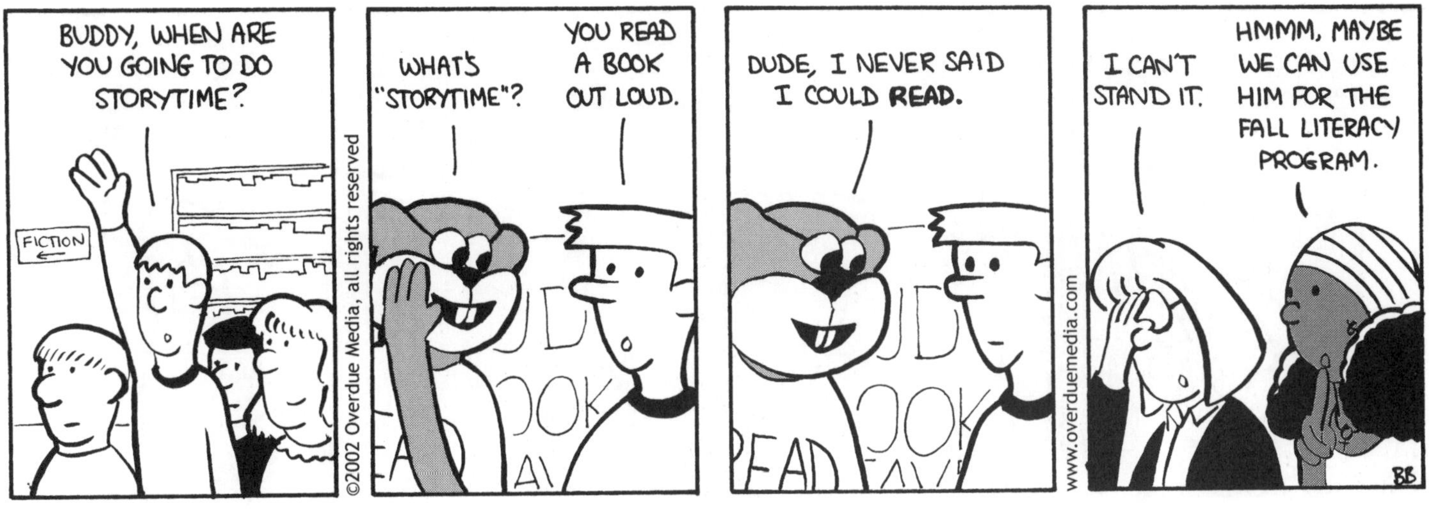
BUDDY, WHEN ARE YOU GOING TO DO STORYTIME?
FICTION
WHAT'S "STORYTIME"?
YOU READ A BOOK OUT LOUD.
DUDE, I NEVER SAID I COULD **READ.**
I CAN'T STAND IT.
HMMM, MAYBE WE CAN USE HIM FOR THE FALL LITERACY PROGRAM.
BB

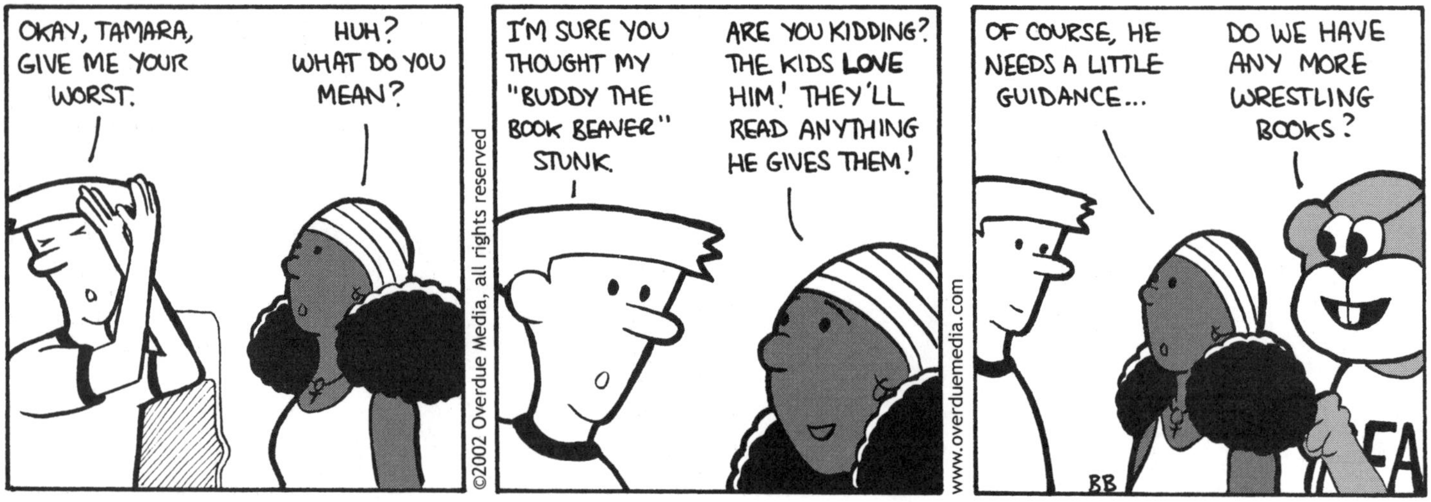
OKAY, TAMARA, GIVE ME YOUR WORST.
HUH? WHAT DO YOU MEAN?
©2002 Overdue Media, all rights reserved
I'M SURE YOU THOUGHT MY "BUDDY THE BOOK BEAVER" STUNK.
ARE YOU KIDDING? THE KIDS LOVE HIM! THEY'LL READ ANYTHING HE GIVES THEM!
www.overduemedia.com
OF COURSE, HE NEEDS A LITTLE GUIDANCE...
DO WE HAVE ANY MORE WRESTLING BOOKS?
BB

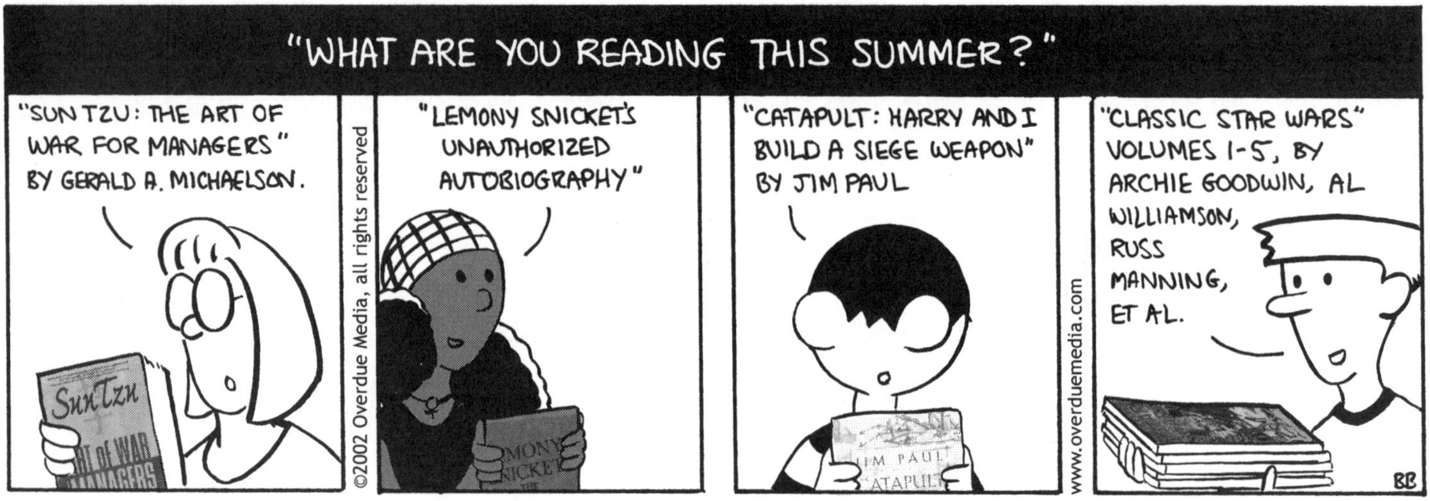
"WHAT ARE YOU READING THIS SUMMER?"
"SUN TZU: THE ART OF WAR FOR MANAGERS" BY GERALD A. MICHAELSON.
Sun Tzu
©2002 Overdue Media, all rights reserved
"LEMONY SNICKET'S UNAUTHORIZED AUTOBIOGRAPHY"
"CATAPULT: HARRY AND I BUILD A SIEGE WEAPON" BY JIM PAUL
www.overduemedia.com
"CLASSIC STAR WARS" VOLUMES 1-5, BY ARCHIE GOODWIN, AL WILLIAMSON, RUSS MANNING, ET AL.
BB

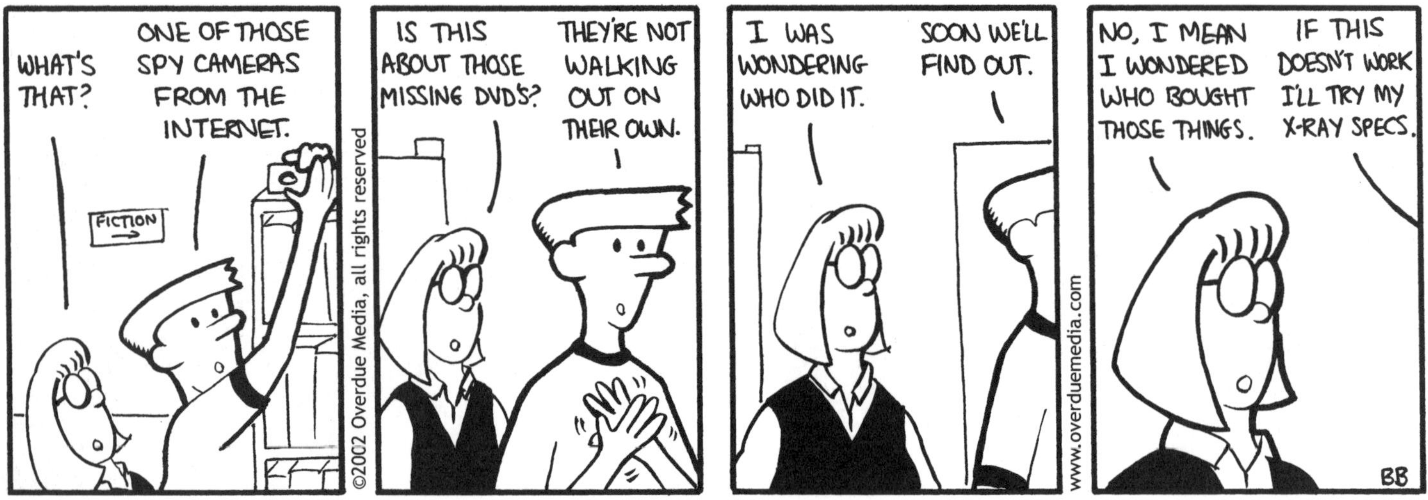
WHAT'S THAT?
ONE OF THOSE SPY CAMERAS FROM THE INTERNET.
FICTION
©2002 Overdue Media, all rights reserved
IS THIS ABOUT THOSE MISSING DVD'S?
THEY'RE NOT WALKING OUT ON THEIR OWN.
I WAS WONDERING WHO DID IT.
SOON WE'LL FIND OUT.
www.overduemedia.com
NO, I MEAN I WONDERED WHO BOUGHT THOSE THINGS.
IF THIS DOESN'T WORK I'LL TRY MY X-RAY SPECS.
BB

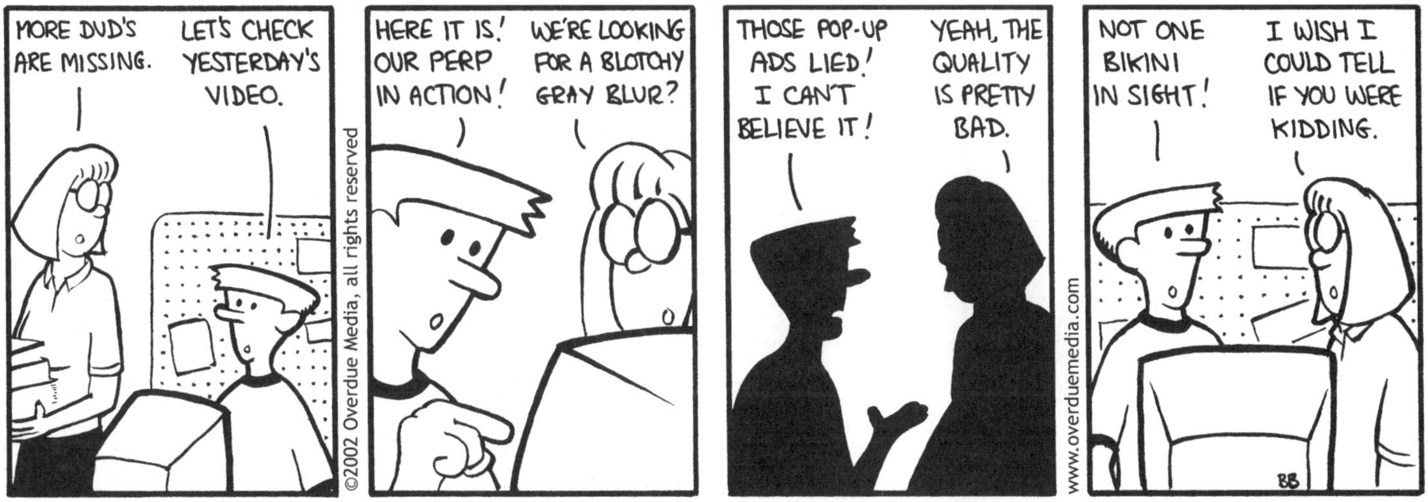
MORE DVD'S ARE MISSING.
LET'S CHECK YESTERDAY'S VIDEO.
HERE IT IS! OUR PERP IN ACTION!
WE'RE LOOKING FOR A BLOTCHY GRAY BLUR?
THOSE POP-UP ADS LIED! I CAN'T BELIEVE IT!
YEAH, THE QUALITY IS PRETTY BAD.
NOT ONE BIKINI IN SIGHT!
I WISH I COULD TELL IF YOU WERE KIDDING.
BB

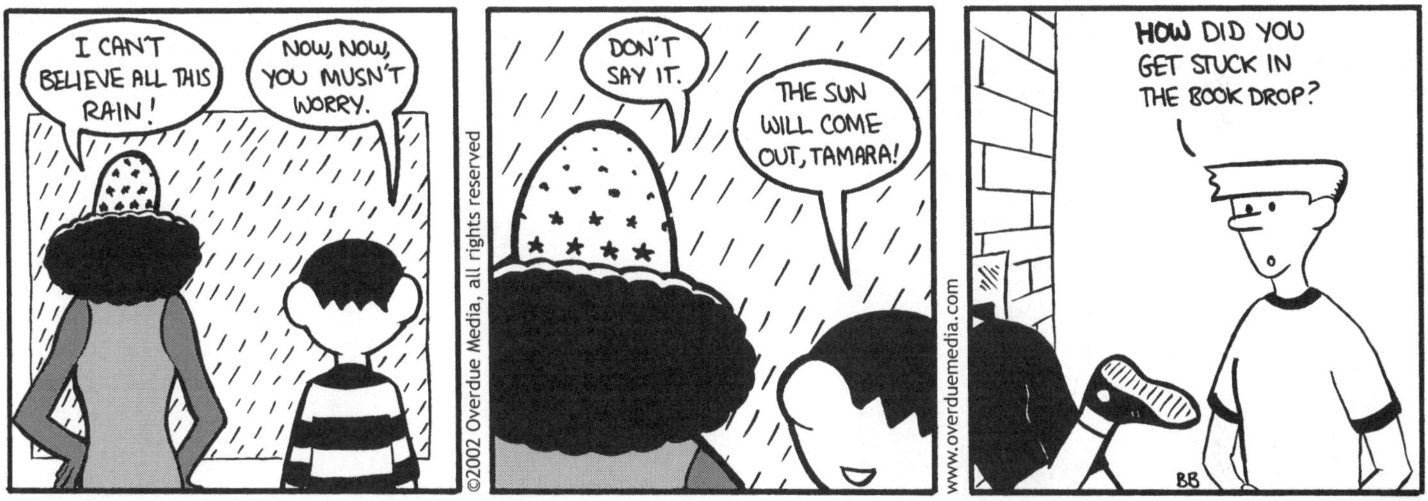
I CAN'T BELIEVE ALL THIS RAIN!
NOW, NOW, YOU MUSN'T WORRY.
DON'T SAY IT.
THE SUN WILL COME OUT, TAMARA!
HOW DID YOU GET STUCK IN THE BOOK DROP?
BB

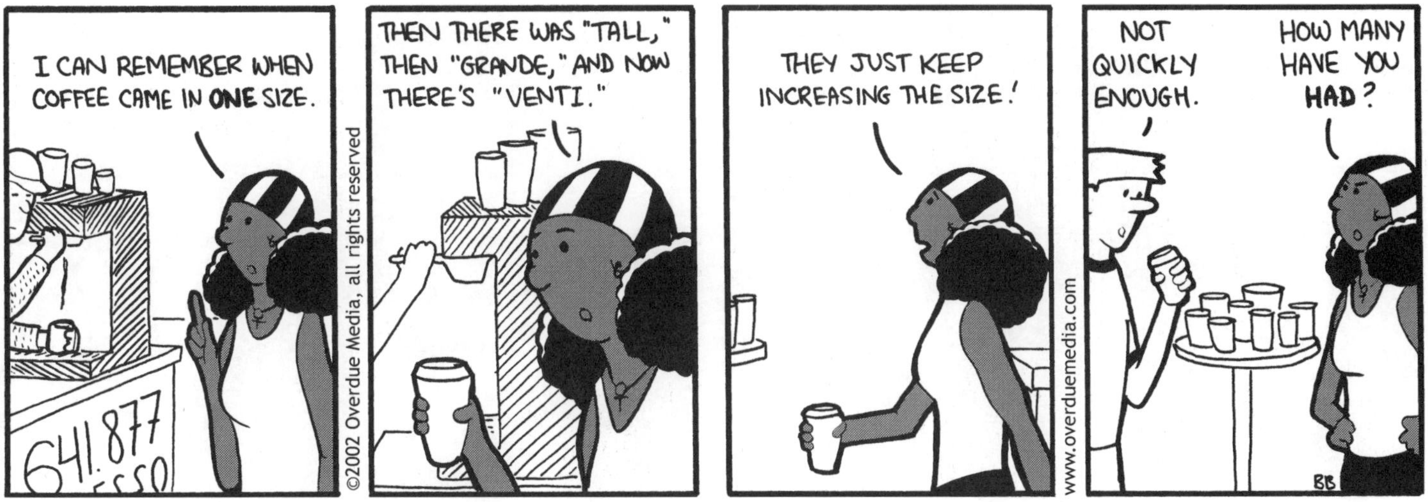
I CAN REMEMBER WHEN COFFEE CAME IN **ONE** SIZE.
641.877
THEN THERE WAS "TALL," THEN "GRANDE," AND NOW THERE'S "VENTI."
THEY JUST KEEP INCREASING THE SIZE!
NOT QUICKLY ENOUGH.
HOW MANY HAVE YOU **HAD**?
BB

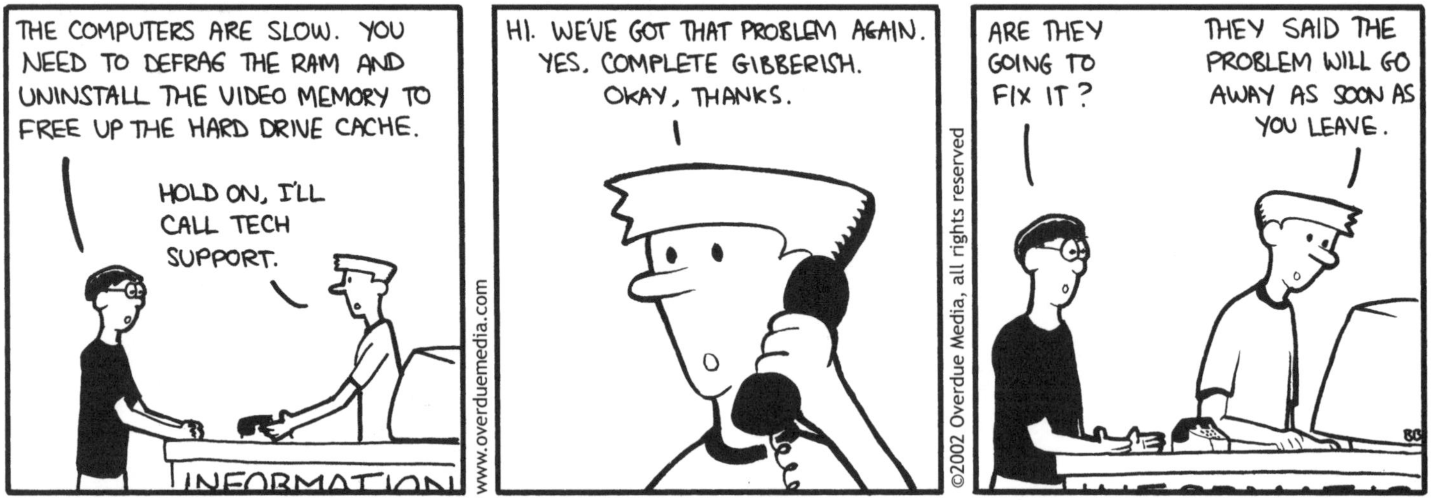
THE COMPUTERS ARE SLOW. YOU NEED TO DEFRAG THE RAM AND UNINSTALL THE VIDEO MEMORY TO FREE UP THE HARD DRIVE CACHE.
HOLD ON, I'LL CALL TECH SUPPORT.
INFORMATION
www.overduemedia.com
HI. WE'VE GOT THAT PROBLEM AGAIN. YES. COMPLETE GIBBERISH. OKAY, THANKS.
©2002 Overdue Media, all rights reserved
ARE THEY GOING TO FIX IT?
THEY SAID THE PROBLEM WILL GO AWAY AS SOON AS YOU LEAVE.
BB

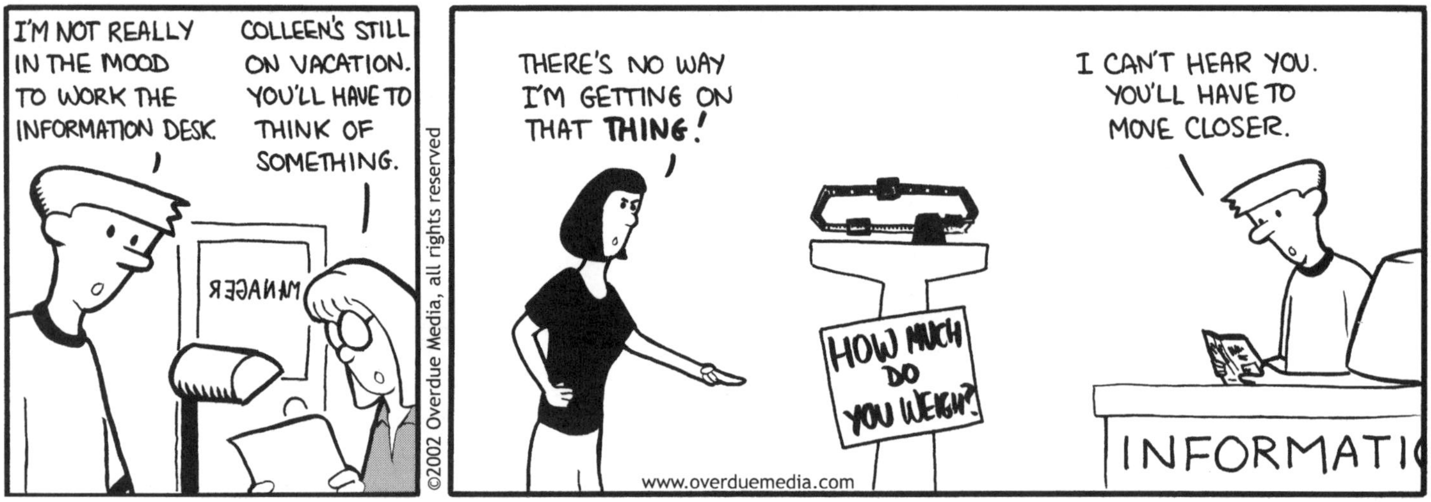
I'M NOT REALLY IN THE MOOD TO WORK THE INFORMATION DESK.
COLLEEN'S STILL ON VACATION. YOU'LL HAVE TO THINK OF SOMETHING.
©2002 Overdue Media, all rights reserved
THERE'S NO WAY I'M GETTING ON THAT THING!
HOW MUCH DO YOU WEIGH?
I CAN'T HEAR YOU. YOU'LL HAVE TO MOVE CLOSER.
INFORMATI
www.overduemedia.com

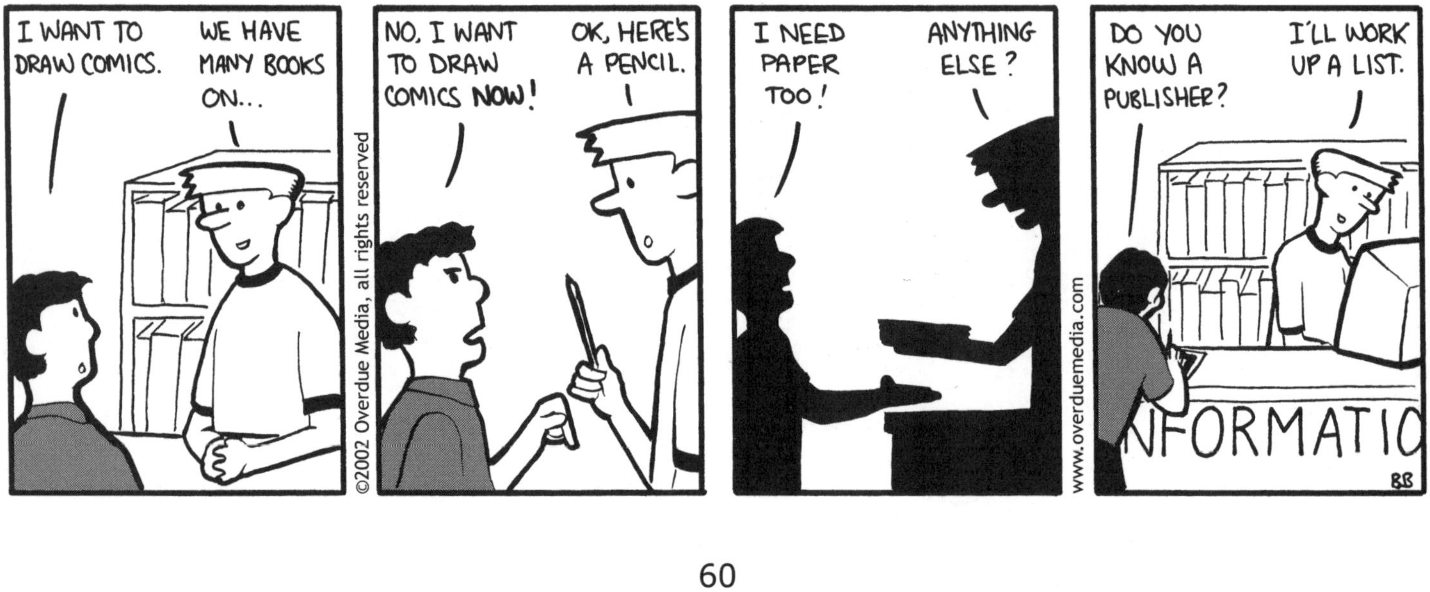
I WANT TO DRAW COMICS.
WE HAVE MANY BOOKS ON...
©2002 Overdue Media, all rights reserved
NO, I WANT TO DRAW COMICS NOW!
OK, HERE'S A PENCIL.
I NEED PAPER TOO!
ANYTHING ELSE?
www.overduemedia.com
DO YOU KNOW A PUBLISHER?
I'LL WORK UP A LIST.
NFORMATIO
BB

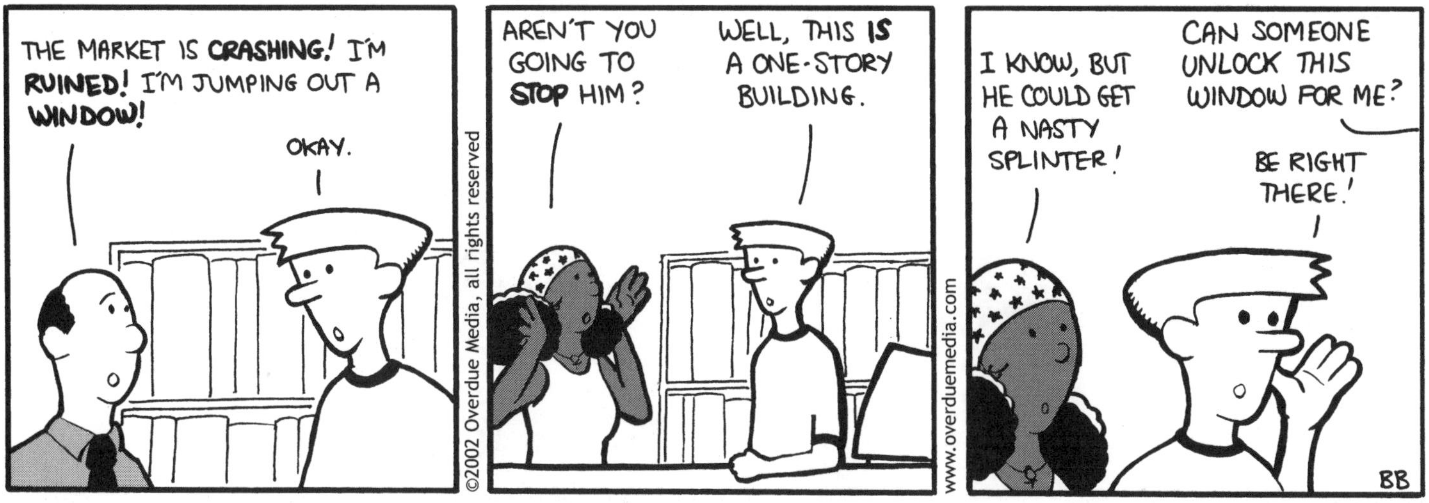
THE MARKET IS **CRASHING!** I'M **RUINED!** I'M JUMPING OUT A **WINDOW!**
OKAY.
©2002 Overdue Media, all rights reserved
AREN'T YOU GOING TO **STOP** HIM?
WELL, THIS **IS** A ONE-STORY BUILDING.
www.overduemedia.com
I KNOW, BUT HE COULD GET A NASTY SPLINTER!
CAN SOMEONE UNLOCK THIS WINDOW FOR ME?
BE RIGHT THERE!
BB

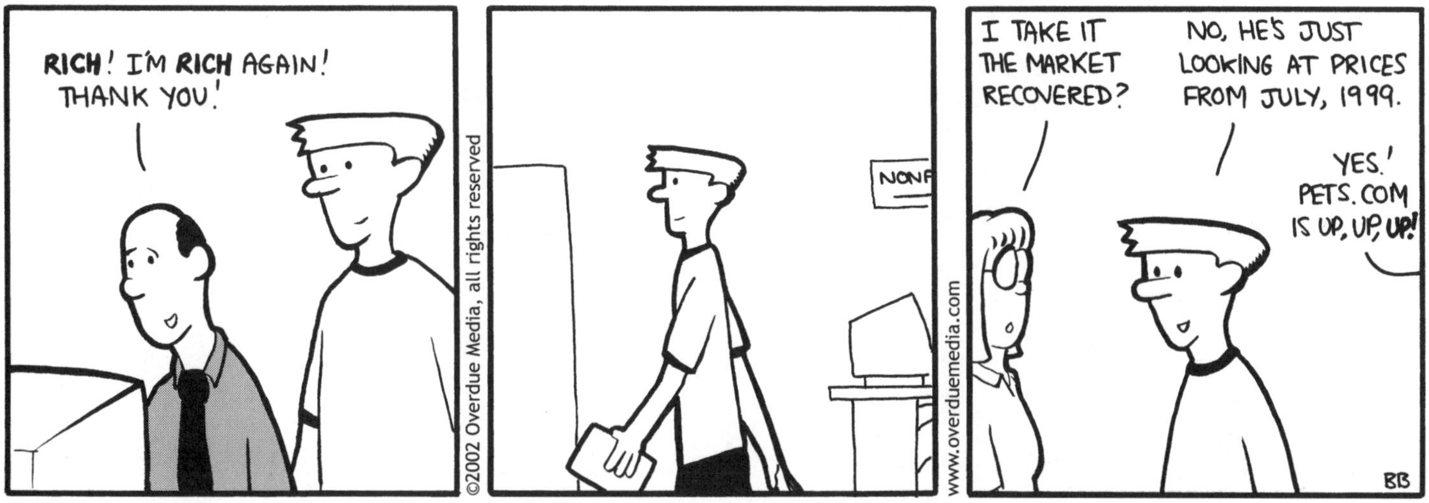
RICH! I'M **RICH** AGAIN! THANK YOU!
©2002 Overdue Media, all rights reserved
NONF
www.overduemedia.com
I TAKE IT THE MARKET RECOVERED?
NO, HE'S JUST LOOKING AT PRICES FROM JULY, 1999.
YES! PETS.COM IS UP, UP, **UP!**
BB

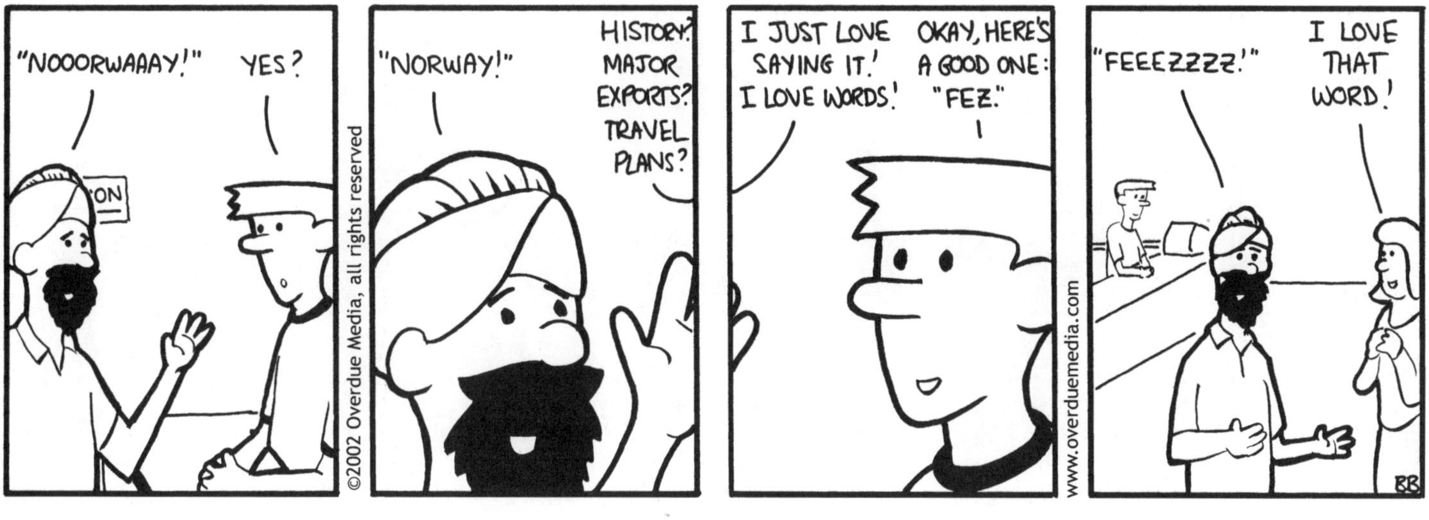
"NOOORWAAAY!"
YES?
ON
©2002 Overdue Media, all rights reserved
"NORWAY!"
HISTORY? MAJOR EXPORTS? TRAVEL PLANS?
I JUST LOVE SAYING IT! I LOVE WORDS!
OKAY, HERE'S A GOOD ONE: "FEZ."
www.overduemedia.com
"FEEEZZZZ!"
I LOVE THAT WORD!
BB

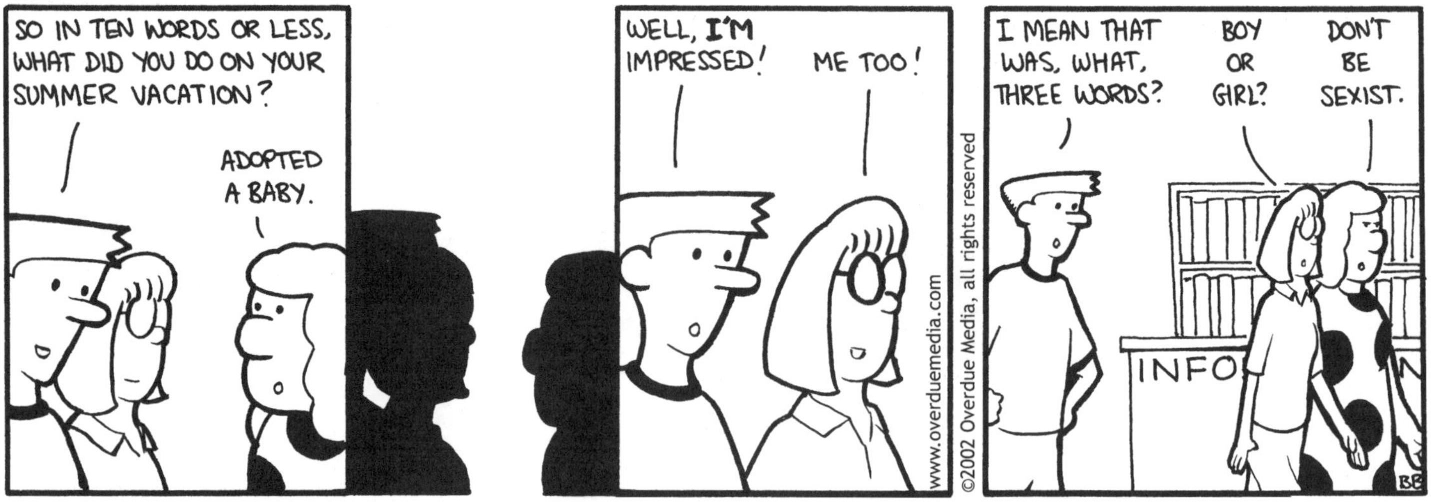
SO IN TEN WORDS OR LESS, WHAT DID YOU DO ON YOUR SUMMER VACATION?
ADOPTED A BABY.
WELL, I'M IMPRESSED!
ME TOO!
I MEAN THAT WAS, WHAT, THREE WORDS?
BOY OR GIRL?
DON'T BE SEXIST.
INFO
www.overduemedia.com
©2002 Overdue Media, all rights reserved
BB

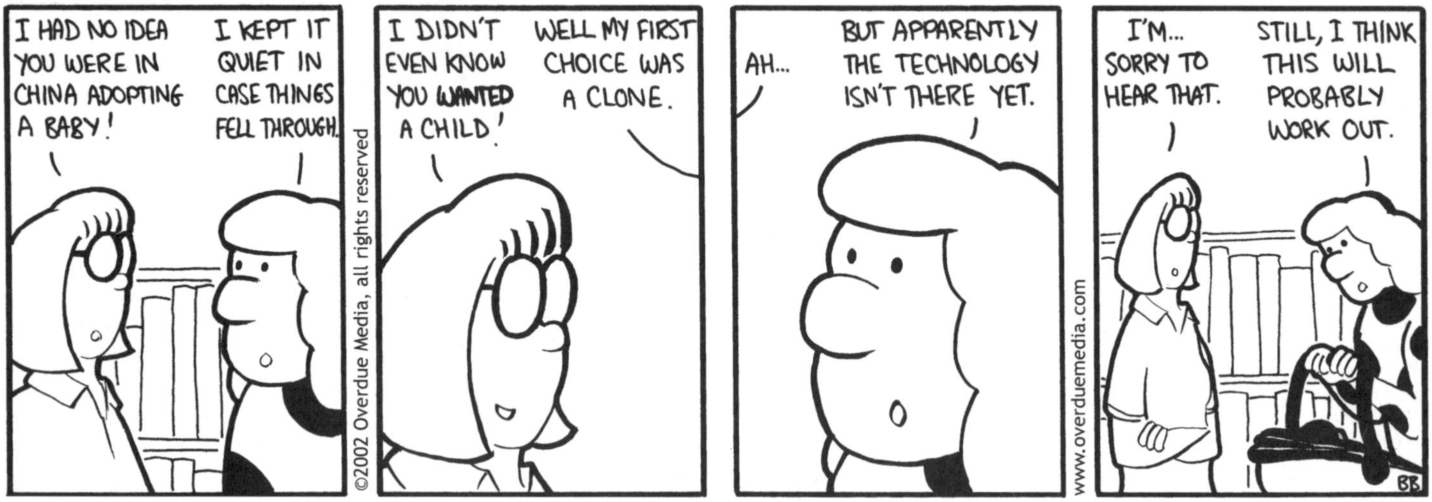
I HAD NO IDEA YOU WERE IN CHINA ADOPTING A BABY!
I KEPT IT QUIET IN CASE THINGS FELL THROUGH.
I DIDN'T EVEN KNOW YOU WANTED A CHILD!
WELL MY FIRST CHOICE WAS A CLONE.
AH...
BUT APPARENTLY THE TECHNOLOGY ISN'T THERE YET.
I'M... SORRY TO HEAR THAT.
STILL, I THINK THIS WILL PROBABLY WORK OUT.
©2002 Overdue Media, all rights reserved
www.overduemedia.com
BB

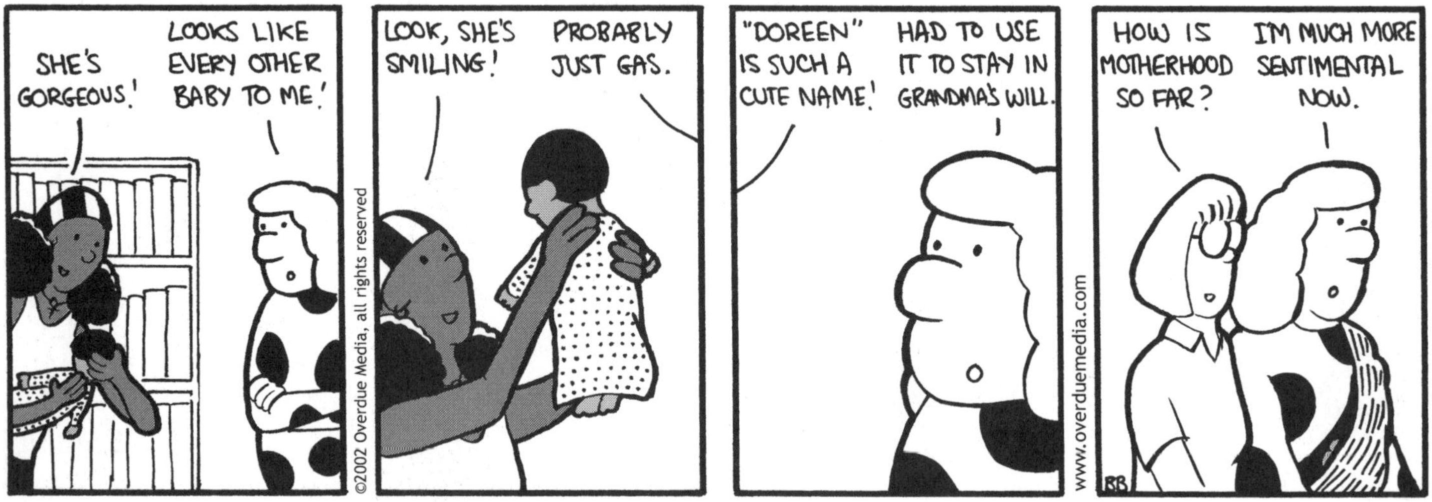
SHE'S GORGEOUS!
LOOKS LIKE EVERY OTHER BABY TO ME!
LOOK, SHE'S SMILING!
PROBABLY JUST GAS.
"DOREEN" IS SUCH A CUTE NAME!
HAD TO USE IT TO STAY IN GRANDMA'S WILL.
HOW IS MOTHERHOOD SO FAR?
I'M MUCH MORE SENTIMENTAL NOW.
©2002 Overdue Media, all rights reserved
www.overduemedia.com
BB

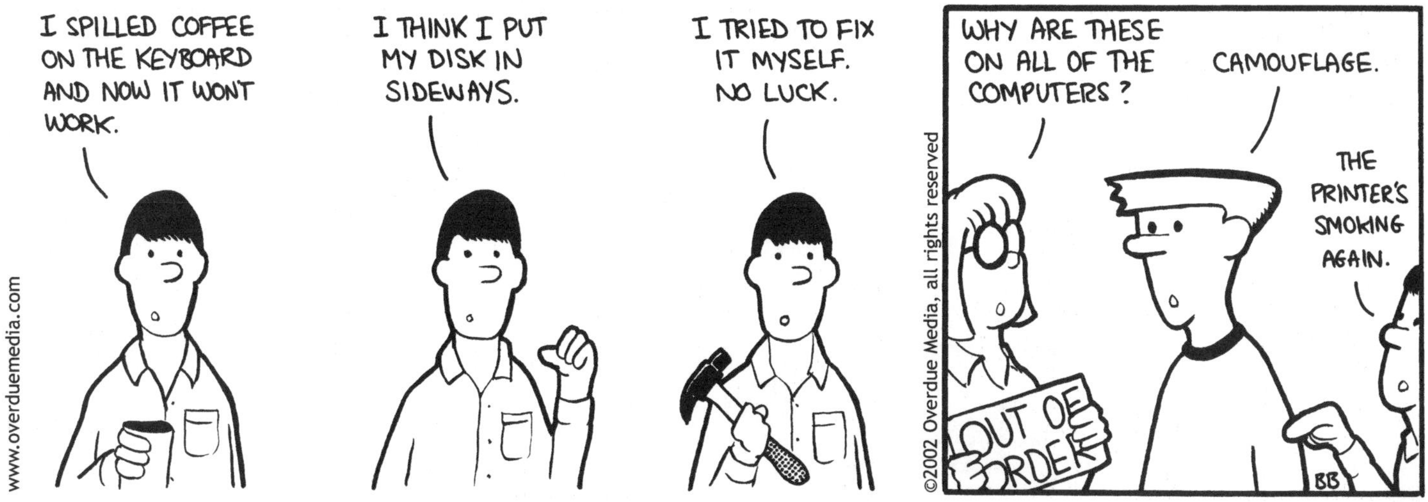
I SPILLED COFFEE ON THE KEYBOARD AND NOW IT WON'T WORK.
I THINK I PUT MY DISK IN SIDEWAYS.
I TRIED TO FIX IT MYSELF. NO LUCK.
WHY ARE THESE ON ALL OF THE COMPUTERS?
CAMOUFLAGE.
THE PRINTER'S SMOKING AGAIN.
OUT OF ORDER
www.overduemedia.com
©2002 Overdue Media, all rights reserved
BB

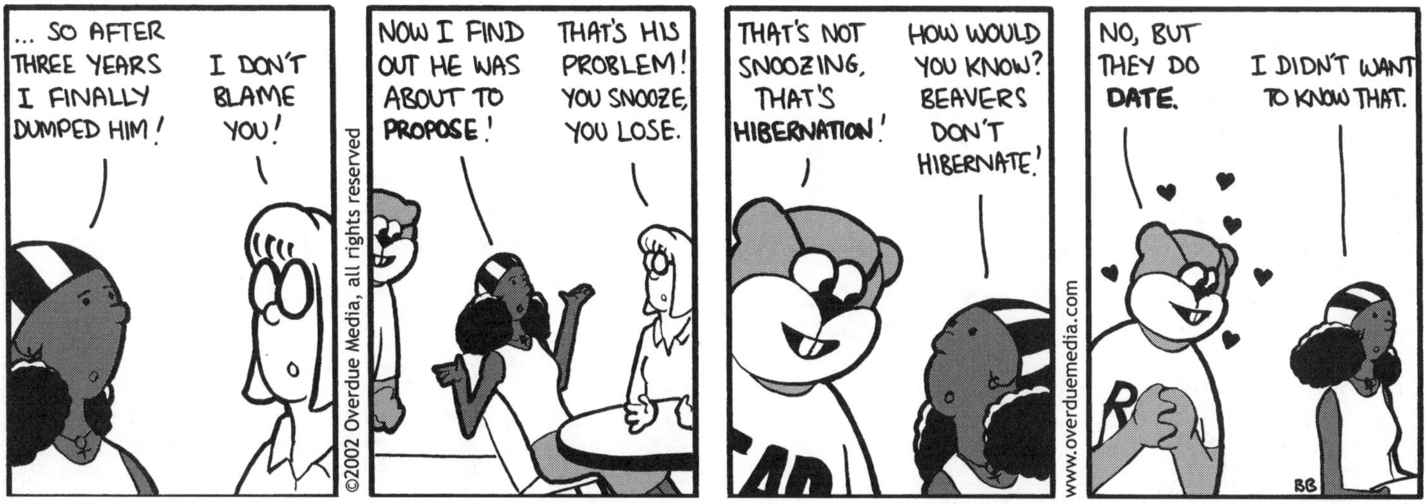
... SO AFTER THREE YEARS I FINALLY DUMPED HIM!
I DON'T BLAME YOU!
NOW I FIND OUT HE WAS ABOUT TO **PROPOSE**!
THAT'S HIS PROBLEM! YOU SNOOZE, YOU LOSE.
THAT'S NOT SNOOZING, THAT'S **HIBERNATION**!
HOW WOULD YOU KNOW? BEAVERS DON'T HIBERNATE!
NO, BUT THEY DO **DATE**.
I DIDN'T WANT TO KNOW THAT.
©2002 Overdue Media, all rights reserved
www.overduemedia.com
BB

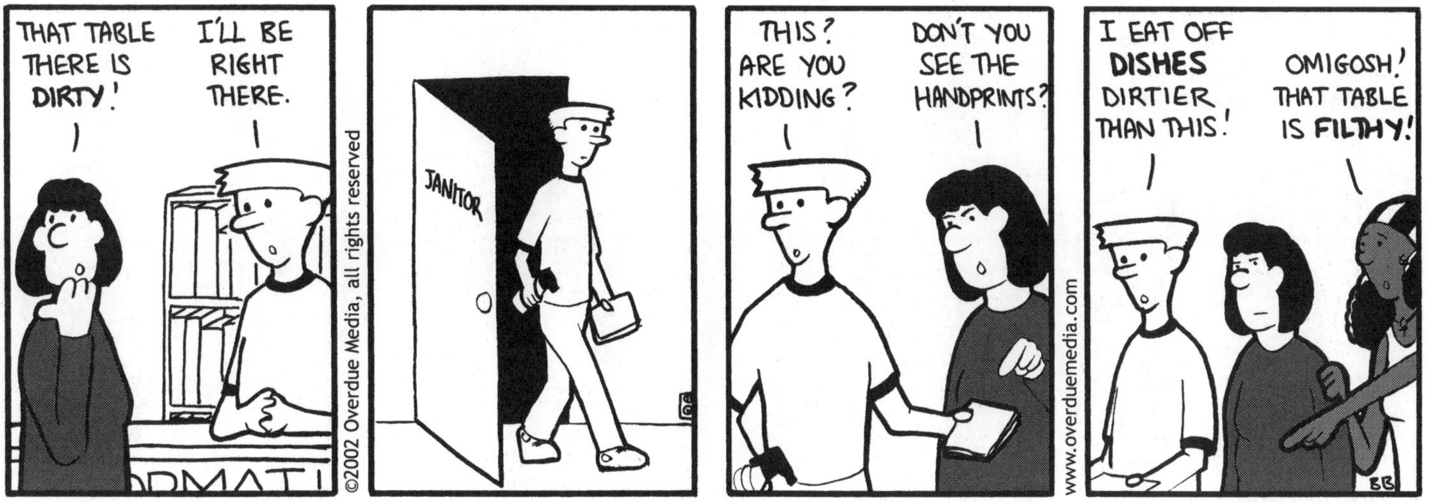
THAT TABLE THERE IS **DIRTY**!
I'LL BE RIGHT THERE.
JANITOR
THIS? ARE YOU KIDDING?
DON'T YOU SEE THE HANDPRINTS?
I EAT OFF **DISHES** DIRTIER THAN THIS!
OMIGOSH! THAT TABLE IS **FILTHY**!
©2002 Overdue Media, all rights reserved
www.overduemedia.com
BB

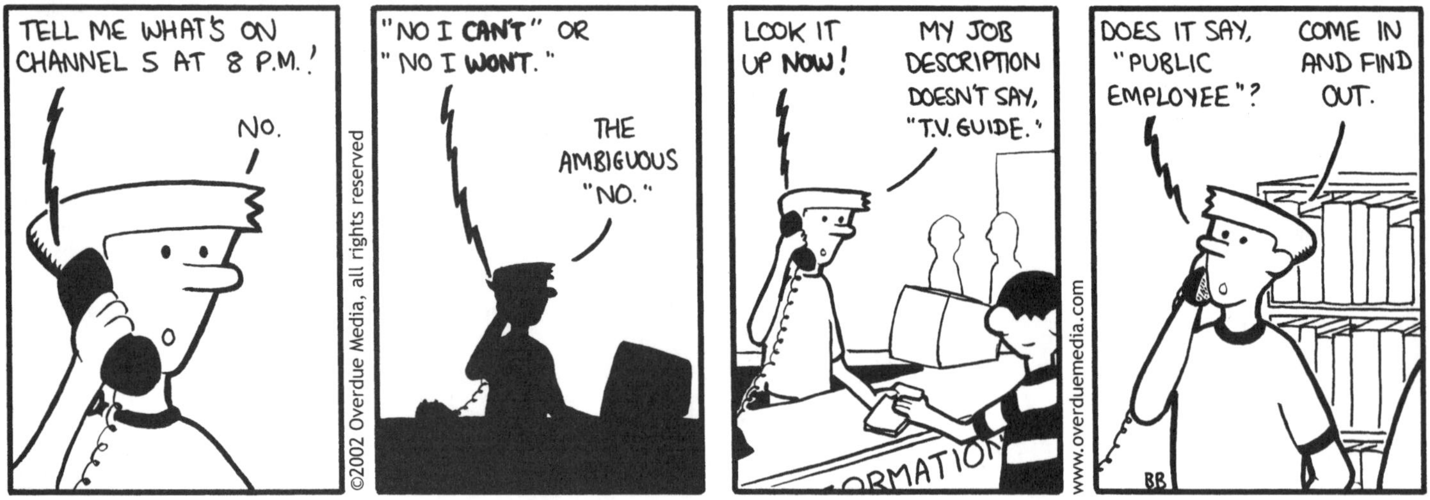
TELL ME WHAT'S ON CHANNEL 5 AT 8 P.M.!
NO.
"NO I CAN'T" OR "NO I WON'T."
THE AMBIGUOUS "NO."
©2002 Overdue Media, all rights reserved
LOOK IT UP NOW!
MY JOB DESCRIPTION DOESN'T SAY, "T.V. GUIDE."
ORMATION
DOES IT SAY, "PUBLIC EMPLOYEE"?
COME IN AND FIND OUT.
www.overduemedia.com
BB

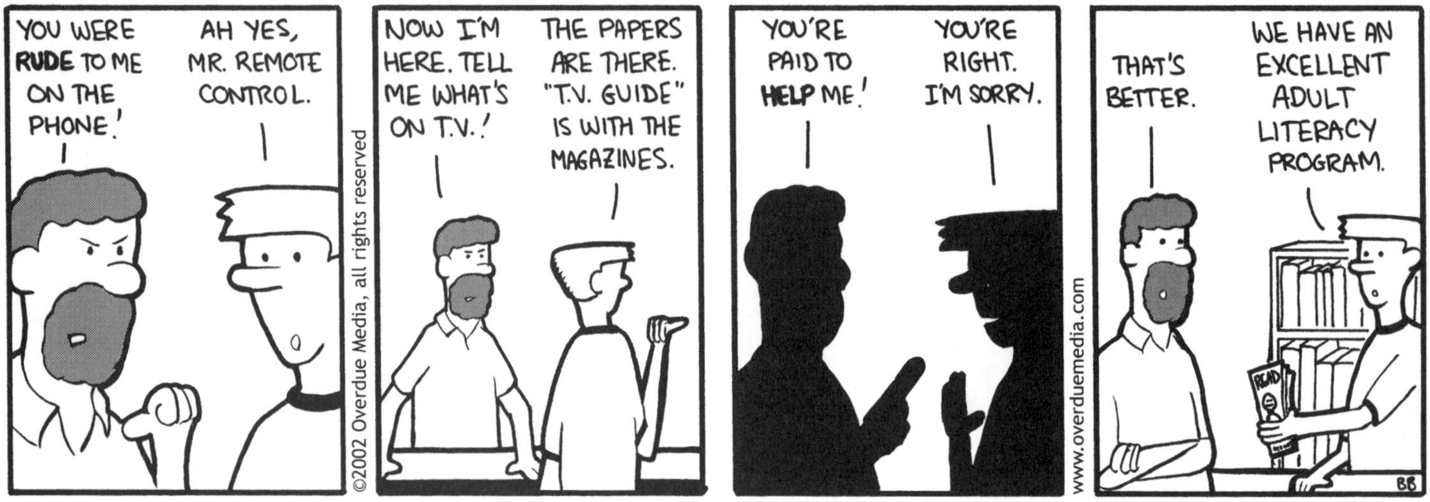
YOU WERE RUDE TO ME ON THE PHONE!
AH YES, MR. REMOTE CONTROL.
©2002 Overdue Media, all rights reserved
NOW I'M HERE. TELL ME WHAT'S ON T.V.!
THE PAPERS ARE THERE. "T.V. GUIDE" IS WITH THE MAGAZINES.
YOU'RE PAID TO HELP ME!
YOU'RE RIGHT. I'M SORRY.
www.overduemedia.com
THAT'S BETTER.
WE HAVE AN EXCELLENT ADULT LITERACY PROGRAM.
READ
BB

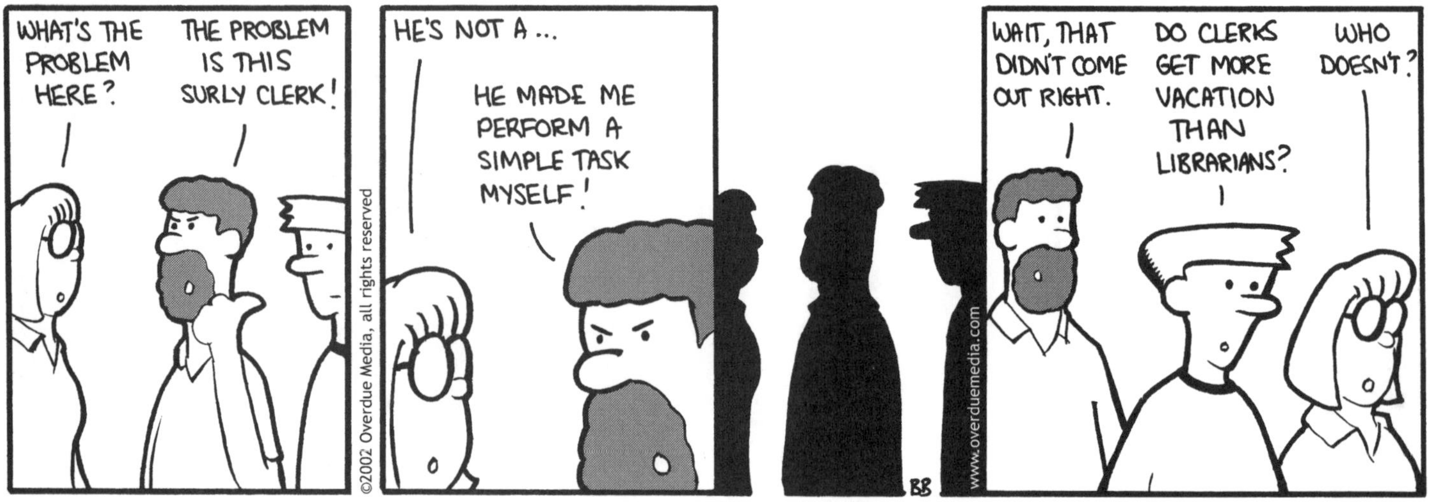
WHAT'S THE PROBLEM HERE?
THE PROBLEM IS THIS SURLY CLERK!
©2002 Overdue Media, all rights reserved
HE'S NOT A ...
HE MADE ME PERFORM A SIMPLE TASK MYSELF!
BB
www.overduemedia.com
WAIT, THAT DIDN'T COME OUT RIGHT.
DO CLERKS GET MORE VACATION THAN LIBRARIANS?
WHO DOESN'T?

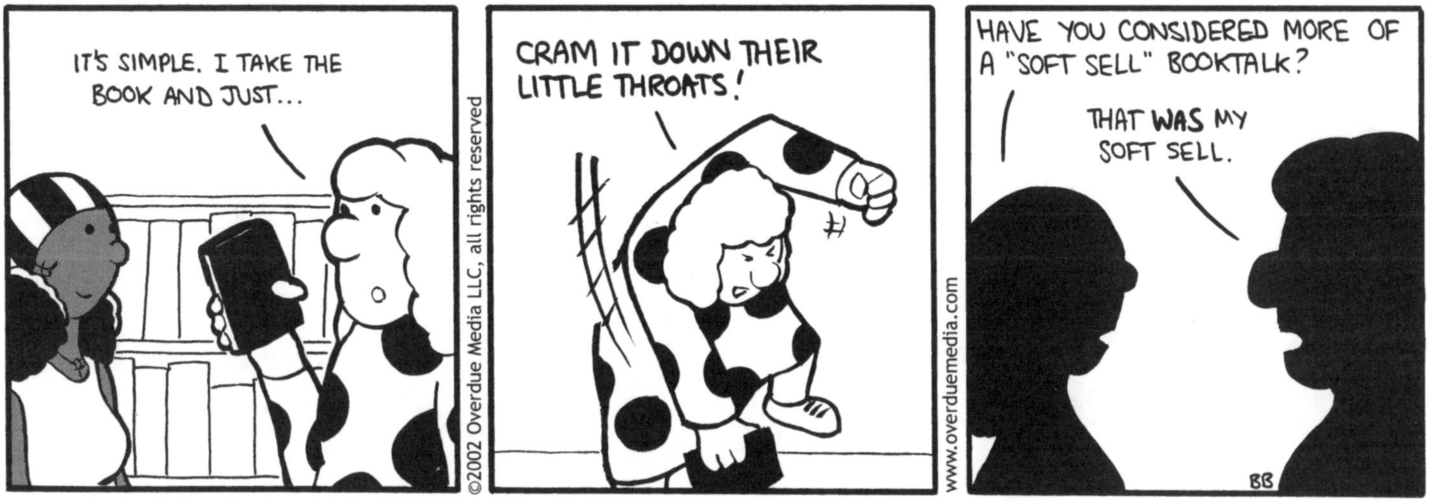
IT'S SIMPLE. I TAKE THE BOOK AND JUST...
CRAM IT DOWN THEIR LITTLE THROATS!
HAVE YOU CONSIDERED MORE OF A "SOFT SELL" BOOKTALK?
THAT WAS MY SOFT SELL.
BB
©2002 Overdue Media LLC, all rights reserved
www.overduemedia.com

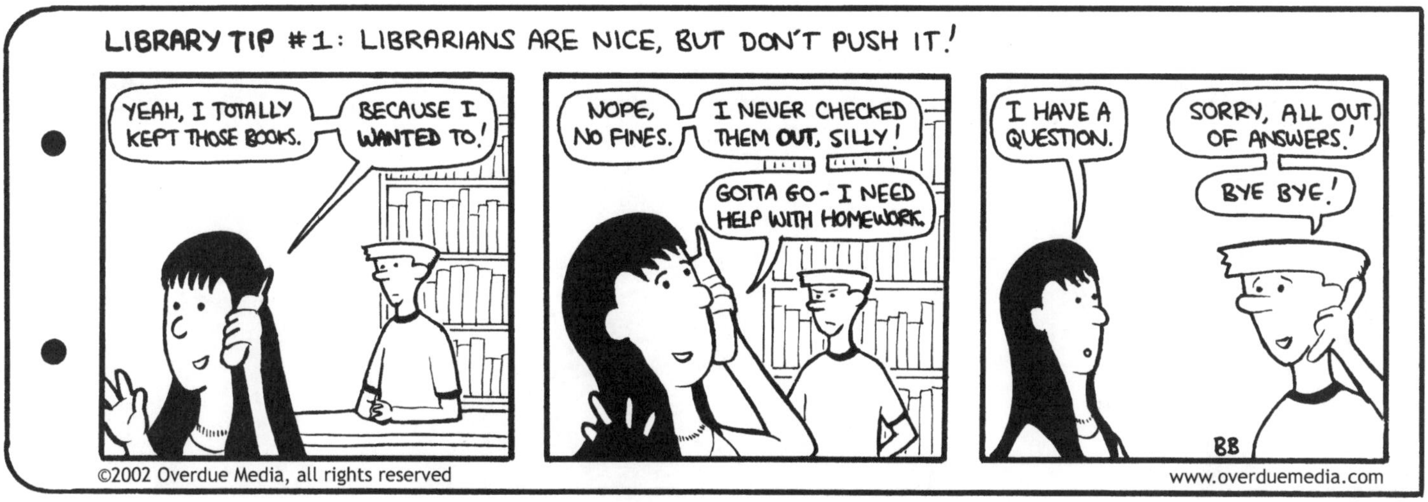
LIBRARY TIP #1: LIBRARIANS ARE NICE, BUT DON'T PUSH IT!
YEAH, I TOTALLY KEPT THOSE BOOKS.
BECAUSE I WANTED TO!
NOPE, NO FINES.
I NEVER CHECKED THEM OUT, SILLY!
GOTTA GO - I NEED HELP WITH HOMEWORK.
I HAVE A QUESTION.
SORRY, ALL OUT OF ANSWERS!
BYE BYE!
BB
©2002 Overdue Media, all rights reserved
www.overduemedia.com

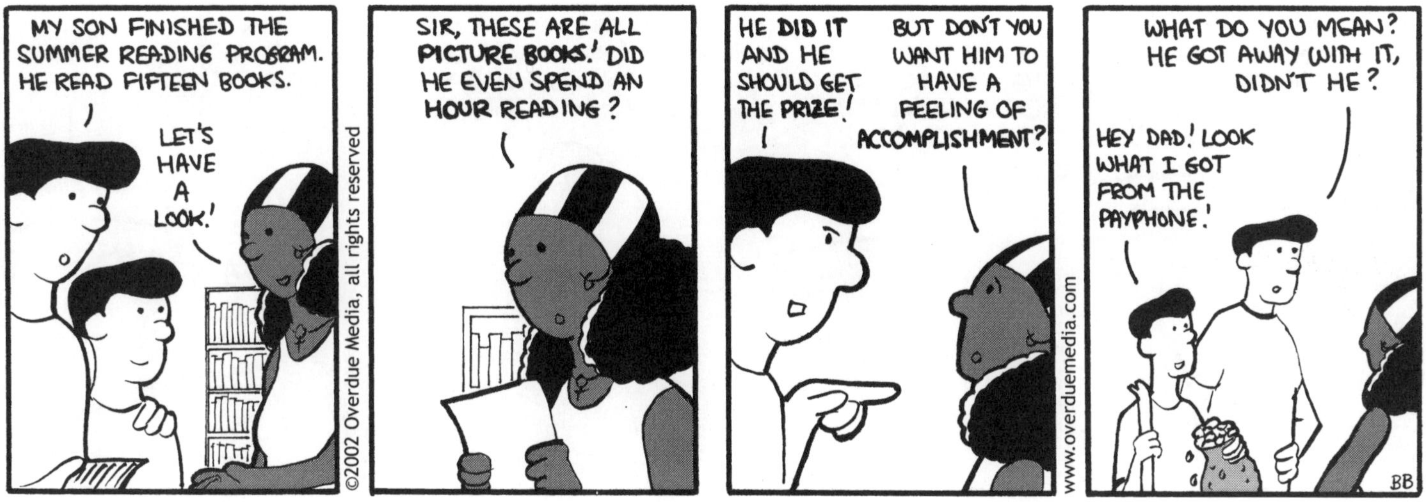
MY SON FINISHED THE SUMMER READING PROGRAM. HE READ FIFTEEN BOOKS.
LET'S HAVE A LOOK!
SIR, THESE ARE ALL PICTURE BOOKS! DID HE EVEN SPEND AN HOUR READING?
HE DID IT AND HE SHOULD GET THE PRIZE!
BUT DON'T YOU WANT HIM TO HAVE A FEELING OF ACCOMPLISHMENT?
WHAT DO YOU MEAN? HE GOT AWAY WITH IT, DIDN'T HE?
HEY DAD! LOOK WHAT I GOT FROM THE PAYPHONE!
BB
©2002 Overdue Media, all rights reserved
www.overduemedia.com

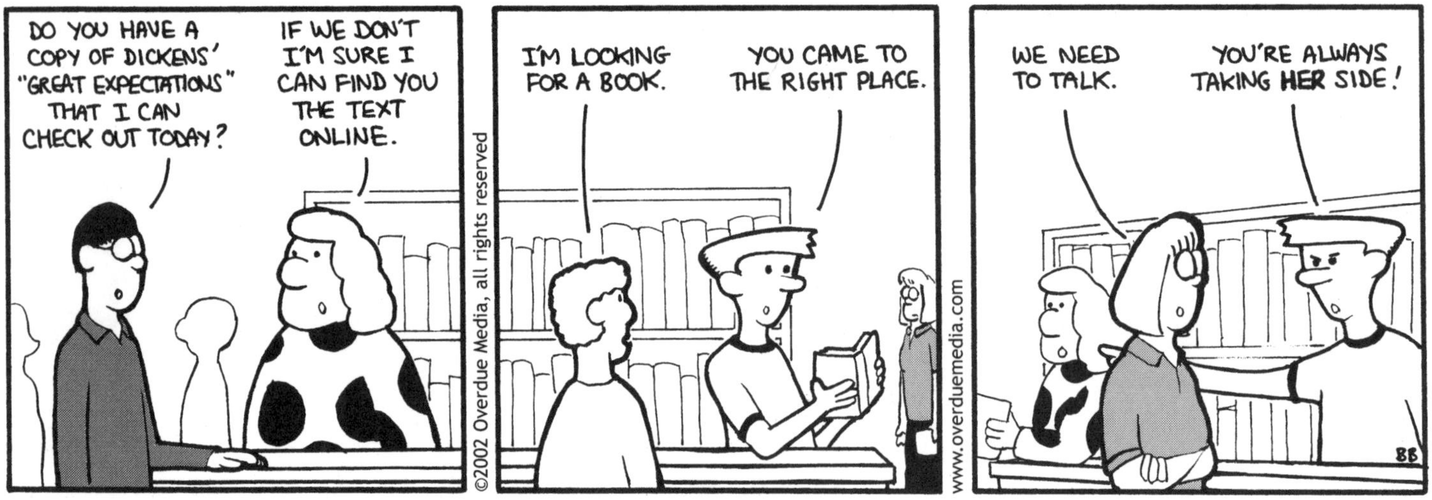
DO YOU HAVE A COPY OF DICKENS' "GREAT EXPECTATIONS" THAT I CAN CHECK OUT TODAY?
IF WE DON'T I'M SURE I CAN FIND YOU THE TEXT ONLINE.
©2002 Overdue Media, all rights reserved
I'M LOOKING FOR A BOOK.
YOU CAME TO THE RIGHT PLACE.
www.overduemedia.com
WE NEED TO TALK.
YOU'RE ALWAYS TAKING **HER** SIDE!
BB

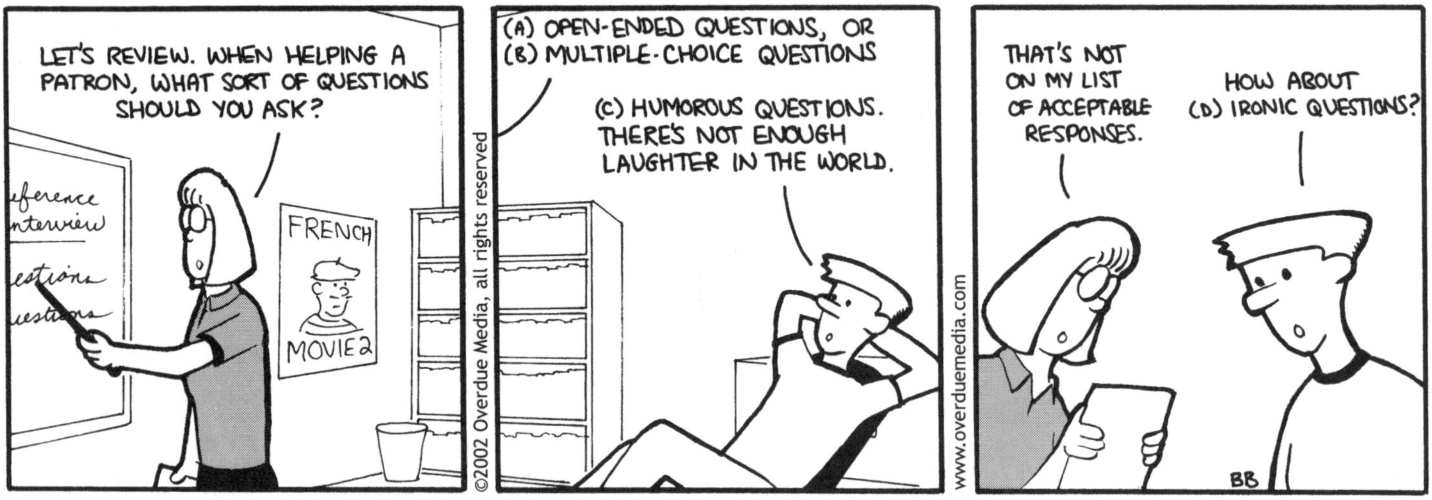
LET'S REVIEW. WHEN HELPING A PATRON, WHAT SORT OF QUESTIONS SHOULD YOU ASK?
FRENCH
MOVIE 2
©2002 Overdue Media, all rights reserved
(A) OPEN-ENDED QUESTIONS, OR
(B) MULTIPLE-CHOICE QUESTIONS
(C) HUMOROUS QUESTIONS. THERE'S NOT ENOUGH LAUGHTER IN THE WORLD.
www.overduemedia.com
THAT'S NOT ON MY LIST OF ACCEPTABLE RESPONSES.
HOW ABOUT (D) IRONIC QUESTIONS?
BB

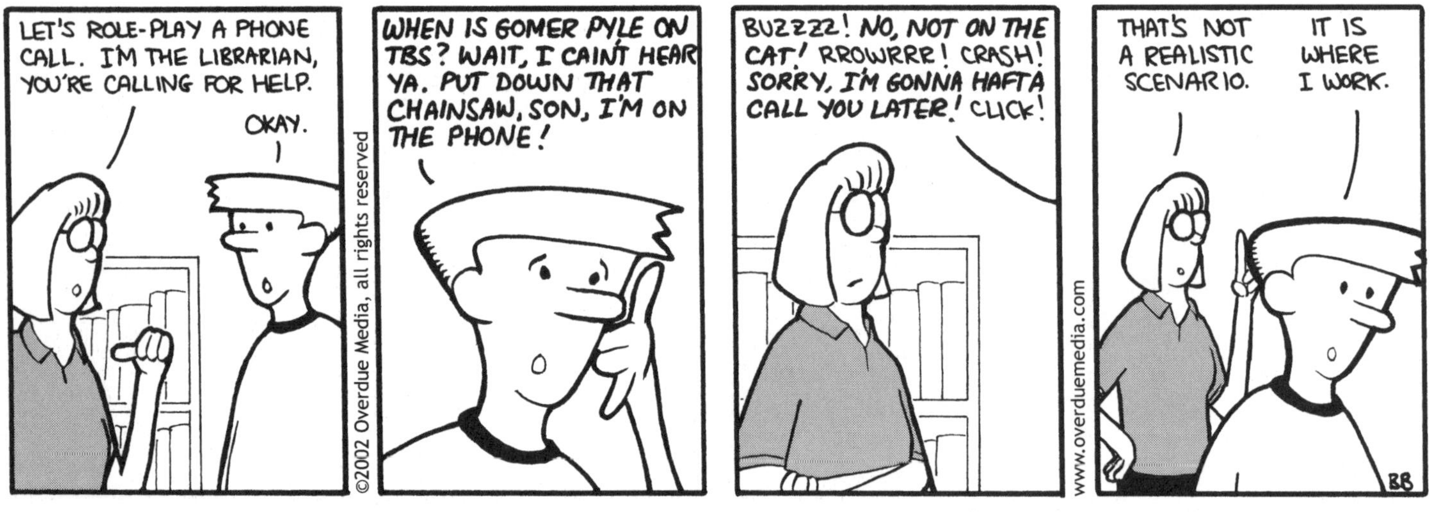
LET'S ROLE-PLAY A PHONE CALL. I'M THE LIBRARIAN, YOU'RE CALLING FOR HELP.
OKAY.
©2002 Overdue Media, all rights reserved
WHEN IS GOMER PYLE ON TBS? WAIT, I CAIN'T HEAR YA. PUT DOWN THAT CHAINSAW, SON, I'M ON THE PHONE!
BUZZZZ! NO, NOT ON THE CAT! RROWRRR! CRASH! SORRY, I'M GONNA HAFTA CALL YOU LATER! CLICK!
www.overduemedia.com
THAT'S NOT A REALISTIC SCENARIO.
IT IS WHERE I WORK.
BB

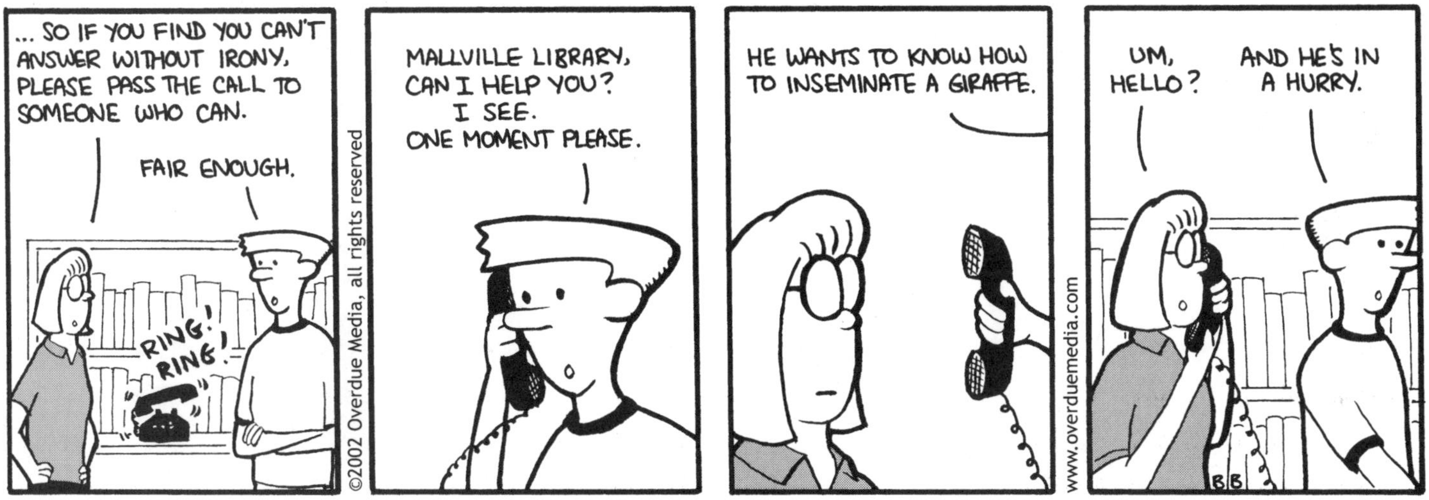
... SO IF YOU FIND YOU CAN'T ANSWER WITHOUT IRONY, PLEASE PASS THE CALL TO SOMEONE WHO CAN.
FAIR ENOUGH.
RING! RING!
MALLVILLE LIBRARY, CAN I HELP YOU? I SEE. ONE MOMENT PLEASE.
HE WANTS TO KNOW HOW TO INSEMINATE A GIRAFFE.
UM, HELLO?
AND HE'S IN A HURRY.
©2002 Overdue Media, all rights reserved
www.overduemedia.com

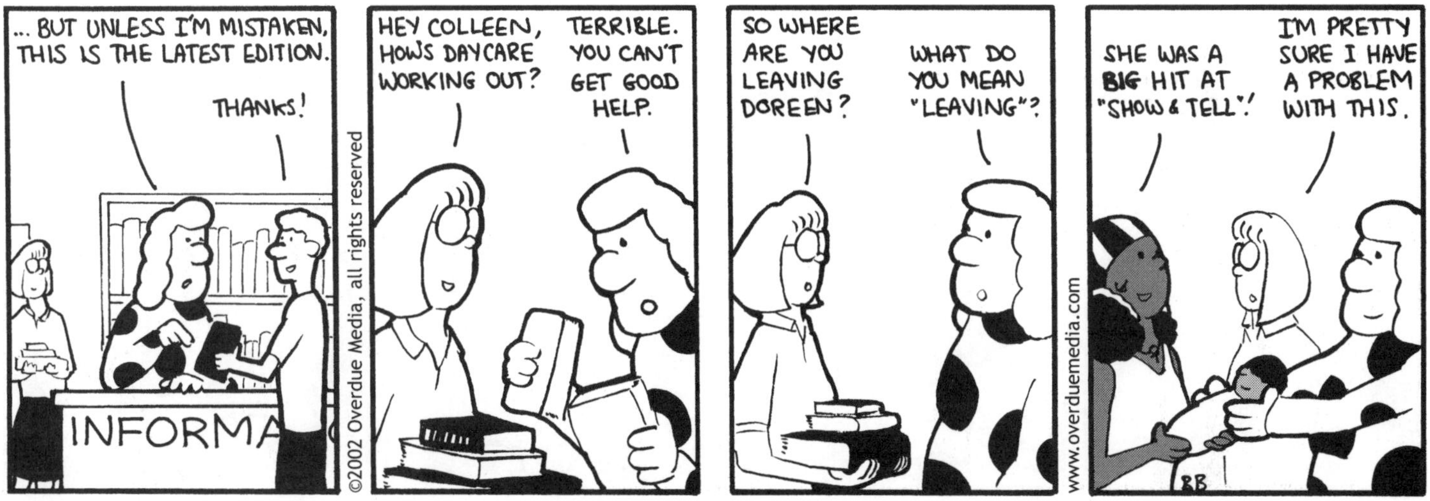
... BUT UNLESS I'M MISTAKEN, THIS IS THE LATEST EDITION.
THANKS!
INFORMA
HEY COLLEEN, HOW'S DAYCARE WORKING OUT?
TERRIBLE. YOU CAN'T GET GOOD HELP.
SO WHERE ARE YOU LEAVING DOREEN?
WHAT DO YOU MEAN "LEAVING"?
SHE WAS A BIG HIT AT "SHOW & TELL"!
I'M PRETTY SURE I HAVE A PROBLEM WITH THIS.
©2002 Overdue Media, all rights reserved
www.overduemedia.com

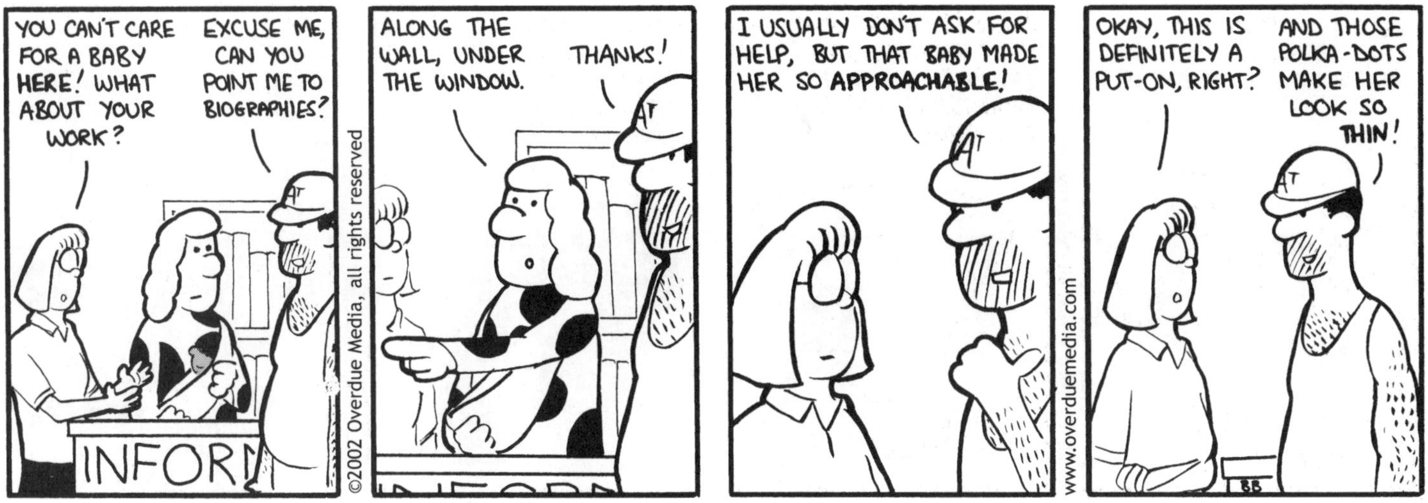
YOU CAN'T CARE FOR A BABY HERE! WHAT ABOUT YOUR WORK?
EXCUSE ME, CAN YOU POINT ME TO BIOGRAPHIES?
INFOR
ALONG THE WALL, UNDER THE WINDOW.
THANKS!
I USUALLY DON'T ASK FOR HELP, BUT THAT BABY MADE HER SO APPROACHABLE!
OKAY, THIS IS DEFINITELY A PUT-ON, RIGHT?
AND THOSE POLKA-DOTS MAKE HER LOOK SO THIN!
©2002 Overdue Media, all rights reserved
www.overduemedia.com

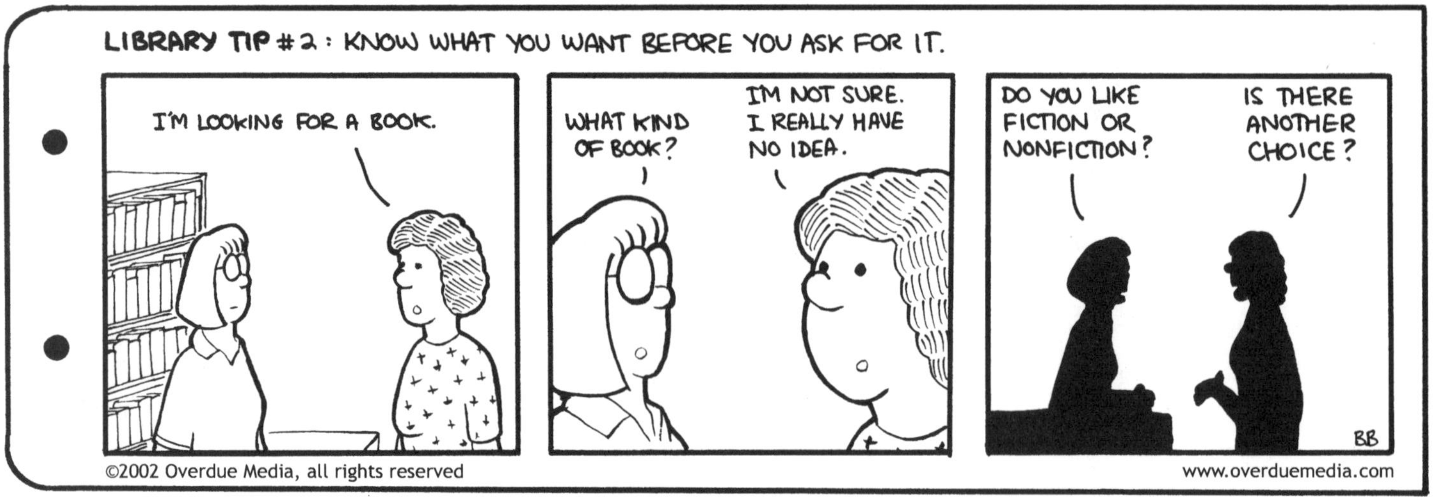
LIBRARY TIP #2: KNOW WHAT YOU WANT BEFORE YOU ASK FOR IT.
I'M LOOKING FOR A BOOK.
WHAT KIND OF BOOK?
I'M NOT SURE. I REALLY HAVE NO IDEA.
DO YOU LIKE FICTION OR NONFICTION?
IS THERE ANOTHER CHOICE?
BB
©2002 Overdue Media, all rights reserved
www.overduemedia.com

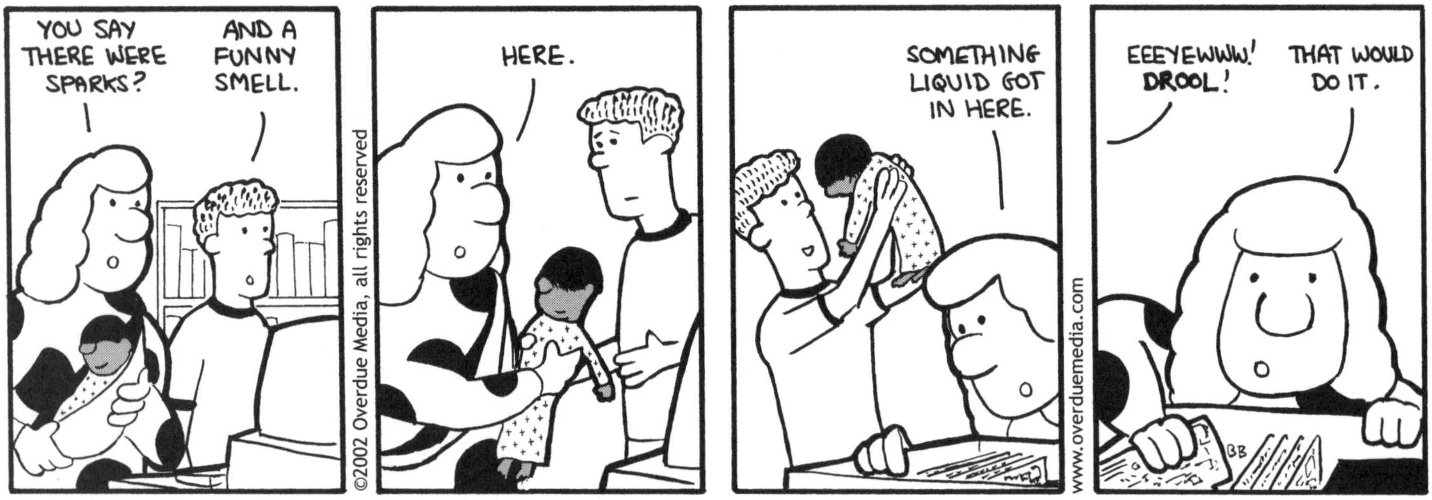
YOU SAY THERE WERE SPARKS?
AND A FUNNY SMELL.
©2002 Overdue Media, all rights reserved
HERE.
SOMETHING LIQUID GOT IN HERE.
www.overduemedia.com
EEEYEWWW! DROOL!
THAT WOULD DO IT.
BB

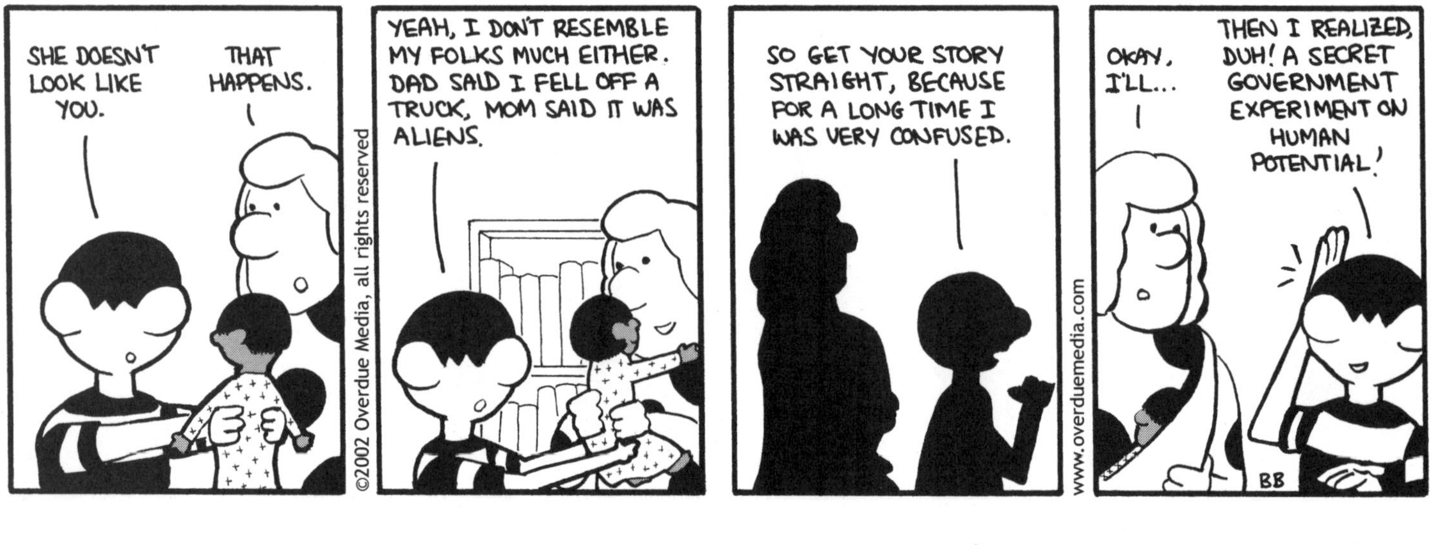
SHE DOESN'T LOOK LIKE YOU.
THAT HAPPENS.
©2002 Overdue Media, all rights reserved
YEAH, I DON'T RESEMBLE MY FOLKS MUCH EITHER. DAD SAID I FELL OFF A TRUCK, MOM SAID IT WAS ALIENS.
SO GET YOUR STORY STRAIGHT, BECAUSE FOR A LONG TIME I WAS VERY CONFUSED.
www.overduemedia.com
OKAY, I'LL...
THEN I REALIZED, DUH! A SECRET GOVERNMENT EXPERIMENT ON HUMAN POTENTIAL!
BB

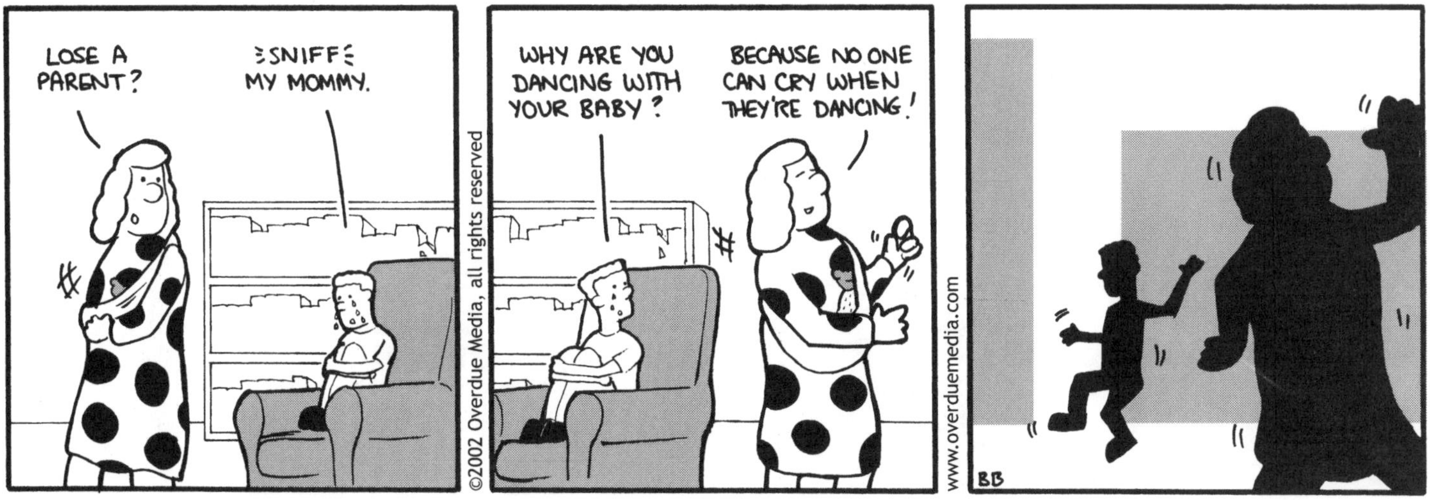
LOSE A PARENT?
SNIFF MY MOMMY.
©2002 Overdue Media, all rights reserved
WHY ARE YOU DANCING WITH YOUR BABY?
BECAUSE NO ONE CAN CRY WHEN THEY'RE DANCING!
www.overduemedia.com
BB

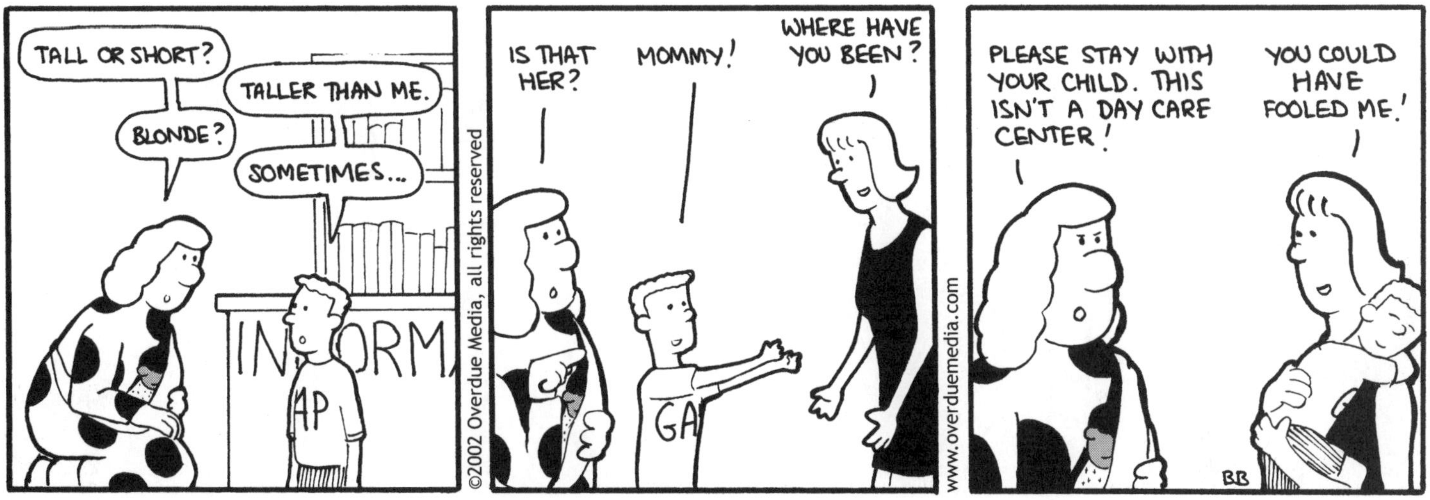
TALL OR SHORT?
TALLER THAN ME.
BLONDE?
SOMETIMES...
INFORM
AP
©2002 Overdue Media, all rights reserved
IS THAT HER?
MOMMY!
WHERE HAVE YOU BEEN?
GA
www.overduemedia.com
PLEASE STAY WITH YOUR CHILD. THIS ISN'T A DAY CARE CENTER!
YOU COULD HAVE FOOLED ME!
BB

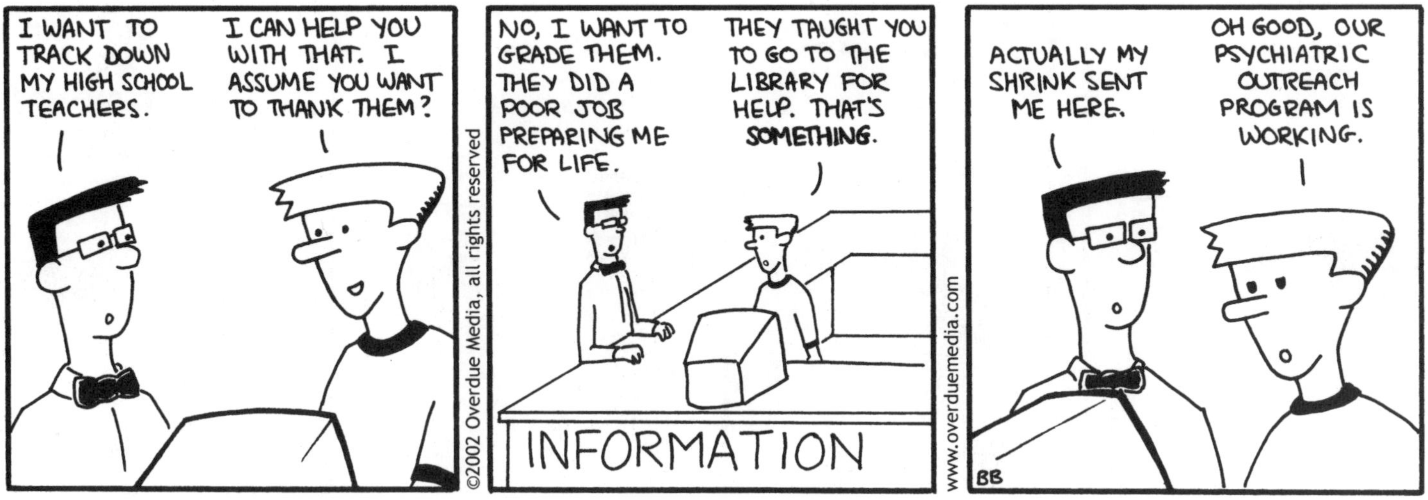
I WANT TO TRACK DOWN MY HIGH SCHOOL TEACHERS.
I CAN HELP YOU WITH THAT. I ASSUME YOU WANT TO THANK THEM?
©2002 Overdue Media, all rights reserved
NO, I WANT TO GRADE THEM. THEY DID A POOR JOB PREPARING ME FOR LIFE.
THEY TAUGHT YOU TO GO TO THE LIBRARY FOR HELP. THAT'S SOMETHING.
INFORMATION
www.overduemedia.com
ACTUALLY MY SHRINK SENT ME HERE.
OH GOOD, OUR PSYCHIATRIC OUTREACH PROGRAM IS WORKING.
BB

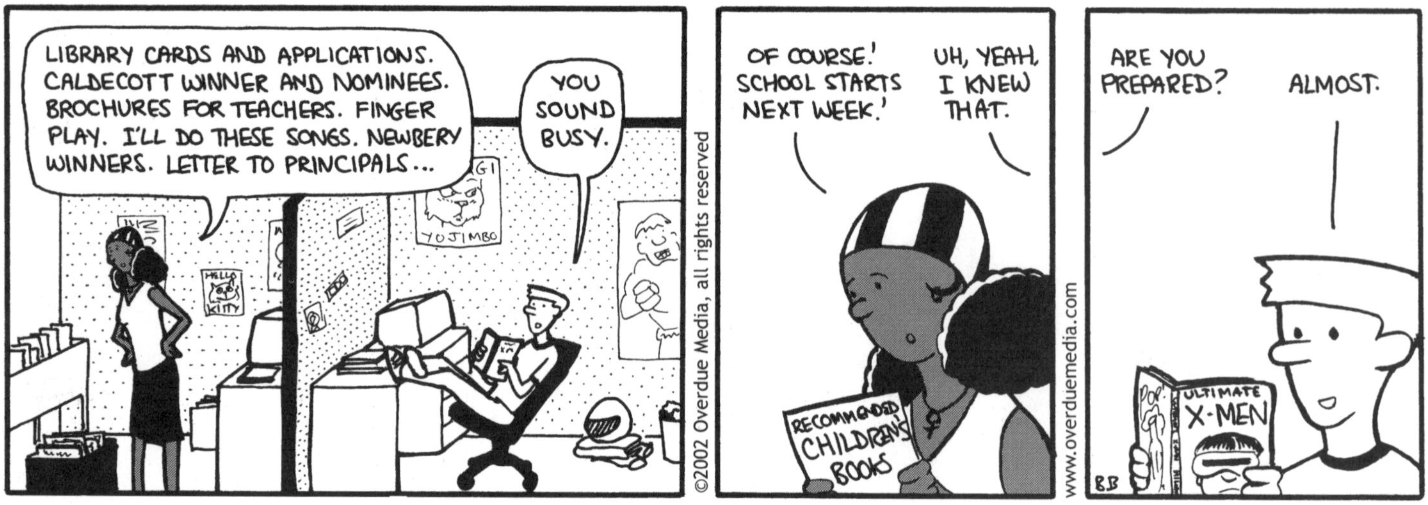

LIBRARY CARDS AND APPLICATIONS. CALDECOTT WINNER AND NOMINEES. BROCHURES FOR TEACHERS. FINGER PLAY. I'LL DO THESE SONGS. NEWBERY WINNERS. LETTER TO PRINCIPALS...
YOU SOUND BUSY.
OF COURSE! SCHOOL STARTS NEXT WEEK!
UH, YEAH, I KNEW THAT.
RECOMMENDED CHILDREN'S BOOKS
ARE YOU PREPARED?
ALMOST.
ULTIMATE X-MEN
©2002 Overdue Media, all rights reserved
www.overduemedia.com

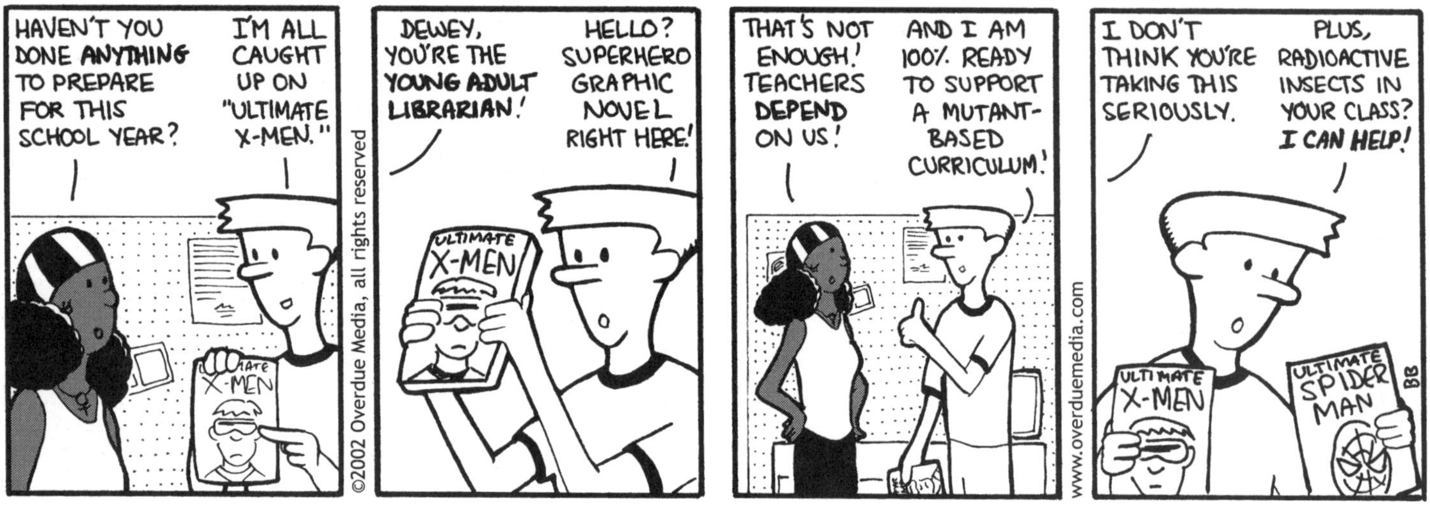

HAVEN'T YOU DONE **ANYTHING** TO PREPARE FOR THIS SCHOOL YEAR?
I'M ALL CAUGHT UP ON "ULTIMATE X-MEN."
DEWEY, YOU'RE THE **YOUNG ADULT LIBRARIAN**!
HELLO? SUPERHERO GRAPHIC NOVEL RIGHT HERE!
ULTIMATE X-MEN
THAT'S NOT ENOUGH! TEACHERS **DEPEND** ON US!
AND I AM 100% READY TO SUPPORT A MUTANT-BASED CURRICULUM!
I DON'T THINK YOU'RE TAKING THIS SERIOUSLY.
PLUS, RADIOACTIVE INSECTS IN YOUR CLASS? ***I CAN HELP!***
ULTIMATE X-MEN
ULTIMATE SPIDER MAN
©2002 Overdue Media, all rights reserved
www.overduemedia.com

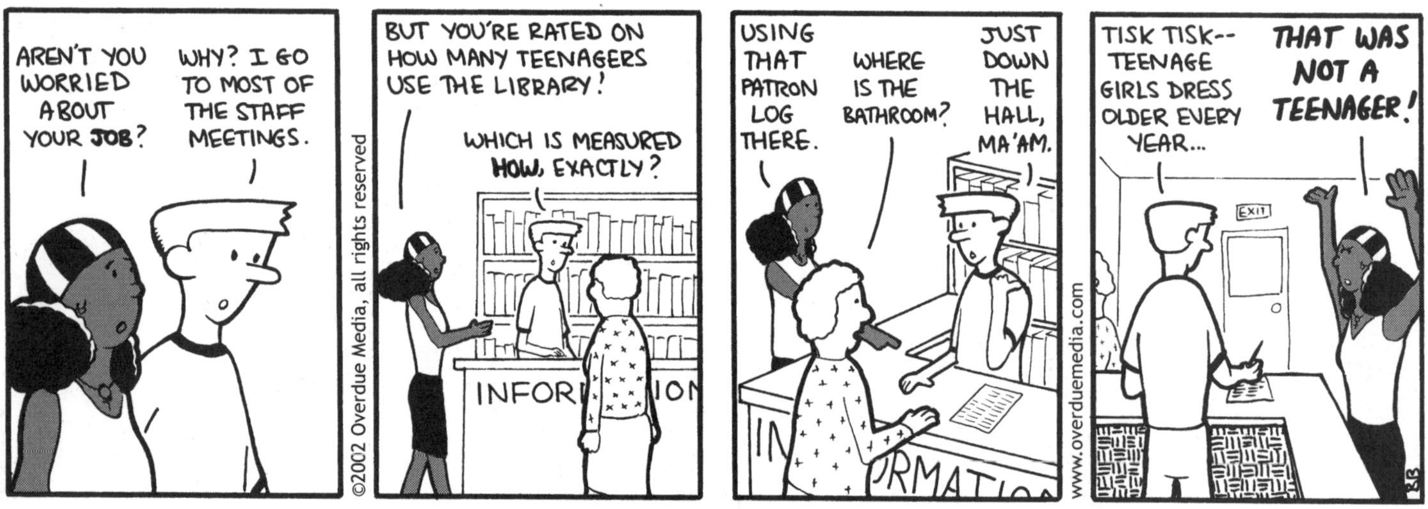

AREN'T YOU WORRIED ABOUT YOUR **JOB**?
WHY? I GO TO MOST OF THE STAFF MEETINGS.
BUT YOU'RE RATED ON HOW MANY TEENAGERS USE THE LIBRARY!
WHICH IS MEASURED **HOW**, EXACTLY?
USING THAT PATRON LOG THERE.
WHERE IS THE BATHROOM?
JUST DOWN THE HALL, MA'AM.
TISK TISK-- TEENAGE GIRLS DRESS OLDER EVERY YEAR...
THAT WAS NOT A TEENAGER!
©2002 Overdue Media, all rights reserved
www.overduemedia.com

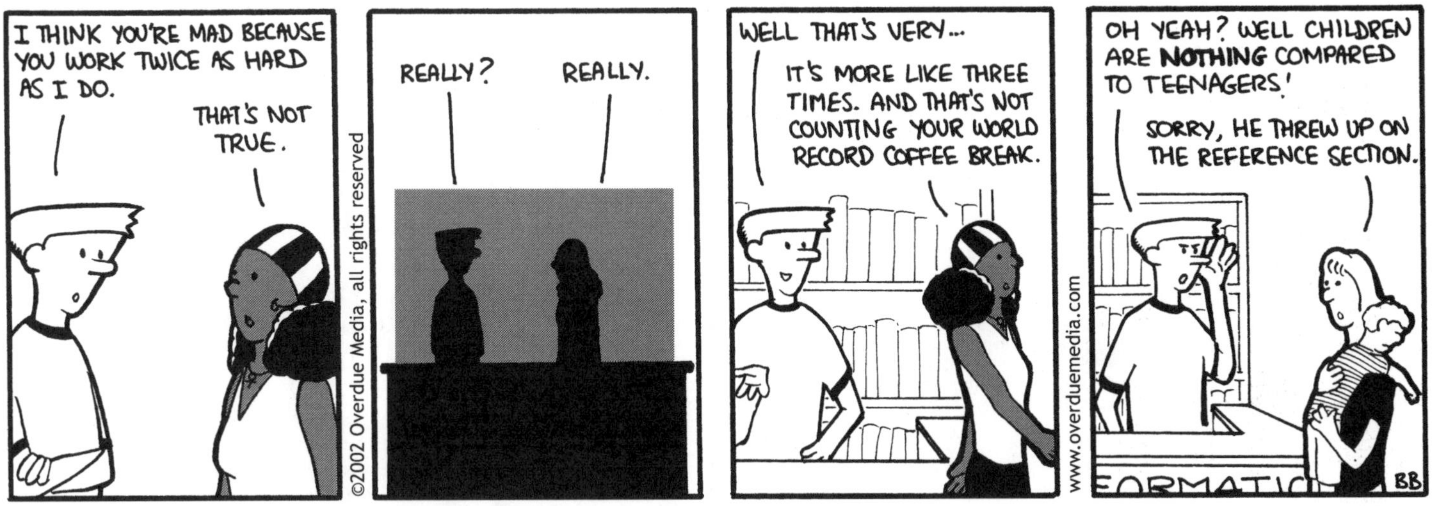
I THINK YOU'RE MAD BECAUSE YOU WORK TWICE AS HARD AS I DO.
THAT'S NOT TRUE.
REALLY?
REALLY.
WELL THAT'S VERY...
IT'S MORE LIKE THREE TIMES. AND THAT'S NOT COUNTING YOUR WORLD RECORD COFFEE BREAK.
OH YEAH? WELL CHILDREN ARE **NOTHING** COMPARED TO TEENAGERS!
SORRY, HE THREW UP ON THE REFERENCE SECTION.
BB

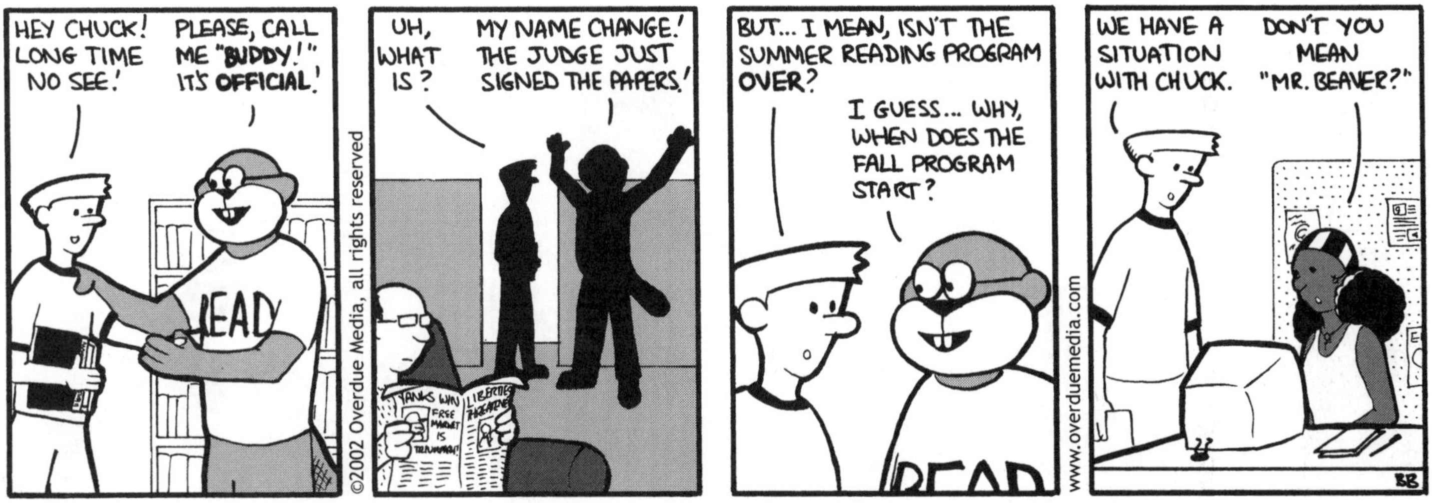
HEY CHUCK! LONG TIME NO SEE!
PLEASE, CALL ME "**BUDDY**!" IT'S **OFFICIAL**!
UH, WHAT IS?
MY NAME CHANGE! THE JUDGE JUST SIGNED THE PAPERS!
BUT... I MEAN, ISN'T THE SUMMER READING PROGRAM **OVER**?
I GUESS... WHY, WHEN DOES THE FALL PROGRAM START?
WE HAVE A SITUATION WITH CHUCK.
DON'T YOU MEAN "MR. BEAVER?"
BB

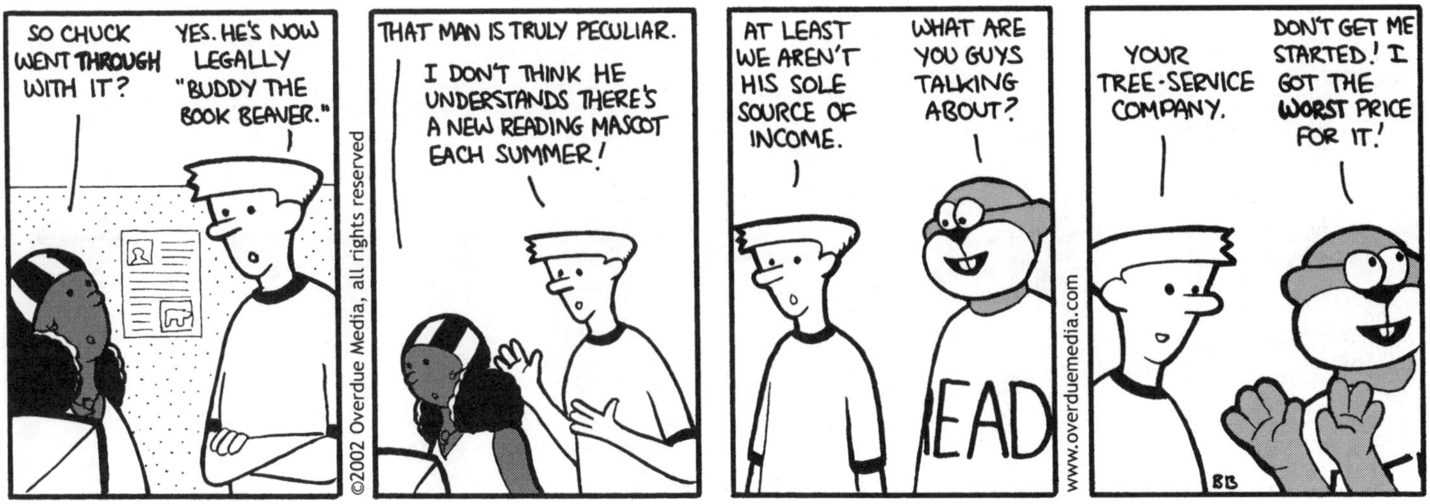
SO CHUCK WENT **THROUGH** WITH IT?
YES. HE'S NOW LEGALLY "BUDDY THE BOOK BEAVER."
THAT MAN IS TRULY PECULIAR.
I DON'T THINK HE UNDERSTANDS THERE'S A NEW READING MASCOT EACH SUMMER!
AT LEAST WE AREN'T HIS SOLE SOURCE OF INCOME.
WHAT ARE YOU GUYS TALKING ABOUT?
YOUR TREE-SERVICE COMPANY.
DON'T GET ME STARTED! I GOT THE **WORST** PRICE FOR IT!
BB

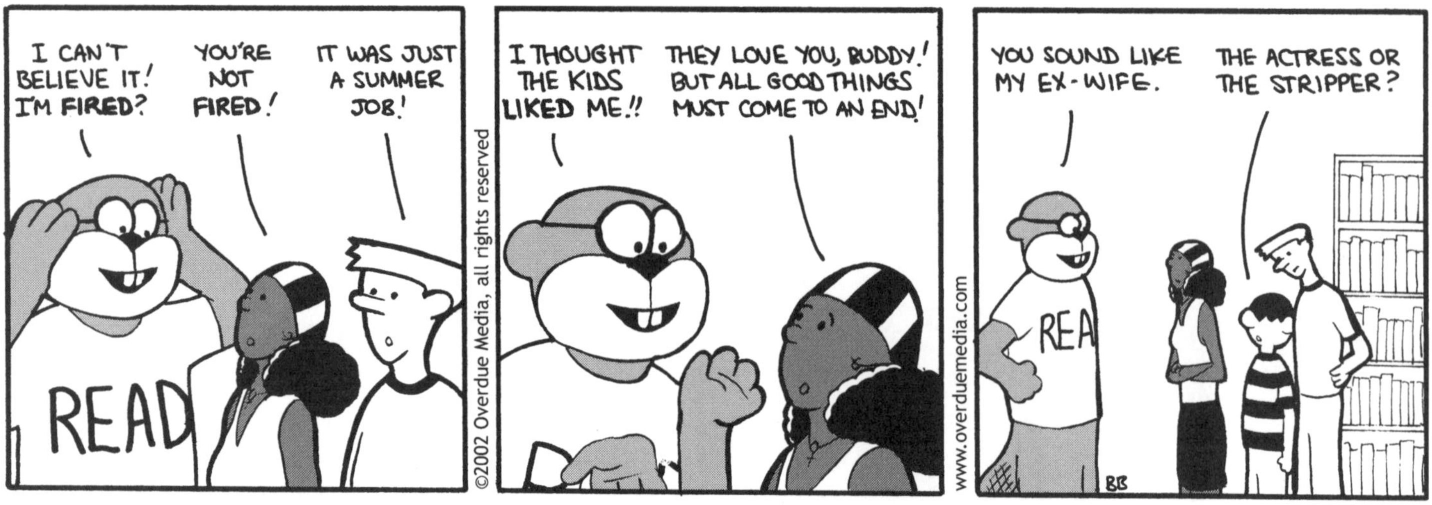
I CAN'T BELIEVE IT! I'M FIRED?
YOU'RE NOT FIRED!
IT WAS JUST A SUMMER JOB!
READ
I THOUGHT THE KIDS LIKED ME!!
THEY LOVE YOU, BUDDY! BUT ALL GOOD THINGS MUST COME TO AN END!
YOU SOUND LIKE MY EX-WIFE.
THE ACTRESS OR THE STRIPPER?
REA
BB

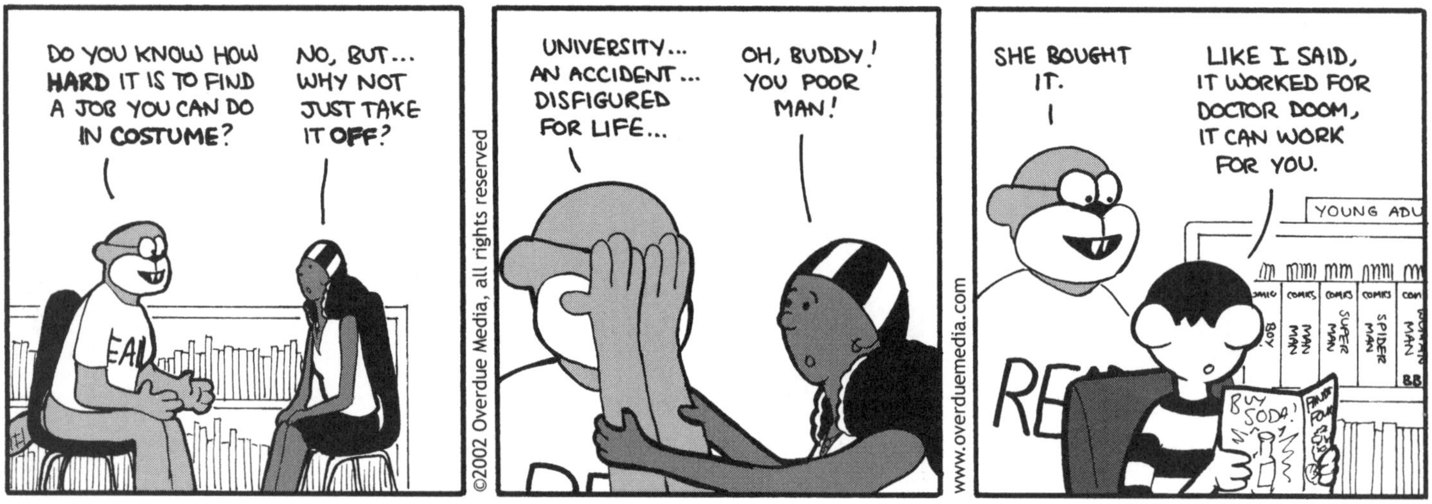
DO YOU KNOW HOW HARD IT IS TO FIND A JOB YOU CAN DO IN COSTUME?
NO, BUT... WHY NOT JUST TAKE IT OFF?
UNIVERSITY... AN ACCIDENT... DISFIGURED FOR LIFE...
OH, BUDDY! YOU POOR MAN!
SHE BOUGHT IT.
LIKE I SAID, IT WORKED FOR DOCTOR DOOM, IT CAN WORK FOR YOU.
YOUNG ADU
BUY SODA!
BB

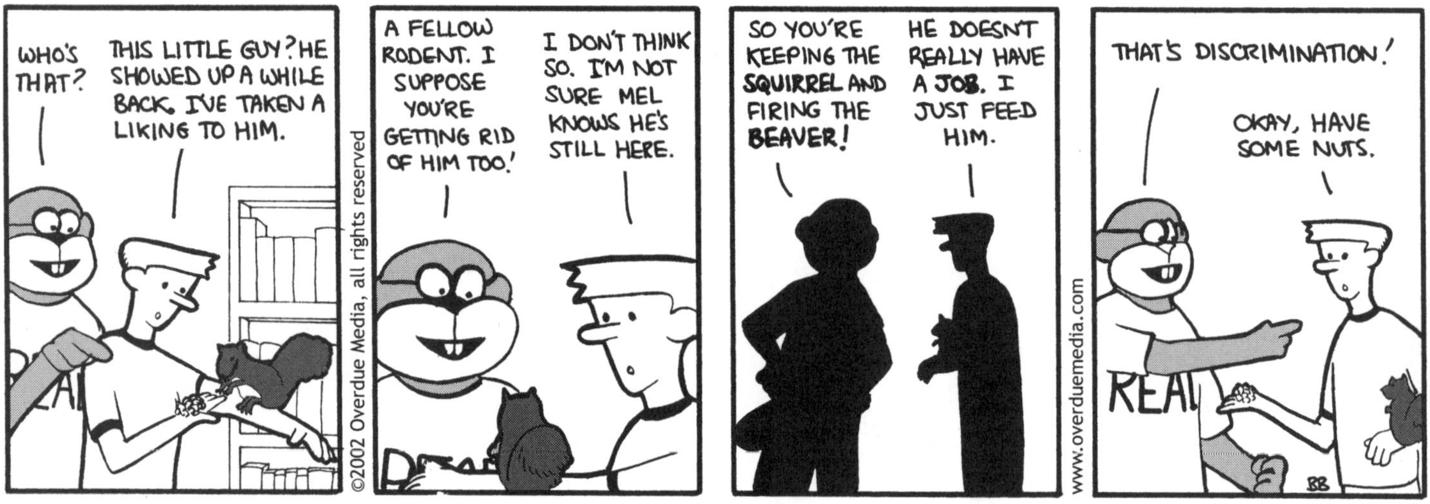
WHO'S THAT?
THIS LITTLE GUY? HE SHOWED UP A WHILE BACK. I'VE TAKEN A LIKING TO HIM.
A FELLOW RODENT. I SUPPOSE YOU'RE GETTING RID OF HIM TOO!
I DON'T THINK SO. I'M NOT SURE MEL KNOWS HE'S STILL HERE.
SO YOU'RE KEEPING THE SQUIRREL AND FIRING THE BEAVER!
HE DOESN'T REALLY HAVE A JOB. I JUST FEED HIM.
THAT'S DISCRIMINATION!
OKAY, HAVE SOME NUTS.
READ
BB

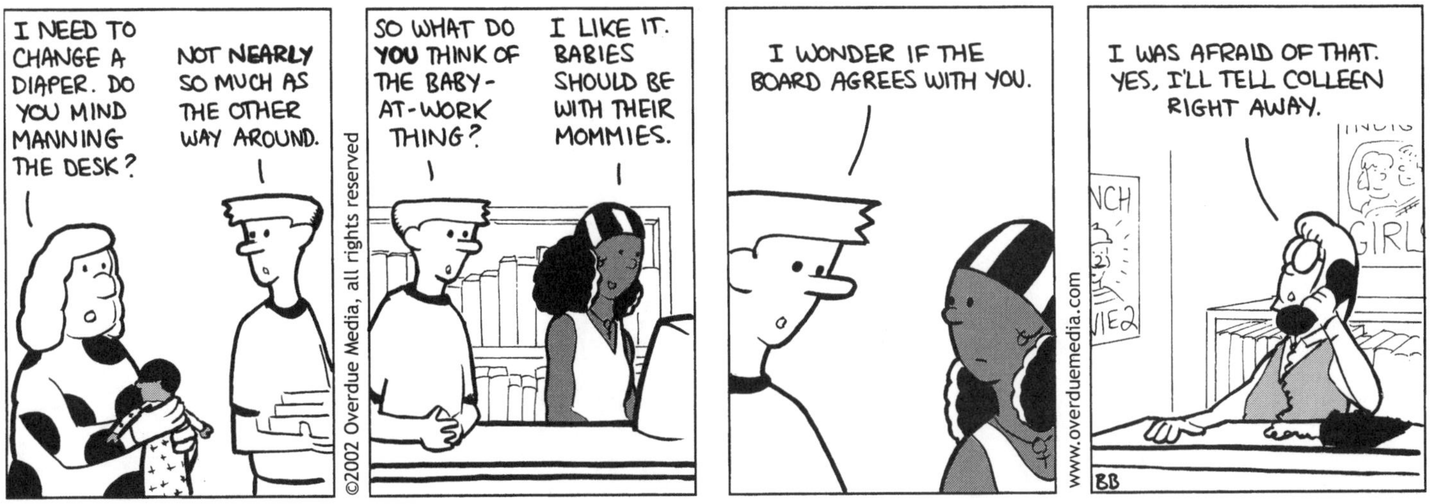
I NEED TO CHANGE A DIAPER. DO YOU MIND MANNING THE DESK?
NOT **NEARLY** SO MUCH AS THE OTHER WAY AROUND.
SO WHAT DO **YOU** THINK OF THE BABY-AT-WORK THING?
I LIKE IT. BABIES SHOULD BE WITH THEIR MOMMIES.
I WONDER IF THE BOARD AGREES WITH YOU.
I WAS AFRAID OF THAT. YES, I'LL TELL COLLEEN RIGHT AWAY.
BB

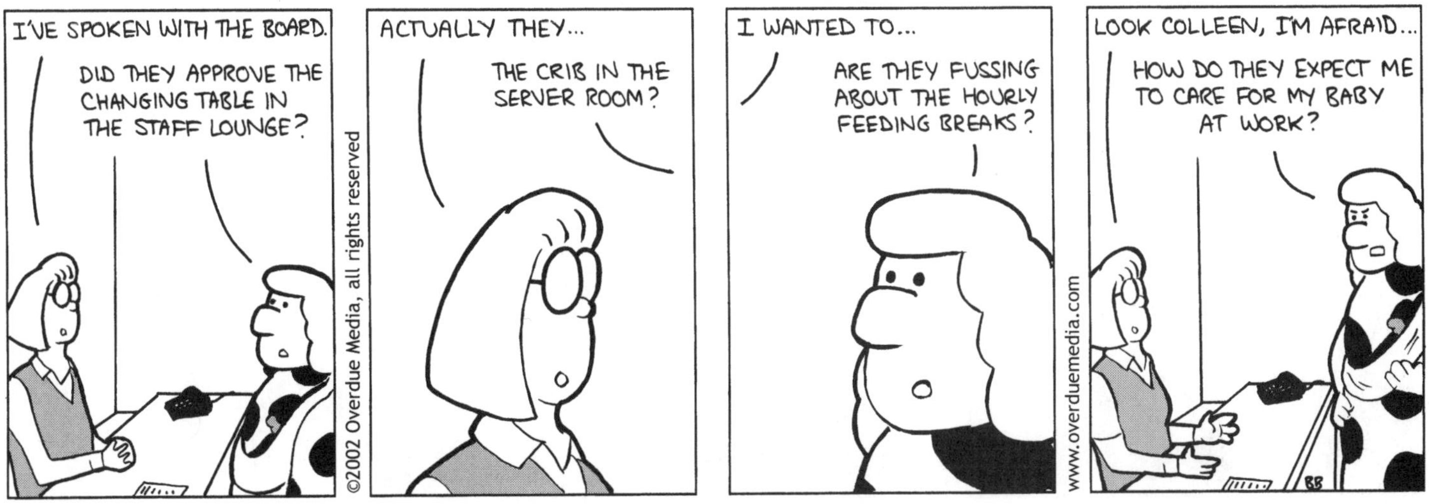
I'VE SPOKEN WITH THE BOARD.
DID THEY APPROVE THE CHANGING TABLE IN THE STAFF LOUNGE?
ACTUALLY THEY...
THE CRIB IN THE SERVER ROOM?
I WANTED TO...
ARE THEY FUSSING ABOUT THE HOURLY FEEDING BREAKS?
LOOK COLLEEN, I'M AFRAID...
HOW DO THEY EXPECT ME TO CARE FOR MY BABY AT WORK?
BB

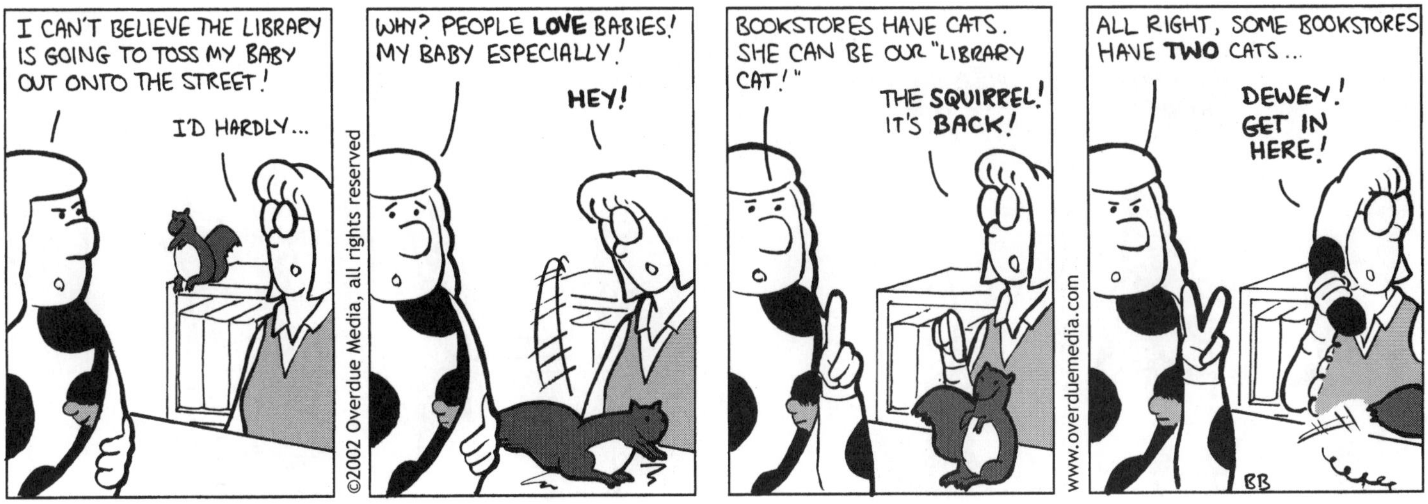
I CAN'T BELIEVE THE LIBRARY IS GOING TO TOSS MY BABY OUT ONTO THE STREET!
I'D HARDLY...
WHY? PEOPLE **LOVE** BABIES! MY BABY ESPECIALLY!
HEY!
BOOKSTORES HAVE CATS. SHE CAN BE OUR "LIBRARY CAT!"
THE **SQUIRREL**! IT'S **BACK**!
ALL RIGHT, SOME BOOKSTORES HAVE **TWO** CATS...
DEWEY! GET IN HERE!
BB

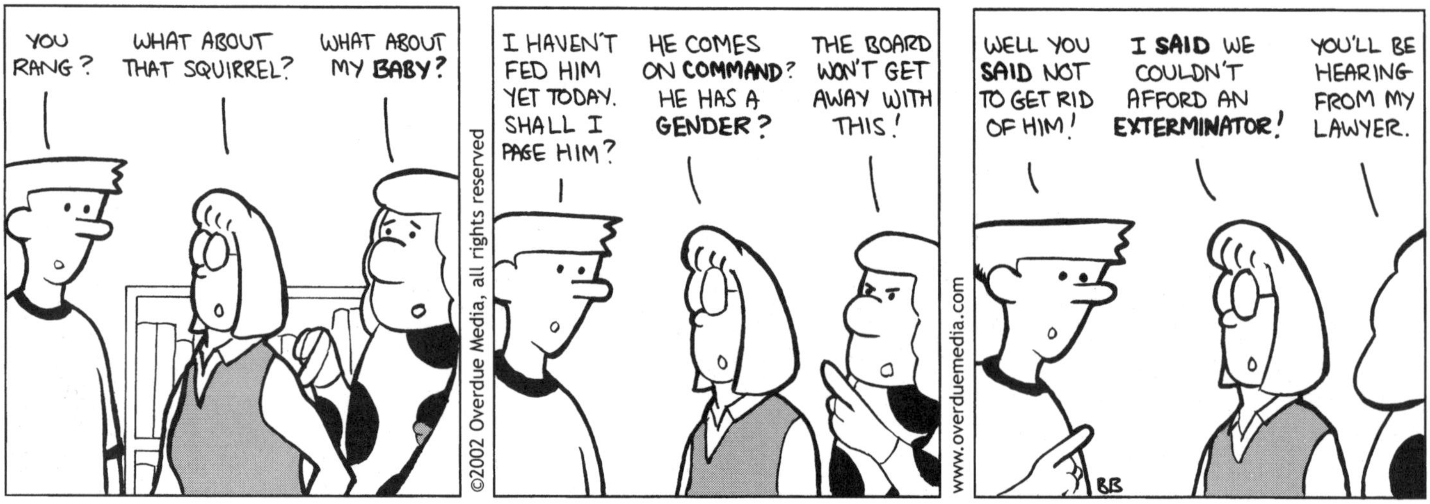
YOU RANG?
WHAT ABOUT THAT SQUIRREL?
WHAT ABOUT MY BABY?
©2002 Overdue Media, all rights reserved
I HAVEN'T FED HIM YET TODAY. SHALL I PAGE HIM?
HE COMES ON COMMAND? HE HAS A GENDER?
THE BOARD WON'T GET AWAY WITH THIS!
www.overduemedia.com
WELL YOU SAID NOT TO GET RID OF HIM!
I SAID WE COULDN'T AFFORD AN EXTERMINATOR!
YOU'LL BE HEARING FROM MY LAWYER.
BB

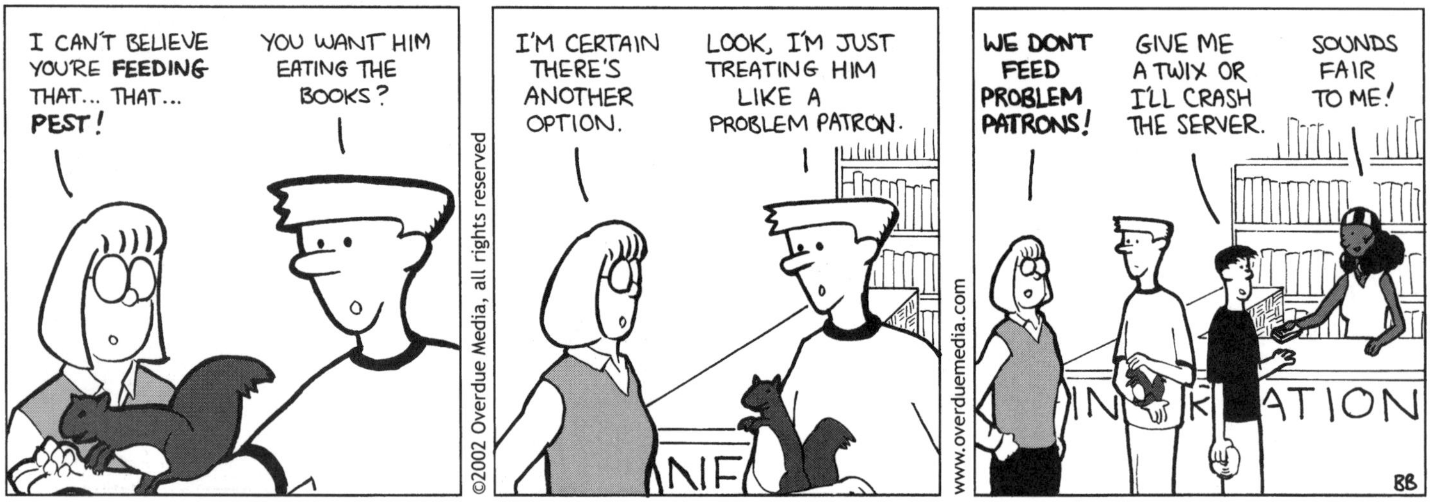
I CAN'T BELIEVE YOU'RE FEEDING THAT... THAT... PEST!
YOU WANT HIM EATING THE BOOKS?
©2002 Overdue Media, all rights reserved
I'M CERTAIN THERE'S ANOTHER OPTION.
LOOK, I'M JUST TREATING HIM LIKE A PROBLEM PATRON.
NF
www.overduemedia.com
WE DON'T FEED PROBLEM PATRONS!
GIVE ME A TWIX OR I'LL CRASH THE SERVER.
SOUNDS FAIR TO ME!
IN ATION
BB

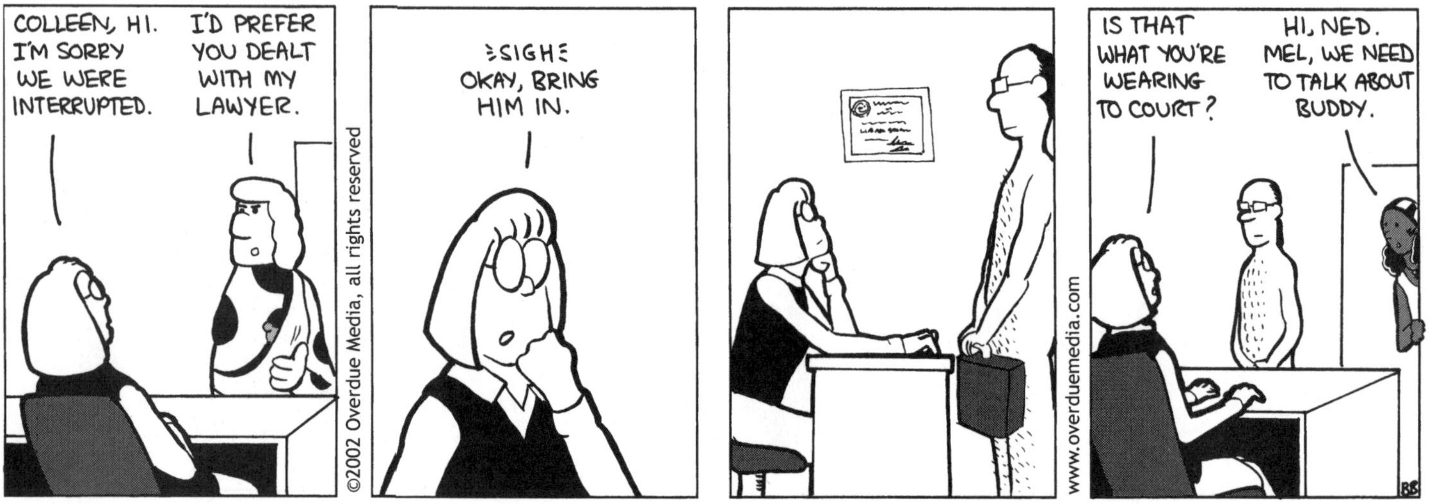
COLLEEN, HI. I'M SORRY WE WERE INTERRUPTED.
I'D PREFER YOU DEALT WITH MY LAWYER.
©2002 Overdue Media, all rights reserved
SIGH
OKAY, BRING HIM IN.
www.overduemedia.com
IS THAT WHAT YOU'RE WEARING TO COURT?
HI, NED. MEL, WE NEED TO TALK ABOUT BUDDY.
BB

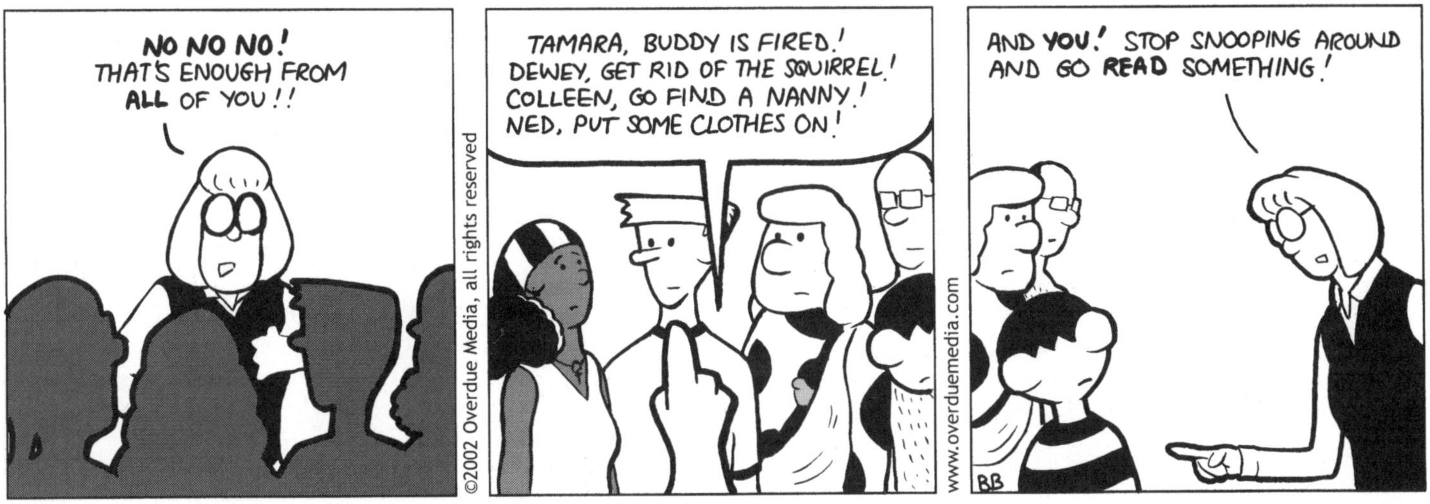
NO NO NO! THAT'S ENOUGH FROM ALL OF YOU!!
TAMARA, BUDDY IS FIRED! DEWEY, GET RID OF THE SQUIRREL! COLLEEN, GO FIND A NANNY! NED, PUT SOME CLOTHES ON!
©2002 Overdue Media, all rights reserved
www.overduemedia.com
AND YOU! STOP SNOOPING AROUND AND GO READ SOMETHING!
BB

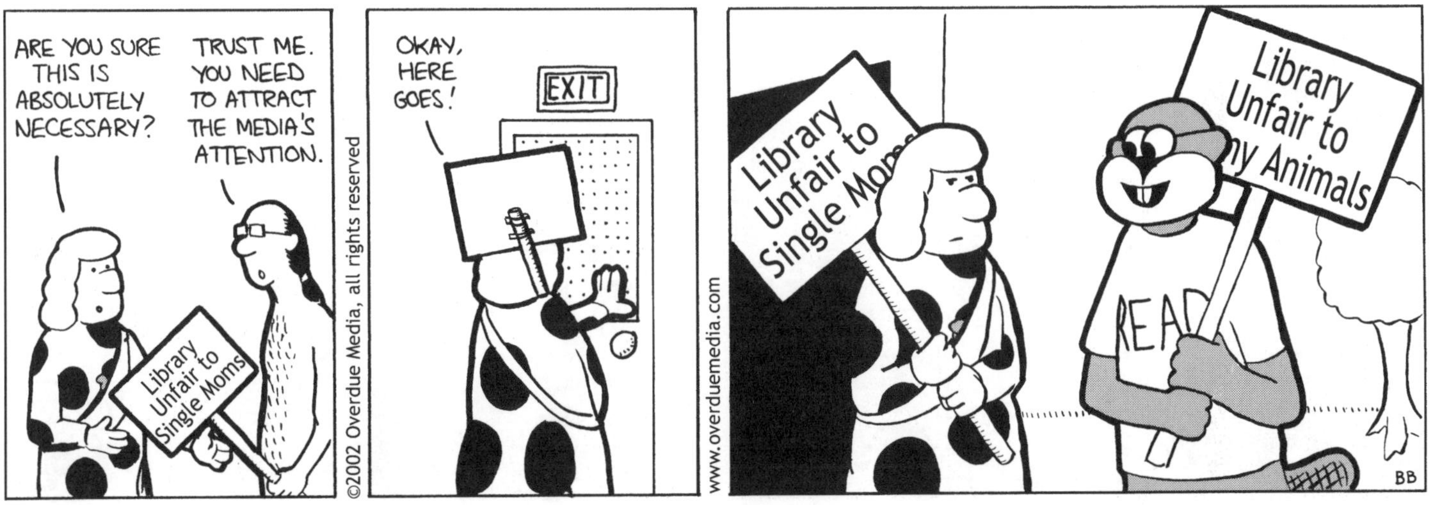
ARE YOU SURE THIS IS ABSOLUTELY NECESSARY?
TRUST ME. YOU NEED TO ATTRACT THE MEDIA'S ATTENTION.
Library Unfair to Single Moms
©2002 Overdue Media, all rights reserved
OKAY, HERE GOES!
EXIT
www.overduemedia.com
Library Unfair to Single Moms
Library Unfair to
READ
BB

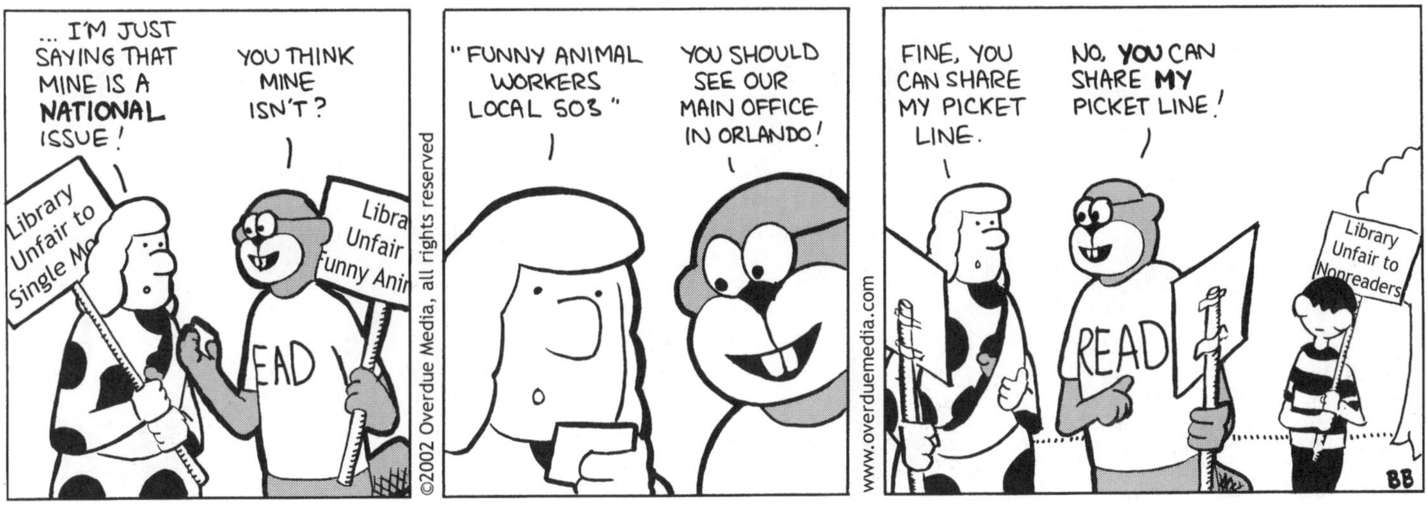
... I'M JUST SAYING THAT MINE IS A NATIONAL ISSUE!
YOU THINK MINE ISN'T?
©2002 Overdue Media, all rights reserved
"FUNNY ANIMAL WORKERS LOCAL 503"
YOU SHOULD SEE OUR MAIN OFFICE IN ORLANDO!
www.overduemedia.com
FINE, YOU CAN SHARE MY PICKET LINE.
NO, YOU CAN SHARE MY PICKET LINE!
READ
Library Unfair to Nonreaders
BB

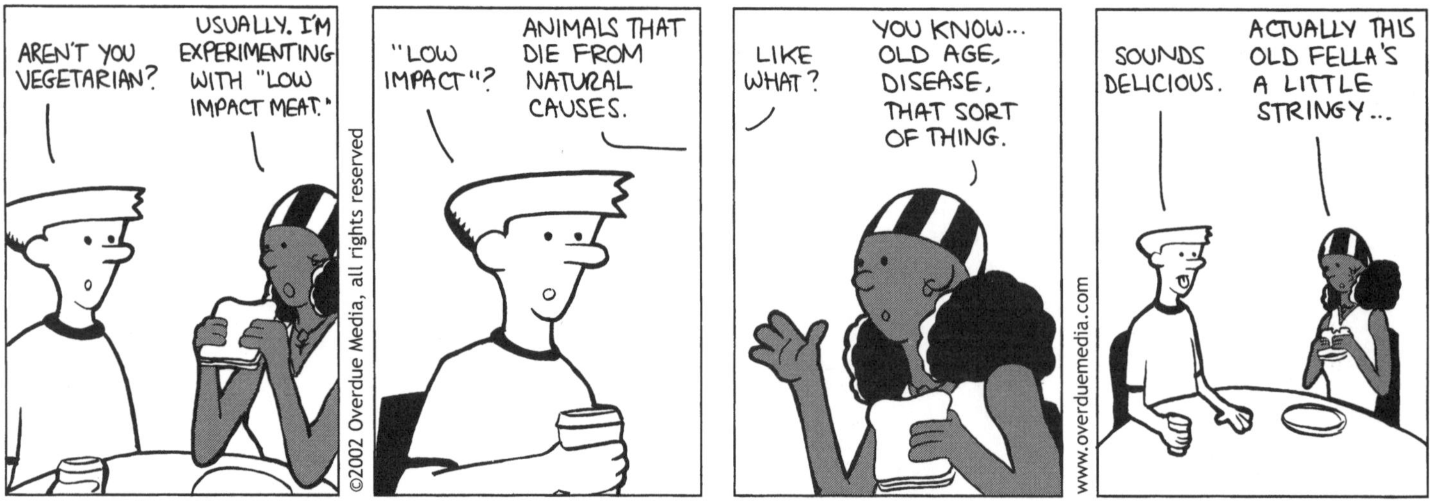
AREN'T YOU VEGETARIAN?
USUALLY. I'M EXPERIMENTING WITH "LOW IMPACT MEAT."
©2002 Overdue Media, all rights reserved
"LOW IMPACT"?
ANIMALS THAT DIE FROM NATURAL CAUSES.
LIKE WHAT?
YOU KNOW... OLD AGE, DISEASE, THAT SORT OF THING.
www.overduemedia.com
SOUNDS DELICIOUS.
ACTUALLY THIS OLD FELLA'S A LITTLE STRINGY...

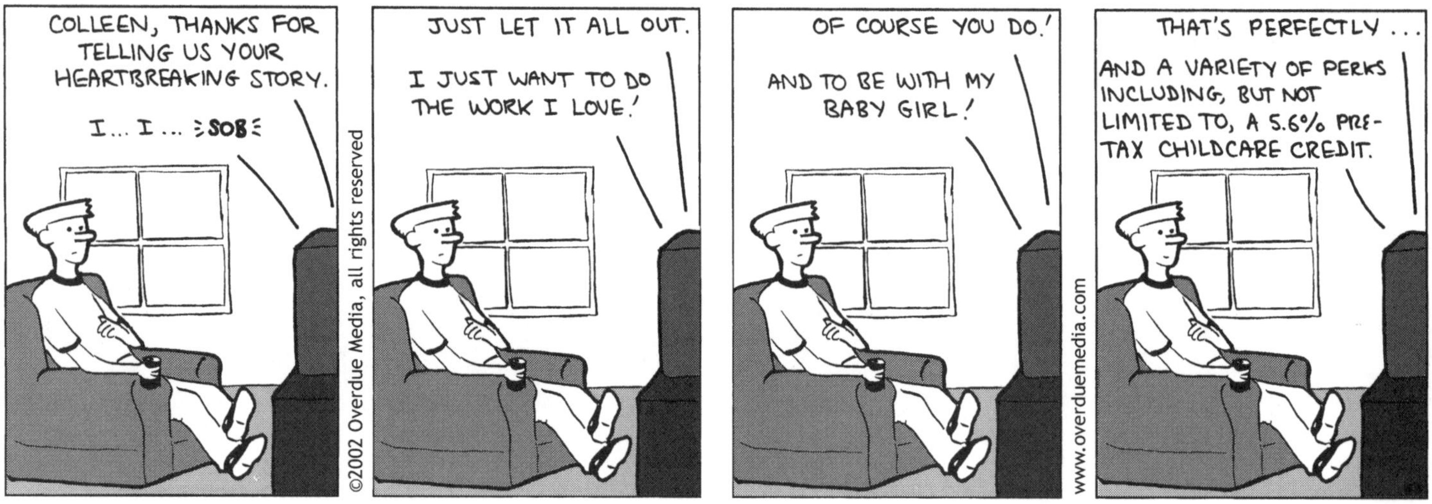
COLLEEN, THANKS FOR TELLING US YOUR HEARTBREAKING STORY.
I... I... SOB
©2002 Overdue Media, all rights reserved
JUST LET IT ALL OUT.
I JUST WANT TO DO THE WORK I LOVE!
OF COURSE YOU DO!
AND TO BE WITH MY BABY GIRL!
www.overduemedia.com
THAT'S PERFECTLY ...
AND A VARIETY OF PERKS INCLUDING, BUT NOT LIMITED TO, A 5.6% PRE-TAX CHILDCARE CREDIT.

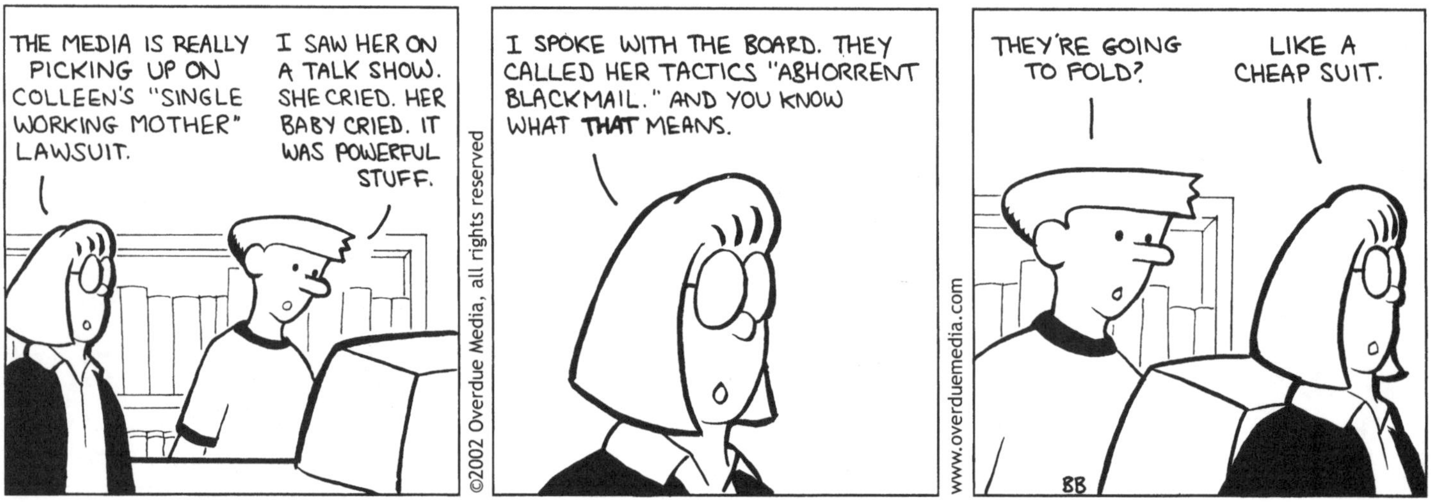
THE MEDIA IS REALLY PICKING UP ON COLLEEN'S "SINGLE WORKING MOTHER" LAWSUIT.
I SAW HER ON A TALK SHOW. SHE CRIED. HER BABY CRIED. IT WAS POWERFUL STUFF.
©2002 Overdue Media, all rights reserved
I SPOKE WITH THE BOARD. THEY CALLED HER TACTICS "ABHORRENT BLACKMAIL." AND YOU KNOW WHAT THAT MEANS.
www.overduemedia.com
THEY'RE GOING TO FOLD?
LIKE A CHEAP SUIT.
BB

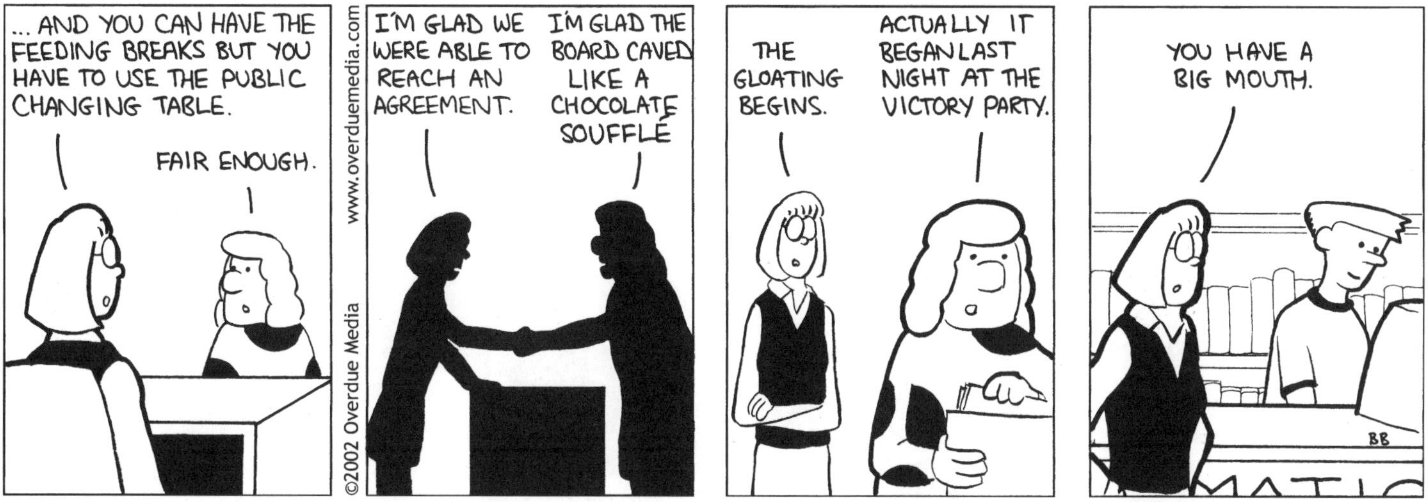
... AND YOU CAN HAVE THE FEEDING BREAKS BUT YOU HAVE TO USE THE PUBLIC CHANGING TABLE.
FAIR ENOUGH.
©2002 Overdue Media www.overduemedia.com
I'M GLAD WE WERE ABLE TO REACH AN AGREEMENT.
I'M GLAD THE BOARD CAVED LIKE A CHOCOLATE SOUFFLÉ
THE GLOATING BEGINS.
ACTUALLY IT BEGAN LAST NIGHT AT THE VICTORY PARTY.
YOU HAVE A BIG MOUTH.
BB

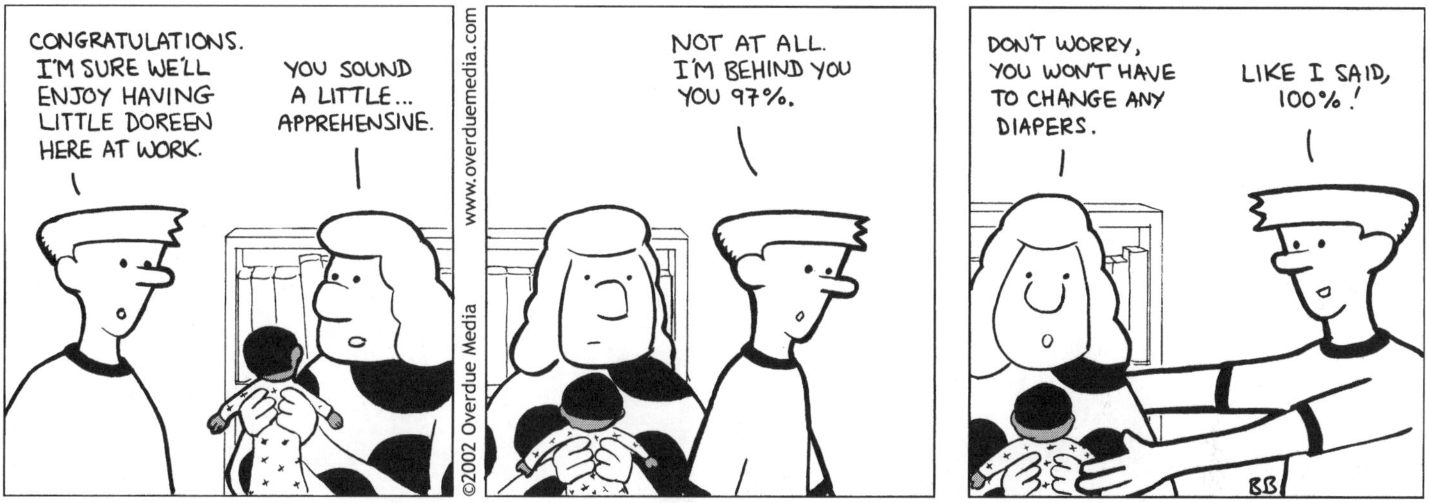
CONGRATULATIONS. I'M SURE WE'LL ENJOY HAVING LITTLE DOREEN HERE AT WORK.
YOU SOUND A LITTLE... APPREHENSIVE.
©2002 Overdue Media www.overduemedia.com
NOT AT ALL. I'M BEHIND YOU 97%.
DON'T WORRY, YOU WON'T HAVE TO CHANGE ANY DIAPERS.
LIKE I SAID, 100%!
BB

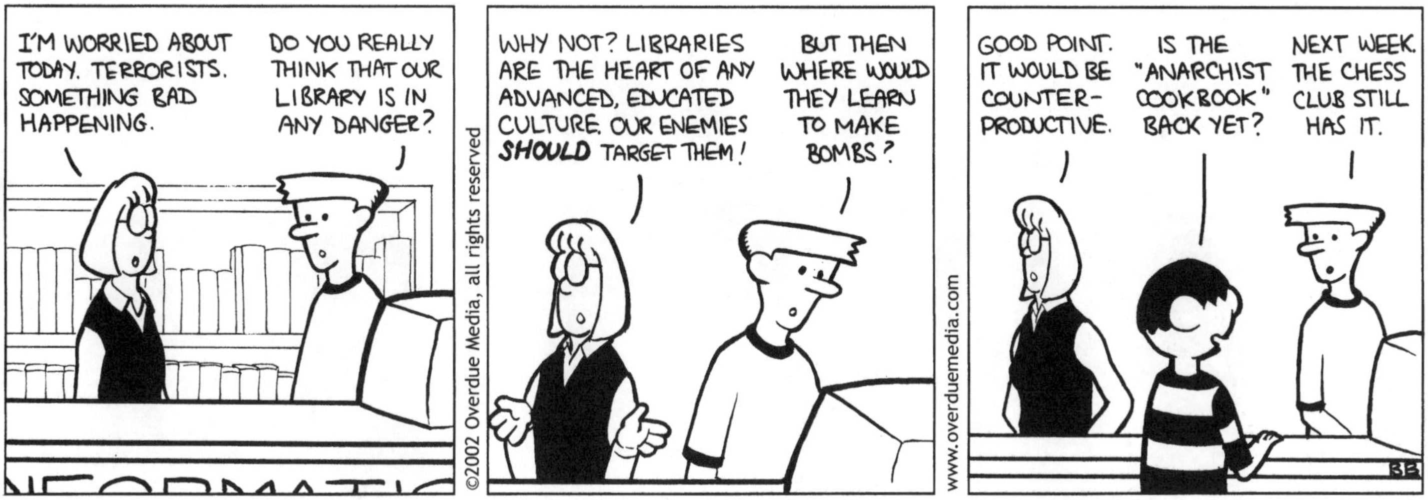
I'M WORRIED ABOUT TODAY. TERRORISTS. SOMETHING BAD HAPPENING.
DO YOU REALLY THINK THAT OUR LIBRARY IS IN ANY DANGER?
©2002 Overdue Media, all rights reserved
WHY NOT? LIBRARIES ARE THE HEART OF ANY ADVANCED, EDUCATED CULTURE. OUR ENEMIES SHOULD TARGET THEM!
BUT THEN WHERE WOULD THEY LEARN TO MAKE BOMBS?
www.overduemedia.com
GOOD POINT. IT WOULD BE COUNTER-PRODUCTIVE.
IS THE "ANARCHIST COOKBOOK" BACK YET?
NEXT WEEK. THE CHESS CLUB STILL HAS IT.
BB

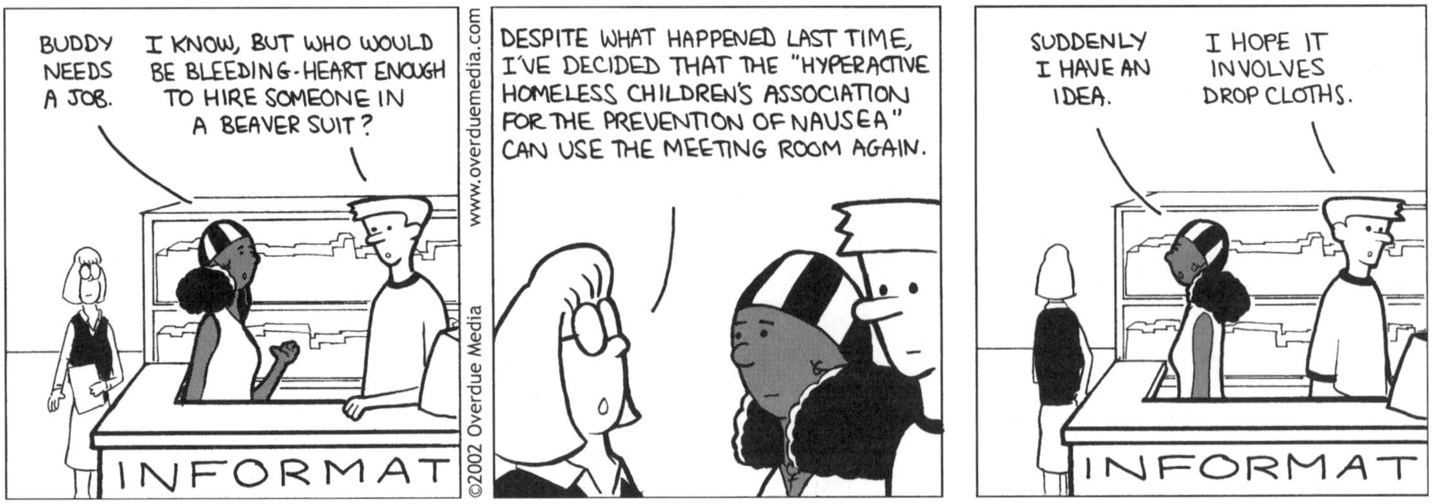
BUDDY NEEDS A JOB.
I KNOW, BUT WHO WOULD BE BLEEDING-HEART ENOUGH TO HIRE SOMEONE IN A BEAVER SUIT?
INFORMAT
DESPITE WHAT HAPPENED LAST TIME, I'VE DECIDED THAT THE "HYPERACTIVE HOMELESS CHILDREN'S ASSOCIATION FOR THE PREVENTION OF NAUSEA" CAN USE THE MEETING ROOM AGAIN.
SUDDENLY I HAVE AN IDEA.
I HOPE IT INVOLVES DROP CLOTHS.
INFORMAT

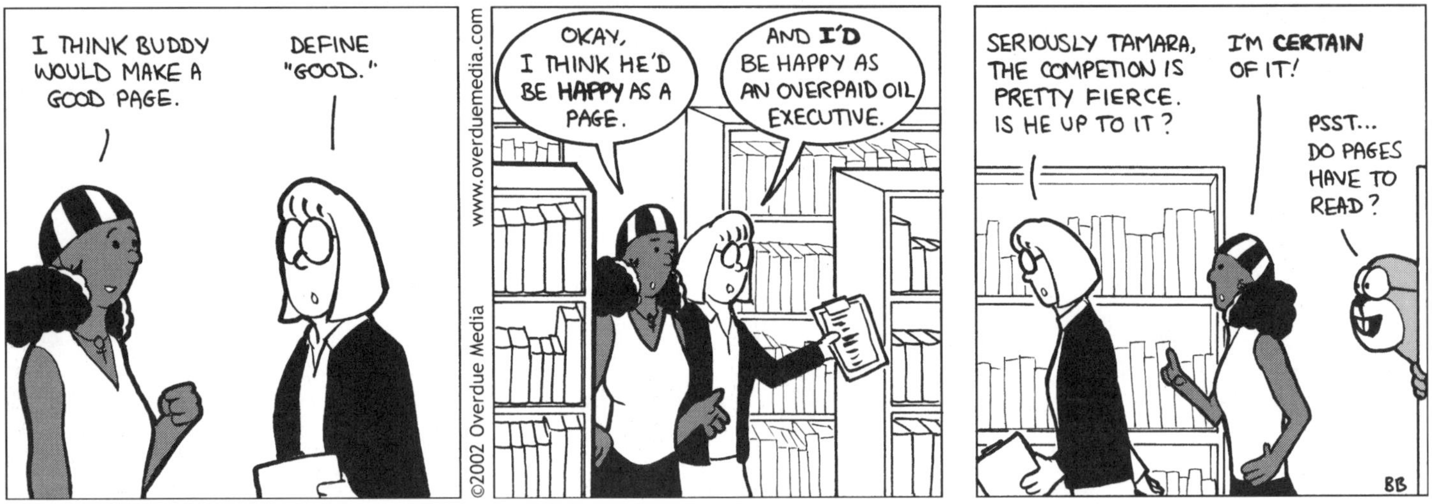
I THINK BUDDY WOULD MAKE A GOOD PAGE.
DEFINE "GOOD."
OKAY, I THINK HE'D BE **HAPPY** AS A PAGE.
AND **I'D** BE HAPPY AS AN OVERPAID OIL EXECUTIVE.
SERIOUSLY TAMARA, THE COMPETION IS PRETTY FIERCE. IS HE UP TO IT?
I'M **CERTAIN** OF IT!
PSST... DO PAGES HAVE TO READ?
BB

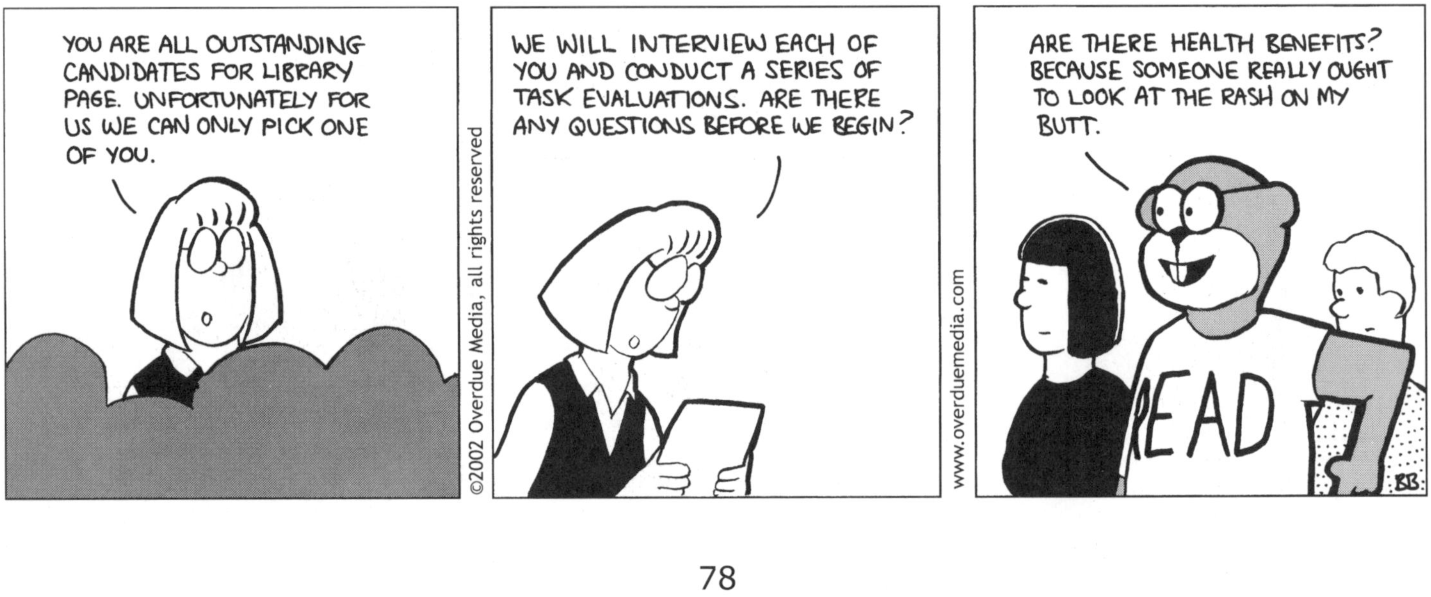
YOU ARE ALL OUTSTANDING CANDIDATES FOR LIBRARY PAGE. UNFORTUNATELY FOR US WE CAN ONLY PICK ONE OF YOU.
WE WILL INTERVIEW EACH OF YOU AND CONDUCT A SERIES OF TASK EVALUATIONS. ARE THERE ANY QUESTIONS BEFORE WE BEGIN?
ARE THERE HEALTH BENEFITS? BECAUSE SOMEONE REALLY OUGHT TO LOOK AT THE RASH ON MY BUTT.
READ
BB

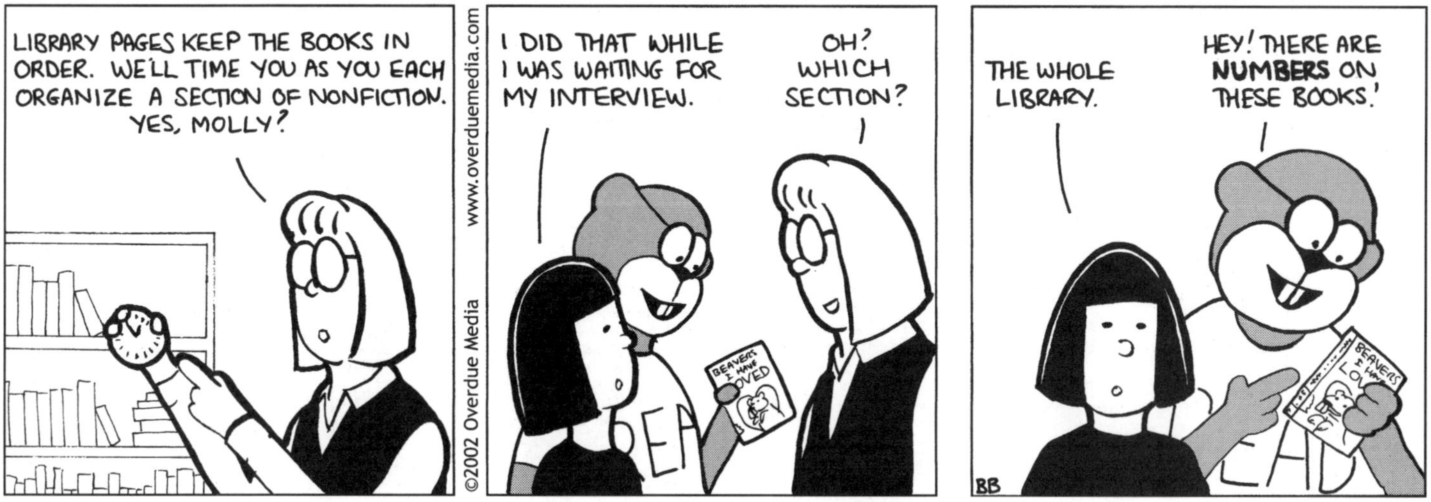
LIBRARY PAGES KEEP THE BOOKS IN ORDER. WE'LL TIME YOU AS YOU EACH ORGANIZE A SECTION OF NONFICTION. YES, MOLLY?
©2002 Overdue Media www.overduemedia.com
I DID THAT WHILE I WAS WAITING FOR MY INTERVIEW.
OH? WHICH SECTION?
THE WHOLE LIBRARY.
HEY! THERE ARE NUMBERS ON THESE BOOKS!
BB

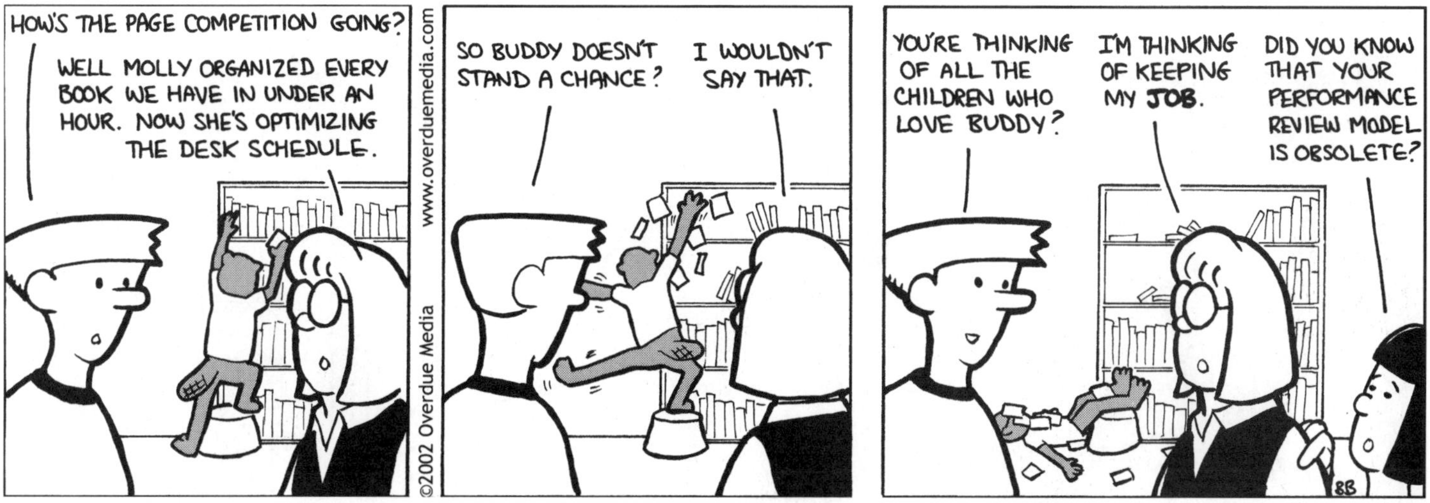
HOW'S THE PAGE COMPETITION GOING?
WELL MOLLY ORGANIZED EVERY BOOK WE HAVE IN UNDER AN HOUR. NOW SHE'S OPTIMIZING THE DESK SCHEDULE.
©2002 Overdue Media www.overduemedia.com
SO BUDDY DOESN'T STAND A CHANCE?
I WOULDN'T SAY THAT.
YOU'RE THINKING OF ALL THE CHILDREN WHO LOVE BUDDY?
I'M THINKING OF KEEPING MY JOB.
DID YOU KNOW THAT YOUR PERFORMANCE REVIEW MODEL IS OBSOLETE?
BB

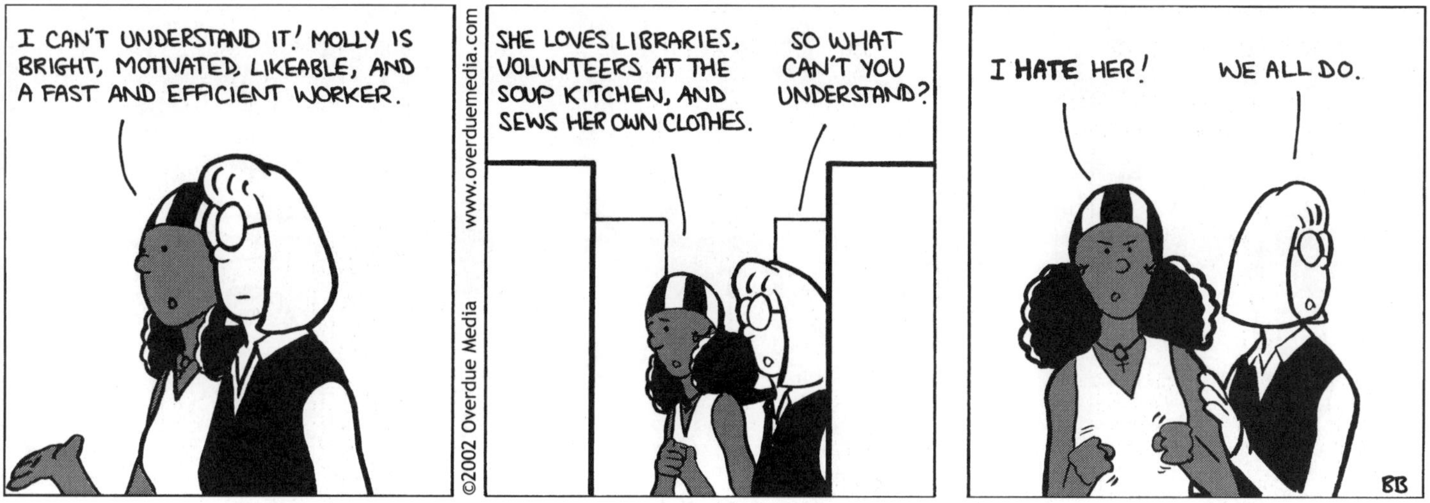
I CAN'T UNDERSTAND IT! MOLLY IS BRIGHT, MOTIVATED, LIKEABLE, AND A FAST AND EFFICIENT WORKER.
©2002 Overdue Media www.overduemedia.com
SHE LOVES LIBRARIES, VOLUNTEERS AT THE SOUP KITCHEN, AND SEWS HER OWN CLOTHES.
SO WHAT CAN'T YOU UNDERSTAND?
I HATE HER!
WE ALL DO.
BB

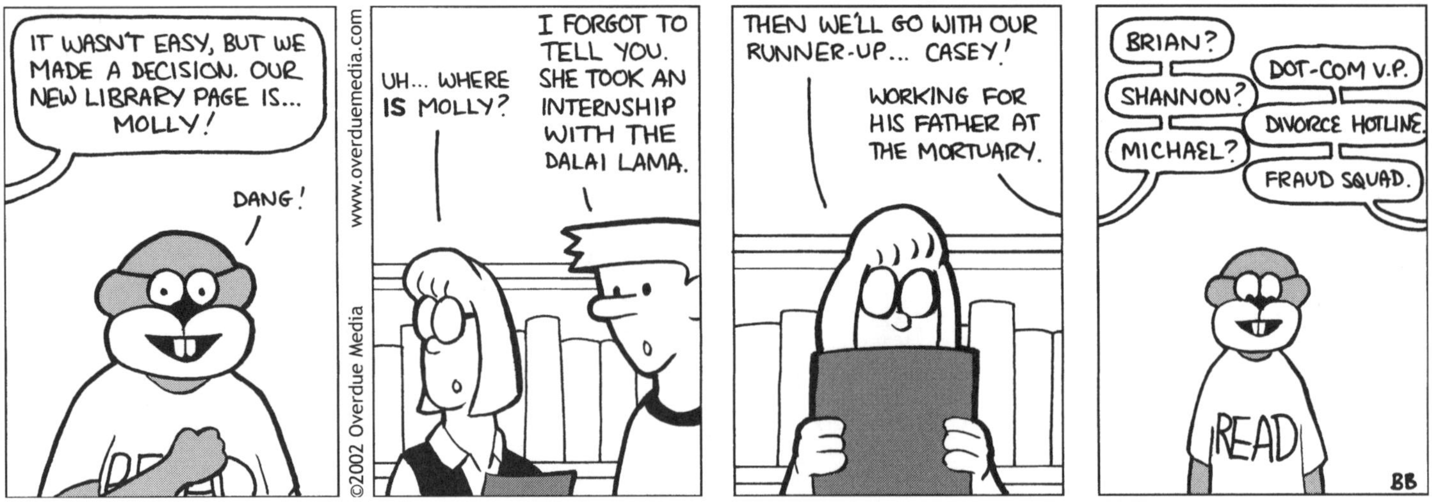
IT WASN'T EASY, BUT WE MADE A DECISION. OUR NEW LIBRARY PAGE IS... MOLLY!
DANG!
www.overduemedia.com
©2002 Overdue Media
UH... WHERE **IS** MOLLY?
I FORGOT TO TELL YOU. SHE TOOK AN INTERNSHIP WITH THE DALAI LAMA.
THEN WE'LL GO WITH OUR RUNNER-UP... CASEY!
WORKING FOR HIS FATHER AT THE MORTUARY.
BRIAN?
DOT-COM V.P.
SHANNON?
DIVORCE HOTLINE.
MICHAEL?
FRAUD SQUAD.
READ
BB

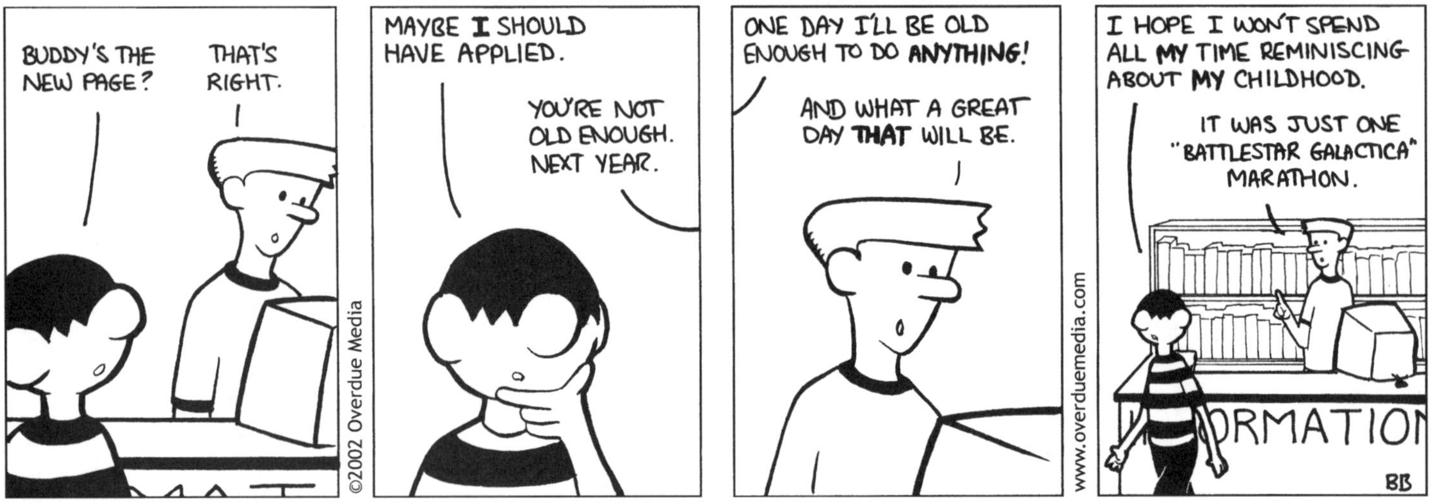
BUDDY'S THE NEW PAGE?
THAT'S RIGHT.
©2002 Overdue Media
MAYBE **I** SHOULD HAVE APPLIED.
YOU'RE NOT OLD ENOUGH. NEXT YEAR.
ONE DAY I'LL BE OLD ENOUGH TO DO **ANYTHING**!
AND WHAT A GREAT DAY **THAT** WILL BE.
www.overduemedia.com
I HOPE I WON'T SPEND ALL **MY** TIME REMINISCING ABOUT **MY** CHILDHOOD.
IT WAS JUST ONE "BATTLESTAR GALACTICA" MARATHON.
BB

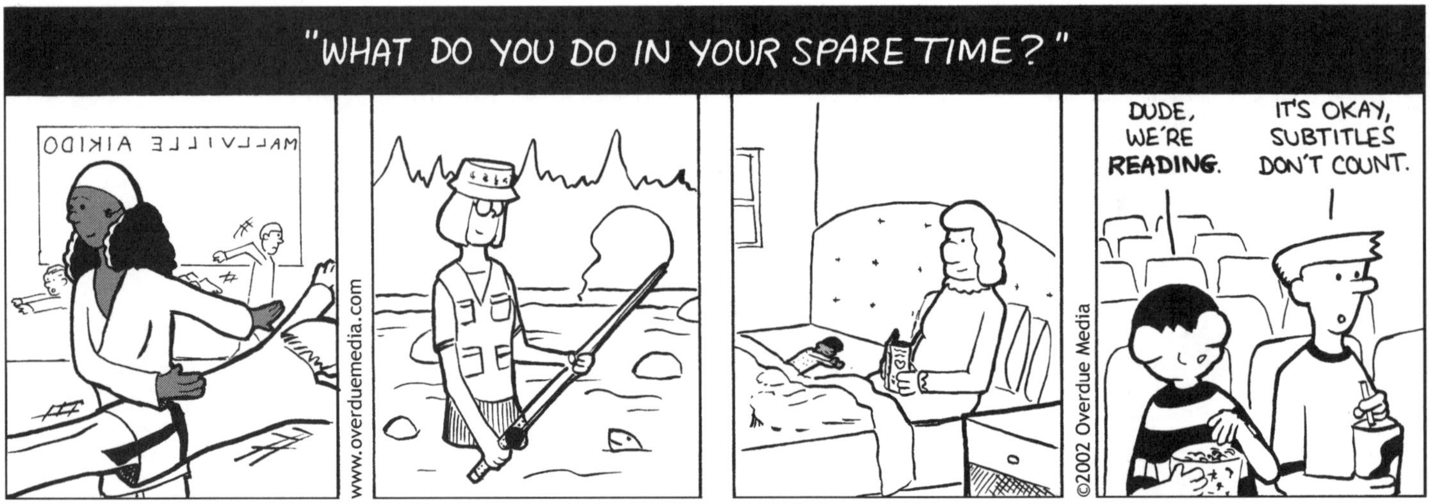
"WHAT DO YOU DO IN YOUR SPARE TIME?"
www.overduemedia.com
©2002 Overdue Media
DUDE, WE'RE **READING**.
IT'S OKAY, SUBTITLES DON'T COUNT.

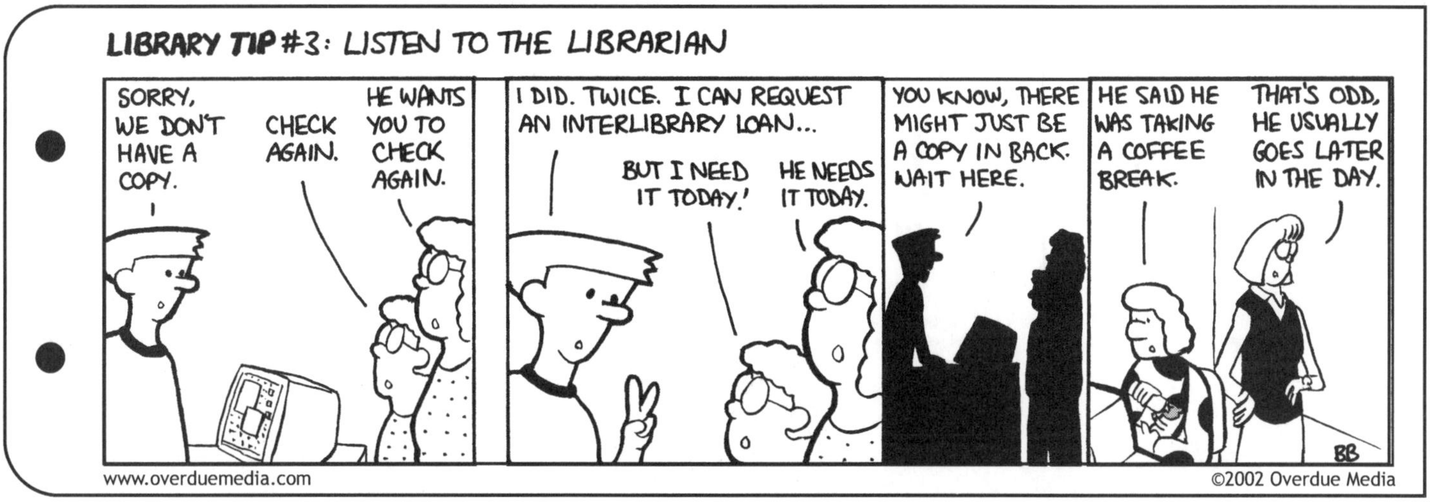
LIBRARY TIP #3: LISTEN TO THE LIBRARIAN
SORRY, WE DON'T HAVE A COPY.
CHECK AGAIN.
HE WANTS YOU TO CHECK AGAIN.
I DID. TWICE. I CAN REQUEST AN INTERLIBRARY LOAN...
BUT I NEED IT TODAY!
HE NEEDS IT TODAY.
YOU KNOW, THERE MIGHT JUST BE A COPY IN BACK. WAIT HERE.
HE SAID HE WAS TAKING A COFFEE BREAK.
THAT'S ODD, HE USUALLY GOES LATER IN THE DAY.
BB
www.overduemedia.com
©2002 Overdue Media

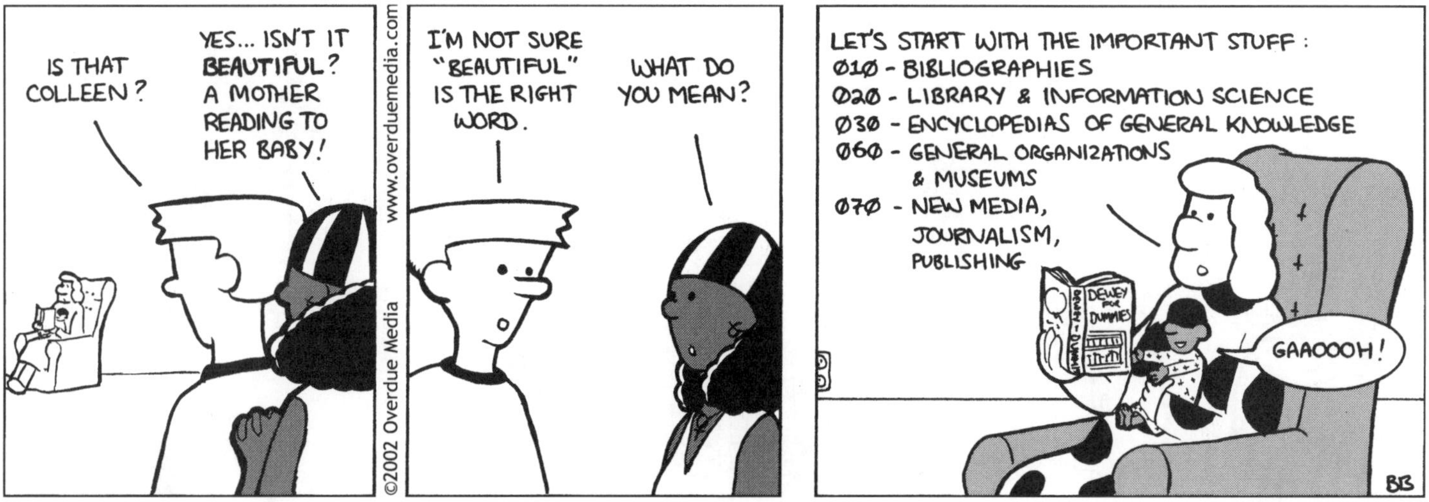
IS THAT COLLEEN?
YES... ISN'T IT BEAUTIFUL? A MOTHER READING TO HER BABY!
www.overduemedia.com
©2002 Overdue Media
I'M NOT SURE "BEAUTIFUL" IS THE RIGHT WORD.
WHAT DO YOU MEAN?
LET'S START WITH THE IMPORTANT STUFF:
010 - BIBLIOGRAPHIES
020 - LIBRARY & INFORMATION SCIENCE
030 - ENCYCLOPEDIAS OF GENERAL KNOWLEDGE
060 - GENERAL ORGANIZATIONS & MUSEUMS
070 - NEW MEDIA, JOURNALISM, PUBLISHING
DEWEY FOR DUMMIES
GAAOOOH!
BB

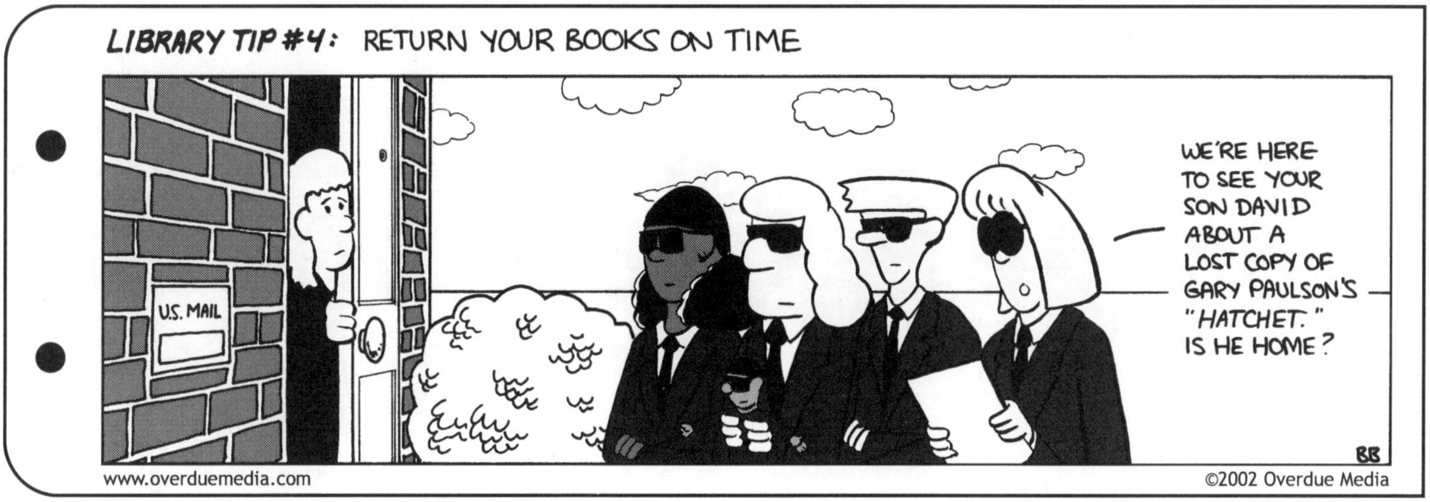
LIBRARY TIP #4: RETURN YOUR BOOKS ON TIME
U.S. MAIL
WE'RE HERE TO SEE YOUR SON DAVID ABOUT A LOST COPY OF GARY PAULSON'S "HATCHET." IS HE HOME?
BB
www.overduemedia.com
©2002 Overdue Media

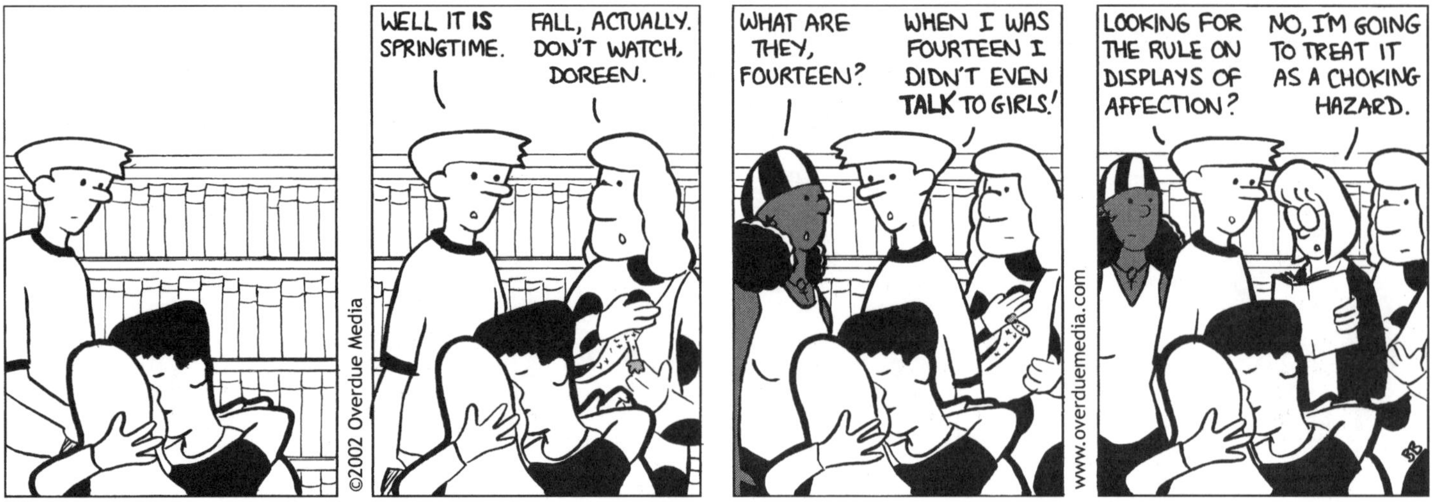
WELL IT IS SPRINGTIME.
FALL, ACTUALLY. DON'T WATCH, DOREEN.
©2002 Overdue Media
WHAT ARE THEY, FOURTEEN?
WHEN I WAS FOURTEEN I DIDN'T EVEN TALK TO GIRLS!
www.overduemedia.com
LOOKING FOR THE RULE ON DISPLAYS OF AFFECTION?
NO, I'M GOING TO TREAT IT AS A CHOKING HAZARD.

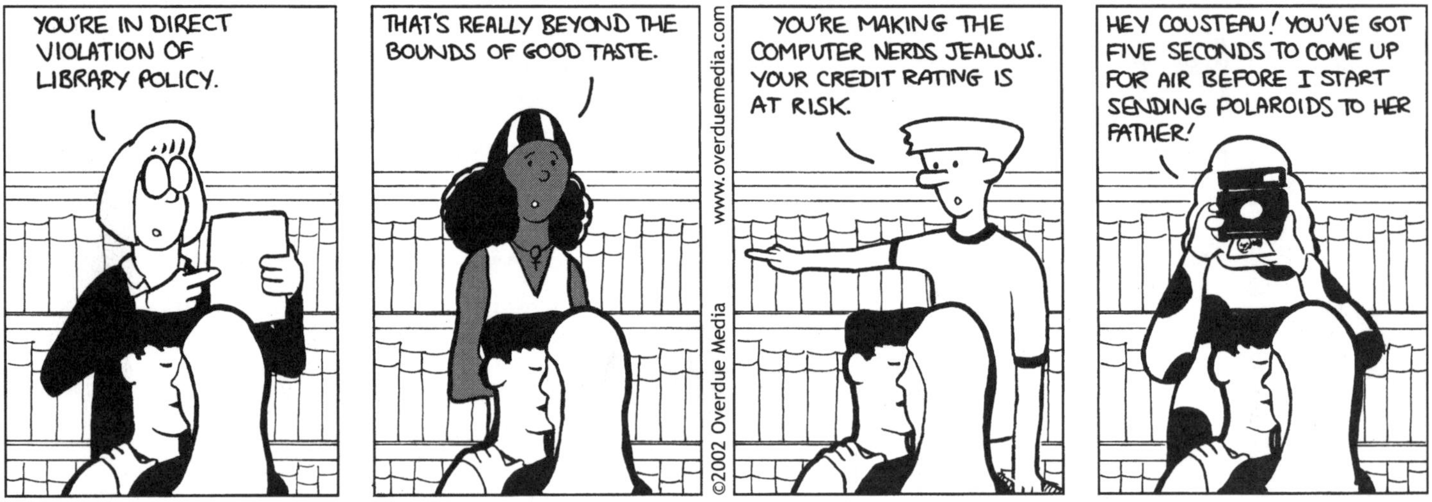
YOU'RE IN DIRECT VIOLATION OF LIBRARY POLICY.
THAT'S REALLY BEYOND THE BOUNDS OF GOOD TASTE.
www.overduemedia.com
©2002 Overdue Media
YOU'RE MAKING THE COMPUTER NERDS JEALOUS. YOUR CREDIT RATING IS AT RISK.
HEY COUSTEAU! YOU'VE GOT FIVE SECONDS TO COME UP FOR AIR BEFORE I START SENDING POLAROIDS TO HER FATHER!

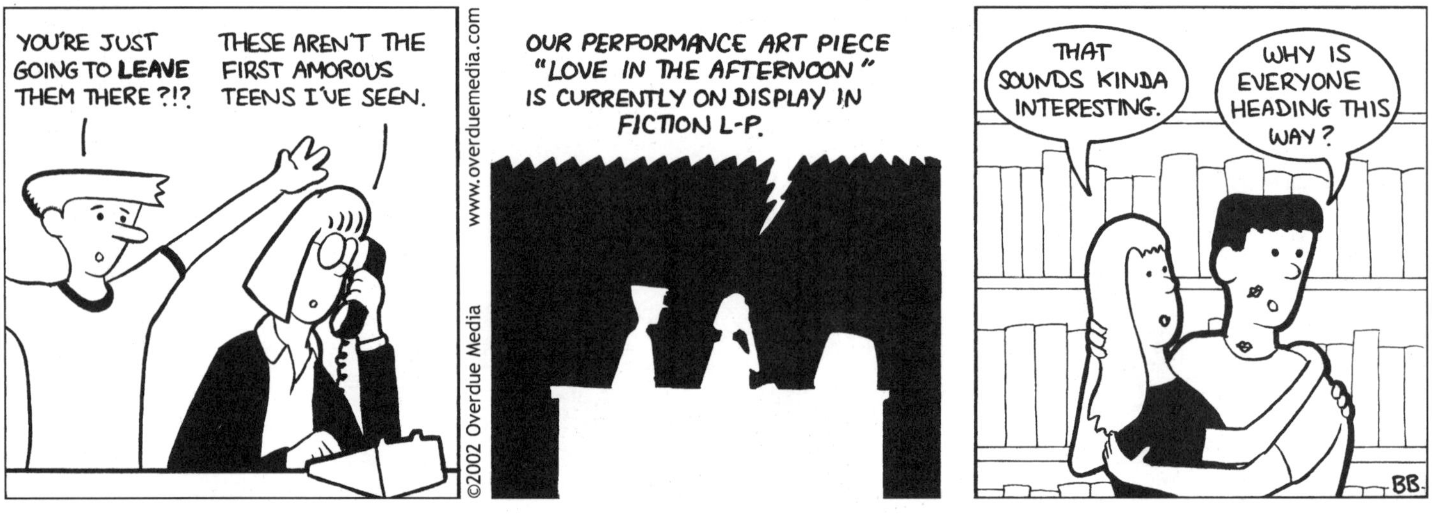
YOU'RE JUST GOING TO LEAVE THEM THERE?!?
THESE AREN'T THE FIRST AMOROUS TEENS I'VE SEEN.
www.overduemedia.com
©2002 Overdue Media
OUR PERFORMANCE ART PIECE "LOVE IN THE AFTERNOON" IS CURRENTLY ON DISPLAY IN FICTION L-P.
THAT SOUNDS KINDA INTERESTING.
WHY IS EVERYONE HEADING THIS WAY?
BB.

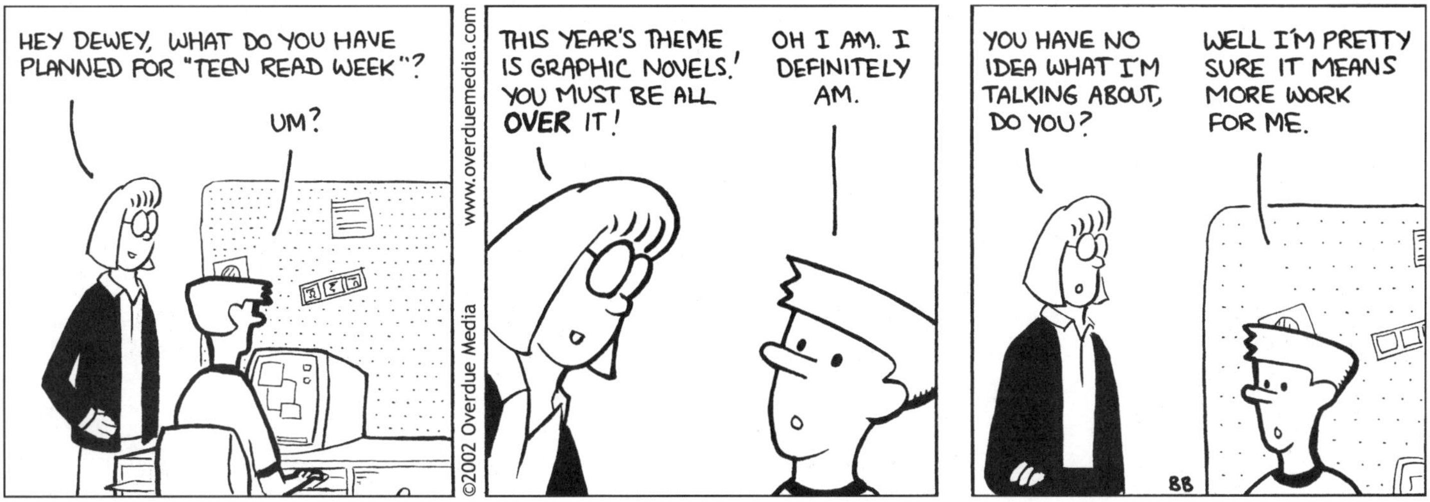
HEY DEWEY, WHAT DO YOU HAVE PLANNED FOR "TEEN READ WEEK"?
UM?
©2002 Overdue Media www.overduemedia.com
THIS YEAR'S THEME IS GRAPHIC NOVELS! YOU MUST BE ALL **OVER** IT!
OH I AM. I DEFINITELY AM.
YOU HAVE NO IDEA WHAT I'M TALKING ABOUT, DO YOU?
WELL I'M PRETTY SURE IT MEANS MORE WORK FOR ME.
BB

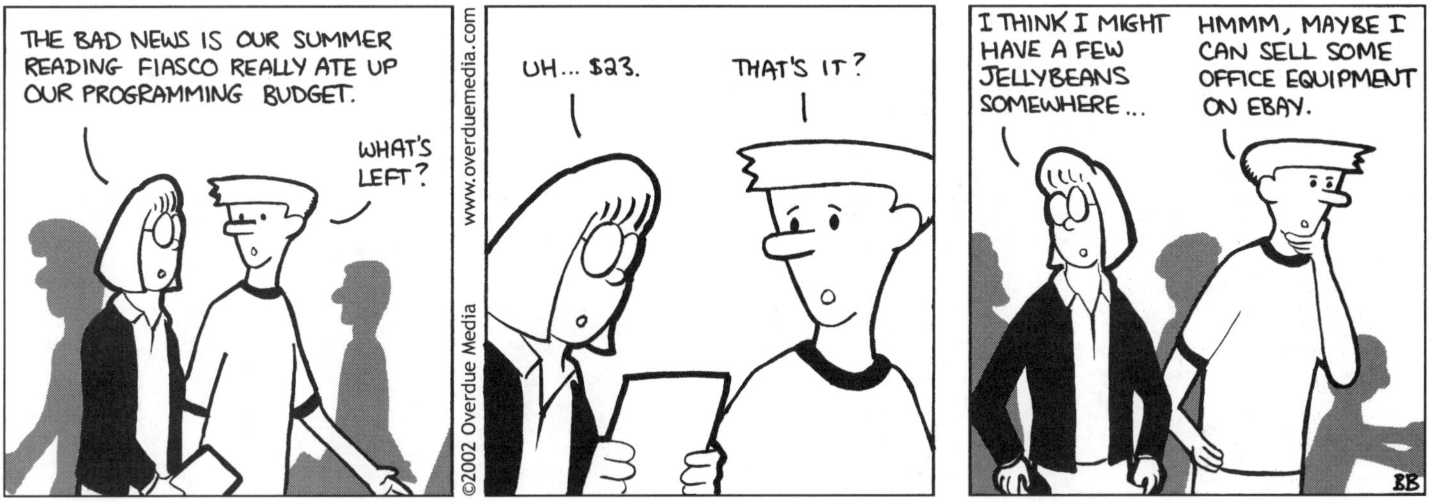
THE BAD NEWS IS OUR SUMMER READING FIASCO REALLY ATE UP OUR PROGRAMMING BUDGET.
WHAT'S LEFT?
©2002 Overdue Media www.overduemedia.com
UH... $23.
THAT'S IT?
I THINK I MIGHT HAVE A FEW JELLYBEANS SOMEWHERE...
HMMM, MAYBE I CAN SELL SOME OFFICE EQUIPMENT ON EBAY.
BB

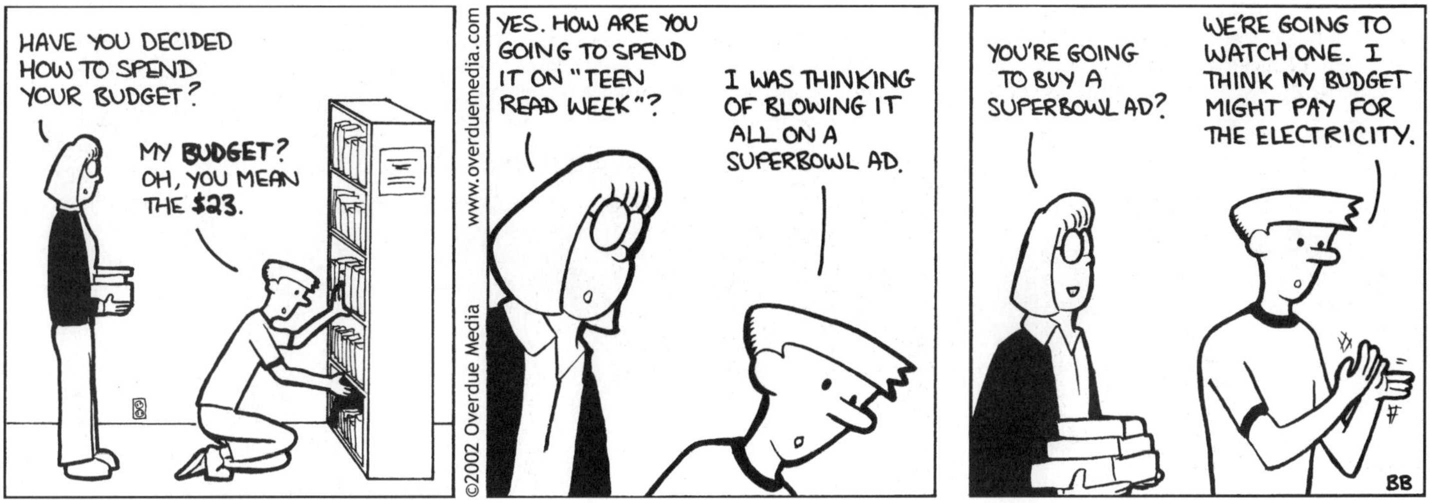
HAVE YOU DECIDED HOW TO SPEND YOUR BUDGET?
MY **BUDGET**? OH, YOU MEAN THE **$23**.
©2002 Overdue Media www.overduemedia.com
YES. HOW ARE YOU GOING TO SPEND IT ON "TEEN READ WEEK"?
I WAS THINKING OF BLOWING IT ALL ON A SUPERBOWL AD.
YOU'RE GOING TO BUY A SUPERBOWL AD?
WE'RE GOING TO WATCH ONE. I THINK MY BUDGET MIGHT PAY FOR THE ELECTRICITY.
BB

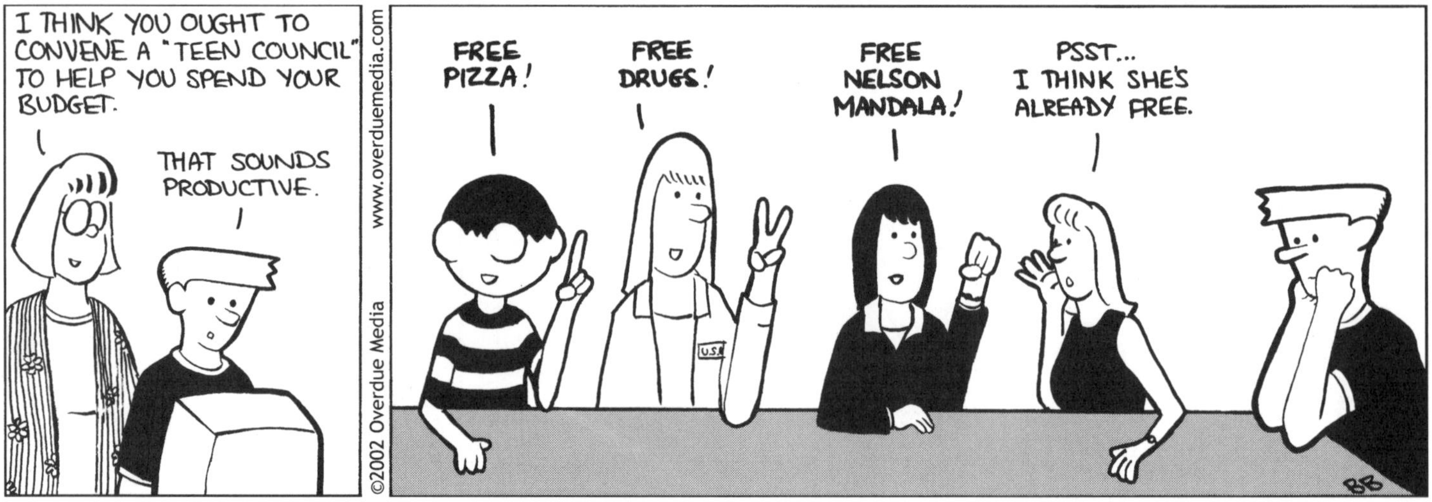
I THINK YOU OUGHT TO CONVENE A "TEEN COUNCIL" TO HELP YOU SPEND YOUR BUDGET.
THAT SOUNDS PRODUCTIVE.
©2002 Overdue Media www.overduemedia.com
FREE PIZZA!
FREE DRUGS!
FREE NELSON MANDALA!
PSST... I THINK SHE'S ALREADY FREE.
BB

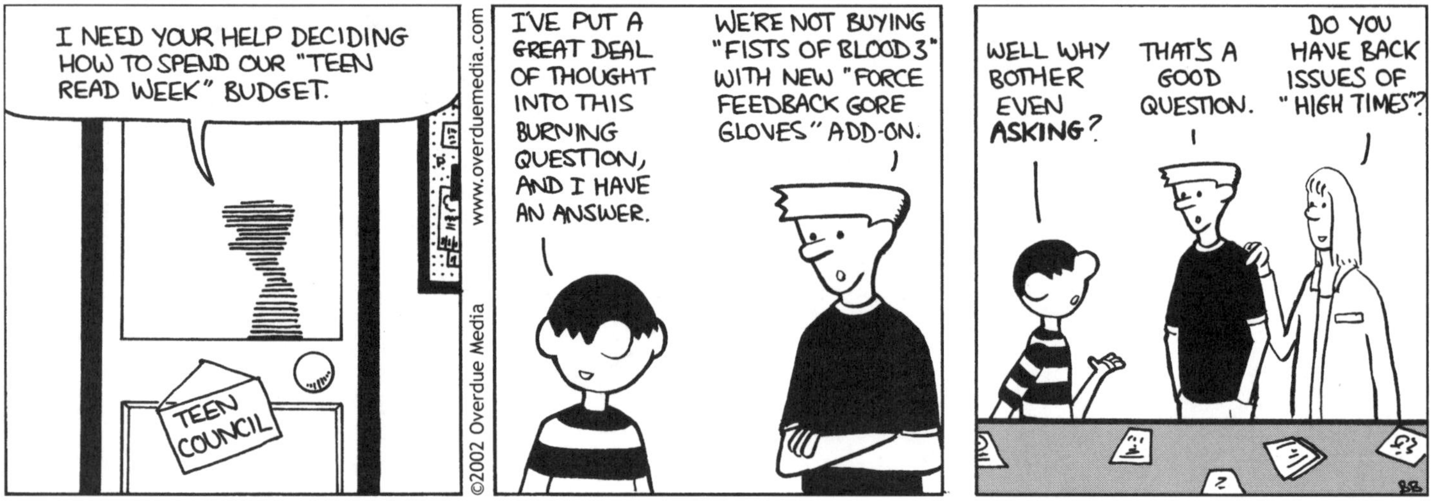
I NEED YOUR HELP DECIDING HOW TO SPEND OUR "TEEN READ WEEK" BUDGET.
TEEN COUNCIL
©2002 Overdue Media www.overduemedia.com
I'VE PUT A GREAT DEAL OF THOUGHT INTO THIS BURNING QUESTION, AND I HAVE AN ANSWER.
WE'RE NOT BUYING "FISTS OF BLOOD 3" WITH NEW "FORCE FEEDBACK GORE GLOVES" ADD-ON.
WELL WHY BOTHER EVEN **ASKING**?
THAT'S A GOOD QUESTION.
DO YOU HAVE BACK ISSUES OF "HIGH TIMES"?
BB

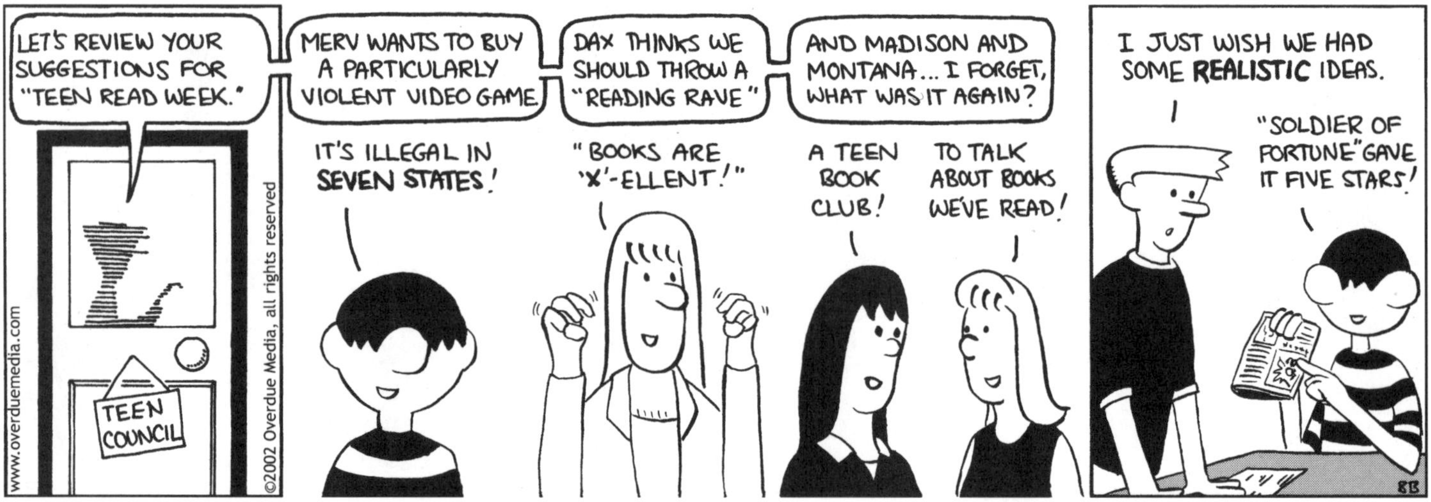
LET'S REVIEW YOUR SUGGESTIONS FOR "TEEN READ WEEK."
TEEN COUNCIL
www.overduemedia.com ©2002 Overdue Media, all rights reserved
MERV WANTS TO BUY A PARTICULARLY VIOLENT VIDEO GAME.
IT'S ILLEGAL IN **SEVEN STATES**!
DAX THINKS WE SHOULD THROW A "READING RAVE"
"BOOKS ARE 'X'-ELLENT!"
AND MADISON AND MONTANA... I FORGET, WHAT WAS IT AGAIN?
A TEEN BOOK CLUB!
TO TALK ABOUT BOOKS WE'VE READ!
I JUST WISH WE HAD SOME **REALISTIC** IDEAS.
"SOLDIER OF FORTUNE" GAVE IT FIVE STARS!
BB

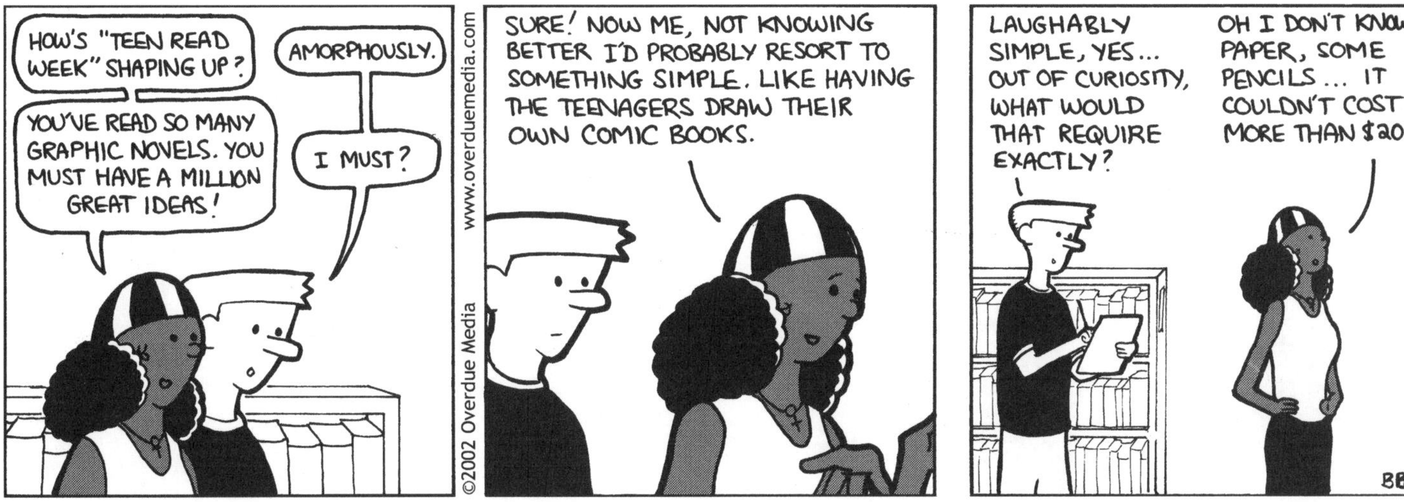
HOW'S "TEEN READ WEEK" SHAPING UP?
YOU'VE READ SO MANY GRAPHIC NOVELS. YOU MUST HAVE A MILLION GREAT IDEAS!
AMORPHOUSLY.
I MUST?
SURE! NOW ME, NOT KNOWING BETTER I'D PROBABLY RESORT TO SOMETHING SIMPLE. LIKE HAVING THE TEENAGERS DRAW THEIR OWN COMIC BOOKS.
LAUGHABLY SIMPLE, YES... OUT OF CURIOSITY, WHAT WOULD THAT REQUIRE EXACTLY?
OH I DON'T KNOW, PAPER, SOME PENCILS... IT COULDN'T COST MORE THAN $20.
BB
©2002 Overdue Media www.overduemedia.com

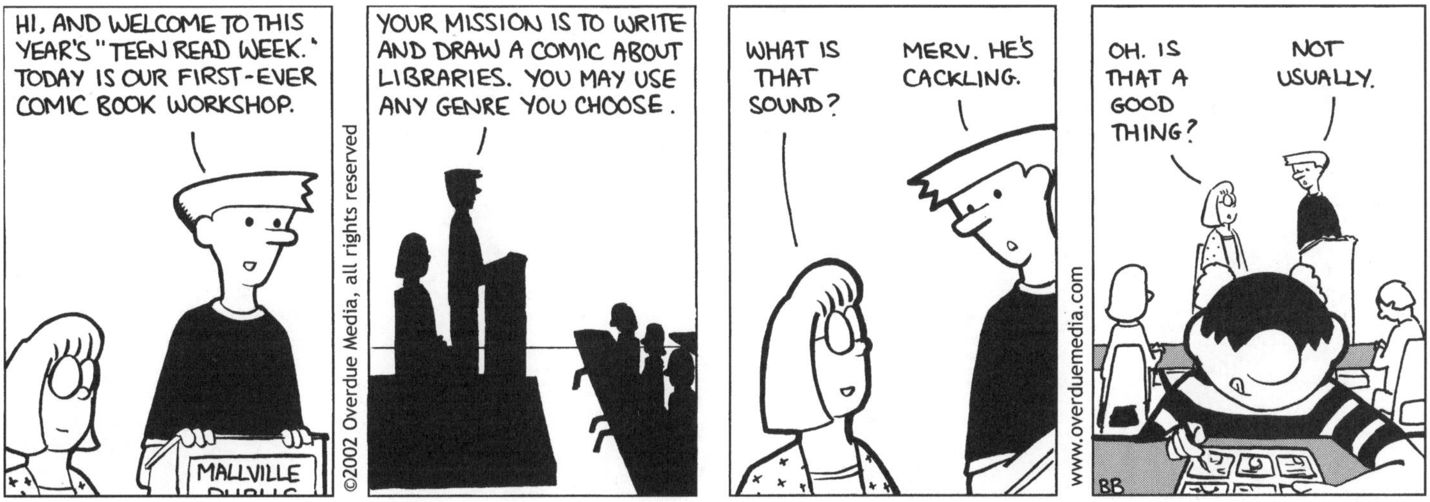
HI, AND WELCOME TO THIS YEAR'S "TEEN READ WEEK." TODAY IS OUR FIRST-EVER COMIC BOOK WORKSHOP.
MALLVILLE
YOUR MISSION IS TO WRITE AND DRAW A COMIC ABOUT LIBRARIES. YOU MAY USE ANY GENRE YOU CHOOSE.
WHAT IS THAT SOUND?
MERV. HE'S CACKLING.
OH. IS THAT A GOOD THING?
NOT USUALLY.
BB
©2002 Overdue Media, all rights reserved www.overduemedia.com

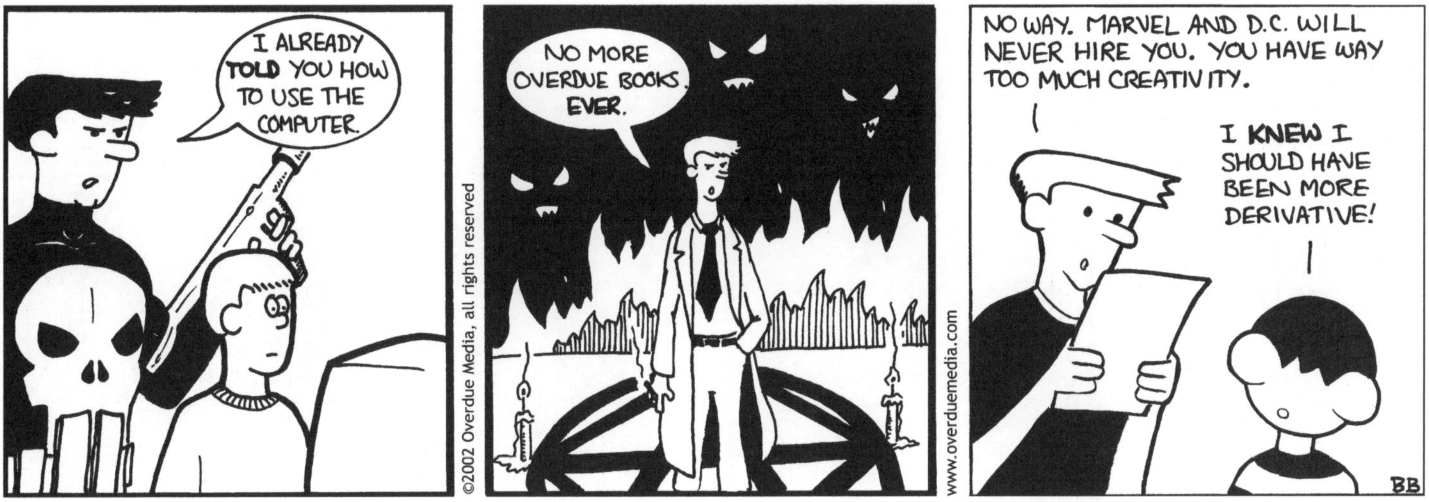
I ALREADY **TOLD** YOU HOW TO USE THE COMPUTER.
NO MORE OVERDUE BOOKS. **EVER.**
NO WAY. MARVEL AND D.C. WILL NEVER HIRE YOU. YOU HAVE WAY TOO MUCH CREATIVITY.
I **KNEW** I SHOULD HAVE BEEN MORE DERIVATIVE!
BB
©2002 Overdue Media, all rights reserved www.overduemedia.com

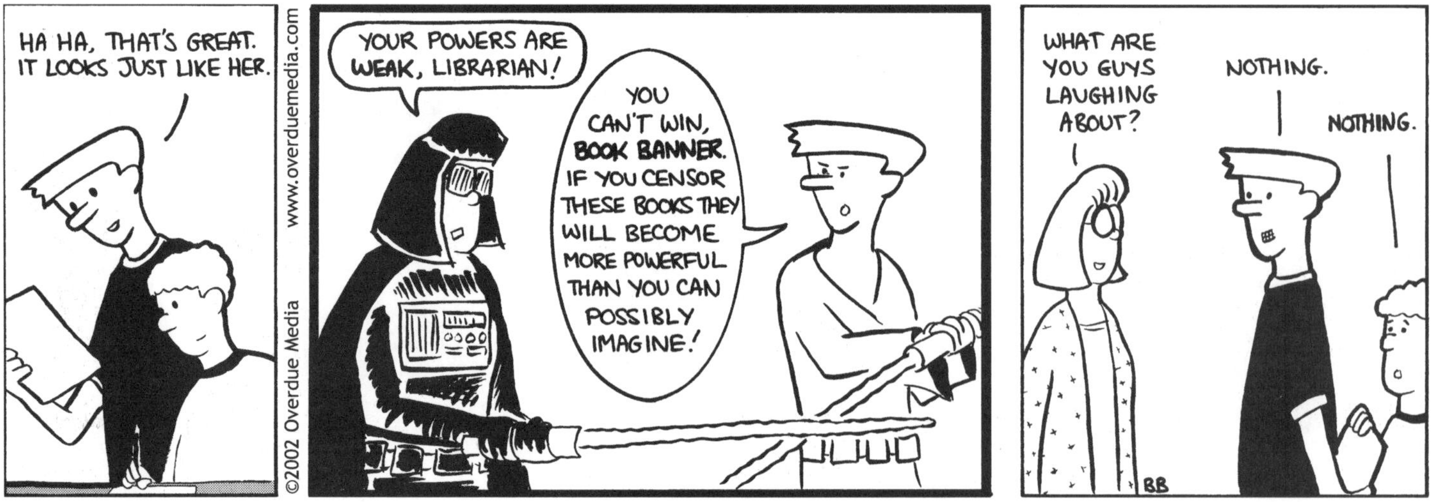
HA HA, THAT'S GREAT. IT LOOKS JUST LIKE HER.
www.overduemedia.com
©2002 Overdue Media
YOUR POWERS ARE WEAK, LIBRARIAN!
YOU CAN'T WIN, BOOK BANNER. IF YOU CENSOR THESE BOOKS THEY WILL BECOME MORE POWERFUL THAN YOU CAN POSSIBLY IMAGINE!
WHAT ARE YOU GUYS LAUGHING ABOUT?
NOTHING.
NOTHING.
BB

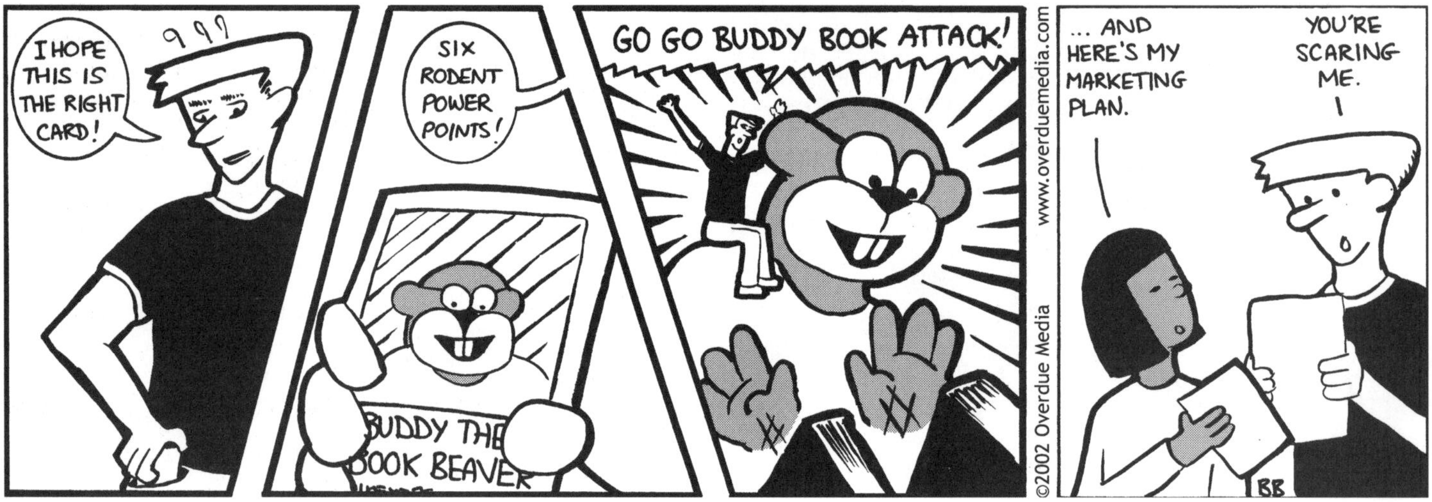
I HOPE THIS IS THE RIGHT CARD!
? ? ?
SIX RODENT POWER POINTS!
BUDDY THE BOOK BEAVER
GO GO BUDDY BOOK ATTACK!
www.overduemedia.com
©2002 Overdue Media
... AND HERE'S MY MARKETING PLAN.
YOU'RE SCARING ME.
BB

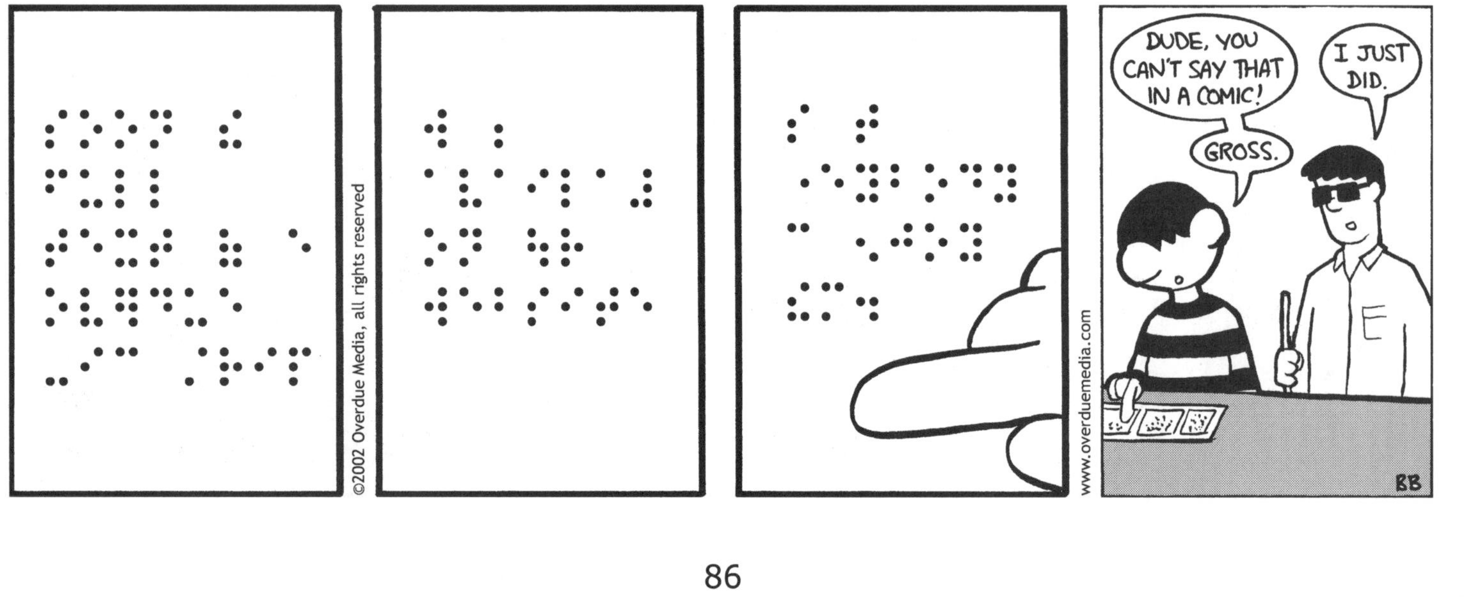
©2002 Overdue Media, all rights reserved
www.overduemedia.com
DUDE, YOU CAN'T SAY THAT IN A COMIC!
I JUST DID.
GROSS.
BB

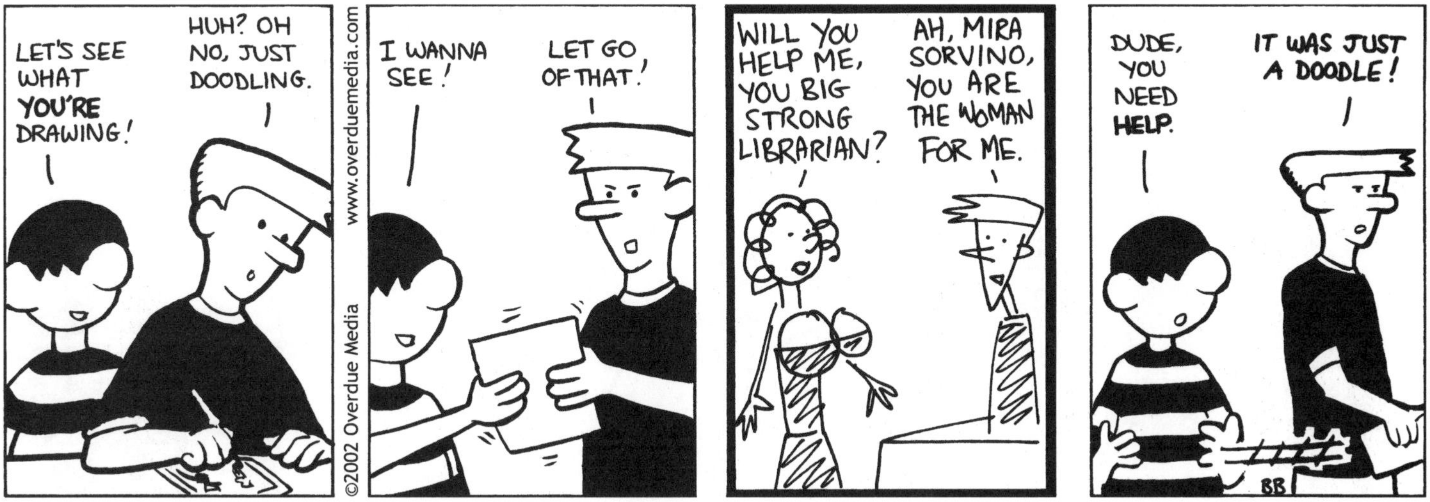
LET'S SEE WHAT **YOU'RE** DRAWING!
HUH? OH NO, JUST DOODLING.
www.overduemedia.com ©2002 Overdue Media
I WANNA SEE!
LET GO OF THAT!
WILL YOU HELP ME, YOU BIG STRONG LIBRARIAN?
AH, MIRA SORVINO, YOU ARE THE WOMAN FOR ME.
DUDE, YOU NEED **HELP**.
IT WAS JUST A DOODLE!
BB

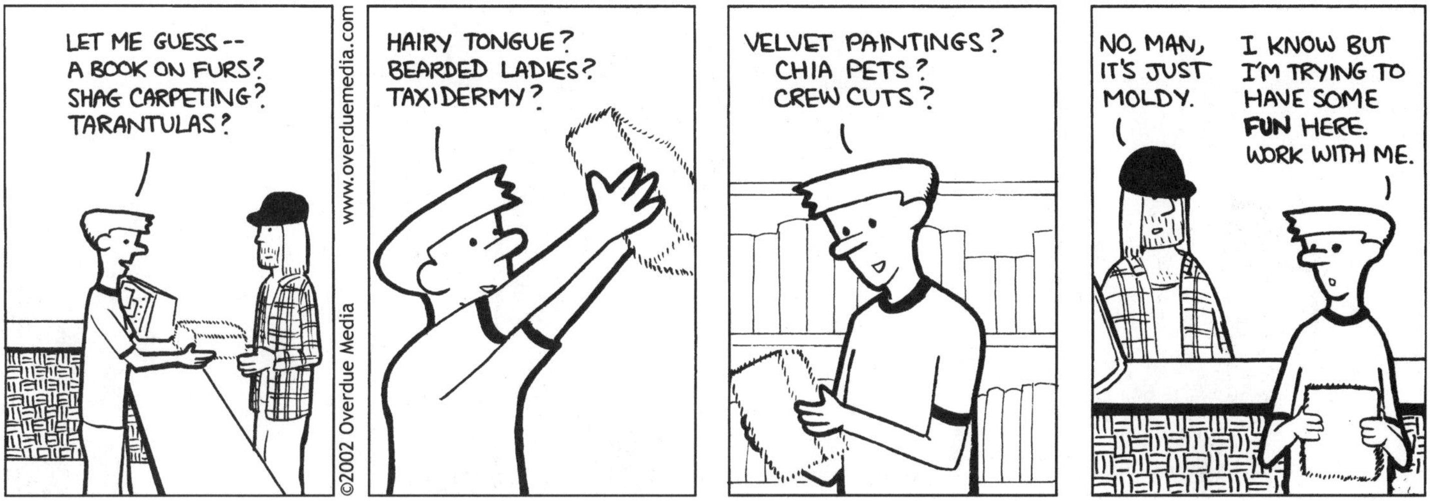
LET ME GUESS -- A BOOK ON FURS? SHAG CARPETING? TARANTULAS?
www.overduemedia.com ©2002 Overdue Media
HAIRY TONGUE? BEARDED LADIES? TAXIDERMY?
VELVET PAINTINGS? CHIA PETS? CREW CUTS?
NO, MAN, IT'S JUST MOLDY.
I KNOW BUT I'M TRYING TO HAVE SOME **FUN** HERE. WORK WITH ME.

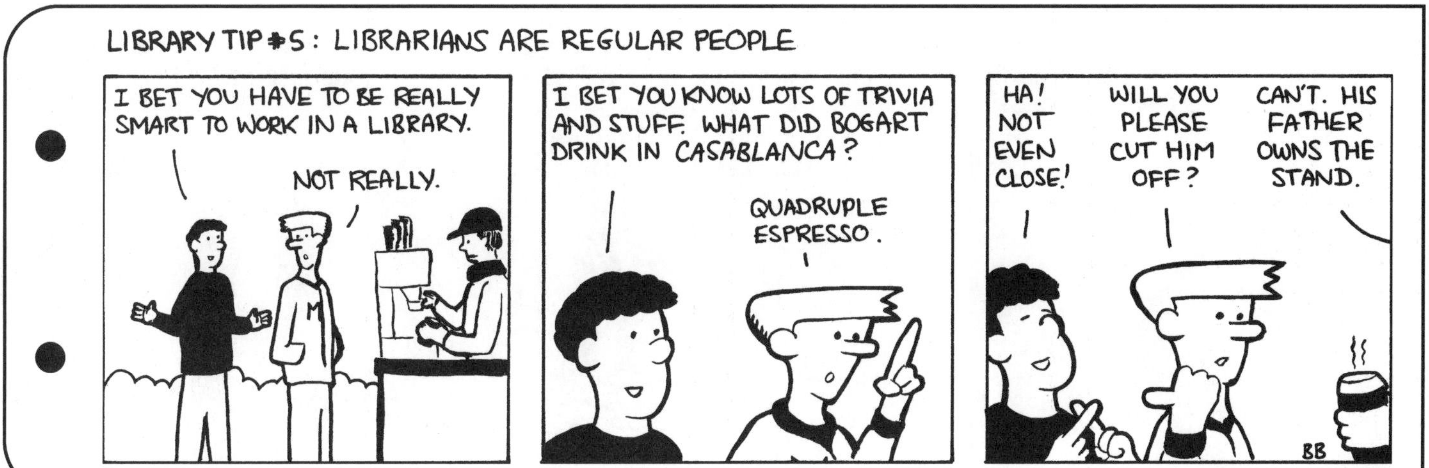
LIBRARY TIP #5: LIBRARIANS ARE REGULAR PEOPLE
I BET YOU HAVE TO BE REALLY SMART TO WORK IN A LIBRARY.
NOT REALLY.
I BET YOU KNOW LOTS OF TRIVIA AND STUFF. WHAT DID BOGART DRINK IN CASABLANCA?
QUADRUPLE ESPRESSO.
HA! NOT EVEN CLOSE!
WILL YOU PLEASE CUT HIM OFF?
CAN'T. HIS FATHER OWNS THE STAND.
BB
www.overduemedia.com
©2002 Overdue Media

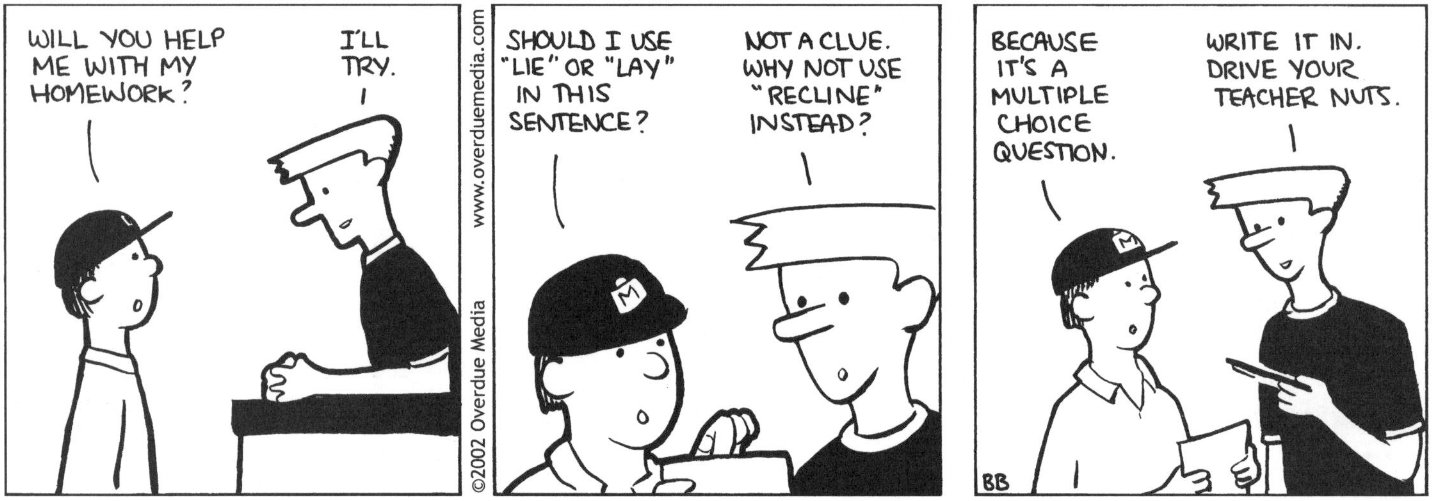
WILL YOU HELP ME WITH MY HOMEWORK?
I'LL TRY.
SHOULD I USE "LIE" OR "LAY" IN THIS SENTENCE?
NOT A CLUE. WHY NOT USE "RECLINE" INSTEAD?
BECAUSE IT'S A MULTIPLE CHOICE QUESTION.
WRITE IT IN. DRIVE YOUR TEACHER NUTS.
www.overduemedia.com
©2002 Overdue Media
BB

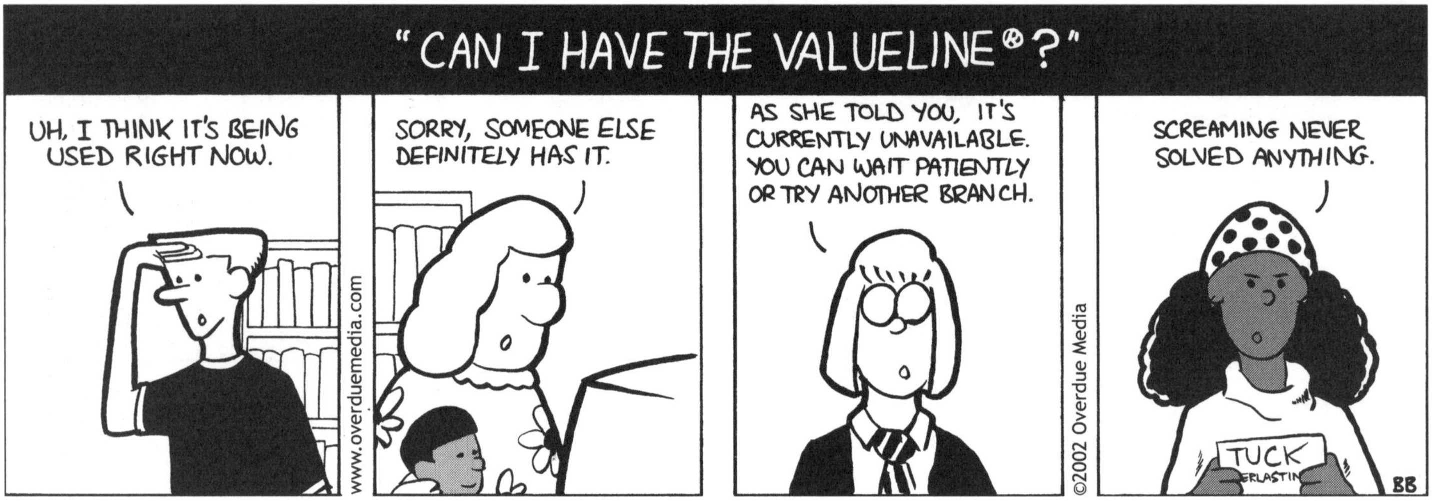
"CAN I HAVE THE VALUELINE®?"
UH, I THINK IT'S BEING USED RIGHT NOW.
SORRY, SOMEONE ELSE DEFINITELY HAS IT.
AS SHE TOLD YOU, IT'S CURRENTLY UNAVAILABLE. YOU CAN WAIT PATIENTLY OR TRY ANOTHER BRANCH.
SCREAMING NEVER SOLVED ANYTHING.
TUCK
www.overduemedia.com
©2002 Overdue Media
BB

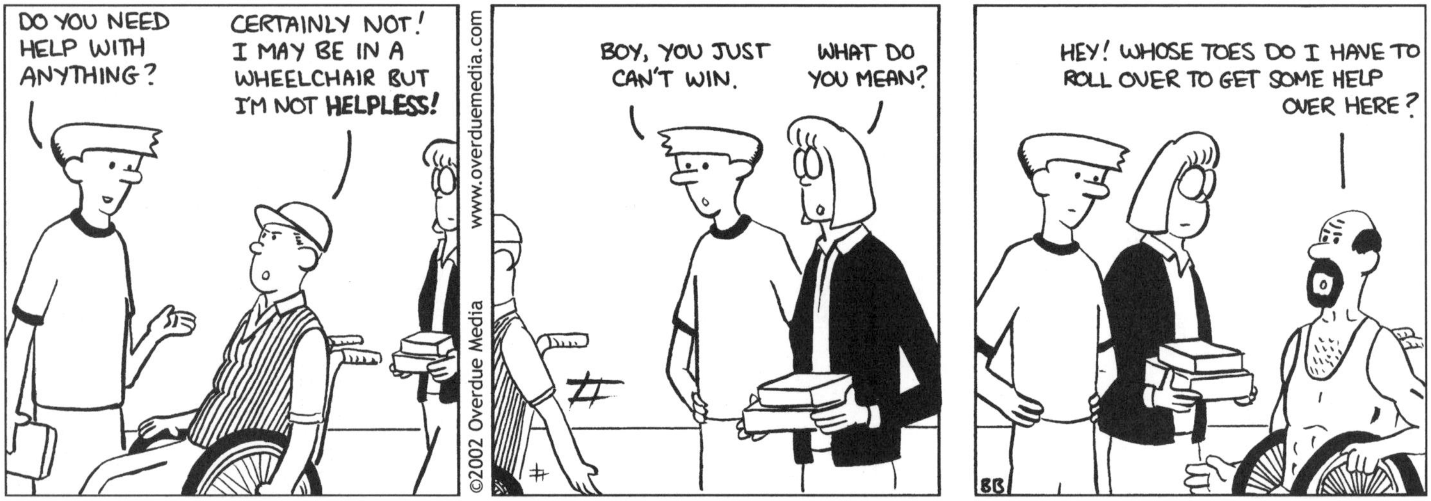
DO YOU NEED HELP WITH ANYTHING?
CERTAINLY NOT! I MAY BE IN A WHEELCHAIR BUT I'M NOT HELPLESS!
BOY, YOU JUST CAN'T WIN.
WHAT DO YOU MEAN?
HEY! WHOSE TOES DO I HAVE TO ROLL OVER TO GET SOME HELP OVER HERE?
www.overduemedia.com
©2002 Overdue Media
BB

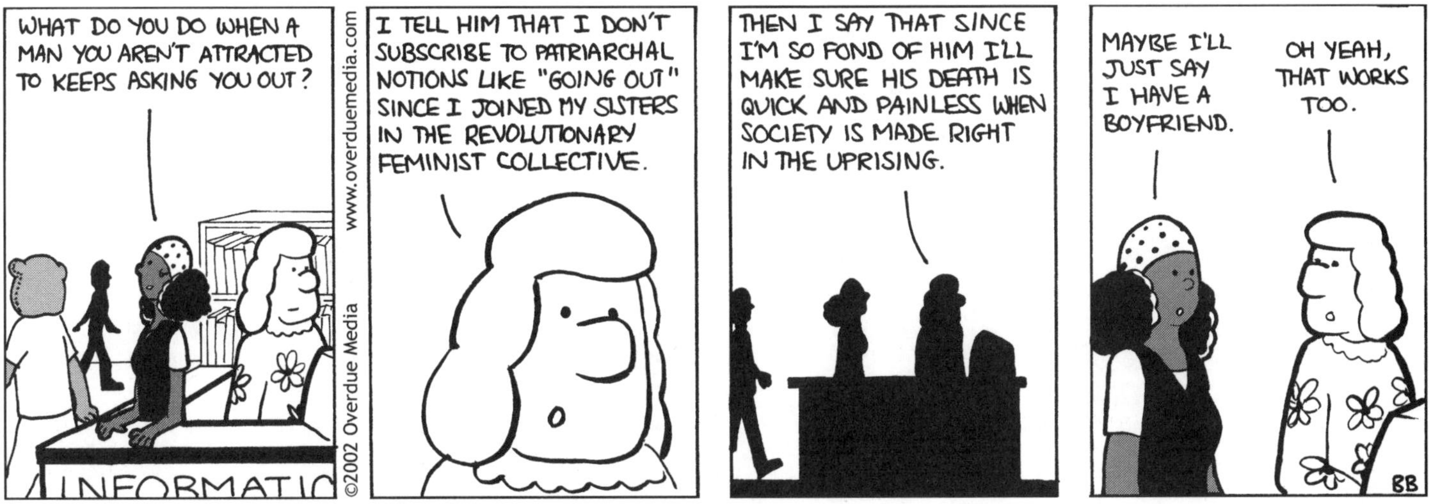
WHAT DO YOU DO WHEN A MAN YOU AREN'T ATTRACTED TO KEEPS ASKING YOU OUT?
INFORMATIC
www.overduemedia.com ©2002 Overdue Media
I TELL HIM THAT I DON'T SUBSCRIBE TO PATRIARCHAL NOTIONS LIKE "GOING OUT" SINCE I JOINED MY SISTERS IN THE REVOLUTIONARY FEMINIST COLLECTIVE.
THEN I SAY THAT SINCE I'M SO FOND OF HIM I'LL MAKE SURE HIS DEATH IS QUICK AND PAINLESS WHEN SOCIETY IS MADE RIGHT IN THE UPRISING.
MAYBE I'LL JUST SAY I HAVE A BOYFRIEND.
OH YEAH, THAT WORKS TOO.
BB

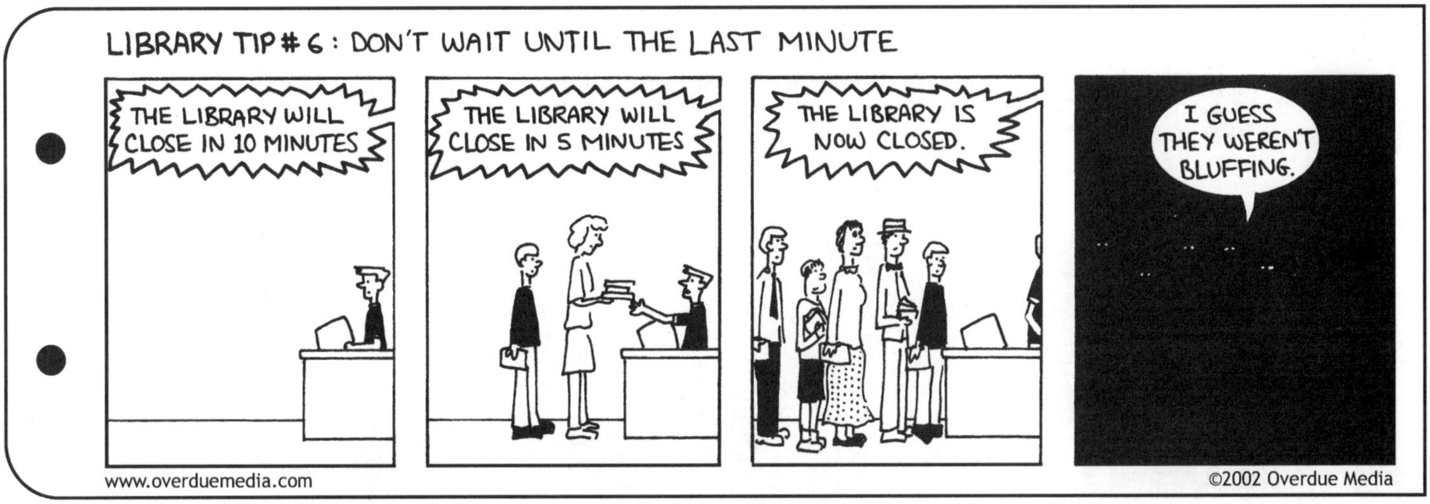
LIBRARY TIP # 6 : DON'T WAIT UNTIL THE LAST MINUTE
THE LIBRARY WILL CLOSE IN 10 MINUTES
THE LIBRARY WILL CLOSE IN 5 MINUTES
THE LIBRARY IS NOW CLOSED.
I GUESS THEY WEREN'T BLUFFING.
www.overduemedia.com
©2002 Overdue Media

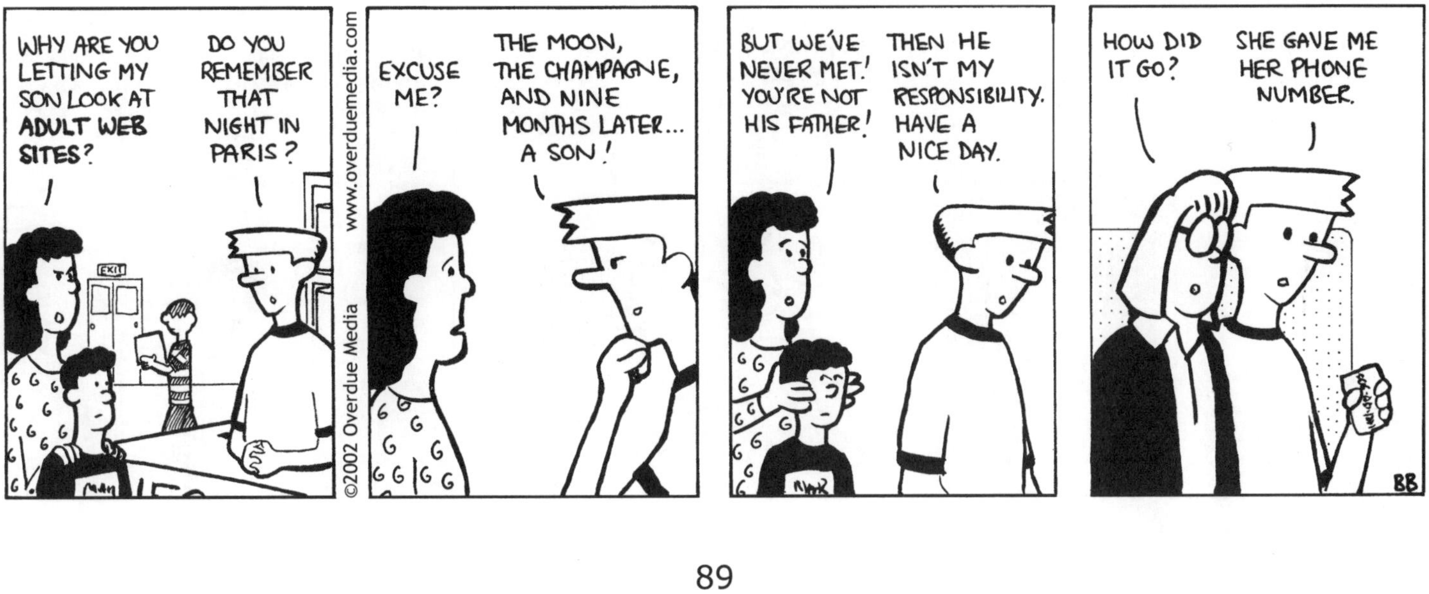
WHY ARE YOU LETTING MY SON LOOK AT ADULT WEB SITES?
DO YOU REMEMBER THAT NIGHT IN PARIS?
EXIT
www.overduemedia.com ©2002 Overdue Media
EXCUSE ME?
THE MOON, THE CHAMPAGNE, AND NINE MONTHS LATER... A SON!
BUT WE'VE NEVER MET! YOU'RE NOT HIS FATHER!
THEN HE ISN'T MY RESPONSIBILITY. HAVE A NICE DAY.
HOW DID IT GO?
SHE GAVE ME HER PHONE NUMBER.
BB

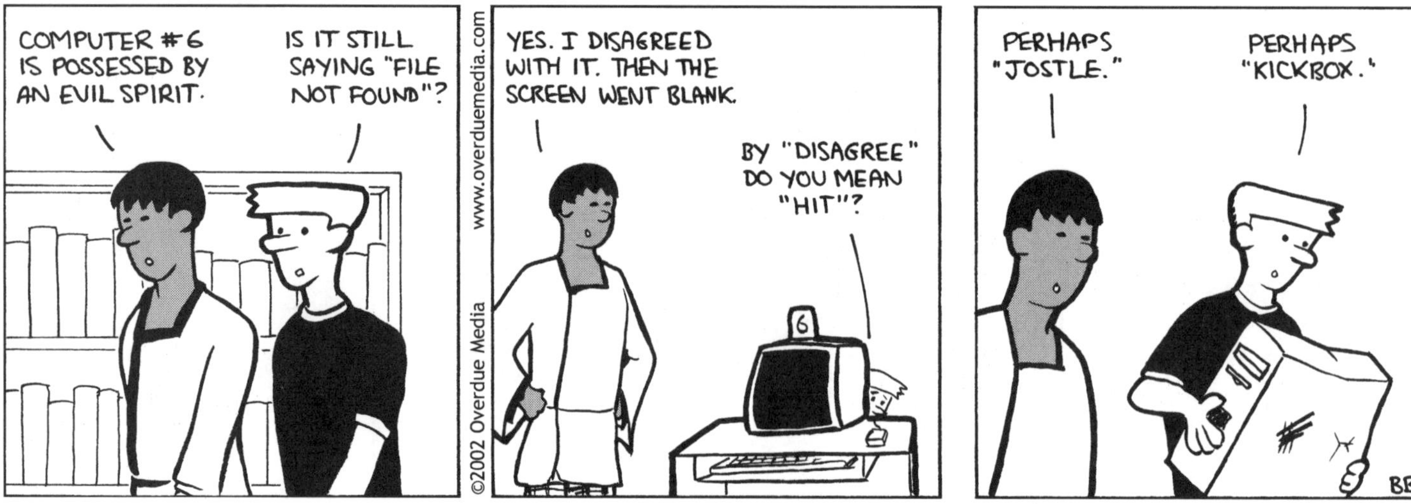
COMPUTER #6 IS POSSESSED BY AN EVIL SPIRIT.
IS IT STILL SAYING "FILE NOT FOUND"?
www.overduemedia.com ©2002 Overdue Media
YES. I DISAGREED WITH IT. THEN THE SCREEN WENT BLANK.
BY "DISAGREE" DO YOU MEAN "HIT"?
6
PERHAPS "JOSTLE."
PERHAPS "KICKBOX."
BB

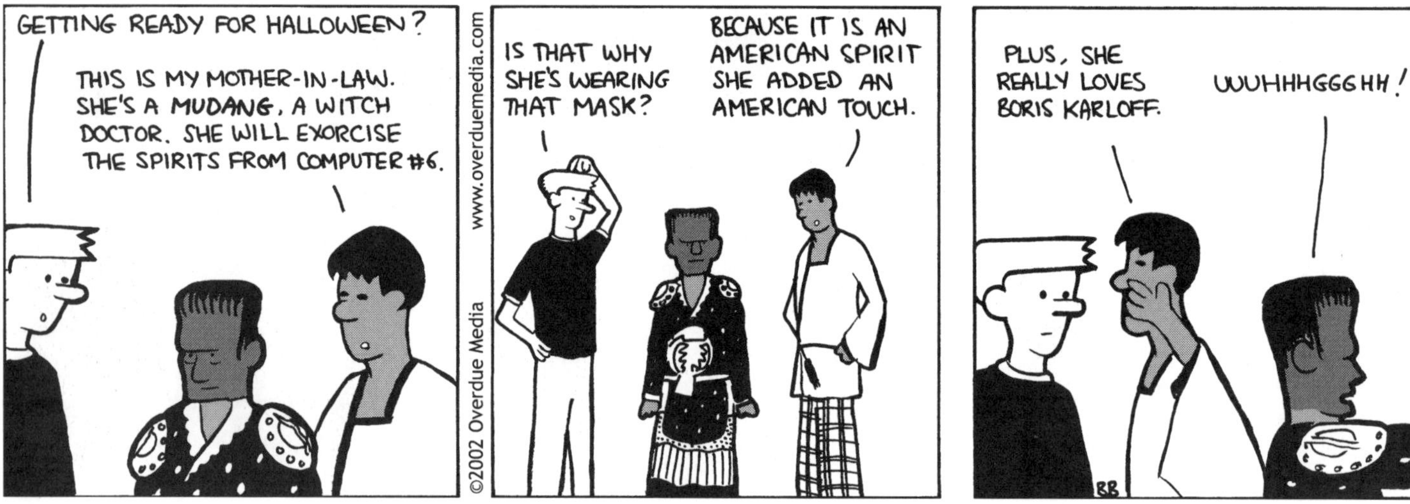
GETTING READY FOR HALLOWEEN?
THIS IS MY MOTHER-IN-LAW. SHE'S A MUDANG, A WITCH DOCTOR. SHE WILL EXORCISE THE SPIRITS FROM COMPUTER #6.
www.overduemedia.com ©2002 Overdue Media
IS THAT WHY SHE'S WEARING THAT MASK?
BECAUSE IT IS AN AMERICAN SPIRIT SHE ADDED AN AMERICAN TOUCH.
PLUS, SHE REALLY LOVES BORIS KARLOFF.
UUUHHHGGGHH!
BB

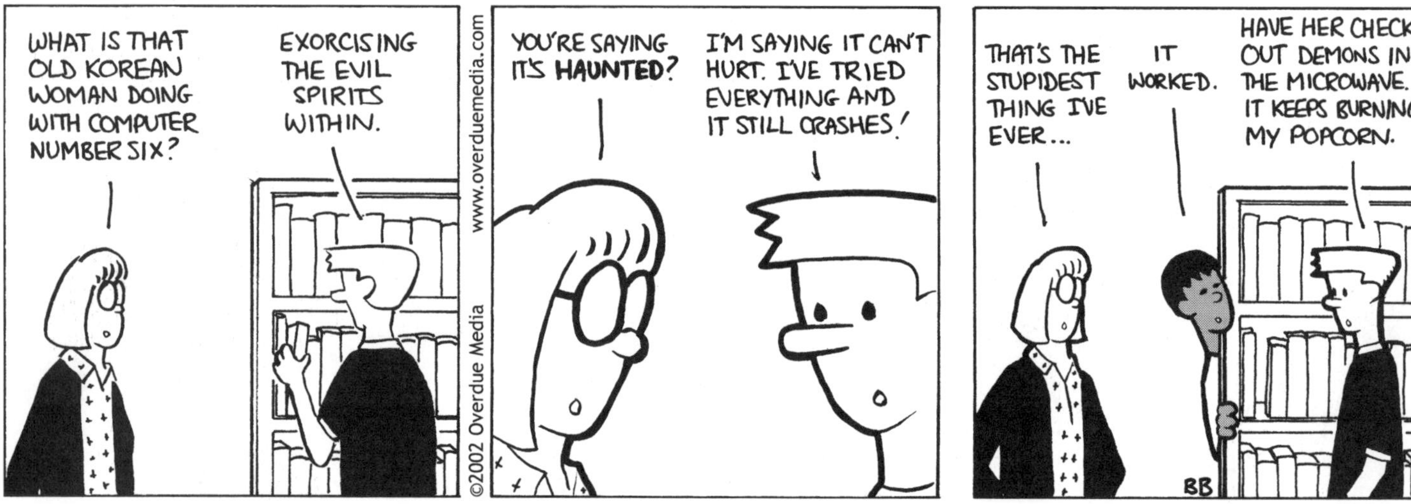
WHAT IS THAT OLD KOREAN WOMAN DOING WITH COMPUTER NUMBER SIX?
EXORCISING THE EVIL SPIRITS WITHIN.
www.overduemedia.com ©2002 Overdue Media
YOU'RE SAYING IT'S HAUNTED?
I'M SAYING IT CAN'T HURT. I'VE TRIED EVERYTHING AND IT STILL CRASHES!
THAT'S THE STUPIDEST THING I'VE EVER...
IT WORKED.
HAVE HER CHECK OUT DEMONS IN THE MICROWAVE. IT KEEPS BURNING MY POPCORN.
BB

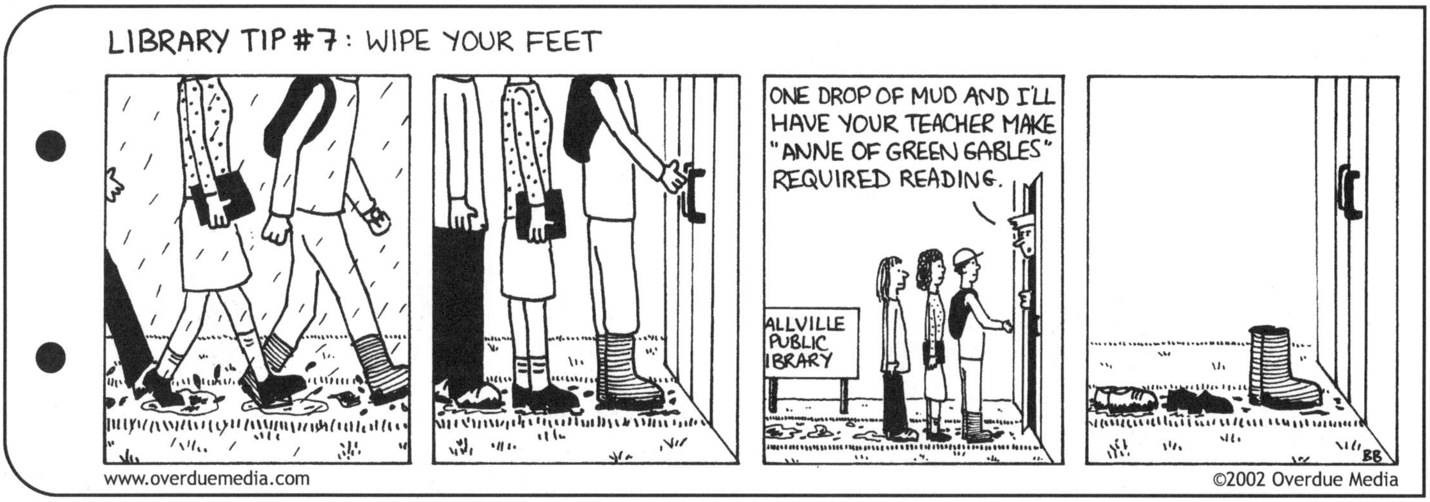
LIBRARY TIP #7: WIPE YOUR FEET
ONE DROP OF MUD AND I'LL HAVE YOUR TEACHER MAKE "ANNE OF GREEN GABLES" REQUIRED READING.
ALLVILLE PUBLIC LIBRARY
www.overduemedia.com
©2002 Overdue Media

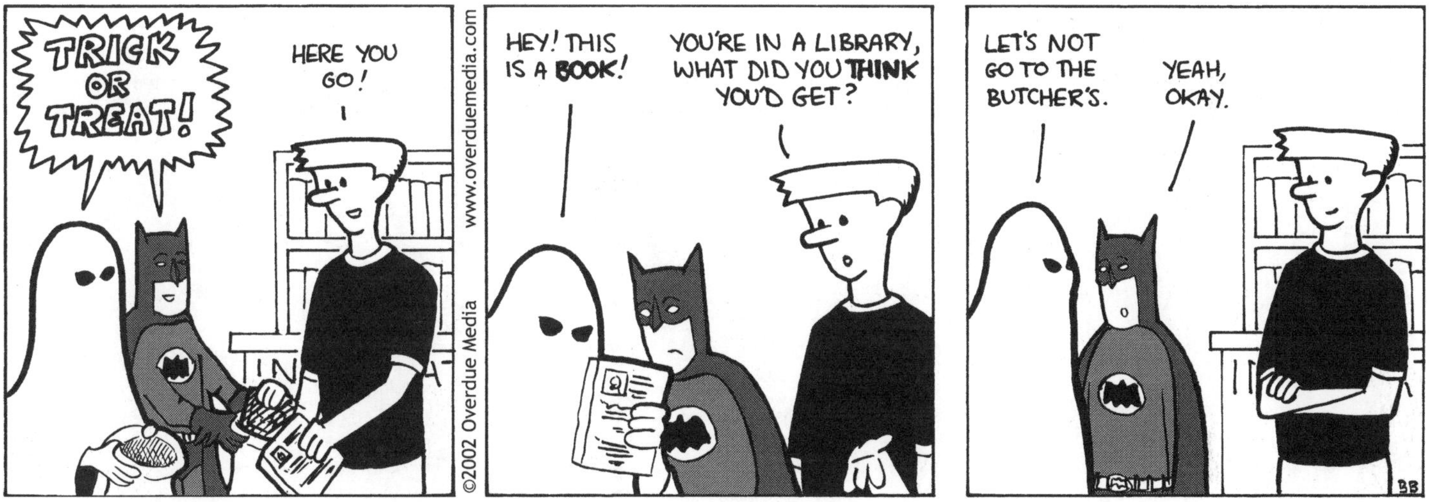
TRICK OR TREAT!
HERE YOU GO!
HEY! THIS IS A BOOK!
YOU'RE IN A LIBRARY, WHAT DID YOU THINK YOU'D GET?
LET'S NOT GO TO THE BUTCHER'S.
YEAH, OKAY.
www.overduemedia.com
©2002 Overdue Media

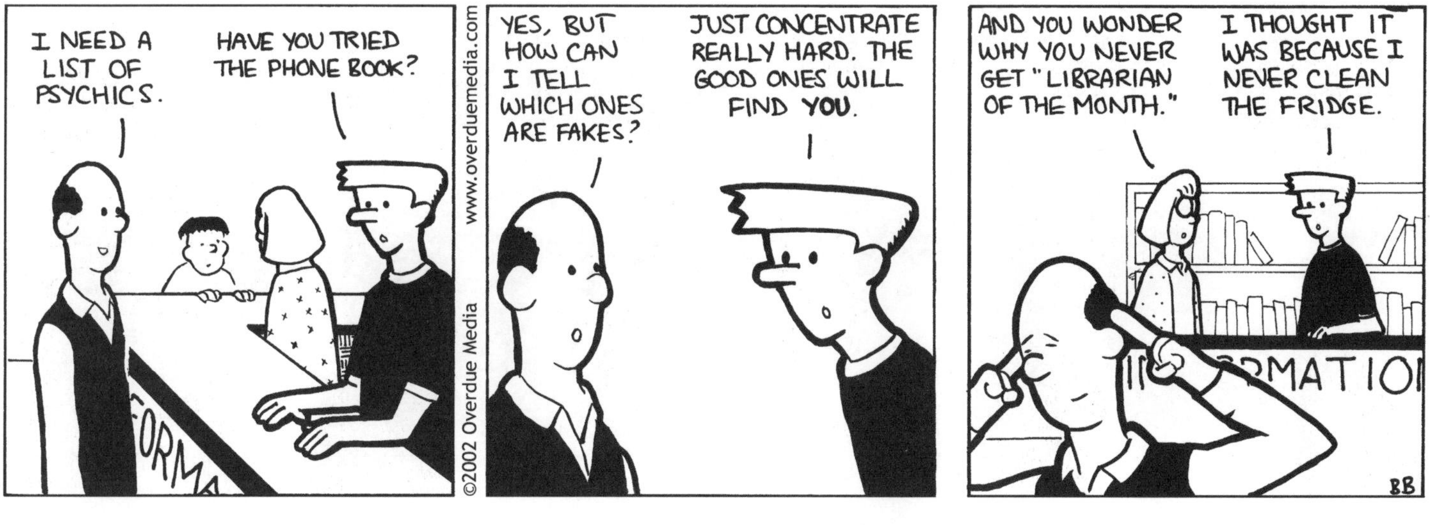
I NEED A LIST OF PSYCHICS.
HAVE YOU TRIED THE PHONE BOOK?
YES, BUT HOW CAN I TELL WHICH ONES ARE FAKES?
JUST CONCENTRATE REALLY HARD. THE GOOD ONES WILL FIND YOU.
AND YOU WONDER WHY YOU NEVER GET "LIBRARIAN OF THE MONTH."
I THOUGHT IT WAS BECAUSE I NEVER CLEAN THE FRIDGE.
www.overduemedia.com
©2002 Overdue Media

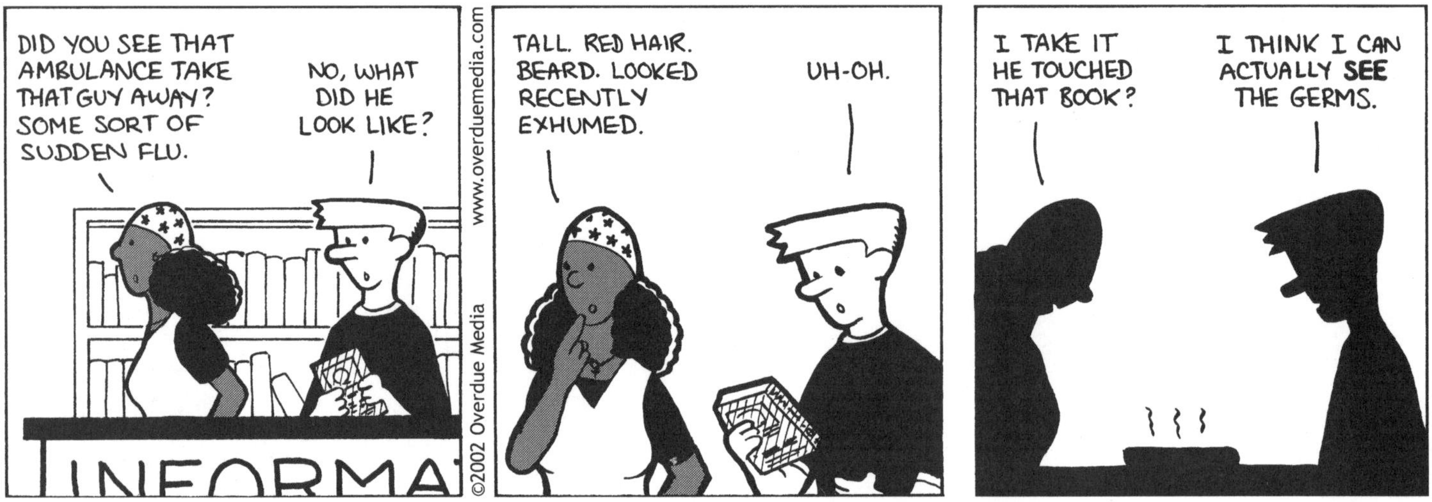
DID YOU SEE THAT AMBULANCE TAKE THAT GUY AWAY? SOME SORT OF SUDDEN FLU.
NO, WHAT DID HE LOOK LIKE?
INFORMA
www.overduemedia.com
©2002 Overdue Media
TALL. RED HAIR. BEARD. LOOKED RECENTLY EXHUMED.
UH-OH.
I TAKE IT HE TOUCHED THAT BOOK?
I THINK I CAN ACTUALLY SEE THE GERMS.

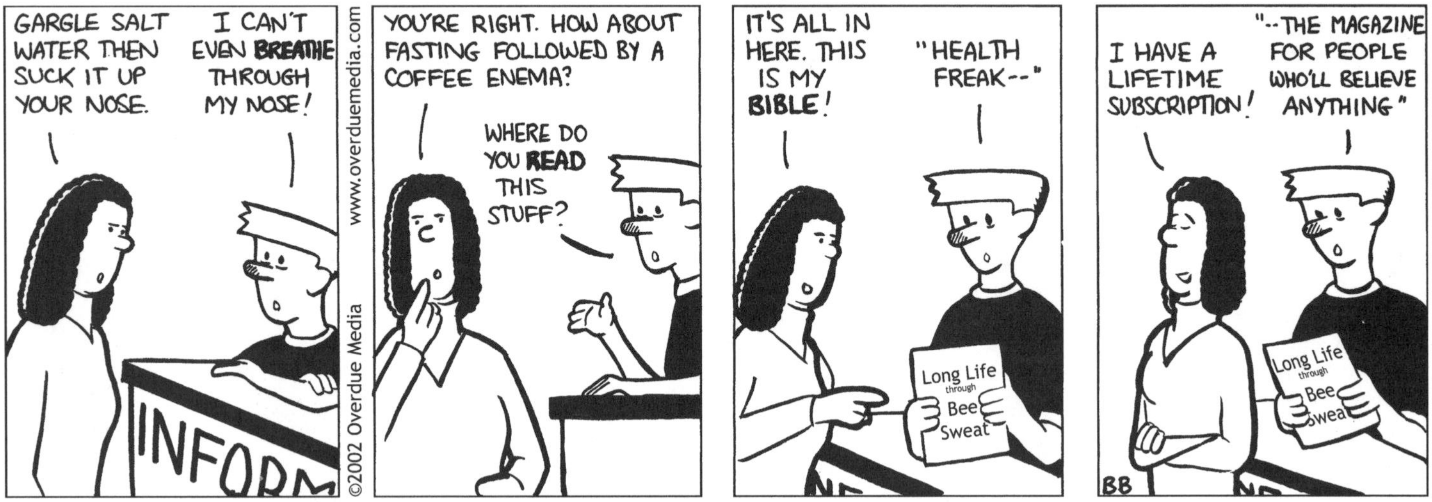
GARGLE SALT WATER THEN SUCK IT UP YOUR NOSE.
I CAN'T EVEN BREATHE THROUGH MY NOSE!
INFORM
www.overduemedia.com
©2002 Overdue Media
YOU'RE RIGHT. HOW ABOUT FASTING FOLLOWED BY A COFFEE ENEMA?
WHERE DO YOU READ THIS STUFF?
IT'S ALL IN HERE. THIS IS MY BIBLE!
"HEALTH FREAK--"
Long Life through Bee Sweat
I HAVE A LIFETIME SUBSCRIPTION!
"--THE MAGAZINE FOR PEOPLE WHO'LL BELIEVE ANYTHING"
Long Life through Bee Sweat
BB

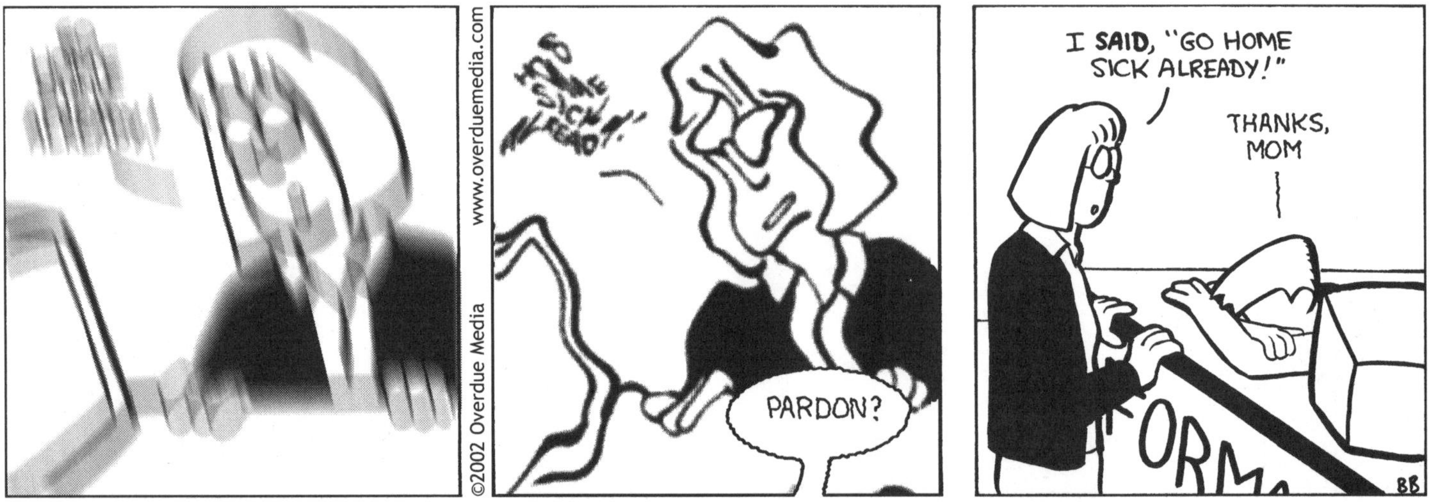
www.overduemedia.com
©2002 Overdue Media
PARDON?
I SAID, "GO HOME SICK ALREADY!"
THANKS, MOM
ORMA
BB

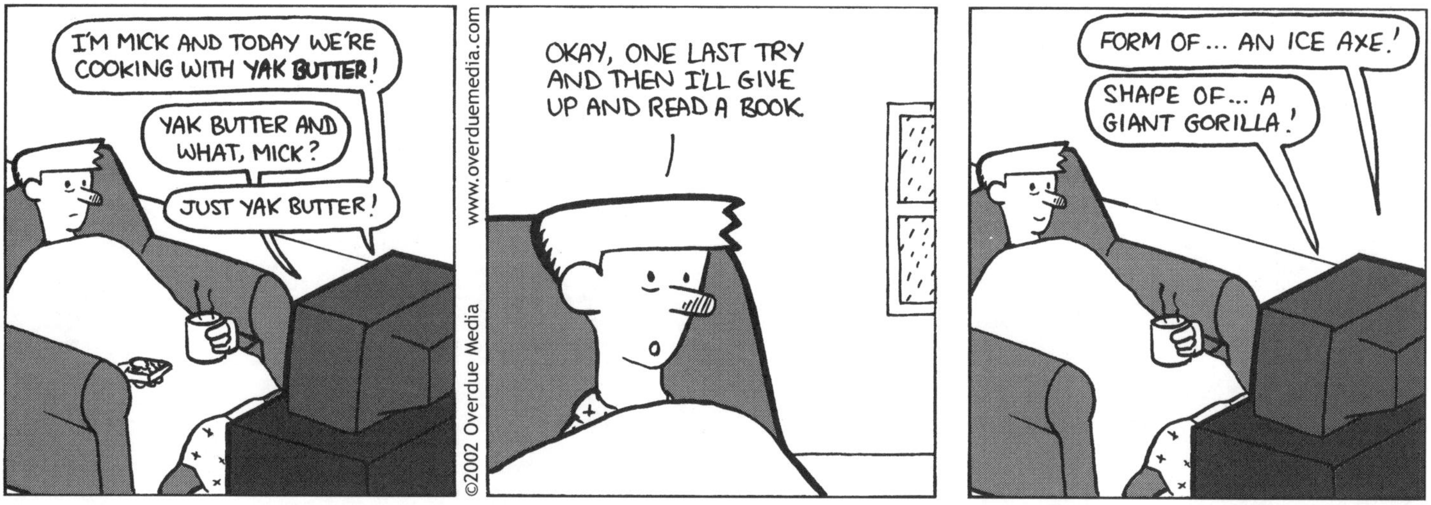
I'M MICK AND TODAY WE'RE COOKING WITH YAK BUTTER!
YAK BUTTER AND WHAT, MICK?
JUST YAK BUTTER!
©2002 Overdue Media www.overduemedia.com
OKAY, ONE LAST TRY AND THEN I'LL GIVE UP AND READ A BOOK.
FORM OF... AN ICE AXE!
SHAPE OF... A GIANT GORILLA!

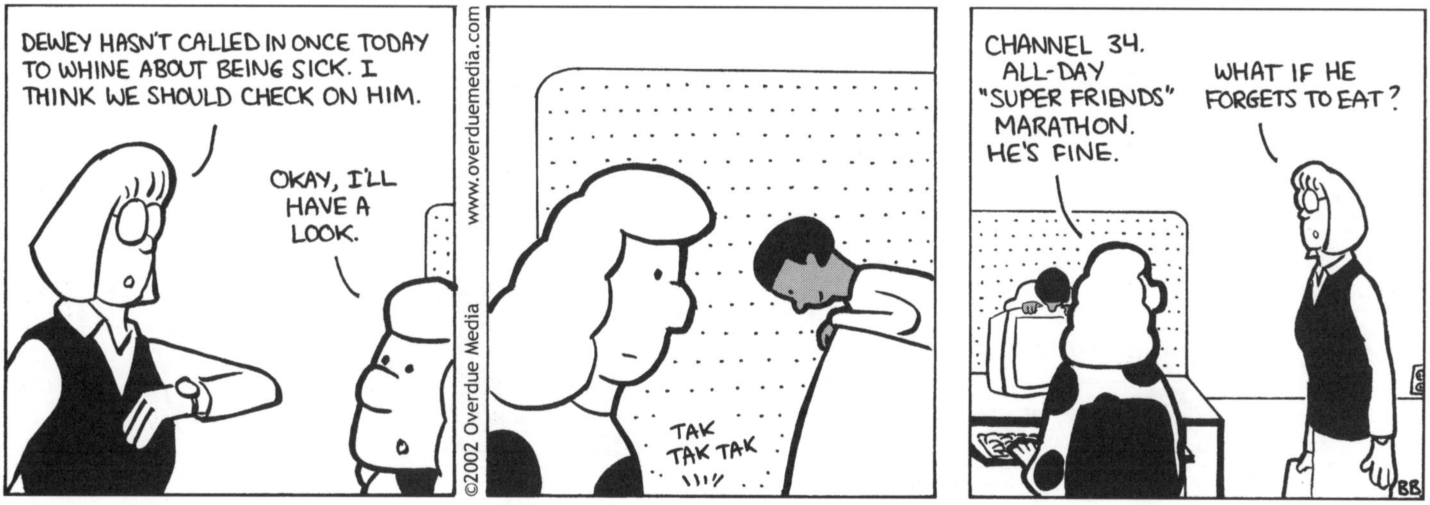
DEWEY HASN'T CALLED IN ONCE TODAY TO WHINE ABOUT BEING SICK. I THINK WE SHOULD CHECK ON HIM.
OKAY, I'LL HAVE A LOOK.
©2002 Overdue Media www.overduemedia.com
TAK TAK TAK
CHANNEL 34. ALL-DAY "SUPER FRIENDS" MARATHON. HE'S FINE.
WHAT IF HE FORGETS TO EAT?
BB

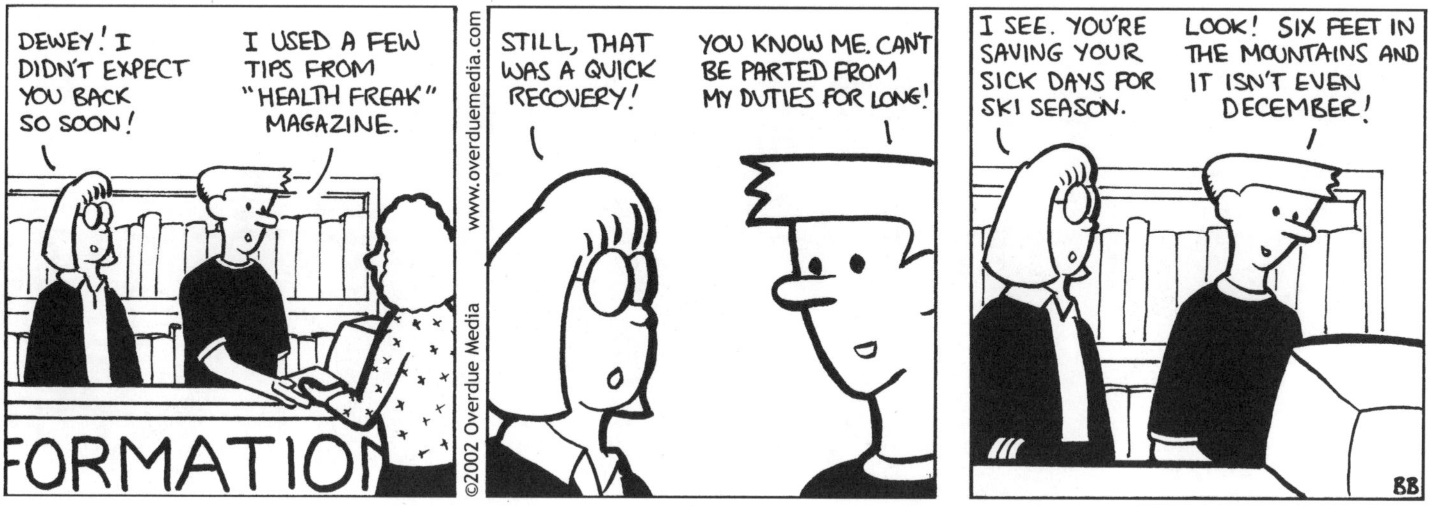
DEWEY! I DIDN'T EXPECT YOU BACK SO SOON!
I USED A FEW TIPS FROM "HEALTH FREAK" MAGAZINE.
FORMATIO
©2002 Overdue Media www.overduemedia.com
STILL, THAT WAS A QUICK RECOVERY!
YOU KNOW ME. CAN'T BE PARTED FROM MY DUTIES FOR LONG!
I SEE. YOU'RE SAVING YOUR SICK DAYS FOR SKI SEASON.
LOOK! SIX FEET IN THE MOUNTAINS AND IT ISN'T EVEN DECEMBER!
BB

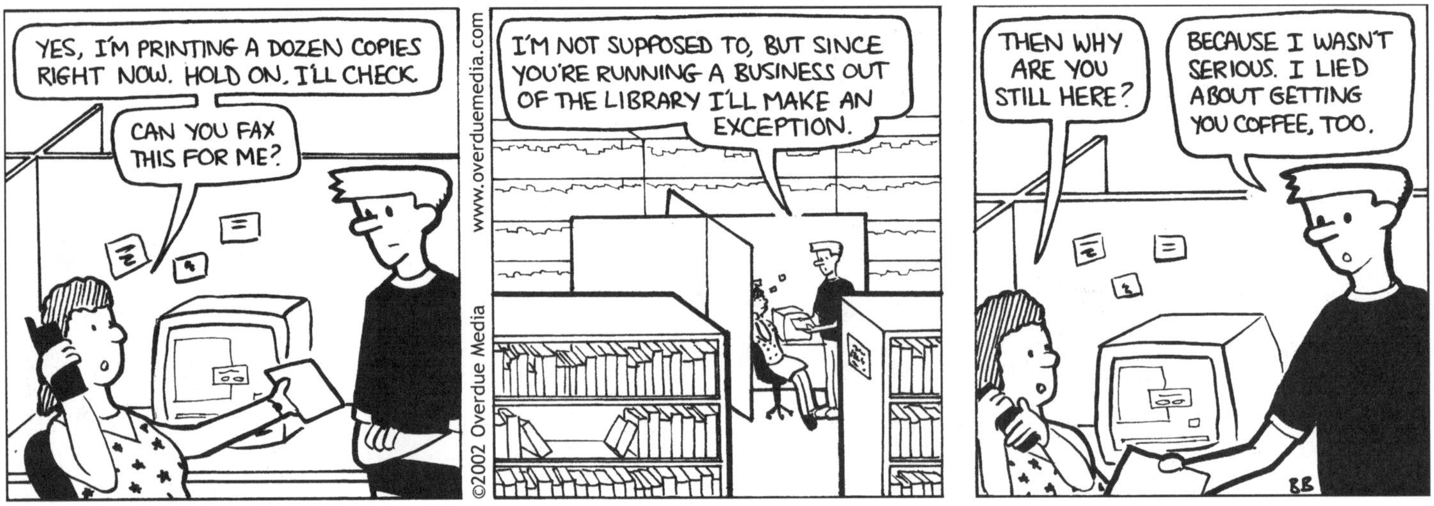
YES, I'M PRINTING A DOZEN COPIES RIGHT NOW. HOLD ON. I'LL CHECK.
CAN YOU FAX THIS FOR ME?
I'M NOT SUPPOSED TO, BUT SINCE YOU'RE RUNNING A BUSINESS OUT OF THE LIBRARY I'LL MAKE AN EXCEPTION.
THEN WHY ARE YOU STILL HERE?
BECAUSE I WASN'T SERIOUS. I LIED ABOUT GETTING YOU COFFEE, TOO.
www.overduemedia.com
©2002 Overdue Media
BB

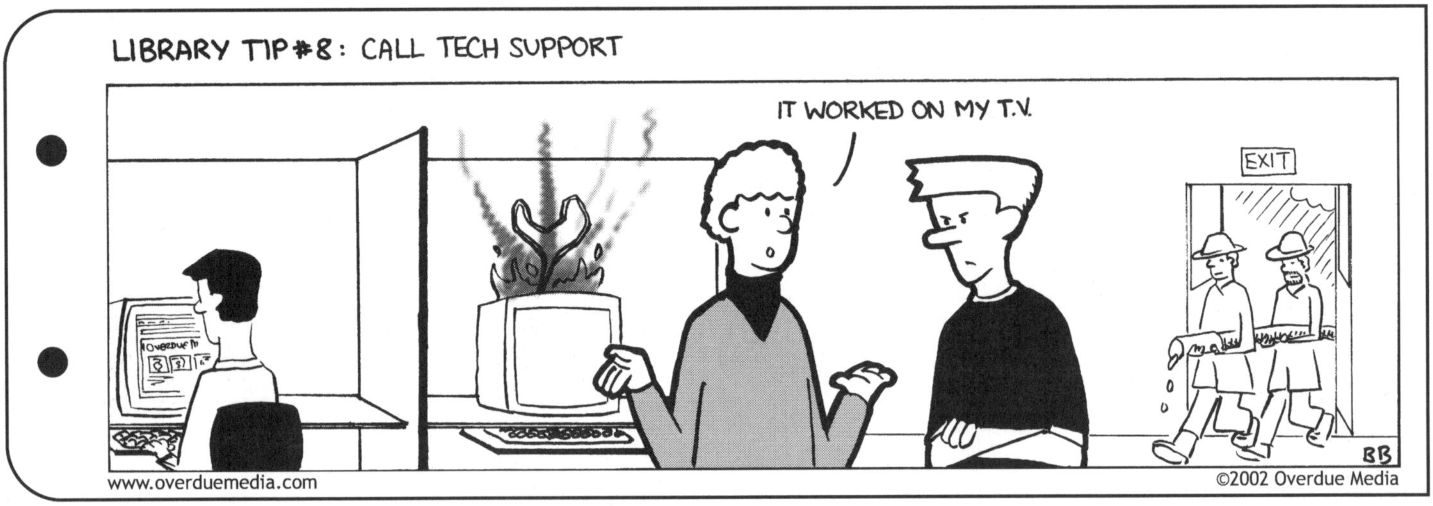
LIBRARY TIP #8: CALL TECH SUPPORT
IT WORKED ON MY T.V.
EXIT
BB
www.overduemedia.com
©2002 Overdue Media

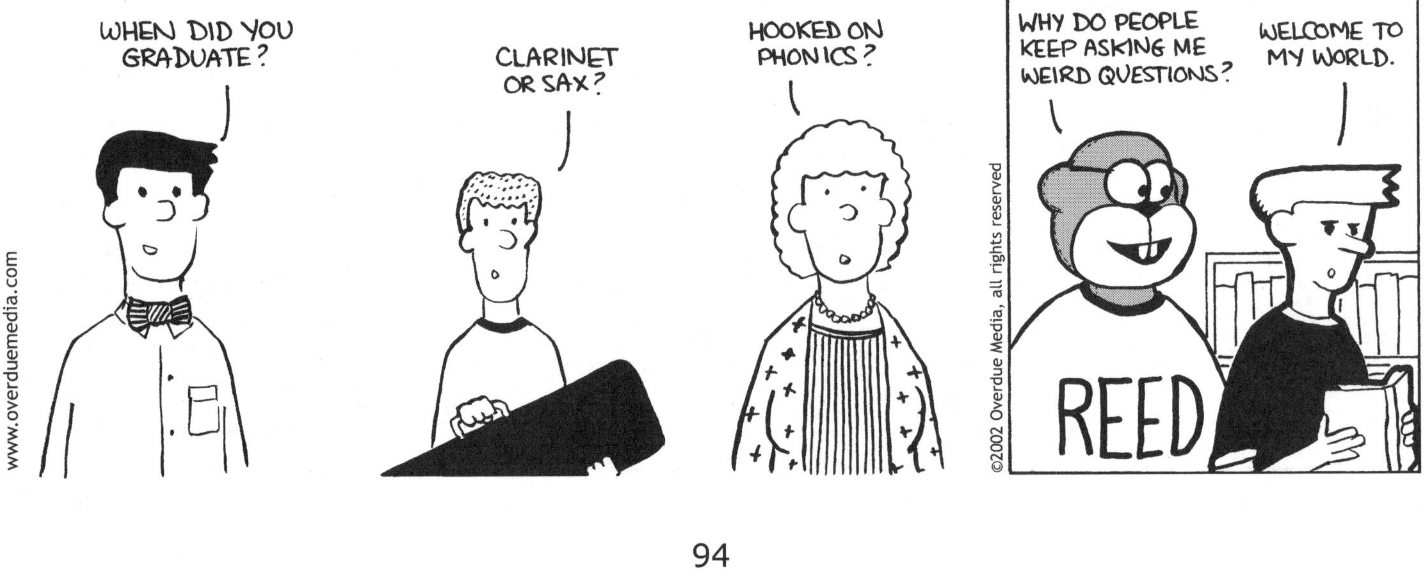
WHEN DID YOU GRADUATE?
CLARINET OR SAX?
HOOKED ON PHONICS?
WHY DO PEOPLE KEEP ASKING ME WEIRD QUESTIONS?
WELCOME TO MY WORLD.
REED
www.overduemedia.com
©2002 Overdue Media, all rights reserved

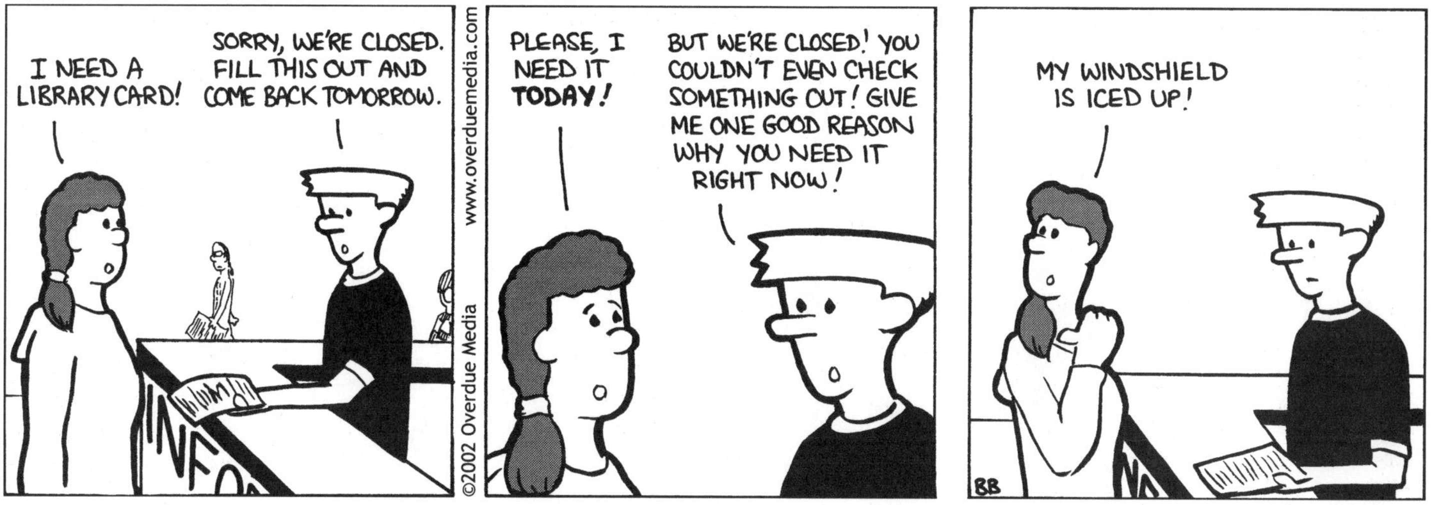
I NEED A LIBRARY CARD!
SORRY, WE'RE CLOSED. FILL THIS OUT AND COME BACK TOMORROW.
www.overduemedia.com
©2002 Overdue Media
PLEASE, I NEED IT TODAY!
BUT WE'RE CLOSED! YOU COULDN'T EVEN CHECK SOMETHING OUT! GIVE ME ONE GOOD REASON WHY YOU NEED IT RIGHT NOW!
MY WINDSHIELD IS ICED UP!
BB

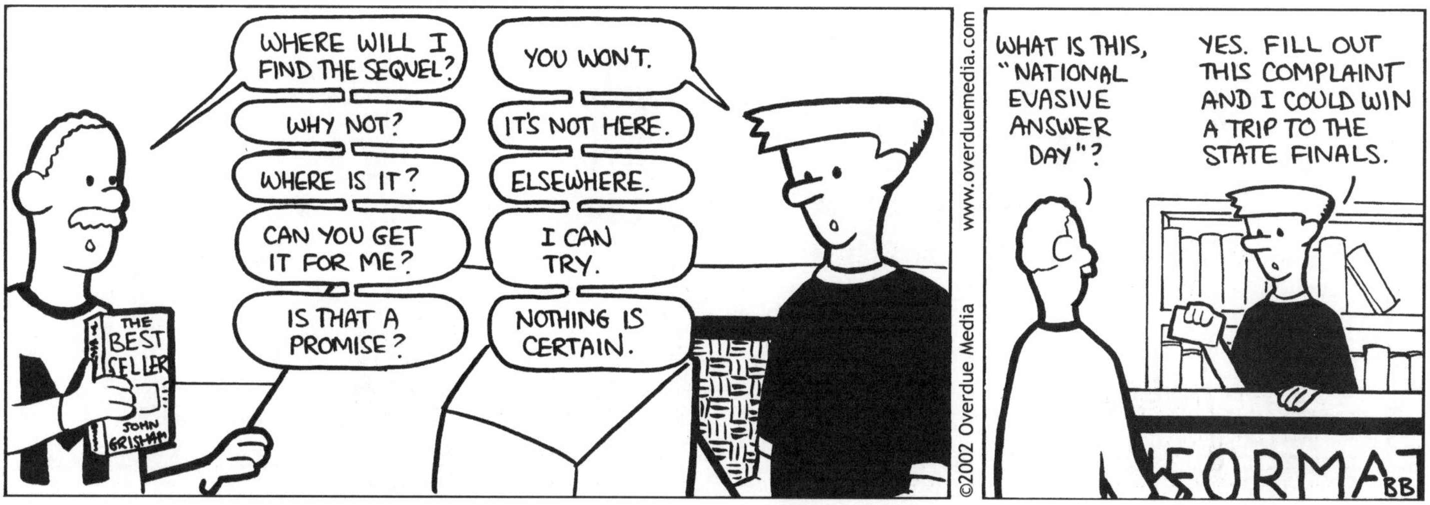
WHERE WILL I FIND THE SEQUEL?
YOU WON'T.
WHY NOT?
IT'S NOT HERE.
WHERE IS IT?
ELSEWHERE.
CAN YOU GET IT FOR ME?
I CAN TRY.
IS THAT A PROMISE?
NOTHING IS CERTAIN.
THE BEST SELLER
JOHN GRISHAM
www.overduemedia.com
©2002 Overdue Media
WHAT IS THIS, "NATIONAL EVASIVE ANSWER DAY"?
YES. FILL OUT THIS COMPLAINT AND I COULD WIN A TRIP TO THE STATE FINALS.
FORMAT
BB

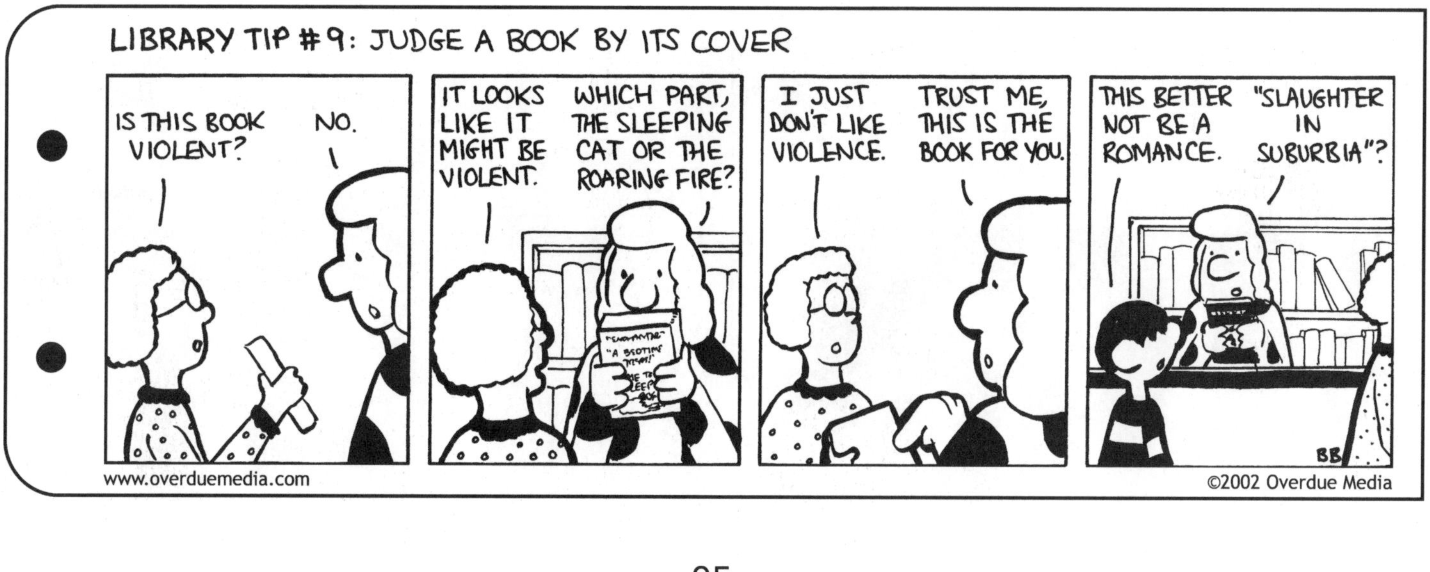
LIBRARY TIP #9: JUDGE A BOOK BY ITS COVER
IS THIS BOOK VIOLENT?
NO.
IT LOOKS LIKE IT MIGHT BE VIOLENT.
WHICH PART, THE SLEEPING CAT OR THE ROARING FIRE?
I JUST DON'T LIKE VIOLENCE.
TRUST ME, THIS IS THE BOOK FOR YOU.
THIS BETTER NOT BE A ROMANCE.
"SLAUGHTER IN SUBURBIA"?
BB
www.overduemedia.com
©2002 Overdue Media

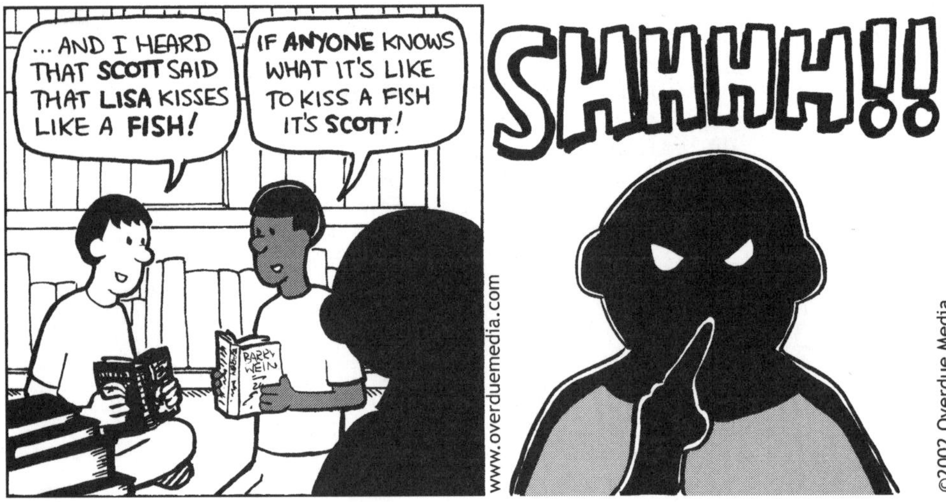

...AND I HEARD THAT **SCOTT** SAID THAT **LISA** KISSES LIKE A **FISH**!
IF **ANYONE** KNOWS WHAT IT'S LIKE TO KISS A FISH IT'S **SCOTT**!
www.overduemedia.com
SHHHH!!
©2002 Overdue Media
WHO **WAS** THAT MASKED MAN?
AND WHY DID HE JUST SPIT ALL OVER US?
BB

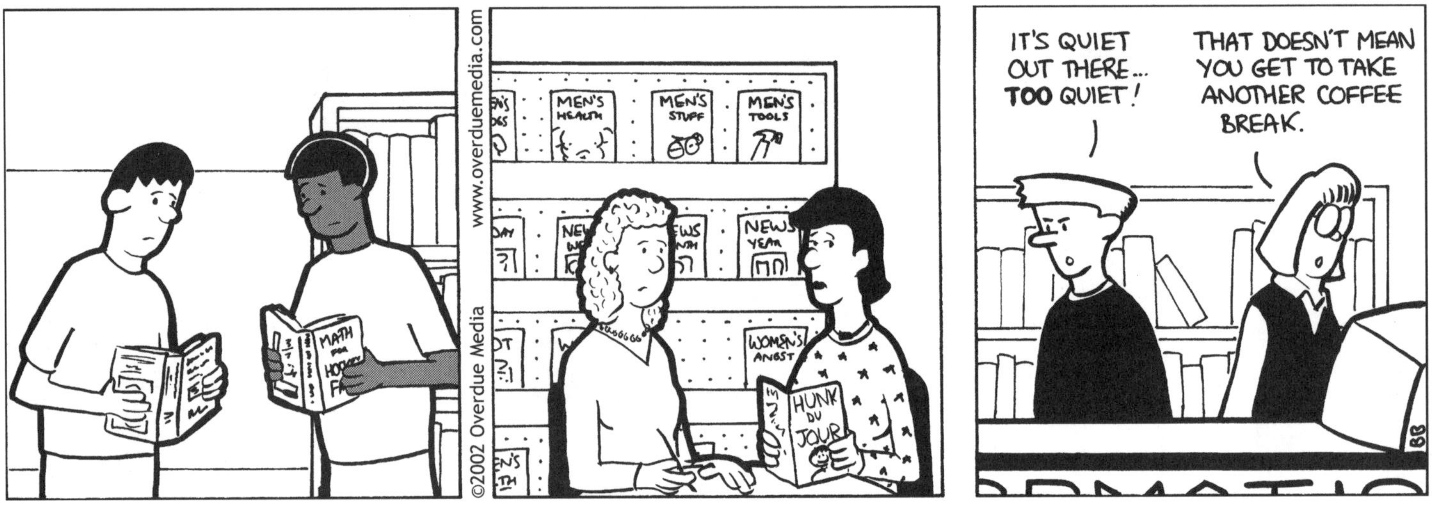

www.overduemedia.com
©2002 Overdue Media
MEN'S HEALTH
MEN'S STUFF
MEN'S TOOLS
NEWS YEAR
WOMEN'S ANGST
HUNK DU JOUR
IT'S QUIET OUT THERE... **TOO** QUIET!
THAT DOESN'T MEAN YOU GET TO TAKE ANOTHER COFFEE BREAK.
BB

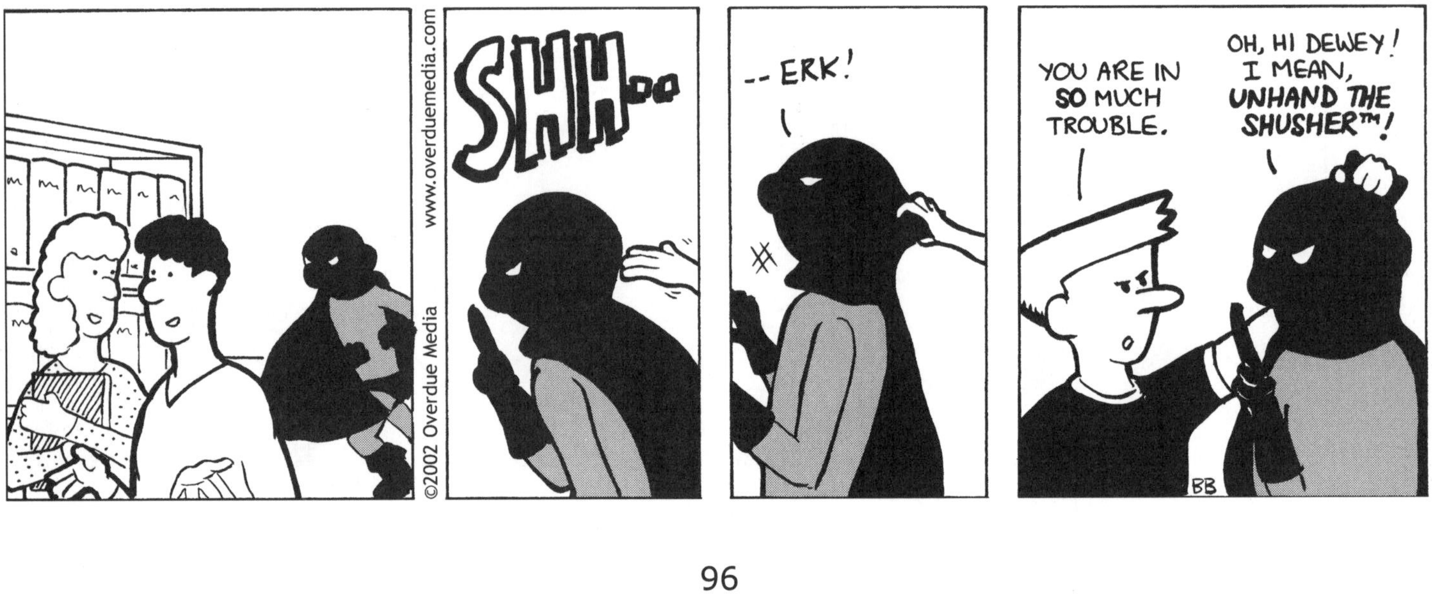

www.overduemedia.com
©2002 Overdue Media
SHH..
-- ERK!
YOU ARE IN **SO** MUCH TROUBLE.
OH, HI DEWEY! I MEAN, **UNHAND THE SHUSHER™**!
BB

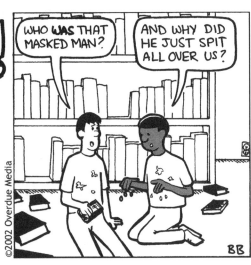

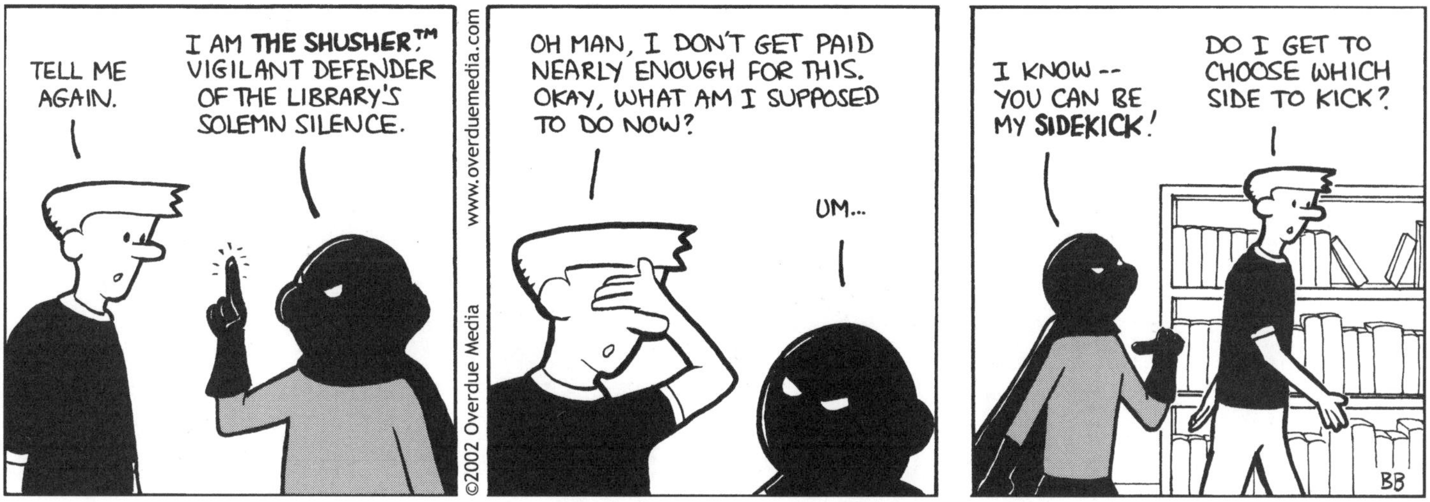
TELL ME AGAIN.
I AM THE SHUSHER™ VIGILANT DEFENDER OF THE LIBRARY'S SOLEMN SILENCE.
www.overduemedia.com
©2002 Overdue Media
OH MAN, I DON'T GET PAID NEARLY ENOUGH FOR THIS. OKAY, WHAT AM I SUPPOSED TO DO NOW?
UM...
I KNOW -- YOU CAN BE MY SIDEKICK!
DO I GET TO CHOOSE WHICH SIDE TO KICK?
BB

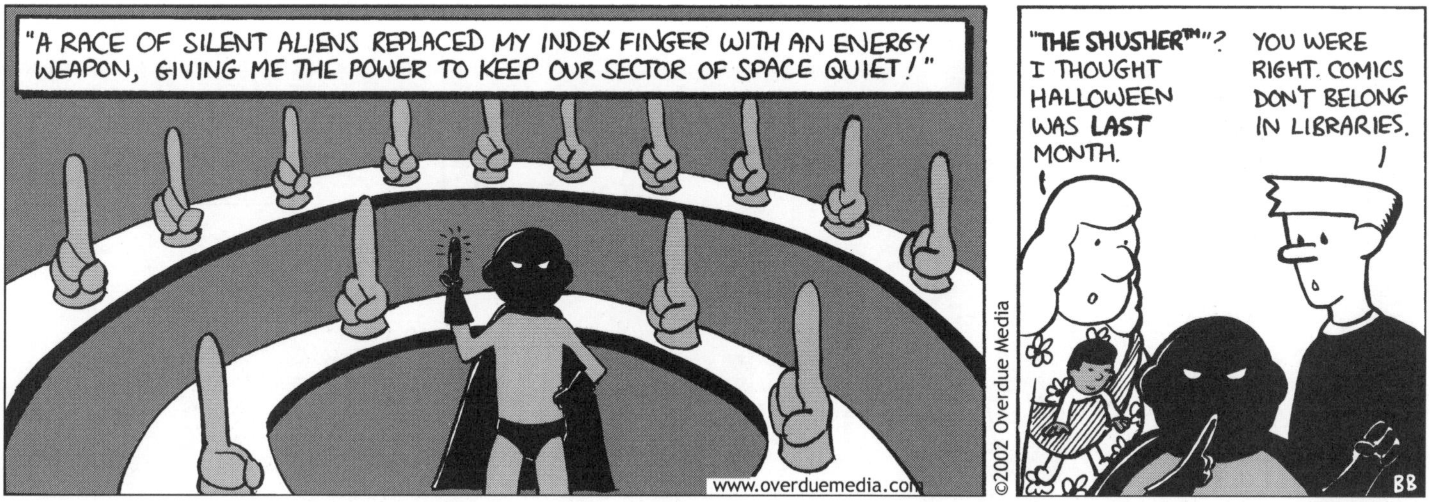
"A RACE OF SILENT ALIENS REPLACED MY INDEX FINGER WITH AN ENERGY WEAPON, GIVING ME THE POWER TO KEEP OUR SECTOR OF SPACE QUIET!"
www.overduemedia.com
©2002 Overdue Media
"THE SHUSHER™"? I THOUGHT HALLOWEEN WAS LAST MONTH.
YOU WERE RIGHT. COMICS DON'T BELONG IN LIBRARIES.
BB

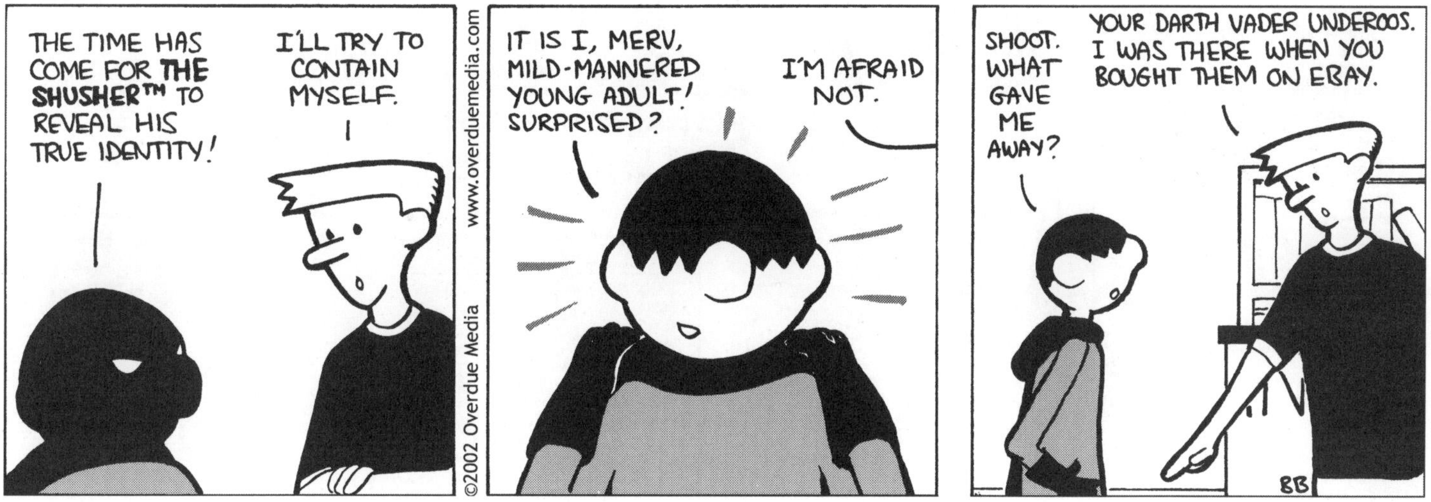
THE TIME HAS COME FOR THE SHUSHER™ TO REVEAL HIS TRUE IDENTITY!
I'LL TRY TO CONTAIN MYSELF.
www.overduemedia.com
©2002 Overdue Media
IT IS I, MERV, MILD-MANNERED YOUNG ADULT! SURPRISED?
I'M AFRAID NOT.
SHOOT. WHAT GAVE ME AWAY?
YOUR DARTH VADER UNDEROOS. I WAS THERE WHEN YOU BOUGHT THEM ON EBAY.
BB

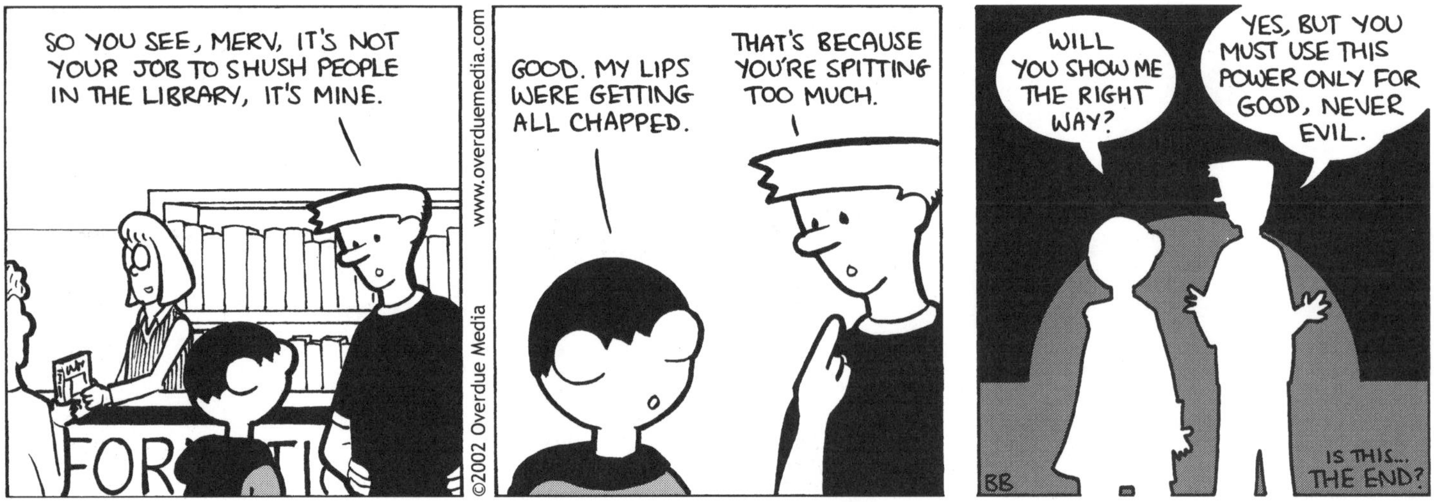
SO YOU SEE, MERV, IT'S NOT YOUR JOB TO SHUSH PEOPLE IN THE LIBRARY, IT'S MINE.
www.overduemedia.com
©2002 Overdue Media
GOOD. MY LIPS WERE GETTING ALL CHAPPED.
THAT'S BECAUSE YOU'RE SPITTING TOO MUCH.
WILL YOU SHOW ME THE RIGHT WAY?
YES, BUT YOU MUST USE THIS POWER ONLY FOR GOOD, NEVER EVIL.
BB
IS THIS... THE END?

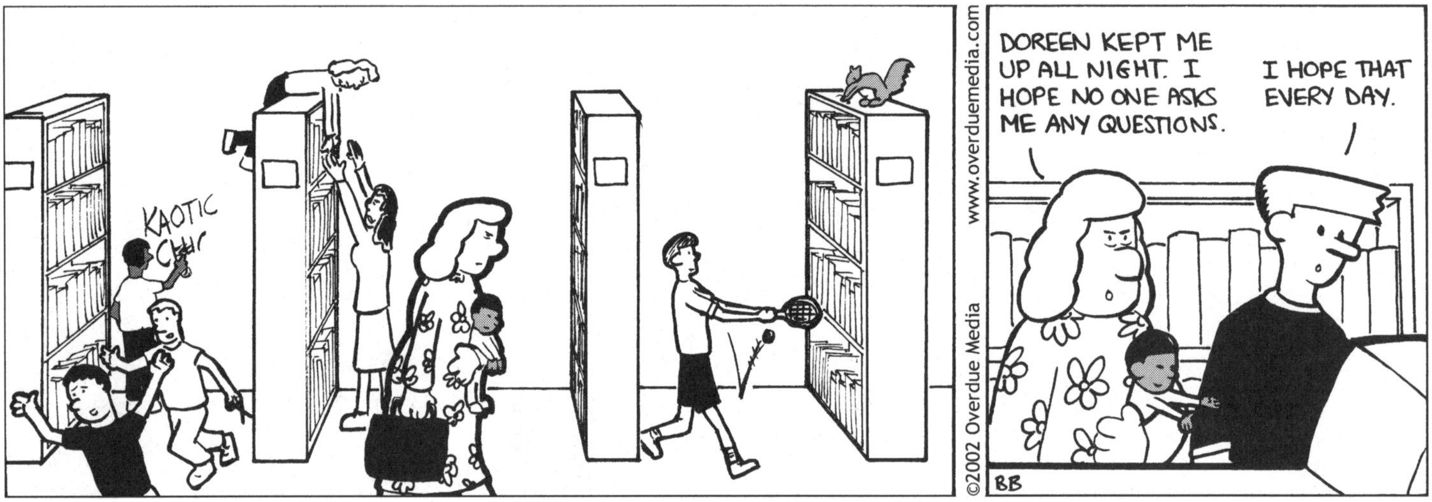
KAOTIC
www.overduemedia.com
©2002 Overdue Media
DOREEN KEPT ME UP ALL NIGHT. I HOPE NO ONE ASKS ME ANY QUESTIONS.
I HOPE THAT EVERY DAY.
BB

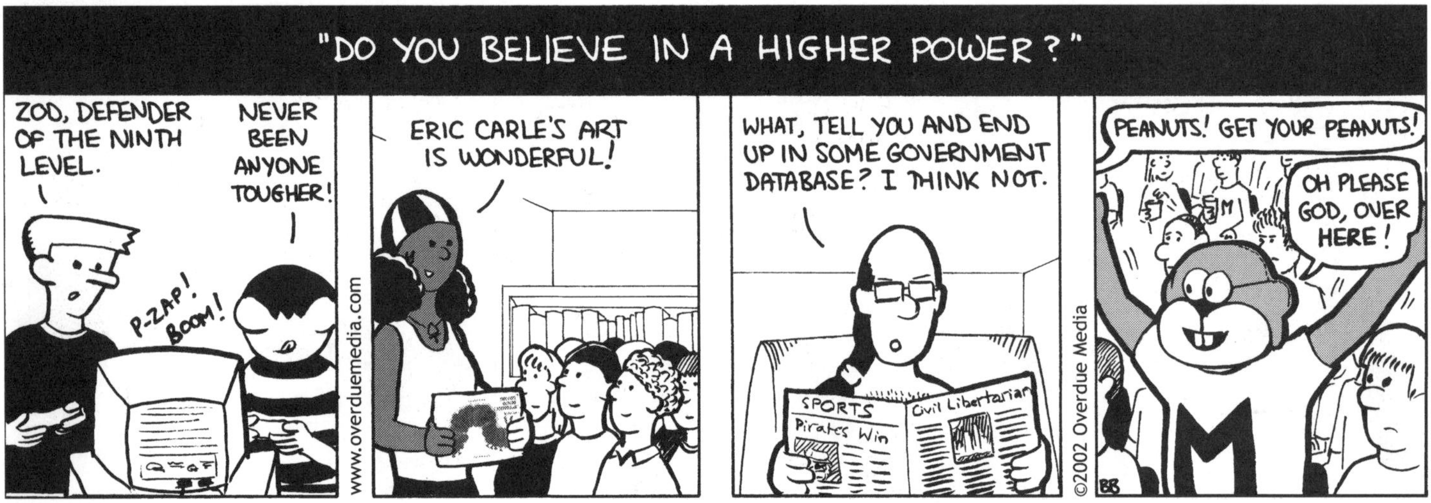
"DO YOU BELIEVE IN A HIGHER POWER?"
ZOD, DEFENDER OF THE NINTH LEVEL.
NEVER BEEN ANYONE TOUGHER!
P-ZAP! BOOM!
www.overduemedia.com
ERIC CARLE'S ART IS WONDERFUL!
WHAT, TELL YOU AND END UP IN SOME GOVERNMENT DATABASE? I THINK NOT.
SPORTS
Pirates Win
Civil Libertarian
©2002 Overdue Media
PEANUTS! GET YOUR PEANUTS!
OH PLEASE GOD, OVER HERE!
M
BB

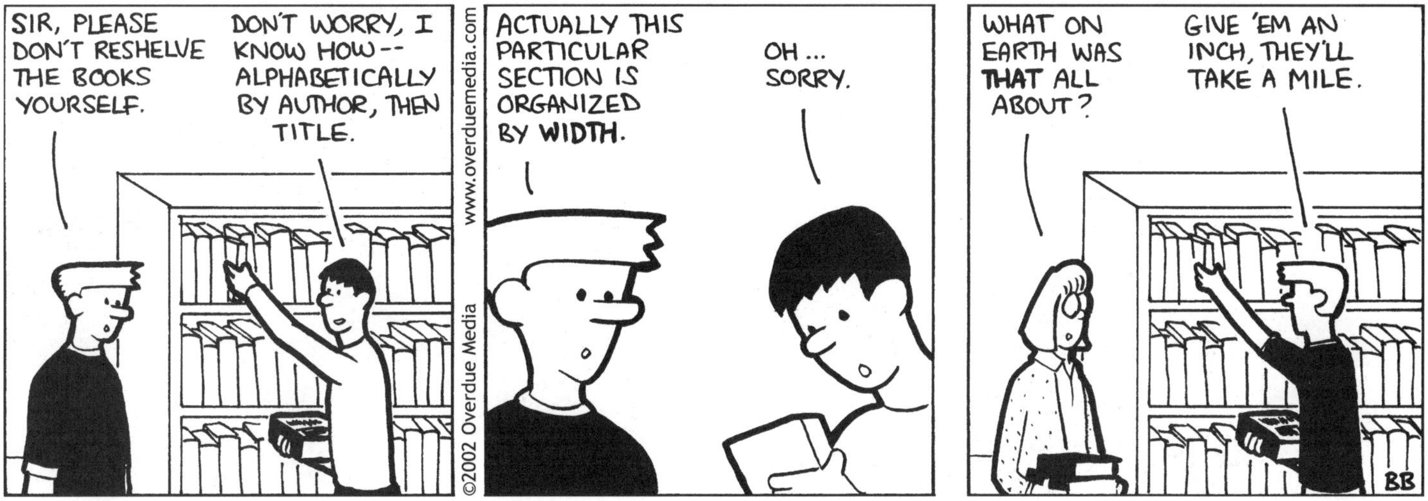
SIR, PLEASE DON'T RESHELVE THE BOOKS YOURSELF.
DON'T WORRY, I KNOW HOW-- ALPHABETICALLY BY AUTHOR, THEN TITLE.
ACTUALLY THIS PARTICULAR SECTION IS ORGANIZED BY WIDTH.
OH... SORRY.
WHAT ON EARTH WAS THAT ALL ABOUT?
GIVE 'EM AN INCH, THEY'LL TAKE A MILE.
©2002 Overdue Media www.overduemedia.com
BB

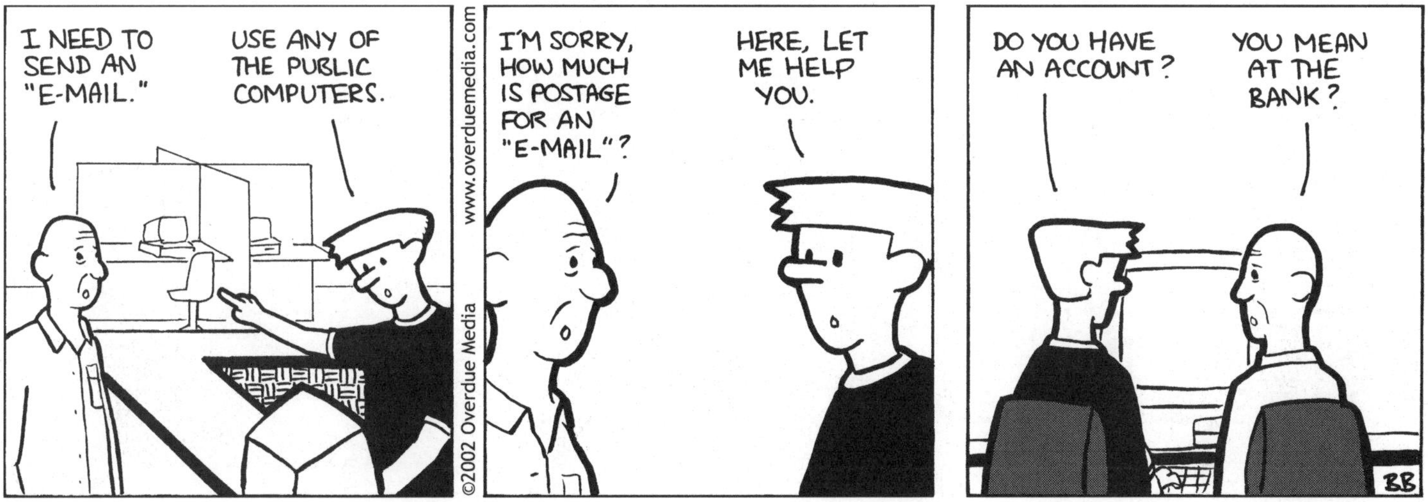
I NEED TO SEND AN "E-MAIL."
USE ANY OF THE PUBLIC COMPUTERS.
I'M SORRY, HOW MUCH IS POSTAGE FOR AN "E-MAIL"?
HERE, LET ME HELP YOU.
DO YOU HAVE AN ACCOUNT?
YOU MEAN AT THE BANK?
©2002 Overdue Media www.overduemedia.com
BB

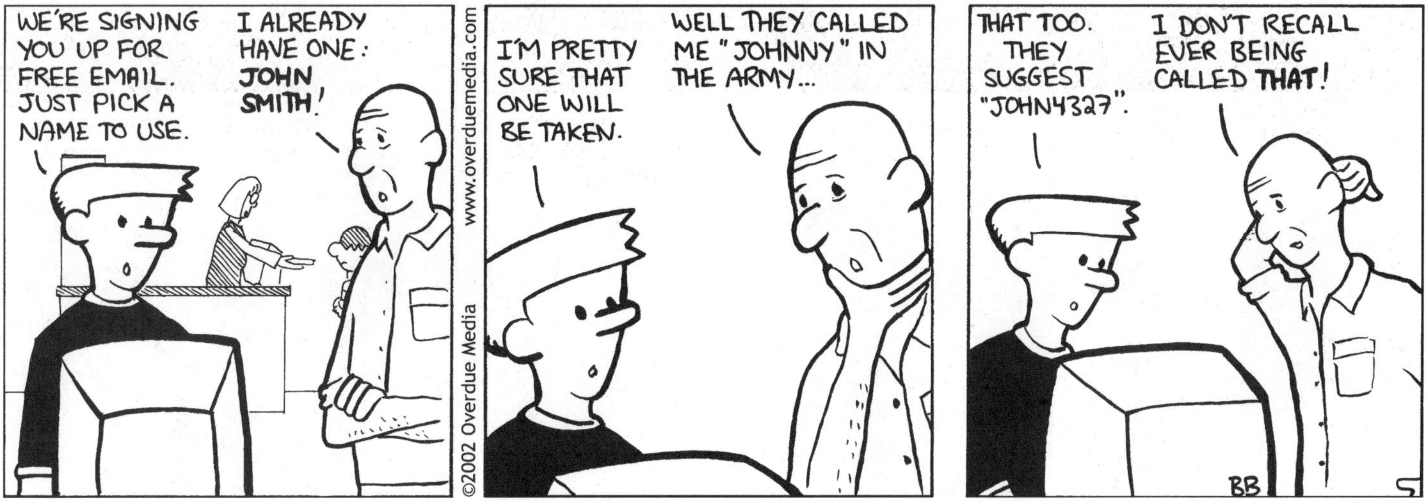
WE'RE SIGNING YOU UP FOR FREE EMAIL. JUST PICK A NAME TO USE.
I ALREADY HAVE ONE: JOHN SMITH!
I'M PRETTY SURE THAT ONE WILL BE TAKEN.
WELL THEY CALLED ME "JOHNNY" IN THE ARMY...
THAT TOO. THEY SUGGEST "JOHN4327".
I DON'T RECALL EVER BEING CALLED THAT!
©2002 Overdue Media www.overduemedia.com
BB

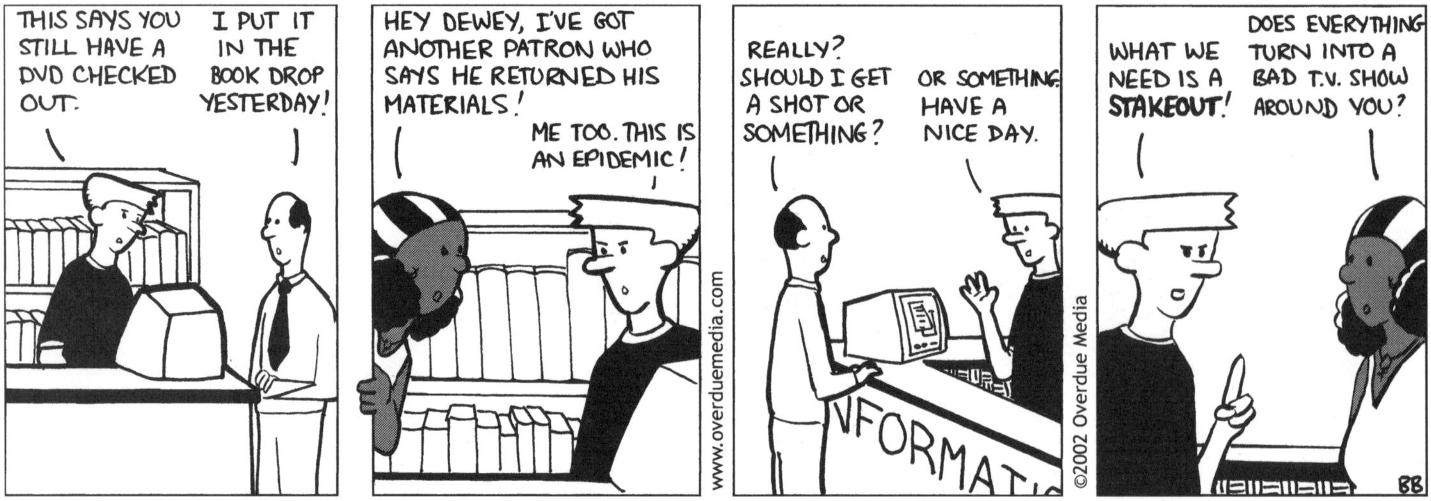
THIS SAYS YOU STILL HAVE A DVD CHECKED OUT.
I PUT IT IN THE BOOK DROP YESTERDAY!
HEY DEWEY, I'VE GOT ANOTHER PATRON WHO SAYS HE RETURNED HIS MATERIALS!
ME TOO. THIS IS AN EPIDEMIC!
www.overduemedia.com
REALLY? SHOULD I GET A SHOT OR SOMETHING?
OR SOMETHING. HAVE A NICE DAY.
NFORMATI
©2002 Overdue Media
WHAT WE NEED IS A **STAKEOUT**!
DOES EVERYTHING TURN INTO A BAD T.V. SHOW AROUND YOU?
BB

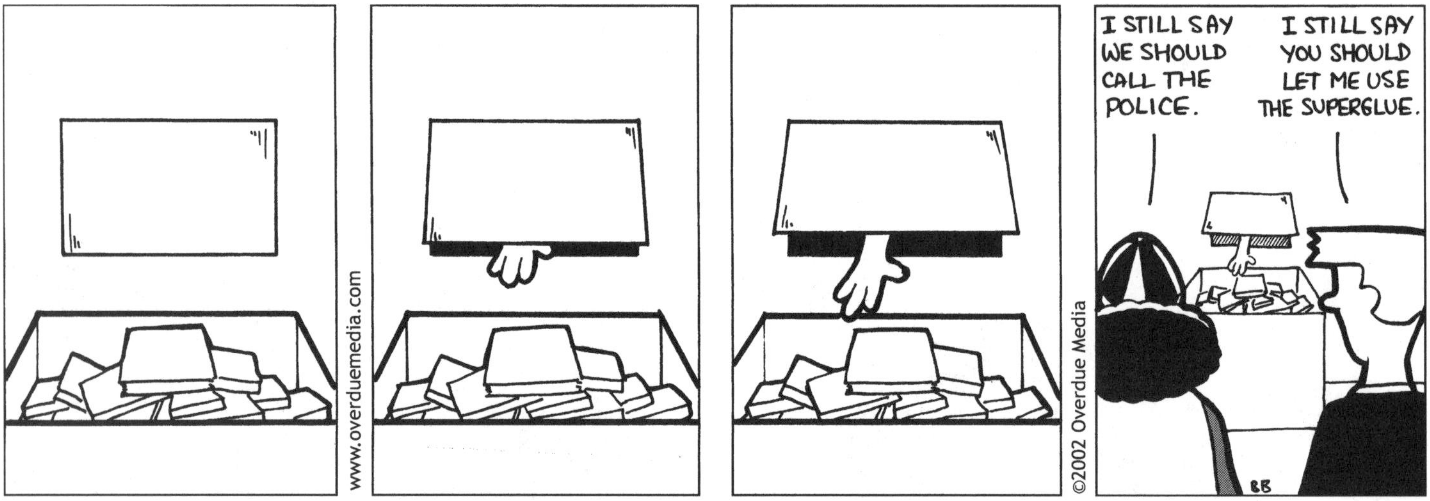
www.overduemedia.com
©2002 Overdue Media
I STILL SAY WE SHOULD CALL THE POLICE.
I STILL SAY YOU SHOULD LET ME USE THE SUPERGLUE.
BB

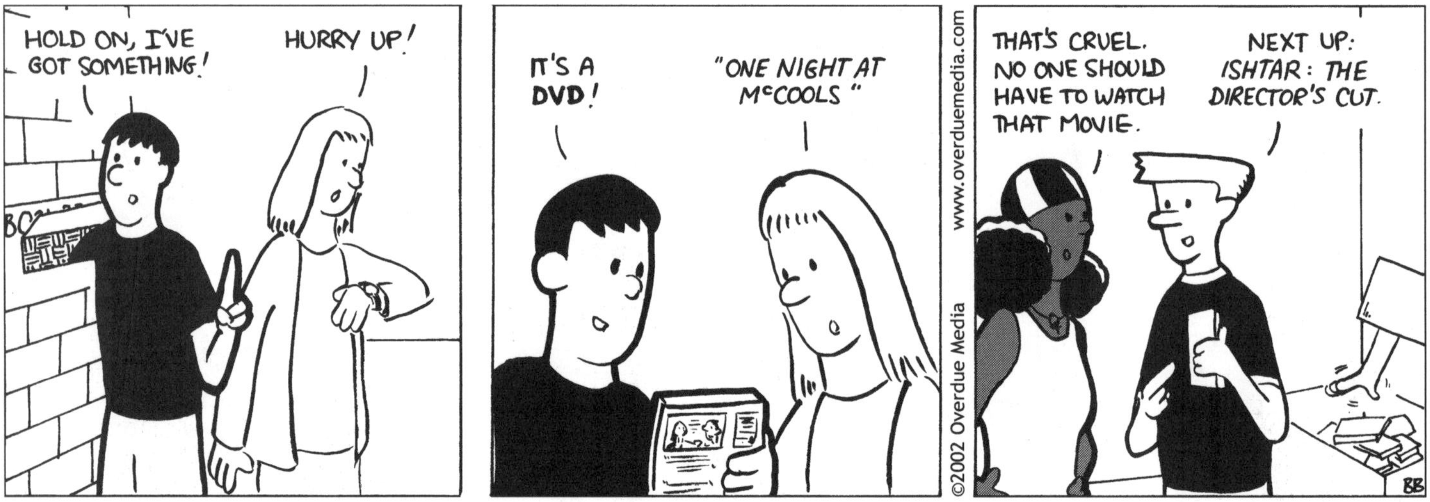
HOLD ON, I'VE GOT SOMETHING!
HURRY UP!
IT'S A **DVD**!
"ONE NIGHT AT McCOOLS"
www.overduemedia.com
©2002 Overdue Media
THAT'S CRUEL. NO ONE SHOULD HAVE TO WATCH THAT MOVIE.
NEXT UP: *ISHTAR: THE DIRECTOR'S CUT.*
BB

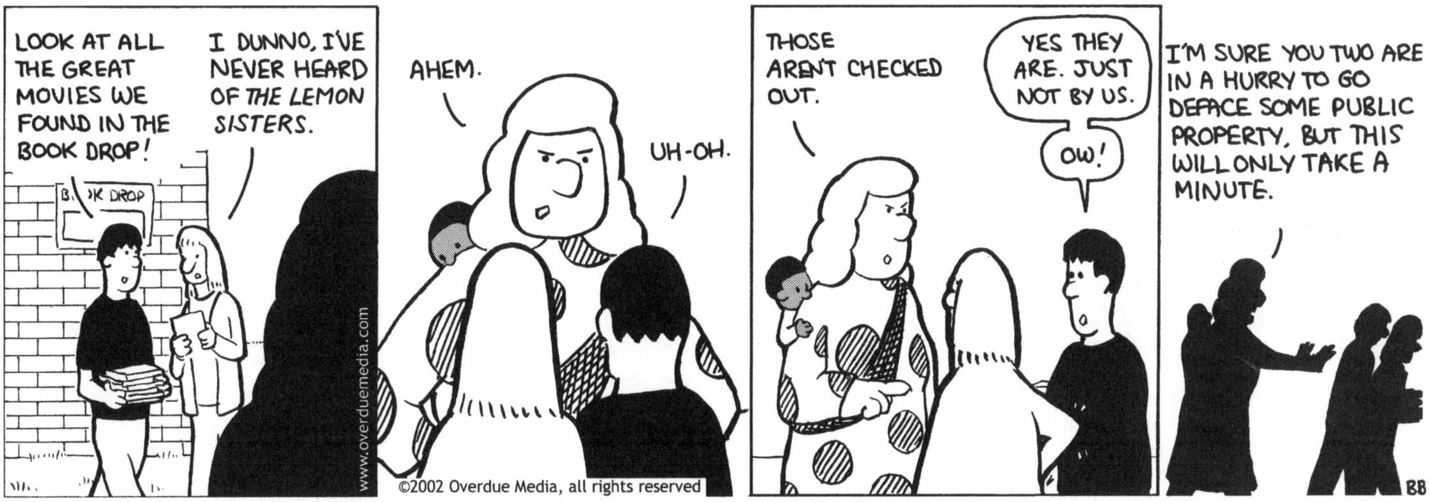
LOOK AT ALL THE GREAT MOVIES WE FOUND IN THE BOOK DROP!
I DUNNO, I'VE NEVER HEARD OF *THE LEMON SISTERS*.
www.overduemedia.com
AHEM.
UH-OH.
©2002 Overdue Media, all rights reserved
THOSE AREN'T CHECKED OUT.
YES THEY ARE. JUST NOT BY US.
OW!
I'M SURE YOU TWO ARE IN A HURRY TO GO DEFACE SOME PUBLIC PROPERTY, BUT THIS WILL ONLY TAKE A MINUTE.
BB

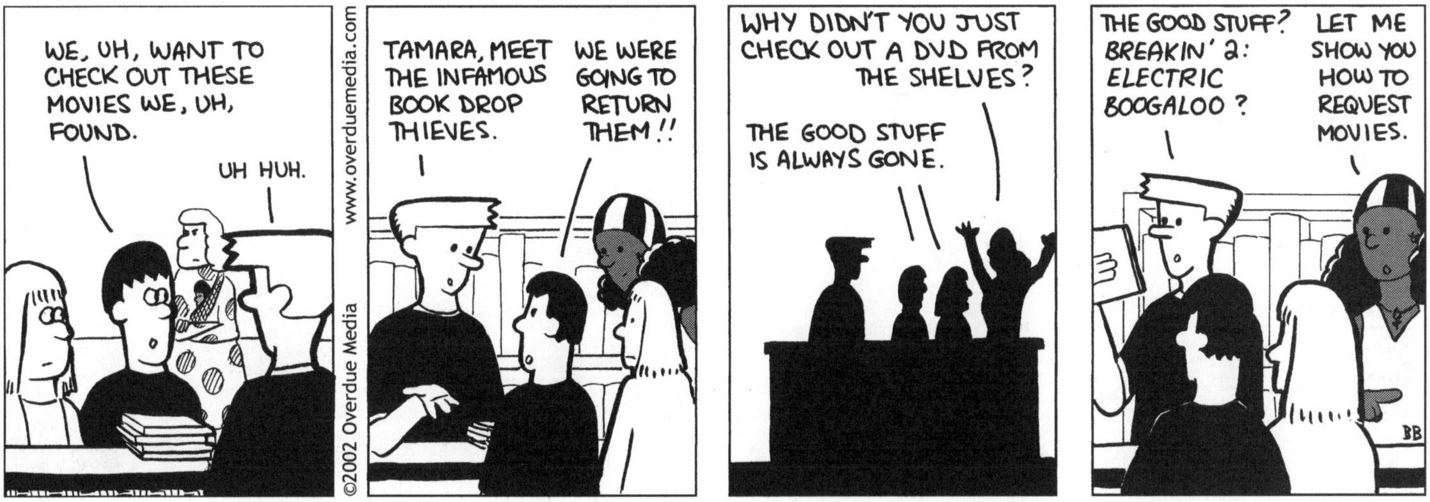
WE, UH, WANT TO CHECK OUT THESE MOVIES WE, UH, FOUND.
UH HUH.
www.overduemedia.com
©2002 Overdue Media
TAMARA, MEET THE INFAMOUS BOOK DROP THIEVES.
WE WERE GOING TO RETURN THEM!!
WHY DIDN'T YOU JUST CHECK OUT A DVD FROM THE SHELVES?
THE GOOD STUFF IS ALWAYS GONE.
THE GOOD STUFF? *BREAKIN' 2: ELECTRIC BOOGALOO*?
LET ME SHOW YOU HOW TO REQUEST MOVIES.
BB

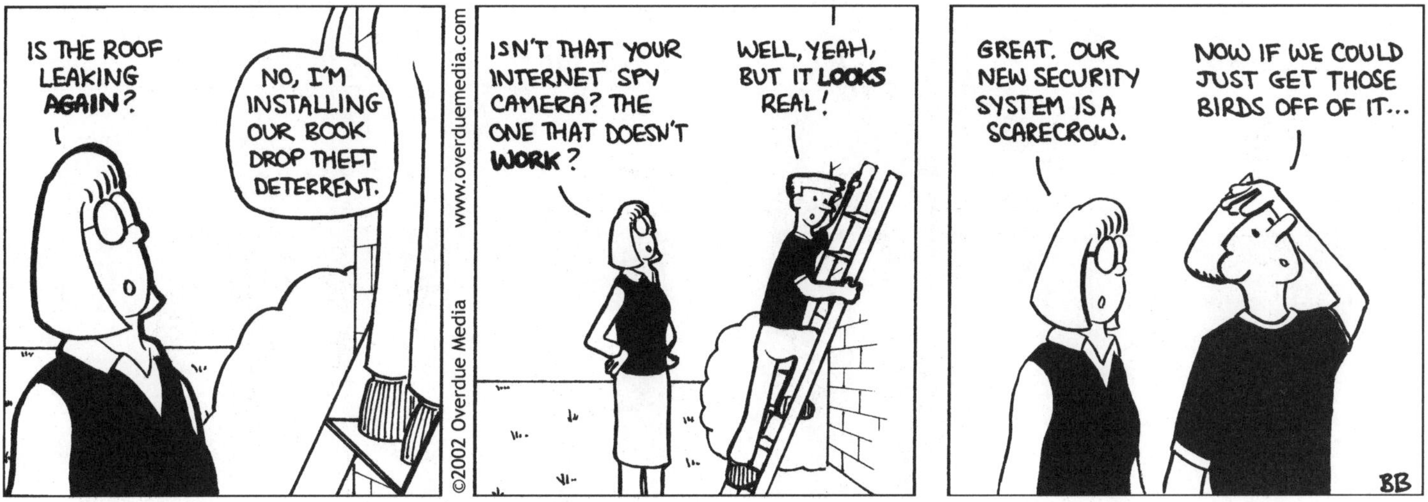
IS THE ROOF LEAKING **AGAIN**?
NO, I'M INSTALLING OUR BOOK DROP THEFT DETERRENT.
www.overduemedia.com
©2002 Overdue Media
ISN'T THAT YOUR INTERNET SPY CAMERA? THE ONE THAT DOESN'T **WORK**?
WELL, YEAH, BUT IT **LOOKS** REAL!
GREAT. OUR NEW SECURITY SYSTEM IS A SCARECROW.
NOW IF WE COULD JUST GET THOSE BIRDS OFF OF IT...
BB

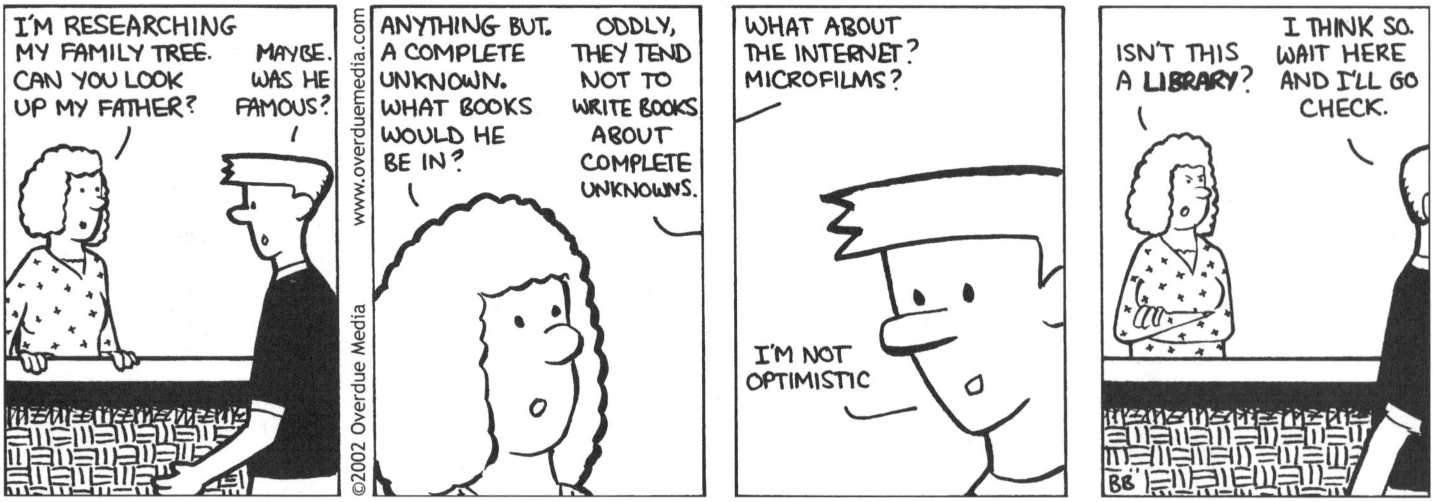
I'M RESEARCHING MY FAMILY TREE. CAN YOU LOOK UP MY FATHER?
MAYBE. WAS HE FAMOUS?
www.overduemedia.com
©2002 Overdue Media
ANYTHING BUT. A COMPLETE UNKNOWN. WHAT BOOKS WOULD HE BE IN?
ODDLY, THEY TEND NOT TO WRITE BOOKS ABOUT COMPLETE UNKNOWNS.
WHAT ABOUT THE INTERNET? MICROFILMS?
I'M NOT OPTIMISTIC
ISN'T THIS A **LIBRARY**?
I THINK SO. WAIT HERE AND I'LL GO CHECK.
BB

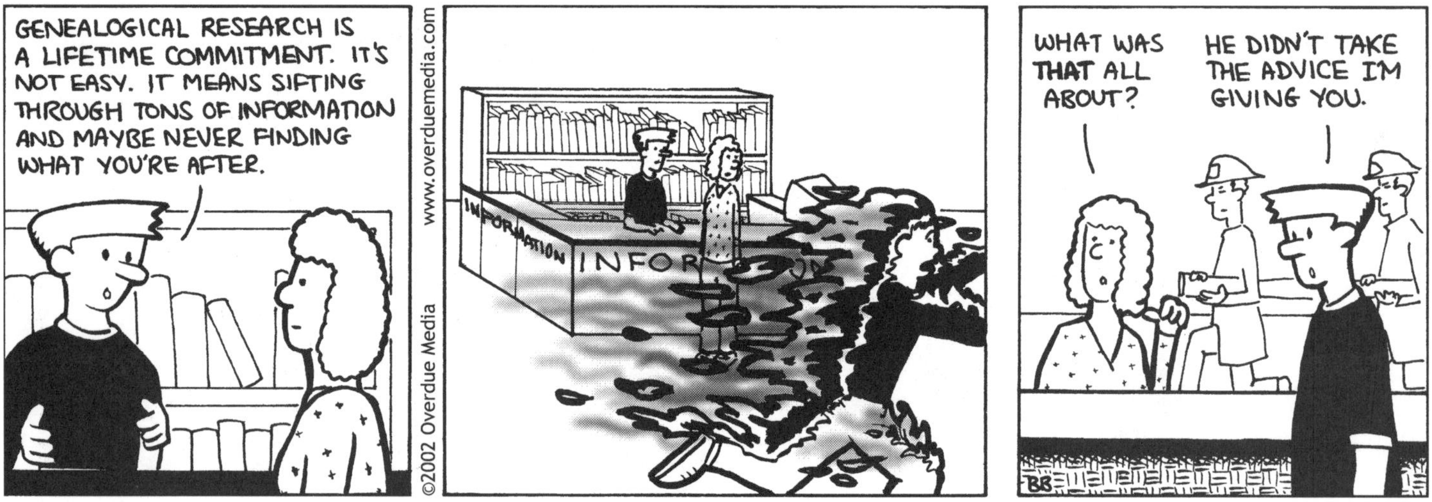
GENEALOGICAL RESEARCH IS A LIFETIME COMMITMENT. IT'S NOT EASY. IT MEANS SIFTING THROUGH TONS OF INFORMATION AND MAYBE NEVER FINDING WHAT YOU'RE AFTER.
www.overduemedia.com
©2002 Overdue Media
INFORMATION
INFOR
WHAT WAS **THAT** ALL ABOUT?
HE DIDN'T TAKE THE ADVICE I'M GIVING YOU.
BB

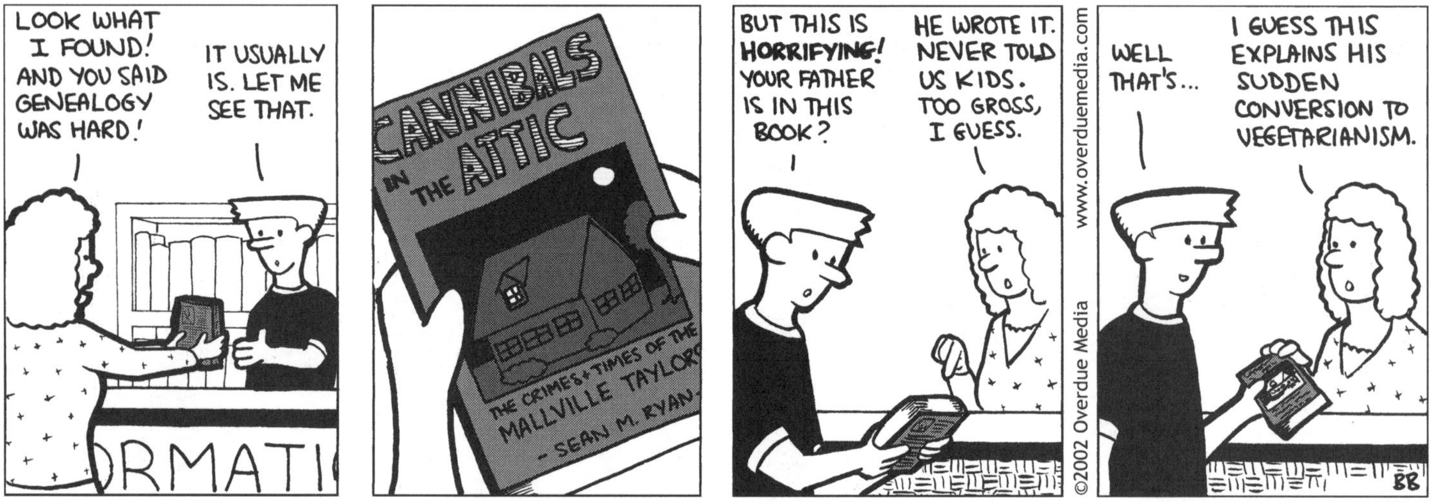
LOOK WHAT I FOUND! AND YOU SAID GENEALOGY WAS HARD!
IT USUALLY IS. LET ME SEE THAT.
RMATI
CANNIBALS IN THE ATTIC
THE CRIMES & TIMES OF THE MALLVILLE TAYLORS
- SEAN M. RYAN
BUT THIS IS **HORRIFYING**! YOUR FATHER IS IN THIS BOOK?
HE WROTE IT. NEVER TOLD US KIDS. TOO GROSS, I GUESS.
www.overduemedia.com
©2002 Overdue Media
WELL THAT'S...
I GUESS THIS EXPLAINS HIS SUDDEN CONVERSION TO VEGETARIANISM.
BB

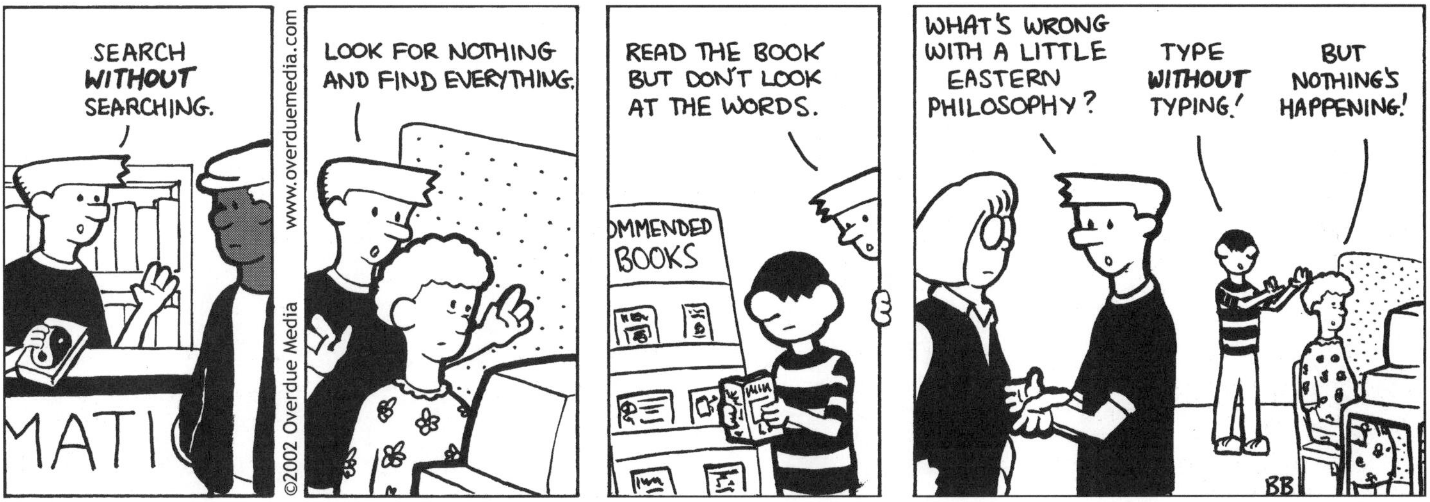
SEARCH WITHOUT SEARCHING.
LOOK FOR NOTHING AND FIND EVERYTHING.
READ THE BOOK BUT DON'T LOOK AT THE WORDS.
WHAT'S WRONG WITH A LITTLE EASTERN PHILOSOPHY?
TYPE WITHOUT TYPING!
BUT NOTHING'S HAPPENING!
MATI
MMENDED BOOKS
www.overduemedia.com
©2002 Overdue Media
BB

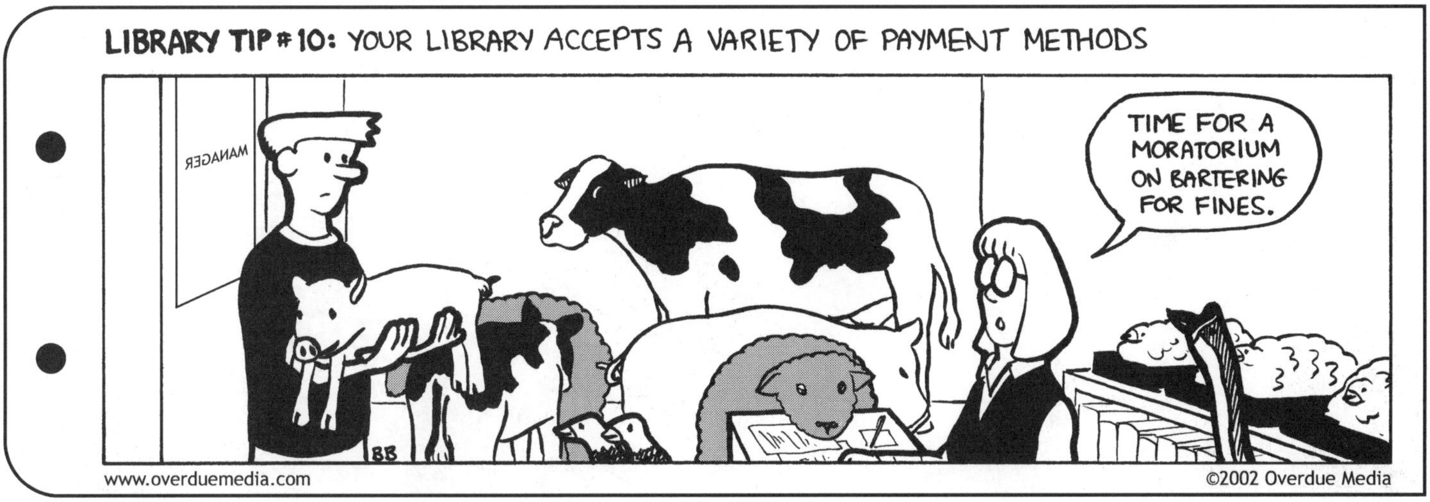
LIBRARY TIP #10: YOUR LIBRARY ACCEPTS A VARIETY OF PAYMENT METHODS
MANAGER
TIME FOR A MORATORIUM ON BARTERING FOR FINES.
BB
www.overduemedia.com
©2002 Overdue Media

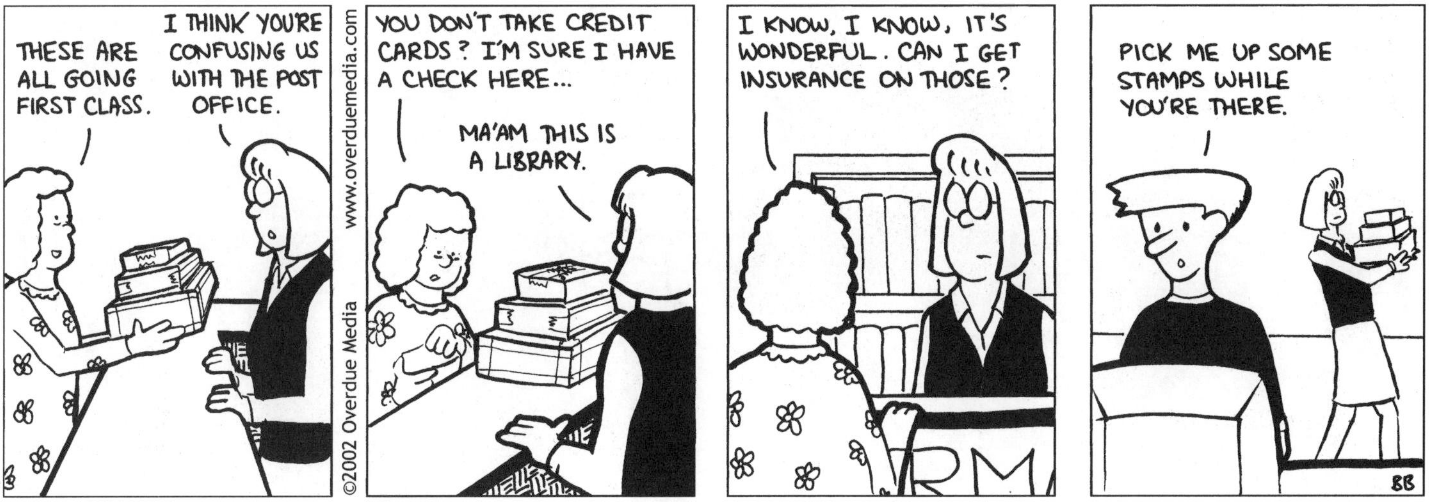
THESE ARE ALL GOING FIRST CLASS.
I THINK YOU'RE CONFUSING US WITH THE POST OFFICE.
YOU DON'T TAKE CREDIT CARDS? I'M SURE I HAVE A CHECK HERE...
MA'AM THIS IS A LIBRARY.
I KNOW, I KNOW, IT'S WONDERFUL. CAN I GET INSURANCE ON THOSE?
PICK ME UP SOME STAMPS WHILE YOU'RE THERE.
www.overduemedia.com
©2002 Overdue Media
BB

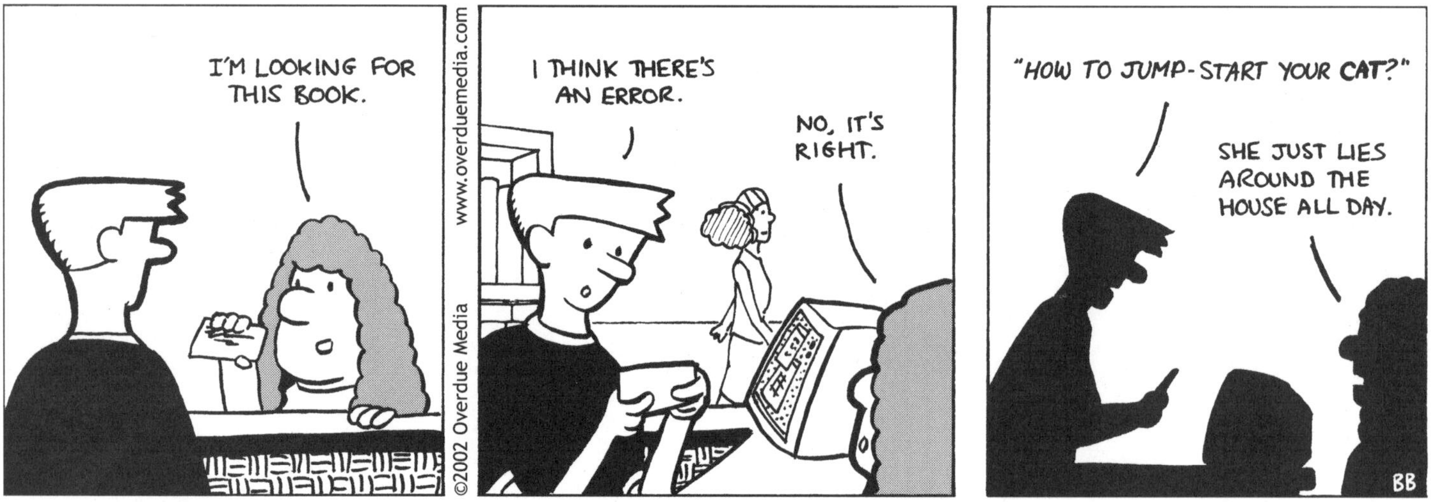
I'M LOOKING FOR THIS BOOK.
www.overduemedia.com
©2002 Overdue Media
I THINK THERE'S AN ERROR.
NO, IT'S RIGHT.
"HOW TO JUMP-START YOUR CAT?"
SHE JUST LIES AROUND THE HOUSE ALL DAY.
BB

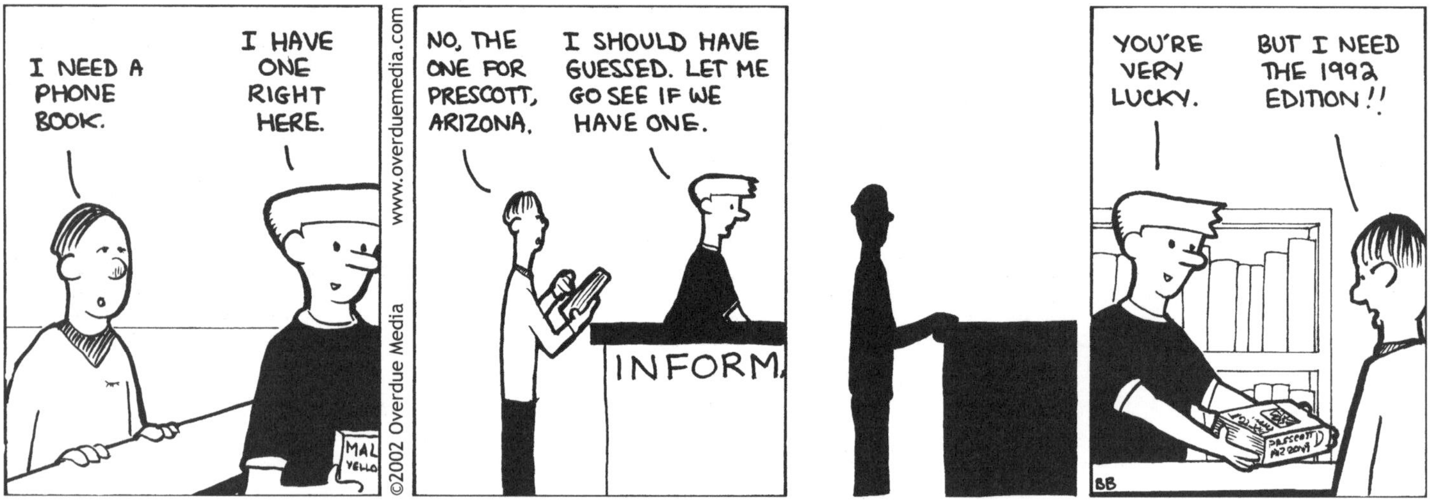
I NEED A PHONE BOOK.
I HAVE ONE RIGHT HERE.
www.overduemedia.com
©2002 Overdue Media
NO, THE ONE FOR PRESCOTT, ARIZONA.
I SHOULD HAVE GUESSED. LET ME GO SEE IF WE HAVE ONE.
INFORM
YOU'RE VERY LUCKY.
BUT I NEED THE 1992 EDITION!!
BB

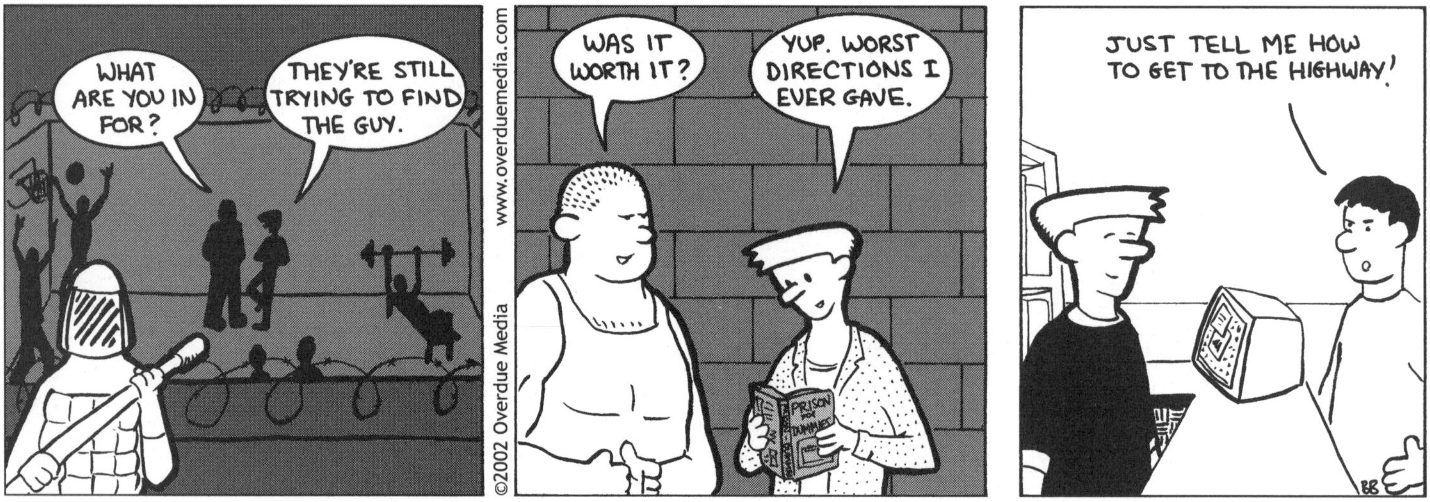
WHAT ARE YOU IN FOR?
THEY'RE STILL TRYING TO FIND THE GUY.
www.overduemedia.com
©2002 Overdue Media
WAS IT WORTH IT?
YUP. WORST DIRECTIONS I EVER GAVE.
JUST TELL ME HOW TO GET TO THE HIGHWAY!
BB

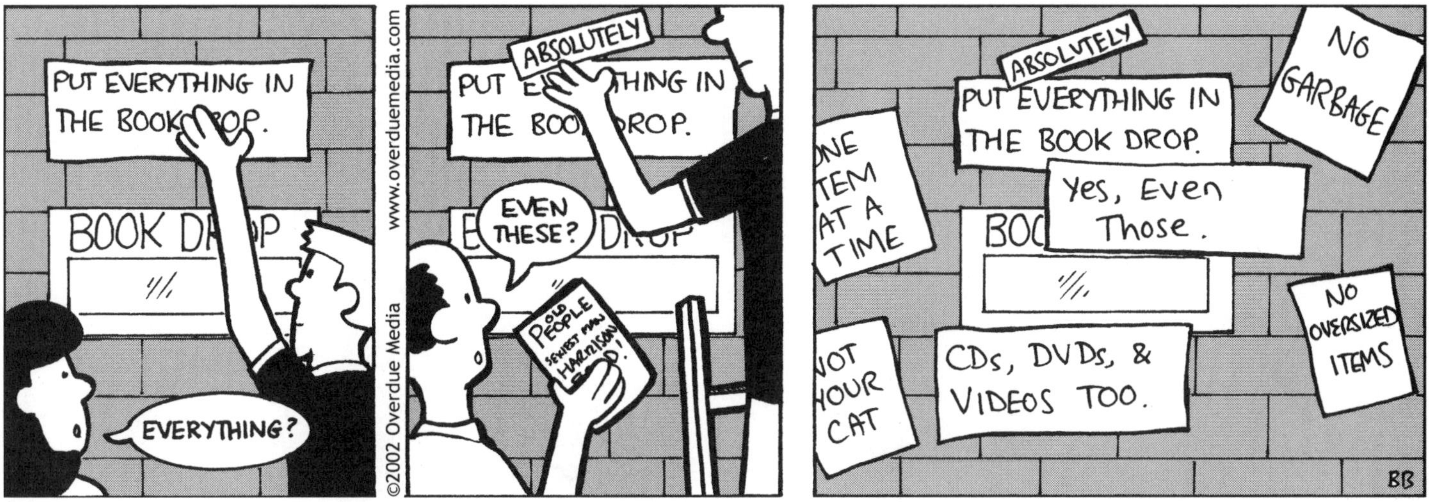
PUT EVERYTHING IN THE BOOK DROP.
BOOK DROP
EVERYTHING?
©2002 Overdue Media
www.overduemedia.com
ABSOLUTELY
EVEN THESE?
OLD PEOPLE
ABSOLUTELY
PUT EVERYTHING IN THE BOOK DROP.
NO GARBAGE
Yes, Even Those.
CDs, DVDs, & VIDEOS TOO.
NO OVERSIZED ITEMS
BB

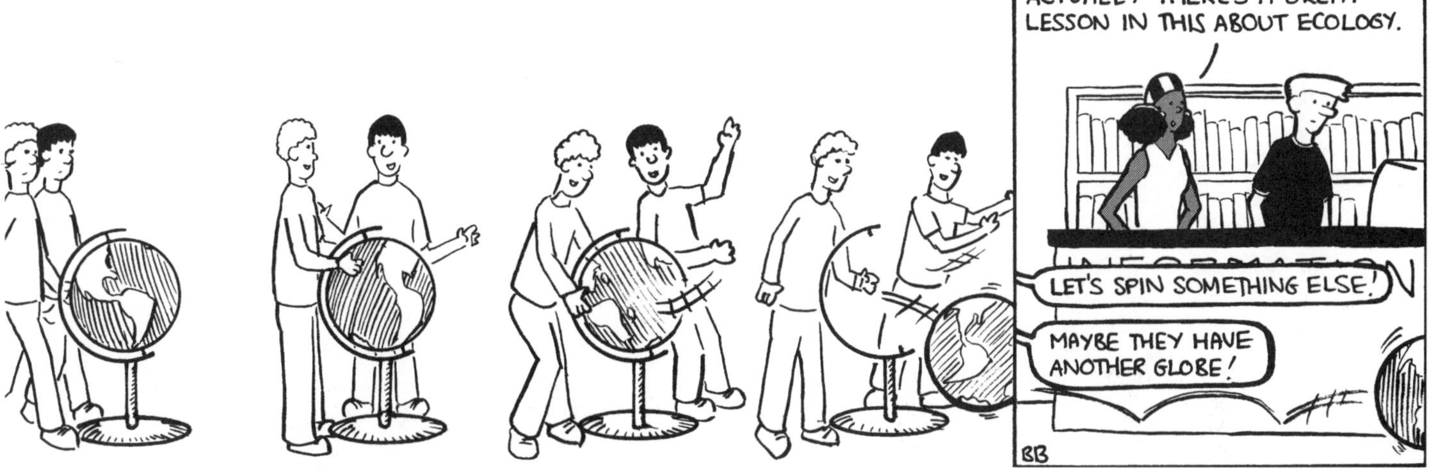
ACTUALLY THERE'S A GREAT LESSON IN THIS ABOUT ECOLOGY.
LET'S SPIN SOMETHING ELSE!
MAYBE THEY HAVE ANOTHER GLOBE!
BB

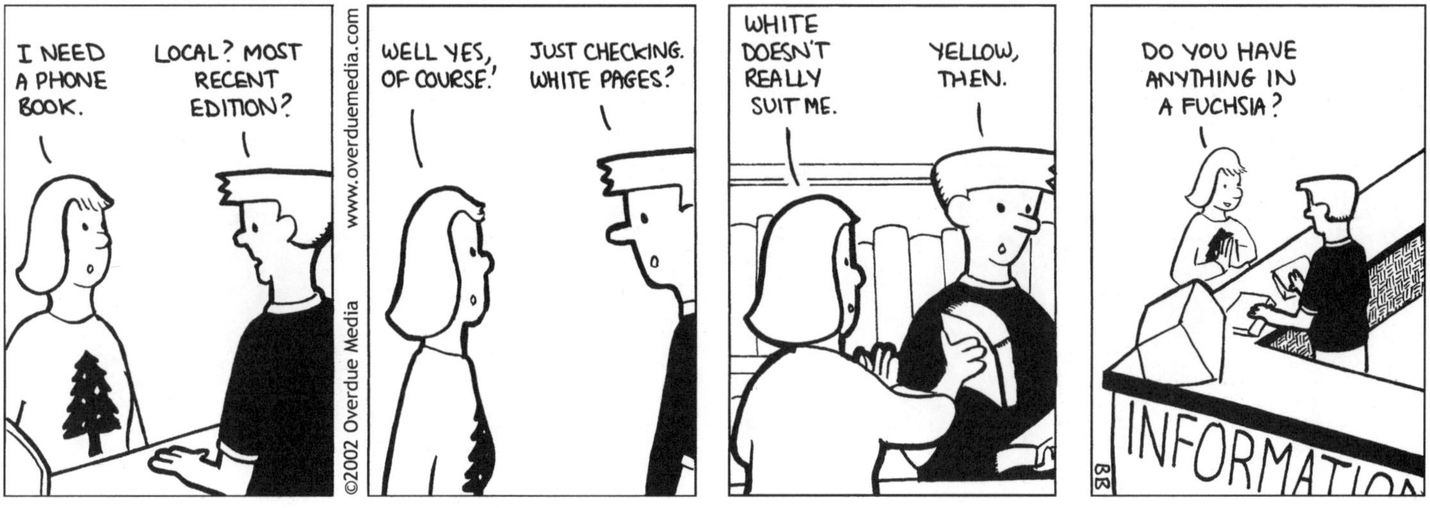
I NEED A PHONE BOOK.
LOCAL? MOST RECENT EDITION?
©2002 Overdue Media
www.overduemedia.com
WELL YES, OF COURSE.
JUST CHECKING. WHITE PAGES?
WHITE DOESN'T REALLY SUIT ME.
YELLOW, THEN.
DO YOU HAVE ANYTHING IN A FUCHSIA?
INFORMATION
BB

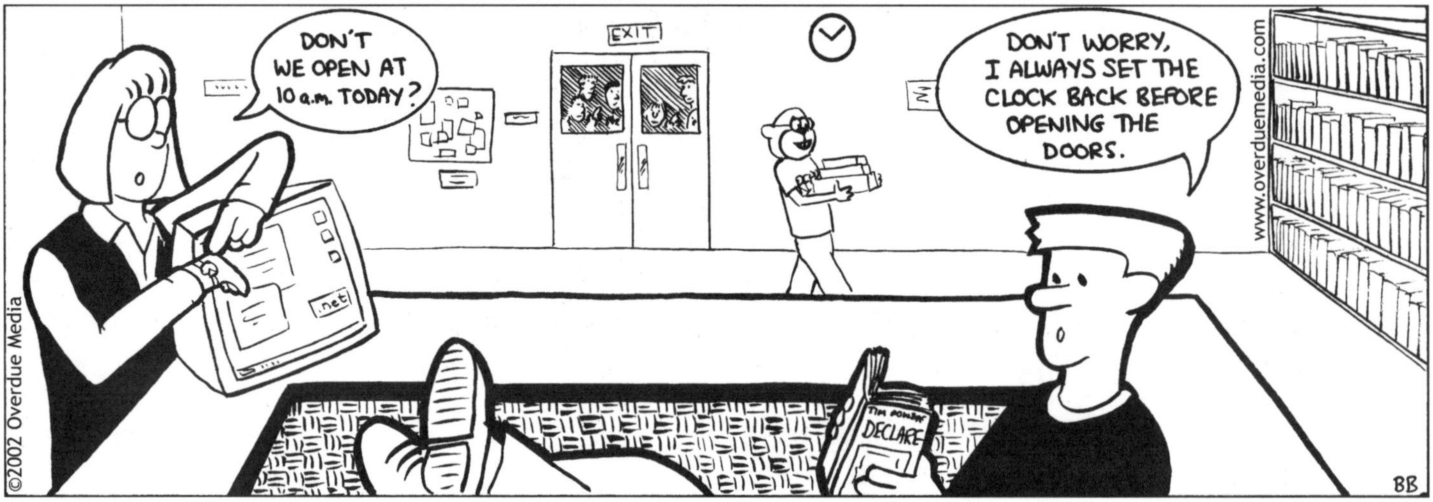
DON'T WE OPEN AT 10 a.m. TODAY?
DON'T WORRY, I ALWAYS SET THE CLOCK BACK BEFORE OPENING THE DOORS.
EXIT
.net
DECLARE
©2002 Overdue Media
www.overduemedia.com
BB

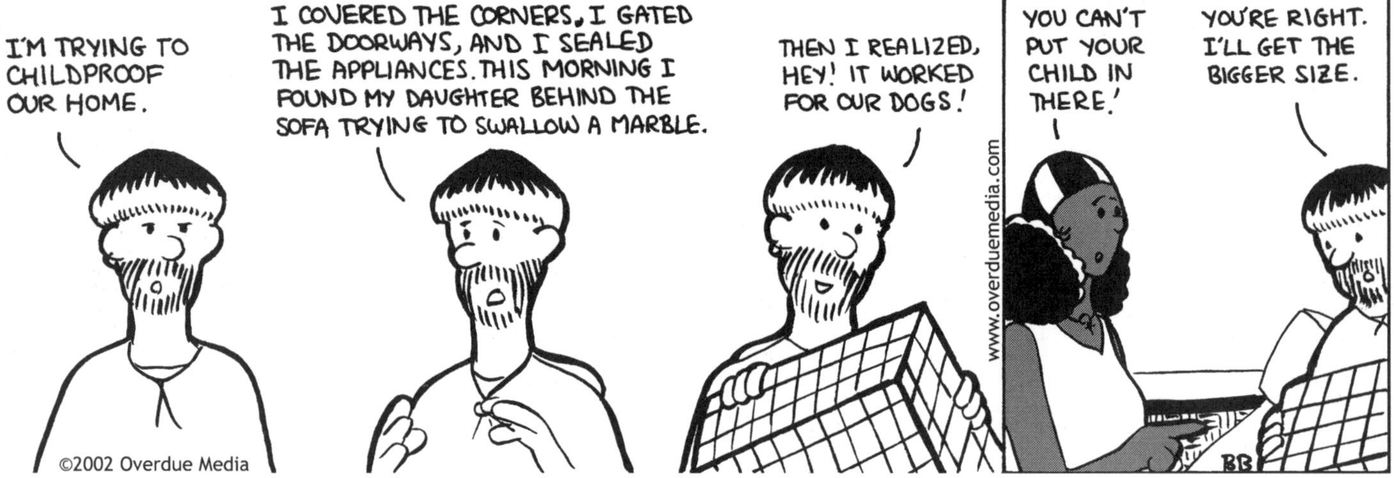
I'M TRYING TO CHILDPROOF OUR HOME.
I COVERED THE CORNERS, I GATED THE DOORWAYS, AND I SEALED THE APPLIANCES. THIS MORNING I FOUND MY DAUGHTER BEHIND THE SOFA TRYING TO SWALLOW A MARBLE.
THEN I REALIZED, HEY! IT WORKED FOR OUR DOGS!
YOU CAN'T PUT YOUR CHILD IN THERE!
YOU'RE RIGHT. I'LL GET THE BIGGER SIZE.
©2002 Overdue Media
www.overduemedia.com
BB

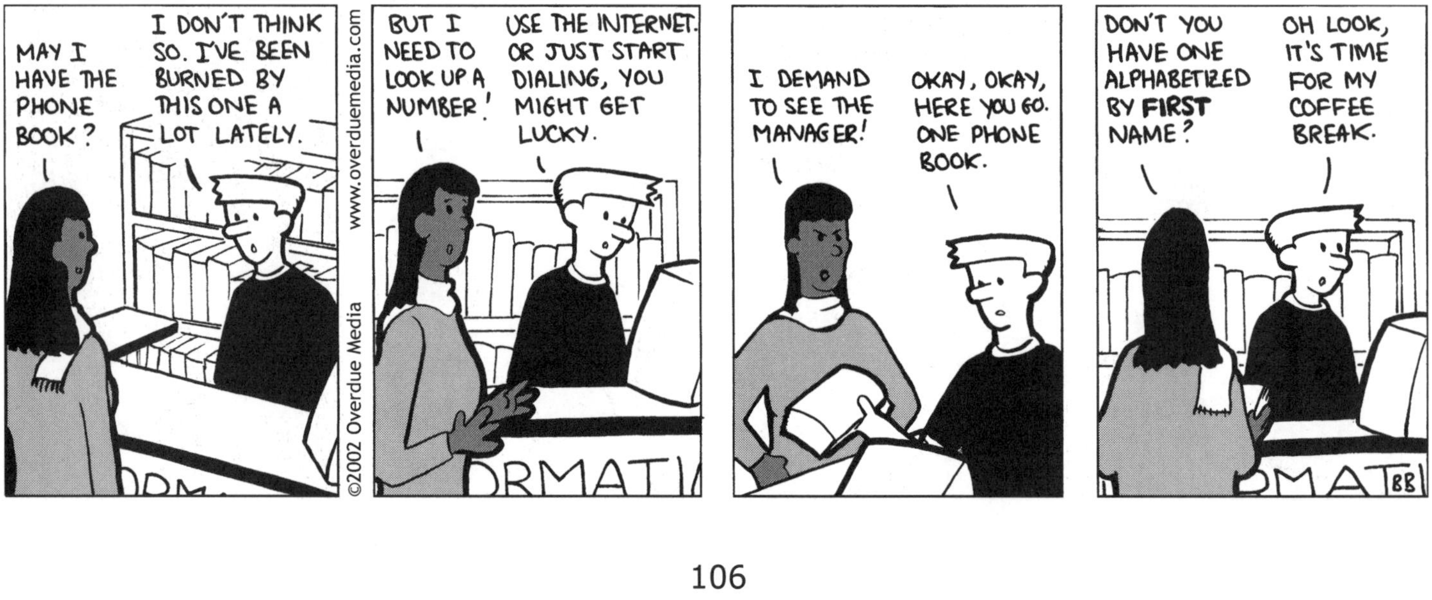
MAY I HAVE THE PHONE BOOK?
I DON'T THINK SO. I'VE BEEN BURNED BY THIS ONE A LOT LATELY.
BUT I NEED TO LOOK UP A NUMBER!
USE THE INTERNET. OR JUST START DIALING, YOU MIGHT GET LUCKY.
I DEMAND TO SEE THE MANAGER!
OKAY, OKAY, HERE YOU GO. ONE PHONE BOOK.
DON'T YOU HAVE ONE ALPHABETIZED BY FIRST NAME?
OH LOOK, IT'S TIME FOR MY COFFEE BREAK.
www.overduemedia.com
©2002 Overdue Media
RMATI
BB

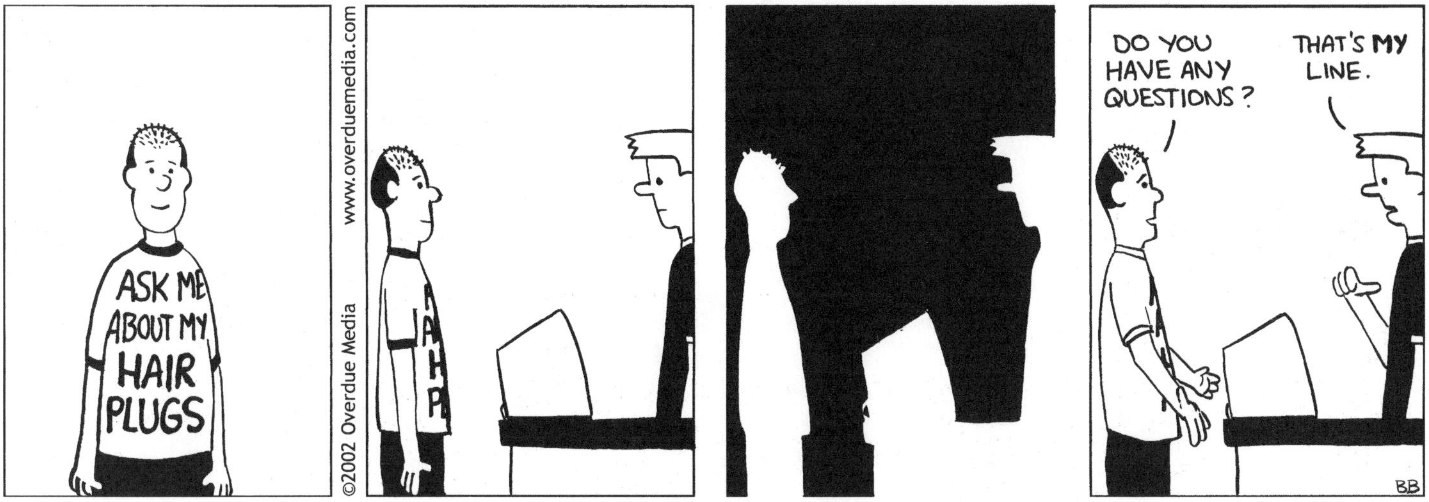
ASK ME ABOUT MY HAIR PLUGS
©2002 Overdue Media www.overduemedia.com
DO YOU HAVE ANY QUESTIONS?
THAT'S **MY** LINE.
BB

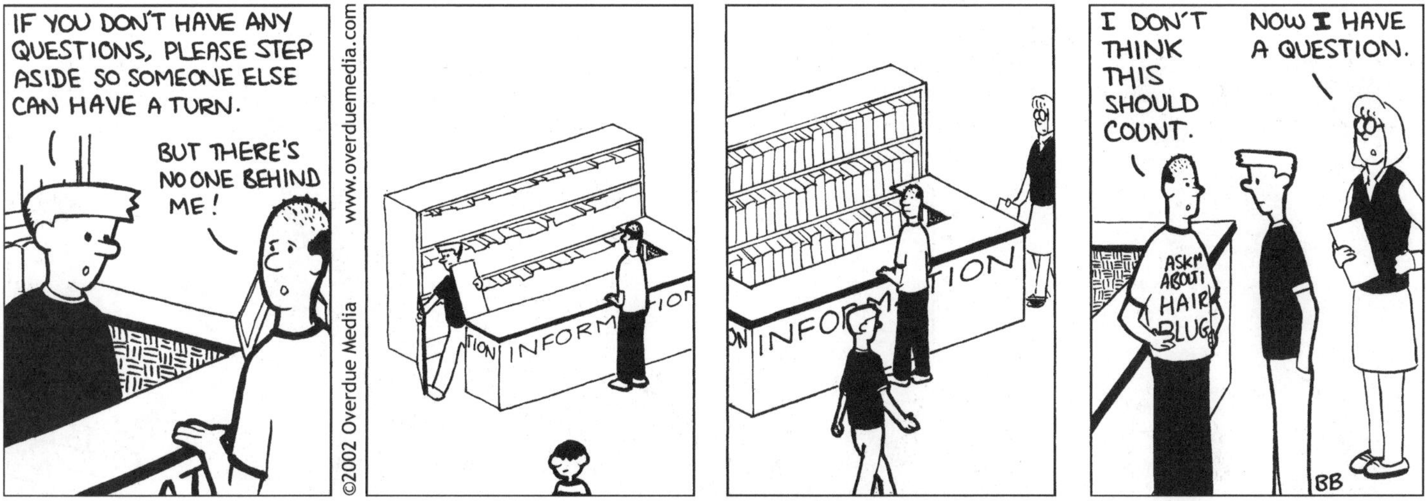
IF YOU DON'T HAVE ANY QUESTIONS, PLEASE STEP ASIDE SO SOMEONE ELSE CAN HAVE A TURN.
BUT THERE'S NO ONE BEHIND ME!
©2002 Overdue Media www.overduemedia.com
INFORMATION
I DON'T THINK THIS SHOULD COUNT.
NOW **I** HAVE A QUESTION.
BB

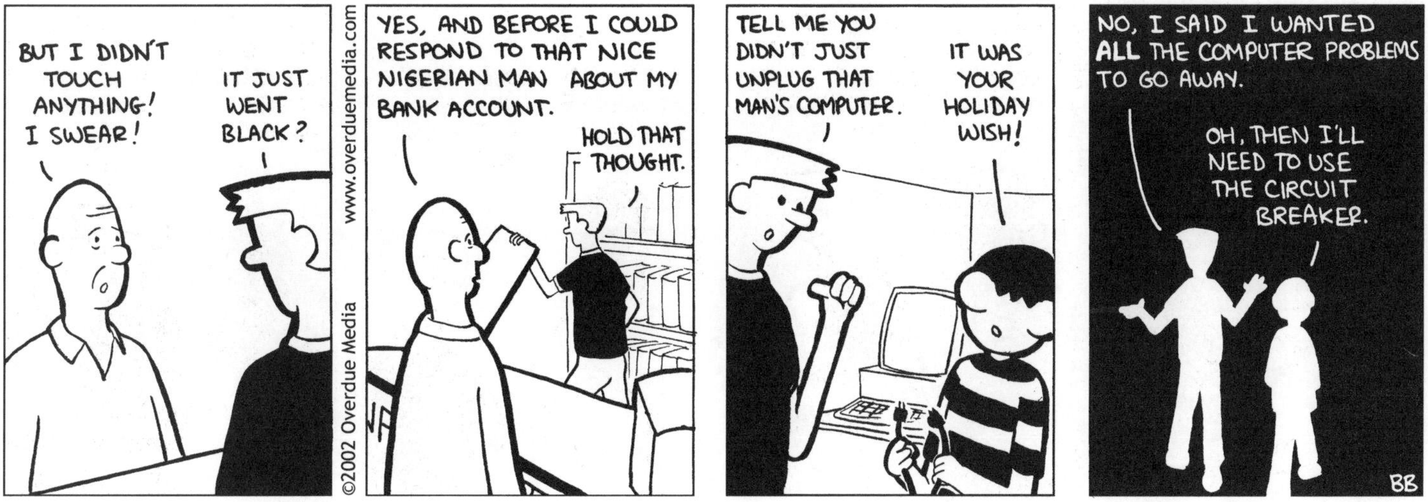
BUT I DIDN'T TOUCH ANYTHING! I SWEAR!
IT JUST WENT BLACK?
©2002 Overdue Media www.overduemedia.com
YES, AND BEFORE I COULD RESPOND TO THAT NICE NIGERIAN MAN ABOUT MY BANK ACCOUNT.
HOLD THAT THOUGHT.
TELL ME YOU DIDN'T JUST UNPLUG THAT MAN'S COMPUTER.
IT WAS YOUR HOLIDAY WISH!
NO, I SAID I WANTED **ALL** THE COMPUTER PROBLEMS TO GO AWAY.
OH, THEN I'LL NEED TO USE THE CIRCUIT BREAKER.
BB

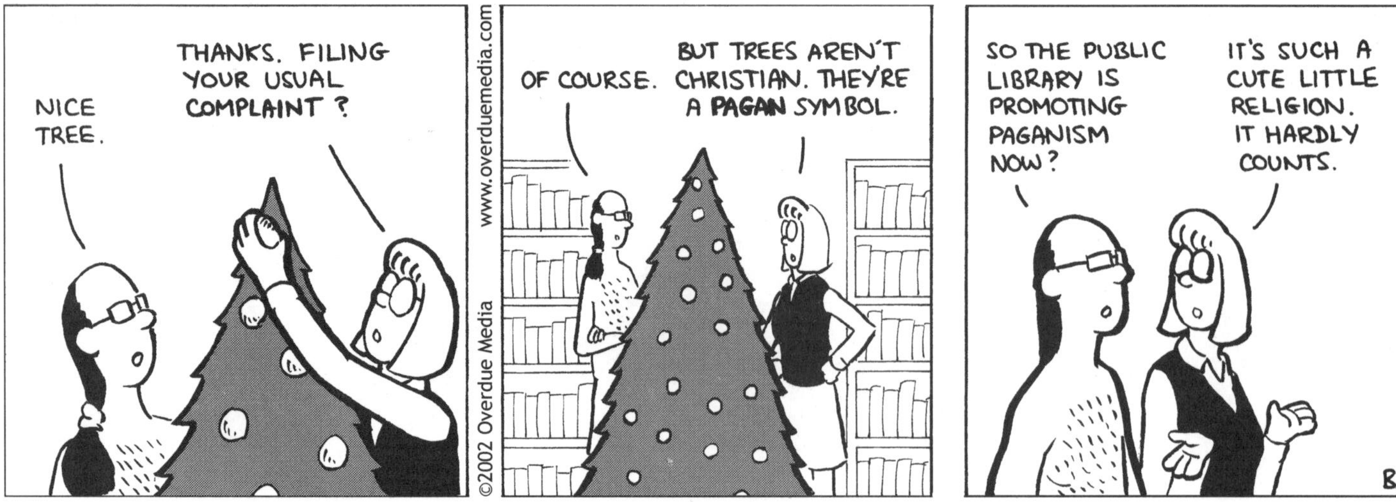
NICE TREE.
THANKS. FILING YOUR USUAL COMPLAINT ?
OF COURSE.
BUT TREES AREN'T CHRISTIAN. THEY'RE A PAGAN SYMBOL.
SO THE PUBLIC LIBRARY IS PROMOTING PAGANISM NOW ?
IT'S SUCH A CUTE LITTLE RELIGION. IT HARDLY COUNTS.
BB
©2002 Overdue Media
www.overduemedia.com

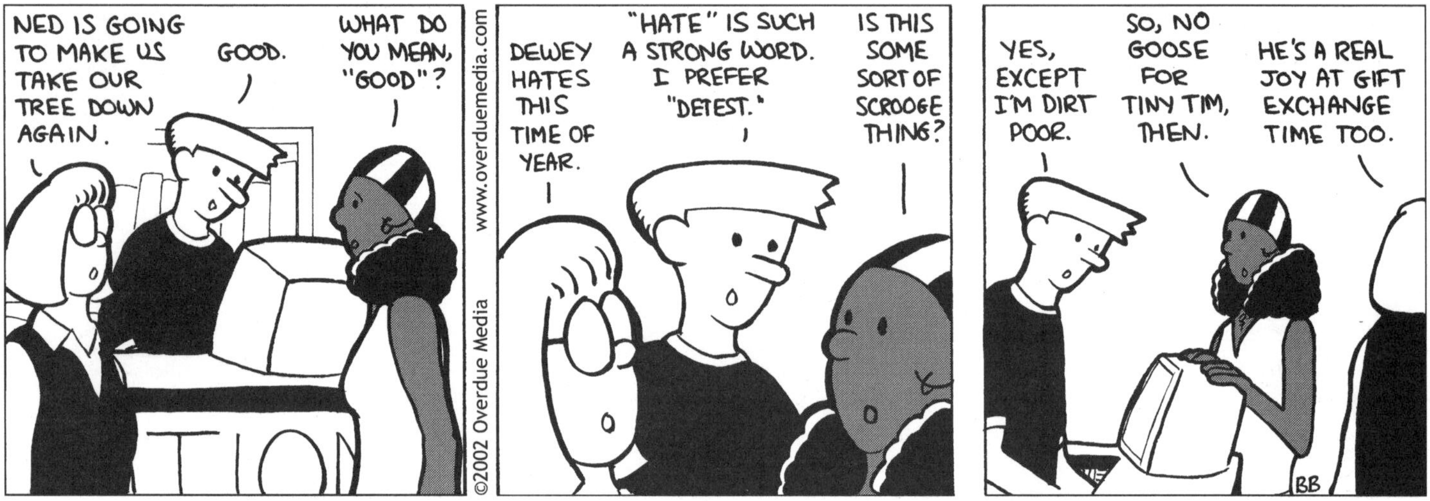
NED IS GOING TO MAKE US TAKE OUR TREE DOWN AGAIN.
GOOD.
WHAT DO YOU MEAN, "GOOD"?
DEWEY HATES THIS TIME OF YEAR.
"HATE" IS SUCH A STRONG WORD. I PREFER "DETEST."
IS THIS SOME SORT OF SCROOGE THING?
YES, EXCEPT I'M DIRT POOR.
SO, NO GOOSE FOR TINY TIM, THEN.
HE'S A REAL JOY AT GIFT EXCHANGE TIME TOO.
BB
©2002 Overdue Media
www.overduemedia.com

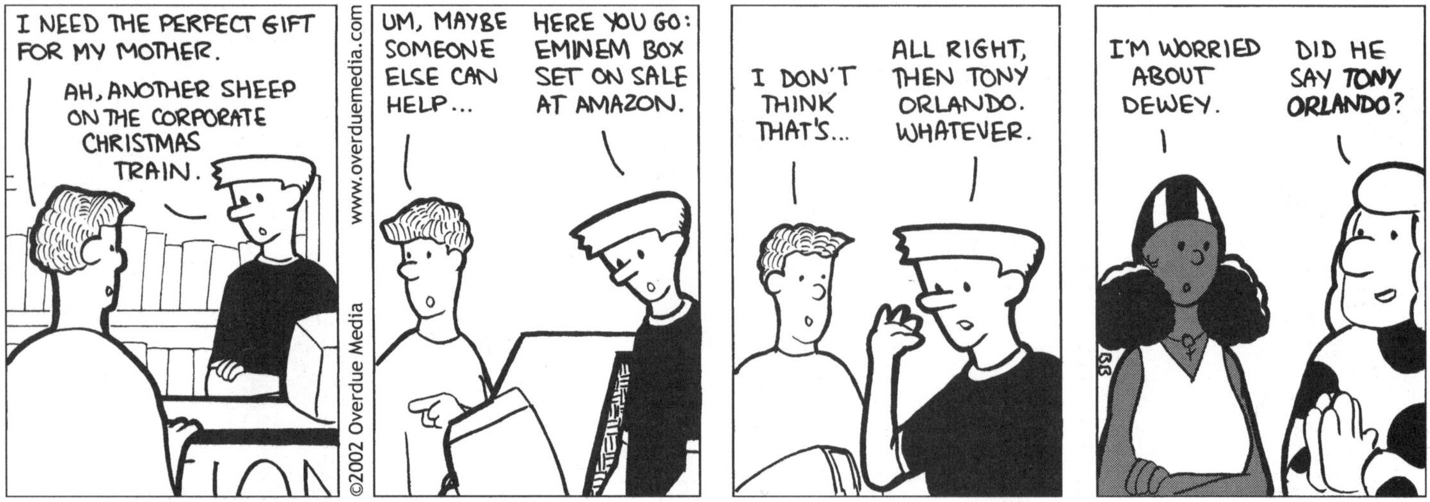
I NEED THE PERFECT GIFT FOR MY MOTHER.
AH, ANOTHER SHEEP ON THE CORPORATE CHRISTMAS TRAIN.
UM, MAYBE SOMEONE ELSE CAN HELP...
HERE YOU GO: EMINEM BOX SET ON SALE AT AMAZON.
I DON'T THINK THAT'S...
ALL RIGHT, THEN TONY ORLANDO. WHATEVER.
I'M WORRIED ABOUT DEWEY.
DID HE SAY TONY ORLANDO?
©2002 Overdue Media
www.overduemedia.com

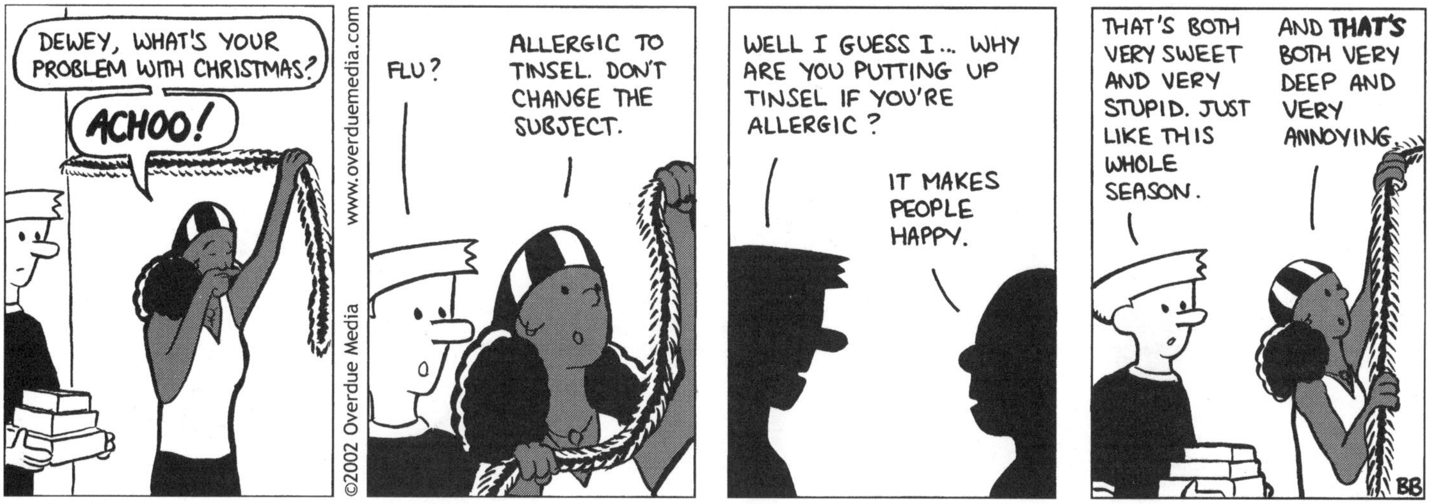
DEWEY, WHAT'S YOUR PROBLEM WITH CHRISTMAS?
ACHOO!
www.overduemedia.com
©2002 Overdue Media
FLU?
ALLERGIC TO TINSEL. DON'T CHANGE THE SUBJECT.
WELL I GUESS I... WHY ARE YOU PUTTING UP TINSEL IF YOU'RE ALLERGIC?
IT MAKES PEOPLE HAPPY.
THAT'S BOTH VERY SWEET AND VERY STUPID. JUST LIKE THIS WHOLE SEASON.
AND **THAT'S** BOTH VERY DEEP AND VERY ANNOYING.
BB

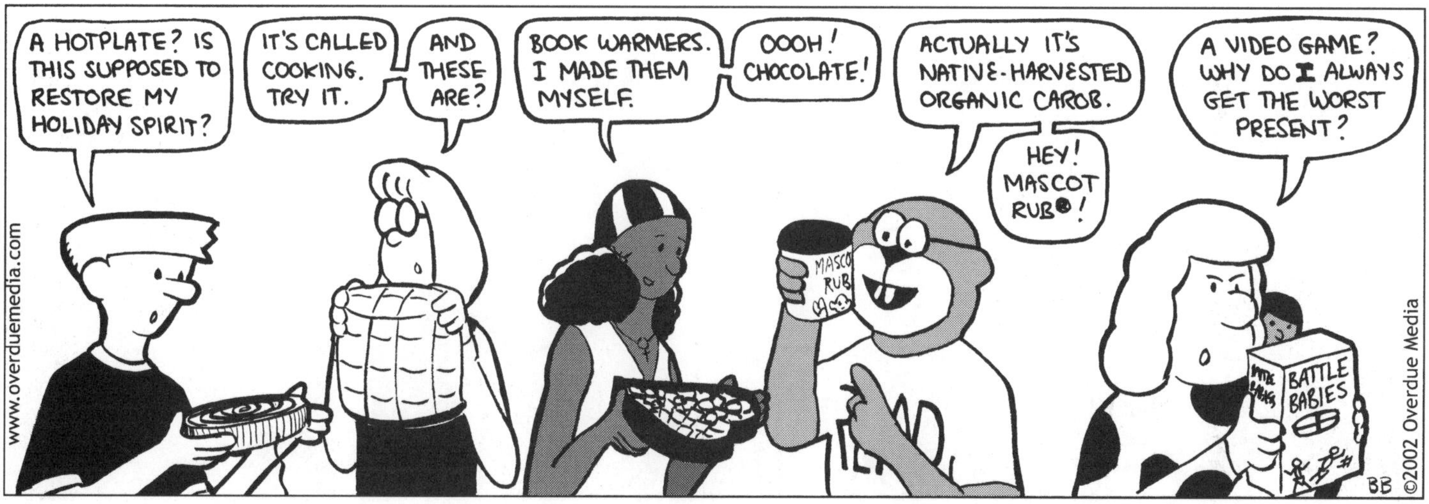
A HOTPLATE? IS THIS SUPPOSED TO RESTORE MY HOLIDAY SPIRIT?
IT'S CALLED COOKING. TRY IT.
AND THESE ARE?
BOOK WARMERS. I MADE THEM MYSELF.
OOOH! CHOCOLATE!
ACTUALLY IT'S NATIVE-HARVESTED ORGANIC CAROB.
HEY! MASCOT RUB®!
A VIDEO GAME? WHY DO **I** ALWAYS GET THE WORST PRESENT?
BATTLE BABIES
www.overduemedia.com
©2002 Overdue Media
BB

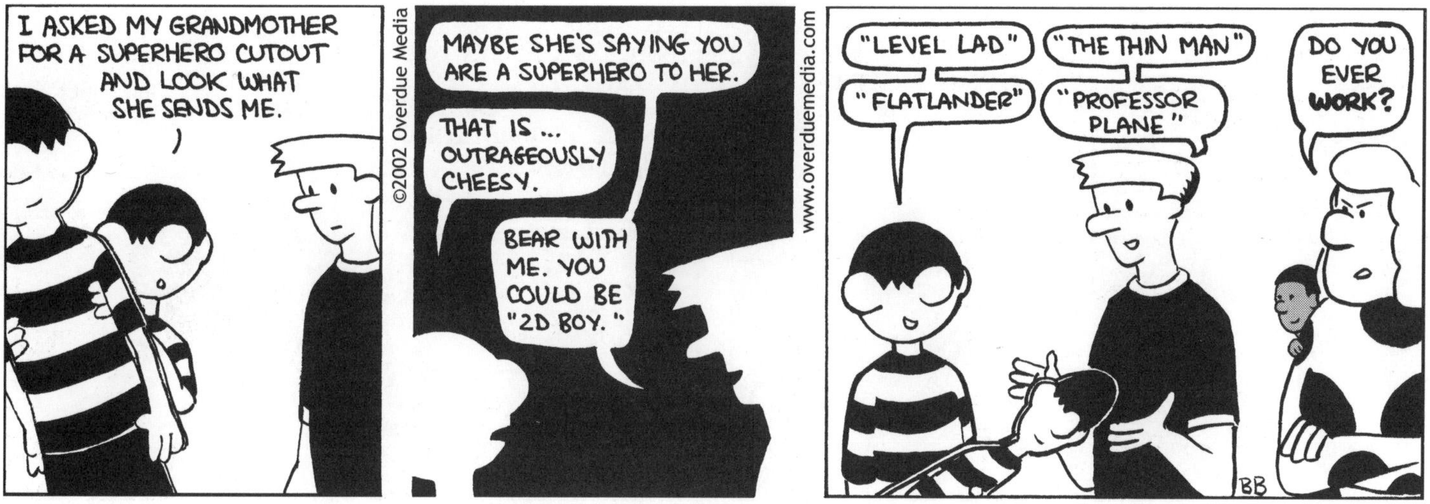
I ASKED MY GRANDMOTHER FOR A SUPERHERO CUTOUT AND LOOK WHAT SHE SENDS ME.
©2002 Overdue Media
MAYBE SHE'S SAYING YOU ARE A SUPERHERO TO HER.
THAT IS ... OUTRAGEOUSLY CHEESY.
BEAR WITH ME. YOU COULD BE "2D BOY."
www.overduemedia.com
"LEVEL LAD"
"FLATLANDER"
"THE THIN MAN"
"PROFESSOR PLANE"
DO YOU EVER **WORK?**
BB

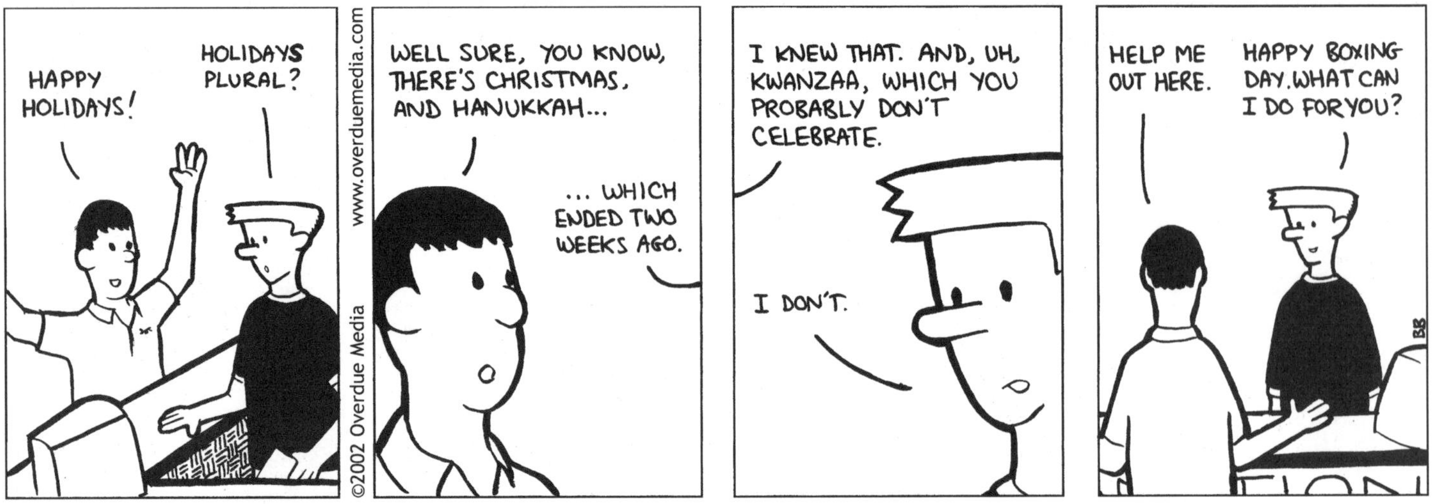
HAPPY HOLIDAYS!
HOLIDAYS PLURAL?
www.overduemedia.com
©2002 Overdue Media
WELL SURE, YOU KNOW, THERE'S CHRISTMAS, AND HANUKKAH...
... WHICH ENDED TWO WEEKS AGO.
I KNEW THAT. AND, UH, KWANZAA, WHICH YOU PROBABLY DON'T CELEBRATE.
I DON'T.
HELP ME OUT HERE.
HAPPY BOXING DAY. WHAT CAN I DO FOR YOU?
BB

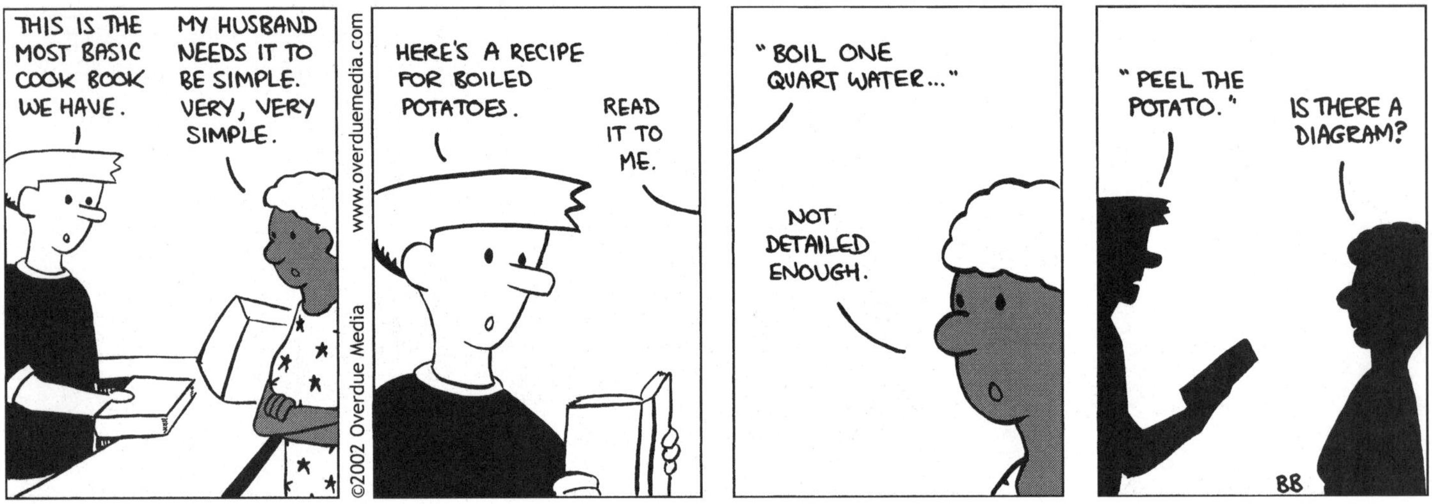
THIS IS THE MOST BASIC COOK BOOK WE HAVE.
MY HUSBAND NEEDS IT TO BE SIMPLE. VERY, VERY SIMPLE.
www.overduemedia.com
©2002 Overdue Media
HERE'S A RECIPE FOR BOILED POTATOES.
READ IT TO ME.
"BOIL ONE QUART WATER..."
NOT DETAILED ENOUGH.
"PEEL THE POTATO."
IS THERE A DIAGRAM?
BB

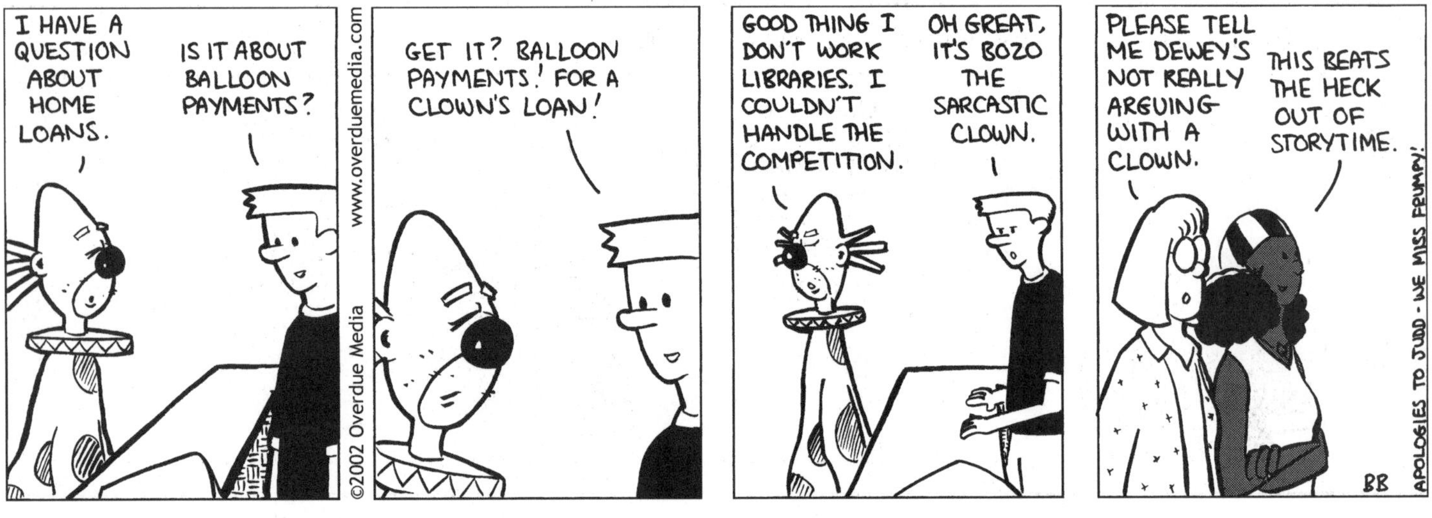
I HAVE A QUESTION ABOUT HOME LOANS.
IS IT ABOUT BALLOON PAYMENTS?
www.overduemedia.com
©2002 Overdue Media
GET IT? BALLOON PAYMENTS! FOR A CLOWN'S LOAN!
GOOD THING I DON'T WORK LIBRARIES. I COULDN'T HANDLE THE COMPETITION.
OH GREAT, IT'S BOZO THE SARCASTIC CLOWN.
PLEASE TELL ME DEWEY'S NOT REALLY ARGUING WITH A CLOWN.
THIS BEATS THE HECK OUT OF STORYTIME.
BB
APOLOGIES TO JUDD - WE MISS FRUMPY!

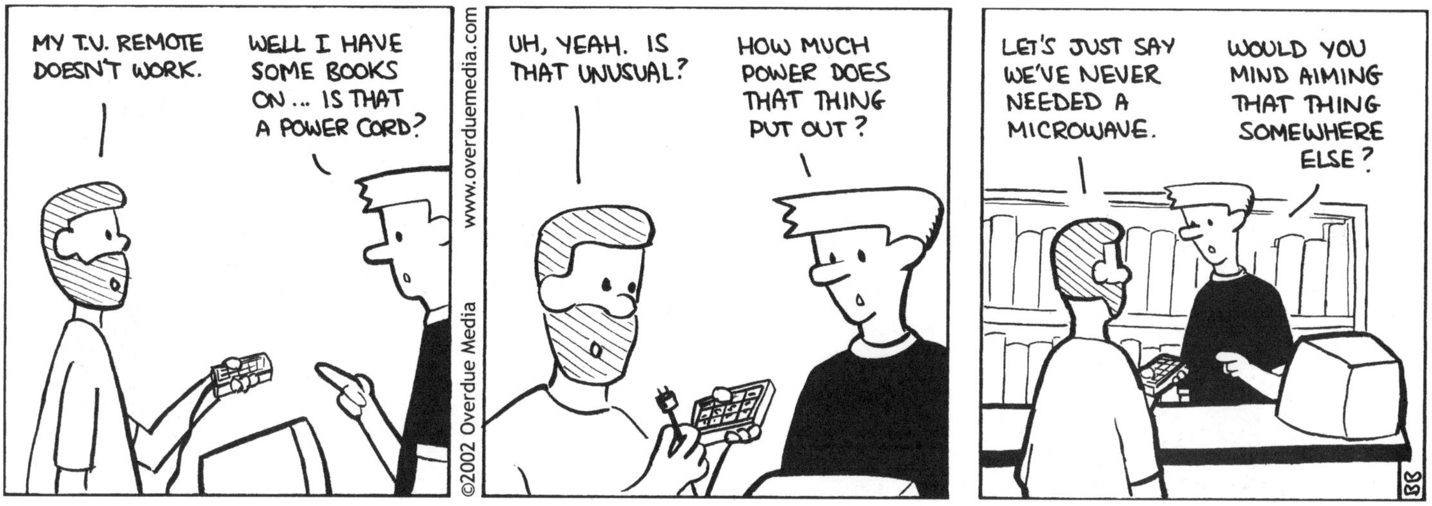
MY T.V. REMOTE DOESN'T WORK.
WELL I HAVE SOME BOOKS ON ... IS THAT A POWER CORD?
UH, YEAH. IS THAT UNUSUAL?
HOW MUCH POWER DOES THAT THING PUT OUT?
LET'S JUST SAY WE'VE NEVER NEEDED A MICROWAVE.
WOULD YOU MIND AIMING THAT THING SOMEWHERE ELSE?
BB

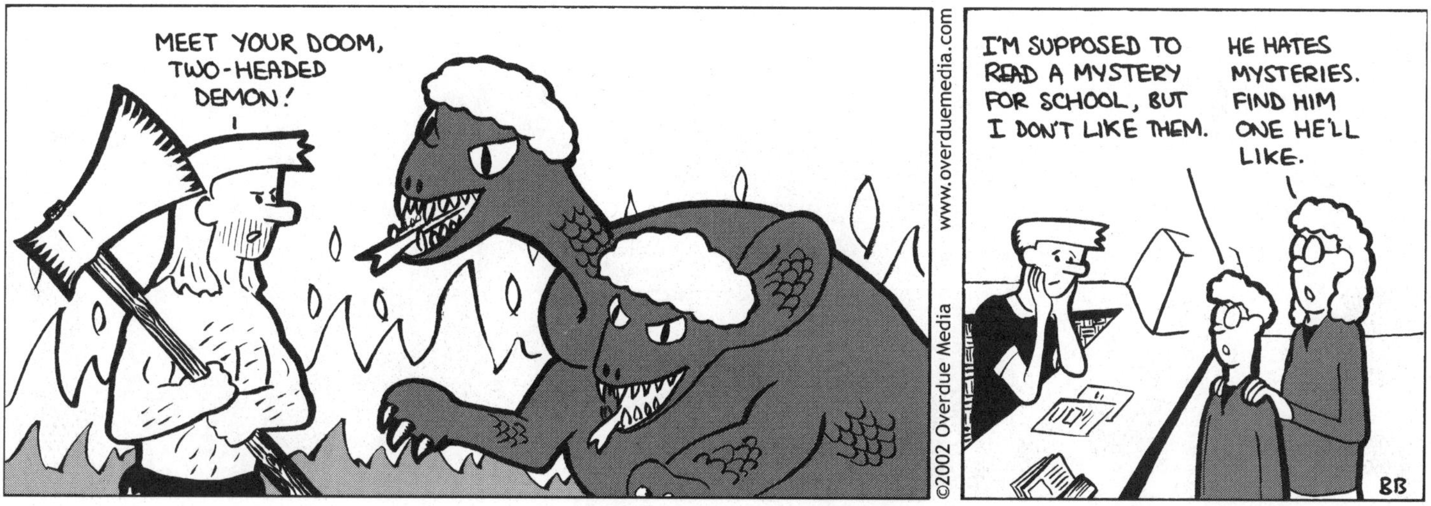
MEET YOUR DOOM, TWO-HEADED DEMON!
I'M SUPPOSED TO READ A MYSTERY FOR SCHOOL, BUT I DON'T LIKE THEM.
HE HATES MYSTERIES. FIND HIM ONE HE'LL LIKE.
BB

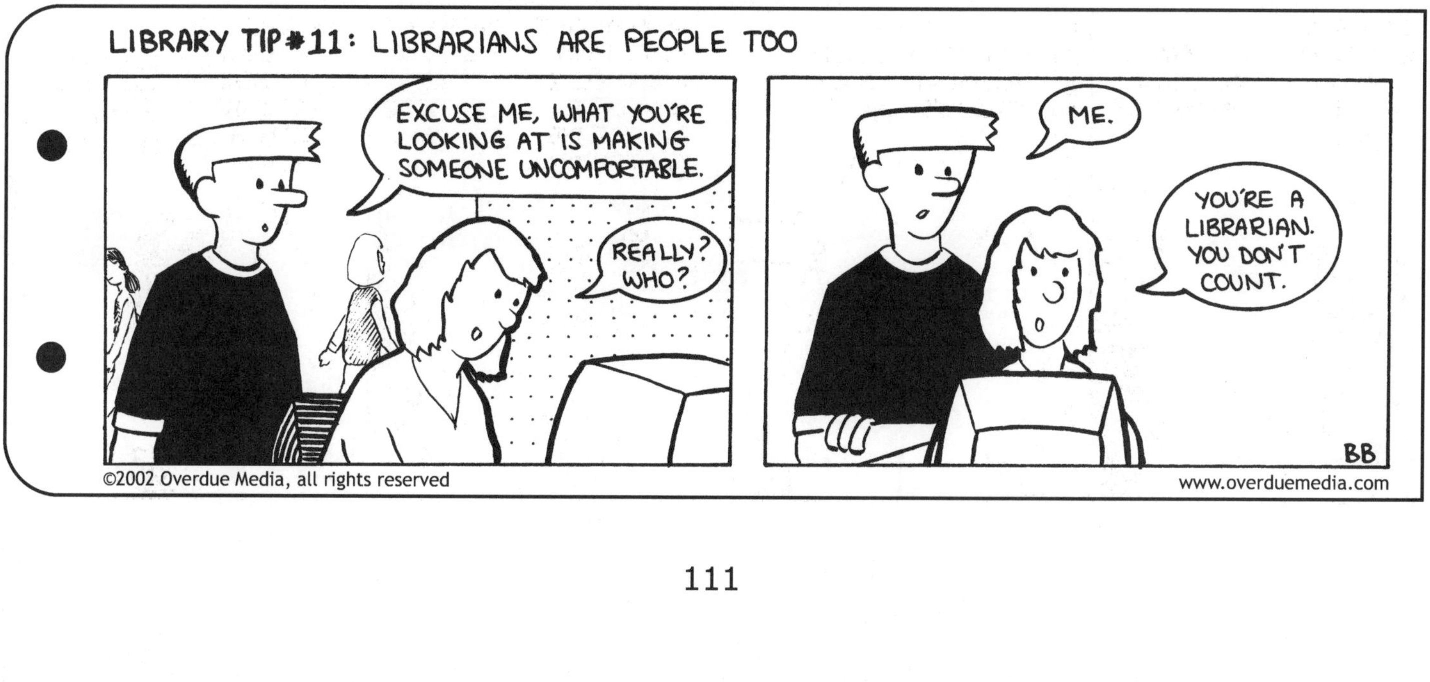
LIBRARY TIP #11: LIBRARIANS ARE PEOPLE TOO
EXCUSE ME, WHAT YOU'RE LOOKING AT IS MAKING SOMEONE UNCOMFORTABLE.
REALLY? WHO?
ME.
YOU'RE A LIBRARIAN. YOU DON'T COUNT.
BB

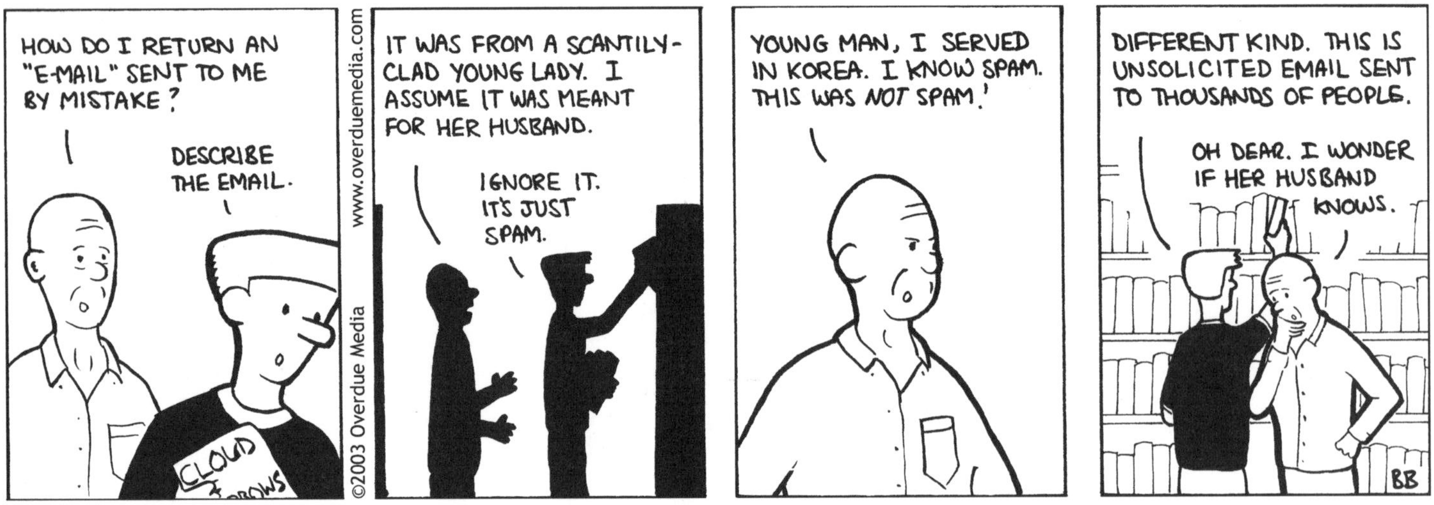
HOW DO I RETURN AN "E-MAIL" SENT TO ME BY MISTAKE?
DESCRIBE THE EMAIL.
©2003 Overdue Media
www.overduemedia.com
IT WAS FROM A SCANTILY-CLAD YOUNG LADY. I ASSUME IT WAS MEANT FOR HER HUSBAND.
IGNORE IT. IT'S JUST SPAM.
YOUNG MAN, I SERVED IN KOREA. I KNOW SPAM. THIS WAS *NOT* SPAM!
DIFFERENT KIND. THIS IS UNSOLICITED EMAIL SENT TO THOUSANDS OF PEOPLE.
OH DEAR. I WONDER IF HER HUSBAND KNOWS.
BB

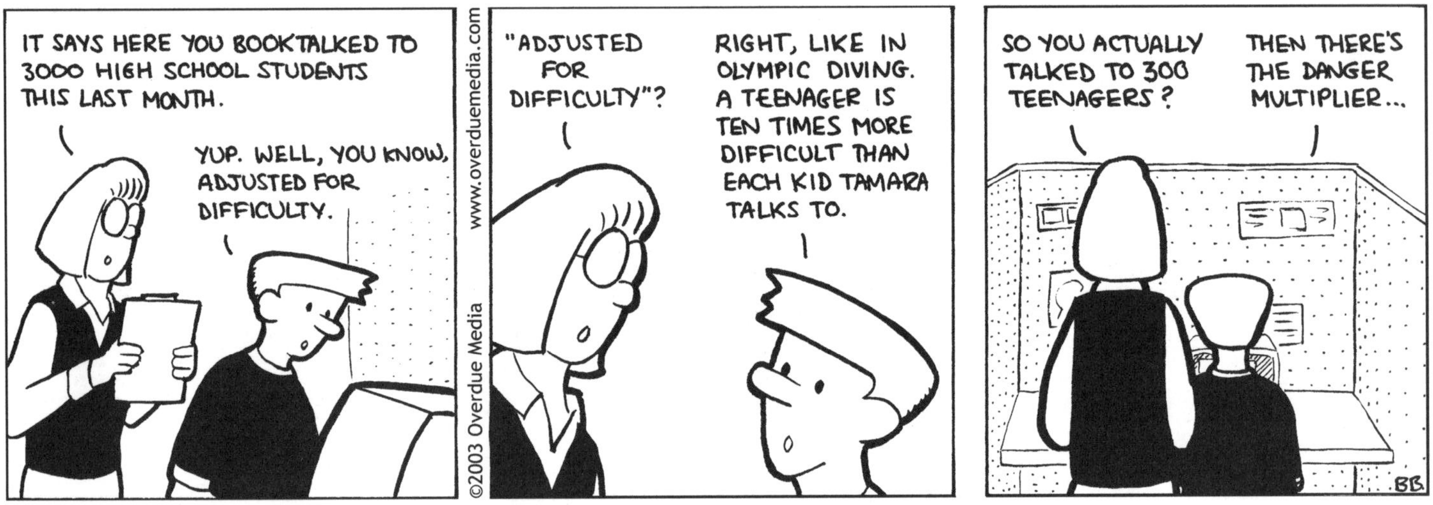
IT SAYS HERE YOU BOOKTALKED TO 3000 HIGH SCHOOL STUDENTS THIS LAST MONTH.
YUP. WELL, YOU KNOW, ADJUSTED FOR DIFFICULTY.
©2003 Overdue Media
www.overduemedia.com
"ADJUSTED FOR DIFFICULTY"?
RIGHT, LIKE IN OLYMPIC DIVING. A TEENAGER IS TEN TIMES MORE DIFFICULT THAN EACH KID TAMARA TALKS TO.
SO YOU ACTUALLY TALKED TO 300 TEENAGERS?
THEN THERE'S THE DANGER MULTIPLIER...
BB

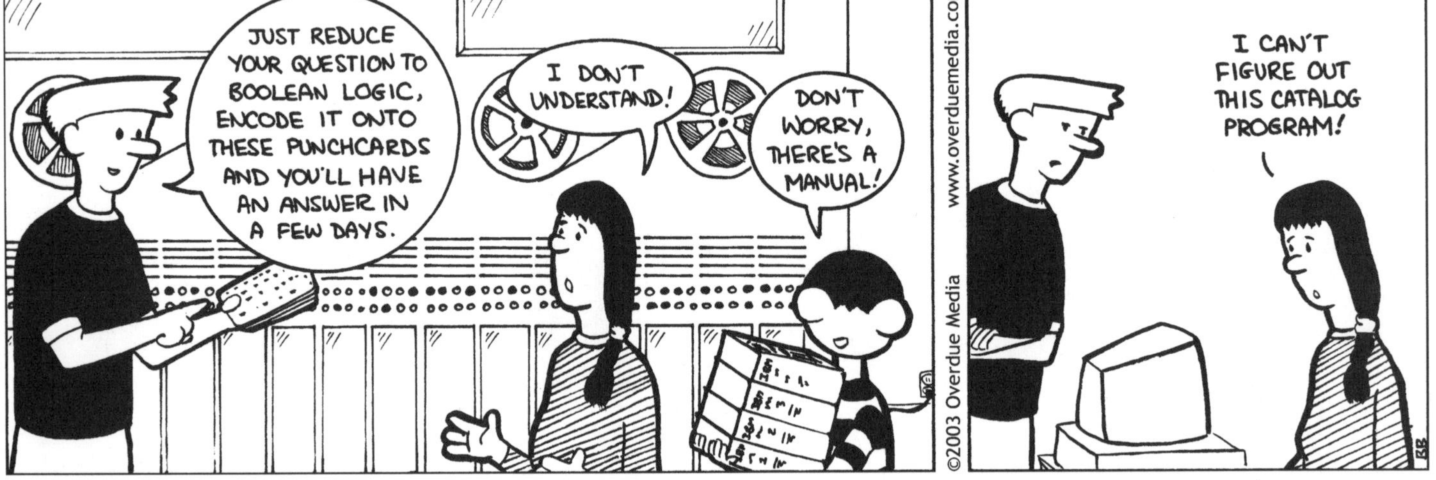
JUST REDUCE YOUR QUESTION TO BOOLEAN LOGIC, ENCODE IT ONTO THESE PUNCHCARDS AND YOU'LL HAVE AN ANSWER IN A FEW DAYS.
I DON'T UNDERSTAND!
DON'T WORRY, THERE'S A MANUAL!
©2003 Overdue Media
www.overduemedia.com
I CAN'T FIGURE OUT THIS CATALOG PROGRAM!
BB

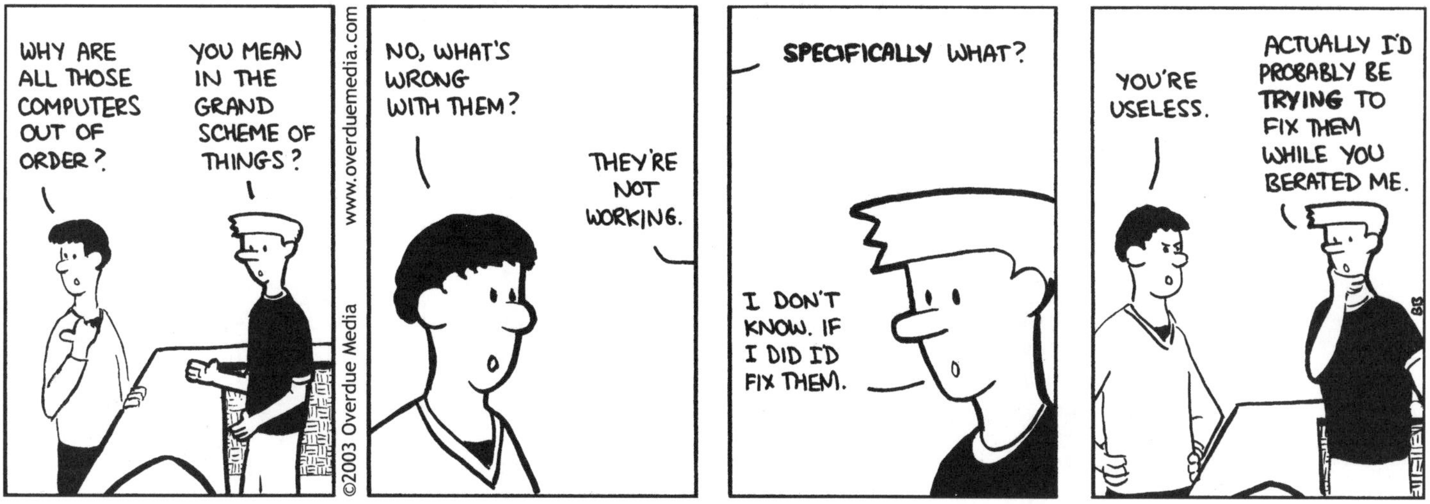
WHY ARE ALL THOSE COMPUTERS OUT OF ORDER?
YOU MEAN IN THE GRAND SCHEME OF THINGS?
www.overduemedia.com
©2003 Overdue Media
NO, WHAT'S WRONG WITH THEM?
THEY'RE NOT WORKING.
SPECIFICALLY WHAT?
I DON'T KNOW. IF I DID I'D FIX THEM.
YOU'RE USELESS.
ACTUALLY I'D PROBABLY BE **TRYING** TO FIX THEM WHILE YOU BERATED ME.
BB

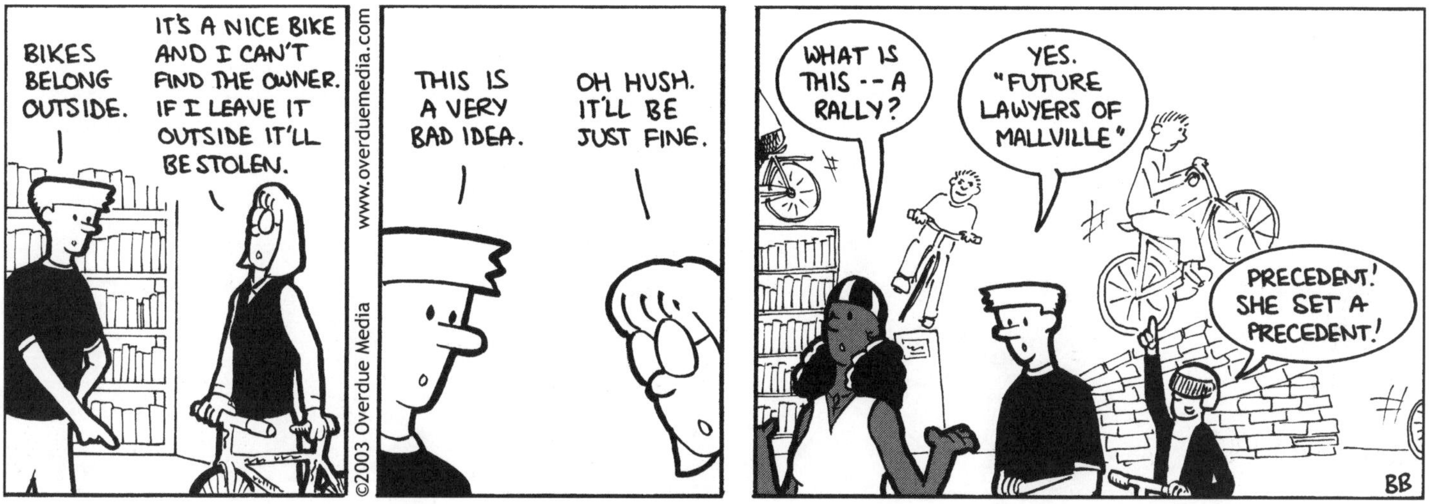
BIKES BELONG OUTSIDE.
IT'S A NICE BIKE AND I CAN'T FIND THE OWNER. IF I LEAVE IT OUTSIDE IT'LL BE STOLEN.
www.overduemedia.com
©2003 Overdue Media
THIS IS A VERY BAD IDEA.
OH HUSH. IT'LL BE JUST FINE.
WHAT IS THIS -- A RALLY?
YES. "FUTURE LAWYERS OF MALLVILLE"
PRECEDENT! SHE SET A PRECEDENT!
BB

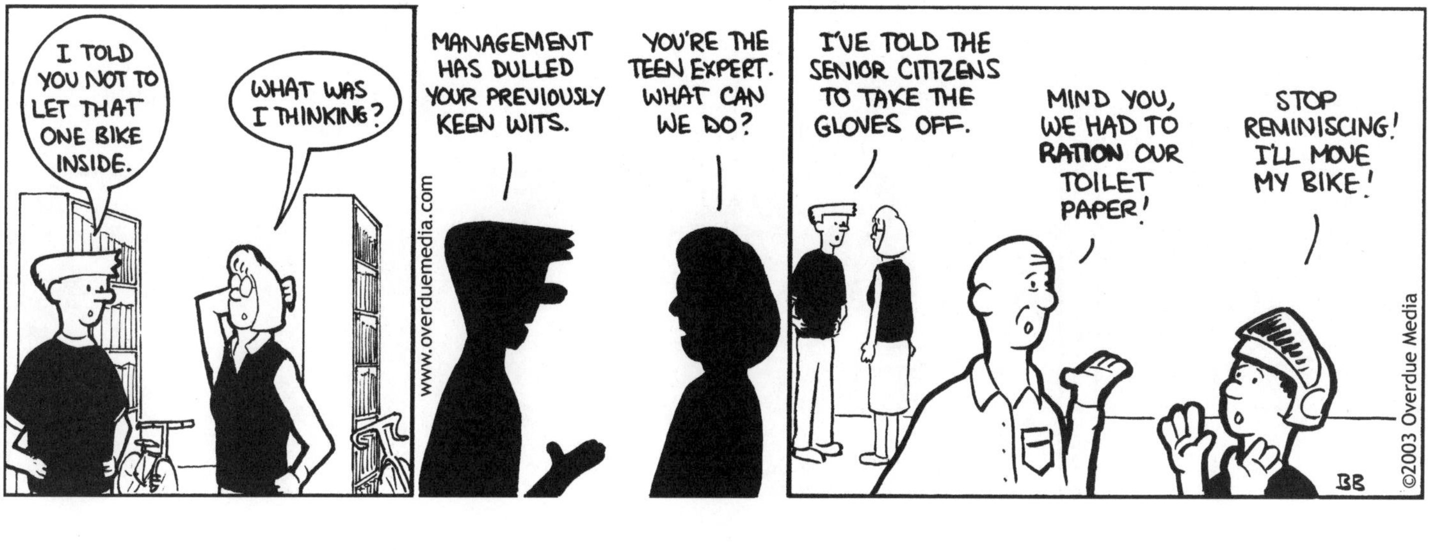
I TOLD YOU NOT TO LET THAT ONE BIKE INSIDE.
WHAT WAS I THINKING?
www.overduemedia.com
MANAGEMENT HAS DULLED YOUR PREVIOUSLY KEEN WITS.
YOU'RE THE TEEN EXPERT. WHAT CAN WE DO?
I'VE TOLD THE SENIOR CITIZENS TO TAKE THE GLOVES OFF.
MIND YOU, WE HAD TO **RATION** OUR TOILET PAPER!
STOP REMINISCING! I'LL MOVE MY BIKE!
BB
©2003 Overdue Media

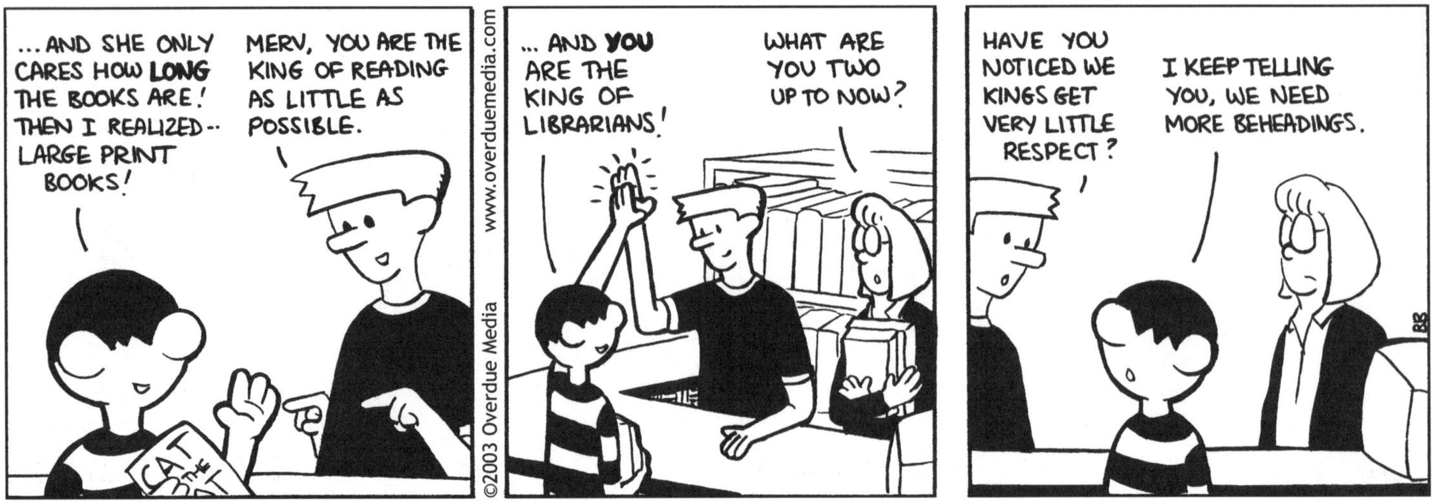
...AND SHE ONLY CARES HOW LONG THE BOOKS ARE! THEN I REALIZED-- LARGE PRINT BOOKS!
MERV, YOU ARE THE KING OF READING AS LITTLE AS POSSIBLE.
www.overduemedia.com
©2003 Overdue Media
...AND YOU ARE THE KING OF LIBRARIANS!
WHAT ARE YOU TWO UP TO NOW?
HAVE YOU NOTICED WE KINGS GET VERY LITTLE RESPECT?
I KEEP TELLING YOU, WE NEED MORE BEHEADINGS.
BB

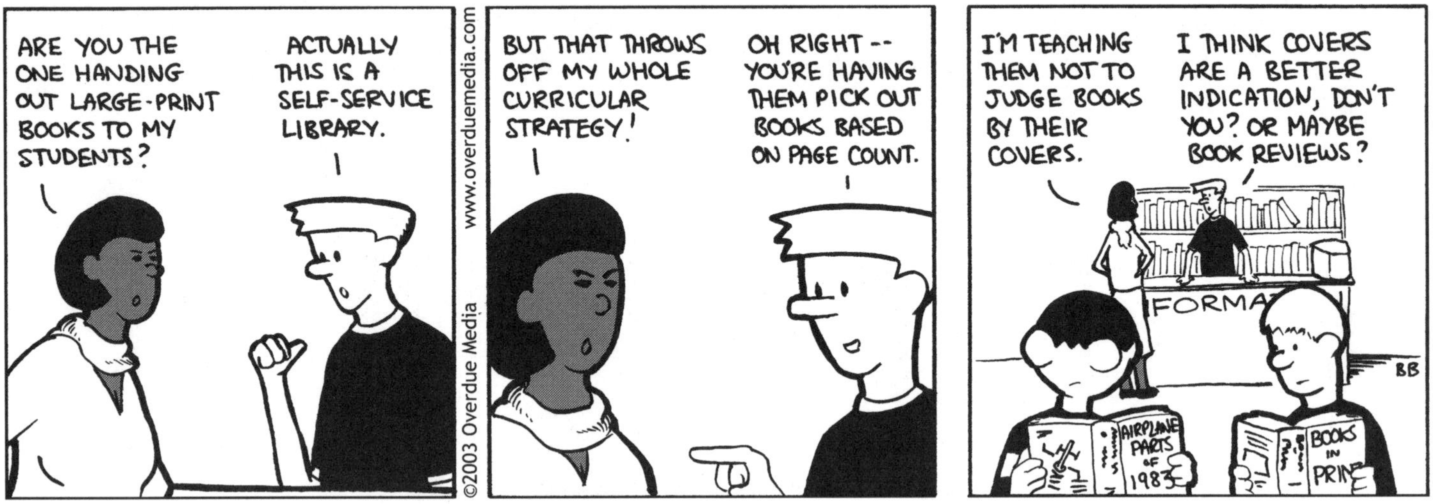
ARE YOU THE ONE HANDING OUT LARGE-PRINT BOOKS TO MY STUDENTS?
ACTUALLY THIS IS A SELF-SERVICE LIBRARY.
www.overduemedia.com
©2003 Overdue Media
BUT THAT THROWS OFF MY WHOLE CURRICULAR STRATEGY!
OH RIGHT -- YOU'RE HAVING THEM PICK OUT BOOKS BASED ON PAGE COUNT.
I'M TEACHING THEM NOT TO JUDGE BOOKS BY THEIR COVERS.
I THINK COVERS ARE A BETTER INDICATION, DON'T YOU? OR MAYBE BOOK REVIEWS?
AIRPLANE PARTS OF 1983
BB

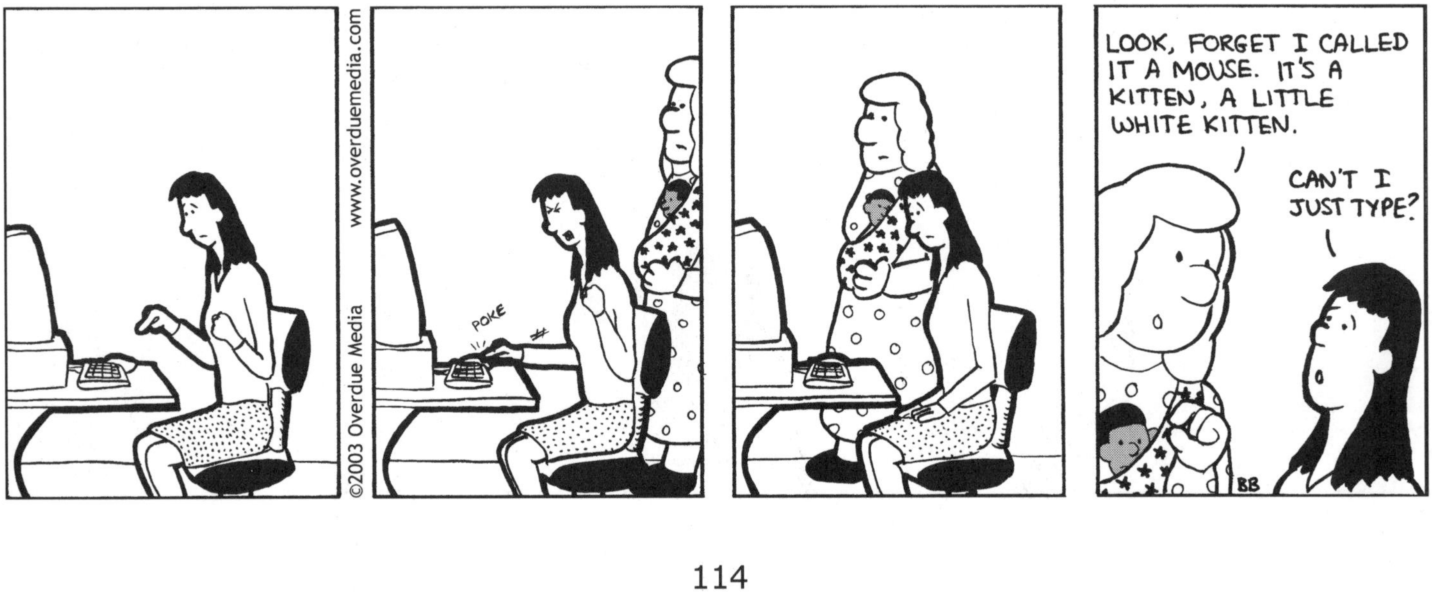
www.overduemedia.com
©2003 Overdue Media
POKE
LOOK, FORGET I CALLED IT A MOUSE. IT'S A KITTEN, A LITTLE WHITE KITTEN.
CAN'T I JUST TYPE?
BB

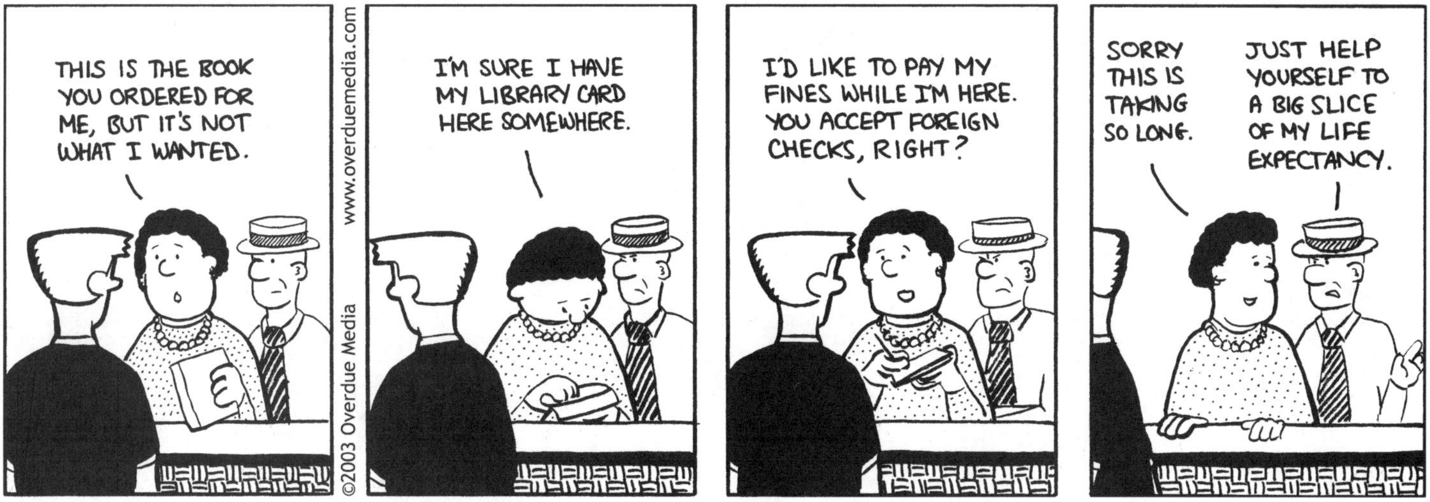
THIS IS THE BOOK YOU ORDERED FOR ME, BUT IT'S NOT WHAT I WANTED.
www.overduemedia.com
©2003 Overdue Media
I'M SURE I HAVE MY LIBRARY CARD HERE SOMEWHERE.
I'D LIKE TO PAY MY FINES WHILE I'M HERE. YOU ACCEPT FOREIGN CHECKS, RIGHT?
SORRY THIS IS TAKING SO LONG.
JUST HELP YOURSELF TO A BIG SLICE OF MY LIFE EXPECTANCY.

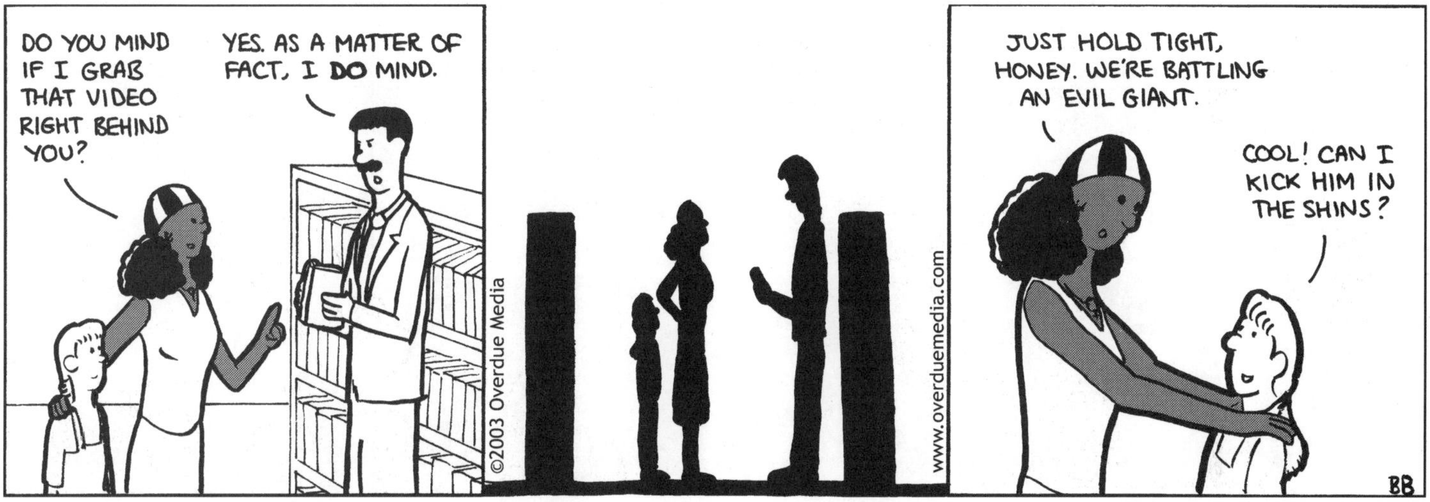
DO YOU MIND IF I GRAB THAT VIDEO RIGHT BEHIND YOU?
YES. AS A MATTER OF FACT, I **DO** MIND.
©2003 Overdue Media
www.overduemedia.com
JUST HOLD TIGHT, HONEY. WE'RE BATTLING AN EVIL GIANT.
COOL! CAN I KICK HIM IN THE SHINS?
BB

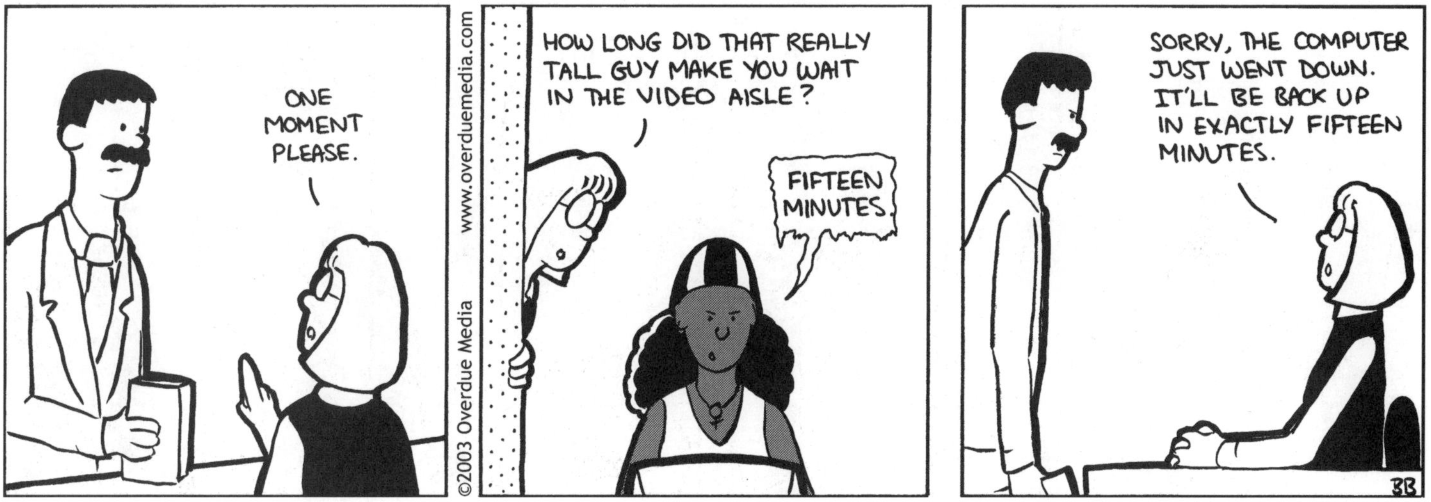
ONE MOMENT PLEASE.
www.overduemedia.com
©2003 Overdue Media
HOW LONG DID THAT REALLY TALL GUY MAKE YOU WAIT IN THE VIDEO AISLE?
FIFTEEN MINUTES.
SORRY, THE COMPUTER JUST WENT DOWN. IT'LL BE BACK UP IN EXACTLY FIFTEEN MINUTES.
BB

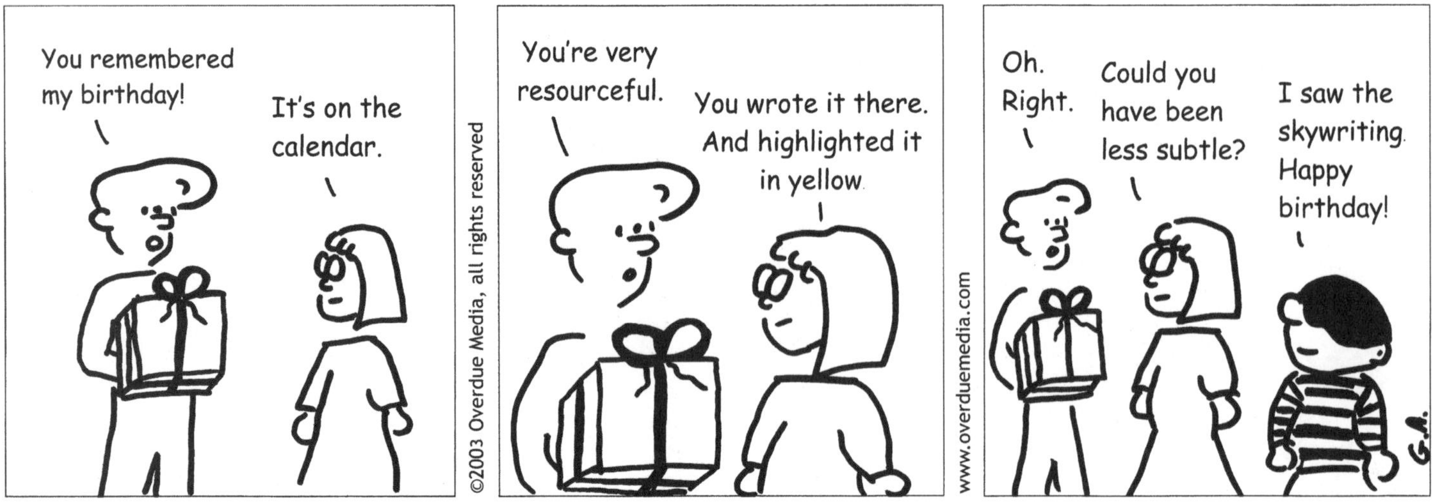
You remembered my birthday!
It's on the calendar.
©2003 Overdue Media, all rights reserved
You're very resourceful.
You wrote it there. And highlighted it in yellow.
www.overduemedia.com
Oh. Right.
Could you have been less subtle?
I saw the skywriting. Happy birthday!

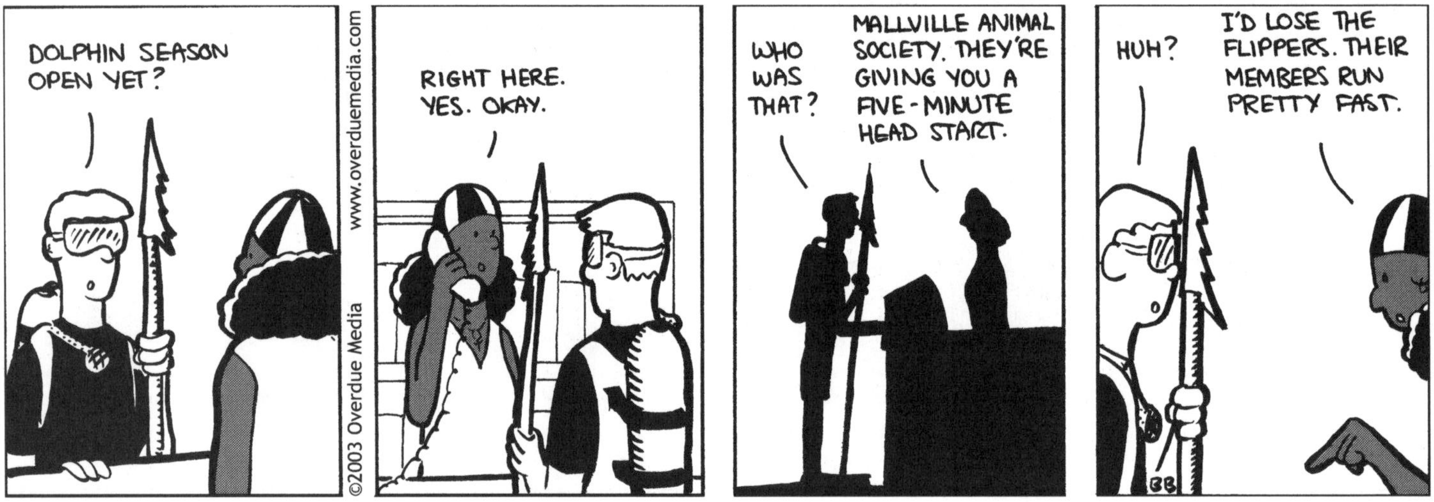
DOLPHIN SEASON OPEN YET?
www.overduemedia.com
©2003 Overdue Media
RIGHT HERE. YES. OKAY.
WHO WAS THAT?
MALLVILLE ANIMAL SOCIETY. THEY'RE GIVING YOU A FIVE-MINUTE HEAD START.
HUH?
I'D LOSE THE FLIPPERS. THEIR MEMBERS RUN PRETTY FAST.

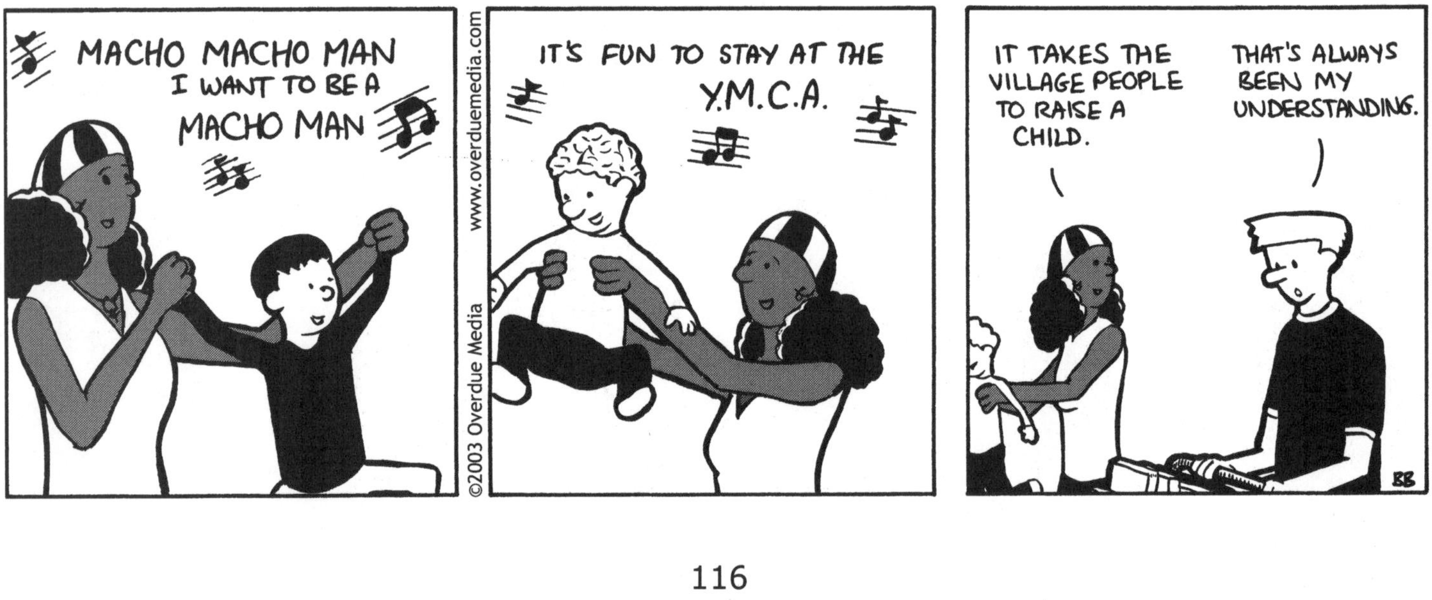
MACHO MACHO MAN
I WANT TO BE A MACHO MAN
www.overduemedia.com
©2003 Overdue Media
IT'S FUN TO STAY AT THE
Y.M.C.A.
IT TAKES THE VILLAGE PEOPLE TO RAISE A CHILD.
THAT'S ALWAYS BEEN MY UNDERSTANDING.

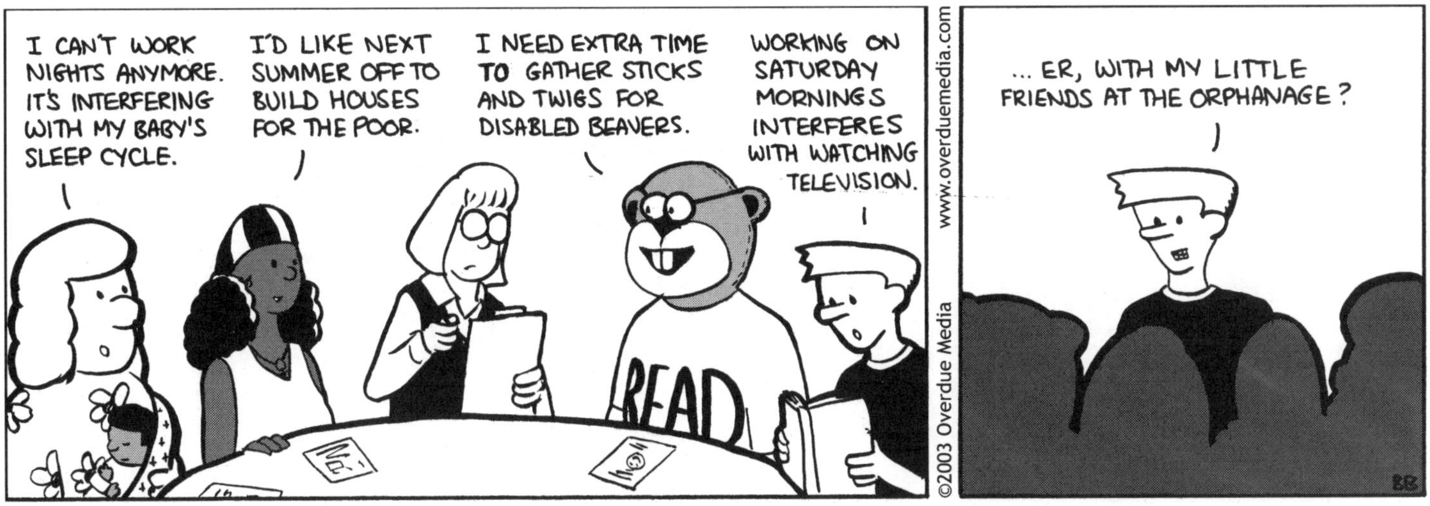
I CAN'T WORK NIGHTS ANYMORE. IT'S INTERFERING WITH MY BABY'S SLEEP CYCLE.
I'D LIKE NEXT SUMMER OFF TO BUILD HOUSES FOR THE POOR.
I NEED EXTRA TIME TO GATHER STICKS AND TWIGS FOR DISABLED BEAVERS.
WORKING ON SATURDAY MORNINGS INTERFERES WITH WATCHING TELEVISION.
READ
www.overduemedia.com
©2003 Overdue Media
... ER, WITH MY LITTLE FRIENDS AT THE ORPHANAGE?
BB

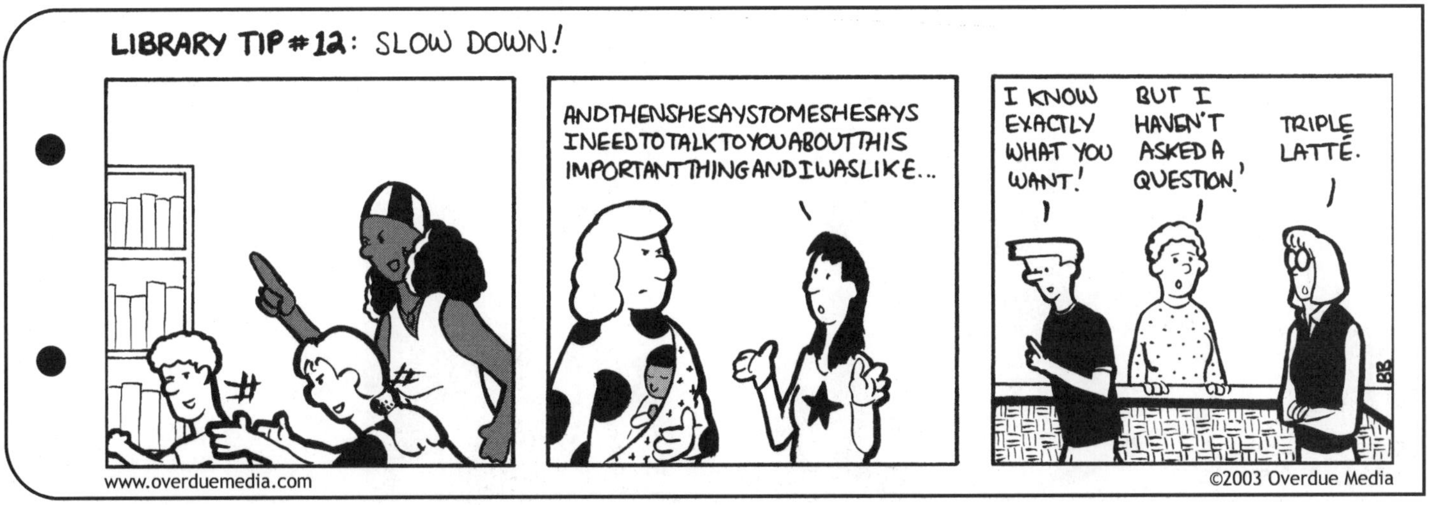
LIBRARY TIP #12: SLOW DOWN!
ANDTHENSHESAYSTOMESHESAYS INEEDTOTALKTOYOUABOUTTHIS IMPORTANTTHINGANDIWASLIKE...
I KNOW EXACTLY WHAT YOU WANT!
BUT I HAVEN'T ASKED A QUESTION!
TRIPLE LATTÉ.
BB
www.overduemedia.com
©2003 Overdue Media

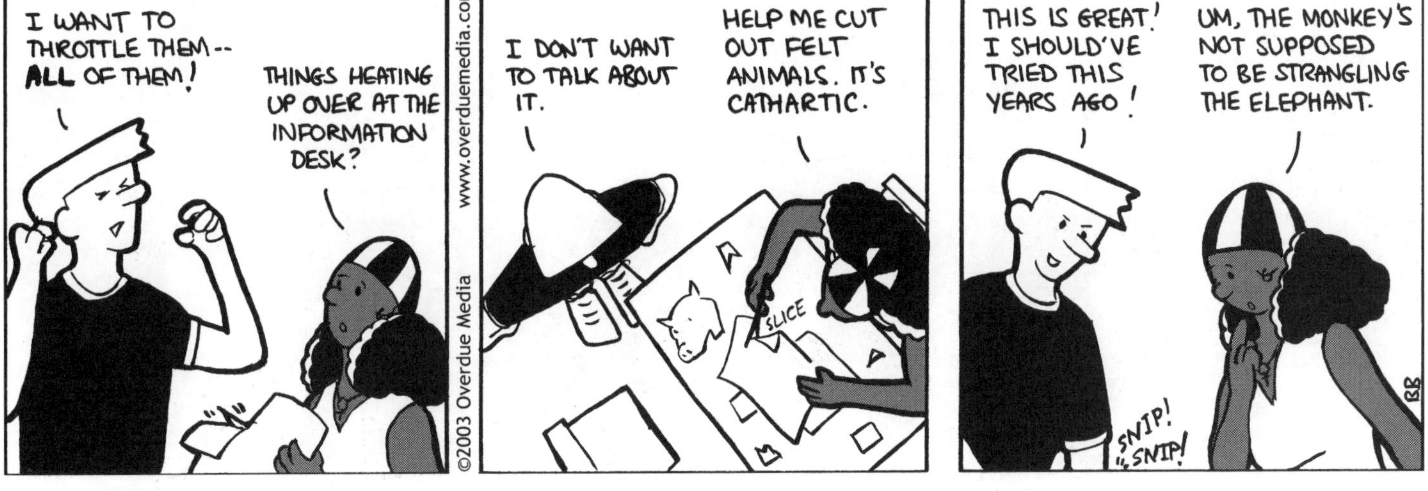
I WANT TO THROTTLE THEM -- ALL OF THEM!
THINGS HEATING UP OVER AT THE INFORMATION DESK?
www.overduemedia.com
©2003 Overdue Media
I DON'T WANT TO TALK ABOUT IT.
HELP ME CUT OUT FELT ANIMALS. IT'S CATHARTIC.
SLICE
THIS IS GREAT! I SHOULD'VE TRIED THIS YEARS AGO!
UM, THE MONKEY'S NOT SUPPOSED TO BE STRANGLING THE ELEPHANT.
SNIP! SNIP!
BB

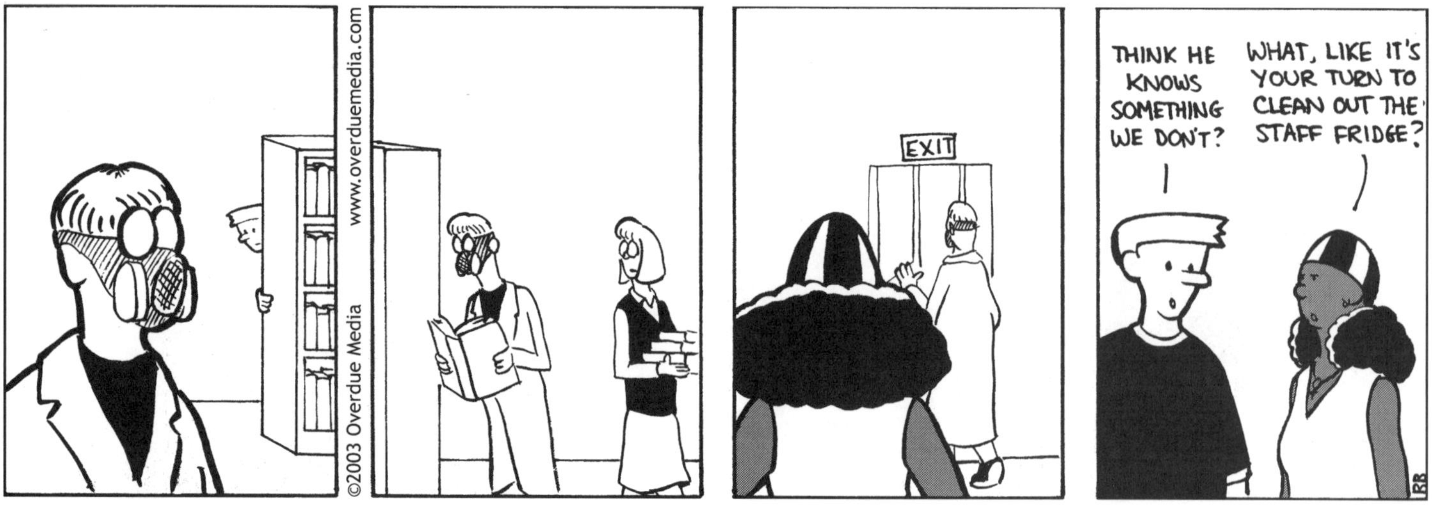
©2003 Overdue Media www.overduemedia.com
EXIT
THINK HE KNOWS SOMETHING WE DON'T?
WHAT, LIKE IT'S YOUR TURN TO CLEAN OUT THE STAFF FRIDGE?
BB

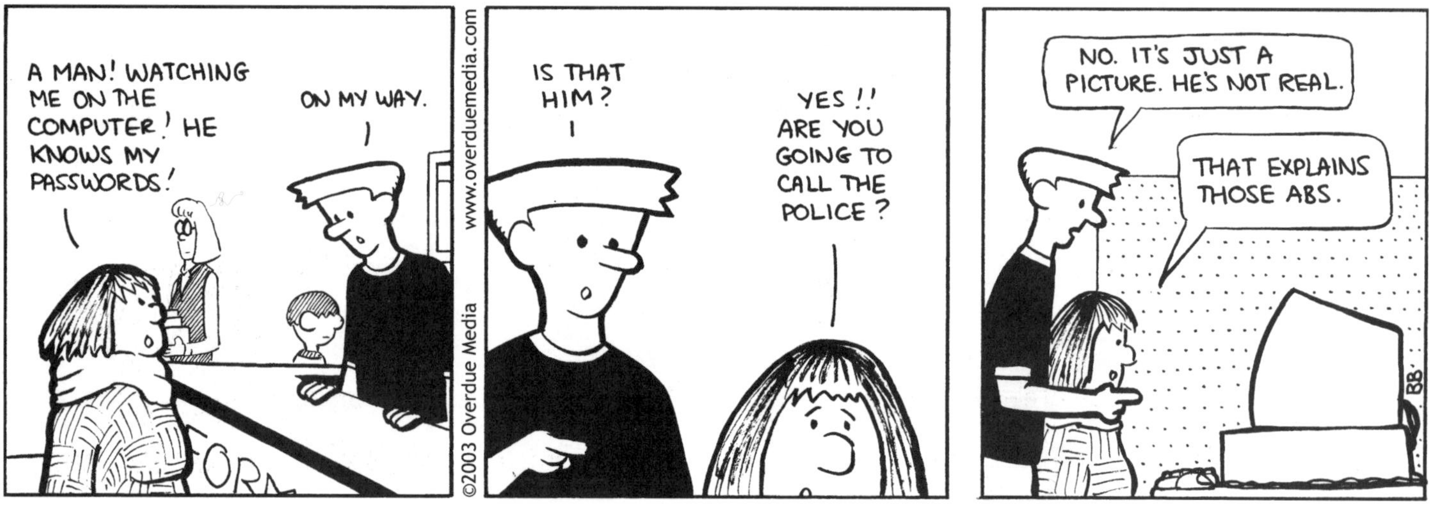
A MAN! WATCHING ME ON THE COMPUTER! HE KNOWS MY PASSWORDS!
ON MY WAY.
©2003 Overdue Media www.overduemedia.com
IS THAT HIM?
YES!! ARE YOU GOING TO CALL THE POLICE?
NO. IT'S JUST A PICTURE. HE'S NOT REAL.
THAT EXPLAINS THOSE ABS.
BB

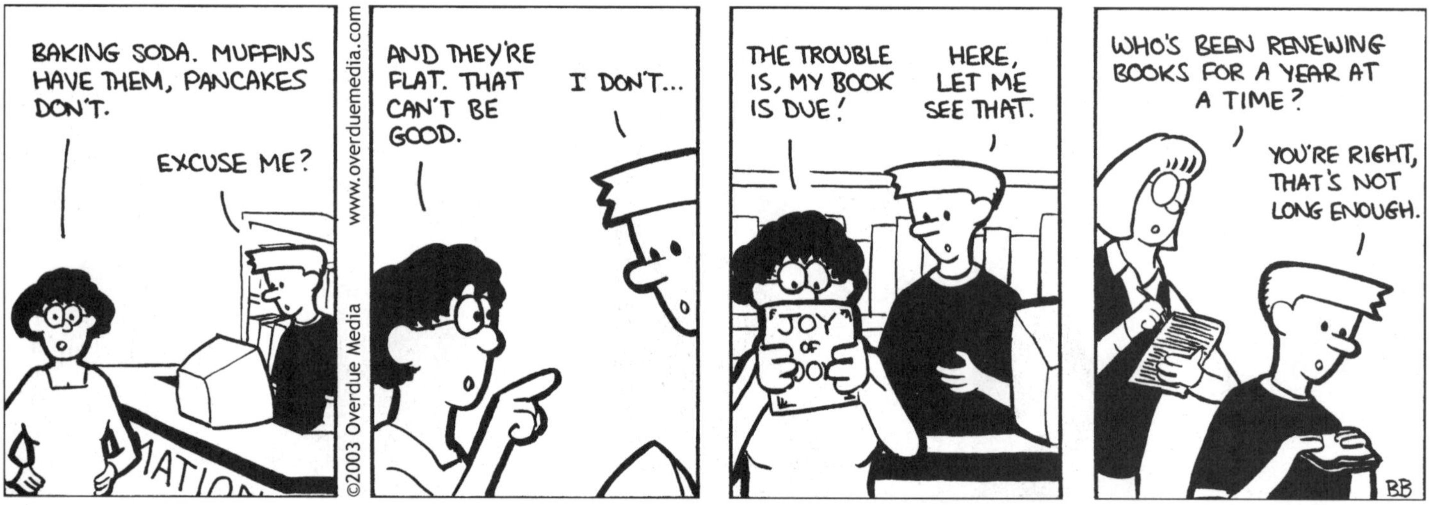
BAKING SODA. MUFFINS HAVE THEM, PANCAKES DON'T.
EXCUSE ME?
©2003 Overdue Media www.overduemedia.com
AND THEY'RE FLAT. THAT CAN'T BE GOOD.
I DON'T...
THE TROUBLE IS, MY BOOK IS DUE!
HERE, LET ME SEE THAT.
WHO'S BEEN RENEWING BOOKS FOR A YEAR AT A TIME?
YOU'RE RIGHT, THAT'S NOT LONG ENOUGH.
BB

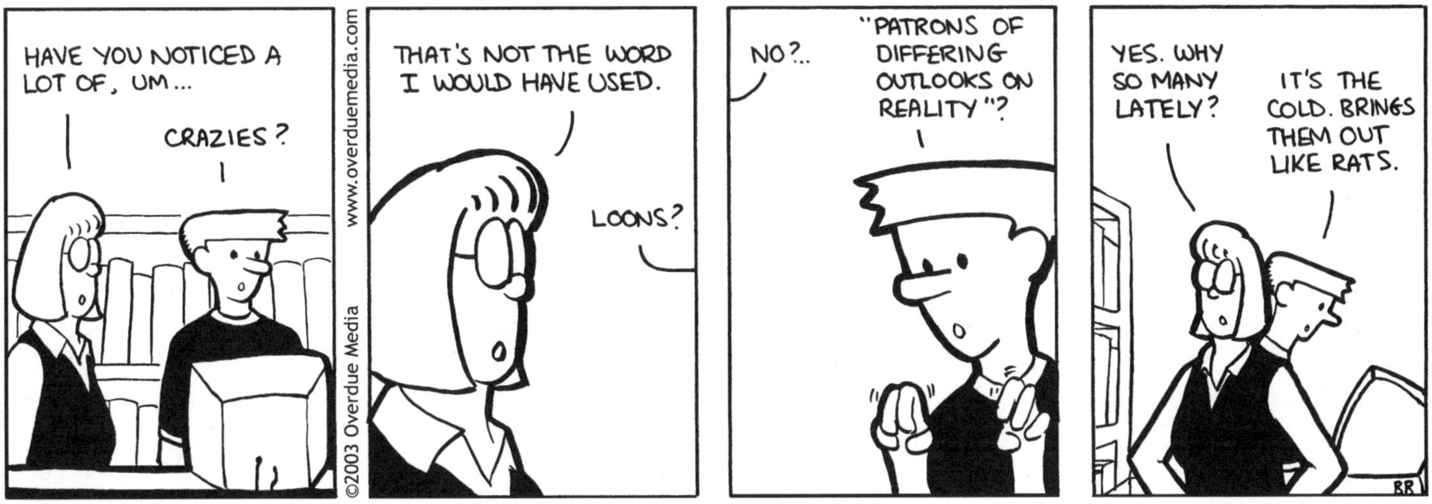
HAVE YOU NOTICED A LOT OF, UM...
CRAZIES?
©2003 Overdue Media www.overduemedia.com
THAT'S NOT THE WORD I WOULD HAVE USED.
LOONS?
NO?..
"PATRONS OF DIFFERING OUTLOOKS ON REALITY"?
YES. WHY SO MANY LATELY?
IT'S THE COLD. BRINGS THEM OUT LIKE RATS.

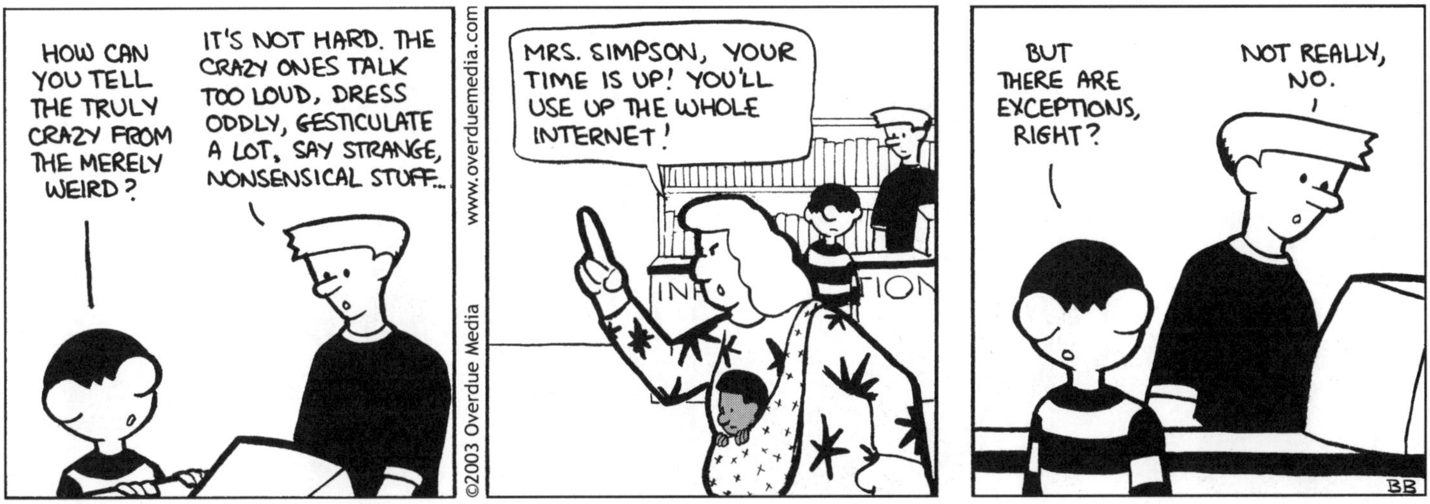
HOW CAN YOU TELL THE TRULY CRAZY FROM THE MERELY WEIRD?
IT'S NOT HARD. THE CRAZY ONES TALK TOO LOUD, DRESS ODDLY, GESTICULATE A LOT, SAY STRANGE, NONSENSICAL STUFF...
©2003 Overdue Media www.overduemedia.com
MRS. SIMPSON, YOUR TIME IS UP! YOU'LL USE UP THE WHOLE INTERNET!
BUT THERE ARE EXCEPTIONS, RIGHT?
NOT REALLY, NO.

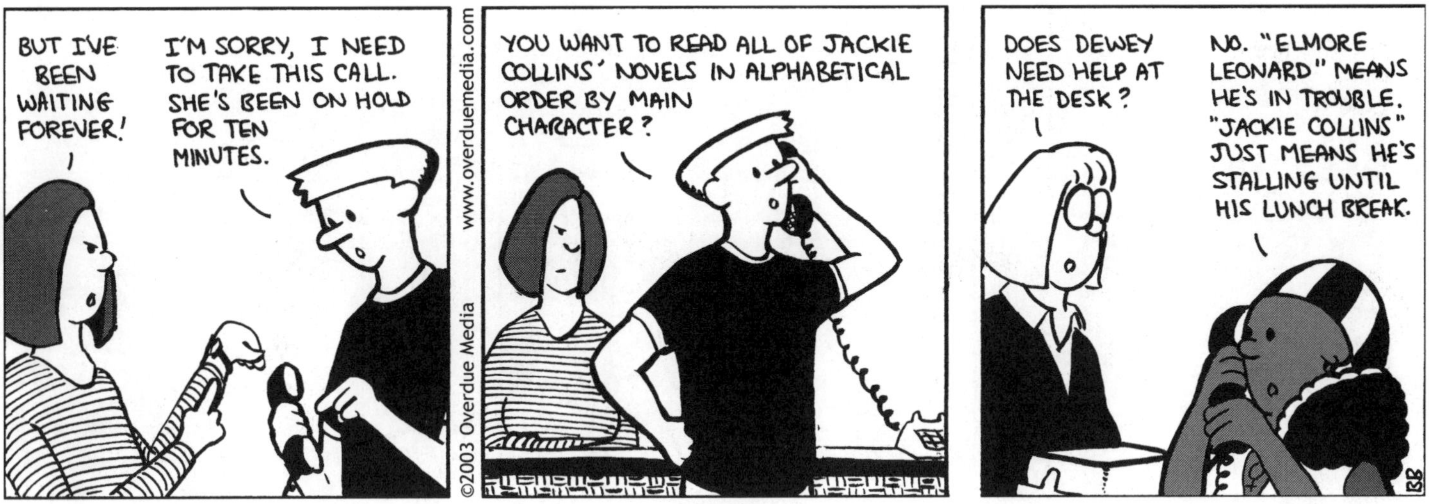
BUT I'VE BEEN WAITING FOREVER!
I'M SORRY, I NEED TO TAKE THIS CALL. SHE'S BEEN ON HOLD FOR TEN MINUTES.
©2003 Overdue Media www.overduemedia.com
YOU WANT TO READ ALL OF JACKIE COLLINS' NOVELS IN ALPHABETICAL ORDER BY MAIN CHARACTER?
DOES DEWEY NEED HELP AT THE DESK?
NO. "ELMORE LEONARD" MEANS HE'S IN TROUBLE. "JACKIE COLLINS" JUST MEANS HE'S STALLING UNTIL HIS LUNCH BREAK.

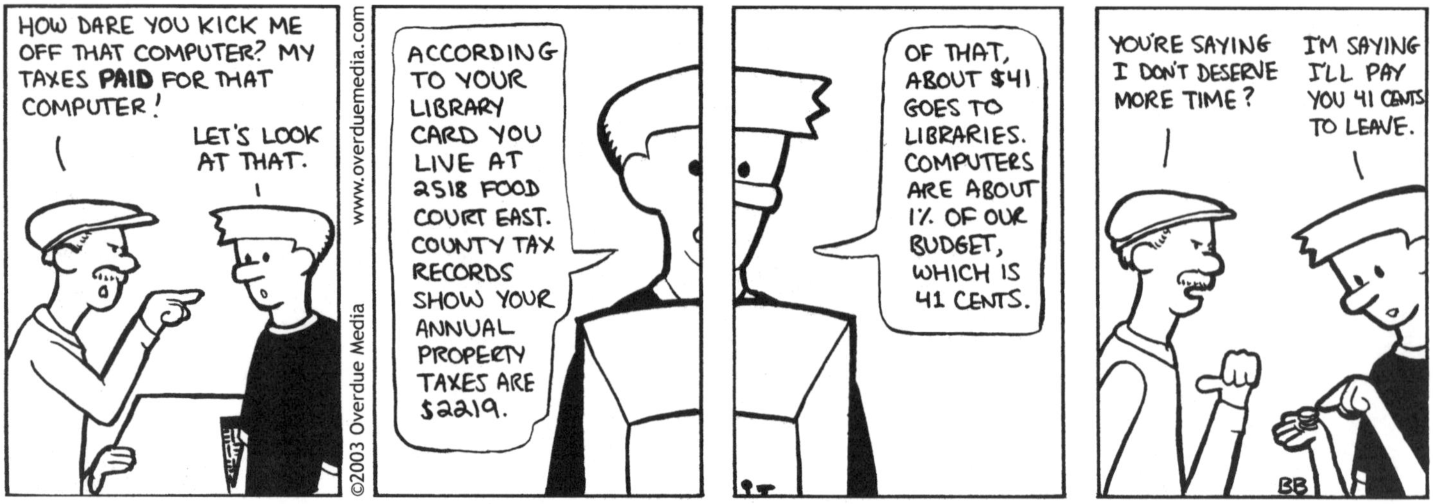
HOW DARE YOU KICK ME OFF THAT COMPUTER? MY TAXES PAID FOR THAT COMPUTER!
LET'S LOOK AT THAT.
www.overduemedia.com
©2003 Overdue Media
ACCORDING TO YOUR LIBRARY CARD YOU LIVE AT 2518 FOOD COURT EAST. COUNTY TAX RECORDS SHOW YOUR ANNUAL PROPERTY TAXES ARE $2219.
OF THAT, ABOUT $41 GOES TO LIBRARIES. COMPUTERS ARE ABOUT 1% OF OUR BUDGET, WHICH IS 41 CENTS.
YOU'RE SAYING I DON'T DESERVE MORE TIME?
I'M SAYING I'LL PAY YOU 41 CENTS TO LEAVE.
BB

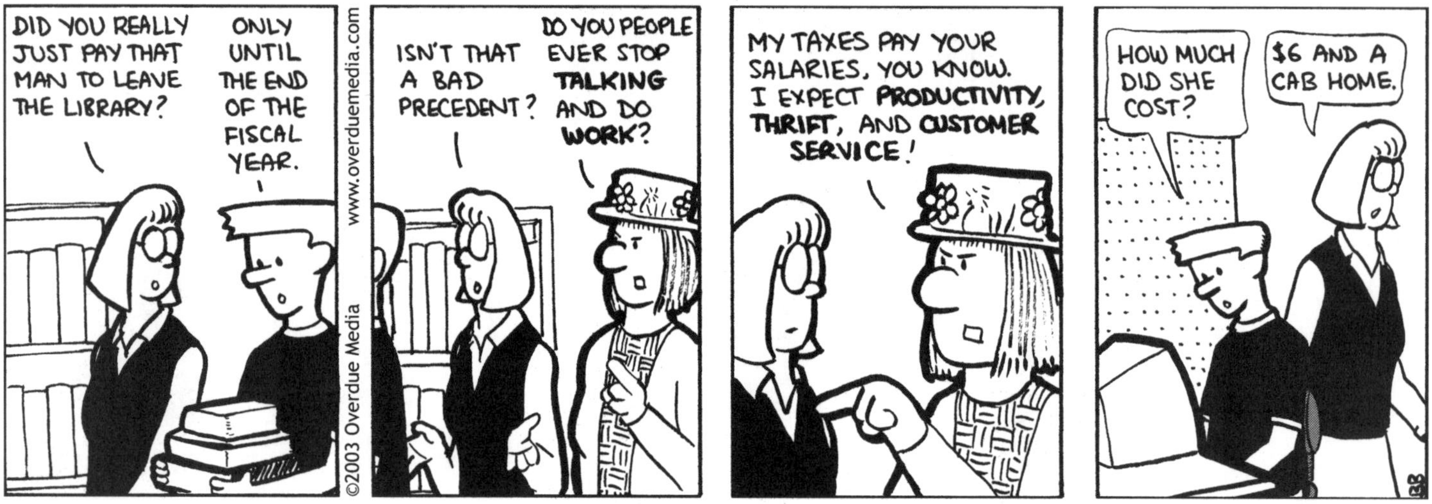
DID YOU REALLY JUST PAY THAT MAN TO LEAVE THE LIBRARY?
ONLY UNTIL THE END OF THE FISCAL YEAR.
www.overduemedia.com
©2003 Overdue Media
ISN'T THAT A BAD PRECEDENT?
DO YOU PEOPLE EVER STOP TALKING AND DO WORK?
MY TAXES PAY YOUR SALARIES, YOU KNOW. I EXPECT PRODUCTIVITY, THRIFT, AND CUSTOMER SERVICE!
HOW MUCH DID SHE COST?
$6 AND A CAB HOME.
BB

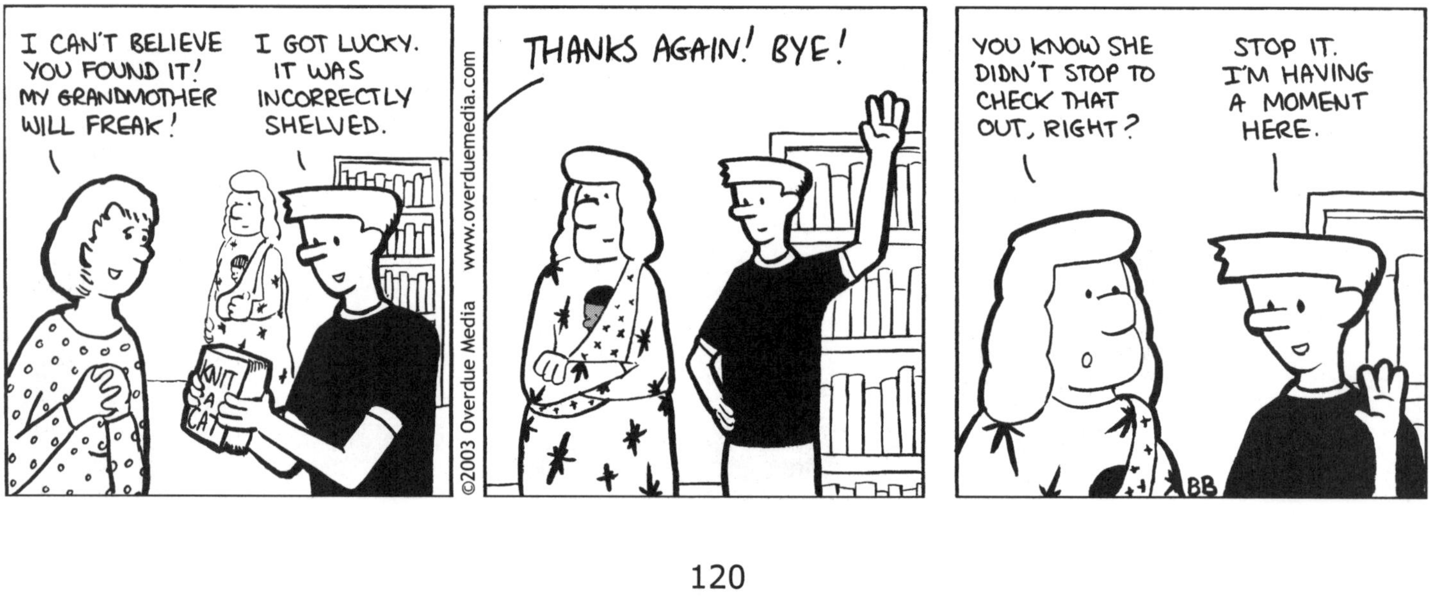
I CAN'T BELIEVE YOU FOUND IT! MY GRANDMOTHER WILL FREAK!
I GOT LUCKY. IT WAS INCORRECTLY SHELVED.
KNIT A CAT
www.overduemedia.com
©2003 Overdue Media
THANKS AGAIN! BYE!
YOU KNOW SHE DIDN'T STOP TO CHECK THAT OUT, RIGHT?
STOP IT. I'M HAVING A MOMENT HERE.
BB

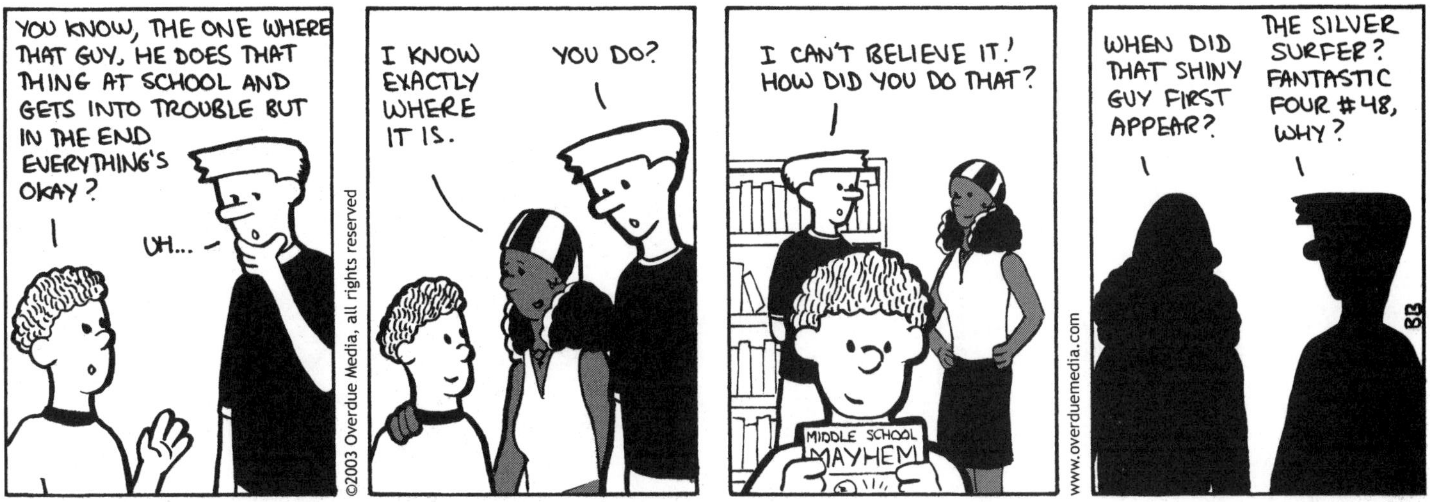
YOU KNOW, THE ONE WHERE THAT GUY, HE DOES THAT THING AT SCHOOL AND GETS INTO TROUBLE BUT IN THE END EVERYTHING'S OKAY?
UH...
©2003 Overdue Media, all rights reserved
I KNOW EXACTLY WHERE IT IS.
YOU DO?
I CAN'T BELIEVE IT! HOW DID YOU DO THAT?
MIDDLE SCHOOL MAYHEM
www.overduemedia.com
WHEN DID THAT SHINY GUY FIRST APPEAR?
THE SILVER SURFER? FANTASTIC FOUR #48, WHY?
BB

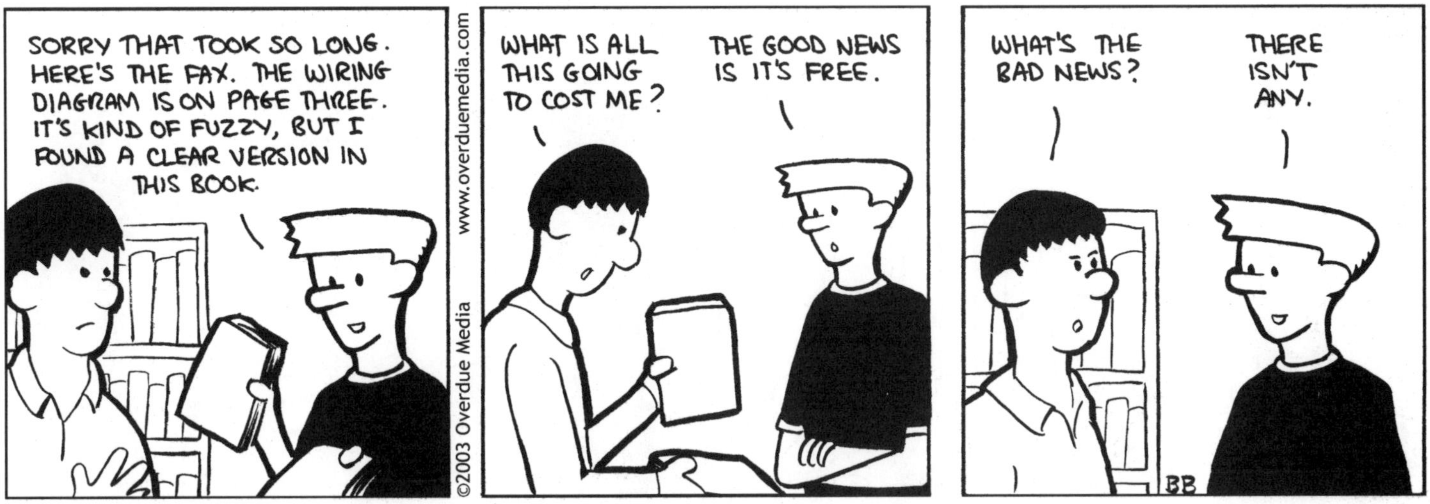
SORRY THAT TOOK SO LONG. HERE'S THE FAX. THE WIRING DIAGRAM IS ON PAGE THREE. IT'S KIND OF FUZZY, BUT I FOUND A CLEAR VERSION IN THIS BOOK.
www.overduemedia.com
©2003 Overdue Media
WHAT IS ALL THIS GOING TO COST ME?
THE GOOD NEWS IS IT'S FREE.
WHAT'S THE BAD NEWS?
THERE ISN'T ANY.
BB

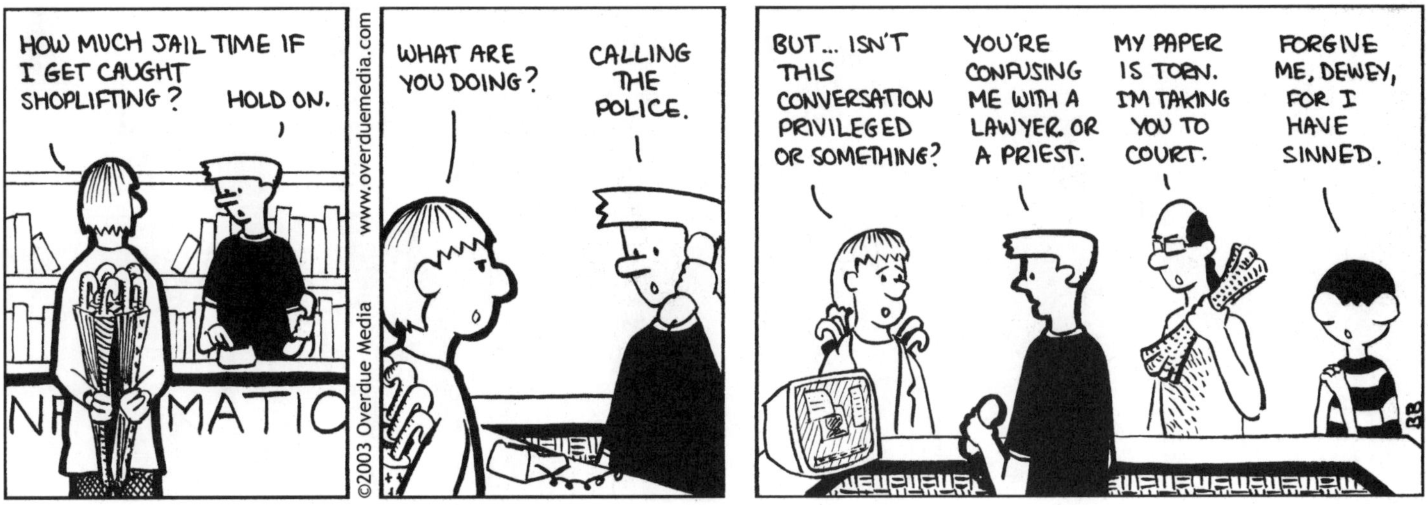
HOW MUCH JAIL TIME IF I GET CAUGHT SHOPLIFTING?
HOLD ON.
NFORMATIO
www.overduemedia.com
©2003 Overdue Media
WHAT ARE YOU DOING?
CALLING THE POLICE.
BUT... ISN'T THIS CONVERSATION PRIVILEGED OR SOMETHING?
YOU'RE CONFUSING ME WITH A LAWYER OR A PRIEST.
MY PAPER IS TORN. I'M TAKING YOU TO COURT.
FORGIVE ME, DEWEY, FOR I HAVE SINNED.
BB

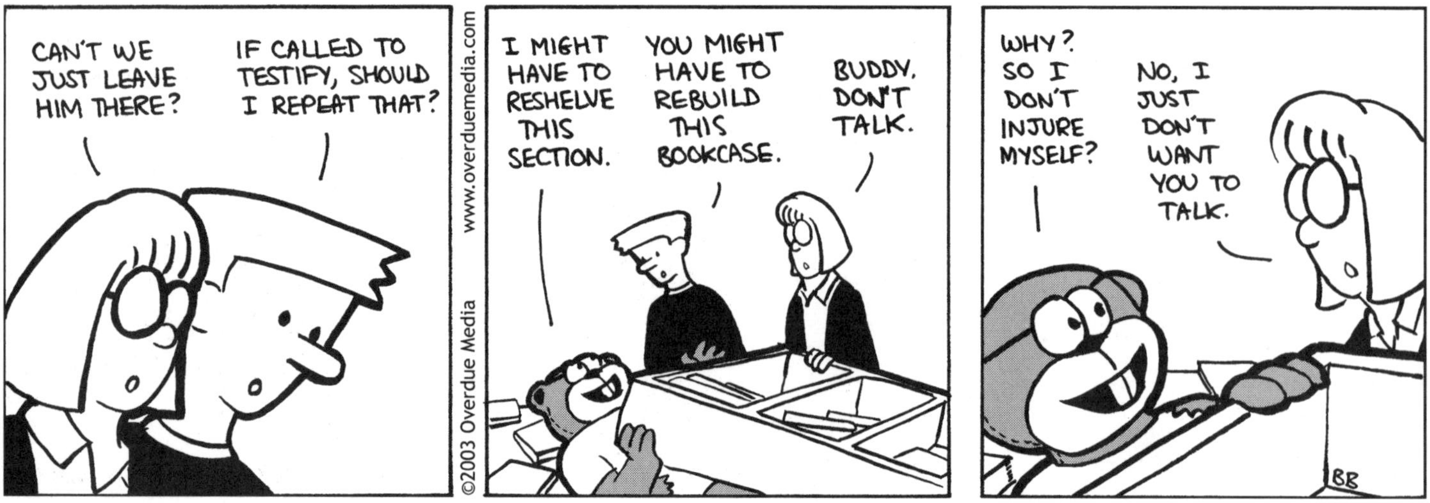
CAN'T WE JUST LEAVE HIM THERE?
IF CALLED TO TESTIFY, SHOULD I REPEAT THAT?
www.overduemedia.com
©2003 Overdue Media
I MIGHT HAVE TO RESHELVE THIS SECTION.
YOU MIGHT HAVE TO REBUILD THIS BOOKCASE.
BUDDY. DON'T TALK.
WHY? SO I DON'T INJURE MYSELF?
NO, I JUST DON'T WANT YOU TO TALK.
BB

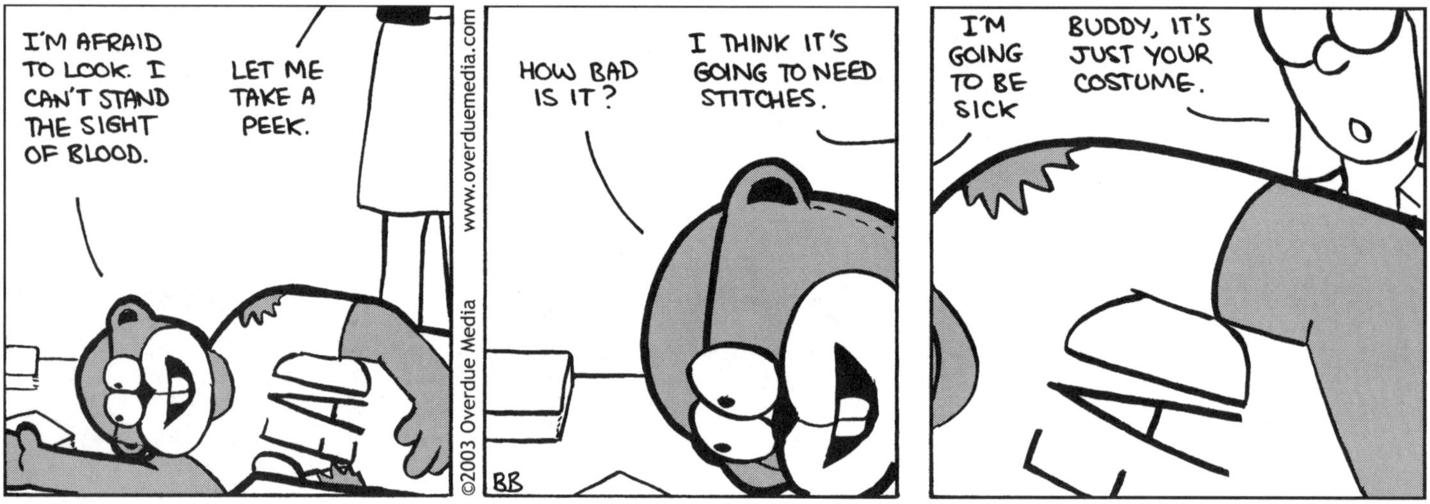
I'M AFRAID TO LOOK. I CAN'T STAND THE SIGHT OF BLOOD.
LET ME TAKE A PEEK.
www.overduemedia.com
©2003 Overdue Media
BB
HOW BAD IS IT?
I THINK IT'S GOING TO NEED STITCHES.
I'M GOING TO BE SICK
BUDDY, IT'S JUST YOUR COSTUME.

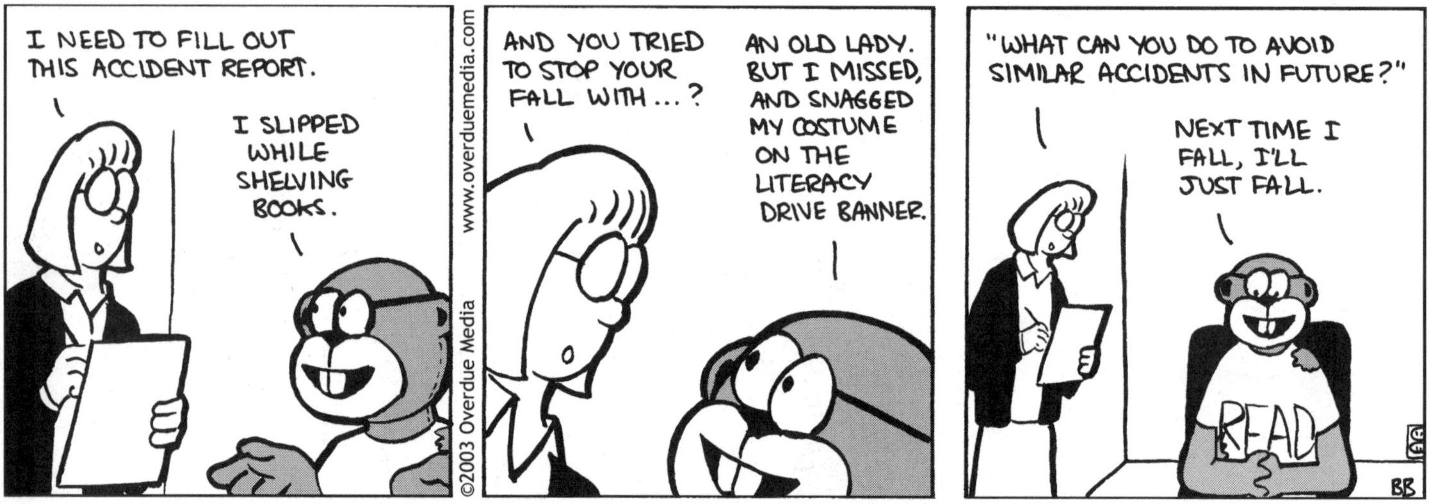
I NEED TO FILL OUT THIS ACCIDENT REPORT.
I SLIPPED WHILE SHELVING BOOKS.
www.overduemedia.com
©2003 Overdue Media
AND YOU TRIED TO STOP YOUR FALL WITH ...?
AN OLD LADY. BUT I MISSED, AND SNAGGED MY COSTUME ON THE LITERACY DRIVE BANNER.
"WHAT CAN YOU DO TO AVOID SIMILAR ACCIDENTS IN FUTURE?"
NEXT TIME I FALL, I'LL JUST FALL.
READ
BB

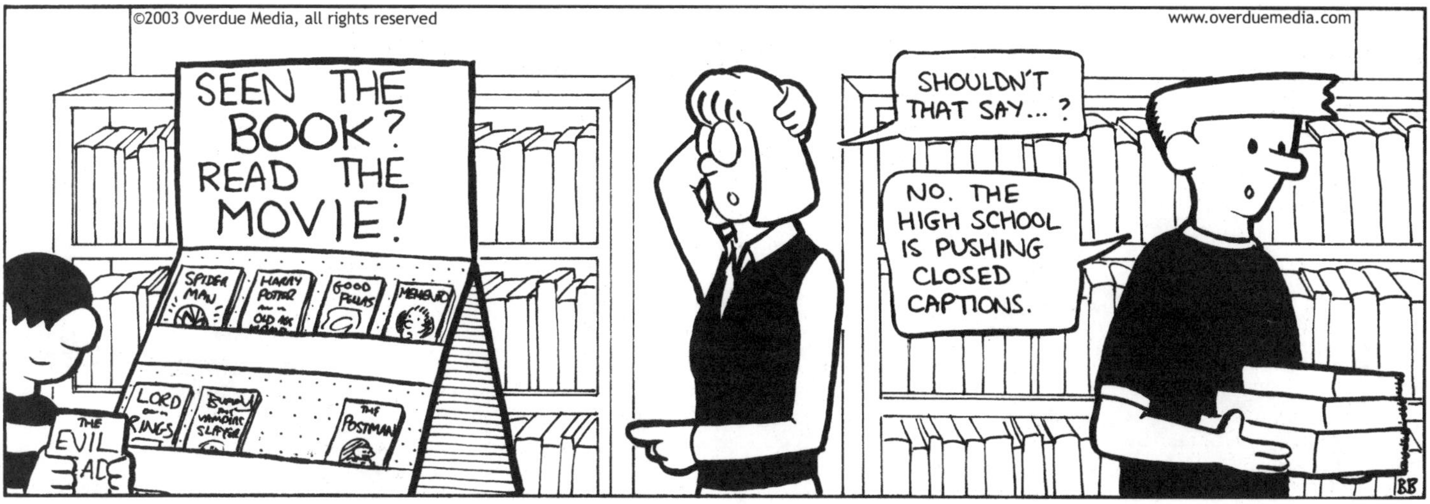
©2003 Overdue Media, all rights reserved
www.overduemedia.com
SEEN THE BOOK? READ THE MOVIE!
SPIDER MAN
GOOD FELLAS
MEMENTO
LORD RINGS
THE POSTMAN
SHOULDN'T THAT SAY... ?
NO. THE HIGH SCHOOL IS PUSHING CLOSED CAPTIONS.
BB

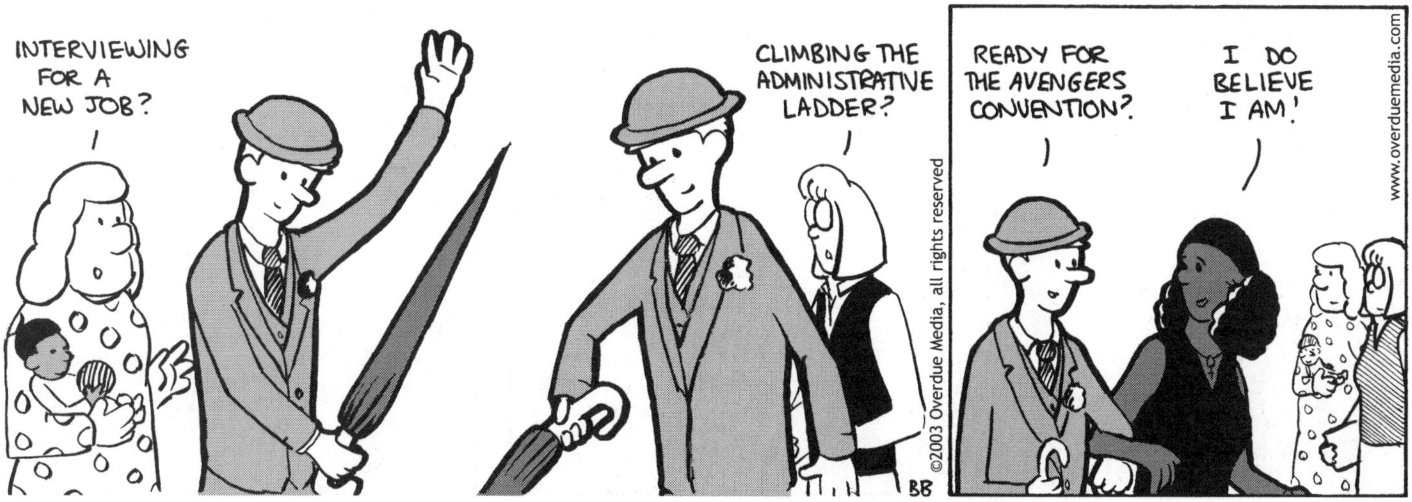
INTERVIEWING FOR A NEW JOB?
CLIMBING THE ADMINISTRATIVE LADDER?
©2003 Overdue Media, all rights reserved
BB
READY FOR THE AVENGERS CONVENTION?
I DO BELIEVE I AM!
www.overduemedia.com

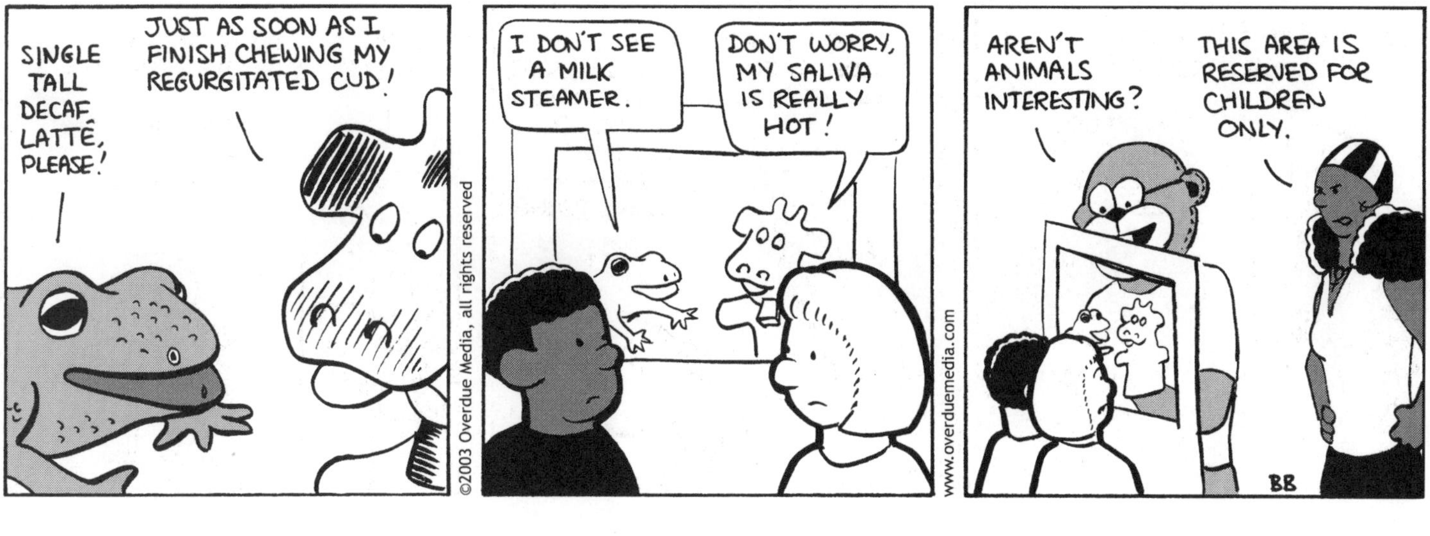
SINGLE TALL DECAF LATTÉ, PLEASE!
JUST AS SOON AS I FINISH CHEWING MY REGURGITATED CUD!
©2003 Overdue Media, all rights reserved
I DON'T SEE A MILK STEAMER.
DON'T WORRY, MY SALIVA IS REALLY HOT!
www.overduemedia.com
AREN'T ANIMALS INTERESTING?
THIS AREA IS RESERVED FOR CHILDREN ONLY.
BB

THIS MUST BE ANOTHER OF YOUR TEACHER'S BRAINSTORMS.
SHE JUST SAID TO WRITE A STORY. THE REST WAS MY IDEA.
www.overduemedia.com
©2003 Overdue Media
"CHOOSE YOUR OWN ADVENTURE"? ISN'T THAT PASSÉ?
A CLASSIC FORMAT READY TO BE REDISCOVERED.
"YOU ARE A HEALTH DEPARTMENT INSPECTOR"
ARE THERE ENOUGH RATS ON THE COVER?
BB

OKAY MISTER INTERACTIVE FICTION. I'M READY FOR MY NEXT CHOICE.
"YOU APPLY TO VOCATIONAL SCHOOL. WHICH CAREER PATH DO YOU PICK?"
www.overduemedia.com
©2003 Overdue Media
LIBRARIAN. NO, WAIT. ROCK STAR!
THOSE AREN'T ON THE LIST.
OH. UM... "ORGAN DONER."
GOOD CHOICE. BETTER BENEFITS PACKAGE THAN "TOXIC WASTE TASTER."
BB

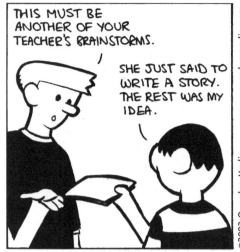

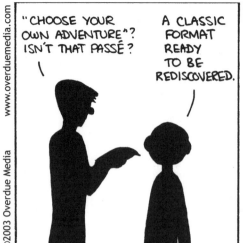

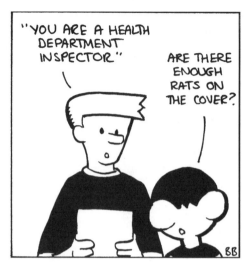

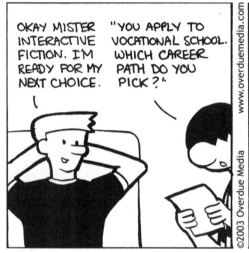

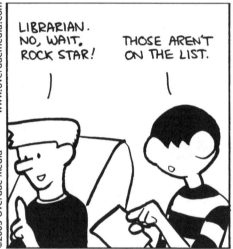

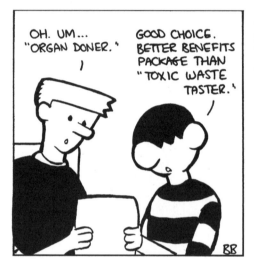

This space intentionally left blank.

WHAT, I DIED AGAIN? THIS IS THE WORST "CHOOSE YOUR OWN ADVENTURE" EVER!
YOU NEED TO MAKE BETTER CHOICES.
I TRIED EVERY CHOICE! I DIED IN ALL OF THEM!
SO IT'S REALISTIC. WE ALL DIE EVENTUALLY.
www.overduemedia.com ©2003 Overdue Media
YOU'RE EITHER VERY PROFOUND OR VERY LAZY.
I LIKE TO THINK I'M BOTH.

SO MERV, DID YOUR STORY GET GRADED YET?
D-
www.overduemedia.com ©2003 Overdue Media
THAT'S A LITTLE EXTREME.
I THOUGHT SO TOO!
MAYBE YOU SHOULDN'T HAVE KILLED OFF THE TEACHER IN THE FIRST CHAPTER.
I REFUSE TO PANDER TO MY AUDIENCE.
CAN I JUST SAY, I LOVE LIBRARIES AND EVERYONE ASSOCIATED WITH THEM!
BB

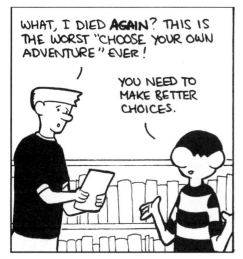

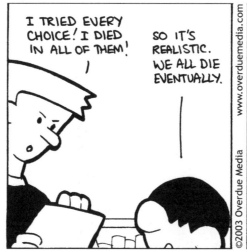

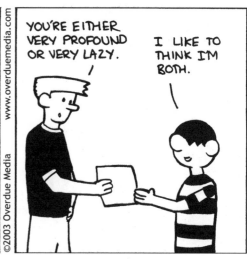

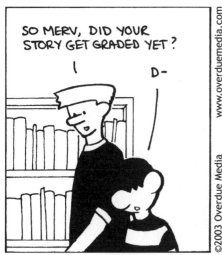

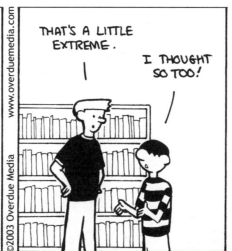

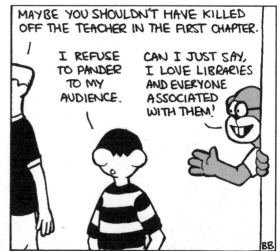

This one too.

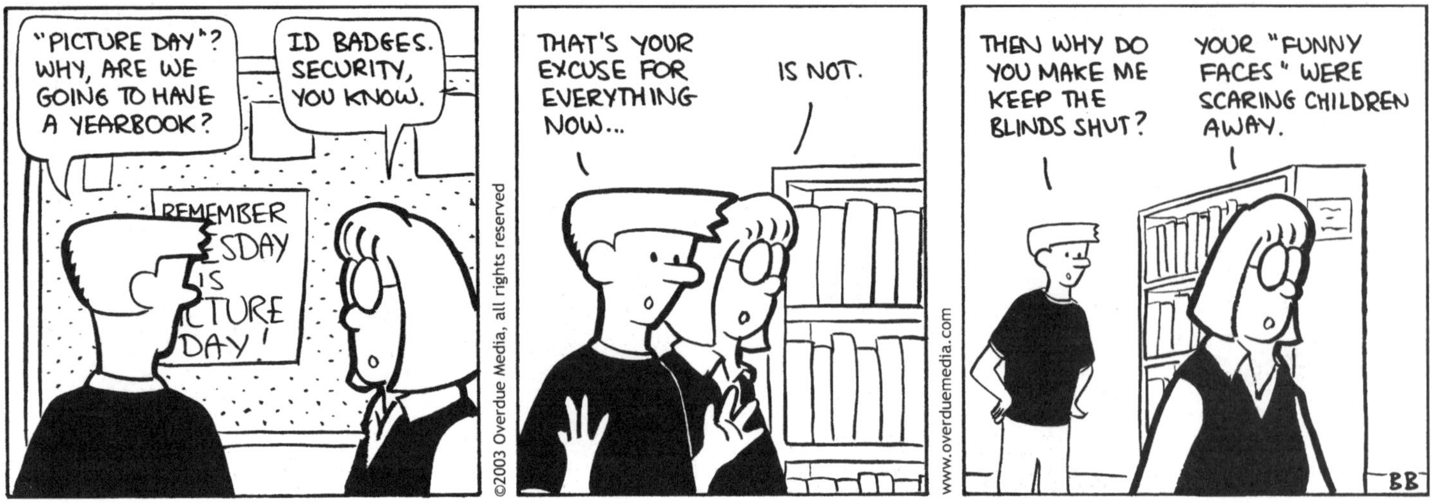
"PICTURE DAY"? WHY, ARE WE GOING TO HAVE A YEARBOOK?
ID BADGES. SECURITY, YOU KNOW.
REMEMBER
THAT'S YOUR EXCUSE FOR EVERYTHING NOW...
IS NOT.
THEN WHY DO YOU MAKE ME KEEP THE BLINDS SHUT?
YOUR "FUNNY FACES" WERE SCARING CHILDREN AWAY.
BB

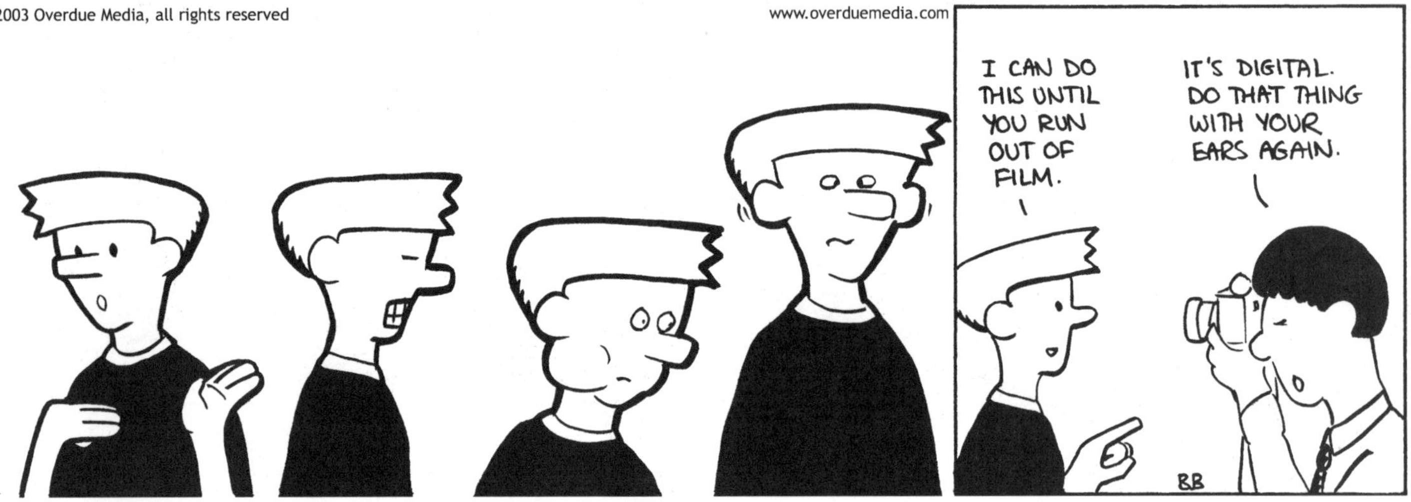
I CAN DO THIS UNTIL YOU RUN OUT OF FILM.
IT'S DIGITAL. DO THAT THING WITH YOUR EARS AGAIN.
BB

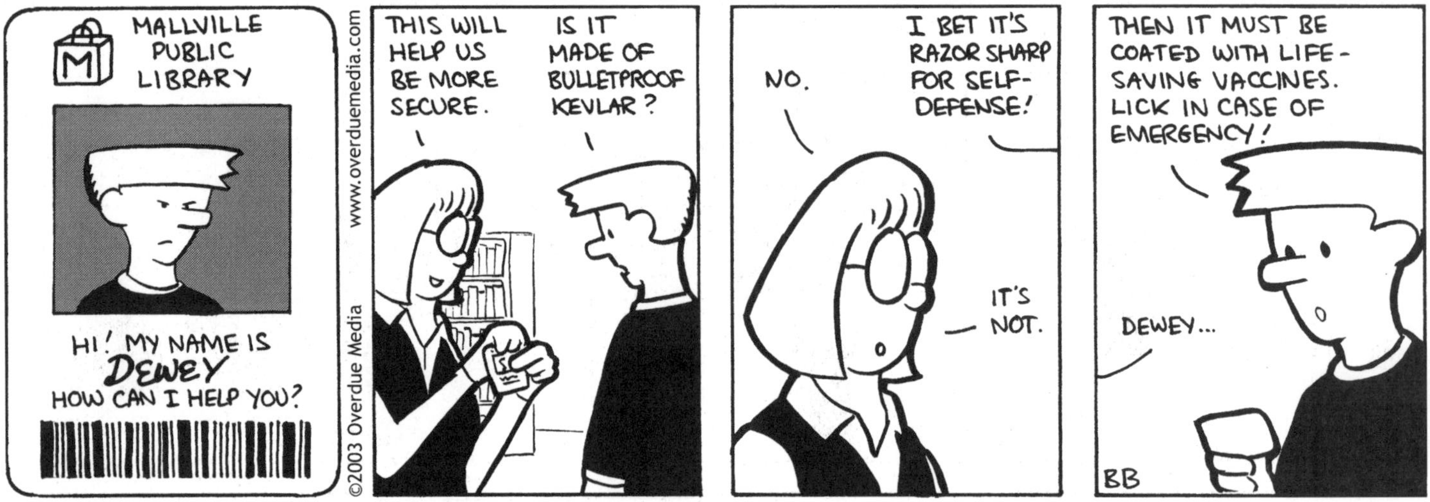
MALLVILLE PUBLIC LIBRARY
M
HI! MY NAME IS DEWEY HOW CAN I HELP YOU?
THIS WILL HELP US BE MORE SECURE.
IS IT MADE OF BULLETPROOF KEVLAR?
NO.
I BET IT'S RAZOR SHARP FOR SELF-DEFENSE!
IT'S NOT.
THEN IT MUST BE COATED WITH LIFE-SAVING VACCINES. LICK IN CASE OF EMERGENCY!
DEWEY...
BB

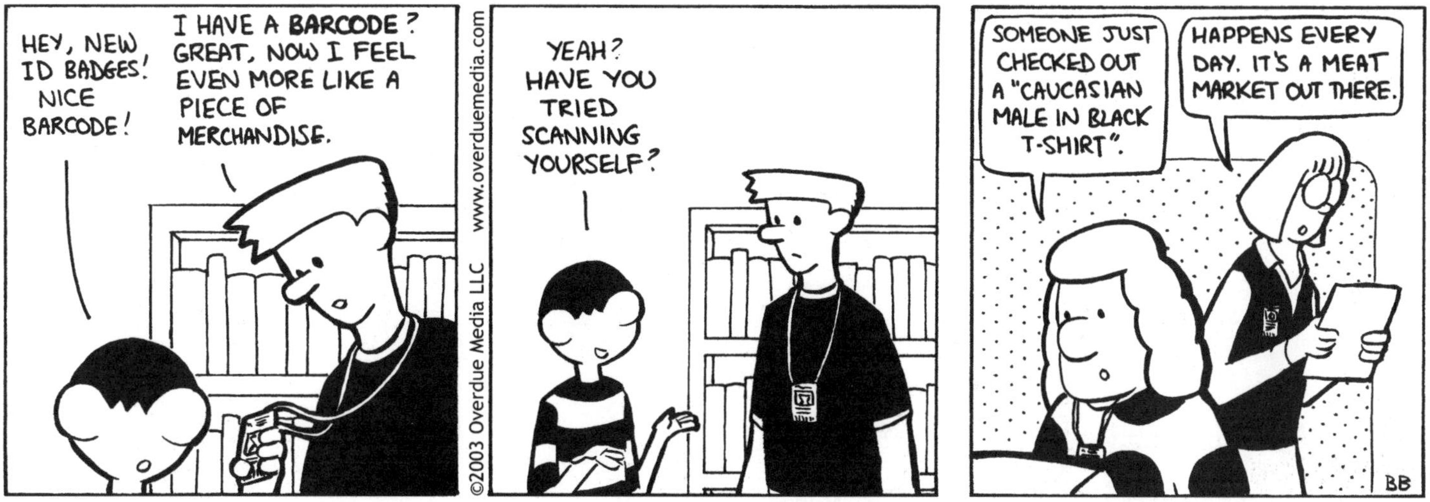
HEY, NEW ID BADGES! NICE BARCODE!
I HAVE A **BARCODE**? GREAT, NOW I FEEL EVEN MORE LIKE A PIECE OF MERCHANDISE.
©2003 Overdue Media LLC www.overduemedia.com
YEAH? HAVE YOU TRIED SCANNING YOURSELF?
SOMEONE JUST CHECKED OUT A "CAUCASIAN MALE IN BLACK T-SHIRT".
HAPPENS EVERY DAY. IT'S A MEAT MARKET OUT THERE.
BB

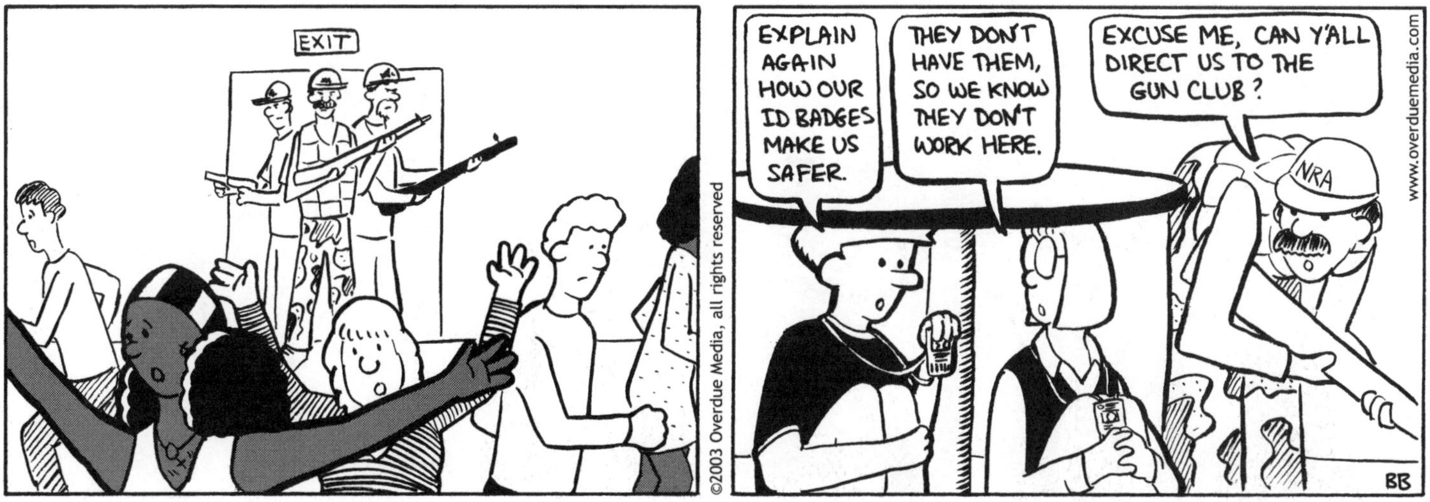
EXIT
©2003 Overdue Media, all rights reserved
EXPLAIN AGAIN HOW OUR ID BADGES MAKE US SAFER.
THEY DON'T HAVE THEM, SO WE KNOW THEY DON'T WORK HERE.
EXCUSE ME, CAN Y'ALL DIRECT US TO THE GUN CLUB?
NRA
www.overduemedia.com
BB

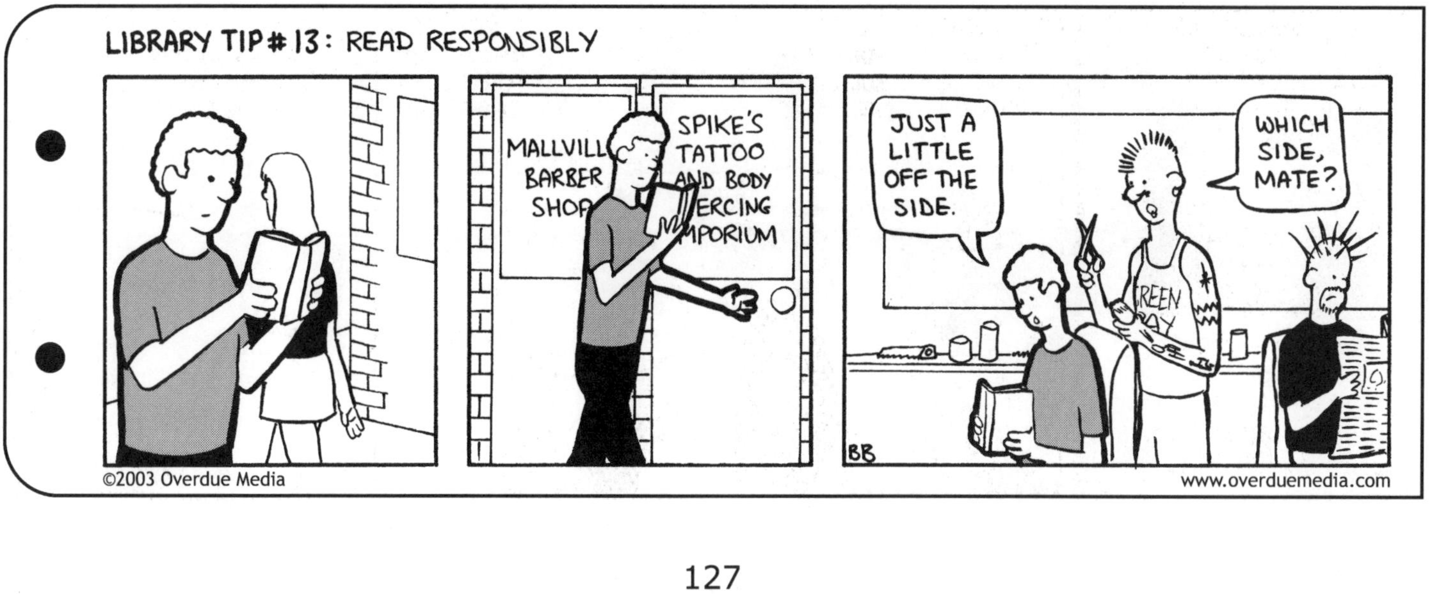
LIBRARY TIP # 13: READ RESPONSIBLY
MALLVILL
BARBER
SHO
SPIKE'S TATTOO
AND BODY
ERCING
MPORIUM
JUST A LITTLE OFF THE SIDE.
WHICH SIDE, MATE?
BB
©2003 Overdue Media
www.overduemedia.com

Read Unshelved™ every day at
www.overduemedia.com

- Strip archive
- Sign up for free daily & weekly email delivery
- RSS and Web syndication
- Buy *Unshelved* books and merchandise
- Authors' blog with news about the strip
- Upcoming appearances by Bill and Gene
- Special features
- ... and much more!

What Would Dewey Do? collects the second year of *Unshelved* in a book that otherwise greatly resembles this one. And what with being a daily comic strip and all, by the time you read this there might be even more books. It's a plague.

You can order our books from our website or your favorite bookseller, comic shop, or library.

drop us a line at
unshelved@overduemedia.com